Handbook of Research on Women's Issues and Rights in the Developing World

Nazmunnessa Mahtab
University of Dhaka, Bangladesh

Tania Haque
University of Dhaka, Bangladesh

Ishrat Khan
University of Dhaka, Bangladesh

Md. Mynul Islam
University of Dhaka, Bangladesh

Ishret Binte Wahid
BRAC, Bangladesh

A volume in the Advances in Electronic Government, Digital Divide, and Regional Development (AEGDDRD) Book Series

Published in the United States of America by
IGI Global
Information Science Reference (an imprint of IGI Global)
701 E. Chocolate Avenue
Hershey PA, USA 17033
Tel: 717-533-8845
Fax: 717-533-8661
E-mail: cust@igi-global.com
Web site: http://www.igi-global.com

Copyright © 2018 by IGI Global. All rights reserved. No part of this publication may be reproduced, stored or distributed in any form or by any means, electronic or mechanical, including photocopying, without written permission from the publisher. Product or company names used in this set are for identification purposes only. Inclusion of the names of the products or companies does not indicate a claim of ownership by IGI Global of the trademark or registered trademark.
   Library of Congress Cataloging-in-Publication Data

Names: Mahtab, Nazmunnessa, editor. | Barsha, Ishrat Khan, 1984- editor.
Title: Handbook of research on women's issues and rights in the developing
   world / Nazmunnessa Mahtab, Tania Haque, Ishrat Khan, Md. Mynul Islam, and
   Ishret Binte Wahid, editors.
Description: Hershey : Information Science Reference, [2017]
Identifiers: LCCN 2017013840| ISBN 9781522530183 (hardcover) | ISBN
   9781522530190 (ebook)
Subjects: LCSH: Women--Developing countries--Economic conditions. | Women's
   rights--Developing countries. | Sex role--Developing countries.
Classification: LCC HQ1870.9 .H36 2017 | DDC 305.409172/4--dc23 LC record available at https://lccn.loc.
gov/2017013840

This book is published in the IGI Global book series Advances in Electronic Government, Digital Divide, and Regional Development (AEGDDRD) (ISSN: 2326-9103; eISSN: 2326-9111)

British Cataloguing in Publication Data
A Cataloguing in Publication record for this book is available from the British Library.

All work contributed to this book is new, previously-unpublished material. The views expressed in this book are those of the authors, but not necessarily of the publisher.

For electronic access to this publication, please contact: eresources@igi-global.com.

Advances in Electronic Government, Digital Divide, and Regional Development (AEGDDRD) Book Series

Zaigham Mahmood
University of Derby, UK & North West University, South Africa

ISSN:2326-9103
EISSN:2326-9111

Mission

The successful use of digital technologies (including social media and mobile technologies) to provide public services and foster economic development has become an objective for governments around the world. The development towards electronic government (or e-government) not only affects the efficiency and effectiveness of public services, but also has the potential to transform the nature of government interactions with its citizens. Current research and practice on the adoption of electronic/digital government and the implementation in organizations around the world aims to emphasize the extensiveness of this growing field.

The Advances in Electronic Government, Digital Divide & Regional Development (AEGDDRD) book series aims to publish authored, edited and case books encompassing the current and innovative research and practice discussing all aspects of electronic government development, implementation and adoption as well the effective use of the emerging technologies (including social media and mobile technologies) for a more effective electronic governance (or e-governance).

Coverage

- Electronic Government, Digital Democracy, Digital Government
- Issues and Challenges in E-Government Adoption
- Knowledge Divide, Digital Divide
- E-Governance and Use of Technology for Effective Government
- Current Research and Emerging Trends in E-Government Development
- E-Government in Developing Countries and Technology Adoption
- Citizens Participation and Adoption of E-Government Provision
- Public Information Management, Regional Planning, Rural Development
- Case Studies and Practical Approaches to E-Government and E-Governance
- ICT within Government and Public Sectors

IGI Global is currently accepting manuscripts for publication within this series. To submit a proposal for a volume in this series, please contact our Acquisition Editors at Acquisitions@igi-global.com or visit: http://www.igi-global.com/publish/.

The Advances in Electronic Government, Digital Divide, and Regional Development (AEGDDRD) Book Series (ISSN 2326-9103) is published by IGI Global, 701 E. Chocolate Avenue, Hershey, PA 17033-1240, USA, www.igi-global.com. This series is composed of titles available for purchase individually; each title is edited to be contextually exclusive from any other title within the series. For pricing and ordering information please visit http://www.igi-global.com/book-series/advances-electronic-government-digital-divide/37153. Postmaster: Send all address changes to above address. © © 2018 IGI Global. All rights, including translation in other languages reserved by the publisher. No part of this series may be reproduced or used in any form or by any means – graphics, electronic, or mechanical, including photocopying, recording, taping, or information and retrieval systems – without written permission from the publisher, except for non commercial, educational use, including classroom teaching purposes. The views expressed in this series are those of the authors, but not necessarily of IGI Global.

Titles in this Series

For a list of additional titles in this series, please visit: www.igi-global.com/book-series

Handbook of Research on Sociopolitical Factors Impacting Economic Growth in Islamic Nations
Suleyman Ozdemir (Bandırma Onyedi Eylül University, Turkey) Seyfettin Erdogan (Istanbul Medeniyet University, Turkey) and Ayfer Gedikli (İstanbul Medeniyet University, Turkey)
Information Science Reference • © 2018 • 472pp • H/C (ISBN: 9781522529392) • US $275.00 (our price)

Urbanization and Its Impact on Socio-Economic Growth in Developing Regions
Umar Benna (Benna Associates, Nigeria) and Indo Benna (Muhammad Al-Mana College of Health Sciences, Saudi Arabia)
Information Science Reference • © 2018 • 404pp • H/C (ISBN: 9781522526599) • US $195.00 (our price)

Sustainable ICT Adoption and Integration for Socio-Economic Development
Charles K. Ayo (Covenant University, Nigeria) and Victor Mbarika (Southern University, USA, and ICT University, USA)
Information Science Reference • © 2017 • 264pp • H/C (ISBN: 9781522525653) • US $180.00 (our price)

Digital Media Integration for Participatory Democracy
Rocci Luppicini (University of Ottawa, Canada) and Rachel Baarda (University of Ottawa, Canada)
Information Science Reference • © 2017 • 259pp • H/C (ISBN: 9781522524632) • US $200.00 (our price)

Digital Governance and E-Government Principles Applied to Public Procurement
Rajesh Kumar Shakya (The World Bank, USA)
Information Science Reference • © 2017 • 323pp • H/C (ISBN: 9781522522034) • US $185.00 (our price)

Politics, Protest, and Empowerment in Digital Spaces
Yasmin Ibrahim (Queen Mary, University of London, UK)
Information Science Reference • © 2017 • 363pp • H/C (ISBN: 9781522518624) • US $180.00 (our price)

Handbook of Research on Sub-National Governance and Development
Eris Schoburgh (University of the West Indies, Jamaica) and Roberta Ryan (University of Technology Sydney, Australia)
Information Science Reference • © 2017 • 625pp • H/C (ISBN: 9781522516453) • US $285.00 (our price)

Agent-Based Modeling in Humanitarian Interventions Emerging Research and Opportunities
John McCaskill (University of Texas at Dallas, USA)
Information Science Reference • © 2017 • 99pp • H/C (ISBN: 9781522517825) • US $115.00 (our price)

701 East Chocolate Avenue, Hershey, PA 17033, USA
Tel: 717-533-8845 x100 • Fax: 717-533-8661
E-Mail: cust@igi-global.com • www.igi-global.com

List of Reviewers

Sara L. Parker, *Liverpool John Moors University, UK*
Sadeka Halim, *University of Dhaka, Bangladesh*
Sharif Af Saber, *RMIT University, Australia*
Shahnaz Khan, *University of Dhaka, Bangladesh*
Fariba Parsa, *George Mason University, USA*
A. K. Firowz Ahmed, *University of Dhaka, Bangladesh*
Suvhendu Das Gupta, *University of Calcutta, India*
Naheem Mahtab, *Independent University Bangladesh (IUB), Bangladesh*
Shahin A. Chowdhury, *College of DuPage, USA*

List of Contributors

Abdel-Hameid, Shahira O. / *Higher Colleges of Technology, UAE* 107
Calvain, Endong Floribert Patrick / *University of Calabar, Nigeria* 281
Chiweshe, Manase / *Chinhoyi University of Technology, Zimbabwe* 170
Chowdhury, Kuntala / *Begum Rokeya University, Bangladesh* 189
Das, Arunima Kishore / *Western Sydney University, Australia* 212
Das, Prabartana / *Jadavpur University, India* 322
Dutta, Sraboni / *Birla Institute of Technology, India* 269
Goswami, Ananya / *Birla Institute of Technology, India* 269
Haque, Tania / *University of Dhaka, Bangladesh* 52
Hossain, Julaikha Bente / *Asian Institute of Technology, Thailand* 69
Islam, Md. Mynul / *University of Dhaka, Bangladesh* 37
Jannat, Gulay / *University of Dhaka, Bangladesh* 37
Jayawardena, Dhammika / *University of Sri Jayewardenepura, Sri Lanka* 19
Kabir, Farah / *ActionAid Bangladesh, Bangladesh* 354
Kamaruzzaman, Mohammed / *BRAC, Bangladesh* 334
Khuntia, Devanjan / *Jawaharlal Nehru University, India* 307
Kousar, Hina / *Jamia Millia Islamia, India* 144
Lakshmi, P. / *Indian Institute of Technology Madras, India* 297
Lutomia, Anne Namatsi / *University of Illinois at Urbana Champaign, USA* 1
Matekere, T. / *Sokoine University of Agriculture, Tanzania* 252
Nasreen, Shagufta / *University of Karachi, Pakistan* 121
Nishat, Khandakar Josia / *University of Queensland, Australia* 235
Parker, Sara / *Liverpool John Moores University, UK* 156
Pathak, Sudha Jha / *Amity Law School, India* 370
Rahman, Md. Shafiqur / *Helen Keller International, Bangladesh* 235
Rombo, Dorothy Owino / *State University of New York, USA* 1
Roy, Parboti / *North South University, Bangladesh* 90
Safa, Noorie / *Asian Institute of Technology, Thailand* 382
Shah, Nasreen Aslam / *University of Karachi, Pakistan* 121
Sikira, A. N. / *Sokoine University of Agriculture, Tanzania* 252
Standing, Kay / *Liverpool John Moores University, UK* 156
Urassa, J. K. / *Sokoine University of Agriculture, Tanzania* 252
Visalakshmi, S. / *VIT University, India* 297
Wahid, Ishret Binte / *London School of Economics and Political Science, UK* 334
Wilson, Elisabeth / *Independent Researcher, UK* 107

Table of Contents

Preface xxi

Acknowledgment xxix

**Section 1
Women and Work**

Chapter 1
Tracing the Rights of Domestic and International Kenyan House Helps: Profiles, Policy, and
Consequences 1
    Dorothy Owino Rombo, State University of New York, USA
    Anne Namatsi Lutomia, University of Illinois at Urbana Champaign, USA

Chapter 2
Patriarchy and (Un)Doing Factory of Women's Collective Identity in Sri Lanka's Localised
Global Apparel Industry: The Glass Ceiling Revisited 19
    Dhammika Jayawardena, University of Sri Jayewardenepura, Sri Lanka

Chapter 3
Care Work vs. Career: Crisis of Middle Class Working Women 37
    Md. Mynul Islam, University of Dhaka, Bangladesh
    Gulay Jannat, University of Dhaka, Bangladesh

Chapter 4
Women-Friendly Working Environment in Bangladesh: Critical Analysis 52
    Tania Haque, University of Dhaka, Bangladesh

Chapter 5
Gendered Organizational Culture: A Comparative Study in Bangladesh and Thailand 69
    Julaikha Bente Hossain, Asian Institute of Technology, Thailand

Chapter 6
Traditional Economic Activities of Indigenous Women in the Chittagong Hill Tracts: Exploring
Indigenous Women's Role in Sustaining Traditional Economic Activities 90
    Parboti Roy, North South University, Bangladesh

Chapter 7
Gender, Organization, and Change in Sudan 107
    Shahira O. Abdel-Hameid, Higher Colleges of Technology, UAE
    Elisabeth Wilson, Independent Researcher, UK

Chapter 8
Emerging Trends and Challenges Faced in Women's Employment and Self-Employment in
Pakistan 121
    Shagufta Nasreen, University of Karachi, Pakistan
    Nasreen Aslam Shah, University of Karachi, Pakistan

Section 2
Women's Education and Health

Chapter 9
Gender Violence in Academia 144
    Hina Kousar, Jamia Millia Islamia, India

Chapter 10
Girls' and Women's Rights to Menstrual Health in Nepal 156
    Kay Standing, Liverpool John Moores University, UK
    Sara Parker, Liverpool John Moores University, UK

Section 3
Vulnerability and Women

Chapter 11
More Than Body Parts: Theorising Gender Within African Spaces 170
    Manase Chiweshe, Chinhoyi University of Technology, Zimbabwe

Chapter 12
Unveiling Barriers and Challenges of Brothel-Based Sex Workers in Private and Public Sphere of
Bangladesh 189
    Kuntala Chowdhury, Begum Rokeya University, Bangladesh

Chapter 13
Women's Commuting Environment in Public Buses in Dhaka City: A Case of Men's
Perspectives 212
    Arunima Kishore Das, Western Sydney University, Australia

Chapter 14
Disaster, Vulnerability, and Violence Against Women: Global Findings and a Research Agenda
for Bangladesh 235
    Khandakar Josia Nishat, University of Queensland, Australia
    Md. Shafiqur Rahman, Helen Keller International, Bangladesh

Section 4
Equality and Empowerment

Chapter 15
Engaging Men in Women's Economic Empowerment in Butiama District, Mara Region, Tanzania 252
A. N. Sikira, Sokoine University of Agriculture, Tanzania
T. Matekere, Sokoine University of Agriculture, Tanzania
J. K. Urassa, Sokoine University of Agriculture, Tanzania

Chapter 16
Empowering Women Entrepreneurs in India With ICT Applications 269
Ananya Goswami, Birla Institute of Technology, India
Sraboni Dutta, Birla Institute of Technology, India

Chapter 17
Advocating the Woman Affirmative Action and Women Empowerment in Rural Cross River State of Nigeria: The Role of the Civil Society and the Media 281
Endong Floribert Patrick Calvain, University of Calabar, Nigeria

Chapter 18
Role of Women Empowerment in Public and Corporate Leadership 297
P. Lakshmi, Indian Institute of Technology Madras, India
S. Visalakshmi, VIT University, India

Section 5
Gender and Media

Chapter 19
Structuring the "Expected": New Social Media Platforms and the Role of Women in Urban Spaces 307
Devanjan Khuntia, Jawaharlal Nehru University, India

Chapter 20
The Role of Media in Perpetuating or Obstructing Gender Equality in the Context of Developing World 322
Prabartana Das, Jadavpur University, India

Section 6
Emerging Challenges and Inclusion of Men on Women's Issues

Chapter 21
Migration, Muslim Women, and Social Reproduction of Gender Inequality: International Migration and Social Remittances in Gender Relations in Bangladesh 334
Ishret Binte Wahid, London School of Economics and Political Science, UK
Mohammed Kamaruzzaman, BRAC, Bangladesh

Chapter 22
Towards a More Gender-Inclusive Climate Change Policy 354
    Farah Kabir, ActionAid Bangladesh, Bangladesh

Chapter 23
Women Painters of Mithila: A Quest for Identity 370
    Sudha Jha Pathak, Amity Law School, India

Chapter 24
Development Interventions and Masculinity in Transition: A Study Among Marma Men Living in
Bandarban Sadar in Chittagong Hill Tracts 382
    Noorie Safa, Asian Institute of Technology, Thailand

Compilation of References 397

About the Contributors 443

Index 450

Detailed Table of Contents

Preface xxi

Acknowledgment xxix

Section 1
Women and Work

Chapter 1
Tracing the Rights of Domestic and International Kenyan House Helps: Profiles, Policy, and
Consequences 1
    Dorothy Owino Rombo, State University of New York, USA
    Anne Namatsi Lutomia, University of Illinois at Urbana Champaign, USA

This chapter traces a history of domestic workers both within, and to a lesser degree without, Kenya. Reading from international policy platforms—including the United Nations and various international non-governmental organizations—as well as academic research, Kenyan government policy documents, and online sources like blogs and periodicals that reveal this history and frame content addressing domestic workers, the authors develop an image of the situation of domestic work in Kenya. We identified missing protections of rights and made other policy recommendations in light of that situation. Using intersectionality to disclose how the different identities of gender, class, socioeconomic status, and ethnic identification (socially imposed or individually emphasized) of domestic workers in Kenya simultaneously clash and collude, workers nonetheless remain embedded within layers of marginalization that make the very circumstance of their work more challenging for upholding the human rights of these employees. By calling attention to the destiny of migrant domestic workers in comparison to local Kenyan domestics and linking to the present international push to protect migrant domestic workers, then, not only discloses but also hints at how the needs and interests of domestic Kenyan workers may be better met, respected, and protected. It suggests future work as well aimed at prompting an acknowledgment of, and policy changes with respect to, the basic human rights of other subaltern populations.

Chapter 2
Patriarchy and (Un)Doing Factory of Women's Collective Identity in Sri Lanka's Localised
Global Apparel Industry: The Glass Ceiling Revisited 19
    Dhammika Jayawardena, University of Sri Jayewardenepura, Sri Lanka

Systemic manifestations of women's subordination, such as the glass ceiling, are still a reality in organisations. Yet, the glass ceiling effect in the Global South is often conceptualised vis-à-vis (white) women's experience in 'gendered organisations' and women's domestic role in the Southern societies.

In this context, this chapter, based on a fieldwork research conducted in Sri Lanka's apparel industry, critically examines the glass ceiling effect of glass ceiling on women's career advancement in the Global South. Alongside the notion of 'universal' patriarchy, it problematises the 'universal' structure of the glass ceiling. And it shows that (un)doing factory women's collective identity—as lamai (little ones)—and the glass ceiling intermingle in the process of women's subordination in the apparel industry. The chapter concludes that, in the apparel industry, the role of managerial women —as well as of men in (un)doing factory women's collective identity—is crucial in keeping the glass ceiling in place.

Chapter 3
Care Work vs. Career: Crisis of Middle Class Working Women 37
    Md. Mynul Islam, University of Dhaka, Bangladesh
    Gulay Jannat, University of Dhaka, Bangladesh

Career is indispensable for woman to ensure their decision-making power to boost up their capability through active voice and participation. However, in Bangladesh most of the middle class working women are facing crisis to manage their double work. Keeping this in mind, this study explains how household related care work costs women's career. It reveals, most of the women have to face multiple problems to maintain their care and office work. Even, a good number of working women sacrificed their career to take care of children and family. Regarding these discriminatory social and institutional systems, most of the working women believe that, positive mind-set can bring a change for women to develop their career.

Chapter 4
Women-Friendly Working Environment in Bangladesh: Critical Analysis 52
    Tania Haque, University of Dhaka, Bangladesh

Work is typically divided along gender lines with men being responsible for paid work and women for unpaid care work. There is a negative correlation between income and level of gender inequalities in unpaid care work. Income can give certain level of independence but reinforces new kinds of dependence and subordination of women in our society in Bangladesh. If women wish to begin their paid work, it means ideologically they want extra jobs and they have to willingly undertake this double burden of household and professional work. The study claims that there is a need of gender responsive rebalancing policies to ensure women friendly working environment to ensure actual empowerment of women in Bangladesh.

Chapter 5
Gendered Organizational Culture: A Comparative Study in Bangladesh and Thailand 69
    Julaikha Bente Hossain, Asian Institute of Technology, Thailand

This study began with the question of what are the factors that lead to different outcomes of women in engineering employment in Bangladesh and Thailand. The primary data for answering this question were drawn from questionnaire surveys with 204 professional engineers, in-depth interviews with 80 professional women engineers, and discussions with employers in construction organizations in Bangladesh and Thailand. The findings identifies several barriers that not only deter women from entering into organizations, but also stopped the stream of women engineering graduates to flow into the engineering job market. The study has shed light on how organizational cultural practices as well as the influence of external factors within organizations affect women's entry and stay in construction organizations in Bangladesh and Thailand. The findings suggest that organizations should develop their own equal opportunity guidelines and policies to provide women with a suitable job and ensure that they remain employed.

Chapter 6
Traditional Economic Activities of Indigenous Women in the Chittagong Hill Tracts: Exploring
Indigenous Women's Role in Sustaining Traditional Economic Activities 90
    Parboti Roy, North South University, Bangladesh

There are about 1% Indigenous population in Bangladeshi and the Chittagong Hill Tracts (CHT) is one of the regions of Bangladesh resided by thirteen indigenous people's communities The indigenous peoples' lives is intrinsically linked to the nature, culture and their tradition. Traditional economic activities are important aspects of subsistence of indigenous people and women play a crucial role in preserving these activities through their knowledge and management skills. However, their traditional economic activities have been hampered by a range of factors. The study concentrates on this issue as it posits that indigenous women in the CHT provide remarkable contributions through the maintenance of their traditional economic activities which not only have traditional and cultural significance but also contain economic value. The study is based on secondary data. It employs theoretical and conceptual framework of post-colonial indigenous feminism and feminist economic analysis of women's domestic and subsistence activities as a means to explore indigenous women's persistent efforts to continue their traditional economic activities. The study argues that indigenous women in the CHT have been able to uphold their traditional economic practices at both an individual and collective level through the assistance of local organizations formed by the indigenous peoples. These efforts by indigenous women manifest the 'solidarity political economy' against the global political economy.

Chapter 7
Gender, Organization, and Change in Sudan 107
    Shahira O. Abdel-Hameid, Higher Colleges of Technology, UAE
    Elisabeth Wilson, Independent Researcher, UK

The position of women and role of gender in Sudan has been researched from anthropological, sociological and economic traditions. This study will review the position of Sudanese women within the formal employment sector, setting this within the specific political, economic and social context of the country. In addition, it will examine women in political and voluntary settings, as these are also important decision making arenas. There has been little published material previously on this topic. The study draws on secondary data from unpublished studies and master's dissertations, and also grey material available in Sudan. In addition, semi-structured interviewing of a purposive sample of selected informants was used. The data were analysed thematically. The findings were that many behavioural patterns seen elsewhere were evident in Sudan, such as stereotyping and discrimination. However, educated Sudanese women sought equality within a man's world, unlike the equal but different gender roles in parts of the Middle East.

Chapter 8
Emerging Trends and Challenges Faced in Women's Employment and Self-Employment in
Pakistan 121
    Shagufta Nasreen, University of Karachi, Pakistan
    Nasreen Aslam Shah, University of Karachi, Pakistan

Women and work is a concept which is still exploratory although various researches have been conducted related to women and work and its related concepts. Women's economic participation has increased in different jobs as compared to the past; however, the question is how much it has been able to fulfill the goal that women economic participation leads to women empowerment. In developing countries, the economic restructuring influenced by globalization policies of trade liberalization, privatization and fiscal austerity has on one hand increased opportunities for economically stable, educated, skilled and urban oriented population excluding the poor, un-educated, un-skilled and rural population. This chapter aims to explore the concept of women and work by comparing the conditions of work women do in formal and informal sector expanding the scope of analysis to focus not only on women inclusion in paid jobs but to review why it is not changing their status and position.

Section 2
Women's Education and Health

Chapter 9
Gender Violence in Academia 144
Hina Kousar, Jamia Millia Islamia, India

This is an exploratory research conducted in three universities of Delhi – University 'X', University 'Y' and University 'Z'. The objective is to study the scope and incidence of various types of sexual violence behaviors experienced by women on campus: undergraduate women; postgraduate women; research scholars; and faculty. This chapter explores types, kind and nature of sexually harassing behaviors; sexual harassment, rape, sexual assault, stalking, and intimate partner violence, experienced by women in campus; the occurrence of different type of behavior among women in age group of 18 to 65 years. Finding indicates 80 percent acknowledged sexual and psychologically offensive behavior. About 70 percent of total sample acknowledged that they were sexually assaulted. A very small percent 2 percent acknowledged of being attempted raped and 89 percent underwent stalking.

Chapter 10
Girls' and Women's Rights to Menstrual Health in Nepal 156
Kay Standing, Liverpool John Moores University, UK
Sara Parker, Liverpool John Moores University, UK

Being able to manage menstruation safely and without stigma is a basic human right which many women and girls in Nepal are denied. Unhygienic and ineffective menstrual hygiene practices have been linked to negative consequences for women and girls, in terms of both reproductive health and social factors such as school attendance. Negative cultural attitudes and taboos around menstruation are widespread in Nepal and basic knowledge of menstruation and menstrual hygiene, especially in rural areas, is limited. The chapter begins to explore the barriers to menstrual health and right and how menstrual Hygiene Management Projects providing education on menstruation and the provision of reusable sanitary pads, are widely used by Non-Governmental Organisations (NGOs) in Nepal to address these problems, with a stated goal of improving girls' reproductive health, educational performance, employment, reducing gender based violence and other psycho-social outcomes.

Section 3
Vulnerability and Women

Chapter 11
More Than Body Parts: Theorising Gender Within African Spaces 170
Manase Chiweshe, Chinhoyi University of Technology, Zimbabwe

This paper questions the reduction of human experience and identity to anatomical determinism in which the category of 'woman' or 'man' becomes a universal concept. Through a review of literature on African gender, feminist and masculinity studies, it highlights how people are more than their body parts. It notes how identities are shaped by an intersectionality of various factors such as education, employment status, class, age, physical condition, nationality, citizenship, race and ethnicity. These factors can be spatial and temporal producing differing experiences of gendered lives. African scholars have built up a rich collection of work that repudiates the univerlisation of gender identities based on Western philosophical schools of thought. This work explores in detail current and historical debates in African gender studies.

Chapter 12
Unveiling Barriers and Challenges of Brothel-Based Sex Workers in Private and Public Sphere of Bangladesh.. 189
Kuntala Chowdhury, Begum Rokeya University, Bangladesh

The value of our society is constructed through different patriarchal organization. Sex workers or prostitutes whatever we call them literally they are stigmatized in our society. Double standard of our society influences us to play double role where a man act like a saint in front of society and at the night they are the regular visitor of a brothel but society respects them and abuse those women who provides sexual pleasure to that men. Most of the sex workers are engaged in this profession because of trafficking, blackmailing or they did not have any other way to earn. They are working in this profession as well as they are serving to the customers to fulfill their sexual demand. However the fact is that stigmatization, challenges and barriers are literally faced by those women who are working as sex workers. The intensity of their life struggle is too much among brothel based sex workers where they are confined to maintain all obligations imposed by Sordarni (Madam) or customers. Though challenges and barriers can be varied from chukri (new girls in brothel) to sordarni (experienced sex workers who control new girls), I tried to put intersectional lenses to understand their challenges. Sex workers in brothels are subjects of different kinds of violence in their public and private sphere and they are objectified as sex object. This chapter is going to show the condition and position of women by examining their barriers in public and private sphere of Bangladesh. This chapter also intends to recommend a few ways to redress these kinds of violence against brothel based sex workers.

Chapter 13
Women's Commuting Environment in Public Buses in Dhaka City: A Case of Men's Perspectives.. 212
Arunima Kishore Das, Western Sydney University, Australia

The constitution of Bangladesh aims to ensure a discrimination free world guaranteeing women equal access to political and public life. The ratification of CEDAW, adaptation of both MDG and SDG by the government also promote this goal. Dhaka requires an efficient transportation system to ensure the freedom of mobility for all. However, the public buses of Dhaka are insecure, unreliable, congested and unsafe. As a result, the women and children suffer the most while boarding a bus. They have to face both physical and emotional pain. This consequently restricts women's mobility rights. As men are responsible for creating a gender insensitive commuting environment inside public buses, their perceptions on the fact is to be explored. This chapter with the help of the researcher' research data (for Masters' thesis) from 2015-2016, highlights on men's perceptions of commuting environment women experience in public buses in Dhaka city. How these perceptions are shaped as an outcome of hegemonic masculinity is also analysed in this chapter using Connell's theory of hegemonic masculinity.

Chapter 14
Disaster, Vulnerability, and Violence Against Women: Global Findings and a Research Agenda for Bangladesh 235
Khandakar Josia Nishat, University of Queensland, Australia
Md. Shafiqur Rahman, Helen Keller International, Bangladesh

Studies of natural disasters have adequately focused on gendered aspect of disaster and women's vulnerability and offered suitable suggestions though only few of these have focused on the issue of the relation between disaster and violence against women. By undertaking meta-analysis of cross-cultural studies, this paper aims to provide an overview of connections between disaster, women's vulnerability and violence against women and to highlight the importance and the relevance of similar researches in Bangladesh. Natural threats are real and moderated by existing socio-economic arrangements and cultural norms in Bangladesh where gender relationships are unequal and violence prone. Therefore it is expected that the lessons of international experiences and insights will help to develop a gendered research framework to understand 'how violence against women is increasing following disasters' in the context of Bangladesh. And finally, that would pave the way for policy options to form a better co-existence for both men and women which would be more equal, dignified and violence free.

Section 4
Equality and Empowerment

Chapter 15
Engaging Men in Women's Economic Empowerment in Butiama District, Mara Region, Tanzania 252
A. N. Sikira, Sokoine University of Agriculture, Tanzania
T. Matekere, Sokoine University of Agriculture, Tanzania
J. K. Urassa, Sokoine University of Agriculture, Tanzania

The chapter addresses women's income poverty using men as active participants in empowering women economically. Butiama district was used as a study area, using 120 women and their husbands who were beneficiaries of the programme dealing with loan provision. As an outcome of the study, men had little participation in women's economic activities, hence, women's economic empowerment was at medium level. Unlike men, women's income was used for fulfilling basic needs of the family, therefore, had little impact on their economic empowerment. By conclusion, men as decision makers have high impact on women's economic empowerment. It is recommended that, awareness creation among men would enhance their participation in empowering women. Improvement of women's access to and control over production resources would improve their income. It is recommended that lobbying and advocacy approaches should be applied to enable women's control over the production resources.

Chapter 16
Empowering Women Entrepreneurs in India With ICT Applications 269
    Ananya Goswami, Birla Institute of Technology, India
    Sraboni Dutta, Birla Institute of Technology, India

In a developing nation like India where the "Gender Digital Divide" is still prevalent, ICT is emerging as a powerful catalyst for women's economic, social and political empowerment. Empowering women entrepreneurs with ICT in this globally competitive environment can have a ripple effect in bettering the social fabric of the nation. Incorporation of ICT has created new opportunities for women entrepreneurs by contributing to knowledge sharing, networking and electronic commerce activities. This study investigates the factors which influence the women entrepreneurs to incorporate ICT in their business firms. It also provides an insight on the barriers towards adoption of ICT applications by these women entrepreneurs. It has been observed that both Government and Non-Government Organizations are working towards ICT awareness programmes, i.e., ICT-related education, training and technical support for the women entrepreneurs so that they can tap the benefit of the applications.

Chapter 17
Advocating the Woman Affirmative Action and Women Empowerment in Rural Cross River State of Nigeria: The Role of the Civil Society and the Media 281
    Endong Floribert Patrick Calvain, University of Calabar, Nigeria

Most media initiatives (particularly radio and television programs) bordering on women empowerment and the woman affirmative action tend to give less attention to the rural woman to the advantage of her urban counterpart who, to a high extent is already abreast of the feminist concept. This more or less "accidental" discrimination is causing the grassroots women to stay somewhat in ignorance and to further be victimized by the viscous patriarchal system which prevails in traditional circles. Based on a documentary analysis and semi structured interviews with experts, this chapter explores the role of the local media and the civil society in the sensitization of the rural woman towards emancipation and socio-economic empowerment in Cross River State of Nigeria. The chapter equally assesses the effectiveness of the advocacy strategies employed by local media houses and NGOs for such purposes. It assesses civil society's use of the media for the women affirmative action in rural Cross River State of Nigeria as well as the local media potential to push this affirmative action in the grassroots.

Chapter 18
Role of Women Empowerment in Public and Corporate Leadership 297
    P. Lakshmi, Indian Institute of Technology Madras, India
    S. Visalakshmi, VIT University, India

The present study attempts to highlight the social and economic benefits of leadership of Indian women based on past evidence; current trends; challenges faced and the path forward in the public and corporate arena. Women empowerment has been a vital issue that has come to limelight in the recent years. Despite numerous government schemes and policy decisions, women in India remain deprived of equal opportunities in terms of education, employment and skill development. Many social scientists have derived that economic independence plays a vital role in ensuring that women get equal opportunities in the society and thereby enjoy and benefit from their other rights. This makes women empowerment as much of an economic issue as a social one. In corporate and public life, success of policies is determined by decisions that incorporate the viewpoints of both men and women. Hence, it becomes essential to understand the nature and extent of gender equality especially in public and corporate leadership and decision making roles. The outcomes of this study from these perspectives will serve to help both sectors in narrowing the gender bias in leadership roles.

Section 5
Gender and Media

Chapter 19
Structuring the "Expected": New Social Media Platforms and the Role of Women in Urban Spaces 307
Devanjan Khuntia, Jawaharlal Nehru University, India

This paper based on empirical research attempts to deal with the question of media imagination and the marginalization of women migrants in Indian Megapolis. Foregrounding on the emerging social fact regarding the urban settings catering to one-third of country's population as migrants of which more than two-thirds are women categorically from non-urban rural areas. Further, in the backdrop of the internet and the new media penetration of rural population by half of total usage in India by 2020, the functions of the mediated imageries of the sexes need to be re-examined within the rural-urban continuum for a better clarity of media-gender relationship. The popular media imageries many of which disseminate unrealistic, stereotypical, and restrictive perceptions resulting in portrayal of women in stereotypical ways contradicts the general perception of non-urban women-emancipation through consumption of media texts which is highly urban centric. Such contestation of media effects raises a need to investigate how women migrant to the urban setting consider, analyse, internalize and utilize such portrayal of themselves in the media thus reflecting the actual consumption pattern of media texts and gender roles fixations. This paper particularly looks at an unexplored area of new media consumption within the non-urban migrants to Indian metropolis. It is an attempt to locate affordable alternative communication technology to understand the renewed social interactions of women migrants via virtual social networks in urban centres and how it infers and shape their social identity formation.

Chapter 20
The Role of Media in Perpetuating or Obstructing Gender Equality in the Context of Developing World.. 322
Prabartana Das, Jadavpur University, India

Media engineers subtle ways in which gender bias can persist in society and ensures the perpetuation of women subjugation in the society. In this chapterI want to excavate the various factors which contributes to the augmentation of gender biases by the media and how the media in developing countries strengthens the cause patriarchy masquerading in the façade of preserving traditions and customs? I also intend to unravel how perennial problems like illiteracy and abject poverty further dents the projectof women empowerment and how deeply entrenched patriarchal values manipulate the media to withhold emancipation in true sense. How women even after being qualified suffers from several negative effects undermining her own status? It will also be interesting to delve into the ways in which gendered media is far more subversive and ubiquitous in the developing world than developed world. And lastly how the gender bias in media can be curbed in the light of social and political awakening in women in particular and the development of humaningenuity and consciousness in general.

Section 6
Emerging Challenges and Inclusion of Men on Women's Issues

Chapter 21
Migration, Muslim Women, and Social Reproduction of Gender Inequality: International
Migration and Social Remittances in Gender Relations in Bangladesh 334
    Ishret Binte Wahid, London School of Economics and Political Science, UK
    Mohammed Kamaruzzaman, BRAC, Bangladesh

Does international migration have a role to reproduce unequal gender relation in a patriarchal society? How does it make such role? How does it further implicate people's religious as well as cultural practices? These are the questions have been addressed in this paper. It takes the case of Bangladesh, a South Asian Muslim-majority country with millions of international labour migrants to different Middle East and Gulf countries including Saudi Arabia, United Arab Emirates, and Bahrain. This international migration makes very positive financial contributions to the migrants and their families at origins, mostly in rural villages. The paper makes it focus on social outcomes, especially on household level gender relations with such migration. Taking up the idea of 'social remittances', it argues that these migrants, mostly men, experience with a range of 'Islamic' norms and practices in destinations, and send back those to origins for religious obligations. These norms and practices largely include discouraging female household members, especially wives, to earn or go outside without purdah in line with the perceived 'Islam'. The paper explains that such 'social remittances' encourage the female household members to be 'good' Muslim women along with the reproduction of gender inequality between women and men.

Chapter 22
Towards a More Gender-Inclusive Climate Change Policy 354
    Farah Kabir, ActionAid Bangladesh, Bangladesh

Climate change is a reality, and poses a serious long term threat to society and to the environment. Much has been written on the negative effects of climate change across the globe focusing on the greater vulnerability of least developed countries and developing countries. Women are often denied of their basic rights due to discriminatory social practices and gender blind policies. Impacts of climate change affect life and livelihood of women, and diverse work responsibilities of women augment their exposure to climate hazards. Due to less access or rights to financial and productive resources, information and services that may help them cope with impacts of stresses and shocks, are not present as a result of the gaps in policies, development agendas, thus leaving women in a greater vulnerable condition. Primarily, these are the reasons slowing the progress on achieving overall gender equality. The objective of this paper is to look at the Post 2015 Arrangements. These are numerous international frameworks and agreements, i.e., SFDRR, SDG and the Paris Agreement, that will determine sustainable development for humanitarian response and climate politics as well as policies for the next fifteen years. They focus on development from a climate change and gender equality point of view, in particular how the policies are enabling 'gender equality', taking common but differentiated responsibilities, and equity, justice and fairness as principles.

Chapter 23
Women Painters of Mithila: A Quest for Identity 370
    Sudha Jha Pathak, Amity Law School, India

The region of Mithila has become synonymous with the beautiful and vibrant Madhubani paintings which are very much coveted by the connoisseurs of art the world over. The women from Mithila have been making these paintings and it is admirable that they have been able to carve out a space and name for themselves amidst the patriarchal set-up of society. Indeed, there is no other parallel anywhere else in the world of a folk-painting being mastered exclusively by women. The progressive commercialization of this art has resulted in the corrosion of this pristine variety of art - in form as well as content. Except a miniscule number of artists, economically the plight of the vast majority of these women painters has remained quite miserable who are forced to sell their artistic pieces for a pittance while a huge profit is earned by the middlemen. The commodification and commercialization of this traditional art form has caused much alarm to the anthropologists, art historians and connoisseurs of art who are sensitive to the cultural origins and solemnity of these art forms, and also made them empathetic to the economic deprivation of the women artists who produce them. These women artists are undermined by the patriarchal social structures of the community and family and also by the market that expropriates traditional knowledge and cultural expressions.

Chapter 24
Development Interventions and Masculinity in Transition: A Study Among Marma Men Living in Bandarban Sadar in Chittagong Hill Tracts 382
    Noorie Safa, Asian Institute of Technology, Thailand

Intent of the study was to trace the shifts in masculinities among three generation's indigenous Marma men due to their increased affiliation with development interventions and its impact on gender relationship in Marma community. Following qualitative methodology, total 28 in-depth interviews and 10 focus group discussions were carried out at Bandarban Sadar, Tigerpara and Balaghata areas. Study covered 70 Marma men of three different generations, where age ranged from 13 to 60 years above. It reflected that to keep pace with modernization or to fill up increased gap with Bengali settlers, indigenous men are moving from primitive non hegemonic order to hegemonic order as existing situation is forcing them to grow up with competitive mind for survival purpose. Gigantic gap among men of three generations, in terms of their perception on what it ought to be a 'real man' signifies how stereotypical gender norms, values, practices are getting engrossed in indigenous Marma communities which is putting serious impact in gender relationships by leaving indigenous women in vulnerable state.

Compilation of References 397

About the Contributors 443

Index 450

Preface

NO RIGHTS, NO IDENTITY: REVEALING UNTOLD AND HIDDEN NARRATIVES FROM DEVELOPING COUNTRIES

You a woman[1]
You a woman, you have a vagina
Can only be our sexual doll
No rights for you rather stigma
Go elsewhere, go wherever
We do not care, but do not come here
Its men's world, we will rule everywhere. (Md. Mynul Islam, 8 April, 2017. Dhaka)

Women consisting half of the population have been treated as weaker sex in all societies of the world. Phrases like, 'discrimination', 'deprivation', 'disadvantaged' 'poorest of the poor', 'identity crisis', 'violence against women' and many more phrases have been widely discussed and debated.

Women issues do not occur in a vacuum, but correspond to and to some extent are determined by the wider social political and environmental perspective of which they form an integral part. The general idea about society and its future, its structure and the role of women and men, entails limitations for the women's issues and concerns.

The present work entitled: 'Women Issues and Rights in the Developing Countries," is unique amidst the existing literature as it provided a panoramic survey of women's issues, based on latest research. The book attempts to present a complete picture of women from different and diverse angles. Within the academic arena and discipline our goal is to promote research and understanding in fighting discrimination, promoting empowerment, dignity and respecting human rights central to our work of eliminating discrimination.

The theme is to advance gender equality and women's empowerment through challenging existing 'orthodox' development discourses and practices, which seeks to ensure that we need to uphold the principles of equality, development and empowerment in dealing with women and gender issues. The ultimate goal of this book is to enhance the efficiency and effectiveness of women in the diverse development areas of concern to be focused in the different chapters of the book.

The book comprises of chapters written by authors from both the developed and developing countries. Countries include, Australia, Bangladesh, India, Nepal, Sri Lanka, Thailand, UK, and USA. The authors have covered a wide range of issues from poverty, education, economy, violence against women, gender equality environment, gender and media migration folk painting and women and climate change.

From modernization to globalization, irrespective of all classes, women are continuously neglected due to the dual policy in the patriarchal global world, though everyday market strategies are upgrading in the name of reducing gender disparities in every sector. In reality, these strategies became more contradictory to improve gender conditions within and outside of the household. Mostly contradiction comes through the insensitive psychological attitude towards women and their working capacities. In our society mostly we are not interested to see women as human being as we want to see them as ideal mothers, ideal daughters, ideal wives, ideal daughter-in-laws, ideal sisters, ideal sister-in-laws and even ideal grandmother, ideal great grandmother, if possible. It resembles cultural expectations from them have no boundary, though the social system socializes them within very limited patriarchal boundary.

By using patriarchal rules and norms, most of the developing countries have social practices that create identical dilemmas to prove our women are always perfect and pure. In this regard, religious misinterpretations are also working to make them more marginal by influencing the power of staying within the home only. However, staying home does not ensure their honor, identity and household decision making power in all aspects. Rather it turns them into a horrible situation, where every day, they have to tolerate that they are doing nothing but cooking or cleaning. Though they are working longer hour than men, as being women, there is no recognition for them to calculate their work or identify them as worker. As a result, these women are facing unrealistic double standard in comparison with men. Men are always indentified as the one and active in the development sector and women mostly identified as passive beneficiaries, as just opposite of them. It causes sexual harassment, rape, marital rape, acid violence, trafficking and other forms of violence against women. In Bangladesh, like other developing countries, we see how most of the women are increasingly isolated from the mainstream development processes day by day due to violence against women.

Due to extreme level of violence against women in our society, a good number of women are missing from the development and globalization projects. It counts their active participation as passive and addressing them as always the beneficiaries not contributors of development initiatives. It influences the imbalanced position between men and women and within and outside the household, everywhere women are rejected to enjoy their rights as men can do. Feminists are not arguing mostly to establish women's rights as men's rights. Rather they are arguing to challenge existing power relations to introduce a new form of it to enjoy everyone's life as they want or wanted to be. As we know, how feminization of poverty disappears their presence in this competitive capitalized world.

Though women's poverty enhances their labor participation in the developing countries, it remains mostly low paid and front desk based job. It mirrors women are representing in these working sectors as either they are cheap or beautiful. No matters how qualified they are, have to be sexually beautiful to entertain male bosses. In addition, a huge number of national and international migrations occur to meet their livelihoods by involving different kinds of income generating activities. Unfortunately, only women are facing problems to become a migrant worker in unknown places. Not only these migrant women, a good number of other professional women are also facing problems to develop their career due to social barriers, security and care work. Against this backdrop, it becomes clear to us that, nowhere in this world, women will be identified as human to enjoy their rights and benefits, if men do not change out patriarchal mentality. Keeping all these facts in mind, this book has been organized in a following manner.

We have tried to divide the book into different sections according to the different themes.

Section 1: Women and Work;
Section 2: Women's Education and Health;

Preface

Section 3: Vulnerability and Women;
Section 4: Equality and Empowerment;
Section 5: Gender and Media;
Section 6: Emerging Challenges and Inclusion of Men on Women's Issues.

In Section 1 there are eight chapters all dealing with various dimensions of women's work. Starting from the paper written by Rombo and Lutomia from USA, there is clear indication in most of the papers as to how women are facing tremendous discrimination with regard to their pay. In their paper they have tried to focus on the rights of domestic workers in Kenya. The authors develop an image of the situation of domestic work in Kenya. The workers remain embedded within layers of marginalization that make the very circumstance of their work more challenging for upholding the human rights of these employees. They have also tried to compare the situation of migrant domestic workers with the local Kenyan domestic workers and tried to focus on the international issue of to protect migrant domestic workers. An important aspect of the chapter is that it entails the situation of domestic workers in the other developing countries. For example, in the case of Bangladesh to, there are many local domestic workers working in homes and also there migrant domestic workers. However, these workers may be staying in an illegal status, or they have accompanied the foreign diplomats family working in Bangladesh. Nevertheless it may be concluded that they suffer from similar discrimination and deprivation as other domestic workers working in other countries.

Next there is a similar finding on the situation of women working in the factory, especially in the apparel industry in Sri Lanka. Here the scenario is comparable to the condition of women working in the garments factory in Bangladesh. Manifestations of patriarchy, causing subordination of women, low paid or under paid, no contractual conditions of their work, no fixed timing, no security, and often open to violence against them have confirmed the notion of 'universal' patriarchy.

The third chapter on care work vs career of middle class working women includes a new dimension of women's work. Here it is revealed how career is indispensable for women to ensure their decision making power in boosting up their capacity to have their voices heard in participation. On the other hand it is also important to manage their family by trying to take proper care and thus maintain a balance between care and career.

Chapter 4 is followed by the notion of how women-friendly environments can be created and how women can willingly undertake the burden of household and professional work, by the need of gender responsive rebalancing policies to ensure women friendly working environment and thus achieve equality and empowerment.

Chapter 5 is quite interesting in the sense that it presents a comparative study of a research on two countries, Thailand and Bangladesh. For a long time the profession of 'engineering' was confined to be mainly a masculine area of study. The study began with the question of what are the factors that lead to different outcomes of women in engineering. By comparing Thailand and Bangladesh, the findings identifies several similar and different barriers that not only deter women from entering in construction organizations, but also stopped the stream of women engineering graduates to enter into the engineering job market. The findings also suggest that despite the concerted efforts of the government, both in Thailand and Bangladesh, in increasing the female engineer's participation in employment, organizations should develop their own equal opportunity guidelines and policies to provide women with a suitable job and ensure that they remain employed make some earnings for the benefit of the family and ultimately achieve equality and empowerment along with men.

Chapter 6 takes the readers into a new area that is more prevalent in India and Bangladesh. Here the author talks about the economic activities of Indigenous Women in the Chittagong Hill Tracts and focuses on their role in sustaining their traditional economic activities. The study concentrates on this issue as it posits that indigenous women provide remarkable contributions through the maintenance of their traditional economic activities. Similar is the case with Indian "Dalits' women, whose activities do not have only traditional and cultural significance but contain economic value.

In Chapter 7, we find an analysis of Gender, Organization and Change in Sudan, where the position of women and role of gender has been researched from anthropological, social and economic traditions. The study reviewed and examined the position of Sudanese women within the formal employment sector, and also examined women in political and voluntary settings, as these are also important decision making arenas. One of the important issues is that educated Sudanese women sought equality within a man's world, unlike the equal but different gender roles found by Metcalfe (2007) in parts of not in the Middle East only, but other developing countries as well.

In Chapter 8, Nasreen Shah and her co-author argues with the issue that Women and Work is a concept which is still exploratory. In developing countries, the economic restructuring influenced by globalization policies of trade liberalization, privatization and fiscal austerity, have on the one hand increased opportunities for economically stable, educated, skilled and urban oriented population, thus excluding the poor, un-educated rural women and women living in urban slums. The chapter also tried to bring out the comparison of the conditions of women working in the formal and informal sectors and emphasizes on the emerging challenges faced by these women. Similar cases are evident in Bangladesh recognized as one of the poorest countries of the South and where are more vulnerable.

Section 2 focuses on women's education and health. Here we have two chapters. Gender Violence in Academia authored by Dr. Hina Kausar from Dallas, USA. Herer she has done an exploratory research in three Universities of Delhi, India. She used anonymous names as University X, Y, and Z. The chapter explores types, kind and nature of sexually harassing behaviours; sexual harassment, rape, sexual assault, stalking and intimate partner violence, experienced by women in campus. At this point it is important to mention that gender based violence is a historical issue and women have been facing these different types of violence through out their live, prior to birth and the phenomenon is present in all countries, developing and developed. However, the chapter is significant in the perspective of making a comparative analysis of different countries and this may be used as a sample study, and so it has been included in the book.

The chapter on girls and women's rights to menstrual health in Nepal is indeed a unique study. It has been written by two Faculty members from UK. Being able to manage menstruation safely and without any stigma is a basic human right which many women and girls are denied. Unhygienic and ineffective menstrual hygiene practices have been linked to negative consequences for women and girls, both in terms of reproductive health and social factors such as attendance in schools.

The chapter focuses on the barriers to menstrual health and menstrual rights. This is important as women of many developing countries are totally unaware of the issue of menstrual problems sand the rights they have. These women are too shy and prefer to be a very private affair to share or discuss. The study leads to the way how these problems may be solved through sharing and discussion.

In Section 3, we have the chapter, "More Than Body Parts: Theorising Gender Within African Spaces," written by Manase Chiwese from Zimbabwe. Here she provides a nuanced analysis on the fragility of the ways gender is inscribed on bodies and the ways in which power is expressed, negotiated and ever present in gendered practices. She rightly argues that gender is an all-encompassing concept

Preface

that affects not only how we live but how we see and perceive our world. She mentions about male/female dichotomy and indicates widespread pathology of people who do not fit into these categories. She claims that women are opposed but not all women are oppressed n the same way. Different factors, such as age, class, ethnicity, location and seniority affect how gender identities are created and performed and applied on women in Africa.

The next three chapters written by authors in Australia are mostly covering issues in the context of Bangladesh. "Women's Commuting Environment in Public Buses in Dhaka City: A Case of Men's Perspectives," submitted by Arunima Kishore das, Western Sydney University, Australia, focuses on the requirement of an efficient transportation system to ensure free mobility of people from all walks of life. Any experience of travelling on a public bus in Dhaka has never been a happy incident for women. As modes of public transport, buses are considered as insecure, unreliable, congested and difficult. It is the women and children who suffer the most while boarding a bus. They have to go through both physical and emotional pains as a part of their daily life experiences of commuting environment. Consequently women are debarred from their mobility rights in the paradigm of a developing country like Bangladesh. Using Connell's theory of hegemonic masculinity the paper also argues how these conditions of women are an outcome of hegemonic masculinity.

Chapter on "Unveiling Barriers and Challenges of Brothel-Based Sex Workers in Private and Public Sphere in Bangladesh," authored by Kuntala Chowdhury, Bangladesh speaks about sex workers or prostitutes as they are stigmatized in our society. She courageously mentions about the double standard/role of a man who acts like a saint in front of society where as at night they are the regular visitor of a brothel and society respects them and abuse those women who provides entertainment and pleasure to meet their sexual desires and aspirations.

"Disaster, Vulnerability, and Violence Against Women: Global Findings – A Research Agenda for Bangladesh," written by Khandakar Josia Nishat from University of Queensland, Australia, focuses on the natural disasters occurring in Bangladesh and how women and affected. It mainly tries to emphasize as to how women become vulnerable in meeting these calamities. However, the paper also tried to show how women can manage and cope and overcome the natural catastrophes like, cyclones, floods, draught, famine by being involved and engaged in development work, and how they can now evade frequent disasters and vulnerability.

Section 4 is on equality and empowerment.

Dealing with equality and empowerment issues, the writers in this section have focused on mainly economic, social and political empowerment. Chapter on "Engaging Men in Women's Economic Empowerment in Butiama District, Mara Region in Tanzania," emphasizes on the need to include men to understand about women's empowerment. It is indeed important that women will not be able to do anything without the support of men. Specially in a developing country like Tanzania. Men here feel that if women are economically empowered in the sense that they have the capacity to earn money it will be to their benefit.

The next paper from Nigeria, written by Endong Flobert and others tries to compare the situation between urban and rural women. Their focus is that the media, particularly radio and television portrays the work of urban women at the disadvantage of rural women. The more or less discrimination is causing the grassroots women to stay somewhat in ignorance and further to be victimized by the universal patriarchal system. Finally the chapter assesses the effectiveness of the advocacy strategies employed by local media and NGOs for affirmative action, and the local media potentials for establishing affirmative action at the grassroots.

Ananya Goswami and Sraboni Dutta from Kolkata discusses "Empowering Women Entrepreneurs in India With ICT Applications." In their paper, they focus on the "Gender Digital Divide," prevalent in India. ICT is emerging as a powerful catalyst for women's economic, social and political empowerment. In the globally competitive environment empowering women entrepreneurs with ICT is having an effect in bettering the social fabric of the nation. They mentioned about the efforts of government and NGOs in working towards ICT awareness programmes and training. So that women can tap the benefit of applications of ICT in their work system.

The last paper in this section deals with political empowerment and leadership. "Role of Women Empowerment in Public and Corporate Leadership," jointly authored by P. Lakshmi and S. Visalakshmi, highlights the social and economic benefits of leadership of Indian women based on past evidence, current trends, future challenges and the path forward. As stated by them, despite numerous programmes, policy decisions by government, women in India remain deprived of equal opportunities in areas of education, employment and skill development. In corporate and public life, the success of policies is determined by the decisions that incorporate the opinion of women.

Section 5 is on gender and media.

This section of the book includes two papers. "Structuring the Expected: New Social Media Platforms and the Role of Women in the Urban Spaces,". written by Devjani Khuntia from India argues the fact the much research work has been done and disseminated through the media specifically on stereotyped issues that reflect and strengthen socially accepted views of gender and normalizing violence against women. In fact nothing positive have been portrayed by the media. This chapter tries to focus on the issue that it is essential to understand renewed social interactions of women via virtual social networks in urban centers and thus shape their social identity formation.

The second paper in this section, "The Role of Media in Perpetuating or Obstructing Gender Equality in the Context of the Developing World," authored by Prabartana Das, India, speaks about the fact the media disseminates in subtle ways in which gender bias can persist and ensures the perpetuation of women's subordination, subjugation and oppression in the society. In her paper she explores the factors that causes gender bias in the media, and how the media portrays the negative attitude of women as a manifestation of patriarchy. She also recommends how the media image may be rectified to present the positive image of women.

Section 6 is on emerging challenges and inclusion of men on women's issues.

The last section of the book deals with few chapters which could not be grouped under any other previous sections. This section therefore concentrates on individual. But very vital issues of contemporary times. For example, the issue of migration, masculinity, climate change are all contemporary matters that needs to be considered in relation with women's issues.

"Migration, Muslim Women, and Social Reproduction of Gender Inequality: International Migration and Social Remittances in Gender Relations in Bangladesh," written by Isret Binte Wahid from London School of Economics and Political Science (LSE) starts with a valid question, does international migration have a role to reproduce unequal gender relation in a patriarchal society like Bangladesh? Bangladesh, a South Asian Muslim majority country with millions of international labour migrants to Middle east and Gulf countries including Saudi Arabia, United Arab Emirates and Bahrain, makes very positive financial contributions to the migrants and their families at their origins. The paper focuses on the social remittances, and argues that these migrants mostly men, practice norms and practices of Islam thus discouraging female headed households especially wives to collect the money without purdah as understood

Preface

in Islam. The paper further explains how the social remittances encourage the female household to be 'good' Muslim women along with the repercussion of gender inequality between women and men. In other words the question remains unanswered, whether social remittances enhances gender inequality or promote gender equality and empowerment of the poor Bangladeshi women, living in the villages?

The next paper, "Development Interventions and Masculinities in Transition: A Study Among Marma Men Living in Bandarban Sadar in Chittagong Hill Tracts," written By Noorie Safa from AIT, Thailand, is more or less a historical study. The intention of the study is to trace the shifts in masculinities among three generation's indigenous Marma men due to their increased affiliation with development interventions and its impact on gender relationship in Marma community. The study found that indigenous men are moving from primitive non-hegemonic order to hegemonic order as the existing situation id pressing them for the need to grow up with competitive mind for survival strategies.

Another very important and very current issue is the relation of women and climate change. Written by Farah Kabir, Bangladesh, the paper, "Towards a More Gender-Inclusive Climate Change Policy," starts with the vital concern that climate change is a reality, and poses a serious long term threat to society and to the environment. It is to long for the clarity of the early days of the modern environmental movement when the problems could be seen and smelled and the results were obvious. Today we are attacked by air and pollution, trees being cut down, stream closing. Much has been written on the negative effects of climate change across the globe focusing on the greater vulnerability of least developed and developing countries. Women are often denied of their basic rights due to discriminatory social practices and gender blind policies in Bangladesh. Impact of climate change affect livelihood of women, and diverse work responsibilities of women augment their exposure to the hazards of climate. However, she mentions about the numerous international frameworks and agreements, like SDG and Paris Agreement that will focus on development from a climate change perspective and gender equality point of view.

The last chapter written by Sudha Pathak from India deals with a very different perspective, that is "Women Painters of MITHILA: A Quest for Identity. Here she portrays the positive aspect of the beautiful and vibrant paintings of Madhubani. These are the paintings of the region of Mithila where the women through their paintings have been successful in carving out a space for them amidst the patriarchal set-up of society. She proudly mentions that there is no other place in the globe to find any parallel world of folk-painting being mastered exclusively by women. Nevertheless she speaks out about the commodification and commercialization of these paintings as concerns of anthropologists, art historians are sensitive to cultural origins and traditions but, the most sympathetic portion is the economic deprivation of these women who painted and produced these.

To conclude, we might ask the question, "Can the world save women?" It is more legitimate and serious than ever before in achieving equality and empowerment of women.

Nazmunnessa Mahtab
University of Dhaka, Bangladesh

Ishrat Khan
University of Dhaka, Bangladesh

Md. Mynul Islam
University of Dhaka, Bangladesh

ENDNOTES

[1] It's a contemporary short poem by Md. Mynul Islam based on women's poor situation and condition of rights around the world, especially from the Asian and African countries.

Acknowledgment

Handbook of Research on Women's Issues and Rights in the Developing Countries is an edited book comprised of contributions from different personalities representing countries from all over the globe. However, since the title entails issues and rights of the developing countries we have received majority of the papers from the developing countries. Countries represented in this book are Australia, Bangladesh, India, Nepal, Sri Lanka, Thailand, Pakistan, African countries like Tanzania, Nigeria and Sudan. As planned, there were to be 15 chapters. However, with the announcement for Call for Papers we were proud to receive about 55 abstracts. Finally, we received 25 chapters covering a variety of issues and concerns and representing different countries.

The book would not have been possible without the contribution of all the respective authors who have submitted their chapters in their areas of specialty and interest. We, the Editorial Board would like to express our sincere gratitude and thanks for contributing to the book and for their sincere dedication and commitment in keeping with the time schedule.

We would like to offer our sincere gratitude to all, our Reviewers who with their expertise have been able to give their comments and suggestions to the concerned authors, and guide them in every step of their journey. We appreciate their concern despite their own busy schedule.

Special thanks are due to the members of my Editorial group, specifically Md. Mynul Islam (My former student), but presently my colleague in the Department who has helped me with great dedication. Determination and commitment to get the task complete within the given time schedule. He also helped me with the intricacies of modern technological devises and its associated problems.

I would like to thank my other members of the team, namely Tania Haque (who joined us later), Ishrat Khan, and Ishret Binte Wahid, who is pursuing her Master's in Development Studies at LSE. She offered her ideas and also contributed a chapter.

I would like to thank my youngest son, Naheem Mahtab, Lecturer, Independent University Bangladesh, who has been a constant assistant to me from the very beginning of the project. I do owe him a lot. Without his help, it would not have been possible to deal with all the 55 abstracts received for the book. I must admit 'Downloading' is indeed a very arduous task.

Acknowledgment

Finally, we the members of the Editorial Board are expressing our deepest gratitude, and thanks to our Coordinator, Courtney Tychinski, at IGI for her constant, continuous, assistance, concern, suggestions, comments, attitude, and full support at all times. We are all indebted to you.

Thanks and gratitude to all at IGI Global Publishers for giving us this grand opportunity to contribute a book.

Nazmunnessa Mahtab
University of Dhaka, Bangladesh

Tania Haque
University of Dhaka, Bangladesh

Ishrat Khan
University of Dhaka, Bangladesh

Md. Mynul Islam
University of Dhaka, Bangladesh

Ishret Binte Wahid
University of London, UK

Section 1
Women and Work

Chapter 1
Tracing the Rights of Domestic and International Kenyan House Helps:
Profiles, Policy, and Consequences

Dorothy Owino Rombo
State University of New York, USA

Anne Namatsi Lutomia
University of Illinois at Urbana Champaign, USA

ABSTRACT

This chapter traces a history of domestic workers both within, and to a lesser degree without, Kenya. Reading from international policy platforms—including the United Nations and various international non-governmental organizations—as well as academic research, Kenyan government policy documents, and online sources like blogs and periodicals that reveal this history and frame content addressing domestic workers, the authors develop an image of the situation of domestic work in Kenya. We identified missing protections of rights and made other policy recommendations in light of that situation. Using intersectionality to disclose how the different identities of gender, class, socioeconomic status, and ethnic identification (socially imposed or individually emphasized) of domestic workers in Kenya simultaneously clash and collude, workers nonetheless remain embedded within layers of marginalization that make the very circumstance of their work more challenging for upholding the human rights of these employees. By calling attention to the destiny of migrant domestic workers in comparison to local Kenyan domestics and linking to the present international push to protect migrant domestic workers, then, not only discloses but also hints at how the needs and interests of domestic Kenyan workers may be better met, respected, and protected. It suggests future work as well aimed at prompting an acknowledgment of, and policy changes with respect to, the basic human rights of other subaltern populations.

DOI: 10.4018/978-1-5225-3018-3.ch001

INTRODUCTION

Domestic work, defined as "work performed in a household(s) as employment" (ILO, 2011), originate in multiple factors, some of which these days include being a product of globalization via colonialism, differences in regional geopolitical economic development trends, and various local/social trends that create the "push" and "pull" of demand for domestic workers. Present-day local domestic work, which morphed from the earlier, historically male-dominated, lower-classform from colonial times, has since become a predominantly female-dominated domain. According to the ILO (2011), the prominence of domestic work worldwide estimates that between 1995 and 2010 the global number of domestic workers rose from approximately 33.2 million to 52.6 million, with 83% of those workers being female. Domestic work is highly dominated by women who account for 83% of domestic workers worldwide (ILO, 2013).

In the chapter we trace the feminization of domestic work in Kenya and examine the role of the human rights approach, both internationally and nationally, around policy, research, and practice that addresses this trend. We explore the role of major entities involved in domestic work through the lens of the United Nations, international agencies, the Kenya government, receiving and destination countries for migrant domestic workers, recruiting bureaus, employers, and employees. Here, intersectionality (Crenshaw, 1991) helps to frame and account for how domestic workers' multiple forms of identity, including gender, race, religion, migration status, class, ethnic affiliation and so on, clash and collude in the shaping of their social worlds, especially in light of the discrimination, oppression, and domination directed at such workers.

The term *domestic worker* partly obscures how such workers are increasingly becoming a core labor force both inside *and* outside of countries; ironically, the domestic has become international. This begins to become evident in how Kenya, as an example, has only limited data on this important group of citizens who contribute to the economy not only by promoting family well-being at home but also through remittances from abroad.

To begin to see this population more fully, this chapter first compiles an image of the Kenyan house help both locally and internationally, particularly in the Middle East, while also identifying and analyzing the policies, or lack of them, that protect this population. As a matter of human rights, witnessing to and analyzing the economic, social, and psychological consequences of house help employment thus opens out on a panorama of recommendations for further research, policy determination, and practice that may offset the negative factors of these consequences and enhance the quality of life for domestic workers.

BACKGROUND

To begin most broadly, the International Labor Organization (ILO) through its member states has identified the key players, along with their roles and shortcomings, with respect to domestic workers, while also advancing policies to protect those workers. This approach, rooted a human rights framework, calls for fair treatment of domestic workers that also upholds their human dignity in every circumstance. More narrowly, the frameworks that Arthur (2009) and Fleury (2016) have explored around the rationales and impacts of migration specifically on women serve to illuminate migrant domestic workers as well. To be sure, while socioeconomic trends have feminized domestic work post-colonially, and while the identities of these workers have equally played a key a role in shaping the experiences of domestic workers, to frame and understand those identities non-intersectionally loses too much explanatory force. Moreover, intersectionality helps to disclose reasons for why domestic workers remain vulnerable despite ILO's (2013) otherwise correctly oriented human rights policymaking.

Intersectionalities

Intersectionality not only recognizes identities as socially constructed but also those social world orders that support discrimination, oppression, and bias (Crenshaw, 1991). Typically from economically disadvantaged backgrounds that include a history of poverty, rural origins, and/or membership in marginalized communities, domestic workers have less, or simply lack any, education compared to their advantaged counterparts, are desperate for employment, and often have little to no family support. While human rights policies are based on an assumption that individuals are able to stand for their rights, domestic workers are predisposed not to. Their identities, rooted as they are in often multiple forms of disadvantage, make it unlikely that they can either collectively organize to agitate for better working conditions or advocate individually for better terms with their employers—all the more so when employers remain confident the government regulations will not be enforced.

Beyond this, the setting of domestic work itself presents challenges to upholding human rights protections. Domestic workers often inhabit informal work settings, are hidden in private homes, so that it is common for them to be isolated and excluded from social and labor policies.

In terms of class, domestic work comprises a so-called lower-class form of labor. Household chores, for instance, which comprise one domain of domestic work, have a history of being undervalued. In patriarchal society, the man's job as bread winner made a wife's unpaid house chores subordinate; even in divorce, the contributions of household chores were not deemed worthy of consideration when dividing matrimonial property. Given the lack of monetary value historically assigned to housework performed by housewives, families of higher socioeconomic status would utilize domestic workers to relieve them of performing such monotonous tasks; that payment should follow for domestic workers seems only grudgingly acknowledged. But whether it is the nature either of the work itself or of who performs it, domestic work has struggled to gain parity with other forms of comparable jobs.

The history of domestic work in Kenya specifically reflects various intersectionalities, with sex or gender foremost. Currently 4 out of 5 of domestic workers in Kenya are women (Biko, 2015, 6 October); those who have migrated as domestic workers to the gulf are also predominantly women (Fleury, 2016). Many also suffer human trafficking (Demetriou, 2015).

The feminization of domestic work results from social trends that allowed women to first migrate locally—from rural to urban centers—and then later internationally. During the previous colonial era, the habit of referring to male domestic workers—who took up these jobs alongside others on farms and at junior positions in government partly to service hut tax that was introduced by the colonial government but also because women and children were banned by law from joining their husbands in the city (White, 2009)—as "boys" emphasized their lack of masculinity and inferiority compared to their "masters" (Sobania, 2003).

After independence, Kenya opened education to both girls and boys, but patriarchal practices like early marriage, and the emphasis on marriage in general, resulted in lower enrollment by girls in schools. Moreover, since public education was not free, families would at times opt to send boys rather than girls to school. In the enthusiasm to take up employment in the wake of the departing colonialists, men who had been "boys" took advantage of the opportunity to obtain other forms of employment. By the 1960s, increased wages to the emergent middle class allowed taking on girls as house helps, typically from disadvantaged families. According to Ondimu (2007), 26% of Kenyan house helps are below the age of 17. Many are likely to be an orphaned or semi-orphaned female, uneducated or only slightly educated, from rural areas, or to be an older sibling from a poor family where the parents are either separated or divorced.

Why Domestic Work Happens

Despite its poor reputation, domestic work is important for both the individuals engaged in it as well as their families and nations. Namuggala (2015) found that domestic work can empower women. More broadly, migrant workers contribute to the social and economic wellbeing of both the sending and receiving countries. For example, the 0.8 million migrant workers from Ethiopia generate 13 billion dollars, or 10-20% of the country's gross domestic product (Fernandez, 2010; Weissbrodt & Rhodes, 2013).

Globalization, economic incorporation, easy access to transportation, increased information flows, and demand for skilled and unskilled labor alike have shaped the process of migration by African women. Motivations for migration have been categorized as "push" or "pull" factors. *Pulls* include economic and/or familial survival, work, attending school, reuniting with spouses. *Pushes* tempt or prompt a person to leave, for example ethnic strife, civil wars, poverty, chronic and mass unemployment, structural adjustments of economics, decline in food production, patriarchal oppression, ecological destruction, grown in informal economy, and the segmentation of labor (Arthur, 2009).

From the turn of the twenty-first century, a scarcity of jobs along with glaring income inequality in Kenya have particularly led to an increased "push" for emigration to the Middle East as one way to cope and improve living standards. At the same time, a some middle eastern countries have initiated a system that allows short-term contracts for specialized recruitment of specialized labor from abroad, the so-called *Khafala*, has increased the "pull" of immigration to the gulf. This allows employers to sponsor an employee thereby facilitating access to a working visa and legal migration (Baldwin-Edwards, 2005). The pay is also another "pull" factor, in some cases amounting to US$450 per month (Fleury, 2016) compared to US$100 per month that local domestic workers get. Since domestic work occurs in the non-formal employment sector, which is prone to exploitation (ILO, 1990), lack of scrutiny from the public and protection through policy often occurs. Human Rights Watch (2015, 30 June) has reported evidence of the injustices workers endure in the Middle East as well as stories how social media has been used both to castigate house helps for their "unbecoming" behaviors and by house helps to share "horror" stories about employment in the Middle East.

While African women form a significant portion of women who move across international boundaries, this fact garners little attention. Arthur (2009) posits that this is because those who study migration assume that migratory decisions are made by men and therefore discuss the migration of women by centering experiences of men and as such not seeing women as agents and initiators of their migration; that labor is seen as male, and excludes domestic work, contributes to this. Arthur (2009) also observes that international migration has given agency and empowerment to female migrants by offering them new directions, new opportunities, and new connections for accessing and creating better economic opportunities for themselves and their families. For most of these women, migrating provides a means for achieving autonomy and independence from the roles set for African women by patriarchal patterns in the society.

Profile of Migrant Domestic Workers

The International Organization for Migration (2015) endeavored to create a country profile of migrants from Kenya. The report observes that there is limited data on human trafficking while acknowledging that children and girls are vulnerable to trafficking. Some of them end up becoming domestic workers.

Common destinations in the Middle East for migrant domestic workers are Saudi Arabia, the United Arab Emirates, and Qatar. From Gikuru's (2013) thesis, which sought to find out why migrant domestic workers from Kenya still left for work after the government had issued a ban on travelling for work to the Gulf region in 2012, it would appear that the profile for migrant domestic workers is different from local ones. Tending to be women, either single or married with and without children, from ages 20 to 40. Some took up domestic work for the first time as migrants and held jobs in the non-formal sector while they lived in Kenya.

One of this study's interviewees was a housewife who had not held a formal job previously. Migrant domestic work appealed to her as a way to enable meeting specific obligations, like paying pay school fees for her children and improve her standard of living. Others had sufficient command of English and income to pay the fees to process travel prerequisites, such as medical exams, recruitment fees, and a passport even in cases when the visa was sponsored. These workers were more likely to be urban folk who had more access to information about recruitment in the first place.

According to Weissbrodt and Rhodes (2013), the Middle East is notorious for discrimination, offering better benefits for natives over migrant workers. While immigrant workers in general suffer, domestic workers are even more disadvantaged. Failed by the sending and receiving country governments, the middle men and recruiting bureaus, and their employers, their own (lack of) education and level of knowledge around their rights does not help their case. Recruiting bureaus will often charge excessive fees and offer fake contracts that are revoked once the worker arrives at the receiving destination. And since the workers come from Africa and Asia with limited to no knowledge of the local language or the cultural terrain, they are privy to exploitation. Employers overwork, underpay, and withhold payment on various pretexts, while making workers live in unsafe conditions or in substandard housing while being subjected to physical, verbal, and sexual abuse. Moreover, Israel, Jordan, Kuwait, Lebanon, Oman, Qatar, Saudi Arabia and United Arab Emirates offer employer-based visas that restrict the migrant worker from leaving bad working terms and conditions to seek something better. Unlike others in construction, or the cleaning industry, domestic workers are isolated, typically to private homes, and can neither demonstrate nor unionize to agitate for better terms and conditions. In some countries, domestic workers are not under the aegis of labor laws at all, thus leaving no legal pathway to seek redress at all. In addition, many of the receiving countries have not ratified the numerous UN conventions on the rights and conditions of domestic workers.

TRACING THE RIGHTS OF DOMESTIC AND INTERNATIONAL KENYAN HOUSE HELPS

Following World War II, the United Nations established the rationale and many of the conventions for human rights. Weissbrodt and Rhodes (2013) track the history of these rights as affording specific protections to women migrant domestic workers in the Middle East. Relatedly, while every pertinent

UN convention has subsequently been ratified by the Kenyan government, upholding those rights has continued to be somewhat elusive.

Kenyan Government Protection of Local Domestic Workers

Kenya has ratified the Domestic Workers Convention of 2011 for domestic workers within the country. In 2009, Kenya had gazetted the *General Wages Order,* which prohibits the employment of any adult for less than minimum wage. However, it was only after the 2011 ILO Convention C189—where members agreed that domestic work deserved protection like any other form of work (Pape, 2016)—that a *monthly* wage for domestic work in Kenya was set at Ksh 9,781 (approximately $89). In 2015, the government announced a 12% pay increase along with new guidelines and penalties for noncompliance for employers of house help. Including weekend time off, an 8-hour work day, an employer contribution to the retirement (NSSF) benefit of Ksh 200 per month, and a hospital insurance (NHIF) contribution of Ksh 400 per month, the wage was set at Ksh 10,945 ($100) per month for live-in employees and Ksh 11,345 ($103) for non-live-in employees, or approximately Ksh 527 per day (Njoroge, 2015, 15 July). This made house help pay equivalent to the predominantly male job domains of private security guards, commercial cleaners, and gardeners.

Wanyama (2015, 14 July) reported in a daily paper *The Star* on support for the proposed minimum wage by the Union of Domestic, Hotel, Educational Institutions, Hospitals and Allied Workers (KUDHEIHA), as well as domestic work training centers, hiring bureaus, and the house helps themselves, even as employers objected that they could not afford the raise. Since, in married households, women often have the responsibility for paying house help, this makes the minimum wage requirement subject to the husband's largesse. But even in dual income households, women tend to earn less. With the average pay for house help at only $50 per month, the proposed $100 minimum was out of reach. Moreover, employers realized that the government could not enforce punishments for those who failed to meet the requirements (i.e., three months of jail time, a Ksh 50,000 fine, or both) and therefore did not feel pressured to pay. Some declared they would simply resort to daycare if house help became unaffordable.

The government policy also did not specify how and how often payment should occur. Payments to house help are often irregular, staggered, and/or not paid directly to them. Some employers only pay out in a lump sum at the termination of employment; for house help supporting their families of origin or other guardians, their pay sometimes goes directly to those beneficiaries. In addition, employers will impose informal, *ad hoc* docking of pay for some damage or destroyed household item, for not performing work to the employer's satisfaction, or simply because they can. Being able to end the work contract at will also erodes job security. Just as house helps have been subjected to losses of income without any possible recourse, house helps have also walked away from jobs without warning leaving families struggling to meet their needs.

The government policy also has not specify how and how often payment should occur. Often, payments to house help are irregular, staggered, and/or not paid directly to them. Some employers only pay out in a lump sum at the termination of employment. For some house help supporting their families of origin or other guardians, their pay might go directly to those beneficiaries. All of this is subject, of course, to informal, *ad hoc* docking of pay by employers for some damage or destroyed household item, for not performing work to the employer's satisfaction, or simply because they can. Being able to end the work contract at will also erodes job security. Just as house helps have been subjected to losses of income without recourse, they have also walked away from jobs without warning, leaving families struggling to meet their needs.

Protecting the Rights of Women Migrant Domestic Workers

Historically, United Nation conventions have framed protections for migrant workers. Weissbrodt and Rhodes (2013), using a human rights perspective, have outlined and evaluated these conventions and the several United Nations bodies that monitor migrant workers in the Middle East. Such a human rights platform guides the creation of laws that member states are encouraged to ratify and adopt to direct national policy and practice. Each convention has a committee pledged with the duty to review country reports on their efforts to attain the rights stipulated in each convention and to then make recommendations, very frequently in light of newly. The Human Rights Convention of 1976, for instance, recognizes civil and political rights. Within that, the International Covenant on Civil and Political Rights (ICCPR) and the International Covenant on Economic, Social and Cultural Rights (ICESCR) emphasize protecting vulnerable groups such as women, children, migrants, persons with disabilities, and urgent situations needing attention such as torture and discrimination.

For migrant workers, the main committee on the convention from 2003 identifies a range of freedoms for leave, non-discrimination, not to be tortured or subjected to ill treatment, no slavery or forced labor, and to have the worker's conscience, opinion, and privacy recognized and respected. Other relevant committees for migrant domestic workers are include the Committee on Elimination of Racial Discrimination (CERD), Committee on the Elimination of Discrimination Against Women (CEDAW), and the Committee against Torture (CAT) of 1984. Despite this, only a few countries—the United States, the Philippines, Lebanon, Uruguay, Sri Lanka (D'Souza, 2010)—have enacted laws to protect migrant workers, but even these laws are poorly enforced leaving employers and employees alike vulnerable to abuse, although the latter still bear far more negative consequences.

The existing global legal framework of human rights to protect migrant workers does not typically articulate specific policy protections. This is partly because there are several players in both the sending and receiving countries that require oversight, but also because specifically *multi*-national employment itself often emerges as a way to avoid or circumvent *intra*-national employment policy-making. While typically more to the advantage of employers, who do not have to adhere to employment regulations because the domestic work is non-formal or occurs out of sight in private homes, it can play to the advantage of employees as well; people previously incarcerated, in some way stigmatized in their local setting, or other somehow unemployable at home can sometimes find work in such an international setting. The situational disadvantages do, however, preclude labor organizing or unionizing. Moreover, in the sending countries, recruiting bureaus and immigration processes control and tax the flow of people, while in receiving countries, the issuance of visas and work permits, and simply access to employers, remain largely out of the direct control of migrant workers. While it is a recognized right of the domestic worker to be protected from exploitation such as trafficking at these different nodes of bureaucratic control, little enforcement exists that workers be provided with clear expectations, with terms and conditions of employment, including benefits, from employers, and assurance of the protection of their rights by receiving countries.

Varia (2011) demonstrated that discrimination based on skin color goes unchecked in the Middle East. Social media discloses the cruel treatment, even murder, that domestic workers can experience there. The Domestic Workers Convention (DWC) of 2011 recognized and made recommendations to protect domestic workers: that domestic workers have a right to work and need social justice for fair globalization; that they contribute to the global economy by providing employment from those countries that have not created enough jobs; that they contribute to the economy of sending countries through remittances; that contribute to the general well-being receiving countries so that their populace lead lives they desire. Nonetheless, domestic workers remain undervalued. The DWC, thus, recommends parity for domestic workers regarding payment, payment schedule, benefits, and explicitly named working conditions. The DWC also specifically outlaws child labor, recommends a minimum age for work, and advocates that work should not interfere with education.

Countries vary in the way that they respond either autonomously or in light of UN conventions to the imperative of protecting migrant domestic workers. For example, according to Human Rights Watch (2015, 30 June), Qatar, the United Arab Emirates, and Oman exclude domestic workers from their labor laws; in contrast, Saudi Arabia, Bahrain, and Kuwait have policies that offer some protection to domestic workers. Specifically, the laws target recruiting bureaus, employers, and employees. Kuwait passed a bill in 2015 stating the conditions of employment for domestic workers, including: a weekly day off, 30 days paid annual leave, a 12-hour working day with rest, and end-of-service benefits. The law recommends replacing recruiting bureaus with public shareholding organizations and requires training to be offered in the sending country, rather than charging the workers to meet that cost. However, the visa sponsorship (khafala) requires the domestic worker not to transfer to another employer before the end of the contract, even in case of abuse, and frames and treats such a transfer as a crime by the worker. Similarly, Bahrain put laws in place in 2012 that mandate an annual vacation and mediation in disputes for domestic workers without offering any protections on working conditions and benefits, once again leaving domestic workers vulnerable to exploitation and abuse and providing no form of recourse. Saudi Arabia passed laws in 2013 that stipulated a 15-hour work day, one day weekly off, and one month of vacation after completing two years of service.

International advocates have also exposed the exploitation and abuse of migrant domestic workers in the Middle East and pressed for better enforcement and improvement of existing or the drafting of protection laws in the first place. These include groups like the International Labor Organization (ILO), the International Office of Migration (IOM), Human Rights Watch, and the Walk Free Foundation (WFF), among others. At one IOM meeting funded by the European Union and the Italian Ministry of Interior working to expose the conditions of migrant workers, out of 162 domestic worker victims, 100% had passports withheld, 87% were confined to their workplace, 76% had wages withheld, 73% experienced psychological torture, and 61% were physically abused(International Organization for Migration, 2015, 11 December).

Varia (2011) reports as well that the long history of Asian immigrants to the Middle East since the 1970s has led to some organizing by community-based groups, by incoming migrant workers and returnees, and by churches and civil societies that have agitated for legal protection or implementation of UN conventions, while also establishing services like hotlines, shelters, and legal representation for migrant workers who are in distress.

Migrant workers from Kenya are some of the latest arrivals in this region and might not benefit directly from the aforementioned organizations, but stand to benefit at least in principle from individual state policies that offer protection to domestic workers. The above suggests that the numbers of extent of such laws or policies in the Middle East is not very extensive.

As such, domestic workers from Kenya, faced with glaring income inequality, limited job opportunities, or working in the ill-regulated informal working sector at home, are thus "pushed" to risk the unchartered territories of the Middle East. In doing so, they leave a country largely without regulations to protect them as migrant workers in order to arrive at destinations that not only similarly lack in protective mechanisms in general but also have cultures of discrimination based on skin color.

On the face of it, local, Kenya, domestic workers appear to have more protection due both to the international UN treaties Kenya has either ratified or has served as a participant in the process of making recommendations for and to actual national policies written into the law. For example, Kenya ratified the UN convention against child labor but also had its own law to protect children from harsh labor. Similarly, Kenyan law, in principle, upholds the economic, civil, and social rights of domestic workers, however well or not those law functions, so that migrant workers to the Gulf are likely to emigrate to areas that have not ratified international UN treaties.

These differences, however, do not imply that local domestic workers are necessarily accorded their rights more often than international domestic workers in the Gulf. The predicament for both remains largely similar, albeit via different mechanisms. For instance, both the Gulf and Kenya are patriarchal,

Table 1. A comparison of united nation human rights treaties and convention locally (in kenya) and abroad (in the middle east)

Un Treaty or Convention	Rights	Local Domestic Workers (Kenya)	Migrant Domestic Workers (Middle East)
Human Rights Convention (HRC) (1976)	Freedom from abuse, arbitrary killing, torture, inhuman treatment, equal treatment before the law, minority right to enjoy culture	Employment Act: Minimum wages, benefits and terms of employment in 2012, but not enforced	Not ratified by some receiving countries. Exploited and abused
Convention on the Elimination of Discrimination against Women (1979)	No. 26 focus on rights of migrant workers protecting women from gender based differences and vulnerabilities	Employment Act: fair pay to females. Paid less than men and others engaged in work similar to domestic work. A fifth have experienced sexual abuse	Subjected to sexual abuse. Culture assumes non-native women are prostitutes and therefore subjected to sexual abuse
International Convention on Civil and Political Rights (ICCPR) 1966	Right to unionize	Limited representation in local unions like KUDHEIHA	Isolated
International Convention on Economic, Social and Cultural Rights (ICESCR)	Right to work in favorable conditions, freedom to join unions, access social security and have fair pay	General Wages Order 2009 sets minimum wage at Ksh. 10,954.70 from May 2015	Restricted from practicing religious rights other than Islam
International convention on the Protection of the Rights of All Migrant Workers and Members of their Families (CMW). 1990	Nondiscrimination, freedom to leave work, no torture, ill treatment, slavery, forced labor. Right to privacy, expression of opinion, religion and conscience	Domestic workers from neighboring countries do not have special protection	Only ratified in 47 countries
International Labor Organization C 189 (2011)	Defined domestic work and called for parity with other forms of labor such set minimum wages, benefits and conditions of labor	The Employment Act 2007 defines employee as "all employed for wages or salaries include apprentice and indentured learners"	Domestic work not included in labor laws. C189 not ratified
Committee on Elimination of Racial Discrimination (CERD)	Equal treatment in private and public	Ethnic chauvinism practiced, though most people employ individuals from the same ethnic group	The Gulf countries have a culture of racial discrimination based on skin color

so that women remain prone to discrimination and unfair treatment in the workplace. As such, although Gikuru (2013) found that migrant domestic workers in the Gulf did not view consider the demand for long hours of work to be abuse, they did consider physical and sexual violence as abuse. For Kenyan international workers, discrimination by race plays a role as abuse. Intersectionally, Kenyan women were often assumed to be prostitutes and are therefore made more vulnerable to sexual abuse. Some Kenyan domestic females were expected to provide sexual favors for males in the household (Gikuru, 2013).

Biko (2015, 6 October), of Kituo cha Sheria—a national NGO in Kenya whose goal is to advocate through education and pro bono representation of the marginalized to protect their rights at every level—outlined the challenges that domestic workers face as well as the laws designed to offer protection to workers at the individual and class-action level, and then analyzes how and why domestic workers remain short-changed in achieving full or adequate protection of their human rights. Importantly, while Kenyan domestic workers in principle have a civil rights to organize, form unions, or participate as one of the 40,000 members of KUDHEIHA—the national Kenyan union representing chefs, hotel workers and cleaners—only 5,000 female domestic workers are members. But even if the interests of domestic workers were not well-represented by greater membership in KUDHEIHA, this would not help international domestic workers, except to whatever extent individuals abroad could successful argue for and advocate for rights otherwise recognized in Kenya.

Biko (2015, 6 October) does not identify why or what mechanism makes KUDHEIHA unattractive for Kenyan domestic workers. A lack of education or a lack of access to information may play an exacerbating role, but it seems, again, that the sheer isolation of the domestic worker to the private sphere of the home is the most determining factor, as also for domestic workers abroad, who are further isolated by language and culture in the home.

As such, despite cultural differences, there is considerable overlap in the domestic workers situation both in Kenya and abroad. Gikuru's (2013) study, for instance, found that the working conditions of the domestic workers in the Gulf were typically left to the discretion of the employer, so that some were treated fairly while the majority were not. The working condition for local, Kenyan domestic workers have been similarly characterized (Biko, 2015, 6 October).

Ultimately, the location of the domestic worker, locally and abroad, in the space of the private home proves the most difficult issue. Located within the domain of the *private*, which is governed particularly by the principles (if not also protected by the laws regarding) property, this enables, if it does not actually enact, forms of treatment toward domestic workers as *property*. Intersectionally, where patriarchy construes women as the property of males, this then overlaps with racially or tribally chauvinistic discourses of slaves as property as well, whether this paradigm of slavery specifically reproduces the "western", trans-Atlantic form of racially explicit slavery or the more world-prevalent forms of tribally chauvinistic slavery that "rationalizes" the indentured servitude of one class of people to another, i.e., the discrimination noted by Gikuru (2013) in the Middle East. A further tension, then, results in that the "western" human rights paradigm itself assumes property as an essential holding for individuals; a tension well in place and, indeed, central to the founding project of the United States. Roediger (2008) points out how Thomas Jefferson's famous formulation *life, liberty, and the pursuit of happiness* in the preamble of the US Constitution is, in fact, a gloss and modification of John Locke's *life, liberty, and property*. As such, an approach to human rights that also values property places it in a contradictory position when advocating for the rights of people otherwise treated as property.

In general, a human rights paradigm does not advocate for the creation of new rights but demands, rather, that pre-existing rights be formally acknowledged and recognized, both socially and as a matter of law. Denial of such rights, then, involves a failure or a deliberate refusal to recognize them. Intersectionality particularly explains how this can occur; in this case, where discourses of women, servants, and property as less than fully human serve to obscure or deny otherwise inalienable human rights. At the intersection of both "woman" and "slave (or servant)", this double dehumanization already begins to marginalize and push the female domestic worker out of the formal world of work from the very beginning and illuminates how she would come to inhabit the non-formal work world—if this marginalization did not, in fact, play a major role in creating the non-formal work world in the first place.

Moreover, the intersection of "woman" and "slave (servant)" as "property" illuminates the treatment of domestic workers as little more than instruments to affect their employer's will: as literally the master's tools. Like a hammer, the domestic worker should be always at hand whenever the employer demands, without complaint (or at least no audible one), to function perfectly and without error (even when mishandled or misused), and to be thrown aside or thrown away once its utility is exhausted. And, of course, never to complain, to always just wait patiently, and, if anything, to express nothing but gratitude for being provided a toolbox to wait in. This intersectionality as a "tool" even illuminates resistance on the part of employers to fairly compensate domestic workers, no matter how much they ask them to do. One pays for a tool in advance (by purchasing it), and after that, the only acknowledged expense would be maintenance costs to repair any defects in the tool. Having already paid the recruiter, the intersectionality of "tool" predisposes them to view all subsequent expenses as unwarranted. Objections by employers to the Kenyan mandate to approximately double the pay of house helps is simply the equivalent of, "that's too expensive" mentality. Similarly, to pay a domestic worker only after the termination of the contract is like paying a rental fee for a machine only upon returning the machine to the lessor.

Of course, no human is literally a tool, and none of this speaks to the experience of being treated as one, except that a human rights approach keeps in the foreground the rights of all people to be treated with dignity. In general, intersectionality discloses in greater detail the predicament of the identity of domestic workers, both in how they experience that identity and how they are perceived by others in the world. It shows the challenges in trying to reach the non-formal places where the use of one's property is generally subject to no public scrutiny, and thus the challenges of a human rights approach to these workers. It suggests a reason why enforcement may be lackluster and why those hiring domestic workers so readily find reasons to avoid recognizing the human rights of domestic workers—since enforcement and recognition directly challenge the property right of "owners" to treat "servants" and other objects in whatever way they see fit. Without an intersection analysis to disclose how "female" and "servant" and "tool" and "property" converge, it becomes difficult, if not impossible, to untangle the situation of domestic workers, the social difficulties in implementing their protection, or offering solutions to these challenges moving into the future.

SOLUTIONS AND RECOMMENDATIONS

Even as the domestic rights of Kenyan workers are largely in the same risk status as domestic workers in the Gulf, the symbolic value of Kenyan protections in the law still has significance. Employers may find ways to circumvent the laws, but they at least know that they are trammeling the rights of human beings to do so. This may mean that they elaborate and contrive even more tortured justifications compared to their Gulf counterparts, but even those justifications themselves are more prone to exposure in the press and the public imagination when it is generally known that domestic workers have rights.

Since these intersectionalities illuminate how and why domestic workers are often denied their human rights, it remains prudent to empower them so that they can to fight for their rights. This may be formally initiated by local unions, such as KUDHEIHA, or NGOs that work with domestic workers by taking cues from the other countries with longer histories of sending domestic workers to the Middle East. One longer-term measure would include making education accessible for vulnerable populations, especially in rural areas. By increasing both enrollment and achievement, this would reduce the number of domestic workers who join the workforce ill-prepared to advocate for their rights. In terms of education, an in-all-likelihood more important objective would be to educate employers, recruiting bureaus, and other similar entities about the civil and economic rights of domestic workers. While enforcement remains a perennial problem, it could require very little money or effort to print a "Know Your Rights" pamphlet that recruiters and so forth must provide to employees and employers. And, because domestic workers may not always have literacy skills, this information can be presented by recruiters, etc., in audio-visual form. In general, the principle by this kind of education is to put people on notice, even as the implementation of Kenyan domestic worker rights in foreign countries remains a problem. Whether as advocacy or education, to know your rights, whether as a Kenyan domestic worker or as a domestic worker in general, might very well predispose you to assert those rights in a situation where an employer is contravening them, but it does not yet guarantee sufficient force to protect those rights. This, of course, is part of the logic of a union, which transforms the isolation of the individual into the force of a collective.

However, the low membership of domestic workers in KUDHEIHA suggests that in some way it does not ideally serve the interests of domestic workers, whether due to a lack of information, a lack of access or availability, or other factors. And, of course, such membership would at present have no binding force on employers in the Middle East in any case. An obvious proposal would be local unions by domestic workers, but there are many factors specific to foreign domestic labor that make this proposal difficult, if not untenable: the isolation of domestic workers, a multitude of different languages, the decentralized setting of domestic work, the turnover of any given domestic worker population who would otherwise agitate for unionization, and, of course, the ominous history of violence directed against unionizing, which becomes more threatening still given the intersectional identity of the generally female domestic worker.

An alternative to this kind of formal organizing in situ, however, is already visible in social networking. Social networking has been used to publicize "horror" stories, by employees and employers of domestic labor alike. For domestic workers, who are distributed "invisibly" throughout the social body of the places they inhabit, their common meeting space can become the virtual site on social media. Not simply to place horror stories before the court of public opinion, but also specifically to argue for and assert the rights of domestic workers, along with assurances of solidarity amongst them, at the very least works against the disempowering isolation that domestic workers face in general. Moreover, the reach of this "space" and solidarity remains international; the Kenyan rights of domestic workers can be professed in Middle Eastern countries where they otherwise have no standing. To what extent any such campaign can prevail against existing discrimination and abuse may, ultimately, be less important than its effect on the mental quality of life for domestic workers abroad. With 73% reporting psychological torture, access to supportive voices, who at a minimum confirm that the abuse is not only unwarranted but a violation of their human rights, not only recommends itself but also draws on trends already being utilized by domestic workers.

Lastly, given that social networking represents a kind of peer-to-peer support network, it may be possible as well to organize physical peer-to-peer support, actual meetings. The logistical difficulties of this remain enormous, but this alone need not rule out the possibility of informal support group meetings by domestic workers abroad as a (politically innocuous) middle ground between active unionizing efforts and remaining utterly isolated and left only to one's devices. Such a proposal, again, is for the sake of the quality of life that domestic workers experience abroad, even if such meetings only have two or three people.

Since the majority of the domestic workers migrants are women who come from one patriarchal nation to another and therefore are socialized to perform submissiveness, they require all hands on deck. They need legal protection, social services, a recognition of their right to association, along with advocacy and policies to govern the process of migrating and working to earn a living. Sending countries require laws to specify how recruiters must inform a recruit of what is required and what is expected of them, and above all that they deserve being treated with dignity and being allowed to make informed decisions about their lives as a matter of human rights. Following the C189 recommendations by ILO, recruiting agents should have confirmed and clear information on minimum wages, working hours, overtime, rent, social security, maternity leave, and special protection laws of the land, along with any other relevant social factors not otherwise addressed by C189. Similarly, receiving agents in destination countries should have contracts that include full contact information of the employer, the method of payment and calculations, benefits, food, accommodation, specifics of work, and any other relevant details. This further requires mechanisms for enforcement, and or international agreements between Kenya and receiving countries to uphold these contracts.

Of course, this formalization can only affect some percentage of the total non-formal domestic labor population. Moreover, a rigorously determined protocol for sending and receiving entities in Kenya and abroad not only does not, of course, guarantee compliance or prevent corrupt efforts to circumvent regulations but also does not reach all of the more informal domestic workers who do not go through these official channels. Also, it creates two classes of domestic workers: those who have the benefits of formal protection, while allowing those without to slip through the cracks. All the more so since a historical risk in establishing procedural protocols is the creation of a black market. And since domestic work is, in many respect, already non-formally as something of a black market anyway, the policy approach taken up should not move forward in ignorance of this.

At a minimum, the "symbolic" value of a top-down framing of domestic workers' rights is to set the framework of discussion. To resolutely declare that all domestic workers have certain inalienable rights, however well or poorly mechanisms designed to ensure those rights operate, when the discourse is set in this way, people who would abuse those rights have less leeway to operate freely. This signal from "on high," as well, can in potential reach the ears and hearts of even the most marginalized domestic, offering the possibility of a cognitive quality of life improvement if nothing else. Further efforts, from the top and bottom alike, would then connect that resolute assertion to actual circumstances in situ, seeking means like unionization, peer-to-peer support groups, or social networking to improve the condition and lessen the abuses of domestic workers abroad.

Since there is limited data on this population, research on how each entity involved would not only specifically shape policy but also influence practice as well remains to be done. For example, the Kenyan government does not yet have comprehensive data on migrants (International Organization for Migration, 2015). Similarly, the role and current form of recruiting bureaus need to be evaluated to isolate best practices. Returnees from domestic labor abroad as well are potentially useful sources of information for researchers to tap into, all the more so since, having "escaped" or "survived" abroad, their stories relevantly illuminate issues named in this chapter.

To proceed with this work, however, seems to demand a recognition of the intersectionality involved. To address the matter only in a legal framework, for example, not only risks missing the black market or even more informalized domestic labor that might result, it also fails to address the underlying attitude—the second-class citizenship of "women" or "servants" or "tools"—that motivate procedural corruption and the necessity of human rights laws in the first place. As such, exploring domestic work from a feminist and migration theory standpoint as described in the next section of this chapter better illuminates an understanding of the issues and lays an improved groundwork for building alliances between governments, human rights advocates, those who benefit in the trafficking of domestic laborers, and domestic laborers themselves.

FUTURE RESEARCH DIRECTIONS

Scholars of global care have long identified the lacunas in research and theory in this area of study. Parreñas (2005) remarked that there has been a repertoire of scholarly work around paid reproductive labor and the articulation of a global division of reproductive labor. This literature has been particularly strong in first theorizing the increasing presence of women in international migration flows, a fact captured in the concept of the "feminization of international migration" (Chammartin, 2002; Morrison, Schiff, & Sjöblom, 2007; Zlotnik, 2005). Second, this literature has also been rather strong in theorizing women's paid reproductive labor, especially as domestic workers and nannies (Hochschild, 2000; Hondagneu-Sotelo, 1997; Parreñas, 2005). Noting the location of immigrant women in the provision of both skilled care work (health, education, religion) and unskilled (domestic work, nannies, sex workers), Yeates (2005) argues for an extension of the theoretical framework of the "global care chain" (Hochschild, 2000), which describes that series of personal links that tie women in poor countries with women in wealthy ones through the commodification of their labor (Hochschild, 2000). One area of future research, then, involves research to understand the effects of the "global care chain" in Kenya.

A systematic gendered approach to migration is important in order to bring to the fore the various forces, whether economic or non-economic, that lead to migration. In *West African Women Immigrants in the United States*, Arthur (2009) explores multiple various realities that influence women's migration, observing that economic factors (poverty, low standards of living) and cultural factors (patriarchal dominance, gendered restrictions of property ownership) are equally critical for thinking about the cheap and abundant supply of women workers. Arthur (2009) notes especially how internal migration in the subregion is important for how it can link to international migration.

Studies focusing on Kenyan house helps, locally or internationally, are few. Generally, anecdotal data on international house helps in Kenya focuses on how they are treated, especially when hurt or killed. Research in Kenya has discussed maids in their ethnic, age, class, gender and rural-urban dimensions, but not much is known about how racial, language, and religious dimensions are contested, locally or internationally. Identity formation as well is important, because it indicates how migrant workers compose transnational identities. Studies along these lines would begin to capture the contributions of Africans in the Gulf away outside of seeing them only as house helps.

Future studies as well could investigate how these women engage politically both in the Arab world and in Kenya, especially in how they raise political consciousness around their lived experiences. The use of platforms like Facebook to engage with those at home represents a key site of this. Studies are also warranted simply to investigate the lived experiences of these women as house helps and as returnees, not simply for the interest in itself but also for how it illuminates intersectional identities in non-formal work generally. To look at the lives of domestic worker returnees especially on how they prepare to return can better inform policymaking for all relevant entities and provide input to planning directives. In so doing the needed assistance can be identified in order to help domestic workers resettle quickly and begin engaging in other activities.

CONCLUSION

The colonial British introduced paid domestic work in Kenya as a lower-class form of employment that became feminized under a patriarchal framework with the onset of political independence and self-governance.

In general, domestic workers come from poor families and have limited education. Those who migrate to the Gulf are relatively more experienced at working in the non-formal sector in Kenya, and show greater demographic diversity. That is, short of illegal immigration, a greater variety and range of resources will more often successfully enable access to international domestic employment, and this manifests as greater demographic diversity in migrant domestic labor.

Although Kenya has several protections provided through policies and ratification of UN conventions, domestic workers in Kenya remain vulnerable to rights violations; those in the Gulf are on average even worse off. Fewer ratified UN conventions, a lack of or poorer domestic worker protection laws, and cultural prejudices dark skin and single females worsen the Gulf setting for domestic workers.

In every sector, especially around recruitment in sending and receiving countries, stricter laws to eliminate the fraudulent or needlessly fee-ridden procedures they adopt to scam domestic workers and employers alike are urgently needed. Employers and house helps alike would benefit from being made aware of their rights.

More conscientious enforcement of existing, and any new, protection laws is in order, but this should come as well with efforts to support existing resources for domestic workers such as social networking, and potentially new ones like, peer-to-peer groups.

In general, it would be a disservice to local domestic workers in Kenya if the United Nations, the Kenyan government, and human rights NGOs address the conditions of migrant domestic workers in the Gulf while leaving them out. The destiny of the two groups should be viewed intersectionally through the same lens, as different sides of the same coin, if for no other reason than to avoid the eventuality of Gulf nations becoming nationalistic when faced with a "foreign" (Kenya) threat of migrant labor.

REFERENCES

Arthur, J. A. (2009). *African women immigrants in the United States: crossing transnational borders.* New York: Palgrave Macmillan. doi:10.1057/9780230623910

Baldwin-Edwards, M. (2005). *Migration in the Middle East and the Mediterranean.* Geneva: Global Commission on International Migration.

Biko, A. (2015, 6 October). *Access to justice for Kenyan domestic workers.* Retrieved from https://kituochasheria.wordpress.com/2015/10/06/access-to-justice-for-kenyan-domestic-workers/

Chammartin, G. (2002). The feminization of international migration. International Migration Programme: International Labour Organization, 37-40.

Crenshaw, K. (1991). Mapping the margins: Intersectionality, identity politics, and violence against women of color. *Stanford Law Review, 43*(6), 1241–1299. doi:10.2307/1229039

D'Souza, A. (2010). *Moving towards decent work for domestic workers: an overview of the ILO's work.* Geneva: ILO.

Demetriou, D. (2015). 'Tied Visas' and Inadequate Labour Protections: A formula for abuse and exploitation of migrant domestic workers in the United Kingdom. *Anti-Trafficking Review, 5*(2015).

Fernandez, B. (2010). Cheap and disposable? The impact of the global economic crisis on the migration of Ethiopian women domestic workers to the Gulf. *Gender and Development, 18*(2), 249–262. doi:10.1080/13552074.2010.491335

Fleury, A. (2016). *Understanding Women and Migration: A Literature Review.* Academic Press.

Gikuru, C. M. (2013). *The Plight of Kenyan Domestic Workers in Gulf Countries.* San Francisco, CA: University of San Francisco.

Hochschild, A. R. (2000). Global care chains and emotional surplus value. In A. Giddens & W. Hutton (Eds.), *On the edge: living with global capitalism* (pp. 130–146). London: Jonathan Cape.

Hondagneu-Sotelo, P. (1997). Affluent players in the informal economy: Employers of paid domestic workers. *The International Journal of Sociology and Social Policy, 17*(3/4), 130–158. doi:10.1108/eb013303

ILO. (1990). International standard classification of occupations: ISCO 88. Geneva: ILO.

ILO. (2011). *Decent work for domestic workers: Convention 189 and Recommendation 201 at a glance.* Geneva: ILO.

ILO. (2013). *Domestic workers across the world: Global and regional statistics and the extent of legal protection.* International Labour Office Geneva.

International Organization for Migration. (2015). *Migration in Kenya: A country in profile.* Nairobi: International Organization for Migration.

International Organization for Migration. (2015, December 11). *Migrant workers suffer exploitation, abuse in Middle East, North Africa: Report*. Retrieved from https://www.iom.int/news/migrant-workers-suffer-exploitation-abuse-middle-east-north-africa-report

Morrison, A. R., Schiff, M. W., & Sjöblom, M. (2007). *The international migration of women*. World Bank Publications.

Namuggala, V. F. (2015). Exploitation of empowerment? Adolescent female domestic workers in Uganda. *International Journal of Child, Youth, and Family Studies*, 6(4), 561–580. doi:10.18357/ijcyfs.64201514288

Njoroge, K. (2015, July 15). Regulations lift pay of househelps to Sh10, 954. *Business Daily, Politics and Policy*. Retrieved from http://www.businessdailyafrica.com/Regulations-lift-pay-of-househelps-to-Sh10-954-/-/539546/2776084/-/178v6nz/-/index.html

Ondimu, K. N. (2007). Workplace violence among domestic workers in urban households in Kenya: A case of Nairobi city. *Eastern Africa Social Science Research Review*, 23(1), 37–61. doi:10.1353/eas.2007.0005

Pape, K. (2016). ILO Convention C189—a good start for the protection of domestic workers: An insiders view. *Progress in Development Studies*, 16(2), 189–202. doi:10.1177/1464993415623151

Parreñas, R. S. (2005). *Children of global migration: transnational families and gendered woes*. Stanford, CA: Stanford University Press.

Roediger, D. (2008). *How Race Survived US History*. New York: Verso.

Sobania, N. W. (2003). *Culture and customs of Kenya*. Westport, CT: Greenwood Press.

Varia, N. (2011). Sweeping changes? A review of recent reforms on protections for migrant domestic workers in Asia and the Middle East. *Canadian Journal of Women and the Law*, 23(1), 265–287. doi:10.3138/cjwl.23.1.265

Wanyama, M. (2015, July 14). To pay or not to pay your house help Sh11,000?. *The Star*. Retrieved from http://www.the-star.co.ke/news/2015/07/14/to-pay-or-not-to-pay-your-house-help-sh11000_c1168337

Watch, H. R. (2015, June 30). Kuwait: New Law a Breakthrough for Domestic Workers: Guarantees Crucial Rights, but Gaps Remain. *Human Rights Watch*. Retrieved from https://www.hrw.org/news/2015/06/30/kuwait-new-law-breakthrough-domestic-workers

Weissbrodt, D., & Rhodes, J. (2013). United Nations Treaty Body Monitoring of Migrant Workers in the Middle East. *Middle EL & Governance*, 5(1-2), 71–111. doi:10.1163/18763375-00501003

White, L. (2009). *The Comforts of Home Prostitution in Colonial Nairobi*. Retrieved from http://www.myilibrary.com?id=207026

Yeates, N. (2005). A global political economy of care. *Social Policy and Society*, 4(2), 227–234. doi:10.1017/S1474746404002350

Zlotnik, H. (2005). International migration trends since 1980. *International Migration and the Millennium Development Goals*, 13.

KEY TERMS AND DEFINITIONS

Domestic Work: Menial tasks such as cleaning, ironing and cooking that is carried out by domestic workers, maids and cleaners.

The Gulf Countries: These are seven countries which border the Persian Gulf namely Kuwait, Bahrain, Iraq, Oman, Qatar, Saudi Arabia and the United Arab Emirates.

Intersectionality: Scholar Kimberlé Williams Crenshaw definition of the superimposing and relatedness of social identities, privileges and oppression.

Kenya: An East African country known for its runners boarded by Uganda, Ethiopia, Southern Sudan, Somali, Tanzania and the Indian Ocean.

Khafala: The practice of Middle Eastern employers to sponsor foreign workers that leads to binding employees to employers. The Khafala system has been criticized for its slave-like conditions.

Middle East: These are mostly Arab speaking nations including Israel, Turkey and Cyprus. In this chapter Middle East implies Saudia Arabia, Kuwait, Yemen, Oman, Bahrain, Qatar, United Arab Emirates and Lebanon.

Migrant: A person who moves to live in another country to seek a better life, work or security.

Recruiting Bureaus: Also known as *agents* these are middlemen who find job, passports, airfare, and provide information for domestic workers while linking them to families in the Middle East.

Returnees: A domestic worker who returns home to settle after working in another country for a longtime.

Chapter 2
Patriarchy and (Un)Doing Factory of Women's Collective Identity in Sri Lanka's Localised Global Apparel Industry:
The Glass Ceiling Revisited

Dhammika Jayawardena
University of Sri Jayewardenepura, Sri Lanka

ABSTRACT

Systemic manifestations of women's subordination, such as the glass ceiling, are still a reality in organisations. Yet, the glass ceiling effect in the Global South is often conceptualised vis-à-vis (white) women's experience in 'gendered organisations' and women's domestic role in the Southern societies. In this context, this chapter, based on a fieldwork research conducted in Sri Lanka's apparel industry, critically examines the glass ceiling effect of glass ceiling on women's career advancement in the Global South. Alongside the notion of 'universal' patriarchy, it problematises the 'universal' structure of the glass ceiling. And it shows that (un)doing factory women's collective identity—as lamai (little ones)—and the glass ceiling intermingle in the process of women's subordination in the apparel industry. The chapter concludes that, in the apparel industry, the role of managerial women —as well as of men in (un)doing factory women's collective identity—is crucial in keeping the glass ceiling in place.

INTRODUCTION

Despite some 'success' stories of (managerial) women, systematic manifestations of women's subordination, such as the 'glass ceiling' or 'sticky floor'—and their effect— are still a reality for women in the Global South (Kiaye & Singh, 2013; Ahmed & Maitra, 2015; Duraisamy & Duraisamy, 2016). The shift of the global assembly line from the North to the South— the 'first global shift,' which took place in the 1970s and 1980s as part of neoliberalisation of the global political economy (Harvey, 2005;

DOI: 10.4018/978-1-5225-3018-3.ch002

Dicken, 2007) —had created job opportunities for (rural young) women in the South Asian region. As a result, during the 1970s and 1980s 'traditionally' unemployed (rural young) women in the region had become 'productive labourers,' mostly in the labour-intensive global apparel industry (Jayaweera, 2002; Khosla, 2009; Jayawardena, 2014).

Even in 'feminised' industries like global apparel industry— such as we see in the case of Sri Lanka's apparel industry, where 80 per cent of employees are (rural young) women— women remain a 'subordinated group' (Jayawardena, 2014): In fact, nearly all 'top-rung,' skilled jobs (on the shop floor) in the apparel industry (*viz.*, factory managers, operations managers, and production executives) are occupied by men. On the contrary, 'low-rung,' unskilled jobs, such as the machine operators/seamstresses, quality checkers, and helpers, remain 'feminine jobs' (Jayawardena, 2010; Hancock et al., 2015). Therefore, as far as the subordination of women in the Global South is concerned, the case of Sri Lanka's apparel industry is significant. Despite the role of the industry as the largest export income generator and one of the major job providers in Sri Lanka (Kelegama, 2005; Jayawardena, 2010; Central Bank of Sri Lanka, 2016), since its emergence in the late 1970s, the apparel industry has been characterised by gender segregated jobs. Yet, the gendered job segregation and women's subordination in the industry cannot be viewed as mere organisational or industrial phenomena. In other words, the policies of the industry alone cannot be accused of 'keeping women down,' particularly on the shop floor of the industry. Rather, the job segregation and subordination are not only imbued with (un)doing factory women's collective identity —as *lamai* (broadly meaning 'little ones') —in the industry. They are also embedded with many adverse socio-organisational forces and processes, such as sexual harassment, unattainable production targets and inhumane punishments at work in the industry, and gender prejudices in wider Sri Lankan society (Devanarayana, 1997; Hewamanne, 2008; Jayawardena, 2010, 2014, 2015; Hancock et al., 2015). Thus, these forces and processes, coupled with (un)doing factory women's collective identity, tend to keep women as a subordinated group in the apparel industry and thereby, hinder their career development (Jayawardena, 2014, 2015).

Despite this complex nature of the subordination of (factory) women in the apparel industries of global south, the literature on the subject often highlights the patriarchal character in corporate culture (David & Woodward, 1998; Hughes, 2002), and in South Asian societies as the main reason for the glass ceiling—and its effect— in the Global South (Bal, 2004; Agrawal, 2013; Kiaye & Singh, 2013; Ahmed & Maitra, 2015; Duraisamy & Duraisamy, 2016). Yet, as some scholars argue, the glass ceiling in the Global South is not an exclusive product of the patriarchy or corporate men (Luke, 1998). Further, the literature shows the historically embedded nature of the patriarchal social relations in the South (Spivak, 1988; Mohanty, 1991; Jayawardena, 2000). Therefore, it is doubtful whether the notion of 'universal' patriarchy, which explains power relations in which women's interests are subordinated to the interests of men (Weedon, 1987), facilitates to understand the subordination of women —in the global apparel industry— in the South. In this context, women's domestic chores and family commitments, which are firmly embedded in the patriarchal social relations in the Southern societies, appear as the main causes that tend to keep the glass ceiling in place in the Global South organisations (Bal, 2004; Kargwell, 2008; Jain & Mukherji, 2010; Kiaye & Singh, 2013). Nevertheless, it is doubtful whether the domestic chores and family commitments of women are crucial in keeping (factory) women down in the global apparel industry as the majority of these women — such as we see in the apparel industry of Sri Lanka—are young and unmarried (Jayaweera, 2002; Hancock et al., 2015).

With this background, based on a fieldwork research conducted in the apparel industry of Sri Lanka, this chapter seeks to reframe the glass ceiling —and its effect — in the global apparel industry in the

South. For this, alongside the notion of universal patriarchy, it revisits and problematises the 'uniform' or 'universal' structure of the glass ceiling. Simultaneously, the chapter critically examines the role of (managerial) women in keeping the glass ceiling in place in the apparel industry. In doing so, it shows that (un)doing factory women's collective identity — as *lamai*— and the glass ceiling intermingle in the process of the subordination of (factory) women in the industry. Thereby, the chapter provides 'new' insight into the glass ceiling effect on women in the global apparel industry in the South.

The chapter is organised as follows. First, alongside the notion of (universal) patriarchy, it critically examines the glass ceiling —and its effect— in the Global South organisations. Second, the chapter creates a 'genealogical account' of Sri Lanka's localised global apparel industry and shows how factory women's collective identity —as *lamai* — is done (and undone) by the various actors in the industry and wider society. Simultaneously, it explains the fieldwork research conducted in the apparel industry. Third, based on the findings of the research, the chapter critically analyses the glass ceiling effect on (factory) women in relation to (un)doing their collective identity. Here, it dissects the role of (managerial) women in keeping the glass ceiling in place in the industry. Finally, the chapter concludes that the glass ceiling in the apparel industry of Sri Lanka is a multifaceted phenomenon where the patriarchal social relations regarding women's collective identity in the industry come into play.

Patriarchy and the Glass Ceiling

The notion of the glass ceiling, which has been coined almost forty years ago in the United States (Beck & Davis, 2005), is still used to metaphorise the 'invisible' barriers that hinder women's advancement in organisations (Agrawal, 2013; Kiaye & Singh, 2013; Ezzedeen et al., 2015; Tandrayen-Ragoobur & Pydayya, 2015; Duraisamy & Duraisamy, 2016). Despite the 'cracks' of the glass ceiling (Ryan & Haslam, 2005), and some 'success' stories of corporate women (Beck & Davis, 2005; Sharif, 2015), the glass ceiling —and its effect— remains an ethico-political issue in contemporary organisations (Gatrell & Cooper, 2007; Powell & Butterfield, 2015): It not only prevents women reaching to the top of their career ladder, but also leads to premature retirement of (managerial) women having experienced that they have almost never moved the glass ceiling (Itzin, 1995; Arfken et al., 2004; Maume, 2004; Bihagen & Ohls, 2006; Pompper, 2011).

In this context, the glass ceiling appears as an invisible barrier which is imbued with patriarchy — societal or institutional— and gendered norms in organisations (Weedon, 1987): Indeed, in (gendered) organisations, work roles are defined vis-à-vis gender, leading to direct discrimination and stereotyping of women (David & Woodward, 1998; Luke, 1998; Hughes, 2002; Terjesen & Singh, 2008). Hence, likewise the notion of (universal) patriarchy or patriarchal power, the metaphor of the glass ceiling— theoretically as well as empirically— is largely based on white women's experience in the Global North; here it is assumed that there is a universal structure of the metaphor. However, when reviewing the literature on the glass ceiling in the Global South, it is questionable whether the experiences of (managerial) women in the Global North manifest women's everyday realities in the Global South.

The Glass Ceiling Effect in the Global South

The literature shows that the glass ceiling effect in the Global South countries (in Asia, Africa, and South America) are embedded in socio-cultural and historico-political evolution of the South. Hence, the Southern women's experience in (and response to) the glass ceiling differs from that of their sisters in the Global North (Luke, 1998; Nath, 2000; Li & Leung, 2001; Omar & Davidson, 2001; Bal, 2004; Yukongdi & Benson, 2005; Kiaye & Singh, 2013; Brumley, 2014; Duraisamy & Duraisamy, 2016). Unlike the Global North women in the global south are still supposed to play the central role in the family. This family-centred social structure and culture often hinders the progression in women's career path in the Global South. For example, Li and Leung (2001) point out that the subordination of female managers in the Asian hotel industry is mostly determined not by corporate practices or policies, but by cultural and societal sanctions. Likewise, Kang and Rowley (2005) show how female employees in South Korea are victimised by the Confucian tradition and domestic responsibilities. As they point out, family and socio-cultural 'burden' compels South Korean women either to give up their jobs to childbirth and care or to choose temporary jobs. If these options are not possible they have to give up or postpone their marriage and childbirth (Kang & Rowley, 2005). Similar findings are reported by Chou et al. (2005) in their exploratory study on Taiwanese female managers. As they show, work-family conflict and Taiwanese cultural values often block the career path progress of Taiwanese female managers.

With this background, reflecting on the patriarchal culture of Indian society, Bal (2004) also shows that family commitments of women scientists in biology hinder their career prospects. As she points out, 'with family responsibilities being culturally their burden, it becomes difficult for women faculty to spend long hours at work. In fact, this issue affects the ability of women both to find and keep faculty positions' (2004, p. 3653). Likewise, Kiaye and Singh (2013) show that, in the South African work context, married women create their 'own' barriers to career advancement. Here the authors highlight gender discrimination and men's domination in the South African organisations and show how women's family commitments hinder their career growth. Similar findings can be seen in research carried out in many other countries in the Global South (for example, Kargwell, 2008; Jain & Mukherji, 2010). In addition, the literature also shows that women's managerial culture in the Global South tends to 'keep women down' in the work settings. For example, according to Luke (1998, p. 247) the systematic manifestations of women's subordination, such as the glass ceiling, in Singapore education sector is also about ''other women' who 'keep women down'.' Hence, she argues that 'It is not only men... who collude 'to keep women down', who downgrade women or take credit for their ideas and work. Career impediments are enacted intergenerationally by women and men' (1998, p. 261).

In this context, we see that not only the glass ceiling effect is imbued with patriarchal social relations in the Global South societies, but also women's domestic chores and family commitments are crucial in keeping the glass ceiling in place in organisations in the Global South. Yet, it is questionable whether the subordination of women in the Global South can be viewed as a 'sole act of a closed male elite' in organisations or 'exclusively men's work' — just like in the Global North (David & Woodward, 1998; Hughes, 2002). Therefore, I argue that, as far as women's subordinations in the Global South are concerned, the uniform or universal structure of the glass ceiling is problematic, although there are similarities among women's subordinations in the Global North and South. Further, I suggest that, to reframe the glass ceiling in the Global South organisations, we need to revisit the role of (managerial) women —in keeping women down— in work settings.

Yet, except a few works, women's role in keeping women down (or in keeping the glass ceiling in place), in the Global South still remains an under-researched area. This lack in the literature induces us to view the glass ceiling in the Global South —likewise in the Global North — as an invisible barrier which is operated through a closed male elite in organisations (David & Woodward, 1998; Hughes, 2002; Gatrell & Cooper, 2007). Nevertheless, as we have seen, women's subordination in the Global South organisations is a result of the complex history of the Southern societies. Further, it has been intensified by the relocation of the global assembly line in the South in the late 1970 and early 1980s which subsequently resulted in an influx of unmarried young women into the assembly line (Jayaweera, 2002; Hewamanne. 2008; Khosla, 2009; Jayawardena, 2014). Thus, as we will see in the following sections, reframing (invisible) barriers like the glass ceiling in the Global South organisations has become a complex process.

Factory Women and the Apparel Industry of Sri Lanka

In the latter part of the 1970s newly elected Government of United National Party (UNP) opened up the economy of Sri Lanka (Wignaraja, 1998). The 'open economic policy,' or economic liberalisation, was probably the 'logical' response to gain advantages from the first global shift and the emerging neoliberal trends in the global political economy during this period (Harvey, 2005; Dicken, 2007). As part of the open economic policy, in 1978 the Government of UNP established the first Free Trade Zone (FTZ) of the country in Katunayake— 26 kilometres from Colombo and close proximity to Sri Lanka's only international airport (at that time) — under the 1978 Greater Colombo Economic Commission Act No. 4. The FTZ created a socio-economic space for global investors and their local partners to (re)locate factories in this exclusive economic zone equipped with attractive tax benefits, sophisticated infrastructure facilities, and relaxed labour laws (Perera, 2008; Jayawardena, 2014).

In this context, the apparel industry of Sri Lanka emerged as the key player in the zone and the nascent liberal economy. Soon after its establishment, the industry had become the largest contributor to the country's export income. Further, since the early 1980s, it has become one of the major job providers in Sri Lankan economy (Kelegama, 2005; Central Bank of Sri Lanka, 2016). In fact, the industry absorbed young peasant women— who migrated to the zone—into its labour-intensive shop floor. This trend not only created an influx of unemployed young peasant women into the FTZ from the late 1970s to early 1980s, but also made them 'productive' labourers in the global apparel industry (Devanarayana, 1997; Jayaweera, 2002).

Feminisation and the Status of Factory Women in the Apparel Industry of Sri Lanka

The influx of women into the zone and the apparel industry was hardly welcome by the actors in the zone area and wider society, such as the inhabitants of the zone area, (traditional) trade unions, opposition and left-wing political parties, media and social critics (Devanarayana, 1997; Lynch, 2002; Jayawardena, 2014, 2015). As a result, the influx of young (peasant) women into the zone was portrayed as a sign of the collapse of moral standards of 'innocent' peasant women (see, for example, Sunday Island, 1991). Also, the role of factory women in the apparel industry was treated as an unskilled, ancillary and perhaps vulgar work: In some instances, it was described with the phrase *suddiyanta jangi mahanawa* (sewing underwear for white women), which denotes both sexual and dirty (Lynch, 2002).

Likewise, neither the Government nor the factory owners provided needed facilities, such as lodgings, healthcare, and transportation, for the migrant women to settle in the zone area. As a result, women were subject to many adverse socio-organisational forces and processes. In the zone environment they had to cope with poor lodgings, sanitary, healthcare and transport facilities mostly provided by the inhabitants of the zone area. For example, most of the lodgings were insecure and unhygienic congested places which were also made out of abandoned hen houses and pig-stays in the zone area (Sunday Island,

1991; Devanarayana, 1997). Likewise, women were often subject to marginalisation and harassment by the inhabitants. For examples, landlords of the lodgings and owners of small shops, where migrant women shopped, charged unfairly for goods and services they provided. On their way to the lodgings and factories, women were often verbally abused with degrading nicknames, such as juki *lamai*, juki *kello* (juki girls)[1], and garment *lamai* or *kello* (garment girls). Further, sexual assault was also reported in the zone area (Devanarayana, 1997; Lynch, 2002; Hewamanne, 2003; Jayawardena, 2014). During this period women's work-life was not different from their social life. Indeed, in work settings, they were subject to unattainable targets, compulsory overtime work, and verbal abuses by the factory supervisors and managers. Sexual harassment and physical punishments were also reported in the factory context (Devanarayana, 1997; Samanmali, 2007; Jayawardena, 2014).

Thus, the influx of women into the zone and, consequently, the 'feminisation' of the apparel industry hardly changed factory women's status as young (peasant) women, although they got opportunities to 'escape' from parental control, and to be financially independent: In wider society as well as in the industry, they were (and are) treated as *lamai* (little ones) — the patronising term which signifies women's collective identity in the industry (Jayawardena, 2014, 2015). Indeed, along with the *lamai* identity, young peasant women have become productive labourers on the labour-intensive shop floor of the industry which has been dominated by men since its emergence in the late 1970s. In fact, top-rung, skilled jobs on the shop floor of the industry, such as factory manager, production manager, production executives, and quality controller/quality assurance executives, are predominantly held by men. On the contrary, low-rung unskilled shop floor jobs (*viz.*, machine operators, quality checkers, and helpers) are treated as typical 'female jobs.' Further, 'smart' men on the shop floor get better opportunity —than their female colleagues —to climb the career ladder, although women remain the majority of the industry and its shop floor (Jayawardena, 2010, 2014; Hancock et al., 2015). Therefore, prevailing gendered norms and job segregation of the apparel industry of Sri Lanka makes the glass ceiling (or sticky floor) a reality for (factory) women in the industry.

Fieldwork and Generating Data

Aligned with this complex nature of the industry and its social actors, I conducted fieldwork of the study in the FTZ and outside it, mostly in two apparel manufacturing companies— ChillCo and HotCo (pseudonyms). ChillCo is situated in a small village 30 kilometres from Colombo, and HotCo is in the FTZ.

Managers and other workers of the companies have become the key participants of the fieldwork. They included the General Manager (GM) and the Human Resource Manager (HR Manager) of both companies, and the Factory Manager (FM), the Assistant Human Resource Manager (Asst. HR Manager), the Floor Manager and a Human Resource Executive in HotCo, and the Operations Manager (OM), and Counsellor of ChillCo. Further, the participants comprised a few shop floor workers, supervisors and production assistants in both companies, and the matron of a boarding-house operated by HotCo. In addition, I conducted interviews with a few social actors in the zone area, such as landlords of lodgings, owners of small shops, and trade union and feminist activists (Jayawardena, 2010, 2014).

Unstructured and semi-structured interviews were the main methods of gathering and generating data. During the interviews, I encouraged the participants to narrate their 'own stories' in relation to managing factory women and (un)doing their collective identity —as *lamai*— in the apparel industry. Here, I asked some situational and follow up questions (Mason, 2002; Bryman & Bell, 2011). Except for my interviews with a few shop floor workers, all other interviews were digitally recorded with the consent of the participants. Observation method— mostly non-participatory— was also used to generate data (Bryman & Bell, 2011), especially in 'socio-spatial arrangements' of the companies, such as shop floor, Joint Consultative Committee —the industrial relations encounter of the zone proposed under the Greater Colombo Economic Commission Act—and cafeterias. Moreover, I participated in one of the regular visits carried out by HotCo's HR staff to the lodgings of absent shop floor workers. During the visit, I observed that the company staff, workers, and social actors in the zone area intermingle in the process of managing shop floor labour and in relation to (un)doing the *lamai* identity (Jayawardena, 2014, p. 291). In addition, during fieldwork, I gathered some secondary data, for example, company prospectus, employee handbooks, and tabloids and newsletters published by trade unions and feminist activists in the zone area. These secondary data also embody (managing) factory women and (un)doing their collective identity in the industry (Jayawardena, 2010, 2014).

WOMEN'S SUBORDINATION AND (UN)DOING FACTORY WOMEN'S IDENTITIES

As we have seen, the subordination of women —and its manifestation via the glass ceiling or sticky floor— in Sri Lanka's apparel industry is an integral part of the gendered norms and patriarchal social relations in Sri Lanka. Further, it is imbued with the discursive formation of factory women's collective identity —as *lamai*— in the industry. Yet, these forces and processes, which keep (factory) women down in the industry, are hard to grasp as they are often mingled with the idea of 'protecting' young women —the patronisation process—in the industry (Jayawardena, 2014).

Factory Women and the Patriarchal Social Relations in Sri Lanka

The idea of protecting (young) women—by their parents, guardians, brothers or fiancé/husband— is still influential in women's social relations and decision-making process, especially in the traditional family milieu (Jayawardena, 1994; Hewamanne, 2008; Herath, 2015). Nevertheless, during the last two decades or so, women have strengthened their role in the economy, education, and employment (Goonesekere, 2000; Jayaweera, 2002). Further, the patriarchal character of Sri Lankan society has changed in different and profound ways, particularly during the British rule of Sri Lanka[2] and as part of the rise of the colonial bourgeoisie, allowing women to control their public and private affairs— hitherto unparalleled extent (Metthananda, 1990; Jayawardena, 2000). Hence, some of the changes introduced by the British rulers, particularly in the field of education, were positive in empowering women, especially bourgeois women in colonial Sri Lanka. As Jayawardena points out, for example:

Capitalism in a colonial context had a liberating effect of some bourgeois women, enabling them to challenge the restraints of patriarchy, abandon feudal and traditional practices and move towards the achievement of equal rights. But the majority of wives and daughters of the bourgeoisie remained family rooted in the patriarchal family with the walls of caste and class; they played the domestic roles of good mother, [and] loyal wife... (2000, p. 297).

Despite these developments, the impact of patriarchy on social relations in contemporary Sri Lanka remains crucial. For example, as Jayaweera argues, 'gender relations have tended to adjust to the economic empowerment of women through employment or education and employment, while the patriarchal roots underpin in the continuing male control of female sexuality in the family and in the society' (2002, p. 367). Indeed, patriarchy in Sri Lanka still affects women in many ways, mostly in relation to their ability to make (independent) decisions (Malhotra & Mather, 1997; Herath, 2015).

Patronising Factory Women

With this background, we see that the idea of protection and care— the patronisation— is a common facet in managing factory women in the apparel industry. Here the age of women and their village roots and gender—young-peasant-migrant-women — and the nature of work they do in the industry allow managers and other social actors in the industry to use patronisation as a means of control of factory women. In fact, this is how Wimala, the matron of HotCo's boarding-house, explains her responsibility — of 'protecting' young women — when I asked Wimala about her role as the matron:

Dhammika: *How is the work?*
Wimala: *It is a huge battle.*
Dhammika: *Why is it called a battle?*
Wimala: *Protecting ganu lamai [girls] is very difficult.*
Dhammika: *Isn't easy?*
Wimala: *Not easy.*
Dhammika: *Why do you say that it's not easy?*
Wimala: *There is a responsibility [of protecting the girls], Sir[3].*
Dhammika: *Does that mean there is an influence of their families?*
Wimala: *No Sir, when [the girls are] sent [to the hostel] I have a responsibility [to their parents].*

Thus, the idea of protecting factory women, or *ganu lamai*, as Wimala explains, is a 'responsibility' that comes not just from women's parents or guardians. Instead, it is also driven by wider social values. Thereby, it intermingles with the formation of factory women's collective identity—as (*ganu*) *lamai*. Indeed, my interview with Wimala exemplifies that the idea of 'protecting women' in the industry often appears with (un)doing the *lamai* identity.

As I continued my fieldwork, this interaction—between protecting women and (un)doing the *lamai* identity— was evident in my encounters with other social actors in the industry, including my interview with the HR Manager of HotCo.

HR Manager: *Most of the time we have 'one to one,' 'eye to eye' relationship with lamai. Like checking absenteeism, every day we go [to the shop floor] and check who has come, who has not come, what are the problems?... A few of us in the human resource division go [to the shop floor]. In the guise of checking absenteeism what we actually do is we practically go there and meet each other.*
Dhammika: *Do you do this for the staff?*
HR Manager: *... We don't do it for the staff as much as for lamai. [We] can't do it 100 per cent or for everyone. But at some point everyone gets covered by this, as [we] continue it for overtime... Truly..., [when we go to] see lamayekwa [a girl/little one] is at home [boarding house] due to sickness, at the boarding [house] without [her] father and mother, [when we go to] see lamayawa [a girl/ little one] in this wooden room, the joy that lamaya feels when we go there, and the words that that*

lamaya utters within the institute [factory] when [she] returns next day, that lamyage [girl's/little one's] own words, we know the reception we have in this production line [due to this].

As the HR Manager narrates, his (and the HR Department's) relationship with factory women is not a mere relationship between the workers and the management. Instead, it is a process where factory women are 'looked after' by the HR staff. Yet, in this process of protection and care, the manager uses the term *lamai* to signify factory women (who are in fact adults) and hence do their collective identity — as *lamai* — in the industry. At the same time, he is careful to separate factory women from the rest of (white-collar) workers whom the manager calls 'staff.' Therefore, alongside the process of patronisation, (un)doing factory women's collective identity— as *lamai* — I argue, allow managers and other executives in the industry to control women (Jayawardena, 2014).

However, use of the term *lamai* to address and signify young boys and girls is common in Sri Lanka. Hence, addressing factory women as *lamai* — and (un)doing the *lamai* identity— appears as a 'innocent' practice (Jayawardena, 2015). Yet, as the manager tells us, the connotation of the term in the *apparel industry somewhat differs from its usage in the family milieu and wider society:*

Dhammika: *... Do you commonly use this term lamai in talking?*
HR Manager: *Do you mean using the term lamai? In a closed environment like this [personal interview in the boardroom], we call them lamai. Actually, this term lamai has derived from the idea of 'little one.' It is not in the same way as Juki kello [Juki girls], mahana kello [sewing girls]. Even though we commonly call them lamai mostly [we call them] nangi [younger sister] or if we know [their] names we call them by names.*
[....]
Dhammika: *Do they [factory women] like or dislike being addressed them as lamai?*
HR Manager: *The term lamai was originally created with the idea [that they are] a group that is in somewhat lower level than the management and [so] should be looked after by the management, as I think lamai... Even at home, we use lamai to [those] who are looked after by us.*

As the HR Manager points out, in the industry context, factory women (*lamai*) are treated as 'a group of people somewhat *lower level* than the management.' Hence, they are treated as *lamai* who 'should be looked after by the management.' Indeed, here we see that the idea of the protection and care — the patronisation — buttresses the discursive formation of the *lamai* identity and vice versa.

Becoming of the *Lamai* Identity

In this context, we see that, in the industry, managers, and other executives, are keen to portray factory women as an 'innocent' and 'feeble' group (Jayawardena, 2010). This is despite the important role that the women play in the industry and Sri Lankan economy (Kelegama, 2005; Central Bank of Sri Lanka, 2016). Therefore, we suggest that portraying factory women as innocent and feeble girls is probably *the* desire of the management— to keep and continue the 'smooth' functioning of the shop floor by making factory women more 'feminine' and 'docile.' Yet, the innocent and feeble disposition of factory women, as the GM of HotCo narrates, is not always the case.

Lamai here [in the zone] are highly corrupted. Now if we take lamai at ChillCo, there are lamai like flowers. Not here. Here.., looking from that angle [they are] very corrupted. They are very stiff girls. ... When newcomers come we can see the difference well. Lamayek [a girl/little one] who has come from village wearing a printed frock which cover [her] legs,[4] the way that that lamaya talks with us, the relationship that is built between us and that lamaya is in many ways different from the responses of a person [woman] who has walked through other factories, who has walked through life.

In his (discursive) formation of the *lamai* identity, the GM demarcates the 'differences' between workers in the FTZ and outside it. For him, 'newcomers' as well as '*lamai* at ChillCo' are 'innocent,' whereas 'old-timers' and the 'zone workers' are 'corrupted' women. Indeed, the way in which the GM portrayed factory women in the zone, echoes how their identity —as *lamai* — is done as a corrupted and lowly group in the zone area (see, Sunday Island, 1991; Hewamanne, 2003). Simultaneously, it also shows the rupture, or becoming, of the *lamai* identity — from 'innocent girls' to 'corrupted women.' This is evident in the following section; in my interviews with social actors in the FTZ area, such as Siril, a landlord in the zone area.

Dhammika: *Within the zone is there a tendency of marginalising lamai?*[5]
Siril: *Within the zone?*
Dhammika: *When compared with other village folks is there a tendency of treating them [the workers] being separated [from the village folks]?*
Siril: *Happen to some extent. There is a thinking of that lowly assessment [among the village folks].*
Dhammika: *Why has it gone to that state, as you think, Mr. Siril?*
Siril: *That would happen perhaps due to some works done by these lamai. So within that group, there are some who do lowly works. Lamai there [in that group], there are some lamai who do that type of works. They do not care much about cleanliness, do not love to the [boarding] place [they] live; perhaps due to the way [they were] groomed in [their rural] villages. When [we] see that type of wrongdoings continually we also happen to think [that] this is the way [they were] groomed in [their rural] villages. Village folks here also think in that way.*

Thus, factory women, whom we confront under the collective identity of *lamai* in the apparel industry, are, on the one hand, innocent and feeble. On the other hand, they are corrupted. Yet, the becoming or double-bind nature of the *lamai* identity —innocent girls and corrupted women— does not make women's lives better in the industry or wider society. Instead, as we will see in the following section, it negatively affects their career advancement.

Keeping the Glass Ceiling in Place: Managerial (Wo)men and Career Advancement

In the apparel industry context, (un)doing factory women's collective identity as *lamai* negatively affects the women's ability to climb up the career ladder. Hence, despite its double-bind nature, the *lamai* identity has become a signification of (factory) women's 'inability' to get promoted to the higher ranks on the shop floor of the industry. As the Factory Manager (FM) of HotCo explains, for example:

FM: Most of the time I see that lamai don't like to take on leadership. Perhaps [they are] afraid, or there are that types of reasons. Sometimes we hire lamayekwa [a girl/little one] to a line and make her a leader. They are afraid to talk about even the problems in the line.
Dhammika: That means they don't come forward?
FM: [They are] afraid to come forward.
Dhammika: What [do you] think about that? Their background or something else?
FM: I think it's their background.
Dhammika: Now, a supervisor is selected from that group?
FM: It's very rarely that a supervisor nagitinne ['stands up' — this means how shop floor workers prepared by themselves to get promoted].

For the FM, factory women or *lamai* are not prepared to take the 'leadership challenge' on the shop floor. The reason for women's failure to prepare for the promotions, as the manager tells us, is the background of the women—young-peasant-migrant-women: They are 'inherently incapable' of taking the supervisory positions in the industry. Therefore, as the FM indicates, women in the industry are probably 'dowry seekers' for their marriage.

FM: What I have seen in the garment trade [industry] is, what lamai are targeting, basically, is marriage.
Dhammika: That means like collecting [their] dowry?
FM: Not exactly, I think that is the situation in Sri Lanka. Women assume that once they get married their problems are over. [They] rarely think about the problems which come after marriage... Generally, when we talk what I see is that most of time women think about marriage. Why I say this is when talking often I have heard lamai saying '[I] am getting married next year and won't come after that.' Marriage is what is in [their] heads. They live until that [marriage]. After that, they hang on that man's neck. And try to live off that man. That is how I see this [the manager is laughing].

Thus, in the (male) discursive formation of factory women's collective identity we often see and face not capable women, who play an important role in Sri Lankan economy, but 'feeble women folks' whose world is the (patriarchal) family. However, in the discursive formation, there was (and is) practically no room for factory women to rise to higher positions —at least to the supervisory level— unless they act assertively.

Factory (Wo)men and Gender-Based Promotion

In this context, we can see that, when making promotion decisions, the *lamai* identity and its double-bind nature — as lowly and corrupted as well as innocent and feeble —as the Operations Manager (OM) explains, gives an advantage to men on the shop floor.

OM: [We] try to promote pirimi lamai [boys], try our best. There are two reasons. One is we try to give this [promotion] chance to pirimi lamai. That is because we need to balance the control of the floor a little. On the other hand..,
Dhammika: What do you mean by that [balance the control of the shop floor]?

OM: *That means if there is any problem that is the place from where it first comes.*
Dhammika: *Is it pirimi lamai [boys] who come out with problems?*
OM: *No, no. It doesn't mean coming out with problems. Really [they] don't bring problems at the moment. If we think about the future, if we think about unions and such things, if there is any problem in any place, they have more power to convince lamai, convince ganu lamai [girls]. Because of that [we] focus a bit and see who leads the team and we promote them. If we want to promote a supervisor, we watch [them] carefully, watch how they work, and promote one person.*
[...]
Dhammika: *Isn't there any need [that would arise] from ganu lamai [girls] that means from a promotional aspect?*
OM: *Should do. Hmm, that is done after a little consideration. That means if we see they [ganu lamai] are progressing we promote [them]. It is rarely that we search for [girls to] promote. That is not discrimination. [We] have given a little better chance to pirimi lamai [boys] ...*

Thus, in the process of promoting shop floor workers, factory men's collective identity—as *pirimi lamai*—is done as 'assertive' and 'capable' men — the (potential) 'trouble makers'— who could convince 'innocent' *lamai*, the factory women. This, subsequently, gives factory men better opportunity to get promoted, although women remain the majority of the industry and its shop floor.

Gender Does (Not) Matter?

However, (un)doing the identities of factory men and women as different 'beings' in the apparel industry is not exclusively (managerial) men's work. On the contrary, as we see in my interview with the Asst. HR Manager of HotCo, (managerial) women in the industry are also keen to do (and undo) the identities of (factory) men and women differently — despite their own gender (consciousness) as women.

Dhammika: *If I suggest there is better chance for boys to get promoted [in the factory]?*
Asst. HR Manager: *Hmm.., now in many times in production, the tendency of women.., in many times tendency of women becoming supervisors are low.*
Dhammika: *But women are the majority of the production [shop floor]*
Asst. HR Manager: *No, that's machine operators...*
Dhammika: *Why have they [women] not been promoted, as you think?*
Asst. HR Manager: *They are, now it is like this, as I said before, why they aren't promoted is to be promoted only knowledge about sewing is not enough. Now she should have the ability to give the required target by controlling the [production] line.*
Dhammika: *Do you think that it is difficult for women to do it?*
Asst. HR Manager: *There are ganu lamai [girls] who do it. It is not impossible. But everyone can't do it...*
Dhammika: *Why more pirimi lamai [boys] are promoted?*
Asst. HR Manager: *That's what I am saying, now that, hmm.., now we think if we hire a supervisor. [Workers] who reach to supervisory level in this trade are pirimi pakshya [men folks].*
Dhammika: *How do you view it? Why is that?*
Asst. HR Manager: *That's.., hmm.., now sometimes women are more sensitive. Now in this work environment, [supervisor] has to work under high pressure. To certain extent women folks might be less able to cope with that pressure.*

Patriarchy and (Un)Doing Factory of Women's Collective Identity

As the Asst. HR Manager narrates, managerial women, like men, view that factory women are 'less capable' to reach (at least) to the supervisory level in the industry. The reason for this (gender) 'incapability,' the manager explains, is the women's sensitivity and their inability to work under pressure. Therefore, she thinks that (assertive) male workers 'naturally' get better chance to get promoted.

With this background, we see that even ex-shop floor workers, who have been promoted to supervisory level, are also keen to keep factory women down. This is exemplified by my interview with a female supervisor of ChillCo, who is an ex-shop floor worker of the company:

... But we [supervisors] tire our brain as well, but lamai tire [their] bodies. We [supervisors] work using our brain... What lamai mean, generally [they] come in the morning [and go] evening, [they work for] eight hours. They have a small part [responsibility] of a small garment. Their responsibility is only for that, restricted there. Their responsibility is only within that area. Now, supervisor means this whole thing. It is us who has to be looking for everything. So this [responsibility] has to be explained to lamai.

Despite her 'erased' identity as a factory woman, or *lamaya* (little one), little progress in career has encouraged the supervisor to portray the role of factory women in the industry as an insignificant and mundane work. Paradoxically, here the supervisor ignores her roots in the *lamai* identity and says that factory women are mere manual workers who use only their body.

In this context, I argue that factory women's 'inability' to climb the career ladder and crack the glass ceiling in the apparel industry of Sri Lanka is firmly embedded (and embodied) in how their collective identity — as 'feeble women folks' or *lamai*— is done (and undone) in the industry and wider Sri Lankan society (Jayawardena, 2014, 2015). Thereby, I suggest that the glass ceiling effect — on (factory) women— in the apparel industry always appears as part of (un)doing factory women's collective identity —as *lamai*— which denotes both feeble and lowly at the same. Ironically, the 'feeble-lowly' identity of factory women, as we have seen, is done (and undone) by both managerial women as well as men. Therefore, keeping the glass ceiling in place in the industry does not appear as exclusively men's work (Luke 1998). Rather, (managerial) women's role — in (un)doing the *lamai* identity— is also crucial in this process.

CONCLUSION

Women's subordination — via invisible barriers, such as the glass ceiling or sticky floor — in gendered organisations in contemporary society has already taken the attention of both policymakers and researchers. Alongside the dynamics in wider society, policies implemented to empower women have created (relatively) better place for women in organisations (Beck & Davis, 2005; Gatrell & Cooper, 2007; Sharif, 2015). However, women still struggle with deep-rooted gendered norms at work. Indeed, the invisible barriers, such as the glass ceiling, which prevent women climbing the career ladder, are still prevalent in organisations in the Global South and North (Agrawal, 2013; Kiaye & Singh, 2013; Ezzedeen et al., 2015; Tandrayen-Ragoobur & Pydayya, 2015; Duraisamy & Duraisamy, 2016).

In the Global South organisations, the subordination of women is often imbued with the historical roots and dynamics of the Southern societies (Spivak, 1988; Mohanty, 1991; Jayawardena, 2000). Yet, the literature on the subject— inspired by (white) women's experience in the Global North— suggests a uniform or universal structure of the glass ceiling. Here, the literature has a tendency of articulating the glass ceiling as an act of a closed male elite in organisations (David & Woodward, 1998; Hughes, 2002). Further, it highlights women's domestic role and family commitments as the major causes of the glass ceiling in the Global South organisations (Bal, 2004; Kargwell, 2008; Jain & Mukherji, 2010; Kiaye & Singh, 2013).

However, the subordination of (factory) women in the Global South — such as we have seen in the case of Sri Lanka's apparel industry — is not exclusively men's work. Rather, (managerial) women as well play an active role in keeping the glass ceiling in place in the industry. Yet, in the apparel industry, it is difficult to argued that the family commitments of factory women are crucial in keeping the glass ceiling intact, as most of these women are young and unmarried (Jayaweera, 2002; Jayawardena, 2014). Further, we see that women's subordination in the apparel industry is deeply embedded (and embodied) in the discursive formation of factory women's collective identity — as *lamai* (Jayawardena, 2010, 2014, 2015). Therefore, (un-doing) the *lamai* identity also appears as a crucial factor that prevents or hinders (factory) women climbing the career ladder.

In this context, I conclude that, the glass ceiling in the apparel industry of Sri Lanka is a multifaceted phenomenon where the patriarchal social relations in Sri Lanka and (un)doing factory women's collective identity — as *lamai* by both managerial men and women— in the industry come into play. Nevertheless, I do not suggest that the role of managerial women in keeping factory women down in the industry is similar to the role of 'queen bee' in organisations (see, for example, Derks et al., 2016). Instead, I argue that whether the strongly patriarchal nature of the apparel industry— where women recognising becoming 'man' in order to 'fit' the requirements of the industry (Mavin, 2006; Jayawardena, 2012) — and managerial women's class consciousness (as the white-collar, petty-bourgeois women) are compelled them to play an active role in keeping the glass ceiling intact in Sri Lanka's localised global apparel industry.

REFERENCES

Agrawal, T. (2013). Are there glass-ceiling and sticky-floor effects in India? An empirical examination. *Oxford Development Studies*, *41*(3), 322–342. doi:10.1080/13600818.2013.804499

Ahmed, S., & Maitra, P. (2015). A distributional analysis of the gender wage gap in Bangladesh. *The Journal of Development Studies*, *51*(11), 1444–1458. doi:10.1080/00220388.2015.1046444

Arfken, D. E., Bellar, S. L., & Helms, M. M. (2004). The ultimate glass ceiling revisited: The presence of women on corporate boards. *Journal of Business Ethics*, *50*(2), 177–186. doi:10.1023/B:BUSI.0000022125.95758.98

Bal, V. (2004). Women scientists in India: Nowhere near the glass ceiling. *Economic and Political Weekly*, *38*(32), 3647–3653.

Beck, D., & Davis, E. (2005). EEO in senior management: Women executives in Westpac. *Asia Pacific Journal of Human Resources*, *43*(2), 273–288. doi:10.1177/1038411105055063

Bihagen, E., & Ohls, M. (2006). The glass ceiling – where is it? Womens and mens career prospects in the private vs. the public sector in Sweden 19792000. *The Sociological Review*, *54*(1), 20–47. doi:10.1111/j.1467-954X.2006.00600.x

Brumley, K. M. (2014). The gendered ideal worker narrative professional womens and mens work experiences in the new economy at a Mexican company. *Gender & Society, 28*(6), 799–823. doi:10.1177/0891243214546935

Bryman, A., & Bell, E. (2011). *Business research methods*. Oxford, UK: Oxford University Press.

Central Bank of Sri Lanka. (2016). *Central bank of Sri Lanka annual report 2015*. Colombo: Central Bank of Sri Lanka.

Chou, W. G., Fosh, P., & Foster, D. (2005). Female managers in Taiwan: Opportunities and barriers in changing times. *Asia Pacific Business Review, 11*(2), 251–266. doi:10.1080/1360238042000291153

David, M., & Woodward, D. (1998). Introduction. In M. David & D. Woodward (Eds.), *Negotiating the glass ceiling: Careers of senior women in the academic world* (pp. 2–22). London: Routledge.

Derks, B., Van Laar, C., & Ellemers, N. (2016). The queen bee phenomenon: Why women leaders distance themselves from junior women. *The Leadership Quarterly, 27*(3), 456–469. doi:10.1016/j.leaqua.2015.12.007

Devanarayana, C. (1997). *A review of Sri Lanka's free trade zone*. Ja-Ella: Dabindu Collective.

Dicken, P. (2007). *Global shift: Mapping the changing contours of the world economy*. London: Sage.

Duraisamy, M., & Duraisamy, P. (2016). Gender wage gap across the wage distribution in different segments of the Indian labour market, 1983–2012: Exploring the glass ceiling or sticky floor phenomenon. *Applied Economics, 48*(43), 4098–4111. doi:10.1080/00036846.2016.1150955

Ezzedeen, S. R., Budworth, M. H., & Baker, S. D. (2015). The glass ceiling and executive careers still an issue for pre-career women. *Journal of Career Development*.

Gatrell, C. J., & Cooper, C. L. (2007). (No) cracks in the glass ceiling: women managers, stress and the barriers to success. In D. Biliomoria & S. K. Piderit (Eds.), Handbook on Women in Business and Management, (pp. 57-77). Glos: Edward Elgar Publishing Ltd.

Goonesekere, S. W. E. (2000). Legal education in independent Sri Lanka: 1948 to 1997. In S. Tilakaratna & H. P. M. Gunasena (Eds.), *University Education since Independence* (pp. 86–110). Colombo: University Grant Commission.

Hancock, P., Carastathis, G., Georgiou, J., & Oliveira, M. (2015). Female workers in textile and garment sectors in Sri Lankan Export Processing Zones (EPZs): Gender dimensions and working conditions. *Sri Lanka Journal of Social Sciences, 38*(1), 63–77. doi:10.4038/sljss.v38i1.7386

Harvey, D. (2005). *A brief history of neoliberalism*. Oxford, UK: Oxford University Press.

Herath, H. M. A. (2015). Place of women in Sri Lankan society: Measures for their empowerment for development and good governance. *Vidyodaya Journal of Management, 1*(1), 1–14.

Hewamanne, S. (2003). Performing dis-respectability: New tastes, cultural practices, and identity performances by Sri Lankas free trade zone garment-factory workers. *Cultural Dynamics, 15*(1), 71–101. doi:10.1177/a033109

Hewamanne, S. (2008). *Stitching identities in a free trade zone; Gender and politics in Sri Lanka*. Philadelphia: University of Pennsylvania Press.

Hughes, C. (2002). *Women's contemporary lives: Within and beyond the mirror*. London: Routledge. doi:10.4324/9780203451618

Itzin, C. (1995). The gender culture in organizations. In C. Itzin & J. Newman (Eds.), *Gender, culture and organizational change* (pp. 30–53). London: Rutledge. doi:10.4324/9780203427965_chapter_2

Jain, N., & Mukherji, S. (2010). The perception of 'glass ceiling' in Indian organizations: An exploratory study. *South Asian Journal of Management, 17*(1), 23.

Jayawardena, D. (2010). *Narratives, lamai and female labour: (Re)narrating the untold story of HRM in Sri Lanka's apparel industry* (Unpublished doctoral thesis). University of Leicester, Leicester, UK.

Jayawardena, D. (2012). Looking through the glass of managerial femininity: A polemic. *Journal of Gender and Justice, 1*, 1–13.

Jayawardena, D. (2014). HRM as a web of texts: (Re)articulating the identity of HRM in Sri Lankas localized global apparel industry. *Organizational Management Journal, 11*(4), 289–298. doi:10.1080/15416518.2014.973794

Jayawardena, D. (2015). On the burden of being-qua-non-being: In between the lines of (working class) writings. In A. Pullen & C. Rhodes (Eds.), The Routledge companion to ethics, politics and organizations (pp. 150-161). London: Routledge.

Jayawardena, K. (2000). *Nobodies to somebodies: the rise of the colonial bourgeoisie in Sri Lanka*. Colombo: Association and Sanjiva Books.

Jayaweera, S. (2002). Women in education and employment. In S. Jayaweera (Ed.), *Women in post- independence Sri Lanka* (pp. 99–142). Colombo: CENWOR.

Kang, H., & Rowley, C. (2005). Women in management in South Korea: Advancement or retrenchment? *Asia Pacific Business Review, 11*(2), 213–231. doi:10.1080/1360238042000291171

Kargwell, S. (2008). Is the glass ceiling kept in place in Sudan? Gendered dilemma of the work-life balance. *Gender in Management: An International Journal, 23*(3), 209–224. doi:10.1108/17542410810866953

Kelegama, S. (2005). Ready-made garment industry in Sri Lanka: Preparing to face the global challenges. *Asia-Pacific Trade and Investment Review, 1*(1), 51–67.

Khosla, N. (2009). The ready-made garments industry in Bangladesh: A means to reducing gender-based social exclusion of women? *Journal of International Women's Studies, 11*(1), 289–303.

Kiaye, E. R., & Singh, M. A. (2013). The glass ceiling: A perspective of women working in Durban. *Gender in Management: An International Journal, 28*(1), 28–42. doi:10.1108/17542411311301556

Li, L., & Leung, R. W. (2001). Female managers in Asian hotels: Profile and career challenges. *International Journal of Contemporary Hospitality Management, 13*(4), 189–186. doi:10.1108/09596110110389511

Luke, C. (1998). Cultural politics and women in Singapore higher education management. *Gender and Education, 10*(3), 245–263. doi:10.1080/09540259820880

Lynch, C. (2002). The politics of white womens underwear in Sri Lankas open economy. *Social Politics, 9*(1), 87–125. doi:10.1093/sp/9.1.87

Malhotra, A., & Mather, M. (1997). Do schooling and work empower women in developing countries? Gender and domestic decisions in Sri Lanka. *Sociological Forum, 12*(4), 599–630. doi:10.1023/A:1022126824127

Mason, J. (2002). *Qualitative researching*. London: Sage.

Maume, D. J. (2004). Is the glass ceiling a unique from of inequality. *Work and Occupations, 31*(2), 250–274. doi:10.1177/0730888404263908

Mavin, S. (2006). Venus envy 2: Sisterhood, queen bees and female misogyny in management. *Women in Management Review, 21*(5), 349–364. doi:10.1108/09649420610676172

Metthananda, T. (1990). Women in Sri Lanka: Tradition and change. In S. Kiribamune & V. Samarasinghe (Eds.), *Women at crossroads: A Sri Lankan perspective* (pp. 41–71). New Delhi: Vikas Publishing House.

Mohanty, T. C. (1991). Under western eyes: Feminist scholarships and colonial discourses. In C. T. Mohanty, A. Russo, & L. Torres (Eds.), *Third world women and the politics of feminism* (pp. 51–80). Bloomington, IN: Indiana University Press.

Nath, D. (2000). Gently shattering the glass ceiling: Experiences of Indian women managers. *Women in Management Review, 15*(1), 44–55. doi:10.1108/09649420010310191

Omar, A., & Davidson, M. J. (2001). Women in management: A comparative cross-cultural overview. *Cross Cultural Management: An International Journal, 8*(3/4), 35–67. doi:10.1108/13527600110797272

Perera, S. (2008). Rethinking working-class literature: Feminism, globalization, and socialist ethics. *Differences: A Journal of Feminist Cultural Studies, 19*(1), 1–31. doi:10.1215/10407391-2007-015

Pompper, D. (2011). Fifty years later: Mid-career women of color against the glass ceiling in communications organizations. *Journal of Organizational Change Management, 24*(4), 464–486. doi:10.1108/09534811111144629

Powell, G. N., & Butterfield, D. A. (2015). The glass ceiling: What have we learned 20 years on? *Journal of Organizational Effectiveness: People and Performance, 2*(4), 306–326. doi:10.1108/JOEPP-09-2015-0032

Ryan, M. K., & Haslam, S. A. (2005). The glass cliff: Evidence that women are over-represented in precarious leadership positions. *British Journal of Management, 16*(2), 81–90. doi:10.1111/j.1467-8551.2005.00433.x

Samanmali, H. I. (2007). Wetup wediwenawita target ekada wediwe [When salaries go up, the target also goes up]. *Dabindu, 23*, 9.

Sharif, M. Y. (2015). Glass ceiling, the prime driver of women entrepreneurship in Malaysia: A phenomenological study of women lawyers. *Procedia: Social and Behavioral Sciences, 169*, 329–336. doi:10.1016/j.sbspro.2015.01.317

Spivak, G. C. (1988). Can the subaltern speak? In C. Nelson & L. Grossberg (Eds.), *Marxism and the interpretation of culture* (pp. 271–313). London: Macmillan Education. doi:10.1007/978-1-349-19059-1_20

Sunday Island. (1991, December 15). Shocking goings on at FTZ. *Sunday Island*, pp. 1, 3.

Tandrayen-Ragoobur, V., & Pydayya, R. (2015). Glass ceiling and sticky floors: Hurdles for Mauritian working women. *Equality, Diversity and Inclusion. International Journal (Toronto, Ont.), 34*(5), 452–466.

Terjesen, S., & Singh, V. (2008). Female presence on corporate boards: A multi-country study of environmental context. *Journal of Business Ethics, 83*(1), 55–63. doi:10.1007/s10551-007-9656-1

Weedon, C. (1987). *Feminist practice and poststructuralist theory*. Oxford, UK: Basil Blackwell.

Wignaraja, G. (1998). *Trade liberalization in Sri Lanka: Exports, technology and industrial policy*. London: Macmillan Press. doi:10.1007/978-1-349-26267-0

Yukongdi, V., & Benson, J. (2005). Women in Asian management: Cracking the glass ceiling? *Asia Pacific Business Review, 11*(2), 139–148. doi:10.1080/1360238042000291225

ENDNOTES

[1] These nicknames suggest that the women have been 'plugged' into Japanese electronic sewing machines—known as Juki (Jayawardena, 2014, p. 290).

[2] Sri Lanka was under the British colonial rule for nearly 150 years. The country gained independence in 1948.

[3] Throughout this chapter I italicise the English terms which are in original Sinhala texts.

[4] In wider Sir Lankan society, this dress is still regarded as a 'decent' outfit for young women, although it is not fashionable.

[5] During my interviews with different actors in the apparel industry, I also used the term *lamai* to refer to factory women. This was either to adapt to the scenario as it emerged or to observe the way in which the participant/s of the interview follow and repeat my utterance.

Chapter 3
Care Work vs. Career:
Crisis of Middle Class Working Women

Md. Mynul Islam
University of Dhaka, Bangladesh

Gulay Jannat
University of Dhaka, Bangladesh

ABSTRACT

Career is indispensable for woman to ensure their decision-making power to boost up their capability through active voice and participation. However, in Bangladesh most of the middle class working women are facing crisis to manage their double work. Keeping this in mind, this study explains how household related care work costs women's career. It reveals, most of the women have to face multiple problems to maintain their care and office work. Even, a good number of working women sacrificed their career to take care of children and family. Regarding these discriminatory social and institutional systems, most of the working women believe that, positive mind-set can bring a change for women to develop their career.

INTRODUCTION

Formal works are very essential for women's economic development, because it gives identity to establish them as economically empowered and independent. Today's market economy enhances more opportunities to ensure gender equality in labor force participation between men and women. In the last decade (1995-2003) women's employment in Bangladesh increases gradually, though they are only 26 percentage of total labor force (Bangladesh Labor Force Survey 2002-2003). Regarding this issue, anthropological work has addressed cultural factors that affected women's market work (Cain *et al.*, 1979). In this perspective, market work tries to improve gender equality in labor force participation between men and women but how far it will be possible for women to continue their market work with the burden of care work?

DOI: 10.4018/978-1-5225-3018-3.ch003

Though working women have to invest huge time to manage their double work (Islam, 2012; Islam and Jannat, 2016), patriarchal expectations prioritize men's career over women's career (Cha, 2010). In addition, most of the working women are feeling guilty to manage their work and family in a proper way due to our socio-cultural practices (Harcar, 2007). In this regard, it is an urgent situation to increase more opportunity for women to participate in a better style to achieve desired position, because there is a close relation between economic empowerment and women's labor force participation (Boserup, 1970; Chaudhuri, 2009), as they are the fifty percent to contribute for overall development (Khan, 1988).

STATEMENT OF THE PROBLEM

From the social definition of women as housewives follows the definition of the men as the breadwinners, the separation between the private sphere of the house, the sphere of production and reproduction and the subordination of the latter under the former (Mies, 2012: 59)

In this regard, Mahtab (2012) stated despite huge investments in time and labor by women, why is there so much discrimination and inequality in terms of women's economic development? However, this is an appropriate time to explore the behind scenario of impact of care work on women's formal work and their coping strategies to manage both the care and formal work.

In addition, there is a long debate between care and formal work, which work is perfect for women and how care work affects on working women's career? Due to our traditional cultural norms and practices, mostly household related works especially cooking, cleaning, and child care are identified as only women's work (Islam and Jannat, 2016). Therefore, gender division of labor operates discrimination not only in reproductive activities within the household but also in productive and community activities for women to achieve targeted position. Besides, to get the desired position, women have to face unequal hiring standards, unequal opportunities for training, unequal pay for equal work, unequal access to productive resources, segregation and concentration in female sectors and occupations, different physical and mental working conditions, unequal participation in economic decision-making and unequal promotion prospects compared with men (Ostin, 2002).

Despite the cultural barriers, due to extreme women's poverty in Bangladesh, we have had some impressive impression for females employment because since 1995 women's work participation rates have doubled though their number is extremely lower than men (Bangladesh Labor Force Participation, 2002-2003), because market work wants to ensure gender equality. In this aspect, market has introduced a lot of new sector to involve more women than previous to ensure women's participation in the labor force (Kabeer, 2012). Having all these facilities, now the question rises why most of the middle class working women failed to exercise their power and agency to get leadership position in the labor market? Because, women's formal work is considered as an extension of household work (Bhasin, 2000). In this regard, UNDP (1995) explores though middle class women are working, hold only 4 percent senior management positions and remain insignificant position within and outside the household. This unexpected situation triggers us to explore the impact of care work on working women to ensure their career.

WOMEN, CARE WORK, AND CAREER: BANGLADESH PERSPECTIVE

According to the Human Development Report 2016, "yet in all regions women consistently have, on average, a lower Human Development Index (HDI) value than do men. The largest difference is in South Asia, where the female HDI value is 20 percent lower than the male HDI value" (UNDP, 2016:5). Many women cannot take the advantage of new opportunities because they are not allowed to participate in paid labor force or, when they do, they do with relatively few skills and little experiences and they cannot bargain for their fair wages or worker benefits (Marilyn et al 1996). As a consequence, around the world we see most of the top positions in different organizations are chaired by men (Cha, 2010).

With the response to the demands of global women's movement and UN mandates to ensure gender equality in every sector, the government of Bangladesh like other developing countries has taken some strategies to bring positive changes (Jahan, 1995). As a result, since 1980s, globally women's participation increases gradually in the labor force but not their managerial position (Cha, 2010). All indicators of development show that women have an unequal share in the benefits of development and they are often negative recipients of the forces of change (Haider, 2000). When resources are stretched thin it is women, the most marginalized in the first place, who suffer first and foremost. Women have the smallest share of the resources pie of the world; when the pie shrinks, women's losses are greatest (Segar & Olson, 1986 cited in Haider, 2000). What happens actually? It is the time to ask what have been the achievements and failure so far and how can we take some further strategies to solve this problem. For middle class families in Bangladesh, there is a common perception and expectation- women should stay at home to do care work no matter whether they are employed or unemployed. Most of the women have to bear many of the marks of a 'disadvantaged minority' in the social, political and economic realms (Mahtab, 2007). According to the labor force survey 2013, the labor force participation rate of the population aged 15 and above at 57.1%, at 81.7% is male and 33.5% for females. In addition, the estimated of female share of overall employment was 29% and while the male share was 71%. Following tables will be helpful to understand the multifaceted discriminatory situation for working women.

From Table 1 and 2, it mirrors that women are still getting low wages and their percentage is very low at different top positions. Different discriminatory socio-cultural expectations like cooking, cleaning, take care of children and old family members are the major obstacles for women to develop their career. As a result, most of the middle class working women are not getting opportunity to access or participate equally to develop their career as men can do. In this aspect, this study especially on middle class women because middle class is a distinct social group with a particular economic bracket, cultivated taste, refined behavior, customs, ethics and idealism (Scrase, 2003 cited in Haque, 2009).

JUSTIFICATION OF THE STUDY

Like many other developing countries, working women in Bangladesh are facing tremendous socio-cultural problem (Mahtab, 2007), because the traditional society is permeated with patriarchal values and norms of female subordination, subservience and segregation resulting from discrimination at birth leading to deprivation and access to all opportunities and benefits in family, social and public life, thus putting them in the most disadvantageous position (Nelson and Chowdhury, 1994). Additionally, our society always ignores the working women's double burden, because care work is not considered as work

Table 1. Average monthly income from employment (wage/salary) by occupation and sex (in Tk.)

Occupations	Male	Female	Total
Managers	21732	18568	21323
Professionals	17687	17203	17531
Technicians and Associate Professionals	18607	15081	17746
Clerical Support Workers	14586	11373	13872
Service and Sales Workers	12072	9520	11458
Skilled Agricultural Forestry and Fisheries	9897	9070	9784
Craft and Related Traders Workers	11302	11784	11482
Plant and Machine Operators and Assemblers	12390	11624	12310
Elementary Occupations	8052	7377	7881
Other Occupations	15232	13248	15147
Total	11621	11136	11493

Source: Bangladesh Labor Force Survey 2013

Table 2. Women's participation in mainstream economic activities and social empowerment

Outcome/impact indicator	Source[1]	Gender	Base Year Year	Base Year Value	Current Year Year	Current Year Value
Unemployment rate	LFS BBS	Female	1999	7.8	2005	7.04
		Male	1999	3.4	2005	3.35
Wage rate by gender for non-agriculture worker	BBS	Female			2009	161
		male			2009	172
Percentage of women in decision making position in public sector	MoE	Female	1999	8.54	2008	18
		Male	1999	91.46	2008	82
Percentage of women in first class government service	MoE	Female	2005	9.6	2007	11.6
		Male	2005	90.4	2007	88.4
Percentage of women in the bar council	Bar council	Female			2008	9.4
		Male			2008	90.6
Percentage of women in the corporate society	Direct. Coop	Female			2007	15.6
		Male			2007	84.4
Percentage of women in the second class government service	MoE	Female			2006	8.4
		Male			2006	91.6

(Islam and Jannat, 2016). Regarding this, working women's problems due to gender division of care work should be considered as a broader part of economic agenda to achieve women's desired career goals.

According to the survey by the Working Mother Research Institute, 79% of working women are responsible for child care, laundry and cooking, according to the survey of more than 1000 working couples. However, working men are responsible for outdoor chores, but both men and women share bill paying jobs. It resembles still working mother handle most of the household work (Holland, 2015). In private patriarchy within household forced women to do more work than men and women are main victims of subordination due to burden of household work (Sultana, 2010-2011). In addition, Ferree (1991), Islam (2012) and Islam and Jannat (2016) found that working women do the lion share of household work. However, a few researchers explained that though the men's participation in household level is increasing gradually, the ratio of their working hour is very lower than women (Blair & Litcher, 1991; Islam, 2012). Hersch and Straton (1994) found the average working hour for men is 7 hours per day. Additionally, household related important activities and decisions are completed by men, as they are head of the family (Sharma, 1986).

Conversely, existing findings on working women mostly focused on workplace related problems like, Azad (2006) explores that sexual harassment at workplace is an unconditional reality in every employed woman's life in Bangladesh. Women have to tolerate sexual harassment at workplace for working in a masculine world. According to Huda (1995) men's sexual harassment, exploitation or embarrassment towards women, it's their superiority and an inherent right. He also analyzed most of the employed remain silent regarding sexual harassment at work place because of losing their job. Besides, Tanjeem and Khan (2009) identified some problem like transportation, accommodation, motherhood and child care and security etc for middle class working women in Bangladesh. However, a very few research focuses on employed women's problem due to conflict between family and work. For instance, in the United States, though women constitute almost 46% of the work force (Heffernan, 2004), nearly 40% of career women take an off ramp and leave work to take care of their families or otherwise at one point in their paths (HBR, 2005). Also, one in three white women who have earned an MBA is not working full time, and only 38% of the female MBA graduates hold full-time careers (HBR, 2005). A significant percentage of women try out the business track for a while, get frustrated with the politics and demands of the workplace, get caught in their desire to have a family, and conclude that the work place is not what it is drummed up to be. They therefore decide to take the easy way out and become fulltime housewives and mothers. Despite the increase in the percentage of working women in households from 59% to 72% in the last 25 years (Geddes, 1998), these working women hold shorter career terms than men and have longer leaves of absences due to their families. These statistics reveal that women continue to desire to put their family first at the expense of their careers. Women pay a high price for this decision, as their average pay continues to be significantly less than men, and their percentage of managerial positions continues to lag. Meanwhile, they continue to hand men the fruits of their labor by giving up their hard-earned positions for men. It is a vicious, treacherous circle of trading equality in the workplace for family. In this regard, we can say, it is the high time to explore working women's problem due to double burden of care work. Because, from Labor Force Survey Bangladesh 2013, we can say that women's participation in labor force has a positive face but still they are less than men both in income and number. Besides, Yao (2015) found that there is a long-standing gap between male and female in terms of their earning. Additionally, International Labor Organization finds in a recent study (2016) that globally employed women have only achieved 'marginal progress' in last 20 years and women's participation is 25.5% less than men in 2015.

GENDER DIVISION OF CARE WORK AND WOMEN'S CAREER: THEORETICAL UNDERSTANDING

Care work includes all activities that directly involve care processes done in services of others (Folbre, 2003), like child care, teaching, health care (England, 2005), and domestic unpaid work, that is disproportionately done by women (Human Development Report, 1999). In this regard, unequal sharing of household responsibilities, child and health care etc between men and women is identified as gender division of care work. Though the unpaid care work is an essential aspect of economic activity and indispensible factors contributing individuals, families and societies (Ferrant *et al.*, 2014), due to sharp sex/gender divisions of labor in households (Mahalingam *et al.*, 2010), mostly it is considered as women's work (Islam and Jannat, 2016). Under the impact of capitalist production relations, the household is defined as only women's place and domestication or housewifisation is the main mechanism by which men achieved the controlling power over women's work (Mies, 2012; Agarwal, 1997). In this aspect, gender division of care work is now considered as a key concept to understand how gender inequalities at household can make obstacles for employed women to develop their career, because due to gender division of labor, employed women have to invest more time and labor to manage their double work (Islam and Jannat 2016; Islam, 2012) and they could not do other formal work than housework (Mies, 2012).

Due to imbalanced gender division of care work, women's career development is generally different from men. It creates a conflict situation between work and household responsibilities only for women. Astin's (1984) developed need based socio-psychological model of career choice and work behavior that attempted to merge both personal (psychological) and social forces as well as their relations. We can identify four key issues in her model: motivation, expectations, sex-role socialization, and structure of opportunity. Both men and women are motivated to use power to ensure primary needs. Though these needs are the same for both men and women, women have to face social dilemmas to fulfill their needs due to maintain their family. In addition, expectations are concerned with the individual's perceptions. They differ for men and women because of sex-role socialization process and the biased structure of opportunity in our society. For instance, distribution of jobs, sex typing of jobs and discrimination in labor market policies cost women's working and leadership capabilities. Though Astin's work has some limitations, regarding our study we found this model realistic to analyze career and care work related issue for middle class working women.

RESEARCH OBJECTIVE

The underlying study entails to investigate the impact of care work on working women's career.

Methodology and Data Collection

This study has a broad focus on feminist research methodology. We have followed qualitative research method to conduct this study. To investigate the impact of care work at household on middle class (defined in terms of income, education, and family member) working women's career, fifteen (15) selected women's (from dual earner households in Dhaka city, aged 25-55) in-depth interviews have been conducted. The in-depth personal interviews were conducted about 2 hours each. Therefore, the interviews were recorded and later transcribed. Secondary sources of data included relevant books, articles, reports of international and national bodies and other similar sources. In our paper, we used pseudonyms of our participants and analyzed only those explanations, which they allowed us to explore.

Care Work, Career, and Crisis of Middle Class Working Women

Gender biased socialization process and family responsibilities make a lot of obstacles to get the proper benefits and opportunities to develop middle class working women's career though they are also qualified. This one eyed household dynamics contributes to maintain middle class women's socioeconomic position more marginal. Even though some of them are aware about their situation, but mostly they failed to challenge the social dilemmas due to fear of husband's negative attitude. Even they have to quit from their job to take care of family members. It creates problems for middle class working women to make balance between their household and job responsibilities equally. Here it becomes clear that cultural practices of our society forced only women to quit or change their job to do household work. Besides, the gender division of care work also contributes to create gender division of market work to dominate working women institutionally.

Unable to Engage for Full Time Job

Household negotiation forced middle class working women to change their job frequently or work as a temporary or part-time worker mostly. Temporary or part-time jobs are not enough defined to improve anyone's career especially for women. Most of the participants informed us that they are unable to do full time work due to household work and child care. In this regard, Aklima Afroz, aged 31, School Teacher, also stated her like following way:

People change their job for better future but I have to change my job to maintain my household work and family. A few days ago I have left my previous job due to my husband's posting in a new district. If I wanted to continue my existing job that will definitely cost my family relationship and working capacity, because I am a mother of two lovely children and one of them is one and half years only.

Rozina Hossain, aged 36, Banker, claimed when husbands and wives are working in a same profession or in a same office, it is unconditionally or naturally expected from wives to work comparatively lower position than husbands. Our social expectations encourage middle class women to work but not to be the boss of their husbands. She stated her opinion like following way:

My bad luck, like me my husband is also working as a banker. Unfortunately his designation is lower than me. It makes him uncomfortable to work.

This patriarchal notion of gender division makes women incapable to work like men. If any woman wants to change the orthodox then it will be sin for her. Like Rozina Hossain, Laboni Akhter, aged 27, Part-time officer claimed that *'society encourages women to take care of family member's instead of full time job'*. Also said like, *'part-time job can protect women from husband's psychological and physical torture'*. Here we can say that, these biased cultural practices contribute middle class working women to remain lower position with minimum income. In this aspect, Tasnim Ara, aged 26, Junior Officer, stated her opinion like following way:

My family members forced me to take an ordinary job to give extra time in house and child care. But I have faith in my capacity that if I get the chance, I will be able to do a better job than now with a standard salary.

Mothers and Wives Will Not Be Accepted to Go Far

Workplaces distance from household can never be long for most of the Bangladeshi women. Family members are highly tensed about their social security and protection. It causes middle class women's lower participation in long distanced jobs in Bangladesh. Ainun Nahar, aged 29, Office Assistant, stated her opinion in this perspective like following way:

Though I had an opportunity to work outside of Dhaka City, my husband requested me to stay with him and children. If I go for there, it will make him anxious all the time.

This socio-cultural norm is one of the major obstacles only for women to achieve their professional success; because men can easily move their places without any family concern for their career and their wives bound to follow their husband's working places to maintain family. In addition, family members are worried for working women's children's future, as our society believes working mothers children's are not growing properly. Like they do not know how to behave properly, how to eat timely, how to talk with elder members and most importantly they are not paying enough time to complete daily study. When working mothers' children's become sick or have any inborn problems, then without any doubt entire family members only raise question to working mothers instead of both mother and father.

Discrimination in Capacity Building Activities

As part of capacity building activities, different kinds of professional training and workshop help employees to be more skilled to challenge the market competition and to direct their future career. Additionally, it gives them to prove their leadership quality and working skills. In Bangladesh, most of the employers are prefer men both as trainer and trainee for training and workshop as they have very less household responsibility. Women are automatically discouraged by their employers because of their household responsibilities and security problems. Furthermore, women are also refused by identifying as less capable to take the appropriate decision for the company's betterment. In addition, men can easily participate in international training but women have to prove their capability twice to be qualified. Regarding this issue, Khadiza Akhter, aged 38, Junior Assistant Officer, stated her opinion as:

In our office only some of my male colleagues have already participated in multiple foreign trainings and meetings. Though I am also qualified, they did not select me. This is because, before selecting female staffs for outside trainings, they think about their family, household responsibilities, and husband's opinion.

Due to these household related issues, a good number of women are now out of these capacity building programs. If they can fully participate in these programs to prove what they can do for working places betterment that may be helpful for them to develop their position. Unfortunately being educated and employed women, most of them are not enough capable to challenge this conventional attitudes. As mostly they learned from their childhood that household responsibilities are solely part of women's life. In addition when working places are also carrying this household discrimination, then it makes them marginal in workplaces as they are now in households.

Women Can Never be Late From Office

Due to official emergency, employees may have to stay quite long at office after working hours and it's a common scenario in everywhere. In reality, how far it would practical for women in the practical societies. Does a patriarchal society allow women to work after their office hours? Need not to wait for a long to get the answer because, the answer is mostly no and never for only women. In addition, if women are married, they have to face huge problems from in-laws. As from childhood, socialization process makes a very clear discriminatory position between boys and girls by transferring the biological differences into the process of their social development like a boy can do anything, but a girl cannot do everything. If we consider their working life and career then it would be clear to us to justify the mature reflection of this biased socialization process. Middle class women are not permitted to work extra hour as they have to be good wives. In this context Sarika Rahman, aged 38, Junior Administrative Officer, stated like:

When I was late from office, my mother-in-law always inquired me the reason by so many irritating questions. Besides, sometime she asked me like whether I want to continue her son's family or not.

Sometime it makes most of the women worried to work properly or to accept extra official responsibilities after their working hours. As they know, it may trouble their family life or sometime it causes domestic violence. Due to this problem, a good of women have to face official problems to get their promotion on time. Regarding this issue, Nishat Pervin, a Junior Administrative Officer, aged 33, Stated as:

If I become late from office, then definitely I will have to face unacceptable behavior from my husband and in-laws. But is it possible to share this fact with my boss? It makes me officially unfit to get promotion or incentives as my male colleagues can do.

Regarding this aspect, Ananya Sharmin, aged 34, Assistant Officer, raised a few questions like: Why always women have to reach home before their husband's? And why only men can enjoy their time after office easily without any household work? The social values and norms believe that only men can do extra official work, as they do not have to pay attention towards household responsibilities and child care. On the other hand, though it gives a chance to work outside for women, still the system is not ready to accept the same situation for women. If women are also started to work like men in their offices, then who will take the household and child care responsibilities.

Questioning Motherhood, Wifehood, and Womanhood

There are some precious connotations related to motherhood, wifehood, and womanhood that makers our women weak to think what they wanted to do and to go where they wanted to go. Society has the ultimate power to dominate women by controlling over their access and opportunities to make them bound to obey. Another thing is that, it is such a sensitive issue, by which patriarchal society not feeling guilty to take chances from women by emotional blackmailing. In this regard, Suraiya Nahar, aged 39, Banker, said like:

You will be surprised to know that, how I am troubling by my in-laws daily due to my strict job times. Often they slanged me that I am not a good mother and not even a good wife, because I am unable to cook for my husband and child daily. Even they said that, I am more concern with my office than my children's well being.

Here we can say how biased socialization process and family learning make working women marginal due to their sexual identity. Additionally, orthodox social practices often creating problems for women to think about their job and children perfectly and they feel guilty maybe they are not giving proper time to them (Harcar, 2007; Austen and Birch, 2000). In addition, unequal sharing of child care among between husbands and wives which results in less time for middle class working women to invest in formal work.

DOUBLE BURDEN AND PSYCHOLOGICAL PRESSURE

For working women, managing all the household and office responsibilities daily is very tough. It costs their healthy life as well their leisure time. Most of the participants shared that, they do not have any leisure time to think about personal necessities and demands. They are just working and working to support their families financially and establish own identities in working sectors. Sometime a good number of them feel anxious like maybe they are not giving proper time towards family members, children and office work as they need to do, because social structures force them to emphasize more on care work than career. It makes a complex situation for middle class women to maintain and satisfy everyone within and outside the family by care and formal work.

Though managing double work is not a new issue for working women, but it becomes heartbreaking reality for most of them, when they do not effort servants in house. From early morning to night, women have to engage themselves in different household works. These responsibilities are becoming more painful and monotonous, when only working women have to maintain and have to hear that they doing nothing at households. Cooking, washing, cleaning etc are not counted as mainstream work in our society as it is identified as women's work. Even some time they are not identified as important financial sources as their husbands by both family members and society.

Though both men and women are working, but before and after office time, men have nothing to do only to get ready and take rest. On the other hand, cooking, cleaning, child care etc are women's responsibilities to maintain their family. Majority of the working women have to work longer hour than men to maintain house work and market work. During working days most of the working women have to work at least 4-5 hours and 13-14 hours for off days. In this perspective Khadiza Akhter, shared as:

No matter women are employed or not, they have to maintain their household work.

In addition, to maintain conjugal life, most of the working women are bound to do their double work. Socio-cultural practices of our society encourage them to look after family first then job. If they do not take their family, society will identify them as not good women. To be good women, most of the working women are doing longer hour work daily. Due to this a good number of women are struggling still to get their desired position in their work places.

POSITIVE MIND-SET: THE ULTIMATE GOAL

Without positive thoughts regarding women's household work and outside work, it would be impossible for them to go far to ensure their development. As the social values of middle class families, household work and care giving work are only women's responsibility no matter whether they are employed or not. Due to this gender division of labor, most of the middle class working women are failed to concentrate their office work and household work properly and at the end they are compromising with their career. The socio-cultural practices forced women to maintain their conjugal life only rather than their career. As a consequence, they have to face a lot of administrative obstacles to get promotion with lucrative salary. Regarding this Ananya Sharmain stated like:

Employers often blame me by saying; you are not perfect here, as you are in your kitchen.

In addition, it would be a difficult situation for working women to participate and communicate properly to take potential decisions, if husbands are not allowed them to go outside willingly. To assure women's identity into the challenging labor markets, most of them want to see a new world with positive thinking perspectives of their husbands. Without changing conventional attitudes towards employed women, women's career development would not be possible. Though a very few husbands have helping attitudes but without social and family support they become helpless to do household work with their wives. It indicates a positive cooperation from men to redistribute household work. Therefore, women are also started to ask that, why household work is only women's responsibility? It should also be men's responsibility to maintain household properly.

However, working women are increasingly becoming more aware about their right and power to ensure their economic development as well as empowerment. In this regard, society has a great role to encourage gender equality based care work distribution between men and women, because patriarchal social values and norms influence religious misinterpretation and cultural dilemmas for employed women to maintain their double burden. Overall it can be assuming that, positive mind-set can reduce this unbearable burden in this modern society. Ishrat Jabin, aged 33, Assistant Officer, stated her opinion in this regard as:

The patriarchal practices of our society and religious misinterpretations are mainly responsible for making this discrimination between working men and women. In this regard, husbands and societies positive attitude towards women's work and care work is an essential issue to develop women's career.

CONCLUSION

In Bangladesh, for middle class families, there is a common patriarchal misconception that husbands have to work outside to maintain their families and wives have to stay at house to manage their household responsibilities and married life. Due to these family responsibilities, a good number of middle class married women have to compromise with their career. Even they have to resign from their lucrative jobs, due to husband's transfer, promotion or new jobs at different places. Our capitalist society offers women to work but not in a higher position like men. In this regard, from this study, it is clear that, unequal care work is the prime obstacle for every middle class employed woman to concentrate their outside work and develop their career. However, to reduce this discrimination, we have to redefine the concept of care work as work between men and women and encourage both men and women to take household and outside work responsibilities equally to manage good and healthy lives. Last but not the least, in our study, we tried to investigate the impact of care work on women's career, need not to be considered sufficient, further research on women, gender, and work and men's perception and attitude toward employed women's career and family is also needed to arrive at a better understanding more thoroughly about women's career and care work.

REFERENCES

Agarwal, B. (1997). Bargaining and Gender Relations: Within and Beyond the Household. *Feminist Economics*, *3*(1), 1–51. doi:10.1080/135457097338799

Astin, H. S. (1984). The Meaning of Work in Womens Lives: A sociopsychological model of career choice and work behavior. *The Counseling Psychologist*, *12*(4), 117–126. doi:10.1177/0011000084124002

Austen, S. E., & Birch, E. R. (2000). *Family Responsiblities and Women Working Lives.* Discussion Paper Series 00/3. Women's Economic Policy Analysis Unit, Curtin University of Technology.

Azad, S. K. (2006). *Sexual Harassment at Work: Experiences with two development organizations in Bangladesh.* Working Paper Series: 1. Department of Women and Gender Studies, University of Dhaka, Bangladesh.

Bangladesh National Labor Force Survey. (2002-2003). Bangladesh Bureau of Statistics.

Bhasin, K. (2000). *Understanding Gender*. New Delhi: Kali for Women.

Blair, S. L., & Lichter, D. T. (1991). Measuring the division of household labor: Gender segregation of housework among American couples. *Journal of Family Issues*, *12*(1), 91–113. doi:10.1177/019251391012001007

Boserup, E. (1970). *Women's Role in Economic Development*. New York: St. Martin's Press.

Cain, M., Khanam, S. R., & Nahar, S. (1979). Class, Patriarchy, and Womens Work in Bangladesh. *Population and Development Review*, *5*(3), 405–438. doi:10.2307/1972079

Cha, Y. (2010). Reinforcing Separate Spheres: The Effect of Spousal Overwork on Mens and Womens Employment in Dual Earner Households. *American Sociological Review*, *75*(2), 303–329. doi:10.1177/0003122410365307

Chaudhury, S. (2009). *Economic Development and Women's Empowerment*. University of Wisconsin-Eau Claire.

Chaudhury, S. (2010). *Women's Empowerment in South Asia and South East Asia: A Comparative Analysis*. MPRA-Munich Personal RePEc Archive. Retrieved from http://mpra.ub.uni-muenchen.de/1968611/

England, P. (2005). Emerging theories of care work, Annual Review of Sociology. *Annual Reviews, 31*(1), 381–399. doi:10.1146/annurev.soc.31.041304.122317

Ferrant, G., Pesando, L. M., & Nowacka, K. (2014). *Unpaid Care Work: The missing link in the analysis of gender gaps in labor outcomes*. OECD Development Centre.

Ferree, M. M. (1991). The gender division of labor in two-earner marriages. *Journal of Family Issues, 12*(2), 158–180. doi:10.1177/019251391012002002

Folbre, N. (2003). Caring labor [Video transcript]. Amherst, MA: Academic Press.

Geddes, D. (1998). CU report: Inequality among women in the workplace is widening. *Cornell Chronicle*. Retrieved from http://www.news.cornell.edu/Chronicle/98/2.19.98/Blau_report.html

Haider, R. (2000). *A Perspective in Development*. Dhaka, Bangladesh: UPL.

Haque, T. (2009). *Household Diplomacy: Access to Income and Women's Agency in Bangladesh*. Working Paper Series: 5. Department of Women and Gender Studies, University of Dhaka.

Harkar, T. (2007). Consequences of work-family conflict for working women and possible solutions: A conceptual model. *Journal of Global Strategic Management, 02*, 60–72.

HBR. (2005). *Harvard business review on women in business*. Boston, MA: Harvard Business School Publishing Corporation.

Heffernan, M. (2004). *The naked truth: a working woman manifesto on business and what really matters* (1st ed.). San Francisco, CA: Jossey-Bass, A Wiley Imprint.

Hersch, J., & Stratton, L. S. (1994). Housework, Wages and the Division of Housework time for Employed Spouses. *The American Review, 84*(2), 120–125.

Holland, K. (2015). *Working moms still take on bulk of household chores*. CNBC. Retrieved from http://www.cnbc.com/2015/04/28/me-is-like-leave-it-to-beaver.html

Huda, S. (1999). Perspectives on Sexual Harassment in Bangladesh: Acknowledging its Existence. *Empowerment*, 6.

International Labor Organization. (2016). *Women at Work: Trend 2016*. Geneva: International Labor Office.

Islam, M. M. (2012). The GDP Matter: Valuing The Fulltime Homemakers Household Work Time. *Modern Social Science Journal, 1*(1), 1–20.

Islam, M. M., & Jannat, G. (2016). Recognition and Redistribution of Household Work: Exploring the Perception of Middle Class Women and Men. Social Science Review, 33(2), 199-214.

Jahan, R. (1995). *The Elusive Agenda: Mainstreaming Women in Development*. Dhaka: UPL.

Kabeer, N. (2012). *Women's Economic Empowerment and Inclusive Growth: Labor Markets and Enterprise Development*. SIG Working Paper, Supported by Dept for International Development (DFID) and International Development Research Center (IDRC).

Khan, S. (1988). *The Fifty Percent: Women in Development Policy in Bangladesh*. Dhaka: The University Press Limited.

Khandker, S. (1987). Labour Market Participation of Married Women in Bangladesh. *The Review of Economics and Statistics*, 69(3).

Labor Force Survey Bangladesh. (2013). *Bangladesh Bureau of Statistics, Statistics and Informatics Division, Ministry of Planning, with support from International Labor Organization*. ILO.

Lorber, J. (1994). *Paradoxes of gender*. New Haven, CT: Yale University Press.

Mahalingam, A. (2010). *Conceptual Guide to the Unpaid Work Module. Gender, Work and Data base*. Retrieved from http://www.genderwork.ca/cms/displayarticle.php?sid=18&aid=56

Mahtab, N. (2007). *Women in Bangladesh: From Inequality to Empowerment*. Dhaka: A H Development Publishing House.

Mahtab, N. (2012). *Women, Gender and Development: Contemporary Issues*. Dhaka: A H Development Publishing House.

Marilyn, C., Martha, C., & Renana, J. (Eds.). (1996). *Speaking Out*. New Delhi: Vistaar Publication.

Mies, M. (2012). Dynamics of Sexual Division of Labor and Capital Accumulation. In S. Padmini (Ed.), *Women and Work*. New Delhi: Orient Blackswan.

Nelson, B. J., & Chowdhury, N. (Eds.). (1994). *Women and Politics World Wide*. New Haven, CT: Yale University Press.

Ostin, P. (2002). Examining Work and Its Effect on Health in Gita. In Engendering International Health: The Challenge of Equity. The MIT Press.

Phillips, A., & Taylor, B. (1980). Sex and skills: Notes towards a feminist economics. *Feminist Review*, 6(1), 79–88. doi:10.1057/fr.1980.20

Sharma, U. (1986). *Women's Work, Class and the Urban Household*. San Francisco: Tavistock Publications Ltd.

Sultana, A. (2010). Patriarchy and Women's Subordination: A Theoretical Analysis. *The Arts Faculty Journal*.

Tanjeem, N., & Khan, I. J. (2009). *Impact of Hegemonic Masculinity at Work Place: An Analysis of Challenges Faced by Today's Middle Class Working Women*. Working Paper Series no. 9. Department of Women and Gender Studies, University of Dhaka, Bangladesh.

UNDP. (1995). Human Development Report 1995. United Nations Development Programme (UNDP).

UNDP. (1999). *Human Development Report 1999*. United Nations Development Programme (UNDP).

UNDP. (2016). Human Development Report 2016: Human Development for Everyone. United Nations Development Programme (UNDP).

Yao, Y. (2015). Pay gap still wide between men and women despite improvements. *China Daily USA*. Retrieved from http://usa.chinadaily.com.cn/epaper/2015-03/13/content_19803414.htm

ENDNOTE

[1] Facts and Figures of Gender Compendium of Bangladesh 2009 (BBS- Bangladesh Bureau of Statistics; LFS- Labour Force Survey; MoE- Ministry of Establishment).

Chapter 4
Women-Friendly Working Environment in Bangladesh:
Critical Analysis

Tania Haque
University of Dhaka, Bangladesh

ABSTRACT

Work is typically divided along gender lines with men being responsible for paid work and women for unpaid care work. There is a negative correlation between income and level of gender inequalities in unpaid care work. Income can give certain level of independence but reinforces new kinds of dependence and subordination of women in our society in Bangladesh. If women wish to begin their paid work, it means ideologically they want extra jobs and they have to willingly undertake this double burden of household and professional work. The study claims that there is a need of gender responsive rebalancing policies to ensure women friendly working environment to ensure actual empowerment of women in Bangladesh.

INTRODUCTION

Over the last two decades, increasing numbers of women have been entering the workforce around the world, particularly in Bangladesh. Gender inequality in labor markets remains a persistent phenomenon where women continue to disproportionately face a range of multiple challenges relating to access to employment, choice of work, working conditions, employment security, wage discrimination, and balancing the competing burdens of work and family responsibilities. Where women's talents are sometimes wasted because they avoid competitive work environments, it seems important to know which types of work environments *are* attractive to them. Traditional gender norms, labor market segregation and unbalanced power relations and access to skills and resources have all led to women as the "*secondary workforce*" – within labor markets, they are treated as flexible and expendable workers and within households as "added workers" (Kabeer, 2008). Although there is no evidence to support the contention that women

DOI: 10.4018/978-1-5225-3018-3.ch004

are less efficient than men, as there are few differences between men and women in cognitive abilities and skills. Bangladesh is experiencing a more than proportionate increase in the female labor force, a process often defined as feminization of the labor force (Standing, 1985).

Though international human rights instruments and national laws have provided right to work in a safe and healthy environment but women still face discrimination in the workplace. However, data shows that women's participation is far from satisfactory and the implementation of the special measures provided by the labor act is questionable. Despite that, women in Bangladesh quite often encounter more obstacles than men in workplaces, and are treated unequally in their terms and conditions of employment. The unequal as well as disempowering environment is explicit both in women's participation in labor market and also in trade unions (Elson, 1999). Gender-balance or women-friendly environment in working world is still a myth in our country. Therefore time has come to chalk out what are the specific obstacles working women are facing in formal and informal sector jobs and what are the specific measures or policies can be taken to ensure women friendly working environment in Bangladesh; which in long run will encourage women to join and climb higher in workforce. Improvement of women's situation cannot be achieved without an understanding of the difficulties they face and the needs they have. This is what this study has attempted to unearth. Therefore the purpose of this paper is to fulfill the need for a comprehensive review of the literature surrounding the issues of equity and access in the workplace from a feminist perspective.

Background of the Study

Government took many policies and measures in promoting women's employment.

- A major problem of giving an accurate picture of the labor market because employment data has not been updated since the Labor Force survey 2010which found an increase in women's labor force participation from 29.2% in 2005 /6 to 36% in 2010. Women have been increasing at a faster rate compared to that of men but still low compared to international standard and women are mostly in low-end jobs. In 2010 the highest number of women 68.84% were engaged in agriculture sector followed by service sector 21.89% and industry sector 13.32%. Government had provisioned separate gender budget to empower women, sanctioned safety net program for poor widows and vulnerable women. From the earlier dim situation, Bangladesh had made a huge jump into the women empowerment. The entire safety net programs are titled towards women.

Women are being recruited into the regular cadre administration services since 1982.

Trends of Female Work Participation in the Labor Market: Gendered Labor Market Patters and Experiences

Employment: Gender Differences

The participation of women in employment has successively increased with the increase of total population in Bangladesh. However, they constitute only approximately 36 per cent of Bangladesh's labor force. The Labor Force Survey (LFS), 2010 found an increase in women's labor force participation (LFP) from 29.2% in 2005/6 to 36% in 2010. Women's LFP has been increasing at a faster rate compared to that of men but women are mostly in low-end jobs. The readymade garment sector continued to the largest sector employing women, though mainly as frontline unskilled workers. In 2010, 68.84% of women were engaged in agriculture sector followed by service sector (21.89%) and industry sector (13.32%). The increase in male internal and external migration, their shifting to non-agricultural activities, and higher crop intensity has resulted in increased women's participation in the agriculture sector. In Bangladesh 3.25 percent of employed women are working in the government sector and 8.25 percent in the private sector. The remaining 89.5 percent are employed in the informal sector. Gender differences in the status of employment was also evident in LFS, which showed that 56.3% women were unpaid family workers compared to 7.1% for men. About 15.7% women were self-employed in agriculture, 8.9% in regular paid employment and 9.4% as self-employed in non-agriculture. There is a higher growth rate of women as unpaid family workers (237% compared to only 35% for males) 15 from the period of 1999-2000 to 2010 and majority of women's economic participation were in informal sector. A good number of women are now engaged in the ICT outsourcing market, in armed forces and in law enforcing agencies.

Unemployment: Gender Differences

The number of unemployed women has regrettably increased at the national level in parallel to the increment in the rate of employment, except in 2002-2003. Unemployed women have increased from 0.7 million in 1999-2000 to 1.0 million in 2010 with an annual rate of 4.28 per cent per annum. During the period of 1999-2000 and 2002-2003, zero growth of unemployment has been shown in the urban areas and a decline of 13.33 per cent has been found in the rural areas. The inequality in employment of women is evident from all labor force characteristics (See Table 1). For example, the unemployment rate is nearly double that of the rate for men, the underemployment rate for women exceeds the rate for men by five per cent, the labor force participation rate of women is only about one-third of men, and the formal sector is clearly male-dominated. It is therefore no surprise that women earn on average 21 per cent less than men.

Table 1. Women's inequality as reflected in key labor force characteristics

Labor force characteristics	Total	Male	Female
Unemployment rate	5	4.1	5.7
Underemployment rate	20.31	14.40	34.15
Labor force participation rate	59.2	82.51	35.98
Male-female labor composition in the total unpaid family labor	21.8	7.01	56.3
Male-female labor composition of the formal sector employment	12.5	14.6	7.7
Male-female labor composition of the informal sector employment	87.5	85.5	92.3

Source: *BBS, LFS 2010*

Women are Overrepresented in the Most Vulnerable, Poorest Forms of Informal Employment

In Bangladesh, women account for only 24 per cent of the employed labour force and three-quarters of all informal workers are males, but 91 per cent of women workers are informally employed as compared to 87 per cent of the men (Rahman, 2002). Most of women workers are suffering from lack of access to property lack of choice work and comfort in Bangladesh. Gender inequality exists not only in the quantity but also the quality informal employment. While there may be more men than women in total informal employment, women are concentrated in the most vulnerable and poorest forms of informal employment – where they have low, irregular or no cash returns, are subject to a high level of job insecurity and do not have safety nets to cover them during periods of low economic demand or when they cannot work or do not have work. The Constitution of the Bangladesh and various international human rights instruments guarantee women the right to an equitable, safe, and healthy working environment. However, de-facto exercises of these rights are absent. Wage gap between women and men still remains and receive almost two thirds of that man. Minimum wages have not been set for all sectors. Lack of gender responsive working environment including inadequate fact working environment including inadequate facilities of child care, transport, accommodation, occupational health and safety are some reasons are need to be focused. Provision for life and disability insurance for women workers need to be ensured The labor law 2013 does not include rights of domestic, agriculture and unpaid homemakers.

Objective of the Study

Most of the research work shows that women are considered as the secondary workforce in the labor market. In spite of women's great contribution, they are still at low ranks and have to face many problems in the professional career. The main objective of this study is to figure out the reason of the untenable position of women in this male dominant filed. This paper mainly aims at demonstrating job situation for working women and, stresses and difficulties that women experience. Therefore the objectives of this study are:

1. To identify the challenges women face in workplaces and provide recommendations to address these challenges.
2. To provide recommendations for creating gender friendly environment in the workplaces.

Sequencing Methodology of Data Collection

The approach used in this study is based on a feminist standpoint, engaging a level of consciousness (Harding, 1987). Articulating experience according to Harding (1992; 178) is a crucial means of creating knowledge for all and all women's lives are valuable for generating feminist knowledge. This process of articulating knowledge is central to consciousness- raising and for women's voices to be heard. Thus there is a need for them to speak from their standpoint, perspective and experience. The analysis is based on the secondary data in nature and relies on multiple resources. Academic contributions in books, journals, government documents as well as published and unpublished works were explored. It represents a timely effort to synthesize the available literature and to shed light of different levels of analysis adopted by researchers. The data has been analyzed by using gender lens. The data has been analyzed by using gender lens. In addition to gender as an analytical category, intersectionality (Davis, 2008) approach has been used to show how the effect of policy on gender relations is intersected with class, age, geographical location, time, language and patriarchy. The notion of intersectionality challenges the notion of layers out and addresses the issues one by one. Multiple discriminations are based on different grounds at different time, whereas intersectional discrimination refers to the intersection of discrimination based on several grounds at the same time (Mackinnon, 2002).

SECTION TWO

A Gender Friendly Working Environment

A gender equitable work environment as one that includes and supports both women and men of diverse backgrounds; stimulates staff members to do their best and find satisfaction in both their professional and personal lives; engages women and men in making decisions that shape the work environment; employs diverse skills, perspectives, and knowledge of women and men; and values diverse contributions and ways of working (Joshi, 2005). A gender friendly working environment will have measures in place to protect the health and safety of woman workers, including reproductive health and ensures non-discrimination in hiring, promotions and remunerations prohibiting sexual harassment (Joshi, 2005). Features of Gender Friendly Working Environment are as follows:

- Includes and supports both women and men of diverse backgrounds. Stimulates staff members to do their best and find satisfaction in both their professional and personal lives.
- Engages women and men in making decisions that shape the work environment; employs diverse skills, perspectives, and knowledge of women and men; and values diverse contributions and ways of working.
- Administrative policy should clearly define position classifications and staff grade levels. Salary should be explicitly tied to grade level.
- Performance reviews should be based on clear and consistent criteria to reduce reviewer bias. Promotions should be based on transparent criteria and processes.
- Both women and men should receive on-going and constructive feedback about their performance. Managers and leaders should understand gender issues and should monitor and guard against the influence of stereotyping gender behaviors or roles in the work place.

Why Women Friendly Working Environment Is a Subject to Analysis

Women's work environment in Bangladesh doesn't begin and end at the workplace. In all the public spaces they inhabit – inside the factory and on the streets -- they must negotiate culturally embedded and highly gendered codes of spatial use and respectability. Women face infinite challenges in their workplace only for their gender. Schooling is more accessible to boys than girls therefore women's access to decent jobs is limited compared to men. In addition, research has consistently shown that organizations that support formal or informal mentoring processes are often more successful in creating work environments where both women and men of diverse backgrounds can develop productive and satisfactory careers. Although the government has invested in social protection, a huge proportion of formal sector workers, the entire informal sector and own account workers are excluded. Women must have access to gender-friendly working environments;

- That enable them first to realize their potential contributions to society and
- To maximize the economic benefits conferred to them and to their families by their employment.

Unequal Path to Ensure Equality: Transparent Barrier

The mainstream economic activities of women can empower and reduce their inequality. Economic opportunity allows women to be independent and lead their lives with dignity. While these changes have undermined established systems of gender difference, they have not provided a clear avenue for creating a new balance between autonomy and connection. To the contrary, a lack of change in other gendered arrangements has created *nonstructural* and *cultural* contradiction. These themes are explored within Bangladesh specifically around the following categories.

Stereotyped Perception Towards Women

Women are perceived as homemaker or housewives. Such expectations and stereotyped perceptions have failed to create a conducive environment for women to work outside. They are sidelined for less important task rather than important one. Employment opportunity bias is a general trend to be noticed in most of the employers' attitude. Biasness towards married women is also another evident in the private sectors where employers prefer hiring an unmarried woman as they think unmarried girls are less occupied with their household duties. As sanctioned by the belief that a good mother must give less effort and priority to work demands, she is therefore seen as a less committed worker.

Gendered Wage Norms: Institutionalized Economic Violence

There are striking differentials in wages and earnings by gender in Bangladesh. Women worker in informal sector are more vulnerable and are not getting general facilities provided by labor law such as equal pay for equal work. Based upon the survey report conducted by Unnayan Onneshan 2012, 33.33 per cent men have got their average daily wage between BDT. 301 and 400, while women did not even receive this wage, even if they worked for the same amount of time like their male counterparts (Hossain, 2012). Therefore the participation of women in the employment sector is seriously low. The presence of pure wage discrimination that is unrelated to skills and efficiency should, in fact, lead to enterprises that de facto practice discrimination by preferring to hire women.

Women's wages typically represent between 70 and 90 per cent of men's wages, entry level wages tend to be lower for women than for men, and there appears to be a persistent pay gap between men and women engaged in similar work, especially in professional and executive-level jobs and skilled trades (ILO 2011, p. 29). The gender differential is much wider in non-agricultural than agricultural employment, in both rural and urban areas. In the garments industry, female wages are on average 86 percent of male's wages, with variations depending on the level of education and category of the worker (UNICEF, 2011). A feature published in the Daily Prothom Alo on March 8, 2010, shows that in such work a female worker receives only 80 Taka after a day's work, whereas, for the same period the male counterpart gets 200 Taka. To reduce the wage gaps between male and female sectors, the Government needs to set wage norms.

Fragile and Insecure Forms of Employment

Though many women have been working for several years most of them are still only in temporary status because of their temporary status they are unable to enjoy many benefits provided to permanent staff. Moreover, several women are working as seasonal workers. The seasonal work demands workers only once or twice in a year for few months. Therefore, garment workers suffer greatly from job insecurity (Paul-Majumder, 2003). Their jobs are insecure not only because of the temporary nature of their jobs, but also because of the informal nature of recruitment. Most of the workers employed in the informal do not receive appointment letters. Therefore, terms and conditions of their employment are unknown to them. They do not know for how long they will be employed, although a temporary worker has the right to know the tenure of his/her employment. Women are unable to find jobs for the whole year round and this has posed a serious threat to the survival of these women. Pregnancy is often grounds for dismissal. Women are dismissed on the grounds that they can no longer meet productivity or time-keeping norms.

Gendered Infrastructure

Lack of gender responsive working environment including inadequate facilities of childcare, transport, accommodation, occupational health and safety are some of the reasons that discourage women from accessing the job market. The Labor Law 2013 does not include rights of domestic and agricultural workers and limits are placed upon union participation in factories. Women entrepreneurs have not yet been able to access institutional financing at a desired level, due to their own lack of capacity to fulfill the requirements and the banks' lack of confidence in women. Communication problem is a major problem faced by most of the female garment workers. A long distance travel is not only physical strenuous but also mentally stressful. No separate toilate for men and women is another practical problem. There is no special facility for working women in night duty.

Sexual Harassment

Sexual harassment in the workplace is a persistent problem. Workingwomen in Bangladesh face a double jeopardy when it comes to sexual harassment. Not only are they vulnerable to physical, verbal and sexual abuse inside the workplace but they are also frequently subjected to harassment in "public" places, as they commute to and from work (Siddique, 2003). Female workers are sexually harassed by their co-workers in the factory or by police or by mastans in the street. The intensity of gali (slang language) and other sexualized disciplinary regimes in garment factories is directly related to the pace of the production. There is no specific law to address sexual harassment in the workplace. Also, there are no procedural guideline for complaint submission and handling. As a result, there is no atmosphere to seek remedies by women in cases of sexual harassment. Women's vulnerability to sexual harassment gets increased due to the informal recruitment practices, lack of documented proof of employment, the fear of losing one's job, fear of retaliatory violence in response to filing a complaint and the absence of woman-friendly legal provisions (Siddiqi, 2003).

The experience of sexual harassment is an affront to a worker's dignity and prevents women from making a contribution commensurate with their abilities. Gendered violence at workplace is an issue that affects all women; however, poor and rural women often have fewer resources to seek protection than middle class and urban women. In hiring, promotions and other employment benefits, women have witnessed sexual harassment in different forms. It is also one of the major obstacles that restrain women taking any type of employment. At the same time the girls not brides movement should be strengthened for continuation of their education.

Inadequate Content and Weak Implementation of Labor Law

The Bangladesh government has introduced several changes in the legal provisions on minimum wage, working time and leave, especially for maternity leave and annual leave. These are only applicable under certain conditions for formal sector workers. This recently revised Act ensures minimum wages (which was not a part of the law earlier) and prohibits discrimination in wages on the basis of sex. It continues to provide maternity benefits to women for up to two children but has increased provision of maternity benefits to 6 months (on 10 January 2011), which was previously 4 months. Criterion for eligibility to receive maternity benefit has been relaxed to include women who have worked for at least six months, which previously included only those who have been working for nine months Maternity benefits are calculated on the basis of the median wage earned in the last three months preceding her maternity leave. This means that women who earn less and women with more than two children get less benefit and no maternity leave, respectively.

- On the other hand the labour laws have protective measures for women, who curtail their rights, a provision provides normal working hours for women from 6 am to 6 pm, and this provision has stopped employers from hiring women for night work. Some of the employers have misinterpreted such provisions and have stopped hiring women in the night interpreting that women should not be hired in the night according to the labor law standard. The Labor Act provides for childcare center in an enterprise where women workers are 50 or more than 50. Such law reinforces that childcare is only a woman's duty and not a man's. Criteria for providing childcare facilities should be on the basis of number of total workers and not only on the basis of the number of women workers ensuring it as a man's responsibility as well. The lack of monitoring system worsens the situation forcing labor into exploitative work conditions.

SECTION THREE

Initiative to Promote Gender: Friendly Working Environment Through Intersectionality Lens

Linked to the issue of substantive equality must be the recognition that women are not a homogenous group. Their heterogeneity requires us to take into account the fact that women do not experience discrimination in the same way. Women are separated by age, class, religion, disability, minority status including sexual orientation. This demands that we take a holistic look at the way societies are organized and the differential impact of discrimination on the various groups within it. Moreover, Bangladesh needs a comprehensive economic growth where participation and anticipation of members should be ensured, employment opportunities must be generated and equal rights will be guaranteed. Furthermore, a sound-working environment for the marginalized portion should be given top priority in all sectors.

The sameness approach cannot protect and promote women's economic rights as women have been in disadvantaged position historically. They need to introduce facilities and support services to help women carry out their jobs more easily, such as childcare, transport to the workplace, working women's hostels and so forth. Existing facilities are not only inadequate; they are also not available to low-income workers. So the issue of concerned the disembodied understanding of work and workplace which proliferates the theorization of an abstract fashion propagating an image of a disembodied universal worker who has no gender, no sexuality, no emotion and no reproductive responsibilities outside work. Creation of short and long-term wage employment for women is essential. Context-specific tailoring of programmes and policies is the only way to ensure that the focus areas of women and decision-making, gender equality in the workplace, gender equitable access to resources, women's entrepreneurship, and reconciliation of work and family responsibilities are each addressed appropriately and effectively. Besides weak implementation of the special measures, the monitoring and supervision mechanism to follow-up on the implementation is virtually absent. The monitoring is not conducted to examine the gender concerns in the workplaces.

Creating Win –Win Situation: Gendering Problems and Engendering Solutions

Ensuring equal opportunities for advancement and career development for women and men is a fundamental element of creating a woman-friendly work environment. Work on this has already begun, with the efforts to establish a comprehensive labor market information system in Bangladesh.

1. Legislation to improve transparency in job advertisement, both within organizations and externally. This might include mandatory advertisement of all vacancies, inside and outside of all organizations, and explicit guidelines with regard to the wording of advertisements to remove gender bias.
2. Legislation for greater transparency in employment policy in organizations, particularly in regard to recruitment, remuneration and mobility. This might involve a set of measurable guidelines for application in organizations.
3. Legislation to ensure greater equality in employment chances between men and women by, equating the costs of employment between them. Thus, maternity leave might be replaced by parental leave and all workplaces are mandatorily equipped with crèches. In order to spread the costs of such measures, a general insurance scheme, similar to the National Insurance (NIS) might be implemented.
4. Self-improvement courses that help to improve or develop marketable management skills in women, to counter the belief, even among them those women are less suitable for management.
5. Greater and more widely disseminated information about the experiences of women in the labor market in order to improve sensitivity and encourage a national culture in this regard.
6. The inclusion of sufficiently punitive measures for breach of laws, and greater attention to enforcement of labor legislation. This might be incorporated under the on-going reform of operations under the Ministry of Labor, through, for example, improved inspectorates.
7. Creation of short and long-term wage employment for women is essential. Support to private sector through finance, policy and encouraging foreign direct investment is essential to address the high

unemployment rate. The private sector has to be regulated and monitored in enforcing equal wage and benefits for women and men as per labor laws and the ILO Conventions.

8. Safety net programs designed to create employment for women and men should support transition to self-employment. Setting target for short-term employment opportunities under construction and development projects for women will facilitate employment.

9. Guaranteeing equal wages will ensure that women benefit equally as men from their labors. Motivation of private sector and oversight for payment of equal wage and support services should continue.

10. Incorporation of a monitoring and regulatory tool to assess the situation of women-friendly working environment in public and private sectors.

11. As employment opportunities are limited self-employment to be prepared with required paper work, tax identification and trade license.

Gender Responsive Rebalancing Policies to Ensure Women Friendly Working Environment

The discussion in this paper has highlighted individual and structural constraints on women's capacity to take up paid work and the resilience of the gender segmented structure of labor markets as constituting two major barriers to women's economic empowerment. Historically and at present women are in disadvantaged position because of prevalent discriminations. Such discriminations need to be addressed and women's biological difference needs to be recognized. Because only women become pregnant, for example, pregnancy may disadvantage women with respect to job opportunity, career seniority and job security. The corrective approach recognizes that in order to redistribute the benefits equally between women and men, reasonable different treatment is required.

De-Feminization of Labor Force: Transforming Masculine Culture to Human Culture

It is argued that gender differences in achievement, which reflect management prefers men's competitive and macho styles, will need to be transformed as organizations will have to adopt a more gender neutral structure to reap the benefits of the changing workforce and to promote gender equality. Gender-responsive measures aimed at enhancing the quality of human resources should be a central component of the rebalancing package.

Gender Sensitization Porogrammes for Employers

One of the reasons of the poor implementation of the special measures provided by the labor laws is the substantial lack of gender awareness and sensitivity among the employers. The labor laws alone have not proved effective in promoting gender friendly environment in the workplaces, therefore, efforts also needs to be directed towards educating the actual implementers. The protection and welfare of migrant workers and their families, as well as increasing their skills, remain a top priority for the government. In addition each organization can introduce cultural adjustment training for men at the very beginning of their employment.

Awareness Among Women Employees

Many women in Bangladesh are illiterate and uninformed of their rights. It is therefore, common that these women are incapable to claim their rights on their own. Civil society need to provide awareness programmes for workers to develop their understanding of rights and make them able to recognize when their rights are curtailed and report to the concerned authority for appropriate actions in cases when the individuals are unable to address the problem themselves.

Gender Responsive Skill Development

To develop a woman-friendly workplace requires the distribution of relevant knowledge and skills among staff at all levels. Gender-responsive skills development should seek to improve the quality of the workforce to meet the needs of today and build and sustain competencies for future development. Bangladesh lacks the skills and productive capabilities that would enable it to take advantage of new economic opportunities and the potential for employment creation through growing global trade. There is a need for designing a strategic medium term trade and employment policy to guide the country towards attaining broad-based development.

Provide Incentives for Employers

In today's dominant patriarchal society, strategic policies are needed to promote women's role in different sectors. One of the strategies can be providing tax exemption to enterprises who hires certain percentage of women or who take actions to promote women in decision-making roles, or in more productive roles etc. Such incentives would acknowledge enterprises contribution for promoting gender equality and ensuring women's economic rights further encouraging the employers.

Flexi Time

Organizations must integrate work and family life by promoting flexible workplace policies that are honestly and effectively implemented to address the specific career needs of women, such as giving them flexible job designs and specialized career path programs. Flexible and alternative work arrangements, such as flex time, job sharing, reduced hours, compressed work-week, family leave options, telecommuting, leaves and sabbatical options.

Gendered Infrastructure Development

Safety Road and Transport System

Infrastructure deficits are likely to have a far more severe impact on female than male earning opportunities because of the greater constraints on women's physical mobility.

In order for women to be able to exercise their right to freedom of movement in cities, public transportation systems should address existing mobility barriers (Peters, 2001). Safe public transit for women and girls must be based on the recognition of women's and girls' distinct roles, needs and experiences. The distinct needs of old and young people, the disabled, and other vulnerable groups also need to be considered in public transportation planning. A significant aspect of women's disadvantage in relation to the labour market relates to the constraints on their mobility in the public domain. This reflects the demands on their time from their domestic and care responsibilities as well as safety and ease of movement outside the home. The absence of infrastructure, particularly road and transport networks, also contributes to the spatial fragmentation of markets.

Housing Facilities

The majority of garment workers are women. The workers are mainly from there mote rural areas. For them it becomes difficult, if not impossible to arrange a secure housing facility with their limited income. In most of the cases, they are to live in the slums which are highly crime pron. Living in the slums involves the highest risk for the women garments worker (Paul-Majumder and Begum, 1997). In addition, the socio-economic condition of Bangladesh has made their condition more vulnerable. Our society, generally, pose a negative impression to the people who are living in the slums; when the slum dweller is a woman and she lives alone apart from her family, the stigma intensify. Taking the advantage of the situation people can easily sexually harass the garment workers. In such a situation, the factory accommodation is the most secure option for the women garments workers. Therefore; the Bangladesh Labor Act may have provision recommending factory supervised housing facilities for the workers.

Toilet at Public and Private Sphere

As an effort to create an enabling working environment for women, the Labor Act requires for separate modern toilets in convenient places for women and men workers. Not only the working place but also factors relating to women working must be improved such as transportation, street lighting, ample windows in rooms etc.

Gendered Health Care Facilities

Health care corners should be established in every magnitude offices to improve the quality of care, strengthen emergency obstetric care and make health services more women friendly. Other initiatives include strengthening supervision and monitoring to improve efficiency, renovating facilities and providing essential drugs and equipment. These medical corners also can provide health information, including the major danger signs of pregnancy, to pregnant workingwomen and new mothers. Reduced absenteeism and turnover, increased productivity, and enhanced worker loyalty; legal compliance and risk mitigation; improved worker satisfaction and worker management communication is highly needed to ensure a women friendly working environment. Each office shall make suitable space available for breastfeeding or expressing breast milk upon request. To enhance comfort and privacy, this room shall be equipped with a suitable chair and a sign indicating that the occupant should not be disturbed.

Adaptation of Women Friendly Technology

There is an emerging literature on the impact of mobile phones on poverty and livelihoods, which suggest that it may be an important route for such change. The introduction of mobile phone coverage in rural areas was associated with a 15% increase in employment, with most of the effect due to increased employment by women. They attributed it to reduced costs of job search (Kabeer,2008).

Address Sexual Harassment

The sexual harassment laws need to be made more specific by correcting the dated language that is couched in terms of a "woman's modesty" (Siddiqi, 2003). The law should protect against all forms of gender-based harassment and not just sexual harassment and at all places, and not just the workplace (Siddiqi, 2003). The Supreme Court has delivered a directive order to develop a Bill on sexual harassment in the workplace in response to a case filed on the issue. A comprehensive law prohibiting sexual harassment at the workplace should be enacted. It should include adequately stringent penalties and complaints' mechanisms. There are no written codes for behavior on the street and in any case 'moral codes of decency' are applied selectively. This is a social reality that must be addressed in the law. Organization must create an enabling culture in which the feeling and threat of power structure does not exist. There is, however, no government monitoring mechanism to track the effectiveness of law. Legal provisions in the Employment of Labour (Standing Orders), Act of 1965 should protect workers from unlawful dismissal. However, enforcement of the law is practically non-existent. "The Nari o Shishu Nirjaton Domon Ain" of 2000 also contains a section on sexual harassment although it does not mention harassment in the workplace specifically.

Gender Sensitive Language

Language should be gender-sensitive rather than gender-blind and/or sexist. This means that it should include both women and men and boys and girls. Gender-sensitive language should be used instead of gender-blind terms, which often results in women and girls becoming invisible. Use gender-sensitive language instead of sexist terms. For example, instead of "man-hours" use "work hours" or "time worked"; instead of "Chairman" use "chairperson".

Paternity Leave: Universal Care Model

Paternity leave needs to be provided to share responsibility of reproductive functioning. Providing paternity leave will also help in breaking the stereotype that only holds women responsible for reproductive functioning. The Labor Rules provides maternity leave of 52 days with full pay for women employees. "Universal Care Model" as characterized by dual earning and care sharing. The right to parental leave differs from paternity leave in that it is addressed to both parents. As with paternity leave it aims to encourage an equal division of unpaid work between parents in the family, which is a pre-requirement of justice in the workplace. Employees on maternity leave are also being able to undertake some paid work without losing their entitlement to statutory maternity pay. Although this is a welcome development for mothers, it has a detrimental effect on fathers who, as a consequence are still seen as 'secondary careers '.

Gender Audit

A gender audit enhances the collective capacity of an organization to examine its activities from a gender perspective and identify strengths and weaknesses in promoting gender equality issues; helps to build organizational ownership for gender equality initiatives; and sharpens organizational learning on gender through a process of team-building, information sharing and reflection. Gender audit provided an opportunity to introduce three indicators into its assessment of programme. The aim of a mainstreaming perspective is to integrate gender issues into all of an organization's objectives, activities, systems, structures, and resource allocation (personnel and financial).

Gender Mainstream in Trade Union

Trade unions are absent in many organizations. Awareness on legal rights could be raised through a trade union. Trade Union should increase women's participation in their policy and decision-making bodies. Trade Union have also been working for women's right, however, they have not been able to extensively cover the private sector. While, an under representation of women in trade unions is explicitly visible, trade union leaders agreed that the number of women members in trade unions has not increased in accordance with increase of female labour force participation in the country.

Research on Gender Friendly Workplace

This study is only indicative; a comprehensive study is necessary to further uncover the impact of discriminatory practices in the workplace. The study needs to focus on bringing out specific problems of government, and concerns of employers and the employees. And a follow-up action plan needs to be developed after the study to implement the recommendations given by the study. On the other hand effectiveness of gender budget and other women development activities in creating women-friendly working environment need to be examined.

Integrating Gender Issues in Planning and Budgetary Process

Despite gender responsive budgeting, the allocation on gender is often curtailed when resources are limited. Ministry of women and children affairs (MOWCA) in Bangladesh must be allocated sufficient resources for fulfilling its advocacy roles and for women's empowerment programmes like training and capacity building. Training needs to be provided also in non-traditional areas such as information and communication technology, driver and vehicle management, etc. Such training should target underprivileged, disadvantaged women who also are from minority groups. In addition to ensuring women's participation in economic sector as employees/workers, a step to empower women to take up roles of employers is vital. Apart from providing information on business planning, account keeping etc, the training should also focus on improving the understanding of market policies, market demands, and gender concerns. It is important to allocate adequate budget for such training programmes and to be provided in a regular basis.

Addressing Care Responsibilities

Women's care responsibilities are among the most pervasive of the constraints that curtail women's ability to participate in the labour market – as well as their ability to participate in the public life of their community more generally. Policies must address women's unpaid care workload that constraints their employment options and underlies stereotypes about women's weaker labor force commitment. It is high time to institutionalization of all informal women activities having given a title for each work as well.

Ensure Monitoring Method

It is important to monitor and supervise the workplaces to ensure worker's right making timely interventions.

ONLY EQUAL PARTICIPATION OF WOMEN AND MEN CAN ENSURE SUSTAINABLE DEVELOPMENT

Economic, social, cultural and environmental concerns need to be approached in an integrated and out of the poverty trap. Women not only constitute the vast majority of the world's poor but they are at a higher risk of poverty compared to men. Women's employment plays a significant role in the socio-economic progress in any country. To achieve sustainable development, women's enrollment in economic activities is urgently needed. Participation of women in the labor force can change the dynamics of the entire labor market. In Bangladesh, the economic contribution of women is substantial but they are not largely acknowledged. A quality labour force – with both women and men contributing to the fullest of their potentials – can foster a virtuous cycle of higher productivity, more and better jobs, income growth, innovation and development. Workers equipped with the knowledge, skills and attitudes required to be competitive, dynamic and performance oriented would be able to effectively and efficiently adjust to shifting labor markets, changing technologies and new threats and opportunities in volatile global markets.

CONCLUSION

The study spells out that patriarchal structures create gender asymmetries endowments, risks and constraints which penalize autonomous behavior for women but also offer them provision to remain within it parameters. It is very important to shift the focus from approaches that treat women as victims of development who are waiting to be rescued. In sum, there is a need for multipronged policies to address the needs of different categories of women in Bangladesh. Thus social dialogue and public debate is more powerful for transforming traditional mentalities or cultural norms. There is no doubt that social dialogue takes different roots, new ideas and brings diversity. Women should engage themselves more actively in a constructive debate with policy makers and negotiate the conceptual and policy issues that affect them directly. What forms of transnational networks, national and local organizations have been most successful in addressing not only in addressing women's interests as workers, women and citizens in national and international policy regimes but have also contributed to making national and international markets work better for women. Gender equality cannot be attained in the absence of equal rights and women themselves have to be the active agents for this change. In essence, promoting gender equality in labor markets not only makes sense but it is also a "smart" policy. The exclusion of women in the workplace and their widespread employment in precarious and vulnerable jobs represent a vast economic and competitive loss for any society. Moreover, creating an enabling environment of equal opportunity and treatment in the labor market for both women and men, would also contribute tremendously to poverty reduction, the achievement of the MDGs and social justice.

REFERENCES

Anker, R., & Hein, C. (1985). Why Third World urban employers usually prefer men. *International Labour Review*, *24*(1), 73–90. PMID:12269173

Bangladesh. (2010). Dhaka: Planning Division, Ministry of Planning, Government of the People's Republic of Bangladesh.

UNICEF Bangladesh. (2011). *A perspective on gender equality in Bangladesh From young girl to adolescent: What is lost in Transition? Analysis based on selected results of the Multiple Indicator Cluster Survey 2009*. Author.

Bangladesh-1999-2000. (n.d.). Dhaka: Planning Division, Ministry of Planning, Government of the People's Republic of Bangladesh.

Bangladesh Bureau of Statistics (BBS). (2004). *Report on the Labour Force Survey, Bangladesh 2002-2003*. Dhaka: Planning Division, Ministry of Planning, Government of the People's Republic of Bangladesh.

Bangladesh Bureau of Statistics (BBS). (2011). *Report of the Labour Force Survey*. Author.

Bergmann, B. (1974). Occupational segregation. Wages and profits when employers discriminate by race or sex. *Eastern Economic Journal*, *1*(2), 103–110.

Chen, M. (2008). Informality and social protection. Theories and realities. *IDS Bulletin*, *39*(2), 18–27. doi:10.1111/j.1759-5436.2008.tb00441.x

Elson, D. (1999). Labour Markets as Gendered Institutions: Equality, efficiency andempowerment issues. *World Development*, *27*(3), 611–627. doi:10.1016/S0305-750X(98)00147-8

Fraser, N. (2003). *Redistribution or recognition? A political-philosophical exchange*. London: Verso.

Ghosh, J. (2009). 'Informalization and women's workforce participation. A consideration of recent trends in Asia. In S. Razavi (Ed.), *The gendered impacts of liberalization: towards 'embedded' liberalism?*. London: Routledge.

Harding, S. (1987) Introduction: Is there a Feminist Method?. In Feminism and Methodology (pp. 1-15). Bloomington, IN: Indiana University Press.

Hossain, N. (2012). *Women's empowerment revisited. From individual to collective power among the export sector workers in Bangladesh*. IDS Working Paper Vol. 2012. No.389. Brighton, UK: IDS.

ILO. (2011). *Report of the Director General. A new era of social justice*. In International Labor Conference, 100th Session, ILO, Geneva, Switzerland.

Joshi. (2005). *Gender friendly environment in the workplace*. Forum for Women, Law and Development, The Asia Foundation.

Kabeer, N. (1994). *Reversed realities. Gender hierarchies in development thought London*. Verso.

Kabeer, N. (1997). Women, Wages and Intra-household Power Relations in Urban Bangladesh. *Development and Change, 28*(2), 261–302. doi:10.1111/1467-7660.00043

Kabeer, N. (2008). Mainstreaming gender in social protection for the informal economy. Commonwealth Secretariat, London.

Lien, B. (2005). Gender, power and office politics. *Human Resource Development International, 8*(3), 293–309. doi:10.1080/13678860500199758

Mahmud, S. (2002). *Informal women's groups in Rural Bangladesh:operation and Outcome. In Group Behavior and Development: Is the market destroying cooperation* (pp. 209–225). Oxford, UK: Oxford University of Press.

Molyneux, M. (2002). Gender and Silences of Social Capital:Lessons Capital:Lessons from Latin America, Developmnet nad. *Change, 33*(2), 167–188. doi:10.1111/1467-7660.00246

Paul-Majumder, P. (2003). *Health Status of the Garment Workers in Bangladesh*. Arambagh, Motijheel, Dhaka: Bangladesh atAssociates Printing Press.

Paul-Majumder, P., & Begum, S. (1997). *Upward occupational mobility among female workers in the garment industry of Bangladesh*. Research Report No. 153 (Dhaka, BIDS).

Peter, F. (2001). Review of Martha Nussbaum's Women and Human Development. *Feminist Economics, 7*(2), 131–135.

Rahman, R. I. (2002). *The dynamics of the labour market in Bangladesh and the prospects of economic development based on surplus labour*. Employment and Labour.

Rahman, R. I. (2002). *The dynamics of the labour market in Bangladesh and the prospects of economic development based on surplus labour*. Employment and Labour.

Sen, A. (1999). *Development as Freedom*. Knopf and Oxford University Press.

Siddique. (2003). Workplace environment for Women: issues of Harassment and need for interventions. *CPD Dialogue Report, 65*.

Standing, H. (1985). Resources wages and Power;The impact of Women's employment on the urban Bengali Household. In H. Afshar (Ed.), *Women, Work and Ideology in the third world*. London: Tavistock Publications.

Chapter 5
Gendered Organizational Culture:
A Comparative Study in Bangladesh and Thailand

Julaikha Bente Hossain
Asian Institute of Technology, Thailand

ABSTRACT

This study began with the question of what are the factors that lead to different outcomes of women in engineering employment in Bangladesh and Thailand. The primary data for answering this question were drawn from questionnaire surveys with 204 professional engineers, in-depth interviews with 80 professional women engineers, and discussions with employers in construction organizations in Bangladesh and Thailand. The findings identifies several barriers that not only deter women from entering into organizations, but also stopped the stream of women engineering graduates to flow into the engineering job market. The study has shed light on how organizational cultural practices as well as the influence of external factors within organizations affect women's entry and stay in construction organizations in Bangladesh and Thailand. The findings suggest that organizations should develop their own equal opportunity guidelines and policies to provide women with a suitable job and ensure that they remain employed.

INTRODUCTION

Organizational culture has been defined in many ways by various authors and researchers. However, the general definition of organizational culture is stated by Arnold (2005:625) is "the distinctive norms, beliefs, principles and ways of behaving that combine to give each organization its distinct character". In other words, it represents the unwritten organizational rules and assumptions that dictate how individuals should act and how things are to be done within the organization.

According to Evetts (1996), an employee's career within the organization is influenced by three cultural factors - stereotypical belief system, behavior or style and power relations. The belief systems and

DOI: 10.4018/978-1-5225-3018-3.ch005

control of social institutions influence career choice. For example, stereotypical beliefs about women in professional positions generate the idea that having traditional male characteristics is a better predictor for success, thus reinforcing the "think manager-think male" belief (Schein as cited in Sauers *et al*, 2002). In the context of an individual's behavior or style in the organization, McILwee and Robinson (1992) contended that cultures create an orderly set of rules, which allow work to be carried out in a particular way. This reflects the differential power of employees to create those practices. Within male-dominated organizations, male power has helped to institutionalize norms culturally associated with men and masculinity (Billing, 2000), therefore, present different kinds of problems for women's professional career.

Engineering[1] is considered to be a men's profession. Thus, not only are there fewer women in engineering profession worldwide, there is also a sharp gender segregation in terms of positions (Wirth, 2004). Careers related to this employment generally provide a higher professional and social status than many other professions; however, the general image of the profession is tough, heavy, dirty and machinery-oriented (Zywno *et al.*, 1998; Ogunlana *et al.*, 1993; McILwee and Robinson, 1992). Hence, any entry by women into this profession is considered an attempt to cross the sex barrier (Jaiswal, 1993).

Further, various schools of thoughts explained the reasons for the relative absence of women in engineering employment. Functionalist and gender-socialization theorists stress socialization and gender role behaviors as major sources of gender inequality and gender segregation in the work force. It stressed that if women are socialized to be more interested in engineering, there will be more women in the engineering workforce; and that gender segregation in the engineering workforce will decrease. However, statistics belie this. Country statistics show a non-linear relationship between the ratio of women in engineering education and the ratio of women in engineering employment. Comparative engineering education and employment statistics in Thailand and Bangladesh show that women have made significant progress in both countries. For instance, in 2015, women constituted 23.7% of the engineering students (in all disciplines) and 22.8% in civil engineering in Bangladesh (Figure 1). In Thailand, the corresponding figures were 17.3% and 9.7% (Figure 2). These figures are a massive leap forward from the early 1990s

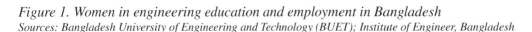

Figure 1. Women in engineering education and employment in Bangladesh
Sources: Bangladesh University of Engineering and Technology (BUET); Institute of Engineer, Bangladesh

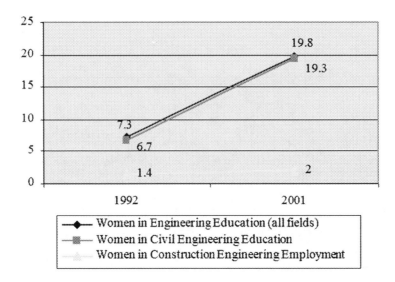

Figure 2. Women in engineering education and employment in Thailand
Sources: Calculated by various Thai universitys' engineering department[2]; The Engineering Institute of Thailand

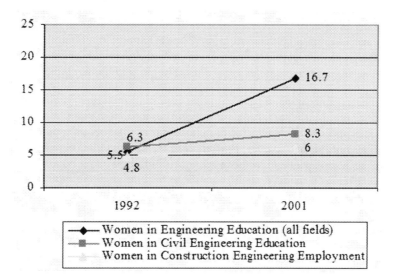

with 7.3% in engineering education (in all disciplines) and 6.7% in civil engineering for Bangladesh, and corresponding figures of 5.5% and 6.3% in Thailand (Figure 1 and Figure 2).

It is noted that women had progressed further in the field of civil engineering in Bangladesh (22.8% in 2015) than women in Thailand (9.7% in 2015). Despite this improvement in civil engineering education in the past decade, there has been little improvement in women's employment in engineering in Bangladesh (3.1%) (Figure 1). In Thailand, on the other hand, while civil engineering education among girls did not improve much, civil engineering employment among women kept pace with civil engineering education (Figure 2) (Hossain and Kusakabe, 2005).

There are few researches conducted on the experience of women engineers in construction organizations, particularly in the Asian region. A study reveals that one of the major problems associated with women engineer's under-representation in civil engineering organizations (e.g., construction organizations) construction organizations is career development obstacles (Ogunlana, et. al., 1993). Empirical research in UK shows that women engineers in construction organizations confronts a greater number of obstacles to their professional career development, which not only limits their career achievements but also prevents them from entering and staying in construction organizations (Dainty *et al.*, 2000).

Many feminist scholars in developed countries (such as in USA, UK) also noted the existence of cultural barriers in their analyses of specific organizations (Rutherford, 2004; Maddock, 1999; Wajcman, 1998; McDowell, 1997; and Gherardi, 1995). Itzin (1995) connects the maleness of organizational cultures to gender inequality that exists in the wider society. Within these workplaces, women were seen as additional competitors for limited career opportunities. A study conducted by Dorsey and Minkarah in USA on "Women in Construction" reveals that 73% of women professional in construction organizations believe that they do not have equal opportunity for their career advancement and 78% say that men with the same qualifications are given greater responsibilities. This study also indicates that women engineers usually get routine assignment, which tends to promote less chance for their career advancement (Dorsey & Minkarah, 1992). Men engineers are given more help, encouragement and support for their career advancement, while women engineers are considered as standbys, without any further promotions and thereby lower ultimate status achieved by women engineers compared to their male colleagues (Parikh & Sukhatme, 1993).

In addition to organizational factors, a number of external environmental factors (such as socio-cultural norms and practices) were recognized as influencing gender differences in career experience, which may account for some gender differences in professional career outcomes (Maddock, 1999; Wacjman, 1998; Itzin, 1995; Flanders, 1994). These external environmental factors shape organizational contexts through their influence on different groups within the organization. The combined result of these factors was that women are found not to have progressed in parity with their male peers. This is likely to lead to their poor retention levels. Rather than see their career progression slow down, many talented women engineers decide to move to another profession altogether (Dainty et al., 2000).

Nonetheless, recently, many researchers and scholars posit that the organizational culture plays a major role in women's career progression (Dainty et al., 2000; McILwee & Robinson, 1992). For instance, research reveals that in response to imminent professional and skill shortages, many organizations in developed countries have been changing/transforming their working pattern from a competitive and hierarchical style to teamwork style of project development that is more collaborative, which could be more attractive to women as well as men (Fletcher, 1999). A study conducted by Dainty et al. (2000) in UK construction organizations also reported that many construction organizations in UK have made considerable efforts today to attract more women to its professions by changing their management work and practices. These changes in the practice of management work might influence the promotional chances of women, at least to junior and middle levels of management (Metcalfe & Alison, 2003).

Similarly, in some developing countries (such as in Bangladesh, India), government has been taking initiatives to promote women's participation in employment, by providing special provision such as quota system for women. This served as a positive incentive for women graduate to embrace a career in the government job (Hossain, 2007). However, some authors argue that the quota system is linked to the concept of reverse discrimination. Under this system an employer would be required (or encouraged) by law to employ a certain proportion from the minority group, such as women. It causes psychological strain on quota appointees as they are generally looked down upon by those selected on the basis of merit (Zafarullah & Khan, 1989).

In sum, the literature suggests that both organizational cultural factors and external environmental factors can account for the low proportion of women engineers within the construction organizations, but the factors are context specific. Thus, the research question is:

- *What are the factors that lead to different outcomes of women in construction engineering employment in Bangladesh and Thailand?*

Importance of the Research

The researcher concentrates on women engineers in engineering employment in Bangladesh and Thailand. The rationales behind the research in these two countries are: (1) Women in Bangladesh have made significant improvement in engineering education, but there has been little improvement in women's employment in engineering employment. While in Thailand, engineering education among girls did not improve much, however, engineering employment among women kept pace with engineering education (Hossain, 2007). It is good comparison, therefore, to investigate the above question.

Construction organizations in both countries play a key role in the nation's economic development, and are a major fount of employment opportunities, due to their labor-intensive nature (Hossain, 2007). Although this profession is highly gender-segregated in both countries to different degrees, careers related to this occupation generally provide a higher professional and social status than many other professions. A wider range of their participation in such prestigious employment will not only increase more female intellectuals, but will also enable women to have more opportunities to engage in high level decision-making and management position as well as change the social outlook about women's lives. It is interesting, therefore, to investigate the factors that are linked to women's advancement in construction organizations of Bangladesh and Thailand.

There has been little empirical comparative evidence that exists concerning what specific factors actually influence women's relative absence from construction organizations in Bangladesh and Thailand. Until now, very few studies have documented the specific constraints that affect women's career development of women engineers in the construction organizations. Almost without exception, these existing literatures have an exclusively Western focus. Furthermore, as far as the researcher is aware, no study to date has jointly examined why the barriers exist in the construction organizations based on the organizational typologies. This is a gap that this study hopes to fill with the survey result. Such information would be extraordinarily valuable to employers, academics, and potential students, amongst others.

The objective of this research is, thus, to examine and identify obstacles, which lead to women's entry and remain in construction organizations in Bangladesh and Thailand. It aims to provide a contemporary understanding of the career experience of women engineers based on organizational cultural typologies, which could lead to better utilizing talented women in current competitive construction organizations in these countries. Understanding is the necessary foundation of constructive social change, and hopefully the research will contribute to both.

This chapter is organized as follows: the preceding introduction (Section one) outlines the background of this research, the problems, research question, importance of the research and research objective. Section two focuses on the methodology and research approach employed during this study, while Section three highlights the major factors related to women's entry into the engineering employment in Bangladesh and Thailand; Section four identifies the factors that deter women's organizational entry and stay in the construction employment. Section five summarizes and concludes the research findings, which will help to signify the insight of women's professional status as well as will generate strategies for women engineers' career progression in construction organizations in Bangladesh and Thailand.

METHODOLOGY AND RESEARCH APPROACH

This study is an exploratory in nature. When the objective is to understand the career experiences of individuals within the organizational culture, then the relevant theoretical issue has to be considered. For this research, a theoretical approach is required and feminist standpoint theory is the best way in this regard.

The Feminist Standpoint: Why Women?

The researcher tries to explore this research in light of feminist standpoint theory or women's voice research, since historically women are the most disadvantaged group in every society. The main contribution of this theory has been to show how women's position in the work place can be seen as part of a whole social system where women are subordinate. Feminist standpoint research has developed a new gender research paradigm, which aimed to change the world. It implies that researchers need not search for the one "truth" but for the multiple "truths" that exist in researching the oppression of women (Harding, 1987). Since the world is constituted by the values and ideas of the ones with power, the oppressed can understand the viewpoints of oppressor (Kusakabe, 1998). Feminist standpoint theorists see the truth of social reality from the systematic analysis of marginalised women's groups, such as their professional career, their formal-informal situation within the organization, interaction pattern, their emotional and intellectual involvement (Harding, 1987).

Today, with economic development, women are now taking more responsibility than ever for the economic support of their families, while the man's role as principal breadwinner is weakening (Safa, 1996:188). But fewer job opportunities, traditional or transitional organizational cultures, carrier development obstacles and other factors have weakened women's position in the work place; which in turn has kept women dependent on men and justified their performing domestic chores for men (Anker and Hein, 1986). Women are in separate, subordinate employee track, with lower opportunities. Feminist standpoint theory suggests the need for a new definition of development in terms of equality, dignity, race, class, religio-cultural practices and alternative development strategies, where development enhances people's lives, life options, and choices, especially appropriate for women. If women's position is improved, the notion of women's separate sphere will be replaced by the notion of individual rights for men and women.

The methodology developed for the study was to 'answer the research question' and how the data is to be collected analyzed.

Since most large and medium construction organizations are located in the capital city, two capital cities - Dhaka (the capital city of Bangladesh) and Bangkok (the capital city of Thailand) were selected as research area for this study. Further, to cover an adequate number of women engineers, fifteen construction organizations (four government organizations and eleven private organizations) in Dhaka, and eleven organizations in Bangkok (one government organization and ten private construction/consulting organizations) were selected. In order to identify construction organizations in both study areas, snowball-sampling[3] techniques were used to identify all types (e.g., private, joint venture and public) of construction organizations, where an adequate number of women engineers are working. Further, the rationale for selecting all types of construction organizations (e.g., private and public organizations) was to determine whether organizations' own policies or the local socio-cultural environment would have most bearing on practices, and attitudes towards women engineers' employment.

The primary data of this study were collected in Bangladesh and Thailand during 2001 through questionnaire surveys with 204 professional engineers (102 each from Bangladesh and Thailand; an equal number of women and men from each organization), in-depth interviews with 80 professional women engineers[4] and informal discussions with employers/representatives. Respondents, who had at least a bachelor degree of Engineering and/or higher level education in engineering, were selected both in Bangladesh and Thailand. The response rate is 68%. To ensure the confidentiality of participants, pseudonyms are used throughout this dissertation for all the studied organizations in both countries. In addition, books, journals, policy papers, project documents and study reports were reviewed as secondary sources. The researcher further revisited the study areas in 2015 in order to find any changes during this period in terms of women engineers' career experience.

Both qualitative and quantitative data were analyzed. For quantitative data, statistical analysis were done by using SPSS computer software packages where appropriate. Qualitative data were used in articulating, interpreting and explaining the facts that researcher has gathered from the field research. This

Gendered Organizational Culture

enabled researcher not only to provide a clear picture of the research findings, but also given way to justify researcher's conclusion. The research findings are presented in descriptive, tabular and graphical forms.

ENTRANCE TO EMPLOYMENT

This section outlines the major factors related to women and men's entry into the engineering employment in Bangladesh and Thailand. It examines the differences and similarities between women engineers in the identified five types of construction organizations in Bangladesh and Thailand as follows: (1) Bangladesh – Private (Owner-centered) Organizations, (2) Bangladesh – Public (Top-down bureaucracy) Organizations, (3) Thai – Private (Informal management) Organizations, (4) Thai – Joint Venture (Team working) Organizations, and (5) Thai –Public (Facilitating bureaucracy) Organizations, with regard to their entry into the engineering employment.

Regarding women's employment in construction organizations in Bangladesh and Thailand, the findings show that the average number of women engineers in all types organizations examined in this study is far below than men engineers (Table 1). The research result also showed that the ratio of women and men engineers in Bangladesh private organizations and Bangladesh public organizations is 1:58 and 1:45 respectively. In contrast, the ratio of women and men engineers in Thai private organizations, joint venture organizations, and public organizations are 1:12, 1:33 and 1:10 respectively (Table 1).

The study shed light to how organizational cultures and its formal and informal practices not only deter women from working in the construction organizations but also stopped the stream of women engineering graduates to flow into the engineering job market in Bangladesh and Thailand.

One mechanism is through hiring and recruitment practices. The study reveals that Bangladesh private organizations and Thai private organizations tend to be more exclusionary to hiring women engineers because of their stereotype attitudes towards women. In Bangladesh, this is further reinforced by additional complicating factors such as over-supply of engineers and socio-cultural restrictions on women's mobility. For instance, because of hostile working environment, until recently, Bangladeshi women are not allowed to work outside the home. This might have influenced construction employers not to recruit women engineers especially at the field level. Neither employer in Bangladesh private organizations and Thai private organizations are found to be under pressure to change this recruitment practices. These

Table 1. Average number of engineers in the studied construction organizations in Bangladesh and Thailand

No. of Engineers	Bangladesh		Thailand		
	Bangladesh – Private Org.	Bangladesh – Public Org.	Thai – private Org.	Thai – Joint Venture Org.	Thai –Public Org.
Women	3.2	15.8	5.1	3.8	30
Men	173.5	712.9	63.3	146.5	300
Total	176.7	728.7	68.4	150.3	300
Ratio (Women: Men)	**1:58**	**1:45**	**1:12**	**1:33**	**1:10**

Source: Field note, 2001

kind of organizational practices may not only influence sex segregation in both private organizations but also reinforce traditional forms of gender ideologies work within the organizations.

On the other hand, the image of Bangladesh public organizations is inviting due to the quota system for women's recruitment in government services, which encourage Bangladeshi women engineers to enter this type of organizations. This may help women in overcoming the entry barrier but due to management's stereotyping attitude towards women, quota does not help women to build a career in Bangladesh public organizations or even to stay employed. Furthermore, due to socio-religious and political pressures, two-third of the quota is not generally met and where they are, the women are regarded as token appointees and assigned secondary roles. It is uncovered that the religious leaders/fundamentalists is another obstacle to women's employment outside the home. In the name of Islam, despite women's mobility, the religious leaders/fundamentalists impose restrictions on women's rights and equality, subject women to strict rules of conduct and dress, and promote the submission of the wife to the husband in the name of social order. All these constraints put women on an unequal footing with men in terms of employment and professional development in the construction organizations.

In contrast, Thai joint venture organizations and Thai public organizations seems to be positive to recruit women because the demand for employment is much higher; and the growth is higher than in Bangladesh. Also, there has been a general shortage of engineers during the economic boom in 1989 – 1996 in Thailand (Thitipaisan, 1999). This might have influenced Thai joint venture organizations to recruit women engineers in order secure enough professionals to meet the construction demand in Thailand. Nonetheless, women engineers experienced many barriers, which not only restrict their entry in the construction organizations, but also affect their career development and stay in the construction organizations in both countries (see following section).

Career Experience of Women Engineers in Construction Organizations

This section set out to explore: (a) the barriers experienced by women engineers in the identified five types of construction organizations based on the organizational culture in Bangladesh and Thailand; and (b) also to draw comparisons among identified five types of construction organizations in Bangladesh and Thailand, where appropriate, with regard to cross-cultural context, for example, the influence of external environmental factors (i.e., social, cultural and political) that influence organizational culture.

The findings reveals that apart from women's less participation rate in construction organizations in Bangladesh and Thailand, a sharp sex segregation in organizations exist in terms of positions in both countries. The findings reveal both horizontal and vertical sex segregation in private construction companies studied in Bangladesh. For example, according to the management of a private construction organization in Bangladesh, of the total 46 engineers, 45 are men and 28 of them are employed at project sites. Twelve are at the top/senior level, 13 at middle level and 20 at junior level. There is only one women engineer in this organization. She works in a junior-level position handling office-based support tasks. Conversely, this study shows highly vertical sex segregation in private companies studied in Thailand, although horizontal sex segregation is not found to be significant. In one of Thai private construction organizations in this study, of the total four women engineers in construction organization, three are employed at a junior level and only one at a mid-level position. The contrast becomes stark when compared with the positions of men. Of the 31 men, ten hold top/senior level positions, 16 are at mid-level and only five are at junior level. Engineers in junior level positions are assigned specific

Gendered Organizational Culture

tasks, whereas mid-level engineers do supervisory and managerial work. Engineers at the top/senior level positions usually help form organizational policies.

By comparing Thailand and Bangladesh, the findings reveals following constraints to professional development encountered by women engineers in both countries.

Management Prejudice Against Women Engineers

Apart from the recruitment barriers discussed in above section (Section three), another constraint reported by women respondents, particularly in Bangladesh private, public organizations and Thai private organizations was management prejudice towards women engineers. Because of such prejudice, women respondents are excluded from any creative and challenging tasks that could help them show their capability and performance. Exclusion from challenging tasks has been argued by many scholars to be a significant factor in women's more general exclusion from influential positions and promotion ladder.

The study reveals that over 80% of the women respondents compared to only 2% men respondents in Bangladesh private organizations reported management prejudices. According to them, they were excluded from any creative and challenging tasks. To quote a 32-year-old woman engineer employed in Bangladesh private organizations:

We are only assigned desk work. Even (though) I am working in my father's firm, I also feel discrimination in terms of site visits and supervision. My supervisor thinks that tough work is not for women. In field visits, I am always second or third preference. We could work hard to prove our capabilities if our supervisor relied on us like our male colleagues; like we sometimes do assignments before being given to them. (Field note, 2001)

Likewise, over 80% of women respondents in Thai private organizations compared to 3.6% of the men respondents reported that despite showing interest, they were not assigned any challenging tasks that could help them show their capability and performance. According to women respondents, supervisors generally believe that men are better suited for technical professions. The management's prejudice against women can affect self-worth of Thai women engineers. To quote a Thai woman engineer employed in Thai private organizations:

I am working in this organization as support staff for more than three-and-a-half years without any reward and promotion. There is no space for me to show my performance and knowledge. I am not assigned to perform any challenging work where I can show my knowledge and ability. My male colleagues get priority as my boss think that we (women) cannot be as competent and efficient as our male counterparts (Field note, 2001)

It seems that workplace discrimination in Thai private organizationsis sustained by myths about the relative abilities of the sexes (e.g., the supposed physical weakness of women) as influenced by traditional gender norms. Within this type of organizations, supervisors "sort" women and men into different jobs or tasks (such as "women's job" and "men's job") based on their traditional gender ideologies and prejudices. Hence, organizational policies and procedures may entail negative consequences for women as a group, irrespective of individual women's capabilities and preferences. Although Thailand have ratified the UN Convention on the Equal Employment Opportunity programs and Elimination of Discrimination against Women policy, none of the Thai private organizations have formal policies relating to anti-discrimination. Without the support of the organization, an equal opportunity program and policy is unlikely to be successful.

In contrast, few women respondents in Thai joint venture organizations reported such management prejudice towards them. Although the cultural image of construction engineering profession as male-oriented still remains very powerful in this type of organizations, this study reveals that Thai women respondents in this type of organizations are in a much better position than women respondents in other types of organizations in this study. The reason might be because the management of Thai joint venture organizationspractices participatory approach through team work. They provide prospective team members with a lot of opportunities to work with each other, to understand each other and to learn from each other. This indeed, gives Thai women engineer's way to explore their potentials and show capabilities. Management value their capabilities and it further enhance and encourage women engineer's participation as well as reduced sex segregation in Thai joint venture organizations. To quote two Thai women engineer working in Thai joint venture organizations:

Team work provided me opportunity to show my technical skills and increased my self-confidence. I have also received good support by interacting with my supervisors and colleagues to carry out work. (Field note, 2001)

Gender Wage Discrimination

Another organizational constraint reported by women respondents in both countries is salary discrimination; an implicit barrier in almost all organizations in this study. To examine gender difference in the earning status of the respondents, the study collected information about the respondent's monthly income in construction organizations in both countries as detailed in Table 2. The findings show that the average monthly salary of Bangladeshi women respondents working in Bangladesh private organizations is comparatively much lower (USD 159.83) than their male counterparts (USD 364.22). The t-test results also show a significant earning difference between women and men respondents in Bangladesh private organizations ($p < .05$).

Likewise, the study shows that the average monthly salary of women respondents working in Thai private organizations and Thai joint venture organizations is USD 541.67 and USD 648.53, while the average monthly salary of male respondents in Thai private organizations and Thai joint venture organizations is USD 794.44 and USD 883.82 respectively (Table 2). The t-test results also show highly significant earning difference between women and men respondents in these types of organizations in Thailand ($p < .05$).

The study uncovered in the discussions with the management of all three types of organizations that one of the reasons for the unequal salary distribution between women and men are due to stereotype attitude of the management towards women. The representative of Bangladesh private organizations and Thai private organizations mentioned that they do not think that women can compete with men in this technical profession.

A common experience among the women respondents in all three types of organizations, i.e., Bangladesh private organizations, Thai private organizations and Thai joint venture organizations is that

Table 2. Respondents' average monthly salary (in US dollar)

Organizations	Women			Men		
	Number (N)	Mean salary	Std. Deviation	Number (N)	Mean salary	Std. Deviation
Bangladesh - Private Organizations*	18	159.83	85.85	18	364.22	194.12
Bangladesh - Public Organizations	33	130.94	30.30	33	131.33	29.01
Thai – Private Organizations*	18	541.67	215.57	18	794.44	314.19
Thai – Joint Venture Organizations*	17	648.53	239.38	17	883.82	244.78
Thai – Public Organizations	16	223.44	87.31	16	257.81	96.49

Note: * Chi-Square Test: $p < .05$
Source: Questionnaire survey, 2001

their starting salary is much lower than their male counterparts in similar positions; even when there is no age and work experience differences among them. They reported that they did not know this kind of pay discrimination before entering the organization. Some of the women respondents further indicate that they have to accept this practice since they do not have other options due to the competitive job market. To quote a woman respondent working in a Bangladesh private organizations:

I accepted the low salary (USD 79) because I waited for one year after my graduation. I thought I will work hard and prove my worth within a short period of time, by which I will get a salary increase. But in reality, it took a long time (three years) to get a salary increase, which is not even satisfactory. My male colleague who joined at the same time received much more salary than me (USD 105) and his salary was increased within one and half year. I cannot protest as the job market is very competitive and employers are reluctant to hire women. (Field note, 2001)

In contrast, this study found less earning difference between women and men respondents in Bangladesh and Thai public organizations. The explanation can be drawn from the fact that the Public Service Commission in Bangladesh and Thailand are responsible for civil service holder's salary in these two types of organizations irrespective of women and men.

Organizational Promotion Process

Another crucial point is that in Bangladesh private organizations, Thai private and joint venture organizations, engineers from field based positions are promoted to top positions more easily and in this way women engineer are systematically excluded from the promotion processes. This is more noticeable in Bangladesh private organizations. Despite social restrictions on women's mobility, management's own interpretation of religio-cultural norms and gender ideological preconceptions reinforce organizational management to undermine women's technical capabilities with respect to men in Bangladesh private organizations. This affects women's professional opportunity, their salary, and exacerbates sex segregation in the Bangladesh private organizations more compared to women in Thai private and joint venture organizations. This does not mean that Thai women are free from such organizational discriminatory practices.

As discussed above, Thai women engineers also suffer from discrimination in their promotion processes due to management's prejudices towards Thai women's roles. This is more noticeable in Thai private organizations. Like in Bangladesh private organizations, they are systematically excluded from involving any challenging assignments and also limits their upward mobility by offering little scope or opportunities for their professional development (such as training). Further, this kind of informal practice within organizations play a major force in the continued dominance of sex segregation and limits women's promotional prospect in the organizations.

On the other hand, although women respondents in Thai joint venture organizations comparatively receive more promotion than women in other organizations, they also receive less promotion than their male counterparts. The reason might be because of their young age and less work experience compared to their male counterpart. According to the representatives of Thai joint venture organizations, technical professionals are assessed mainly on their merit and work experience for promotion. They usually provide skill development program for their technical professionals irrespective of gender in order to enhance their promotion prospects. Nonetheless, none of these Thai joint venture organizations have specific programs in place to encourage women to apply for promotion. The reason provided by organization representatives is that to enact programs to specifically help women would be viewed as "actually encouraging inequity and discrimination". To quote a representative in a Thai joint venture organizations:

We do need to conform to the local environment. That means that we cannot actively help women's promotion prospects. We can encourage them for their work performance but we cannot provide a specific program only for women professionals. Our entire skill development program is for any professionals irrespective of women or men for their progression. We cannot go beyond the social system operating in the local environment. (Field note, 2001)

Differences in Interpersonal Relationships

Interpersonal relationships can be conceptualized by the social network theory as the informal associations and connections that link the organizational members together and interact with each other, which provide ways for organizational members to gather information and introduce new ideas and opportunities. This has long been established as a critical element of success in a professional career. Many prior researches reveal that interpersonal relationships is a vital route to senior management level as the key benefits associated with it include access to visibility, support and upward mobility, and recognition within the organization (Bozionelos, 2004; De Janasz and Sullivan, 2004; Ensher et al., 2003). Dainty and Lingard (2006) posit that interacting forms an essential dimension of organizational life and individuals who excel at interacting/communicating with each other generally excel within the organizations in which they work. In this regard, lack of access to interpersonal relationships resulted in a lack of access to contacts, information and professional opportunities.

The findings show that women respondents in Thai private, joint venture and public organizations have more interpersonal relationships as men respondents than in Bangladesh. The reason might be because all types of construction organizations in Thailand are more open and have less restriction in terms of Thai women's visibility, personal freedom and interaction with other staff, as the system operating in the local environment. Whereas protective and top-down management system in both private organizations and public organizations in Bangladesh systematically discourage entrances of women engineers as well as affect women's career development in organizational employment in Bangladesh. Further,

Gendered Organizational Culture

conservative nature of Bangladeshi society may influence construction organizations to pose restrictions on women's visibility, personal freedom and interaction with other staff in the male-dominated working environment. Nonetheless, majority of the respondents (both women and men) pointed out the importance of interpersonal relationships in building their self-confidence and providing them access to interactions, information and opportunities. To quote a woman engineer in a private organization in Bangladesh who lacks interpersonal relationships in her organization:

My boss (supervisor) helps me if I have problem in understanding some tasks but I cannot communicate with him easily like my male colleagues do. Moreover, as a woman there are some problems. For instance, we cannot go to our colleague' room freely to discuss some important work like male colleagues. In this profession, consulting with supervisor/colleagues is very essential, which is not possible all the time due to lack of interpersonal relationships with them. (Field note, 2001)

Professional Development Opportunity

Professional development opportunities i.e. training is crucial to enhance the ability of women and men to achieve and function effectively in their respective positions and to ensure that they have the skills required for career advancement.

This study reveals that very few Bangladeshi private organizations offer professional development opportunities (e.g., training) for their professionals; and women respondents are far behind for those opportunities. Most of women respondents mentioned that they are not offered any training opportunities which could help them show their capabilities and performance. Further discussion with the management representatives in Bangladeshi private organizations reveals that only some of larger organizations offer training opportunities with a limited number and on the basis of each organizational division's/unit's own judgment. Since the ratio of women to men is found to be 1:58 in Bangladesh private organizations, a woman engineer in this type of organizations has to compete with at least 58 male colleagues within her work team in order to avail training opportunities. Moreover, they are systematically excluded from these opportunities since the majority of women respondents in Bangladesh private organizations are involved in support tasks.

Although the Bangladesh Constitution grants equal employment opportunity to women, this study reveals that none of the organizations studied in Bangladesh private organizations have formal policies relating to equal employment opportunity. Progression was seen to be much more in the hands of one's line manager than to be determined by formal organizational system in this type of organizations. Regarding human resource development, the Bangladesh private organizations are not very committed to invest on staff development, especially for women professionals. The reason is not only because of their limited access to financial resources for staff development but also their stereotype attitudes towards women in this type of organizations.

On the other hand, Bangladesh public organizations provide training opportunities and study leave to their employees on the basis of seniority, length of service to the organization, both locally and in foreign countries. Apart from political influence, there exists subtle gender discrimination in terms of training and higher studies, especially if the higher studies are in a foreign country. Therefore, the future of employment in these organizations is intimately dependent not only on bureaucratic organization policy but also in political pressure and internal organizational culture and its practices.

Likewise, Thai private organizations also offer professional development opportunities (e.g., training) for their professionals. However, it is revealed that women respondents in this type of organizations are far behind such opportunities. Lack of career development opportunities has also been cited as a career constraint of Thai women engineers in Thai private organizations. Among 18, 13 women respondents (72.2%) in Thai private organizations reported that they were not actively encouraged to participate in career development activities (e.g., training opportunity) because of their supervisor's prejudice. The supervisors believe that men are more appropriate and capable than women for technical profession and get priority over women; even when they (female) are in the same rank and have equal work experience with their male counterparts. Such attitudes not only deprive women engineers but also affect their promotional prospect. To quote a Thai woman engineer employed in a Thai private organization:

Every year our company offers three trainings for the junior and mid-level engineers for their professional development. But we were always excluded from this opportunity, except those who have family connections with the management. To get the opportunity, we have to be a daughter or spouse of our boss. (Field note, 2001)

In Thai public organizations, this study found less sex segregation in these organizations as working in these organizations is seen as more women-friendly because of its flexibility in terms of working hours and workload. However, the central issue for Thai women engineers working in Thai public organizations is the scope of work and promotion. The majority of Thai women respondents working in Thai public organizations also reported dissatisfaction in their present jobs. One of the reasons cited is the smaller scope for creative work; government organizations usually outsourced the major part of the engineering work. Further, in terms of opportunity to use professional skills in Thai public organizations, 8 out of 16 or 50% of Thai women respondents reported that supervisors sometimes offered them some works that did not match their position. For example, one of the female engineer in Thai public organizations reported that although she is a fully qualified engineer and was appointed as office engineer, her professional responsibilities at the workplace is public relation. She is mainly entrenched in the public relation aspects of the organization even outside official working hours, often entertaining official foreign delegates to the organization. This kind of constraints not only affects women's career advancement but also undermine women's technical skills and knowledge in Thai public organizations.

In contrast, only 11.8% women respondents in Thai joint venture organizations reported that they were not actively encouraged to participate in career development activities (e.g., training opportunity) due to their short-term contract with the organization. Since construction is a project based business, most Thai joint venture organizations usually appoint engineers on a project basis; and usually do not offer professional development opportunity to employees with short term contract (less than one year) with the organization.

Hostile Organizational Environment

For construction engineers, it is important to have site experience in order to be promoted to managerial positions. In Thailand, women in all organizations are getting more opportunities to go to sites as compared to Bangladeshi women, because construction sites are better organized and more secure for women to work in Thailand. Another advantage for Thai women is their greater mobility than Bangladeshi women. Thus, Thai women are getting more opportunities to go to sites compared to Bangladeshi women. This shows that even though sites are generally seen to be dangerous for women, it is possible to improve the security situation in order to allow women to work. On the other hand, hostile and insecure working conditions are another major barrier of women's employment in both Bangladeshi private and public organizations. They faced more threats from extortionists compared to their male counterparts at the workplace and also from colleagues aligned to religious fundamentalist forces. Moreover, the social norms of seclusion of women are tighter in Bangladesh which influences Bangladesh private organizations to exacerbate horizontal sex segregation in these organizations.

According to women respondents in Bangladesh public organizations, terms are set for women working at the project site i.e. they must wear a veil, must leave before sunset, etc. Buckling under the pressure, women engineers either quit their jobs from Bangladesh public organizations or move to office-based desk work in Bangladesh private organizations; thus limiting their prospects for promotion. A 35-year-old woman engineer worked in a Bangladesh public organizations reported that she was threatened by some people at the project site. She reported:

At the project site, I was responsible to supervise the execution work. One day a group of people came to our site and asked me why I was working here. (They said) If I work, I have to follow their rules such as for this project we have to buy some construction/building materials from them and compromise with them. I told them that my job is only to supervise work and not to be involved in other matters. They told me to communicate with the person in-charge of buying materials. I refused. One evening they came to my house when I was not home. They threatened my family. After that, my family members, especially my spouse, did not allow me to work in any construction organization. To avoid family conflict, I had to sacrifice my career and quit the job. Now I am just doing my household duties. (Field note, 2001)

Insecure working conditions are a major barrier of women's employment in Bangladesh. The law and order situation of Bangladesh is much worse than Thailand but there are no government regulations to protect Bangladeshi women against such harassment.

Due to prevailing insecure working conditions in Bangladesh, many families are reluctant to encourage women's outside field-based work, which affect women's occupational career. To avoid family conflict, they more likely prefer to go into teaching, research and development institute rather than engineering organizations. Some of the women engineers interviewed planned to work in the constructions organizations in Bangladesh but was discouraged by their family because of the persistent insecure working conditions. For example, *Samina*, a 33-year-old engineer, is a lecturer in an engineering academic institute in Bangladesh. Her father was a professor in the same profession and she was the only daughter. She was inspired by both her engineer father and only brother. To quote her:

In my secondary schooling, I planned to be an engineer and was one of the few lucky girls who got support from my family for my future career. My father and brother are both engineers and encouraged me to study in the engineering field. But after graduation, I had to wait six months to look for a job not only because I was a fresh graduate but also because employers do not like to hire women engineers in our country. My engineering GPA (Grade Point Average) was much higher than my elder brother but my brother got job without waiting for graduation.

Later, I had the opportunity to work in the same private organization where my brother is working. I worked in that organization for only four months and had to quit the job because after I got married, my in-laws' family strongly discouraged me to continue work in the organization. During my engineering academic life, I planned to work some years in a private construction organization to get practical experience and then planned to start my own business. But after got married, I had to change my future prospect. To avoid family conflict, I had to quit that job and continued higher education. I completed master's degree in structural design and am now teaching engineering students. (Field note, 2001)

However, the experience is not only with lower level engineers in public and private organizations in Bangladesh. Women respondents in high-level positions (such as design engineers or project engineers) in Bangladesh private organizations also experienced problems working with their subordinates and colleagues as men are reluctant to accept women as superiors. To quote a senior male engineer in a private organization in Bangladesh:

Bangladeshi people (men) are not used to work under female supervisors and our society also doesn't encourage women to be in the leading position in any profession. (Field note, 2001)

The above statement reflects gender ideologies and patriarchal exclusionary practices within organizations in Bangladesh, which excluded women from influential positions and exacerbated sex segregation in the construction organizations.

The above findings in Bangladesh are consistent with some previous research by Maddock (1999), Wajcman (1998), Itzin (1995), and Flanders (1994). They argue that hostile working environment lead to specific behaviors within an organization and help to curb gender discrimination.

DISCUSSION AND CONCLUSION

This chapter summarizes the research findings on career experience of women engineers in construction organizations in Bangladesh and Thailand. The findings suggest that both organizational culture and other factors (such as social norms, work environment, family obligation, etc.) can account for women engineers' career constraints within the construction organizations in both countries.

The study revealed significant differences among the five types of organizations in Bangladesh and Thailand, particularly in terms of organizational culture and its practices. For instance, the dominant characteristics of Bangladesh – Private (Owner-centered) Organizations are: highly centralized but low formal modes of operation; top-down command and control of management system; decisions are taken on the basis of influence rather than procedures or logical grounds. For instance, the reward system (i.e., promotion and salary increase) is based more on knowing and impressing than on formal systems of assessment of one's ability. The dominant characteristics of Bangladesh – Public (Top-down bureaucracy) Organizations are: hierarchical nature of structure and old-fashioned management systems in which high authority (usually men) maintain patriarchal power relations; jobs are secure, but give little room to contribute one's talents and abilities, where members of the management also tend to adopt a paternalistic approach, by keeping their subordinates under close supervision.

In contrast, the dominant characteristics of Thai – Private (Informal management) Organizations are: highly competitive and result-oriented organizations, but an informal favoritism overshadows the formal management systems. The dominant characteristics of Thai – Joint Venture (Team working) Organizations are: participation, team work orientation; maintaining good inter-personal relationships among organizational members; innovation, and opportunity for professional development. While Thai – Public (Facilitating bureaucracy) Organizations are described as: low risk, slow feedback organizational environment; bureaucratic management style; top-down systems of communication; work is controlled by formal procedures and policies; predictability and continuity are the basic values; non-innovative, but cooperative.

In conclusion, although the research findings provide insights into a variety of factors that account for women engineers' entry and career progression in the construction organization in both countries, the following themes seem to be particularly important and deserving of further discussion:

- The study has shed light on how organizational cultural practices as well as the influence of socio-cultural norms and gender ideologies within the organizations affect women's entry and continued employment in construction companies, in both countries. Some scholars like Gherardi (1995), and Hearn (1992) also indicate that organizational culture has consistently been identified as a source of attitude and behavior which not only reinforces sex segregation at the workplace, but also maintains barriers to women's professional advancement.
- Participatory approach through teamwork in Thai joint venture organizations was encouraged in order to ensure high quality of work and maintain rapport and credibility with their clients. This gave women the opportunity to do work that would not be assigned to them as individuals. Through teamwork, the participatory working pattern enhances and encourages women engineers' professional development as well as reduced sex segregation in joint venture construction organizations in Thailand.
- Previous research in other countries indicated that teamwork can lead to changes in work attitudes and orientation to work and such changes allow women more space in organizations (Metcalfe and Alison, 2003; *Cianni* and *Wnuck, 1997)*. If women get the opportunity to use their skills and work performance as well as if their work is valued by the organization, women engineers, like their men counterparts, will be able to develop their professional career in construction organizations.
- The other theme of particular consequence relates to the importance of establishing inter-personal relationships among members within organizations. The findings of the study suggest that inter-personal relationships among organizational members are instrumental in helping women advance to higher level positions. This finding lends support to arguments by Mueller et al. (1994) that organizations need to integrate employees so as to create group cohesion among employees. In Thailand, inter-personal relationships within the organization facilitates Thai women engineers' visibility, personal freedom and interaction with other colleagues in Thai private, joint venture and public organizations. Thus, Thai women are getting more opportunities to develop their identity, which could strengthen their self-confidence as well.
- In contrast, the restricted nature of inter-personal relationships within organizations in Bangladesh limits women engineers in using their abilities, and has a negative impact on their visibility, personal freedom and interaction with other colleagues. This kind of subtle discrimination not only undermines their capacity to compete on an equal footing with men, but also makes their status inferior in both private and public organizations in Bangladesh.

- Apart from organizational practices, Bangladeshi women engineers' situation within organizations is further reinforced by the country's traditional religio-cultural norms and gender ideologies. For construction engineers, it is important to have site experience in order to be promoted to managerial positions. In Thailand, women are getting more opportunities to go to sites compared to Bangladesh, not only because the social norms of seclusion of women are tighter in Bangladesh, but also because sites are better organized and more secure for women to work. This shows that even though sites are generally seen to be dangerous for women, it is possible to improve the security situation in order to allow women to work.

In short, the findings underline the importance of organizational policies, practices and culture in creating a women-friendly environment in both countries. The wider society's culture and norms do guide the way women and men expect each gender to behave and act. However, organizations are able to create their own culture and practices that does not necessarily reinforce the societal gender expectation. The Thai example shows that even though sites are generally seen to be dangerous for women, it is possible to improve the security situation in order to allow women to work. Consequently, participatory working pattern (through team work) introduce its technical professionals to new ways of working in joint venture organizations in Thailand. These changes in the practice of management work not only open more space for Thai women in organizations but could also enhance their self-confidence, credentials and credibility as well. The respondents in both countries expressed their desire to be in more challenging positions and a high level of enthusiasm to work on development projects even at sites, to gain valuable experience which will help them build their professional careers. In order to utilize talent, women's potential and also to maintain a highly productive and creative workforce in construction organizations, there is an increasing need to employ women engineers in construction engineering organizations in both countries. In order to achieve this, it is important for construction managers to review their organizational culture from a gender perspective.

REFERENCES

Anker, R., & Hein, C. (1986). *Sex Inequality in Urban Employment in the Third World*. London: Macmillan Press. doi:10.1007/978-1-349-18467-5

Arnold, J. (2005). *Work Psychology: Understanding Human Behavior in the Workplace* (4th ed.). London: Prentice Hall Financial Times.

Billing, Y. (2000). Organizational Cultures, Families and Careers in Scandinavia. In L. Haas, P. Hwang, & G. Russell (Eds.), *Organizational Change and Gender Equity*. Thousand Oaks, CA: Sage.

Bozionelos, N. (2004). Mentoring Provided: Relation to Mentors Career Success, Personality, and Mentoring Received. *Journal of Vocational Behavior, 64*(1), 24–46. doi:10.1016/S0001-8791(03)00033-2

Cianni, M., & Wnuck, D. (1997). Individual Growth and Team Enhancement: Moving toward a New Model of Career Development. *The Academy of Management Executive, 11*(1), 105-111.

Dainty, A. R. J., Bagilhole, B. M., & Neale, R. H. (2000). A Grounded Theory of Womens Career Under-achievement in Large UK Construction Companies. *Journal of Construction Management and Economics, 18*(2), 239–250. doi:10.1080/014461900370861

Dainty, A. R. J., & Lingard, H. (2006). Indirect Discrimination in Construction Organizations and the Impact on Womens Careers. *Journal of Management Engineering, 22*(3), 108–118. doi:10.1061/(ASCE)0742-597X(2006)22:3(108)

De Janasz, S. C., & Sullivan, S. E. (2004). Multiple Mentoring in Academe: Developing the Professorial Network. *Journal of Vocational Behavior, 64*(2), 263–283. doi:10.1016/j.jvb.2002.07.001

Dorsey, R. W., & Minkarah, E. (1992). *Women in Construction. A report to The Construction Industry Institute*. The University of Texas at Austin.

Ensher, E. A., Heun, C., & Blanchard, A. (2003). Online Mentoring and Computer-mediated Communication: New Directions in Research. *Journal of Vocational Behavior, 63*(2), 264–288. doi:10.1016/S0001-8791(03)00044-7

Evetts, J. (1996). *Gender and Career in Science & Engineering*. London: Taylor & Francis.

Flanders, M. L. (1994). *Breaking through: The Career Woman's Guide to Shattering the Glass Ceiling*. London: Paul Chapman.

Fletcher, J. K. (1999). *Disappearing Acts: Gender, Power and Relational Practice at Work*. Cambridge, MA: MIT Press.

Gherardi, S. (1995). *Gender, Symbolism and Organizational Cultures*. London: Sage.

Harding, S. (1987). Rethinking Standpoint Epistemology: What is Strong Objectivity? In L. Alcoff & E. Potter (Eds.), *Feminist Epistemologies*. New York: Routledge.

Hearn, J. (1992). *Men and organizational culture*. Paper given in IRRU Workshop, Warwick Papers in Industrial Relations, No. 48, University of Warwick.

Hossain, J. B. (2007). *Women Engineers in Construction Industry: A Comparative Study in Bangladesh and Thailand*. AIT Diss. no.GD-07-01. Asian Institute of Technology, Bangkok.

Hossain, J. B., & Kusakabe, K. (2005). Sex segregation in construction organizations in Bangladesh and Thailand. Journal of Construction Management and Economics, 23(6).

Itzin, C. (1995). The Gender Culture in Organizations. In C. Itzin & J. Newman (Eds.), *Gender, Culture and Organizational Change: Putting Theory into Practice* (pp. 30–53). London: Routledge. doi:10.4324/9780203427965_chapter_2

Jaiswal, R. P. (1993). *Professional Status of Women: A comparative study of women and men in science and technology*. New Delhi, India: Rawat Publications.

Kusakabe, K. (1998). *Women's Participation in the Market: A Case Study of Women Retail Traders in Phnom Penh, Cambodia.* AIT Dissertation No. GD-98-01. Asian Institute of Technology, Bangkok.

Linda, W. (2004). *Breaking through the glass ceiling: Women in management (Updated).* Geneva: ILO.

Maddock, S. (1999). *Challenging Women: Gender, Culture and Organization.* London: Sage.

McDowell, L. (1997). *Capital Culture: Gender at Work in the City.* Oxford, UK: Blackwell. doi:10.1002/9780470712894

McIlwee, J. S., & Robinson, J. G. (1992). Women in Engineering: Gender, Power, and Workplace Culture. Albany, NY: State University of New York Press.

Metcalfe, B., & Linstead, A. (2003). Gendering Teamwork: Re-Writing the Feminine. *Gender, Work and Organization, 10*(1), 94–119. doi:10.1111/1468-0432.00005

Mueller, F. (1994). Team between Hierarchy and Commitment: Change Strategies and the Internal Environment. *Journal of Management Studies, 31*(3), 383–403. doi:10.1111/j.1467-6486.1994.tb00623.x

Ogunlana, S. (Ed.). (1993). Women in the Thai Construction Industry. AIT Women Study Circle and structural Engineering and Construction Program (AIT WSC), Asian Institute of Technology, Bangkok.

Parikh, P. P., & Sukhatme, S. P. (1993). *Women Engineers in India. A Study on the Participation of Women in Engineering Courses and in the Engineering Profession.* Bombay: Indian Institute of Technology.

Rutherford, M. D. (2004). The effect of social role on theory of mind reasoning. *British Journal of Psychology, 95*(1), 91–103. doi:10.1348/000712604322779488 PMID:15005870

Safa, H. I. (1996). Gender Inequality and Women's Wage Labor: A Theoretical and Empirical Analysis. In V. M. Moghadam (Ed.), *Patriarchy and Economic Development: Women's Positions at the End of the Twentieth Century* (pp. 184–219). Oxford, UK: Clarendon Press. doi:10.1093/acprof:oso/9780198290230.003.0009

Sauers, D., Kennedy, J. O., & Sullivan, D. (2002). Managerial sex-role stereotyping: A New Zealand perspective. *Women in Management Review, 17*(7), 342–347. doi:10.1108/09649420210445794

Thitipaisan, A. (1999). *Strategies for Improving the Construction Industry in Thailand.* AIT Thesis No. ST-99-52, Asian Institute of Technology, Bangkok.

Wajcman, J. (1998). *Managing Like a Man: Women and Men in Corporate Management.* Oxford, UK: Polity Press.

Zafarullah, H. M., & Khan, M. M. (1989). Toward equity in public service employment: the Bangladesh experience. In Equity in public employment across nations. Lanham, MD: University Press of America.

Zywno, M. S., Gilbride, K. A., Hiscocks, P. D., Waalen, J. K., & Kennedy, D. C. (1998). *Attracting Women into Engineering - A Case Study.* IEEE. Retrieved from http://www.ieee.org/

ENDNOTES

[1] Engineering is the art or science of creatively applying mathematical and scientific knowledge to solve practical problems which affect people, our communities and our environment. Engineers find innovative solutions to contemporary problems and manage the wise use of the earth's resources, both human and natural.

[2] Chulalongkorn University, Chiang Mai University, Khon kaen University, Thamasat University, Kasetsat University and Mahidol University.

[3] In this method, informal contacts with company representatives/human resource personnel were made in the first instance and on their suggestions, new companies where adequate number of women graduate engineers were working, were identified and contacted for interview.

[4] Among the 80, 40 (20 from each country) were exiters, i.e., who quit working in construction organizations. Some of them are now working with other engineering organizations (i.e., computer engineering) or academic institutes/universities, some of them have taken up other professions altogether and have their own business, some of them are engaged in higher studies, and some of them are engaged in household duties.

Chapter 6
Traditional Economic Activities of Indigenous Women in the Chittagong Hill Tracts:
Exploring Indigenous Women's Role in Sustaining Traditional Economic Activities

Parboti Roy
North South University, Bangladesh

ABSTRACT

There are about 1% Indigenous population in Bangladeshi and the Chittagong Hill Tracts (CHT) is one of the regions of Bangladesh resided by thirteen indigenous people's communities The indigenous peoples' lives is intrinsically linked to the nature, culture and their tradition. Traditional economic activities are important aspects of subsistence of indigenous people and women play a crucial role in preserving these activities through their knowledge and management skills. However, their traditional economic activities have been hampered by a range of factors. The study concentrates on this issue as it posits that indigenous women in the CHT provide remarkable contributions through the maintenance of their traditional economic activities which not only have traditional and cultural significance but also contain economic value. The study is based on secondary data. It employs theoretical and conceptual framework of post-colonial indigenous feminism and feminist economic analysis of women's domestic and subsistence activities as a means to explore indigenous women's persistent efforts to continue their traditional economic activities. The study argues that indigenous women in the CHT have been able to uphold their traditional economic practices at both an individual and collective level through the assistance of local organizations formed by the indigenous peoples. These efforts by indigenous women manifest the 'solidarity political economy' against the global political economy.

DOI: 10.4018/978-1-5225-3018-3.ch006

INTRODUCTION

There are 370 million indigenous and tribal people in the world with distinctive cultures and traditions and in Bangladesh there are 45 groups of indigenous peoples reside both in different districts of the plains and in the Chittagong Hill Tracts (CHT) region (Vinding&Kampbel 2012 pp. 8- 11). The indigenous peoples in the CHT have diverse cultures and traditions different from the dominant Bengali population in Bangladesh. The CHT is located in the south-eastern part of Bangladesh which is comprised of three districts named Rangamati, Bandarban and Khagrachori. This hilly region of the country is a home to eleven indigenous groups. These groups arethe *Chakma, Marma, Tripura, Lushai, Mro, Khumi, Pankhoa, Bawm, Chak, Tanchangya and Khyang*. The CHT was historically a part of the British colony for nearly two hundred years. Studies reveal that the British colonized the CHT in order to exploit the natural resources and dominate the indigenous peoples (Uddin 2008 p. 39). As part of their imperialistic project, the British started interfering in the economy of the CHT indigenous peoples by imposing restrictions on the traditional mode of production called '*jum* cultivation' or slash-and-burn or shifting cultivation (Nasreen and Togawa 2010 p. 93). Such profit maximization projects continued in the Pakistan period and current Bangladesh too by implementing multiple development initiatives in the name of modernization that impacted upon the livelihoods of indigenous peoples (Clarke 2001 p. 424; Barua 2010 p. 372) and ignored indigenous local knowledge. Likewise, the traditional economic activities of indigenous peoples were hampered. Traditional economies are an important part of indigenous people's lives not only for their economic value but also for the existence and sustenance of traditional activities (Koukkanen 2011 p. 215). The study explores how indigenous women in the CHT resiliently practice their traditional economic activities despite multiple challenges. More precisely, the purpose of the study is to examine the degree to which indigenous women's participation in traditional economic activities has persisted or been eroded or transformed as a consequence of multifaceted changes in the CHT.

Purpose and Methodology

The major objective of the study is to analyze the persistence of traditional economic activities of indigenous women in the CHT. To fulfill this purpose the study demarcates several specific objectives as follows:

- To analyse impact of development intervention on indigenous women from the post-colonial indigenous feminist perspective, More specifically, to examine indigenous women's economic status through the British colonial period followed by the postcolonial government of Pakistan and most recently the government of Bangladesh which was installed after the British colonial and Pakistan period.
- To assess the state of indigenous women's traditional economic activities in the contemporary period.
- To explore indigenous women's persistent practise of traditional economic activities in the mainstream setting.
- The study is based qualitative method of employing secondarydata source. The following quantitative materials will be examined-

- Surveys and studies conducted on CHT indigenous women's participation in different economic activities or engagement in income-earning by Government and Non-government organizational reports, papers, and books.
- Yearly reports and studies by local and International or transnational agencies.

The qualitative materials are:

- Book, journals and scholarly articles on in diverse economic activities
- Any source of popular culture, for example- newspaper, online articles, and magazines about CHT women relevant to the thesis.
- Articles published in local magazines and journals on indigenous peoples.

Rationale and Limitations

Women constitute half of the indigenous population in Bangladesh and are considered to be the custodians of its culture and tradition (Roy C 2004 p.3; Dewan I 2010 p.190). Indigenous women play a key role in their communities by undertaking various forms of traditional economic activities to preserve their cultural practices from generation to generation and they contribute to the economy, often through unpaid labor. It is important to focus on the role and impact of changes in women's traditional activities and/ or adaptation of economic activities as a consequence of a globalized market as there is lack of substantial studies or specific research on this particular issue. Further, the study prioritizes the importance of the interwoven relationship between indigenous women and their traditional economic activities. This is because the current study recognizes that tradition is one of the important mechanisms to preserve culture and sustain indigenous economy and women are key players in this regard. Furthermore, it is assumed that this study may direct for further feminist economic studies as well as development research as there have been no feminist studies on indigenous women's economic contribution through their participation in traditional activities in the CHT.

The major limitation of the paper is it lacks primary source and concentrates on indigenous women in the CHT excluding indigenous women living in the plains due to dearth of adequate secondary data on traditional economic activities and time limitation. Moreover, the study provides a general overview on indigenous women rather than focusing on a specific indigenous group or groups in the CHT.

CONCEPTUAL AND THEORETICAL FRAMEWORKS

Traditional Economic Activities

It is important to define the nature of economic activities before considering traditional economic activities. Conventional economic paradigms identify economic activities as being based on monetary values, limiting it to activities which contribute directly to a country's Gross Domestic Product. A number of feminist economists have challenged this narrow definition because it ignores the invisible and unpaid contributions that women and children make to economic survival (Waring 1988 p.21). Margaret Reid (cited in Waring 1988 p. 21) re-defines economic activity as any activity to accomplish any service or product which one can purchase or hire someone to do with or without payment. In addition, several international development organizations such as the United Nations and the ILO have outlined criteria to define economic activities as well as economically active persons. The International Labour Organisation (ILO), for example, defines economically active persons as:

The economically active population comprises all persons of either sex who furnish the supply of labour for the production of economic goods and services as defined by the United Nations systems of national accounts and balances during a specified time-reference period. According to these systems the production of economic goods and services includes all production and processing of primary products whether for the market for barter or for own consumption, the production of all other goods and services for the market and, in the case of households which produce such goods and services for the market, the corresponding production for own consumption (International Labour Organization 1982).

The term traditional economic activities generally refers to the activities that have been followed by successive generations of indigenous peoples and their communities and have a profound relationship to their own customs and cultural practices (Roy RD2000 p. 80). The paper analyses the traditional economic activities undertaken by indigenous women in the CHT and their contribution through paid or unpaid or underpaid labor in sustaining the local economy for the greater welfare of their communal traditions and cultures.

Jum Cultivation

Jum cultivation is the primary source of subsistence for indigenous peoples in the CHT. *Jum* or shifting or swidden cultivation or or slash-and-burn cultivation is a major traditional mode of cultivation by indigenous peoples. Primarily, a plot is selected for *jum* cultivation on the hill slopes in January or February. After that the plot is cleared by cutting the forests and vegetation. However, the large trees remain uncut. The cut *jum* is then dried in the sun and burnt prior to the monsoon rain in April or May. The land is then cleared of charred logs and debris. When the monsoon begins various seeds of different crops are sowed. Different produce is harvested in different seasons. The plants are then weeded from time to time until they mature. A *jum* land can be cultivated two or three years in a row and it takes 10 more years to rejuvenate the soil fertility (Gain 2000 p. 22).

Postcolonial Indigenous Feminism

Postcolonial feminism is a critique of Western feminist notion on the universal experience of women in the South. It concentrates on the multiple subjective position and experiences of women in the south that covers different intersectional forces of power, race, class, ethnicity, gender, sex, caste in the context of power, knowledge, culture and voice (Briggs and Sharp 2004 pp. 5-6; Haraway cited McEwan 2011 pp. 97-98; Rajan and Park 2000 pp. 53-71). It is also known as 'third world' feminism that contains variety of names and 'indigenous' feminism is one of them. Being an indigenous woman researcher and from the standpoint of postcolonial indigenous feminist perspective, I considers the importance of incorporating this theoretical perspective as it brings indigenous women's experiences intertwined with their ethnicity, indigeneity, culture, tradition and economic activities in the colonial, postcolonial period and the contemporary period to scrutinize the changes and or persistence of their traditional livelihoods.

Feminist Economics

Feminist economics have made a significant contribution in challenging conventional economic theory that undervalues women's economic contribution in fields of micro and macroeconomics. One of the crucial contributions of feminist economists is analysis of the gendered division of labour and gender relations in the household and in the subsistence production economy. Ester Boserup's epoch-making study on rural women's role in economic development makes a significant contribution to the feminist economics and women in development approach (WID) and later on in gender and development. She documented women's contribution to the subsistence economy and asserted the importance of including rural women's work in production and income statistics. Boserup also identifies the importance of the skill and knowledge development of training for women in income generating sectors. She identifies rural women's contribution to subsistence economies in the developing countries to integrate them into development (Beneria 2001 pp. 249-251). However, Boserup's assumption of the integration of women into subsistence and domestic activities has been criticized by Beneria (2001 p. 268) who claim that she overlooks the reproductive role of women. Moreover, Margaret Reid is a pioneer feminist who articulated the need to include women in domestic activities and the production and supply of basic necessities in the rural economy in her *Economics of Household Production (1934)*. Marylyn Waring's book *If women counted* in 1988 extended this phenomenon in a broader way (Beneria 2001 p.249). She identified women's invisibility in the national income accounting, and specifically the non-recognition of the economic value of women's service in household production (Postner 1992 p. 238). Women's domestic labour, for the purposes of household consumption and economic activities for selling and bargaining in rural areas is invisible in national censuses, and in the agricultural labour force statistical data in many developing countries (Jain et al. cited in Dixon 2001 pp. 221- 223). Based on feminist economic analysis to address women's role in household, traditional, paid and unpaid economy, the paper draws attention toward indigenous women's contribution in preserving traditional economic activities in their respective communities.

Indigenous Women's Role in Traditional Economic Activities

Indigenous women in the CHT play a substantial role in the traditional economy directly and indirectly for the greater welfare of the society. Indigenous women are the de facto managers of household (Roy RD 2004 p. 10) They collect wood, prepare food, take care of children and the elders and fetch water for the daily support of the family (Roy C 2004 pp. 10-11; Khan Md. 2005; p. 56;) and contribute significantly to family income through engaging in homestead agricultural production (Wazed 2012 p. 205). Furthermore, indigenous women are the custodians of culture and tradition as they weave traditional indigenous cloths and possess ecological knowledge and skills to make herbal medicine from the trees and plants for the cure of sick people. Apart from collecting ingredients for medical purposes in the forest, women also collect bamboo shoots, mushrooms, yams and fruits for daily nutritional supplements (Roy RD2000p. 83). As mentioned in the first chapter the indigenous peoples in the CHT are collectively characterized as the *Jumma* peoples because they are traditionally dependent on the subsistence economy of '*jum* cultivation' or swidden/ slash-and-burn cultivation for their livelihood (Roy R D 2000 p. 78; Hossain 2013; Mallick& Rafi 2008 p.12). The other traditional economic activities of indigenous peoples of the CHT are basketry, and hunting, forestry, and wine making are all closely linked to *jum* cultivation (Roy RD2000 p.82; ChakmaK & Hill G 2013 p. 154). Some traditional economic activities are gender neutral where both men and women are engaged in basketry, hunting, animal rearing and poultry raising (Roy RD2000 pp. 83-84; Nath Inoue &Chakma 2005 p. 135). Even though studies on the CHT describe both men and women equally participate in the *jum* fields (Women's Resource Network 2010 p. 5), there are gendered distinctions in tasks. In the *jum* field women predominantly sow seeds, weed, harvest and preserve seed (Khisa 2011 p. 4), whereas cutting wood and burning the forest is solely men's responsibility (Chakma KG 2010 p.31). Other traditional economic activities of indigenous women include weaving, midwifery and childbirth attendant. Handloom weaving is one of the vital parts of female traditional economic activities through which indigenous women preserve the culture and pass the knowledge of weaving to future generations (Roy AD2005 p.35; Roy RD2000 p. 85). Further, a small number of elderly indigenous women still practice midwifery and birth attendance in rural remote areas of CHT (Islam RM 2010 p.70; Roy RD2000 p. 83) especially where maternal health care facilities are not available. At present, many indigenous women in the CHT contribute considerably to the local economic sector through the production of vegetables for sale in the markets. However, studies reveal that indigenous women have less access to credit and capital compared to indigenous men and Bengali women (Barkat et al. 2009 p.103) because they have limited ownership of resources in their communities (Vinding&Campbel 2012 p. 26; Chakma BP 2010 p.47). Despite limited ownership to resources Indigenous women's contribution to household income comes mainly from the multiple crop production in the *jum* field and selling of products from the forests (Barkat et al. 2009 p.90).

Impact of Colonial and Postcolonial Development Projects on CHT Indigenous Women

The multiple development projects from the period of the British colonization and the result of globalization with neoliberal economy have transformed the CHT people's livelihood options and income generating activities. Historically the CHT was part of the British colony from the 1860. Colonization is one of the prime factors that have had a huge impact on the socio-economic lives of indigenous people (Roy RD 2000 p. 89). The British colonization of the CHT in the mid nineteenth century deflected the subsistence economic pattern of indigenous population in the CHT through the introduction of Reserve Forest Policy and decreased indigenous people's access to forest land. The British government further introduced plough cultivation as a strategy to exclude the Hill peoples from their traditional economic activities (Mohsin cited in Chowdhury 2008 p. 65; Mitchell 2011 p.94; Van Schendel cited in Gerharz 2001 p. 78). Various development projects on forests including reforestation and deforestation programs in the postcolonial then Pakistan period and after the independence of Bangladesh, severely hampered indigenous women's daily activities through intensifying their workloads in the collection of water, foods and fuel and other daily necessities to remote areas (Mitchell 2011 p. 121; Dhali 2008 p. 236; Khan FC 2005 p. 47). During the Pakistan period, the then government segregated indigenous women from their traditional *jum* practice by falsely declaring CHT lands as unsuitable for shifting cultivation. It is notable that the indigenous people have a very intimate relationship with *jum* cultivation as it is a part of their tradition and the primary means of livelihood. The establishment of a paper mill and a hydroelectric project on the *Karnaphuli* River in 1960 relentlessly impacted on the livelihood status of indigenous women by submerging the best part of arable land and reduced them to poverty by displacing them from their native lands. Therefore, many indigenous women became victims of internal and external displacement as the then Pakistani government did not provide sufficient compensation to the affected hill families (Nasrin & Togawa 2010 p. 94).Following the British colonial legacy, the Pakistani government had continued to promote plough cultivation and imposed horticulture or fruit gardening programs on indigenous peoples (Nasrin&Togawa 2010 p. 94; ChakmaK 2011 p.3)I the name of development which did not bring any substantial changes in the livelihoods of hill peoples. Vandana Shiva (1989 p. 1) contends that 'development' is a 'colonial project' which is grounded in the domination of western knowledge and westernization of economies by rejecting the traditional economies and the exploitation of natural resources for the capitalist accumulation and commercialization of economy. Shiva's contention is similar with the case of the CHT in which Hill women's traditional economic activities became threatened by multiple development projects.

The traditional occupations of indigenous women in the CHT have undergone several critical changes in the decades since the independence of Bangladesh. Some factors which were present in the colonial and post-colonial Pakistan period continue in the contemporary setting of the CHT. These predominant factors are population growth, state-sponsored population transfer programs, militarization, pressure on lands and forests, expansion of education, violence against indigenous women and various development programs and projects as a consequence of globalization and neoliberal political economy.The population transfer program by successive governments led to ethnic conflict between settler Bengalis and Hill peoples after the independence of Bangladesh, especially in the late 1970s. The Bengali settlers who were moved into the CHT mostly belong to landless, poor and homeless day laborers and some of them were alleged criminals. The ethnic conflict further increased violent attacks by the Bengali settlers on indigenous families, including burning the houses and farms of indigenous villagers and sexual violence against indigenous women (Chakma K &D'Costa 2013 p. 143). These led Hill to people being evicted from their ancestral lands and homesteads. The population transfer program was led by the government in association with the establishment of militarization of the CHT in the late 1970s as part of controlling the indigenous leaders' led armed wing named '*Shanti Bahini*'. '*Shanti Bahini*' was formed by the indigenous political party named *Parbatya Chattagram Jana Samhati Samiti* (PCJSS) to fight against state's discriminatory attitudes towards indigenous people and non-recognition of indigenous people's rights. The insurgency movement in the CHT by the indigenous peoples continued for more than two decades (1975-1997). At the end of 1997, ending two decades long conflict the *Chittagong Hill Tracts Accord*, also known as CHT Peace Accord was signed between the PCJSS and the government of Bangladesh. Despite this agreement the government has not yet fully implemented the fundamental provisions of the Accord. Population growth in the CHT not only roused ethnic conflict between the Bengali settlers and the *Jumma* peoples over land but also increased the trading monopoly of Bengalis in the markets as well as increased vulnerability of swidden lands and reduced profitability of *jum* cultivation (Roy RD 2012 p.11).Due to the decreased land entitlement for *jum* production indigenous men and women, especially from the working poor started to work as wage laborers for their neighbor's *jum* and other sources of non-traditional activities like wet rice cultivation, agroforestry, tree plantation, poultry, retailing, horticulture, commercial fishing, homestead gardening and domestic service. Nath and his colleagues (Inoue &Chakma 2005 pp. 137-139; Adnan 2004 p. 115; Roy RD cited in Roy RD 2006 p. 39) assert that despite delivering more labor than males in the *jum* fields females get less payment than their counterparts. The constant presence of military camps in the CHT rural areas affected the natural environment and caused harm to trees and led to deforestation (Gain 2000 p. 21) and vulnerability of indigenous women. Indigenous women are prone to being sexually harassed and oppressed by the dominant Bengali settlers and armed forces while they go to collect water, food or firewood in the isolated forest areas or crop lands (Ala Uddin 2009 p. 20; Halim 2010 p. 189). Moreover, the research of Guhathakurta and others (2000 p. 80; Ahmed 2011 p. 6; Halim 2007 p. 120; Levene 1999 p. 344; Khan FC 2005 p. 226) shows that ever since the insurgency period Hill women in the CHT are harassed when they go to local markets to sell their commodities produced in *jums* and Village Common Forests(VCF). VFC are community forests where the community people maintain these forests to meet their daily necessities as a means to natural resource management. Other studies (Halim 2007 p. 120) reveal that indigenous are sometimes compelled to accept low prices in order to sell their goods prior to dark due to the fear of being sexually harassed by the Bengali armies and settlers. Furthermore, Hill women have less knowledge about the market economy and thus the Bengali traders have ubiquitous control in the market of CHT (Gain 2000 p. 16; Roy & Halim 2007 p. 47). It is also clear that, the militarization hampered indigenous women's productive activities and increased the social stigma on women through sexual harassment, rape and forced marriage (The Chittagong Hill Tracts Commission 1991).

The combination of globalization and neoliberal economic policies has forced indigenous women to pursue non-traditional occupations. The expansion of education as one of the instrument of globalization has had a profound impact on Hill women's traditional economic activities. Educational advancement allowed middle class indigenous families in the CHT to take up alternative occupations. However, it cannot be wholeheartedly argued that the development of education propelled all indigenous women to engage in non-traditional occupations.

In addition, although the government endorsed numerous international instruments to ensure equal rights and opportunities for indigenous peoples, these are not implemented and the government continues to ignore indigenous peoples' concerns and needs which are reflected in the constitutional non-recognition of indigenous peoples, less or no voice in the national development policies and plans for women in Bangladesh.

Furthermore, in the post-Accord period, a number of international organizations in partnership with government organizations launched development projects for the economic development of indigenous population (Asian Development Bank 2013; Chittagong Hill Tracts Development Facility United Nations Development Facility 2010). Some of these development projects worked to promote a few traditional economic activities, like weaving. In addition, entrepreneurship programs launched by the partnership of government and international agencies and local Non-Governmental Organizations tend to prefer demonstrating the success stories of microcredit (Asian Development Bank 2010). In contrast to this, other studies (Roy C 2010 p. 89; Roy RD& Halim 2007 p. 17) articulate that the micro-finance programs are not beneficial for the indigenous peoples as they are not familiar to such 'non-traditional' schemes and cash economy. As women's traditional economic activities are restricted by the aforementioned multidimensional factors, many indigenous women are forced to migrate to city areas to look for alternative work to support themselves and their families and most find work in garment factories and beauty parlours (Halim 2007 p.119). Studies underline rape and sexual harassment cases of indigenous female garment workers and domestic workers in the cities (Roy RD 2000 p. 108).

PERSISTENCE OF TRADITIONAL ECONOMIC ACTIVITIES: CHALLENGES AHEAD

Despite the pervasive influence of globalization associated with postcolonial hegemonic state policies and programs, socio-political, economic and cultural factors indigenous women still practice their traditional economic activities. However, these activities have become peripheral in the mainstream Bangladeshi economic context. In some arenas several traditional economic activities have become a supplementary source of income but some have remained as primary occupations. It is clear from the previous section that the traditional economic activities of indigenous women are located in a complex set of relationships in the current period. Some of the traditional activities are nearly extinct or some are integrated with the modern ones which have severely impacted their income earning options in order to cope with the global economy. The multiple factors associated with globalization and neoliberal economy have obliged indigenous women to engage in alternative economic activities and income earning options. As discussed previously, that almost all the traditional economic activities in indigenous societies of the CHT are directly or indirectly associated to *jum* or shifting cultivation. As shifting cultivation is no longer practiced widely, as a result of multifaceted events, most of the traditional activities have now been integrated with mainstream agricultural methods. For instance, *jum* cultivation is practiced alongside plough and fertilizer based methods. Raw materials like cotton has nearly become extinct in *jum*, women now have to buy cotton and threads from the markets. Therefore, it is clear that traditional activities are no longer a source of primary income for the indigenous peoples. Despite the reduced access to access to land, the indigenous peoples continue to practice *jum*. This is because their strong belief that it is the main source of their subsistence, the key symbol of their identity, and their traditional culture and customs.

Studies show that the main source of the CHT economy is agriculture with 64 per cent of households and approximately 90 per cent of indigenous women contribute to the agricultural economy (Dutta cited in Hossain 2013 p.27; UNDP cited in Women's Resource Network 2010 p. 2). Hill women contribute to the CHT agricultural economy through their unpaid and paid labor in their households, homesteads, in *jum,* as well as VCFs and in USFs. Many rural Hill women are involved in vegetable, firewood and fruit selling produced in *jums* and forests although they do not get fair prices for their commodities in the market (Chakma et al. 2007, p.36; Women's Resource Network 2010 p.8).

In addition, indigenous women still practice weaving also known as blackstrap loom for both personal consumption and marketing even though they encounter financial shortcomings as a result of the market expansion for traditional woven cloths (Raju 2013 p.2). Current media reports show that indigenous women contribute 95 per cent of their labour in the production and marketing of indigenous traditional cloths (Chakma HK 2013). Weaving is mostly practiced by rural indigenous women although some women in the town areas of the CHT are engaged in this practice. While indigenous women have become engaged in non-traditional jobs and activities, for example, in local administration, day laborer, domestic worker, petty trader, teaching, garment jobs, horticulture, wet rice cultivation, poultry and in NGOs (Roy RD& Halim 2007 p. 39). The influence of Bengali culture remains intense on the indigenous communities of the CHT. The Bengali settlement can be considered as a dominant feature of globalization which impacts on many of the cultural practices of Hill peoples. Women's traditional clothing is one of them. The settlement of Bengalis in CHT has discouraged indigenous women from wearing their traditional attire because mainstream Bengali cultural values particularly in the urban and the plains area, support the ridicule of Hill women and treat them as primitive and sexually promiscuous. The majority of Bengali people in Bangladesh are Muslims and religiously adhere to a conservative dress code for women including the practice of *purdah* or seclusion (Sultana A 2009 p.13). However, within indigenous societies, whether in the CHT or the plains, women are not bounded by such restrictions as Bengali women. *Caritas* Development Institute (cited in Gain 2000 p. 94) found that about 83 per cent of Hill women work in the public domain. *Jumma* women have tended to adopt Bengali attire such as, *sari* and *salwar kamiz* to avoid harassment or being ridiculed by Bengali men. Hence, it can be seen that the Bengali cultural aggression on indigenous women's physical appearance is intense in Bangladesh (Dewan, 2002; Roy A 2005 p.; Ala Uddin 2009 pp.21-22; Vinding&Campbel 2012 pp. 12-13). Despite their adoption of Bengali dress code indigenous women play proactive roles in maintaining their culture through wearing traditional fabrics and weaving these dresses for use themselves as well as for sale. Hill women's persistence in sustaining their cultural traditions despite these factors indicates their commitment to the movement for 'cultural resurgence' (Chakma K & Hill 2013 p. 135).

There are a number of indigenous individuals who have been able to develop the indigenous tradition of weaving at an entrepreneurial level and *Manjulika Khisa* is one of the *Chakma* indigenous women who has been involved in the development of indigenous textiles in the CHT. She is the first indigenous *Chakma* women entrepreneur in the CHT and has made handloom products popular in the market. She was inspired by her mother's various items made from back strap weaving and as a result she established *Bain Textile*. She organized Hill women from her locality to engage in collective activities like handloom weaving for marketing. The main purpose of this initiative is to develop indigenous handloom products with the use of advanced marketing. Her textiles produce mainstream Bengali dresses and traditional *Chakma* female apparel called *pinonhadi* as well (Nasrin 2007 p. 65; Roy A 2005 p. 43). She also assists indigenous women to engage in income generating activities and to become economically independent through the advancement of her textile business. Even though *Manjulika*'s textiles makes some mainstream Bengali dresses it equally retains the traditional culture of indigenous peoples by producing traditional dresses which are profoundly linked to indigenous identity and survival. It is noteworthy that *Manjulika* not only sustains indigenous traditional weaving practices through her business but also by provides income generation opportunities to other indigenous women in her business.

At the collective level, indigenous peoples' grassroots organizations play a key role in supporting and preserving the traditional economic activities of indigenous peoples. After the Peace Accord, many international, national and local development organizations were set up in the CHT. The local NGOs in the CHT concentrate on the development of livelihoods for indigenous communities. Despite receiving minimal funds from national and international NGOs, the local NGOs are likely to follow their own organizational goals to promote traditional economic activities of rural indigenous populations and reinstatement of their traditional economic activities and culture. One of the local NGOs in the CHT named *Trinamul Unnayan Sangstha* (TUS), deals with the empowerment of indigenous peoples through traditional activities. TUS has programs to support the grassroots communities and ex-*jum* cultivator to improve their economic status through a variety of economic activities including traditional handloom weaving and handicrafts. The traditional handicraft program of TUS was initiated in 2009 and it is still continuing to improve skills and marketing strategies for women weavers and handicraft makers. The Community Action on Resource Management for Decent Living (CANDL) initiatives of TUS also encourages indigenous women to continue to practice their nearly extinct unique weaving style to revive them and assist female weavers to market their handloom products in contrast to machine loom cloths. Additionally, the organization operates projects on developing indigenous knowledge and practice, especially indigenous women's role and knowledge on natural resource management in community forests (TrinamulUnnayanSangstha Annual Reflections 2012 pp. 18, 26).

Some local NGOs of local peoples in the CHT advocate the planting of traditional herbal medical plants. This is because herbal medicines are of great importance to the local peoples. Indigenous people in the remote areas mostly prefer to receive health services from the traditional healers rather than modern technological nurses as the traditional system is more familiar to them (Sayem N.D. Pp.7-8; Nath Inoue &Chakma 2005 p. 136). Even though the practice of traditional healing is dominated by indigenous men in the CHT, women play the key role in maintaining herbal plants in *jums*, homestead gardens and VCFs for traditional healing practice (Khan NA& Rashid M 2006 p.39). Some local NGOs support the plantation of herbal medicine in the context of the socio-economic and cultural development of Hill people and the Centre for Integrated Programme and Development (CIPD) is one of them. CIPD solely focuses on the participation of indigenous communities in development and emphasizes indigenous knowledge and the economic empowerment of grassroots communities (CIPD nd.). *Taungya*, another local NGO, focuses on the socio-economic development of the VCF communities, emphasizes indigenous knowledge systems, gender equity, women's empowerment and forest resource management (Halim & Roy RD 2006 pp. 16-18; Taungya nd.). Even though these NGOs receive funds from international and national development organizations they tend to follow indigenous values to restore the capacities of indigenous communities.

Such initiatives through individual efforts and local NGOs' activities in the CHT seem to reflect a commitment towards the 'solidarity political economy'. Solidarity political economy is a network which holds principles against the neo-liberal economy. It was identified by Brazilian academic *Luis Razeto* in 1990 as denoting "Factor C; corporation, co-responsibility, communication and community" as a type of alternative economy (Alfred *et al.*cited in Ferguson 2009 p. 113). The attempt of local NGOs and female entrepreneurship in the CHT indicate the importance of collective economic development of community people, especially women. Their activities manifests resistance against global economy while reinforcing agency to sustain the traditional economic activities of indigenous women.

It can be seen that indigenous women's individual and collective actions and stances, through individual or organizational actions, actively resist the impact of global capitalism. Despite the resilient nature of globalization as well as the postcolonial development agenda, indigenous women somehow continue to pursue their efforts to sustain their traditional economic activities. Indigenous women's persistent practices of traditional economic activities are economically significant but, perhaps more important to sustain indigenous identity, culture and traditions to which women have remarkable contribution. Therefore, it is crucial to integrate indigenous women's traditional economic activities into national statistics to formally recognize their contribution the development of policy to further support and sustain these.

CONCLUSION

The paper has explored the extent to which indigenous women in the CHT of Bangladesh have been able to sustain their traditional economic and cultural practices in the context of the changes that national and global forces have brought to their region. The study shows that Indigenous women in the CHT continue to play a key role in maintaining their traditional economic activities in the contemporary period in spite of colonial influence, postcolonial development interventions, and globalization and neoliberal

Traditional Economic Activities of Indigenous Women in the Chittagong Hill Tracts

development policies. It has focused specifically on CHT indigenous women rather than on indigenous Bangladeshi women who are dispersed throughout different districts in the plains of Bangladesh due to lack of time constraint to collect primary data and lack of literature on women in the plains in terms of traditional economic activities. There is dearth of particular studies on indigenous women and their contribution to the maintenance of traditional activities. The study aimed to explore this particular concern which is intrinsic to indigenous women's identity, development and the preservation of indigenous knowledge from the postcolonial indigenous feminist perspective and researcher's location as indigenous woman. The paper entails the theoretical perspectives of feminist economics and conceptual frameworks on traditional economic activities and *Jum* cultivation to consider indigenous women's contribution in traditional economic activities. This study endeavored to fill the research gap using the framework of feminist economics and postcolonial indigenous feminist approach to analyze the impact of colonial and postcolonial development interventions on indigenous women of the CHT and their individual and collective persistent effort to revive traditional economic activities as part of resistance from their respective location of indigeneity.

The colonialism and post-colonial interventions have had a huge impact on the traditional economic lives of indigenous people. The hegemonic influence of the British colonizers in the CHT not only disrupted indigenous peoples' access to their ancestral lands and forests but also restricted their access to *jum*. The *jum* or slash-and-burn cultivation is a crucial part of indigenous women's economic activity economy and closely tied to the other traditional economic activities including weaving, vegetable production and the collection of forest products including wood for family and communal consumption and herbal medical plants. The paper has shown that the dispossession of women from traditional lands has disrupted or destroyed all these traditional roles.

Moreover, the detrimental projects of the postcolonial Pakistani government in the name of economic development displaced indigenous peoples from their lands and the legal restrictions on communal forests disempowered indigenous women socio-economically followed by the population transfer program, militarization of the CHT, land grabbing of indigenous peoples of the consecutive Bangladeshi government regimes and multiple development projects in the CHT eroded the Hill people's capacity for self-sufficiency even further. The monopolization of Bengali traders in markets controlled indigenous women's traditional activity of selling vegetables. Thus, all these factors forced indigenous peoples to take up alternative occupations.

It is noticeable that current government development plans, policies and projects on women tend to follow the postcolonial ideology that ignores indigenous peoples' right to their lands and to practice traditional economic activities. At the same time such attitudinal tendency led to increased monoculture in agriculture and plantations which has reduced bio-diversity and exacerbated environmental degradation. These changes have led to the socio-economic deterioration of indigenous population, reduced *jum* practice and increased sexual violence against indigenous women and adaptation of alternative occupation. Hence, the intense influence of globalization, postcolonial ideologies and neoliberal economy has forced indigenous women to take up alternative occupations. The dominant Bengali culture in the CHT adversely impacts many intangible aspects of women's everyday lives such as such as their attire and mobility in the public sphere. In addition, due to the development of formal education, many indigenous women do not pass on their traditions to the younger generation. Despite the persisted challenges to their traditional economic activities indigenous women have been able to preserve and continue to practice a number of their traditional economic activities in combination with their involvement in wage labor.

Anecdotal sources reveal that a significant number of indigenous women individually practice weaving. Some women continue to produce and sell vegetables and firewood and indigenous herbal medicines in markets. Therefore, the traditional practices of indigenous women whether from individual or collective level are being sustained through the profound effort of women in the CHT to preserve their traditions and to resist the worst excesses of the global economy.

REFERENCES

Tarafder, T. (2014). Reproductive health beliefs and their consequences: A case study of rural indigenous women in Bangladesh. *Australian Journal of Regional Studies*, *20*(2), 251–374.

Jahan, M. (2008). The impact of environmental degradation on women in Bangladesh: An overview. *Asian Affairs*, *30*(2), 5–15.

Chakraborty, E. (1993). *Marginality, modes of insecurity and indigenous women of Northern Bangladesh*. Retrieved from http://calternatives.org/resource/pdf/Marginality,%20Modes%20of%20insecurity%20and%20Indigenous%20Women%20of%20Northern%20Bangladesh.pdf

Chakraborty, E., & Sarkar, C. (2014). *BangladesherAdibashiNari: shamajikobosthan o biponnotarchalchitro*. Dhaka: Banglaprakash.

Chakma, K. G. (2010). *'Shifting cultivation as traditional livelihood and impacts of climate change in Bangladesh',Traditional Livelihoods and Indigenous Peoples*. Thailand: Asian Indigenous Peoples Pact Foundation.

Chakma, H. (2013). *Indigenous women's role in the market economy*. Prothom Alo.

Adnan, S. (2004). *Migration, land alienation and causes of poverty in the Chittagong Hill Tracts*. Dhaka, Bangladesh: Research and Advisory Services.

Ala Uddin, M. A. (2009). Cultural assimilation and survival strategy of ethnic people in Bangladesh: Bengali dress on ethnic physic in Chittagong Hill Tracts. *Canadian Social Science*, *5*(1), 16–23.

Asian Development Bank. (2010). *Women thrive in local business*. Retrieved from: http://www.adb.org/features/women-thrive-local-business

Asian Development Bank. (2013). *Closing the gender gap*. Retrieved from: http://www.adb.org/themes/gender/overview

Barkat, A., Halim, S., Poddar, A., Osman, A., Khan, S. M., Rahman, R., … Bashir, S. (2009). Socio-Economic baseline survey of Chittagong Hill Tracts. United Nations Development Program.

Beneria, L. (2001). The enduring debate over unpaid labour. In L. Beneria & S. Bisnath (Eds.), Gender and Development: Theoretical, Empirical and Practical Approaches. Edward Elgar.

Chakma, B. P. (2010). *The economy of the Indigenous people of CHT: some myths and realities*. Paper presented at the Conference on Development in the Chittagong Hill Tracts, Rangamati, Bangladesh.

Chakma, K. (2011). *(In)equality and (In)difference: indigenous women of the Chittagong Hill Tracts in post-colonial Bangladesh*. Paper presented at a workshop on Gender, militarization and endemic conflict: new research agendas, Radcliff Institute of Harvard University.

Chakma, K., & Hill, G. (2013). Indigenous women and culture in the colonized CHT of Bangladesh. In K. Visweswaren (Ed.), *Everyday Occupations: Experiencing Militarism in South Asia and Middle East*. University of Pennsylvania.

Chakma, K., & D' Costa, B. (2013). *The Chittagong Hill Tracts: diminishing violence or violent peace?*. London: Routledge.

Chittagong Hill Tracts Development Facility United Nations Development Program. (2010). *Economic Development*. Retrieved from: http://www.chtdf.org/index.php/focus-areas/economic-development

Chowdhury, K. (2008). Politics of identities and resources in the Chittagong Hill Tract, Bangladesh: Ethnonationalism and/or Indigenous identity. *Asian Journal of Social Science*, *36*(1), 57–78. doi:10.1163/156853108X267567

Chittagong Hill Tracts Commission. (1991). *Life is not ours: Land and human rights in the Chittagong Hill Tracts*. Retrieved from: http://www.iwgia.org/iwgia_files_publications_files/0129_Life_is_not_ours_1-108.pdf

Chakma, G. K., Chakma, B., & Tripura, S. P. (2007). *The occupation of shifting cultivation and indigenous peoples: a case study in the Chittagong Hill Tracts, Bangladesh*. Dhaka, Bangladesh: ILO.

Centre for Integrated Program and Development. (n.d.). Retrieved from: <http://www.cipdauk.org/index.php/about-cipd>

Clarke, G. (2001). From ethnocide to ethno development? Ethnic minorities and indigenous peoples in Southeast Asia. *Third World Quarterly*, *22*(3), 413–436. doi:10.1080/01436590120061688

Dewan, I. (2010). *Women in Hill society. In Between Ashes and Hope: Chittagong Hill Tracts in the Blind Spot of Bangladesh Nationalism* (pp. 190–191). Dhaka: Drishtipat Writers Collective.

Dewan, A. (2002). *Woven textiles as art: an examination on the revival of weaving in the Chittagong Hill Tracts* (Master thesis). Concordia University, Montreal, Canada.

Dhali, H. H. (2008). Deforestation and its impacts on indigenous women: A case from the Chittagong Hill Tracts in Bangladesh. *Gender, Technology and Development*, *12*(2), 229–246. doi:10.1177/097185240801200204

Dixon, B. R. (2001). Women in agriculture: counting the labour force in developing countries. In L. Beneria & S. Bisnath (Eds.), *Gender and Development: Theoretical, Empirical and Practical Approaches* (Vol. 1). Edward Elger Publishing Limited.

Ferguson, A. (2009). Alternative economies Mexican women left behind: Organizing solidarity economy in response. In L McGovern & I. Wallimann (Eds.), Globalization and Third World Women: Exploitation, Coping and Resistance. Ashgate.

Gain, P. (2000). *Life and nature at risk. In The Chittagong Hill Tracts: Life and Nature at Risk* (pp. 1–41). Dhaka, Bangladesh: SEHD.

Gain, P. (2000). *Women in the CHT: some facts. In The Chittagong Hill Tracts: Life and Nature at Risk* (pp. 94–95). Dhaka, Bangladesh: SEHD.

Gerharz, E. (2001). *Ambivalences of development co-operation in post-conflict regions: ethnicity in the Chittagong Hill Tracts Bangladesh* (Diploma Thesis). Bielefeld University.

Guhathakurta, M. (2000). Women's survival and resistance. In P. Gain (Ed.), *The Chittagong Hill Tracts: Life and Nature at Risk* (pp. 79–93). Dhaka, Bangladesh: SEHD.

Halim, S. (2007). Situation of indigenous women and ILO Convention on discrimination. *Solidarity.* Bangladesh Indigenous People's Forum.

Halim, S., & Roy, R. D. (2006). *Lessons learned from the application of human rights-based approaches in the Chittagong Hill Tracts, Bangladesh: A case study of the village common forest project implemented by Taungya.* United Nations Development Programme. Retrieved from: http://hrbaportal.org/wp-content/files/bangladesh_forestry-sector.pdf

Halim, S. (2010). Insecurity of indigenous women. In N. Mohaiemen (Ed.), Between Ashes and Hope: Chittagong Hill Tracts in the Blind Spot of Bangladesh Nationalism. Drishtipat Writers' Collective.

Hossain, M. D. (2013). Socio-economic situation of Indigenous people in the Chittagong Hill Tracts (CHT) of Bangladesh. *Middle-East Journal of Business*, *7*(3).

Islam, R. M. (2010). *Maternal morbidity and mortality among Indigenous peoples in Bangladesh: a study of the Mru community* (MPhil Thesis). University of Tromsø, Norway.

Khan, F. C. (2005). Gender violence and development discourse in Bangladesh. *International Social Science Journal*, *57*(184), 219–230. doi:10.1111/j.1468-2451.2005.546.x

Khan, N. A., & Rashid, M. (2006). *A study on the indigenous medical plants and healing practices on Chittagong Hill Tracts (Bangladesh)*. Academic Press.

Khisa, S. (2011). *The women of the Chittagong Hill Tracts and their experiences on climate change. In Indigenous Women, Climate change & Forests* (pp. 127–140). Baguio City, Philippines: TEBTEBBA Foundation.

Koukkanen, R. (2011). Indigenous economies, theories of subsistence, and women: Exploring the social economy model for Indigenous Governance. *American Indian Quarterly*, *35*(2), 215–240. doi:10.5250/amerindiquar.35.2.0215

Levene, M. (1999). The Chittagong Hill Tracts: A case study in the political economy of creeping genocide. *Third World Quarterly*, *20*(2), 339–369. doi:10.1080/01436599913794 PMID:22523784

Mallick, D., & Rafi, M. (2008). *Are the female-headed households more food secure? Evidence from Bangladesh*. Working Paper, Deakin University, Australia.

Mitchell, S. (2011). Falling far from the tree: How forestry practices in Bangladesh leave women behind. *Heinonline, 24*, 93–122.

Nasrin, J. (2007). *Leading Indigenous (Adivasi) Women* (J. Nasrin & B. Chakaborty, Eds.). Dhaka, Bangladesh: Oxfam GB Bangladesh Program.

Nasreen, Z., & Togawa, M. (2010). Politics of development. *Journal of International Development and Cooperation,* 93-97.

Nath, K. T., Inoue, M., & Chakma, S. (2005). Shifting cultivation (jhum) in the Chittagong Hill Tracts, Bangladesh: Examining its sustainability, rural livelihood and policy implications. *International Journal of Agricultural Sustainability, 3*(2), 130–142. doi:10.1080/14735903.2005.9684751

Roy, A. D. (2005). *Indigenous Textiles of the Chittagong Hill Tracts*. Rangamati, Bangladesh: Charathum Publishers.

Roy, C. (2004). *Indigenous women: a gender perspective*. Resource Centre for the Rights of Indigenous Peoples.

Roy, R. D. (2000). *Occupations and economy in transition: A case study of the Chittagong Hill Tracts. In Traditional Occupations of Indigenous and Tribal Peoples: Emerging Trends: Project to Promote ILO Policy on Indigenous and Tribal Peoples*. International Labour Organization.

Roy, R. D., & Halim, S. (2007). Populaton transfer, minoritization and ethnic conflict in Bangladesh: the case of the Chittagong Hill Tracts. In *Indigenous Communities and Settlers: Resource Conflicts in Frontier Regions of South and Southeast Asia*. Department of Social Anthropology, University of Zurich. (Unpublished)

Sayem, D. R. (n.d.). *Best practices and alternative integrated community based model in delivering primary health care service for Chittagong Hill Tracts of Bangladesh*. Retrieved from: http://www.google.com.au/url?sa=t&rct=j&q=&esrc=s&source=web&cd=1&ved=0CCkQFjAA&url=http%3A%2F%2Fwww.dghs.gov.bd%2Flicts_file%2Fimages%2FOther_publication%2FHealth_System_in_Chittagong_Hill_Tracts.pdf&ei=fWGDUrSoOoSpiAeo74CQBg&usg=AFQjCNGl9rMzv6RcKF8jPStnqNs9Okd5mw&bvm=bv.56343320,d.dGI

Shiva, V. (1989). *Staying Alive: women, ecology and development*. London: Zed Books.

Sultana, A. (2009). Patriarchy and women's subordination: A theoretical analysis. *Asian Journal of Social Science, 37*(4), 599–662.

Taungya. (n.d.). *Activities*. Retrieved from: http://www.taungya.org.bd/Activities.aspx

Sangstha. (2012). *Annual Reflections 2011*. Khagrachari, Bangladesh: Academic Press.

Vinding, D., & Kampbel, E. R. (2012). *Indigenous Women Workers with case studies from Bangladesh Working Paper, Nepal and the Americas*. International Labour Standards Department, ILO Bureau for gender Equality, Switzerland.

Waring, M. (1988). *Counting for Nothing: What Men Value & What Women are Worth*. Allen & Unwin New Zealand Limited. doi:10.7810/9780868615714

Wazed, S. (2012). *Gender and Social Exclusion: A Study of Indigenous Women in Bangladesh* (Unpublished PhD Thesis). Institute of Applied Social Sciences, University of Birmingham.

Women Resource Network. (2010). *Draft Report on the Situation of Indigenous Women in Bangladesh*. Rangamati, Bangladesh: Author.

The United Nations Statistics Division. (2013). *Economic activity*. Retrieved from: http://unstats.un.org/unsd/demographic/sconcerns/econchar/econcharmethods.htm#A

McEwan, C. (2001). Postcolonialism, feminism and development: Intersections and dilemma. *Progress in Development Studies*, *1*(2), 93–111. doi:10.1191/146499301701571390

Briggs, J., & Sharp, J. (2004). Indigenous knowledge and development: A postcolonial caution. *Third World Quarterly*, *25*(4), 661–676. doi:10.1080/01436590410001678915

Rajar, S. R., & Parl, Y. (2000). *Postcolonial feminism/postcolonialism and feminism*. In H. Schwarz & S. Ray (Eds.), *A Companion to Postcolonial Studies* (pp. 53–71). Blackwell Publication.

Chapter 7
Gender, Organization, and Change in Sudan

Shahira O. Abdel-Hameid
Higher Colleges of Technology, UAE

Elisabeth Wilson
Independent Researcher, UK

ABSTRACT

The position of women and role of gender in Sudan has been researched from anthropological, sociological and economic traditions. This study will review the position of Sudanese women within the formal employment sector, setting this within the specific political, economic and social context of the country. In addition, it will examine women in political and voluntary settings, as these are also important decision making arenas. There has been little published material previously on this topic. The study draws on secondary data from unpublished studies and master's dissertations, and also grey material available in Sudan. In addition, semi-structured interviewing of a purposive sample of selected informants was used. The data were analysed thematically. The findings were that many behavioural patterns seen elsewhere were evident in Sudan, such as stereotyping and discrimination. However, educated Sudanese women sought equality within a man's world, unlike the equal but different gender roles found by Metcalfe (2007) in parts of the Middle East.

INTRODUCTION

The position of women and role of gender in Sudan has been researched from anthropological, sociological and economic traditions. A noticeable gap is gender applied to formal organizations. As female graduates have recently exceeded male graduatesand more educated women move into formal employment, this chapter will review the position of Sudanese women within employment,as well as in political and voluntary settings, setting this within the political, economic and social context of the country.

DOI: 10.4018/978-1-5225-3018-3.ch007

BACKGROUND

The Sudanese Context

Until the 2011 secession of the South, Sudan was the largest country in Africa, ranging from desert in the north to tropical rain forest in the south. The Nile river is an important source for irrigation and settlement (Badri, 2008a). In excess of 40 percent of the Sudanese population identify themselves as Arabs, although rarely resembling Arabs from the Levant or Gulf (Clammer, 2007). The dominant group is described as Riverine Arabs, overwhelmingly Muslim. In the South (now independent) there are ethnic links with Kenya and Uganda, as well as the Dinka, the largest non-Arab group (Clammer, 2007). There are other smaller ethnic groups, both Arab and non-Arab. The Sudanese are over 70% Muslim, with generally southern Christians, and some indigenous religions (Clammer, 2007).

Sudan gained its independence in 1956 from a British-Egyptian administration. It then declined to join the (then 'British') Commonwealth, instead embracing the Arab League, later changing its principal official language from English to Arabic. Awareness of this political orientation is crucial to understanding the national identity of the country. Sudan had both democratic and military regimes after independence, culminating in the 1989 military coup. Long-running conflict between the north and south, principally about the distribution of resources but also with ethnic and religious elements, erupted into a lengthy civil war, leading to 4.9m internally displaced persons by 2009 (UNDP, 2009).. The Comprehensive Peace Agreement (CPA) signed in 2005 set up a devolved government in the South and a power sharing administration for the country as a whole (Foreign and Commonwealth Office, 2009). The United Nations had a peace support mission throughout Sudan (UNMIS), particular focused on the south (Foreign and Commonwealth Office, 2009). The conflict in Darfur had not been satisfactorily resolved at the time of writing, and the UN had a humanitarian mission (only) to that region. In March 2009 the International Criminal Court issued an arrest warrant for President Bashir, for alleged crimes against the inhabitants of Darfur. In April 2010 there were the first multi-party elections for 24 years (Guardian, 2010), from which the SPLM and Umma (nationalist) parties withdrew in protest at alleged irregularities; President Bashir won. After an overwhelming referendum the South seceded in 2011.

Sudan has recently exported agricultural crops, and also imported food (Clammer, 2007). The commercial exploitation of oil started in 1999, leading to infrastructure developments. The long-standing US and EU embargo on foreign direct investment led to significant Chinese, Malaysian and Arab investment. In 2008 Sudan was ranked near the bottom of middle income countries according to the UNDP Human Development Report, with average income at US$1,887. However as 90% of the population were said to live on a dollar a day, there were large economic disparities. Post conflict 87% of government income was spent on security, with deleterious effects on health and education services. Urban/rural differences were particularly evident in relation to lifestyle and infrastructure.

As in MENA countries, there were three contradictory sources of law relating to individuals: civil, Sharia, and customary. Before 1983 women entered higher education, worked, travelled and had freedom to pursue different lifestyles and dress (Badri, 2008b); then the legal presumption changed and Sharia became pre-eminent (Badawi, 2003), The 2005 interim constitution gave equal rights for all citizens regardless of religion, race, ethnicity, class, sex, language, political or other opinion, national or social origin, property or other status (Al Fatih, 2005). Sudan has ratified a number of UN Conventions including on the Rights of the Child, but not CEDAW (the Convention for the Elimination of Discrimination against Women). There are various departments at state and Federal level concerned with women, and several universities have programmes focused on women's development, health and other aspects (Nouh & Badri, 2008).

Badri (2008a) surveyed civil society in Sudan, indicating a variety of traditional indigenous civil society groups (mostly religious), and NGOs concerned with peace, reproductive health and female genital mutilation (FGM), human rights, environment, anti-poverty, HIV/AIDS, and development and relief. Some NGO activity had been curtailed by government regulation and co-option. Specific groups focused on women included women's sections in political parties and the Sudanese Women Union, theoretically for all women, but government controlled and of limited effectiveness. Thirty four out of 140 registered NGOs were concerned with women, with other NGOs having women-focused programmes. In addition there were community based organizations (CBOs) at local level. U.N. agencies and foreign donors had programmes to promote women's empowerment (Nouh & Badri, 2008).

From this brief overview it can be seen that there are many sources of difference and diversity in Sudan before gender is considered: ethnicity, religion, political orientation, and socio-economic status.

METHODS

This chapter offers a review of gender and organization in Sudan, drawing on secondary data from unpublished studies and masters dissertations, conference papers and also grey material available in Sudan. In addition to secondary data, primary data collected using semi-structured interviewing of a purposive sample of informants (see Table 1).

The interview started with biographical and career information. Explaining the authors interest in women in decision-making positions, the authors enquired first about interviewees' organizations: where men and women were found in relation to levels, departments and jobs. The authors were interested in any change in the last five years, and likely in the next 5 years. Questions probed perceived differences between public and private sectors, Sudanese and foreign-owned companies, and local non-governmental organizations (NGOs), international NGOs(INGOs) and the UN. Because the authors suspected that there might be ignorance and also cultural taboos about exercising legal remedies, specific questions were asked: 'There are many ways in which women have equal rights in the workplace in Sudan. If a woman has a complaint, what can she do?' Questions about women in society were kept to the end of the interview to avoid influencing earlier answers. The authors asked about societal changes, and views about potential legal changes in relation to women's social and work status. Open-ended questions followed about what helps and hinders women to be accepted as colleagues and managers. Finally, the authors probed into issues related to the influence of religion on working women.

The primary data, which were collected utilizing semi-structured interviews were undertaken in English and Arabic (the Sudanese researcher was bilingual Arabic/English). Informants were informed of the purpose of the study and proposed outputs, and all data were anonymised. Additional data is included from participants on programmes held at Ahfad University, Sudan. All data were analysed thematically and combined with the secondary data.

Table 1. Purposive sample: Interviewees

Name	Role	Organization
Civil service		
Public figure	Member	Civil service commission
Civil servant	Middle rank civil servant	Ministry of social welfare (worked in conflict zone)
Political/diplomatic		
Opposition activist	Member of central political committee	Umma party
Southern activist	Communication officer	SPLM (Southern Peoples Liberation Movement)
Diplomat	Principal political officer	Foreign embassy
NGO sector		
Expatriate NGO manager	Country representative/director	Humanitarian organization
NGO director	NGO director	Local NGO for women's rights
Private sector		
Industrialist	Chairman	Manufacturing company
Human resources manager	HR manager	Manufacturing company
Consultant	Freelance financial consultant	Self employed
Women's organisations		
Civil society activist	Chairperson	Women's peace organisation
General overview		
Academic	Professor and director of Institute	Not-for-profit university
Donor agency manager	Senior Social Development Adviser	Foreign donor government

DISCUSSION: WOMEN AND WORK IN SUDAN

Family Life

Historical records indicate that some Sudanese women held important positions of power and influence. Recently daughters have been valued less than sons, with 63 percent of girls attending primary school in 2003, compared to 71.3% of boys (Badri, 2008a), and less likely to complete their education (El Fatih & Badri, 2008). FGM was widespread, leading to psychological and physical consequences (Badri, N., 2008b). El-Tahir (1999) described how children's games led towards different gender roles, assumed innate, preparing boys and girls for the public and private domains respectively. Girls were brought up to be feminine and submissive (Abdel/Hameed, 1998), and virginity expected (though not of boys) (Alarabi, 2001), with patriarchal power exercised over female sexuality (Dousa, 1999).For young women early marriage was prevalent, and the ideal role was as wife and mother (Osman, 2008b).Stereotypes and gender differentiated roles were reinforced by the school curriculum and media (El Fatih and Badri, B 2008). Girls were less likely to go to technical schools or pursue science subjects at university (Badri and El Fatih, 2008 B). Some young men extended their subordination of women outside the family, as in Islamic youth movements (Elrahman Abdien, 2001).

Gender, Organization, and Change in Sudan

Women also had differences of ethnicity, age, marital status, education, socio-economic background and political affiliation. They worked overwhelmingly in the informal sector, in roles such as hairdressers, domestic work, henna, tea stallholders, market sellers and less often factory workers (Badri, 2008a). This chapter is concerned principally with the educated urban elite, mainly Riverine Arabs, as they act as markers for the emancipation of women in general.

Although only a privileged few had the opportunity to go to university, young women were outnumbering young men (El Fatih & Badri, 2008). Abdel/Hameed (1998) found marriage a goal for 90% of female university students. Consent of both families was required, and socio-economic status took precedence over emotional considerations. Educated parents were more likely to let their daughter choose(Abdel/Hameed, 1998). The professor and other informants shared the view that young Sudanese women could be go-getters, but often inhibited by social norms.

The professor expressed her concern at the growth of 'secret marriages' in universities, which were not legally recognized. The pair did not live together, they just had sex. The Sudanese Religious Council had issued a fatwa stating that this marriage should be legal, but this gave women almost no rights. Divorce was increasingly common among the urban elite (activist and opposition politician). There was some disagreement amongst interviewees about the degree of stigma, as divorcees could remarry. Widowhood was not uncommon, and most women relied on family support. It was estimated that 27% of households were headed by women, rising to 58% among internally displaced families affected by conflict (Badri, 2008a). As well as widowhood and divorce, men emigrated in search of work, for instance to the Gulf (Abdel Rahmen, 1999), or just disappeared.

The professor said that employment was a secondary goal. Until recently it had been acceptable to study but not to work(NGO director), especially after children. However, a husband might encourage his wife to continue working, for instance, if she had a higher salary than him (the professor) or a secure job in an embassy (female diplomat). Abdel Rahmen (1999) explored work-life balance for educated working wives, describing not only a 'double shift' of paid work and domestic responsibilities, but also an expected third community role. A persistent gender division of labour within the household, reinforced by laws and media, was attributed to patriarchy by Abdel Rahmen (1999). This was challenged in some families with working wives, where there were husbands helping with homework, playing, shopping, and doing maintenance, but significantly not with basic care such as feeding, bathing and changing (Abdel Rahmen, 1999). The NGO director pointed out that there were no proper nurseries. She stated that whilst supportive men were rare, some educated women did not want their husbands involved in domestic work. Where children helped, more was expected of girls than boys (Abdel Rahman, 1999, Yassin, 2006). Working wives had various strategies including hiring additional help (Yassin, 2006). Although most wives worked for financial reasons, increasing numbers cited self fulfilment (Yassin, 2006). Both Abdel Rahmen (1999) and Yassin (2006) found ambiguity about working wives' contribution to household expenses, even when they were the main breadwinner, so entrenched is the male breadwinner role (El Fatih & Badri, 2008). The Quran states that a husband should meeting all basic expenses for his wife and children. Thus working wives tended to make irregular cash contributions to the household(Abdel Rahman, 1999).

There were aspects of the law where women were treated as minors. Under Sharia law women had to obey their husbands and accept polygamy, however they had rights for maintenance for themselves and their children (Badawi, 2003).All women were required to have a male 'guardian', a close relative. Only the guardian could conclude a marriage contract, and a woman could not travel without permission unless she was with a close male relative or over 50. There were no laws against gender-based violence against women (Badawi, 2003, Malik, 2008).

Women tended to associate socially with kinship groups across generations (El Tahir, 1999), and might also socialise with close neighbours, even from conservative families. Men on the other hand tended to socialise with men of a similar age outside their kinship group (El Tahir, 1999). If a woman tried to act differently, she risked being ostracised, as men defined strangers and the 'other' (Badri, 2002). As described above there were clear gendered power relations in Sudan, and women had differential treatment, both symbolic and material (Dousa, 1999). Interviewees observed that mixing of the sexes was regulated by social norms. However, men and women were not segregated in the same way in Sudan as in other Arab countries, for instance on the local minibuses in Khartoum. Men and women danced together in groups at celebrations such as weddings (authors' observations).

History of Feminism in Sudan

A survey of feminist perspectives in Sudan was undertaken by Badri (2008b), and is summarized here. Women's associations were founded before independence leading to the formation of the Sudanese Women Union in 1951. After independence the ability of feminists to influence the government depended on the regime. After 1971 some NGOs dedicated to empowering women were registered, including significantly the Babbiker Badri Scientific Association for Women's Studies, which promoted integrated rural development for women and initiated campaigning against FGM. From 1989 to 2005 the fundamentalist military regime restricted NGO activity. In 2003 there were however 37 registered NGOs concerned with women's issues, and five women's networks focusing on peace. Badri (2008 p.54): noted that the theoretical bases of feminism in Sudan varied widely:

Only those who engage in legal issues of violence against women have the discourse that includes issues of gender relations or addresses the structural causes of women('s) subordination.

First, she identified academic feminists who since the 1970s had used frameworks to analyze gender relations and engender mainstream disciplines. This work was spearheaded by Ahfad University for Women, and extended to lobbying and influencing policymakers. The second group was civil society feminists, a less coherent group. Third, feminists were active in formal institutions such as the government, UN agencies and international organizations. Those working in government or pro-government institutions have been criticized by Badri (2008b) as focusing on economic empowerment only, lacking in gender analysis, and generally sympathetic to the government's Islamist view, so there were few tangible gains for women. Fourth, Badri (2008b) acknowledged women and men who opposed subordination of women at a personal and familial level.

Badri (2008b) made further distinctions between Islamist and secular feminists in Sudan. The first group included pro-government Islamists, conservative Islamists and Islamic feminists, the last relying on a re-interpretation of the Quran to promote women's equality. Secular feminists were more broadly based, and looked to international conventions and recommendations. Northern based secular feminists were concerned with women's rights, legal reform, FGM, and building a grassroots network. They also had contact with the international community as advocates and networkers. Southern based secular feminists had similar concerns but had worked alongside men for the liberation of the South. They focused on public and political emancipation, and the integration of women's needs into peace building.

Gender, Organization, and Change in Sudan

Women at Work

Workforce participation by women had increased in recent decades, including in the formal sector, prompted by rising educational attainments and male emigration (Badawi, 2010).Ali (2008) reviewed women's employment in Table 2, noting that working women were more likely to be found in the informal sector. Market liberalisation had led to increased agricultural imports, affecting rural livelihoods, but gender differentiated statistics were unavailable (Ali, 2008).

Legislation relating to women at work was informed by both sameness and difference, with women viewed both as responsible adults and also dependent minors. On the one hand the Labour Act 1997 guaranteed the right to employment, giving the wife an independent identity whilst enacting some protective legislation(the professor). In addition, there was the right to equal pay and promotion according to competence (Badawi, 2010). On the other hand, wives needed permission of their husbands to work under Sharia law, there was insufficient maternity leave (Badawi, 2008), and little equal opportunity in the private sector. The labour laws were criticised: first, for supporting prevailing gender norms; second, women's lack of awareness of their rights (Badawi, 2003, Mohammed, 2007); third, the lack of coverage of women in the informal and agricultural sectors (Badawi, 2003) and small businesses; fourth, no institution for monitoring effectiveness (the professor); and fifth, lack of effective legal remedies (Yassin, 2006, and the professor). All respondents mentioned that Islam respects women working, but the problem lay in the interpretation and implementation of Islamic doctrines (see Elrahmen Abdien, 2001). Informants agreed that the number of working women was increasing, accepted by family and community. Reasons were: female headed households; economic pressures on family income; and the migration of many men in the 1970s, leaving vacancies for women.

Dress

As in other countries there was an asymmetric dress code. Women were expected to wear traditional dress, covering head and body, whereas urban men changed from Galabya (long sleeved shift) to trousers and shirt at the beginning of the 20th century (Dousa, 1999). For a time after 1989 there was a public order allowing police officials and self-appointed 'moral guardians' to harass women considered inappropriately dressed (Osman, 2008). Younger women were more likely to wear long skirts and long sleeved tops and add a hijab, older women wearing a 'tobe', a length of diaphanous material over the head and

Table 2. Women's share of different types of employment

Employment	% of Women
Top management	5
Professional	44
Technical	24
Clerical	70
Traditional agriculture	78
Informal sector	85

Source: Bureau of civil Affairs (2004) and MOLAR (1996), cited in Ali (2008)

long skirts and blouses. The professor said many used not to wear either. Some women covered all their hair under the tobe; niqabs were rare.

A visiting anthropologist commented on the 'fashion' for Arab clothes previously regarded as outmoded (Boddy, 2009). At the time of writing there was a requirement for the hijab or tobe to be worn for women to enter government institutions, universities, or work in the public sector (Badri, 1998). Badri's (1998) interviewees thought that the hijab was ordered from the Quran, but nevertheless saw it as a personal choice (as in Omair, 2009). Badri (1998) noted that female sexuality was considered dangerous, and therefore concealed. Noting that women in the 19th century were unveiled Dousa(1999) considered dress was symbolic language, a form of social control. The freelance consultant added that young women wearing trousers were subject to harassment by the police, because wearing trousers was viewed as western culture. On the other hand evening dresses at private functions were sleeveless (the professor).

Sexual Harassment

There have been two studies of sexual harassment, the first of female students (Alarabi, 2001), and the second of women working in the formal and informal sectors (Abdel-Hameid and Abdel Rahman, 2007). Although the hijab was constructed as protection from male attention (Badri, 1998), harassment occurred regardless of dress when female students entered public space (Alarabi, 2001). Abdel-Hameid and Abdel Rahman (2007) found that sexual harassment was perceived by the targeted women as unwelcome, unaccepted and harmful. The key harassers were bosses and managers in organisations, and in the marketplace clients, suppliers, tax-collectors and policemen (Abdel-Hameid and Abdel Rahman, 2007).

Sexual harassment was an issue of concern in many organizations, but participants from the public and private sectors indicated that sexual harassment policies were usually not explicit, so employees did not know their rights. The HR manager asserted that if a woman applied from a foreign-owned company, it was often because of sexual harassment. Although there were laws against it:

Who would go and complain? For a Sudanese lady to do this would be like a revolution. So she will quit (HR manager, 2016).

He stated that it was less likely to happen between Sudanese because of social links. In general sexual harassment was a silent issue.

Stereotyping and Gendered Jobs

Educated women were traditionally thought suited to clerical and banking jobs, along with teaching and to a lesser extent nursing. However by the 1990s they had entered professions including medicine, veterinary surgery, engineering, pharmacy and law (Abdel Rahmen, 1999). Stereotyping persisted: the civil servant said that the Department of Petroleum Engineering at Khartoum University would not admit women, citing travel away from urban areas. Yet as pointed out by the public figure, women worked as teachers and nurses in rural areas. The civil servant observed that Sudanese women were excluded from industries such as petroleum and some banks. Even when both sexes were recruited, stereotyping persisted. Male and female management students in Khartoum offered internships by a company had similar qualifications and experience; however, the men were designated as salesmen and met customers, and the women were designated merchandisers and did administration (Ahfad student, personal communication).Nevertheless informants said that attitudes towards gendered jobs and roles were changing, an inconsistent and fluid situation.

The informants unanimously agreed that there were socio-cultural values that could constrain women in managerial positions. Frequently cited were cultural and family pressure about marriage, lack of opportunities for training and promotion; lack of husbands' support, and undervaluation of women's reproductive work (see also Badawi. 2010). The expatriate manager specifically cited women being viewed as second class citizens without potential; some being out of the labour market; and the lack of legal structures and policies to promote women. The NGO director stated that:

Women are suffering too much in the workplace. All the time they are seen as not ready for a higher position. They think she is busy with her reproductive role. Women have no facilities to help balance career and duties at home (NGO Director, 2016).

Similar to Nyambegera's (2002) study, ethnicity in Sudan was an issue contributing to job segregation, and the donor agency manager mentioned that professional jobs were dominated by elite northern women.

HRM Policies and Practice

When discussing HR policy and practice, there was a clear distinction made between international and Sudanese organizations. The former had equal employment and gender equality policies, such as maternity leave. However, a donor agency manager drew attention to a problem of finding suitable women; as no allowance was made for their reproductive roles.

In Sudanese organizations similar policies hardly existed. The civil servant observed gender inequality in recruitment policies in institutions that excluded women, including the Faisal Islamic bank. The Omdurman Islamic bank had two branches in one building; the female run branch dealt with women and the male run branch with men. The recruitment process for all banks, included certain elements.

They will not say it publicly but it is there. They will expect the female to be dressed in a certain way ... the hidden agenda is there (Civil Servant, 2016).

He added applicants would also be asked about Islam and the Quran, opining that this is quite unrelated to banking. In contrast the professor believed that in her institution gender equality HRM policies existed. Some firms were introducing new HRM policies; the HR manager declared that they had recently introduced flexi-time to encourage female recruitment.

Reviewing training opportunities, Badawi (2010) found that women were 20% of attendees on a leadership program at Sudan Academy for Administrative Sciences, but 71% of those attending a clerical college. This general pattern was confirmed by interviewees. Badawi's (2010) informants considered that gender bias in promotion existed but might be decreasing, particularly in the public sector. She significantly found that tribal and political connections were salient in promotion (Badawi, 2010). Similar gendered human resource processes in recruitment, selection and promotion have been documented in other Gulf countries (see chs XXX in this volume).

Women in Decision Making Positions: Perspectives

Almost all the informants in this study emphasized that top positions were dominated by men as indicated in Table 1, even when women's participation had increased at lower levels (Badawi, 2010).For instance, women constituted 50% of public service employees but were concentrated in lower grades (Bureau of civil affairs, 2007, cited in Badawi, 2010).The Southern activist highlighted that the many women in the public sector in hospitals and teaching were not decision makers. No woman had been president of a university, board or corporation(Malik, 2008), and there were only 3-13% at the top of trades unions (Bashier, 2000).In relation to the private sector there was little data, with estimates of 3.7% to 10% female employees (Badawi, 2010). The NGO director asserted that difficulties such as career breaks for children and prejudices were serious barrier to women's promotion.

Many interviewees regarded UN, international and foreign government bodies as more favourable. There were increasing numbers of female senior officers (consultant), and many UN agencies had female directors. The industrialist and Southern activist remarked that INGOs had policies to put women into senior positions; however, it was only recently that Sudanese women had joined INGOs. Even in international organisations, there were constraints on women reaching the top. The humanitarian organization manager drew attention to the problem of finding women for higher positions, again citing provision for reproductive roles. The donor agency manager mentioned that women were increasingly found at the top of her government's civil service, with encouragement at middle and senior management:

The professor and the diplomat revealed that women used to go into the public sector but perceived that the private sector now offered opportunities. The activist indicated that husbands preferred their wives to work in the private sector (particularly foreign companies). This was because they were less likely to be harassed (see contrary point above), had a good salary and access to training. The Southern activist commented that some women were more concerned about pay than the actual job. Nevertheless there were constraints in the private sector, the NGO director stating that one could not find a woman director unless she was the owner. The professor stated that it was easier for self-employed women who belonged to business families, although women faced with a marital crisis might consider a professional business.

Women in business had increased since 1989. A study of Sudanese banking investigating women and men in high positions found that positive influences on women included: first, family support (parents, husband, brother); second, academic attainment; and third, single status (Alim, 1999). Women still had to contend with gender stereotypes (Alim, 1999). A later study of 16 Sudanese women-owned large scale enterprises found that some belonged to or attended formal networks, (Alsarraj, 2008). However women had been excluded from formal meetings on the grounds of 'talking too much' (Alsarraj, 2008). One Sudanese woman had started the first real estate agency, before moving into the petroleum sector (the professor)

INGOs had increased in number and type of activity between 1995 and 2008, but the expulsion of selected INGOs in March 2009 by President Bashir led to a decrease in activity and employment. However the local NGO sector was regarded as potentially more open to women (the professor). The Southern politician stated that:

When women lack opportunities in (political) parties, they go back to NGOs' (Female Politician, 2016).

Gender, Organization, and Change in Sudan

She believed NGOs provided better opportunities for being decision-makers. Nevertheless, the professor pointed out that NGOs tended to be managed by educated people in their 50s and 60s, mostly men. When the government became aware of the international focus on NGOs, it created 'GoNGOs' (Government run NGOs) with evident tokenism (the diplomat); for instance a woman from a disadvantaged region used as an example.

A significant factor for all sectors in Sudan was influence, regulation or control by the government. Under the Bashir regime a government employee was closely observed if affiliated to another political party, and could find him or herself fired or imprisoned (activist).The activist noted privileges granted to private sector companies associated with government supporters. The professor further elaborated that many women in business had connections with the ruling party, with a politician father, husband, or brother really in control.

Although there was also a boom in the media, which had:

open(ed) up a public space for women. There were no women at a higher level, and media was controlled by the government (Female Activitst, 2016).

Malik (2008) reviewed women in decision-making positions, noting low political participation in government, and at lower levels in rural areas. The interim constitution included an equality clause referring to colour, language, political opinion and ethnic origin, but significantly excluded gender; in addition there were no laws against gender-based violence (Malik, 2008). Sudanese Islamic movements had varying discourses about women's rights (Elrahmen Abdien, 2001), but were generally not supportive of empowerment.

Most informants depicted a gloomy picture regarding the political situation. This included: tokenism, and female Parliamentary representation insufficient to enable empowerment(Mohammed (2007). Both Ali (2008) and Badawi (2010) noted few female Ministers. The professor explained that to achieve the 25% quota there was a big struggle between 2005 and 2008, with northern and southern organizations working together. Prior to the 2010 election, concern was expressed about the quality of female candidates (SuWEP, 2009), a view shared by the Southern activist. There were few issues over which women would collectively unite (the professor).

When asked about what changes could or should take place, there were varying views. The donor agency manager stated that she did not anticipate any legal changes in relation to women's social and work status, as she considered that the current government was too busy with other political challenges. The civil servant said that Sudan had not signed CEDAW, and that talk about gender was seen as imitating the West, with little practical understanding of gender.

There was a curious disjuncture for some interviewees between their feminist analysis and their proposed solutions. For instance, the NGO director stated that women needed to demonstrate seriousness in their work and in developing careers, exert more effort to be accepted as equal partners, and change the perspective of the men. The activist declared that women themselves needed to be strong and confident and ask for their rights, now they were working alongside men. Both seemed to be suggesting a personal solution to a structural problem.

CONCLUSION

Those familiar with literature in relation to gender and organization in the North and the South will recognise many organizational arrangements and behavioural patterns seen elsewhere. The authors have described a fluid situation in relation to the position of women in decision-making positions in Sudanese organizations. Generally women were absent from important arenas where policymaking and planning were discussed, and there was ambiguous progress. On the one hand the fundamentalist, militarist government was antagonistic to all but the token empowerment of women. On the other hand internal and particularly international political pressure was creating spaces for women where they could make their mark, such as foreign companies and NGOs. In this latter respect this was similar to Moghadam and Sadiqui's (2006) account of changes in the public sphere in MENA countries, and accompanying feminization of civil society.

The political regime appeared the most salient influence on women's status and progress. In Sudan the production and reproduction of gender, and institutionalized patriarchy(Acker, 2006) extended beyond the usual boundaries of the state to businesses and 'GoNGOs'. The ruling party influenced identification with the Arab world and culture and a particular interpretation of Islam. Some of the undesirable practices described by Nyambegera (2002) were evident in the superiority of the Riverine Arabs. The influence of Arab culture was however different to that described by Metcalfe (2007) in that gender equality was not generally sought through separate streams. Relationships between men and women, in both the social and working context, were more relaxed than described in other Arab cultures. The Islamic culture as imposed by the government placed patriarchal ideals at the centre of family law, restricting women's freedom, in a similar way to that described by Moghadam (2006). This had however been challenged and loosened following the CPA. We suggest that Sudan was both similar to and different from other Arab and African countries, and itself an intersection of culture.

The strengths of this chapter are that it is the first study of gender and organization in Sudan that attempts to be comprehensive. Second, the authors have drawn on a wide variety of Sudanese sources, many unpublished or unavailable outside Sudan. Third, the authors have thus drawn attention to both descriptive and theoretical research undertaken in Sudan in relation to gender and organisation. Fourth, using both foreign and Sudanese investigators offers both insider and outsider perspectives. Fifth, the authors believe to have offered new insights into a changing situation, with implications for Arab and African countries. Last, it gives a foundational starting point for more research in this field in Sudan. The main limitation of the study identified by the authors is the fact that they cannot claim that this is a comprehensive account and review of literature, and in addition the empirical work had a small sample size.

REFERENCES

Abdel Hameid. (1998). *The attitude of university women students towards the selection of a spouse* (Unpublished Masters dissertation). Ahfad University for Women.

Abdel Rahman, W. A. (1999). *Employed Women and Domestic Responsibilities: Perceptions, Challenges and Strategies* (Unpublished Masters dissertation). Ahfad University for Women.

Alarabi. (2001). *Ahfad University Students' Opinions on Sexual Harassment* (Unpublished Masters dissertation). Ahfad University for Women.

Al Fatih, T. (2005). *Participation in Decision Making Processes in the Local Government after the Comprehensive Peace Agreement of 2005: Case Study pf South Kordofan and Upper Nile States (PhD Proposal).* Ahfad University for Women.

Asjarraj, A., & Abdel Mageed, A. (2008). *Sudanese women owned large scale enterprises: opportunities and perspectives* (Unpublished Masters dissertation). Ahfad University for Women.

Alim, L. O. (1999). *Women Executive Managers in the Sudanese Banking System: Experience and Challenges* (Unpublished Masters dissertation). Ahfad University for Women.

Ali, W. (2008). A Brief Overview on Women Economic Participation and Employment. In *Sudanese Women Profile and Pathways to Empowerment.* Ahfad University.

Alim, L. O. (1999). *Women executive managers in the Sudanese banking system: Experience and challenges* (Unpublished Masters dissertation). Ahfad University for Women.

Badawi. (2010). *Factors affecting women's promotion into top managerial positions in the Sudan.* Population Council Final Dissemination Conference on Gender and Work in the Mena Region, Cairo, Egypt.

Badawi, Z. A. (2003). *Gender sensitivity in Sudanese labour and employment laws: working women views and experiences* (Unpublished Masters dissertation). Ahfad University for Women.

Badri, A., & Elfatih, T. (2008). Sudanese girls and Women Educational Attainment. In Sudanese Women Profile and Pathways to Empowerment. Ahfad University for Women.

Badri, B. (2008a). Introducing Sudan. In Sudanese Women Profile and Pathways to Empowerment. Ahfad University for Women.

Badri, B. (2008b). Feminist Perspectives in Sudan. In Sudanese Women Profile and Pathways to Empowerment. Ahfad University for Women.

Badri, L. I. (2002). *Agency and negotiating restrictions in creating space for women within the household.* Preliminary PhD proposal.

Badri, N. (1998a). *State Power over the Female Body* (Unpublished Masters dissertation). Ahfad University for Women.

Badri, N. (2008b). Sudanese Women Health Profile. In Sudanese Women Profile and Pathways to Empowerment. Ahfad University for Women.

Bashier, M. A. (2000). *The Position of Women Unionists in the High Echelons of the Sudanese Trade Unions* (Unpublished Masters dissertation). Ahfad University for Women.

Dousa, M. H. (1999). *Gender Identity Formation and its impact on the status of women in Zaghara tribe* (Unpublished Masters dissertation). Ahfad University for Women.

El-Tahir, G. H. (1999). *Children games: Towards different gender roles* (Unpublished Masters dissertation). Ahfad University for Women.

Elrahman. (2001). *The Sudanese Islamic Movements' Perceptions to Womens Rights* (Unpublished Masters dissertation). Ahfad University for Women.

Foreign and Commonwealth Office. (2009). *Sudan country profile*. Retrieved from: http://www.fco.gov.uk/en/travelling-and-living-overseas/travel-advice-by-country/sub-saharan-africa/sudan1?ta=all

Kallefalla. (2000). *Towards gender sensitive policies in Sudan: A Case Study: Sudan National Comprehensive Strategy (1992-2002)* (Unpublished Masters dissertation). Ahfad University for Women.

Malik, S. A. (2008). Women Political Rights, Decision Making, Representation and Good Governance. In Sudanese Women Profile and Pathways to Empowerment. Ahfad University Press.

Mesh'a. (2002). The influence of traditional culture on attitudes towards work among Kuwaiti .... *Women in Management Review*, *17*(5/6), 245.

Metcalfe, B. D. (2007, January). Gender and human resource managementin the Middle East. *Int. J. of Human Resource Management*, *18*(1), 54–74.

Moghadam, V. M. (2006). Maternalist policies versus women's economic citizenship? Gendered social policy in Iran. In Gender and social policy in a global context: Uncovering the gendered structure of 'the social'. Basingstoke, UK: Palgrave Macmillan and U.N. Research Institute for Social Development.

Moghadam, V. M., & Sidiqui, F. (2006). Women's activism and the public sphere: An introduction and overview. *Journal of Middle East Women's Studies, 2*(2).

Mohamed. (2007). *Educated Sudanese Women Knowledge about Women rights in the Constitution in Khartoum State* (Unpublished Masters dissertation). Ahfad University for Women.

Nouh, I., & Badri, B. (2008). Social Capital and Women institutions in government and Non Government bodies. In Sudanese Women Profile and Pathways to Empowerment. Ahfad University for Women.

Nyambegera, S. M. (2002, November). Ethnicity and human resource management practice in sub-SaharanAfrica: The relevance of the managing diversity discourse. *International Journal of Human Resource Management*, *13*(7), 1077–1090. doi:10.1080/09585190210131302

Omair, K. (2009). Arab women managers and identity formation through clothing. *Gender in Management*, *24*(6), 412-431.

Osman, M. E. (2008). Overview of Women's Social Positioning in Sudan. In Sudanese Women Profile and Pathways to Empowerment. Ahfad University for Women.

UNDP. (2008a). *Human Development Indices: A statistical update 2008 - HDI rankings*. Retrieved from http://hdr.undp.org/en/statistics/

UNDP. (2008b). *Human Development Report: Sudan country factsheet*. Retrieved from: http://hdrstats.undp.org/countries/data_sheets/cty_ds_SDN.html

UNDP. (2009). *Human Development Report 2009*. Retrieved from: http://hdr.undp.org/en/media/HDR_2009_EN_Complete.pdf

Yassin, U. E. (2006). *Women and Work: An examination of how women manage their triple roles* (Unpublished Masters dissertation). Ahfad University for Women.

Chapter 8
Emerging Trends and Challenges Faced in Women's Employment and Self-Employment in Pakistan

Shagufta Nasreen
University of Karachi, Pakistan

Nasreen Aslam Shah
University of Karachi, Pakistan

ABSTRACT

Women and work is a concept which is still exploratory although various researches have been conducted related to women and work and its related concepts. Women's economic participation has increased in different jobs as compared to the past; however, the question is how much it has been able to fulfill the goal that women economic participation leads to women empowerment. In developing countries, the economic restructuring influenced by globalization policies of trade liberalization, privatization and fiscal austerity has on one hand increased opportunities for economically stable, educated, skilled and urban oriented population excluding the poor, un-educated, un-skilled and rural population. This chapter aims to explore the concept of women and work by comparing the conditions of work women do in formal and informal sector expanding the scope of analysis to focus not only on women inclusion in paid jobs but to review why it is not changing their status and position.

INTRODUCTION

I am doing my work while my daughter sleeps on my lap (A woman worker)

This chapter explores the concept of women and paid employment in the context of globalization. Women and work is a concept which is still exploratory because of the changing economic and political conditions of the world although various researches have been conducted related to women and work and its

DOI: 10.4018/978-1-5225-3018-3.ch008

related concepts. Women's economic participation has increased in different jobs as compared to the past; however, the question is how much it has been able to fulfill the goal that women economic participation leads to women empowerment? In developing countries, the economic restructuring influenced by globalization policies of trade liberalization, privatization and fiscal austerity has one hand increased opportunities for economically stable, educated, skilled and urban oriented population excluding the poor, un-educated, un-skilled and rural population. To evaluate the status of women, this paper aims to explore the concept of women and work by comparing the conditions of women's work in formal and informal sector. The first part of the chapter is based on review of literature on women's economic status in the global economy. The second part is based on the findings of two researchers one is about socio-economic conditions of self-employed and home-based women workers of Karachi and second is about female workers in industrial sector of Karachi in context of economic globalization. The third part is based on discussion and conclusion.

BACKGROUND

Feminist scholars and researchers have contributed a lot in analysis and redefining of the concepts of work, development and the impact of economic policies on women. Work done by women, whatever might be its nature has been much debated in recent feminist scholarship. They strongly advocate that women's work spans community and industry and 'the social relations of work, its cognitive and affective domains, and its sexual divisions are structured around gender' (Maggie, 1989, p.311). Women constitute half of the world population and are majority of the world poor bearing triple burden of unpaid household work, low wage market and community activities. Although historically women have always remained active generators of income, research regarding the gendered nature of economic development is very recent (Braunstein, 2007). Most of the studies related to women and work tend to focus on women experiences of work in relation to their childcare and family responsibilities and thus ignore the structures and social relations which keep women at a certain place in employment (Coyle, 1988).

Lewenhak, S. (1992) explores the classifying of some human activities as work and giving them a value. It is the domination of middle and upper class men who defined 'work' ignoring some activities that are performed by women. The definition of work has been narrowed to only activities which bring in cash income emerged in the change from subsistence to exchange economies. The concept of work as consisting of all the tasks involved in gaining a livelihood was superseded by the concept of paid employment in a single job. The change happened most extensively in the eighteenth and nineteenth centuries in countries where the industrial and agricultural revolutions developed. Lewenhak (1992) stress on need of revaluation of work because the overall trend for provision of goods of services by human resource is declining due to a range of technologies.

Ward (1988) synthesized that during development women's economic status relative to men has stagnated and women's position continue to decline because it's shaped by the global capitalist economy. The economic growth in developing countries is dependent on core countries which has resulted in income inequality and lowered the status of women. Another strong argument of feminist theory is that women's work must be seen in the context of the family economy. Frank (2008) observes that the 'prevailing definition of 'work' is waged labour in a formally structured relation – a definition based upon a masculine ideal of 'work'. She further adds that in order to understand the concept of work what is 'equally important is that what is regarded as work is a result of both social and statistical definition which have a variety of meanings (Maggie, 1989, p.16). The term 'women workers' also needs to be explained a little in view of the growing scholarship about the co-relation between women and work. An interesting argument is advanced by feminist theorists claiming that the working woman wage earner is 'likely to be more radical than the housewife. This is because women workers see the reality of wage differentials and therefore know that women's rights do not exist in practice' (Maggie, 1989, p. 313).

Despite research spread over the past several decades, women's economic role and their participation in increasing family income remains marginally recognized. Stephanie Barrientos and Naila Kabeer, observe that 'women's earnings are often a crucial element in household survival, they are not 'secondary earners' as depicted in more traditional employment models, and they can accrue many advantages from their employment' (Barrientos & Kabeer,2004).

The work is categorized on gender bases. 'The tendency for men and women to be employed in different occupations is known as occupational segregation by sex' explains Debra Barbezat, (2003). This gendered nature of work and segregation is not limited to the traditional societies but as Richard Anker observes 'it is extensive in every region, at all economic levels, under all political systems, and in diverse religions, social, and cultural environments (Barbezat, 2003,p.177)'.

Women economic participation is an important indicator of human development. It shows increase over the period of time but the percentage of women in employment is stagnated, low income and mostly informal as we compare it with the population growth rate and economic indicators. Traditional development economists and modernization theorists have viewed economic development as process in which economic growth and women's incorporation into the labour force go hand in hand. Others however argue that the process of industrialization and economic development is accompanied by marginalization of women (Bhattacharya, 2007).

Economic Restructuring (Globalization) and Women's Work

To understand the role of women in the economy we need to trace the changes in economic policies that have shaped the global economy. The 'development' process carried out after the Second World War is highly influenced by the international financial institutions the World Bank, the International Monetary Fund (IMF) and the General Agreement on Tariffs and Trade (GATT) which was reviewed in 1995 as WTO (World Trade Organization). The term globalization was used in the 60's in the context of the establishment of transnational corporations; the term however gained wider usage by mid 80s. Globalization has many aspects as Friedman (2000) explains it as inexorable integration of markets, nation states and technologies, enabling individuals, corporations and nation states to reach around the world farther, faster, deeper and cheaper than ever before. Kingsbury (2008) draw upon various authors and sources concludes that it is a process or series of linked processes leading to greater interaction and integration. Chow (2002) defines that globalization refers to the compression of the world in spatial and temporal terms, describing the ever-changing and intensifying networks of cross border consciousness, human interaction, system interdependence and transformation on a world scale. Anthony Giddens (1990) explains that globalization is the intensification of worldwide social relations through time /space destination. It is multifaceted concept that encompasses a variety of meanings and dimensions (Giddens, 1990). Arjun Appadurai (1990) suggest that current global flows occur in and through the growing integration and disjuncture of different landscapes-finanscapes (e.g. money and trade) technoscapes (e.g. technology and information) ethnoscapes (e.g. people through international migration and travel) medias capes (e.g.

mass media and communication) and ideoscapes (e.g. ideas, images and ideology) (Appadurai, 1990). Feminist scholarship has explored its meaning in a different way.

Rege maps three overlapping perspectives of feminist studies about globalization. She categorizes them as the first, gender and political economy of the development perspective focusing the Structural Adjustment Programs (SAP) programs in South Asia, Africa and Latin America. The second transnational feminist perspective draws upon postcolonial analyses of uneven and dissimilar circuits of culture and capital. The third perspective draws upon women experiences living through the post-communist transitions. She further states that feminist analysis has sought to unmask the gendered character of the neo-liberal discourse. Deregulation has been accompanied by an increased regulation of reproduction, austerity by consumerism and a feminised workforce with increased level of malnutrition and violence against women. Analyses of women's labour bring into focus the four areas of labour generally overlooked: subsistence, unpaid work, domestic production and voluntary work. She suggest at this point that only differences between men and women should not be analyzed rather including complex relations of power in different class, caste, and ethnic locations.

The increased trade and economic integration has not been beneficial for people around the world especially for women in developing countries. Feminist criticize that the process of industrialization and economic development is accompanied by marginalization of women (Bhattacharya, 2007) and restructuring, as a result of globalization, tends to reinforce and exacerbate existing gender inequalities (Marchand & Runyan 2000). Mies (1998) pointed out coercive job losses of women in developed countries and creation of low paid jobs for women in developing countries by capitalism. Afshar and Berrintos explain that women of the world are being effected by globalization and 'the effects have been multiple and contradictory, inclusionary and exclusionary'. They identify its main features increasing economic liberalization, free trade and more deregulated labour, goods and financial markets and dominance of Transnational Corporations (TNCs) (Afshar & Barrientos, 1999). Momsen (2004) analyze that due to globalization integration has occurred between countries and people and it has been utilized by TNCs. At present the number of women in paid jobs has increased but we need to understand the quality of this change.

Susan Horton observes changes in employment patterns after globalization. It has become urban centred, industries have changed as well as occupations and the wage gap between men and women has reduced due to increase in women education and experience. But at the same time she notes some exploitation especially for those who have migrated from rural areas. In the process of globalization gradually the state control over resources declines and corporations capture the markets which usually lead to suppression of union organization and degradation of environment. Koggel (2003) analyze the increase labour force participation of women and its linkage to freedom and choices. Women's freedom and agency are not always improved when they enter the work force so the need is to take 'Informed discussion of development processes and policies must include accounts of global forces of power and their intersection with and utilization of local systems of oppression. Fussell (2000) explore another aspect that MNCs exploit the women workers of third world countries because of absence or ineffectual labour laws. Sparr (1994) analyze Structural Adjustment Programs (SAP) introduced in 1990s in developing countries increased in labour in some parts, mostly urban areas but they are unable to move up the level, they are able to survive but not empowered. A lot of paid work done in Informal sector is invisible because they are not counted in the workforce. Women and men are not politically or economically equal and house hold has a great connection with macro economy. If a women and a men earns in household their spending patterns are different.

Economic Globalization in Pakistan and Female Labour Force Participation (LFP)

Pakistan is not an exception when it comes to influences of international economic changes and restructuring. Like other developing countries, in Pakistan the process of globalization started along with other developing countries. Analysts observe a shift of policies from 1988 and 1990 when Pakistan signed agreements with IMF, World Bank and Asian Development Bank (Irfan 2008; Sayeed, 2001; Zaidi,1999). Irfan (2008) argue that a shift in policies of the development sector squeezed its expenditure, compounded by the occasional unpredictable weather conditions adversely affecting the growth in agriculture, the major sector of the economy. The conjunctive influence of tariff rationalization, financial sector reform and privatization led to closure of factories and downsizing which in turn resulted into substantial job losses. The state ceased to be the employer of the last resort rather assumed the role of the auctioneer wherein a number of the public sector units were disinvested and sold to the private sector having adverse implication for employment generation. It may be added that poverty related expenditure of the government drastically reduced as a percentage of GDP during the decade of 1990s till 2003 thereby crucifying the poor at the altar of macro stabilization (Irfan, 2008). Kemal (1999) summarize from his findings that privatization has not been able to reduce the fiscal deficit. Qamar Abbas and Unsa Hussain argue that labour unions in Pakistan represent only 2.5% of the labour force of Pakistan and privatization has lead to further decrease in it (Abbas & Hussain, 2008).

Pakistan is a developing country and mainly non-industrial country, where the range of unpaid home and family work is greater as compared to developed countries. In rural areas they are the main providers of food, water and fuel. In urban areas women are educated, doing jobs and have access to better health facilities. As a Islamic country, segregation is a mark of class, privilege and adequate financial circumstances. Poor women work outside their homes in farming, herding, factories and offices. But their conditions vary greatly.

In the context of economic changes that occurred, studies show that simultaneously with the introduction of SAP, especially the liberalization policies, poverty has increased in Pakistan (Kemal & Amjad, 1997) (MHCHD,1999). Poverty led to an increase in labor supply, especially of women who have never worked before (Khattak & Sayeed, 2000). This changing trend is observed in national surveys and other studies as we compare it to the past. At the time of independence participation of women in paid jobs was low. Slowly and gradually number of women increased in paid jobs but in limited sectors. Sabeeha Hafeez quote according to 1951 census 20.2 percent women workers of the non-agricultural labour force were found in the manufacturing sector. In 1961 the definition of labour force was revised and the labor force participation was raised to 42.1. The overall percentage of women in industries was found to be very low 1.4 percent against 98 percent men. Later, Hafeez in her study argued that findings of her study showed higher number i.e. 8 percent against the LFS 1986-87 which showed 0.97 females in manufacturing. Studies in 1980's show that women were mostly employed in the formal sector jobs in textile, garments and clothing. However, changing economic policies and globalization brought a lot of changes in urban areas and rural areas. The gradual increase persisted at a slow rate as Pakistan Employment Trends 2009 illustrated that in the last decade women's labour force participation grew to a large extent in Pakistan. Majority of females work in agricultural sector with little or no economic security and the share of employment for females increased from 69.9 to 71.1 percent in informal sector. A recent report of Female Employment Trends, 2012-13 shows an increased Female participation in labor force as compared to male LFP rate, which remains in the close vicinity of 83% during the period with spike in 2005-06 (84%). It states that Female participation Rates curve up from (16.2%) rates in 2001-02 to about (24.3%) thereof in 2012-13. Similarly, the economic survey of Pakistan accept that in some major sectors male participation rate is up to 100% while female LFP is lower than 30 percent in some sectors. It signifies that in manufacturing and construction sector total participation rate has increased while female participation rate has declined in 2012-13 as compared to 2009-10.

There are various problems identified related to counting females as a work force. As discussed in beginning these problems are first of all related to defining work and worker (ADB, 2008), (Nayyar & Sen, 1987) (Mumtaz & Shaheed, 1987) (Shah, 1986). Pakistan NGO Alternative Report on CEDAW, 2012 states that the Country report provides a generalized view of women in working in formal and informal sector. It does not provide substantiate data on working women. Further, country labor laws exclude agricultural workers, formal sector, domestic workers and home-based workers while majority in this sector are women workers.

The distribution of female work force vary province wise and restricted to few sectors. Hisam's (2009) comparative study about female workers in Bangladesh and Pakistan shows an estimated 30 percent of workforce in textile consisting of females. Within this sector, women workers are concentrated in low paid, labour intensive, downstream production. A comparative study by Nayyar and Sen in 1987 explored similar trends explained above which shows that much has not changed. The employment of women in the organized manufacturing sector was low; mainly women were confined in textile and garment industries. A sample survey of 10 percent of the women employed at these factories revealed that the majority of them preferred factory work to agriculture work, probably because of the regular flow of income assured by the former. The study shows that women participation in workforce is need based and traditional set up exist in these countries (Nayyar & Sen, 1987, p. 129).

Paid employment for women in Pakistan became acceptable by women themselves and by their families due to pushing economic conditions rather than a choice. It is accepted only because it increases economic contribution to family income. Most of the women in paid jobs are from middle and lower class. The condition and choice of work for upper class are very different. Mirza (2002) categorize the gendered structure of the labour market as women from upper and upper middle class heavily concentrated in teaching and medicine and choosing new careers like banking, journalism, law; lower class women commonly employed as home-based piece-rate workers, starting to join as traders in Sunday bazaars or as hawkers in upper class shopping areas. She identify a change in the women of lower-middle-class as increasingly entering in office sector as receptionists, secretaries, telephone operators, computer operators etc.

Country Gender Profile (CJP) of Pakistan, 2008 explain that poverty and economic restructuring has increased women's demand in labour force but the conditions are putting them in to triple burden. Women have to fulfil their reproductive role regardless of her involvement in paid activities. It also highlights the concern regarding increase in female labour force participation and its link to "greater happiness on the part of women due to the enhancement in financial autonomy" (SDPI, 2008, p.78). Khattak (2001) find that the sexual division of labour has by and large not changed due to increased participation of women in employment. The study shows that household responsibilities are shifted to other female members. Women are taking part in productive as well as reproductive 'responsibilities'.

Job dissatisfaction and increase of work burden has gained attention of many researchers in Pakistan. Ali and Haq (2006) conclude that labour force participation is not making women 'happy' in the context of Pakistan. It seems that the majority of Pakistani women seek work out of need and the money earned by them is used either for the household needs or is taken over by the husband. Not only this, women in Pakistan in most cases bear the double burden of house and work and economic independence rarely leads to individual independence (Ali & Haq, 2006). Some researchers also identify that the wage gap and confinement of women to some jobs is not due to 'glass ceilings' because there is little evidence for it however the major hindrance in the way of women moving upward are gender discrimination on account of cultural restrictions, household responsibilities and low levels of education and skills (Hyder & B, 2005).

Several factors influence the participation of women in paid jobs. Culture and social relations is major subject related to women and paid employment in Pakistan. Pakistani society is patriarchal in its structure limiting the women's mobility and creating a dichotomy of public and private sphere (Papanek, 1971, p.519, 528). This representation of Pakistani woman has changed a lot. Syed (2008) argues that there are socio-cultural and economic differences in Muslim majority countries therefore conventional equal employment opportunity approach is inappropriate to analyze it. In Islamic societies there are both cases; women closed, isolated and voiceless on the other hand women with freedom of work, expression and in control of their own lives. *Purdah* in form of *hijab* or *chador* or segregation is taken as a norm and in many cases women themselves find it difficult to work with men. Basic Islamic sources do not restrict women to engage in paid activities however it is the interpretations which strengthen the gender differences. The basic source of Islamic injunctions i.e. Quran says

In Quarn 4: 32

To men is allotted what they earn and to women what they earn

... and offer prayer, and give zakat (Alms-tax) and obey Allah and His Messenger (33:33)

In another verse Allah (T) says

O you who believe! Spend of the good things which you have earned (2: 267)

These verses clearly show that women and men can earn, must pay *zakat*[17] and are asked to spend from their earnings. Naseef (1999) discusses that this verse has been translated by some Muslim scholars in terms of obedience to Allah and punishment for disobedience. In other interpretations it is referred to 'work'. But it is clear that women are eligible for ownership because they are ordered to pay *zakat* (Naseef, 1999, p. 162)

Women's economic participation is significantly influenced by factors such as their age, education and marital status. Study of Naqvi and Shahnaz identifies that in Pakistan the chances of a woman to be paid and productive member of the society increases with education. Thus women of rural background because of their lack of education usually get involved in low paid economic activities. Older better educated women can take decision about their doing paid job in contrast to younger poorly educated women (Naqvi & Shahnaz, 2002). Similar findings were reported by Hafeez and Ahmed that female labour force participation increase with the rise education attainment. Family structure is another important determinant of whether a woman can or cannot undertake paid activities. 33 Studies from South Asia also show that with the growth of world trade and finance, labour force participation is increased in numbers but the working conditions are hazardous with fear of insecurity and low wages (Hafeez & Ahmed, 2002).

A number of small scale studies related to women and work in formal and informal sector are conducted in Pakistan which shows that life cycle patterns considerable changed. Why women enter the workforce and why they leave it. Why women enter into paid activities is a complex question because it is not about just increasing the number of women in paid activities but the change it brings into the life of women, the reasons women choose to do paid work, available opportunities, its legal condition and safety of environment. As discussed earlier that studies of developed and developing countries show that the number of jobs for women is clearly increasing. The reasons may be poverty, socio cultural changes, and increase in level of education for women, international community and its efforts for gender equality and so on. But the effect on women of overall changes in the structure of the economy depends not only on the number of women's jobs available, but also on the quality of these jobs. Furthermore, the economy affects different women in different ways, so that the impact of these changes varies for women depending, for example, on their marital status, number of dependents, race, and class (Kuhn & Bluestone, 1987).

Sharma and Sharma also analyze the choice of female employment. They identify many causes for choice of 'work' in particular cultural context such as mobility, education, poverty and marital status. Marriage does influence the value of time in the home. The value of time of married women / single women depends on household structure. In general, marriage_ related market mechanism creates a mutual dependence between men and women who want to work, buy or reproduce. Marriage is assumed to be an exchange of household labour between the spouses. Hence, there are two aspects of labour within the household and in the labour market. There are interesting insights regarding labour supply, consumption, fertility and marriage. A prediction of the theory is that income changes have differential impact on wives' and husbands' labour supply and the female's labour supply curve is more backward bending then male's (Sharma & Sharma, 2006).

Hussain (2008) explains the working problems of women in Karachi. She categorized her respondents into three main socio-economic groups' domestic workers, sales and clerical jobs and managerial jobs. Women's work experience is related to the socio-economic status of their families. Women from families with little or no education usually take domestic work or very low-level jobs. Women from moderately educated and/or religious backgrounds are often found working in traditional jobs, and women from well-educated and socially advanced families have the opportunity to pursue non-traditional jobs and careers, where they compete with males. Parents' encouragement plays a very important role for girls pursuing male-dominated occupations. It was found that parental support was one of the strongest predictors of young women's career aspirations and motivations: those who were career oriented girls f faced less pressure from their parents to marry early and have children.

Women and Work: Experiences From Formal and Informal Sector From Karachi

This part of the chapter is based on a comparison of two studies conducted in Karachi, Pakistan; one is about socio-economic conditions of self-employed and home-based women workers of Karachi and second is about female workers in industrial sector of Karachi in context of economic globalization. Both of the studies are concerned with women and work related concepts including work conditions, occupational health, job security, harassment at work place and control and decision making about socio-economic aspects of their lives. By comparing the findings of both these researches it is attempted to create a broader scope of analysis for women and work in the context of Pakistan and in general for developing countries. The basic aim of the chapter is to understand the changing trends of women's employment because women are increasingly joining paid jobs. Many influencing factors such as globalization, modernization, urbanization and corporal mobility; in country migration, social transformation, gender relations; change in family patterns from joint to nuclear and amendments in laws regarding marriage, divorce and violence against women have played an important role in bringing this change. Therefore, it is important for policy makers to make gender sensitive policies rather than focusing only on increasing the number of women in different sectors.

METHODOLOGY

The study of female work in industrial sector of Karachi in context of economic globalization was conducted in selected[2] Industries from the three industrial areas of Karachi[3] namely SITE Karachi, SITE North Karachi and Korangi Industrial area. The first task was to identify the number of industries in which women are employed. From earlier studies it is noted that mostly women are employed in textile and food industries, and drugs and medicine industry (Hafeez, 1989). To identify the total number of industries of Karachi, concerned governmental departments namely Industries and Commerce Department, Government of Sind, Sindh Small Industries Corporation, Sindh Bureau of Statistics, Sindh Employees Social Security Institution (SESSI), Employers federation of Pakistan (EFP) and Sindh Technical Education & Vocational Training Authority (STEVTA) were contacted. All of these departments have data about number of industries and workers in factories and industries of Karachi. During the process a problem come about that they do not have sex segregated data. During meetings they informed that garments and pharmaceuticals have more women workers and the ratio of male to female is 80 – 20 percent in the workforce. However STEVTA employment exchange provided the data which supported this argument. After that the selection of industries was very difficult task. Direct contact with these industries revealed that they were not willing to share any information regarding workers and many of them refused to conduct interviews with women workers. So the process of selecting the industries was changed. In Karachi Non Governmental Organizations (NGOs) were contacted which are working with labour unions in these areas. With the help of contact persons the researcher was allowed to fill the questionnaires from women workers. Another strategy adopted was to contact the female women councillor of the area and with her reference women workers were contacted. For this study probability sampling technique was used because it was not possible to study entire population women workers in industries of Karachi. Total 200 women workers were interviewed from 13 garments industries located in different industrial areas of Karachi. With the help of prepared questionnaire women respondents were asked the questions which were recorded on the questionnaire itself in the presence of the respondents. Secondary analysis research method was used to study official data and recent reports of government to relate the employment with selected macroeconomic indicators in the period of 1980- 2008. The raw data obtained from the questionnaire filled by the respondents was converted into statistical form of tables and graphs.

The second study was based a study of experiences of home-based and self-employed women of 900 women from 9 towns of Karachi. The towns included New Karachi, Liaquatabad, SITE, Orangi, Lyari, Gulberg, Gadap, Baldia and North Nazimabad. The towns are sub-divided into 178 localities governed by elected union councils (UCs). From these towns, home based women were selected on the basis of prior information by using random sampling method. It took four years to collect data, observing the life patterns of these women at their houses. The data were gathered through a survey. For this study a team including two M.Phil students and the researcher collected the data with the help of interviewing schedule. Primary data was collected through a household sample survey. The questionnaire-cum interview method was used. With the help of prepared questionnaire women respondents were asked the questions which were recorded on the questionnaire itself in the presence of the respondents. Once the data was complete, it was manually fed into tables. The data collected from the home-based women workers, selected randomly, through questionnaires and personal narratives reveal that they do work within the walled spaces of their homes but their lives are neither bounded by space nor they live in isolation.

In this chapter findings of both of the studies mentioned above are compared to identify the similarities and differences in the work conditions of women working in formal and informal sector.

RESULTS AND DISCUSSION

Analysis of macroeconomic indicators of Pakistan during the period of 1980 to 2009 shows the changes occurred due to the policies of economic globalization. Results show that inflation has increased, GDP growth rate is very unstable, expenditure on health and education has not shown any increase, external debt has increased and people living below poverty line has increased. Table 1 shows selected macroeconomic indicators from 1981- 2009. The reason of taking this time period is to take a quick look at the before and after impact of change in economic policies. The aim of these economic policies was based on the idea of economic growth, openness of markets, improving efficiency of public institutions by privatization and reducing fiscal deficit.

Table 1 shows that these policies couldn't make the changes promised. GDP growth rates show fluctuations. Rather than improving the standard of living the economic policies adopted under the premise of liberalization along with political instability and law and order situation of Pakistan, inflation increased manifolds increasing the cost of daily use items. Often quoted by Pakistani economists and common people is the prices of diesel and petrol. In 1999 it was Rs.10.80 and in early 2010 the cost was high as Rs. 73 per litre. The prices of daily use items rise discreetly with increase in the price of fuel directly affecting the life of people especially poverty stricken population. It is important to note that according to a news report in 2011, 40 percent population in Pakistan was living below poverty line.[4]

Table 1. Key macroeconomic indicators: 1981-2009

Years	GDP	Current Account deficit	Inflation (Consumer Price Index)	Budget deficit	Public Investment	Total investment	Exports (Goods and Services)	Foreign direct investment
	Growth % per annum	% of GDP	Growth % per annum	% of GDP	% of GDP	Growth % per annum	Growth % per annum	net inflows (% of GDP)
1981	6.4	4.3	12.0	n.a.	9.1	18.4	12.31	0.38463493
1985	8.7	3.1	5.2	n.a.	8.9	17.99	10.42	0.421864139
1990	4.6	4.51	12.7	7.18	8.58	19.52	15.53	0.612997637
1995	4.1	4.5	13	6.46	6.4	17	16.70	1.19175194
2000	3.9	2.13	3.6	4.1	4.63	16.97	13.44	0.416484258
2005	9.0	3.1	12.2	4.3	4.07	21.95	15.68	2.008211679
2009	4.1	2.0	17.9	n.a.	n.a.	18.9	12.84	1.473547967

Sources:
1. Hand book of Statistics on Pakistan Economy, 2010, http://www.sbp.org.pk/departments/stats/PakEconomy_HandBook/index.htm
2. Economic Survey of different years
3. World Bank http://data.worldbank.org/country/pakistan

Emerging Trends and Challenges Faced in Women's Employment and Self-Employment in Pakistan

The years 2000-2003 have witnessed the introduction of such policies as promotion of liberalization, deregulation, and reduction in the cost of doing business; these policies have laid equal emphasis on encouraging a stable macro economic framework in terms of inflation, interest rate and exchange rate. Further, they have also concentrated on the promotion of export of services, which had not received proportional attention in the past. In fact, they made the promotion of services an integral component of the overall trade policy of the country.

Table 2 shows a decline in exports of goods and services and a marked increase in external debt.

Table 3 shows that the population of Pakistan has doubled from 1980 to 2009 but the expenditure on health and education has not changed, it has rather reduced. For accessibility of health, education people are being pushed towards private sector which has created two types of qualities of health and education. The private is affordable for the rich and to some extent middle class while public sector is affordable for poor classes.

In the backdrop of economic conditions explained above, the impact of macroeconomic policies on women can be analyzed according to her gender roles. In Pakistan women are almost fifty percent of the

Table 2. Macro economic indicators

Years	Exports of goods and services (% of GDP)	External debt stocks, total (DOD, current US$)
1990	15.53830689	20589310000
2000	13.44132462	32953615000
2007	13.21461341	42006027000
2010	13.51626785	64003295000
2014	12.27708535	62184234000
2015	10.94612705	n.a.

Source:
World Bank (http://databank.worldbank.org/data/reports.aspx?source=2&country=PAK#)

Table 3. Comparison of social and economic indicators

Year	Population	Education Expenditure (% of GNI)	Health Expenditure, Total (% of GNP)	Labour Participation Rate		
				Female (% of Female Population Ages 15+)	Male (% of Male Population Ages 15+)	Total (% of Total Population Ages 15+)
1981	85096000	1.5	0.6	12.3	86.4	51.6
1985	94794433.82	2.0	0.7	11.6	85.7	50.7
1990	107975060.2	2.3	0.7	13.5	84.5	50.7
1995	122374952.6	2.4	0.8	12.5	83.3	49.4
2000	138080000	2.3	0.7	16.1	84	51.3
2005	155772000	1.51	0.4	19.4	84.4	52.9
2009	169708302.6	2.15	n.a.	21.7	84.9	54.3

Source: World Bank http://data.worldbank.org/country/pakistan

population. Her primary role is considered her reproductive role although it has changed a lot in the last decade. Unfortunately her paid work is underreported making her invisible from the productive domain and giving her also a feeling that she is not doing 'work' but a supportive activity to survive. In the formal sector she is confined to some specific sectors and it was thought that may liberalization policies would generate more employment for women. But this study shows that results have not changed. The data shared by Sindh Employment Exchange shows that garments, pharmaceutical, food industries remain the dominant sector for women and they are only few in numbers in management level jobs. One reason quoted for this situation is that as to reduce labour cost the work shifted from work place to sub-contract jobs expanding the informal sector and increase in casual employment. (Khattak & Sayeed, 2000) (Petras & Veltmeyer, 2001) (Sadeque, 2003) (Sayeed, 2001). In this research interviews with women workers and activists clearly mentions that majority of women workers are on contract bases.

Invisibility and Recognition

In both studies, women working in formal and informal sector, a common feature noticed is invisibility and under representation of women workers. Although, women workers in industries are selected from the formal sector statistically they remain invisible, for instance The "Development Statistics of Sindh 2008" shows that number of manufacturing establishments in Sindh was 1852 in the year 2005-06 with average daily employment 290,376. It is in total with no distinction for male or female workers. To identify the number of industries in Karachi, those with high female employment and ratio of male and female workers became quite difficult. All the major sources such as Industries and Commerce department, Government of Sindh, Sindh Bureau of Statistics, EOBI, STEVTA and NILAT were visited to collect this data. They all had generalized data. During informal interviews and conversation they all agreed that the ratio of male and female in industry is 80 and 20 percent as workers in industries. The detailed information was provided by STEVTA. It showed that in heavy industry such as motor companies and Ghee industries there are no women workers because it is considered heavy work, require more skill and women are never tried for such work. In textile mills, women if employed are in office/administrative jobs while in manufacturing area women are not employed. Pharmaceuticals and garments are the main industries where women are employed and the ratio of workers there is fifty percent for females.

Studies reviewed in earlier part of this chapter shows that women in informal sector face invisibility and under representation problem. In case of Pakistan, C 177, the convention of home-based workers is not yet ratified, however, ILO has been working with Federal and Provincial Governments, who show interest, in developing and implementation policies related to HBW. According estimates of ILO there are 12.5 million HBW in Pakistan and their number is increasing due to shrinking of the formal sector, more than 80% of these are women working more than 12 hours a day (ILO, 2016).

The study conducted by one of the author, confirms the under representation of women in informal sector. In this study terms home-based working women and self-employed woman has been used interchangeably. There are multiple reasons for this. The field experience and discussion with self-employed women were convincing enough that instead of coping with words and phrases and labels for determining the category and nature of work women are engaged in, one must listen to the voice of women themselves. During the research when they were asked about the nature of their work that 'What difference does it make?' they asked instead of answering any question:

Emerging Trends and Challenges Faced in Women's Employment and Self-Employment in Pakistan

Call it whatever you fancy; we work because it brings us money. We are not beggars. (A woman working in Informal sector)

As Lewenhak (1992) argued that the changing economic conditions changed the concept of work excluding the tasks in gaining the livelihood and focusing only on employment in a single job. This change of definition ignored the social impacts and the importance of person involved in these tasks, in this case they are women. Similarly, as Shahid (2010) analyze the efficacy of proposing a law for women domestic workers in Pakistan, which is also part of informal sector, she argues that the law can only be effective if it recognizes the experiences of women and existence of other factors such as race, ethnicity, class, religion and gender that constitute women's multiple identities.

Work Conditions

I discontinued my education because of financial problems. Although I am a position holder in my educational period and I won many debate competitions. Since I was the eldest of all my sisters and brothers I had a strong intention to support my parents financially and emotionally. We had weak financial conditions. My father was jobless and my mother was housewife that's why I couldn't continue my education.

During interviews majority of the women shared that joined the paid work due to economic problems. Increased poverty has pushed these women into these jobs rather than making choices.

They were unaware of liberalization policies, however, employers and supervisors were aware of the changes in industrial sector after liberalization. They considered it beneficial because they thought these policies attracted the foreign companies and corporations which created employment opportunities in Karachi. These are women of young age (28-32 years), majority unmarried, literate with not more than ten years of education. Majority have high number of dependents due to which more than one member is engage in income generation activities. They are earning below minimum wage level and doing paid job to fulfil economic needs of the household. Interestingly they were the first woman from their families to enter into paid jobs. Majority of them are spending their income at home. They are working for eight hours per day and are not satisfied with their wages and nearly half of them do over time to increase their income. In industrial sector their wages are equal to males. As expected and revealed by other studies, women are mostly in hosiery, readymade garments, bed sheets and towel industry. Males are in ginning, spinning and weaving. In textiles and garments 90 percent are on contract bases.

Similar responses were given by self-employed and home based women workers. They are mostly huddled in slums of metropolitan city of Karachi. Here they are living a ghetto style life. Belonging to the lower-strata of income (and this also means lower social hierarchy) these females of all ages remain engaged in income generation. These women are really struggling hard to thrive and boost their livings by supporting their families before or after marriages. Some of them are working from the age of 15, 16 or 20 years and then they never looked back. Thus a never ending fight against poverty starts once they step in the establishment of their businesses. The reasons for not recognizing the work of self employed women is that majority of them are illiterate and lack of confidence. The inequalities in the lives of these women start at the very young age. It is amazing to watch little girls busy in helping their mothers and grandmothers in a variety of work. As little girls they do not go to school and like their mothers and grandmothers one day would be counted in the list as adult illiterates and as self-employed women.

As told by themselves, these women do not complete their primary or secondary education because of poverty and also because of the gender hierarchies. Being a working woman they have dreams regarding their family and children. Sadly, very few of them can hardly provide even the primary education to their children and at last they would also become the part of this scuffle.

Field visits have shown how the self-employed women suffer from the constraints caused by lack of knowledge and information, social skills and networking. With no education and no formal training, these women would have no chance to find employment in the formal sector and therefore, would remain engage in generating their own income and employment within their homes with allusive resources and diminishing capital in view of accelerating poverty. According to the findings of this research very few self-employed women of Karachi are able to take up vocational training.

Multiple Roles

When I leave for work in the morning I cook food and leave home at 8:00am and when I come back home at 6:00 pm, I cook for the night, my husband is jobless, he is at home but it's my work to do home chores.

Women have to perform role of a mother, a wife, a home maker, worker and a citizen. A women engaged in paid work also have to look after domestic work. This dual responsibility has overburdened working women, thereby leading to multidimensional problems. Where joint family exists she is expected to fulfil the demands of her role as a daughter in law. She has a much larger are of social interaction. So her informal work increases more if she is a part of voluntary associations. Due to her multiple roles she has no time to relax. Chronic fatigue, weakness, is some of the results of such high level stress. Some other factors related to job are monotonous work, poor ventilation, unfriendly working atmosphere and discrimination at work place. Although Karachi is considered a modern city but traditional attitudes and behaviours exist. Since her primary responsibility is considered home and children they require to work at home and outside the home. Mothers have to face quite a lot of problems if she is going for paid job she leaves her child with someone which means additional expenditure if it is a day care. Children also feel neglected she suffers from guilt and find torn between the two. Even they are doing house work and do not get help from their husbands or male members of the family.

Occupational health is another very important aspect of women's work. During interviews with women workers in industries, most of the women complained about effect on their health. It has physical as well as psychological impacts. Usually they are in stitching and continuously doing this work causes back pain, head ache, eye sight problems. From field observation it was noted that in majority of work places the conditions were difficult with low lighting facility and uneasy seats.

I usually feel stress and pain in my back and want to quit the job but I don't have a choice

When I go back home I get tired and feel pain in my legs because most of the time I stand to supervise the work

Even an employer said that "Women come to work in factory in better condition but during their employment they seem to lose their health day by day."

Self Confidence

Women economic participation is considered a tool for women's empowerment. The business of self employment has brought some positive change in the lives of the self employed women in Karachi. It has raised their respect in the family and in the neighborhood. The business has also boosted the self-confidence in these women.

During interviews women workers of industries also told that they have become confident after doing job because they can take decisions by themselves, their mobility has increased, they can spend money as they wish, they have become important for the family and their self esteem is high. Others who thought no change has occurred think that males are dominant so they have to follow their decisions. Few of them think that 'elders can make better decisions for us' and they have internalized the subordinate role of women. One of them also think that traditional and norms of society do not allow women to show their confidence. An overwhelming majority (92.50 per cent) responded that they have become confident after doing job because they can take decisions by themselves, their mobility has increased, they can spend money as they wish, they have become important for the family and their self esteem is high. Others who thought no change has occurred think that males are dominant so they have to follow their decisions. Few of them think that 'elders can make better decisions for us' so they have internalized the subordinate role of women. One of them also think that traditional and norms of society do not allow women to show their confidence. Another assessment of empowerment is spending of income. Similar answers were received when they were asked about savings.

A part from the achievement of self-confidence, more than half of these women (53.50 per cent) said they are unable to save from their income. They worked for family survival because in most of the cases head of the family was unemployed, money was needed to pay school fees of siblings, house rent was paid from it or other needs of the family were fulfilled from it. Those women who saved money deposit it in form of committee.[5] Others are saving it for dowry of their daughter or for their own marriage. However four of them said they are saving it in bank. The major reason of low saving is high level of poverty. Those who do save are spending it on necessities. So the incomes they generate are very limited and give them little access and control over resources. These finding shows on one hand slight improvement in their status and position but for long term and sustainable equitable position they need to be economically independent and make their own decisions.

Level of awareness about laws was very low among women workers. It is an indicator of awareness of her rights and legal structures. Majority (95 per cent) women workers were unaware about labour laws. Lack of awareness of his or her rights is the first barrier to fight for their rights. They were further asked about promotions, night shifts, labour laws and minimum wages. Surprisingly more than half (58 per cent) women were aware of minimum wage fixed by the government. This is good sign because they were aware of wages. On the other hand it shows that women workers were only concerned about payments and were unaware of other legal protections which they could avail from laws. They were also asked regarding night shifts for women workers. All of them replied negatively that night work is not allowed in the industry for women, but they gave varied answers. They said there is no permission from home for night work or due to less security, distance from home and work place. Only 10 percent women knew that it is not part of the labour policy that women work in night shifts is not allowed

All of the women workers from industries were from the formal sector but 56 per cent replied negative to the existence of a trade union. Because they are working on contract jobs and it confirmed the earlier studies that after liberalization policies trade unions are absent or declining. Those who were members of trade unions can be categorized as two types. One who was active members because they thought it is their right to be a part of a trade union; it helps in approval of their demands, or just for the sake of membership. According to women who were not part of a trade union, they thought

it is not useful because whatever policy comes is implemented even if it faces any resistance. (A women worker in industry)

They were also unaware about organizations working for women's rights. Most of the women were unaware about organizations which provide credit facility. Out of 200, only 16 women were aware about NGOs and they were contacted in the past by an NGO working for labour rights. These finding poses two important ideas, one, organizations working for labour rights can play an important role in raising awareness among women workers. Secondly that government role is very important because NGOs have limited access and outreach. By developing linkages between these two the pace of development can be increased. Another major problem they were facing is contract based jobs. Many facilities can be availed if the job is permanent. This is one of the reasons of job insecurity. It also leads to lower bargaining power of workers. Another demand was provision of transport facility. The public buses used for transport are not easy, they are over loaded giving less space for women, become a cause of sexual harassment and high bus fares cost them very much. In case of government the complain was about increasing inflation due to which living conditions are becoming difficult for middle and lower class of the society. They also demanded increase in wages, and job security. Other demands were implementation of labour laws. Few of them asked for security which was showing their fear of harassment. Others who didn't ask for anything believe that 'demands are made where they are being fulfilled'. It shows their feeling of uncertainty and mistrust on institutions. Majority (95 per cent) women workers were unaware about labour laws. Others who knew had very little knowledge.

The impact on the economy directly impact on women. With high prices more women are pushed into jobs. These jobs are not improving their standard of living but fulfilling their basic needs. That is the reason in this research it was identified that women decision making power has not changed. The reason is lack of acceptance for female working outside the home due to social norms and customs. Even though many households are being financially headed by females but socially and politically they do not have choices and opportunities as much as males have. During interviews with activists it was revealed that due to globalization policies the formal sector has not expanded. Furthermore, the workers are on contract based jobs. They are waiting for their confirmation letters. Case studies revealed that women are working for more than three years and they are yet not permanent whereas, according to the labour laws the probation period is three months.

On the other hand self-employed and home-based women workers are already part of informal sector and they were facing the problems of irregularity of work, low wages, and long working hours. It questions then what's the difference in lives of women engaged in income generating activities at home and those working outside the domain of home?

As discussed in earlier part of this chapter, women and work is complex and changing concept due to integration of economies and nations. It is on one level increasing the number of women in paid jobs but on the other hand it is not changing their status and position as assumed by traditional theorists. In this study an attempt was made to compare the working conditions of women in formal and informal sector which showed many similarities. They are earning low and living at a subsistence level. It shows that women workers with low literacy level, low skilled jobs working in factory have similar earnings as to a home-based worker. Their 'working hours' including time spent for the paid activity vary but their domestic roles and responsibilities remain the same. Despite all the hardships they are struggling had for themselves and their families. They have gained self-confidence and have a feeling of independence. The interviews of these women suggest that their work gives them a sense of achievement and pride as they are able to contribute to their family income. Unfortunately, they are not organized and are unaware of the organizations which can help them improve their knowledge and skills.

CONCLUSION

In conclusion the present day Pakistani society women roles are changing. This change is brought by many factors and globalization is one of it. Women are too much caught in thinking about improving their families' economic conditions that they become unaware of the policies that are planned for them by governments or international institutions. For many their first priority has become the survival for which they accept all conditions of employment. Women in this case are more affected in discharging her dual role at home and work place and to strike an optimal balance amongst them, her satisfaction level varies. They are victims of poverty that has a central role to join industries. They are concerned about bad working conditions, bad environment, and harassment but they have no choice rather than accepting it due to poverty. They are not usually active in unionization. Policy makers continue to the policy of liberalization, austerity and privatization because they think it is the only way to improve the economy. But in this process they only count women in labour force participation rates. At the time of decision making or budgeting the priority is not gender bases but increase in GDP growth and other macroeconomic indicators.

RECOMMENDATIONS

Based on the findings there are some general and some specific recommendations. First of all a country level study needs to planned for women workers both in formal and informal sector because invisibility remains the first problem when it comes to the research regarding women and work. Secondly, more and more new categories of work have emerged and women are joining new fields therefore it is necessary to count all these women and analyze their experiences within their context. Many organizations are working for women's rights and gender equality but there is a need to work in collaboration with Government and non-governmental organizations. There is also a lack of linkage between academic research and policy making that gap needs to be bridged up.

For informal sector the first important step is recognize them as a worker and bring them within the scope of labour laws. Gender equality, improvement in work conditions, job security and availability of decent jobs can only be achieved by identifying the needs and problems from women workers and taking their suggestions for bringing a change. Some specific recommendations for home-based workers would be:

1. Formulation of a National Policy and a Plan of Action in consultation with provincial governments for home based women workers by the Government of the Pakistan.
2. Data regarding home based women workers and their contribution to national economy should be incorporated into official statistics.
3. Minimum protection from the exploitation of middleman should be provided.
4. An investigation of the problems of home based working women at home should be undertaken.
5. Access to markets and economic resources including raw materials, technology, and credit information should be made easily available.
6. Micro-finance system should be provided.
7. Monitoring system for women borrowing loans should be introduced.
8. Information on occupational health and safety, statutory social protection, pregnancy, childbirth and child-care be provided
9. Skill development and literacy programmes be made available
10. Home based women be encouraged to form their organization/collectives.
11. Home based women's work should be projected by holding periodical displays of their products.
12. More research is needed on the issue of women's work in the informal sector.

REFERENCES

Abbas, Q., & Hussain, U. (2008). *Globalization, Privitization and Collective Bargaining of Labour: A Time Series Analysis of Pakistan 1973- 2004. 8th Global conference on Business and Economics*, Florence, Italy.

ADB. (2008). *Rleasing Women's Potential Contribution to Inclusive Economic Growth, Country gender Assesment Pakistan*. ADB.

Afshar, H., & Barrientos, S. (1999). *Women, Globalization and Fragmentation in the Developing World*. London: Women Studies at York. doi:10.1057/9780230371279

Ali, M., & Haq, U. (2006). Women's Autonomy and Happiness: The Case of Pakistan. *Pakistan Development Review*, *45*(1), 121–136.

Appadurai, A. (1990). Disjuncture and Differences in the Global Cultural Economy. In M. Featherstone (Ed.), *Global Culture: Nationalism, Globalization and Modernity* (pp. 295–310). Newbury Park, CA: Sage.

Aurat Foundation, Pakistan NGO Alternative Report on CEDAW, 2012. (2012). Aurat Publication and Information Service Foundation.

Ayub, N. (1994). The Self-Employed Women in Pakistan: A Case Study of the Self-Employed Women of Urban Informal Sector in Karachi. Karachi, Pakistan: Association for Women's Studies & News.

Barbezat, D. (2003). Occupational Segregation around the World. In Women, Family, and Work: Writings on the Economic of Gender. Blackwell Publishing.

Bhattacharya, R. (2007). Gender and Employemnt in the Context of Globalization: Some Facts and Figures. In R. Ghadially (Ed.), *Urban Women in Contemporary India*. Sage.

Braunstein, E. (2007). *The Efficiency of Gender Equity in Economic Growth: Neoclassical and Feminist Approaches*. The International Working Group on Gender, Macroeconomics, and International Economics, Working Paper Series. Retrieved from www.genderandmacro.org

Braunstein, E. (2009). *Women's Employment, Empowerment and Globalization: An Economic Perspective*. Retrieved September 23, 2010, from World Survey on the Role of Women in Development, Expert Papers EC/WSRWD/2008/EP.3: http://www.un.org/womenwatch/daw/ws2009/first_experts.html#expert1

Chow, E., & Lyter, D. (2002). Studying Development With A Gender Perspective: From Main stream Theories to Alternative Frame Works. In E. Chow (Ed.), *Transforming Gender and Development in East Asia* (pp. 25–30). New York: Routledge.

Coyle, A. (1988). Continuity and Change: women in paid work. In Women and Work: Positive Action for Change. Macmillan London

Frank, A. K. (2008). Key feminist concerns regarding core labor standards, decent work and corporate social responsibility. WIDE Network. Retrieved from www.wide-network.org

Friedman, T. (2000). *The Lexus and The Olive Tree*. Anchor Books.

Fussell, E. (2000). Making Labor Flexible: The Recomposition of Tijuanas. *Feminist Economics*, 6(3), 59–79. doi:10.1080/135457000750020137

Giddens, A. (1990). *The Consequences of Modernity*. Cambridge, UK: Polity Press.

Government of Pakistan. (2009). *Pakistan Employment Trends for Women: Series No.5*. Islamabad: Ministry of Labour, Manpower, Labour Market Information and Analysis Unit.

Hafeez, A., & Ahmed, E. (2002). *Factors Detremining the Labour Force Participation Decision of Educated Married Women in District of Punjab*. Islamabad: SDPI, Working Paper No. 74.

Horton, S. (1996). *Women and Industralization in Asia*. New York: Routledge. doi:10.4324/9780203434369

Humm, M. (1989). *The Dictionary of Feminist Theory*. London: Prentice Hall.

Hyder, A., & B, R. (2005). The Public and Private Sector Pay Gap in Pakistan: A Quantile Regression Analysis. *Pakistan Development Review*, 44(3), 271–306.

ILO. (2016). Retrieved from http://www.ilo.org/islamabad/info/public/pr/WCMS_233379/lang--en/index.htm

Irfan, M. (2008). *Pakistan's Wage Structure, During 1990/91 - 2006/07*. Retrieved March 13, 2011, from PIDE: http://www.pide.org.pk/pdf/pws.pdf

Kemal, A., & Amjad, R. (1997). Macroeconomic Policies and their impact on Poverty Alleviation in Pakistan. *Pakistan Development Review*, 36(1).

Kemal. (1999). *Privatization in South Asia: Minimizing Social Effects Through Restructuring* (G. Joshi, Ed.) Retrieved April 19, 2011, from ILO Publications: http://www.ilo.org/public/english/region/asro/bangkok/paper/privatize/index.htm

Khattak, S. G. (2001). *Women, Work and Empowerment*. Working Paper No. 4. Karachi: PILER & SDPI.

Khattak, S. G., & Sayeed, A. (2000). *Subcontract Women Workers in the World Economy: The Case of Pakistan*. Islamabad: SDPI.

Kingsbury, D. (2008). Globalization and Development. In D. Kingsbury (Ed.), *International Development: Issues and Challenges*. Palgrave.

Koggel, C. M. (2003). Globalization and Womens Paid Work: Expanding Freedom. *Feminist Economics*, 9(2-3), 163–183. doi:10.1080/1354570022000077935

Kuhn, S., & Bluestone, B. (1987). Economic Restrcturing and the Female Labour Market: The Importance of Industrial Change on Women. In L. Beneria & C. R. Stmpson (Eds.), *Women, Households and the Economy*. Rutgers University Press.

Lewenhak, S. (1992). The Revaluation of Women's Work. Earthscan Publications Limited.

Marchand, M. H., & Runyan, A. S. (Eds.). (2000). *Gender and Global Restructuring: Sightings, Sites and Resistance*. London: Routledge.

MHCHD/UNDP. (1999). A Profile of Poverty in Pakistan. Islamabad: Author.

Mies, M. (1998). *Patriarchy and Accumulation on a World Scale: Women in the International Division of Labour*. London: Zed Books.

Mirza, J. (2002). Between Chaddor and The Market. Oxford, UK: Karachi.

Momsen, J. H. (2004). *Gender and Development*. London: Routledge.

Mumtaz, K., & Shaheed, F. (1987). *Diversification of Women's Employment and Training: Country Study Pakistan, Unpublished Report*. Retrieved April 17, 2011, from www.researchcollective.org/Documents/Women_Paid_Work.pdf

Naqvi, Z. F., & Shahnaz, L. (2002). How Do Women Decide to Work in Pakistan. *Pakistan Development Review*, 41(4 Part II), 495–513.

Naseef, F. U. (n.d.). *Women in Islam: A discourse in rights and obligations*. New Delhi: Sterling Publishers Pvt. Ltd.

Nasreen, S., Shah, N. A., & Ali, A. (2012, December). Ascertaining Impact of Economic Conditions of Pakistan on Women Working in Industrial Sector of Karachi. *Pakistan Journal of Gender Studies*, 6.

Nayyar, R., & Sen, S. (1987). The Employment of Women in Bangladesh, India and Pakistan. In United Nations Economic & Social Commission for Asia and the Pacific (p. 125). United Nations Economic & Social Commission for Asia and the Pacific.

Pakistan Employment Trends. (n.d.). Retrieved from http://www.pbs.gov.pk/sites/default/files/Labour%20Force/publications/Pakistan_Employment_2013.pdf

Rege, S. (2007). More than Just Taking Women on to the Macro- Picture: Feminist Contributions to Globalization Discourses. In R. Ghadially (Ed.), *Urban Women in Contemporary India*. Sage.

Sayeed, A. (2001). *Structural Adjustment and Its Impact on Women.* Working Paper No. 1. Karachi: PILER & SDPI.

SDPI. (2008). *Pakistan: Country Gender Profile.* Retrieved September 12, 2010, from http://www.jica.go.jp/activities/issues/gender/pdf/e08pak.pdf

Shah, N. M. (1986). *Pakistani Women: A Socioeconomic & Demographic Profile.* Islamabad: PIDE & East-West Population Institute.

Sharma, S., & Sharma, K. (2006). *Women's Employment.* New Delhi: Anmol Publications.

Sparr, P. (1994). Feminist Critiques of Structural Adjustment. In P. Sparr (Ed.), *Mortgaging Women's Lives* (pp. 20–29). London: Zed Books.

Syed, J. (2008). A context-specific perspective of equal employemnt oppurunity in Islamic socities. *Asia Pacific Journal, 25*(1), 135–151. doi:10.1007/s10490-007-9051-6

Ward, K. B. (1988). Women in the Global Economy. In Women and Work an Annual Review (Vol. 3). New York: Sage Publications.

Wilkinson-Weber, C. M. (2001). Gender, Handicrafts, and Development in Pakistan: A Critical Review. *Pakistan Journal of Women's Studies: Alam-e-Niswan, 1&2,* 91-103, 98.

Zaidi, A. A. (1999). Issues in Pakistan Economy. Karachi: Oxford.

ENDNOTES

[1] Purdah, Hijab, Chaddor are different words used for religious sanctions about segregation of sexes, the covering of one's face and body from men who are not immediate relatives.

[2] Karachi has a projected population of 15 million, which is at present growing at about 5% per year, mainly because of rural-urban internal migration. (For details see City District Government Karachi, http://www.karachicity.gov.pk/).

[3] Karachi accounts for the majority share of national GDP and revenue. Seventy percent (70%) of income tax and 62% of sales tax collected by the Government of Pakistan comes from Sindh Province and of this 94% is generated in Karachi, while it produces about 42 percent of value added in large scale manufacturing. In its formal sector, the city has 4,500 industrial units. However, there are no estimates available for the informal sector. For details see (Hasan, 2003).

[4] *"Ifraat-e-zar, Mulk ki Chaalis fi sad aabadi khat-e-ghurbat say neechay chali gayee"* (Translation. Inflation: 40 per cent population is living below poverty line) July 19 2011, Daily Jang, p. 4.

[5] Committee is an informal local system of pooling money on monthly bases for a specific time–period with one member of the collective taking the money each time. By lottery system, initially the list of member to receive money is decided in ascending order. Every member receives it once in the given time period.

APPENDIX

Table 4. Selected key indicators of the labor market: Pakistan (%)

Indicators	2001-02	2003-04	2005-06	2006-07	2007-08	2008-09	2009-10	2010-11	2012-13
Labour force participation rate									
Both sex	50.5	50.7	53.0	52.5	52.5	53.1	53.5	53.4	53.1
Male	82.7	82.7	84.0	83.1	82.4	82.0	81.7	81.9	81.1
Female	16.2	18.0	21.1	21.3	21.8	23.1	24.1	24.4	24.3
Employment-to-population ratio									
Both sex	46.5	47.0	49.7	49.8	49.9	50.3	50.7	50.4	49.9
Male	77.6	77.6	79.6	79.6	79.1	78.5	78.3	78.0	77.0
Female	13.6	15.6	19.0	19.4	19.9	21.0	21.9	22.2	22.1
Unemployment rate									
Both sex	7.8	7.4	6.1	5.1	5.0	5.2	5.3	5.7	6.0
Male	6.2	6.2	5.2	4.2	4.0	4.2	4.1	4.8	5.1
Female	16.4	12.9	9.6	8.6	8.7	9.0	9.2	9.0	9.1
Share of industry in total EMP									
Both sexes	21.0	20.6	21.2	21.4	20.6	21.0	21.4	21.8	22.8
Male	22.0	21.7	22.7	23.5	22.7	23.1	24.1	24.6	26.2
Female	14.8	14.9	15.1	12.6	12.2	12.7	11.6	11.5	11.3
Share of agriculture in total EMP									
Both sexes	41.1	41.8	41.6	42.0	42.8	43.3	43.4	43.5	42.2
Male	37.2	37.0	35.6	35.0	35.2	35.7	35.2	34.9	33.1
Female	64.5	66.6	67.7	71.4	73.8	72.7	73.9	74.2	74.9
Share of services in total EMP									
Both sexes	38.0	37.6	37.1	36.6	36.6	35.7	35.2	34.7	35.0
Male	40.8	41.3	41.8	41.5	42.2	41.2	40.7	40.5	40.7
Female	20.7	18.4	17.3	16.0	13.9	14.6	14.5	14.2	13.8
Share of wage and salaried workers in total EMP									
Both sexes	40.4	38.5	38.4	38.3	37.1	36.8	36.5	36.9	39.7
Male	40.9	39.8	41.2	41.5	40.6	40.5	40.7	41.2	43.8
Female	37.1	31.5	26.6	25.1	22.9	22.6	20.8	21.6	24.9
Share of own account workers in total EMP									
Both sexes	39.9	38.6	36.8	36.0	35.9	34.8	35.6	36.3	34.9
Male	43.7	42.9	41.5	41.1	41.2	40.1	41.3	41.8	40.1
Female	16.5	17.0	16.2	14.3	13.9	14.0	14.5	16.6	15.9
Share of EMP in the informal economy									
Both sexes	63.8	69.4	72.3	71.5	72.4	73.0	72.9	73.5	73.3
Male	64.1	69.9	72.2	71.6	72.4	73.1	73.0	73.9	73.6
Female	60.8	64.5	73.1	69.9	71.7	71.6	72.7	70.6	70.9
Share of EMP working 50 hours or more									
Both sexes	40.7	42.7	41.0	40.0	39.3	38.0	39.5	38.5	36.3
Male	45.2	48.9	48.3	47.8	47.0	46.3	48.0	46.9	44.4
Female	13.4	11.6	9.4	7.7	7.6	6.0	7.8	8.4	7.3
Share of EMP in agriculture working 50 hours or more*									
Both sexes	38.2	38.3	33.0	29.3	28.5	26.6	28.7	28.6	24.3
Male	45.0	47.8	44.0	40.4	40.0	38.5	41.3	41.0	36.0
Female	14.3	11.3	8.3	6.4	6.1	4.0	6.4	7.7	5.9
Share of EMP in trade working 50 hours or more*									
Both sexes	62.8	69.4	68.4	70.3	69.5	68.8	70.1	67.7	67.1
Male	63.5	70.3	69.3	71.5	70.5	69.5	71.1	68.4	67.8
Female	26.0	22.2	38.8	30.0	32.6	32.9	35.7	35.3	38.2

Source: PBS, various years, *Pakistan Labour Force Survey*; * Share has been calculated from respective sector

Source: http://www.pbs.gov.pk/sites/default/files/Labour%20Force/publications/Pakistan_Employment_2013.pdf

Section 2
Women's Education and Health

Chapter 9
Gender Violence in Academia

Hina Kousar
Jamia Millia Islamia, India

ABSTRACT

This is an exploratory research conducted in three universities of Delhi – University 'X', University 'Y' and University 'Z'. The objective is to study the scope and incidence of various types of sexual violence behaviors experienced by women on campus: undergraduate women; postgraduate women; research scholars; and faculty. This chapter explores types, kind and nature of sexually harassing behaviors; sexual harassment, rape, sexual assault, stalking, and intimate partner violence, experienced by women in campus; the occurrence of different type of behavior among women in age group of 18 to 65 years. Finding indicates 80 percent acknowledged sexual and psychologically offensive behavior. About 70 percent of total sample acknowledged that they were sexually assaulted. A very small percent 2 percent acknowledged of being attempted raped and 89 percent underwent stalking.

INTRODUCTION

Violence against women alternatively referred to as gender-based violence. Gender violence include physical, sexual, or psychological harm or suffering to women occurring at different points in their life. Many women experience multiple episodes of violence in their life cycle that may start in the prenatal period and continue through childhood to adulthood and old age. Therefore violence against women is a serious health and human right issue condoned throughout the world, but this Violence operates as a means to maintain and reinforce women's subordination.

Lawry (2011) has broadened the definition to include any harm including sexual violence to an individual that is perpetrated against their will and is a result of power imbalances. Gender-based violence on campus includes rape and sexual assault, but also dating and domestic violence, stalking, and sexual harassment. Person affected by gender-based violence are women and girls, because of power disparity between women and men. They also suffer a series of consequences on their sexual and reproductive health, including forced and unwanted pregnancies, unsafe abortions and resulting deaths, traumatic fistula, and higher risks of sexually transmitted infections (STIs) and HIV." (UNFPA Strategy and Framework for Action to Addressing GBV, 2008-2011, p. 7).

DOI: 10.4018/978-1-5225-3018-3.ch009

Gender Violence in Academia

Violence against women owes much to poverty, deprivation and social exclusion made worse by globalization, and commodification of women. Although it is a gross violation of women's human right but it is present in all social and economic class, every religion, race and ethnicity. In a male dominated society men perceive women as objects, and that legitimizes violence as a tool to achieve personal goals. In early childhood, boys and girls first learn that women are expected to perform the domestic roles, and men's responsibilities are associated with strength and power. MacKinnon (1979) stated that the hierarchy of gender: men dominate women, not just in traditional male hierarchies, but by virtue of their being men. This is visible in workplaces where sexual harassment by supervisors of subordinates is common; in education, by administrators of lower level administrators, by faculty of students. But it also happens among coworkers, from third parties, even by subordinates in the workplace, men who are women's hierarchical inferiors or peers. Basically, it is done by men to women regardless of relative position on the formal hierarchy. Gender violence is most underreported crime with horrifying rate and unsatisfactory conviction rate.

Definition

"Gender-based violence is the general term used to capture violence that occurs as a result of the normative role expectations associated with each gender, along with the unequal power relationships between the two genders, within the context of a specific society." (Bloom 2008, p14). UN Convention on the Elimination of All Forms of Discrimination against Women (CEDAW) in year 1992 adopted General Recommendation No. 19 on VAW (GR 19). This clarifies that GBV against women is a form of discrimination and therefore covered by the scope of CEDAW. GBV is defined as "violence that is directed against a woman because she is a woman or that affects women disproportionately", thereby underlining that violence against women is not something occurring to women randomly, but rather an issue affecting them because of their gender. Further, GBV is defined as including "acts that inflict physical, mental or sexual harm or suffering, threats of such acts, coercion and other deprivations of liberty." GR 19 also specifies that GBV may constitute a violation or women's human rights, such as the right to life, the right to equal protection under the law; the right to equality in the family; or the right to the highest standard attainable of physical and mental health. (Source: CEDAW General Recommendation No. 19 on Violence against Women)

The UN Declaration on the Elimination of Violence against Women (DEVAW) adopted by the UN General Assembly in year 1993 has been influenced by CEDAW General Recommendation No. 19. It defines VAW as: "Any act of gender-based violence that results in, or is likely to result in, physical, sexual or psychological harm or suffering to women, including threats of such acts, coercion or arbitrary deprivations of liberty, whether occurring in public or in private life." (Article 1) The declaration encompasses all forms of gender-based violence against women (physical, sexual and psychological), no matter in which context or setting they occur:

- Family (such as battery, marital rape; sexual abuse of female children; dowry-related violence; ; female genital mutilation/cutting and other traditional practices harmful to women);
- General community (such as rape, sexual harassment and intimidation at work, in school and elsewhere; trafficking in women; and forced prostitution), and

- Violence perpetrated or condoned by the state, wherever it occurs (Article 2).
- Further, DEVAW specifies that violence against women is a manifestation of unequal power relationships between men and women and a violation of women's human rights (preamble). Article 3 lists examples of these rights, such as the right to life, the right to equality, the right to the highest standard attainable of physical and mental health, or the right not to be subjected to torture, or other inhuman or degrading treatment or punishment. (Source: 1993 UN Declaration on the Elimination of Violence Against Women)

Violence Against Women on Campus

Gender violence on campus is an umbrella term both pervasive and interconnected; it includes Rape, sexual assault, sexual harassment, stalking, intimate partner violence. The common characteristic shared by all forms of sexual violence is lack of consent. There is notably high rate of sexual violence among college students (Black et al., 2011; Fisher, Cullen, & Turner, 2000). Studies of college samples depict sexual assault rates at 21 to 42 percent among female samples (Combs-Lane & Smith, 2002; Easton et al., 1997; Fisher, Cullen, & Turner, 2000; Gross et al., 2006; Kalof, 2000a; Nasta et al., 2005; Synovitz & Byrne, 1998; Krebs et al., 2007). A major large-scale study has estimated a national prevalence for rape or attempted rape of women at approximately 18 percent (Tjaden & Thoennes, 2000). A 1987 study of 3,000 college women surveyed indicated that more than 50 percent reported being sexually victimized and 15 percent were victims of rape. The statistics were re-affirmed by subsequent 1997 and 2006 studies (Franiuk, 2007).

A significant amount of the research describing interventions has also been conducted in educational settings. There is little evidence that students per se experience or perpetrate violence against women disproportionately, although campuses provide concentrations of young adults that may well result in a higher incidence of stranger rape and date rape (see Koss, 1994). Researchers have consistently reported that a sizable percentage of women are sexually assaulted during their college years, with, on average, at least 50% of their sexual assaults involving the use of alcohol or other drugs by the perpetrator, victim, or both (Abbey, 2002; Fisher et al., 2000; Testa & Parks, 1996). Studies researching sexual harassment on campus, found quid pro quo sexual harassment between 19 and 40 percent have experienced a sexually harassing incident by a professor or instructor (Kalof, Eby, Matheson, & Kroska, 2001; Kelley & Parsons, 2000; Runtz & O'Donnell, 2003). Even the lowest sexual harassment rate in these findings encompasses one in five women on college campuses that have been victimized by professors through quid pro quo sexual harassment (Kelly & Parsons, 2000).

Our knowledge of the magnitude and the nature of the problem of sexual violence are limited in India. Data are available for few types of sexual violence. Very little research has been conducted on men's risk of perpetration of different forms of sexual violence as well as the social context in which it occurs. In India study based on the National Family Health Survey (3) (NFHS, 2007:100) was carried out in 2005-2006 across households in India with a sample size representing 124,385 women. It showed that 39% of married women between the ages 15-49 years old reported having experienced sexual, emotional or physical violence. (Martin 1999) stated that the Indian state of Uttar Pradesh, in a representative sample of over 6000 men, 7% reported having sexually and physically abused their wives, 22% reported using sexual violence without physical violence and 17% reported that they had used physical violence. Metha and Simister's study showed statistics of increasing prevalence of violence against women concerning the crimes of rape, sexual harassment and cruelty by husband or relatives in India between the years 1995-2007.

The data on rape showed figures of an increase of prevalence from 11.7 rapes per million people in 1990 to 18.2 per million in 2007. The other crimes investigated saw double prevalence increase as stated by Metha and Simister, (2010). According to a 2007 research report by Akshara, a Mumbai-based NGO, finding out prevalence and impact of sexual harassment that covered 44 city colleges, 61 percent of the 533 women students interviewed had been sexually harassed in college, either by their peers or by staff. The Ernst and Young survey (2015) conducted through an online questionnaire hosted on EY's website in India. The nature of complaints: 47 percent were for physical contact and advances, 13 percent over demand or request for sexual favors, 37 percent over sexually colored remarks, and four percent over display of pornographic content.

Quantitative research on sexual violence is particularly weak in theoretical development. This may reflect its concentration on measuring sexual violence; however the hypotheses underlying this research and the theoretical assumptions which inform survey questions need to be made more explicit and further developed. The continuing problem of defining sexual violence is constantly debated, and the progress in prosecuting crimes using different definitions is documented (Weiner & Hurt et al., 1997). The literature is heavily concentrated in western settings, all forms of sexual violence against women need to be given consideration in research agenda's, not merely those forms that are most visible, as all form of sexual violence are criminal acts and involve the violation of women's right to freedom from violence. The researches lend support to the notion that the prevalence of sexual violence is very high in both educational and workplace settings and many researchers stipulate that one of the reasons sexual violence is so pervasive is due to the acceptance of myths surrounding not only sexual harassment, but violence against women in general.

PRESENT STUDY

This research was an attempt to provide the full examination of sexual violence in education, the issues raised by the definition given by the student and faculty respondents of the three universities of Delhi. An exploratory research on sexual violence is made in the three Universities of Delhi – 'X', 'Y', 'Z'. The data for such is to determine the scope and incidence of various types of unwanted sexual behaviors experienced by four groups of women on campus: undergraduate women; post graduate women; research scholars; women faculty members all in age group of 18 to 65 years. The Universe of study has been NCT of Delhi because of high rate of sexual violence.

The purpose of this research is to explore the nature, kind and types of sexually violent behavior experienced by women in each group; the occurrence of each type of behavior. The rationality of this research finding will be of value in two ways as to contribute to greater understanding of the occurrence of gender violence among Women College and university students and women faculty and secondly to provide university administration with information which could be used in designing program preventing gender violence. The sample is purposively selected because researcher needs to reach a targeted sample. Hence forth sampling was on recommendation of Women Studies Centre and it is applicable to all the three universities. In this study semi-structured interview was used, which was conducted with a fairly opened framework based on themes to be explored. Study has been directly taken from 400 subjects in campus by a semi-structural interview consisting of open ended questions.

In order to study the kinds of behaviors which falls in the category of unwanted sexual behavior includes various conducts, whether they are verbal, visual, or physical, and are severely sexual in nature. In the same context, we disclosed from the analysis of data from the three universities, the kinds of sexually harassing behavior perceived as well as experienced in university campuses. Collecting data on unwanted sexual behavior, students were asked about the rate of sexual assault and sexual misconduct. The following behavior were revealed-

Sexual looks, staring, teasing in abusive language (calling a women doll, babe, sweetie etc.), stalking, SMS, placing comments with sexual overtone, personal gifts, making difficult for girls to come to the university by gang of boys, making a love proposal and exerting pressure to accept it, facial expression, touching, pinching, grabbing, holding, rubbing. Dirty words written on toilets and on T-shirts or on any other places, sexually colored conversation, jokes, letters, phone calls, Email, vulgar gesture, unwanted attempt to stoke or fondle or kiss. Sexist comments which degrade women status (e.g. women cry more, suggesting that women should be barefoot and pregnant etc.), teachers discussing sex in class room (out of context), taking photograph for blackmailing or video voyeurism, attempted rape and sexual assault.

Sexual violence is often conceptualized as a continuum, with rape (forced sex without consent) and physically brutal forms of sexual violence at the extreme end of the continuum, sexual assault, including a broader range of unwanted and forced sexual contact, in the middle of the continuum, and sexual harassment at the opposing end of the continuum. Sexual harassment - including non-physical forms of abuse such as threats and intimidation, verbal slander, unwanted sexual advances and attention, stalking, and sexual humiliation - is represented as a lesser form of violence.

Present study revealed that in Quid pro quo situation where sexual relations were demanded by senior professors for a particular professional benefit. The victim in these situations were research scholars / M Phil, ad-hoc teachers and contractual employee are major target of the unwanted sexual harassing behavior. The research scholars in majority said that they were asked by their research guide for sexual relation in return of completion of thesis. Most of the proposals of compromises were received by young temporary or guest lecturers of the three universities. The permanent faculty members denied in majority about any kind of sexually harassing behavior other than less severe form of harassment like sexual looks. As far as gender harassment is concerned, the faculty member of three universities stated instances of gender harassment which are more in number in University 'Z'.

Present study reveals that Women aged 16-24 experience the highest percent of intimate partner violence. To measure this kind of violence among student of three universities it was intended to capture violence associated with relationships that are consensual in nature. These questions were administered to respondent who said they had been in any "partnered relationship" since enrolling in college. This was approximately 75 percent of the student respondents who were in romantic relationship. A partner relationship included: causal relationship or hook-up ν steady or serious relationship ν marriage, or live in. To be classified as a victim, respondents said that their partner had controlled them or often tried to control. A 50 percent said that they were stopped from going to classes or pursuing their educational goals. A student from university Z said that "my live-in partner did not allow me to see or talk with friends or family – made decisions for me such as, where i go or what i wear or eat and at times he threatened me physically to harm me" Another research scholar of university Z said "It's painful to see that someone whom you love, using physical force against you because you were talking with other guy". About 30 percent student said that they were violently attacked by their boyfriends on date out of which 10 percent bent their fingers or bit them another 5 percent were choked, slapped, punched or kicked the other 5 percent were hit with something other than a fist – attacked with an object, and

10 percent otherwise physically hurt or injured them. In the present research large number of students told the researcher that they took their own car on date with their boyfriend. They often have a backup network of friends ready to rush up, if need arises. Some students of university Y said they stay sober on date and only go to public places. Some student said of university Z said that they decide with their boyfriend about their sexual limits. Few students said that they took training on self-defense so that can remain safe. A undergraduate student said "we women take many cautions by keeping chili powder in our purses, as dating with men is very dangerous undertaking". A few post graduate students stated that "I ask my boyfriend to have a simple date rather than an expensive one so that he may keep his expectations low". This is supported by Basow, Susan and Minieri, Alexandra (2011) includes a unique study on the different perceptions of date rape according to the type of date and how expensive it was decides the sexual expectation of male partner.

Overview of this research work reveals high incidence rate of sexual harassment, dating, domestic violence, sexual assault in university campuses of Delhi.

The following statistics reveals:

- 50 percent of victims of dating violence were abused by a current or former boyfriend.
- 20 percent of Undergraduate students reported having experienced dating violence by a current partner. 34 percent experienced dating violence by a pervious partner.
- 10 percent of university women reported that they were asked to have sex by a dating partner.
- Among university students who were sexually assaulted, 5 percent of attempted rapes occurred on dates, 22 percent of threatened rapes occurred on dates, and 2 percent of completed rapes occurred on dates.
- 1 percent of domestic violence in college campuses occur in casual or steady dating relationships.
- Over 89 percent of college women report they have been stalked. Of these, 40 percent were stalked by a boyfriend or ex-boyfriend. The stalking behavior reported by students were; someone made unwanted phone calls, sent emails, voice, text or instant messages, or posted messages, pictures or videos on social networking sites.
- Around 80 percent acknowledged mailed, texted, tweeted, phoned, or instant messaged offensive sexual remarks, jokes, stories, pictures or videos.
- About 70 percent of total sample acknowledged that they were sexually assaulted (like hit on breast).
- Approximately 90 percent of victims of sexual assault on college campuses know their attacker.
- 99 percent of sexual assault victims on university campuses do not report the assault.
- 80 percent of students acknowledged street sexual harassment which caused disappointment with college experience.
- 20 percent said peer sexual harassment caused inability to concentrate in class.
- 60 percent of women faculty has experienced sexual harassment at work at some point their lives which was unwelcome sexual advances, requests for sexual favors, or other verbal or physical conduct of a sexual nature.
- 80 percent research scholars were asked for sexual favors by their research supervisor to complete their thesis.
- 80 percent of women reported significant short-term or long-term impacts such as post-traumatic stress disorder.

Constrains of College Students

Sexual violence affects college women and impedes their ability to participate fully in campus life because college students face a variety of obstacles in accessing services that may assist them in escaping sexual violence. Studying the impact of sexual violence on victims, as majority respondents of the three universities said that it has psychological impact, others called health related, or on mobility and few said change in career plans. The respondents' response related to coping strategies where counseling which is considered appropriate by most of the respondent of two universities 'X' and 'Z'. Other indirect methods used by respondents of three universities are missing classes by avoiding / joking / ignoring the harasser which is used by major respondents. Very few believed in direct confrontation with harasser. The majority of respondents of the three university said that women is blamed for her harassment because it is a social failure which do not recognize sexual harassment as an abuse at all. The majority of people enjoy gossip on such issue. Marx (2005) describes sexual assault as a life altering event with "pernicious effects" experienced long after the incident. Nagel et al. (2005) may have negative attitudes toward sexual assault victims. There is also a societal negative effect of sexual assault, described by Post et al. (2002), for example. Their research enumerates both the tangible (medical and mental health services costs; loss of economic productivity; police, prosecution, and correctional costs) and intangible effects (psychological pain and suffering and generalized fear of victimization in society) of sexual assault.

Most of the student respondents of the present study reported that they lacked social comfort and support after sexual violence but those who remain silent become isolated but those who reveal the incident of sexual violence to their family and friend often get rejected, blamed, or not believed, rather than provided support and comfort that they needed. Students may feel isolated from their personal support networks and resources for help because the student is away from home for the first time. This is especially true if the student is also from a different state or country. Sometimes college students feel trapped by the social networks and/or the closed environment of many campuses. They may have a small or limited social network due to the college campus atmosphere. Therefore students may fear the assailant. Often times, due to a somewhat isolated atmosphere of a college campus, it is easier for an assailant to stalk his or her partner. And many students were doubtful and confused to classify the behavior as abuse or may not define their experience as abusive. They deny out of fear that their parents will find out and will take them out of college. Administrators may not understand the scope of the problem and not reacting appropriately (i.e. if professors and/or teachers are notified about a domestic violent relationship between two students).

Typically, the attitude of society is that it dismissed such incidents as trivial, isolated, and personal or as universal natural or biological behaviors. The women response to sexual harassment came across women's docility, passivity by ignoring it, denying it, and avoidance of being at risk. Only a very small fraction said that one should confront at all frequency of harassment and the harasser should be asked to stop the behavior, threatened him with consequences. A small percent said that they asked friend or family to intervene. Only a very low percent of respondents believed in direct confrontation only small percent of the total sample asserted that they confront it. This study argues that all kind of sexual violence will decrease when the nature and extent of the problem is fully understood as well as potential victims and law enforcement understand the protections necessary under the law. Therefore Ngo's should come up and play important role in disseminating information and supporting national efforts in prevention of and response to violence against women.

Recommendations

Prevention approaches aim to reduce risk factors and promote protective factors for sexual violence. In addition, comprehensive prevention strategies should address factors at each levels that influence sexual violence—individual, relationship, community, and society. Campus climate survey is the right step in this direction. College campuses can begin to take steps to implement sexual violence prevention strategies based on the best available research evidence which reveal it's extend. Evaluation of prevention strategies with college-aged students is needed to better understand the nature of sexual violence on their campus.

It is important that sexual assault prevention strategies be designed such that students, especially fresher's are educated after enrollment about sexual harassment policy and about resource center. Programs should focus on both primary prevention for women who have not experienced sexual assault and secondary prevention in an effort to prevent re-victimization. Sexual assault prevention programs for women could: Provide accurate information on legal definitions of sexual assault, the extent and nature of sexual assault among college women, and risk factors for sexual assault. Strategies that try to equip the victim with knowledge, awareness, or self-defense skills are referred to as "risk reduction techniques." Strategies focused on the harasser attempt to change risk and protective factors for sexual violence to reduce the likelihood that an individual will engage in sexually violent behavior.

NGO's should take up social media campaigns as a prevention strategy designed to raise awareness and change social norms related to sexual violence as victim support services Educate women about different types of sexual assault, especially since there appears to be continuity in the type of sexual assault experienced over time (physically forced or incapacitated sexual assault); Workshops should be implemented for the entire campus community to sensitize and educate staff, faculty, and administrators. Teaching effective sexual assault resistance strategies to reduce harm, particularly with respect to strategies for protection from men that women know and trust; Educate women about how to increase their assertiveness and self-efficacy; Convey knowledge about how to report to police or to University administration availability of different types of services on and off campus; Stress the importance of reporting incidents of attempted and completed sexual assault to mental and/or physically health service providers and security/law enforcement personnel on campus, and the importance to seeking services, especially given the well-documented negative impacts sexual assault can have on psychological and physical functioning. In addition, gender sensitization programs for men to prevent sexual assault perpetration.

Victim should be protected from all kind of retaliation. Counseling services is provided for victim other services relating to sexual assault and intimate partner violence will be approached from a "victim/survivor advocacy" perspective. Advocacy consists of responding to immediate, crisis driven needs, safety, and requests for services from the campus and community. Further university women studies center should provide accurate information on legal definitions of and legal penalties for sexual violence; educating men that they are ultimately responsible for determining whether or not a women has consented to sexual contact, and whether or not a women is capable of providing consent; and educate men about confirming consent.

All of these prevention programs should be tailored to include risk factors that both college women and men encounter in common college social situations. Moreover, the programs should be designed as continuing educational curriculums rather than brief, workshops since research suggests that the former approach is more helpful. The Campus Sexual violence is a safety, and public health problem that affects men and women across the country. The Study data suggest women at universities are at considerable risk for experiencing sexual assault, especially sexual assault occurring after the consumption of alcohol, and that a number of personal and behavioral factors are associated with increased risk. It is our hope that universities can take the information produced by research Study and use it to reduce the prevalence of sexual assault, as well as improve the resources for and response to sexual violence victims.

Study Limitations

Being an exploratory study the author recommends caution in interpreting and generalizing findings to other contexts and populations. Future research should attempt to replicate this study with larger and more geographically diverse samples because there is a paucity of research on the impact on women's victimization, and specifically, sexual assault, intimate partner violence, and stalking. Future study can be, to consider the impact of lifestyle variables and how situational and individual constructs can strengthen property, personal, effect of self-control on victimization and sexual security and victims accountable for their own victimization. Thus, important directions for future study include the integration of concepts derived from traditional victimization theories (e.g., routine activity, self-control) with feminist explanations of sexual assault victimization.

CONCLUSION

The foremost need of this hour is to promote the need for changing minds set and behavior of men through gender sensitization and should also advocate for gender equality and women's rights. Victim spoke of personnel pain while narrating their experience related to sexual violence and researcher putting it publicly aim not to gain sympathy or to claim their absolute status as oppressed but to provoke debate about the between speech and conduct and to examine the ways of perception of harm are socially construct. Ultimately, the given research demonstrates the pressing need for experts and advocates to work on providing with alternative ways of thinking about the causes, outcomes and appropriate interventions to sexual violence. Only strong implementation can ensure women empowerment and their pursuance of economic independence can become safer and smoother. It is important that the nation rises not just to support the law but also to support its effective implementation.

Violence is, however, preventable. Although no formula will eliminate it, a combination of multiple efforts that address enhances income, education, health, effective laws and infrastructure can reduce violence and its tragic negative consequences for women and their family. We have to encourage survivors to come forward by regarding the truth. The more we ignore the truth, and disregard survivors' experiences, the more this epidemic will grow. Every time when we refuse to believe a survivor, the harasser wins. Rationally believing them, we can instill hope and healing with the approach on therapeutic jurisprudence which emphasize the role of citizens, community groups and civil society institutions. Dealing with the cases of sexual violence in the social context of the victim and by the therapeutic potential of the legal intervention and integration of victim services with judicial intervention with the involvement, and collaboration with non- government organizations.

REFERENCES

Abbey, A. (2002). Alcohol-Related Sexual Assault: A Common Problem among College Students. *Journal of Studies on Alcohol. Supplement*, (14): 118–128. doi:10.15288/jsas.2002.s14.118 PMID:12022717

Basow, S., & Minieri, A. (2011). You Owe Me: Effects of Date Cost, Who Pays, Participant Gender, and Rape Myth Beliefs on Perceptions of Rape. *Journal of Interpersonal Violence, 26,* 479.

Black, M. C., Basile, K. C., Breiding, M. J., & Smith, S. G. (2011). *The national intimate partner and sexual violence survey(NISVS):2010 summery report.* Atlanta, GA: National Center for Injury Prevention and Control, Centre for Disease Control and Prevention. Available at www.cdc.gov/violence prevention/pdf/misvs_executive_summeryapdf

Bloom, S. (2008). *Violence against Women and Girls: A Compendium of Monitoring and Evaluation Indicators.* Chapel Hill, NC: MEASURE Evaluation.

Combs-Lane, A. M., & Smith, D. W. (2002). Risk of Sexual Victimization in College Women: The Role of Behavioral Intentions and Risk-Taking Behaviors. *Journal of Interpersonal Violence, 17*(2), 165–183. doi:10.1177/0886260502017002004

Fisher, B., Cullen, F., & Turner, M. (2000). *The sexual victimization of college women.* Washington, DC: US Department of Justice. Available at www.ecrs.gov/pdf files/nij/182369.pdf

Fisher, B. S., Cullen, F. T., & Turner, M. G. (2000). *The Sexual Victimization of College Women.* Washington, DC: National Institute of Justice and Bureau of Justice Statistics. doi:10.1037/e377652004-001

Franiuk, R. (2007). Discussing and defining sexual assault: A classroom activity. *College Teaching, 55*(3), 104–107. doi:10.3200/CTCH.55.3.104-108

Gross, A. M., Winslett, A., Roberts, M., & Gohm, C. L. (2006). An Examination of Sexual Violence against College Women. *Violence Against Women, 12*(3), 288–300. doi:10.1177/1077801205277358 PMID:16456153

IIPS. (2007). National Family Health Survey (NFHS-3), 2005–06: India Volume I. International Institute for Population Sciences (IIPS).

Jewkes, R., Sen, P., & Garcia-Moreno, C. (2002). Sexual Violence. In E. Krug, L. Dahlberg, J. A. Mercy, A. B. Zwi, & R. Lozano (Eds.), World Report of Violence and Health (pp. 147–181). Geneva, Switzerland: The World Health Organization. Available at http://www.who.int/violence_injury_prevention/violence/global_campaign/en/chap6.pdf

Kalof, L. (2000). Vulnerability to Sexual Coercion among College Women: A Longitudinal Study. *Gender Issues, 18*(4), 47–58. doi:10.1007/s12147-001-0023-8

Kalof, L., Eby, K. K., Matheson, J. L., & Kroska, R. J. (2001). The influence of race and gender on student self-reports of sexual harassment by college professors. *Gender & Society, 15*(2), 282–302. doi:10.1177/089124301015002007

Kelley, M. L., & Parsons, B. (2000). Sexual harassment in the 1990s: A university-wide survey of female faculty, administrators, staff, and students. *The Journal of Higher Education, 71*(5), 548–568. doi:10.2307/2649259

Koss, M. P., & Cleveland, H. H. III. (1996). Athletic Participation, Fraternity Membership, and Date Rape: The Question Remains—Self-Selection or Different Causal Processes?. *Violence Against Women, 2*(2), 180–190. doi:10.1177/1077801296002002005 PMID:12295458

Lawry, L. (2011). *Research study on sex and gender based violence*. Retrieved from www.africom.mil/news room /transcript/7957/transcript-research

MacKinnon, C. A. (1979). *Sexual harassment of working women: A case of sex discrimination*. New Haven, CT: Yale University Press.

Martin, S., Kilgallen, B., Tsui, A., Maitra, K., Singh, K., & Kupper, L. (1999). Sexual behaviors and reproductive health outcomes: Associations with wife abuse in India. *Journal of the American Medical Association, 282*(20), 1967–1972. doi:10.1001/jama.282.20.1967 PMID:10580466

Martin,, S. L. (1972). Sexual behaviour and reproductive health outcomes: Associations with wife abuse in India. *Journal of the American Medical Association*.

Marx, B. P. (2005). Lessons learned from the last twenty years of sexual violence research. *Journal of Interpersonal Violence, 20*(2), 225–230. doi:10.1177/0886260504267742 PMID:15601796

Marx, B. P. (2005, February). Lessons Learned from the Last Twenty Years of Sexual Violence Research. *Journal of Interpersonal Violence, 20*(2), 225–230. doi:10.1177/0886260504267742 PMID:15601796

Mehta, P. S., & Simister, J. (2010). Gender Based Violence in India: Long-term Trends. *Journal of Interpersonal Violence, 25*(9), 1594–1611. doi:10.1177/0886260509354577 PMID:20068114

Nagel, B., Matsuo, H., McIntyre, K. P., & Morrison, N. (2005). Attitudes Toward Victims of Rape: Effects of Gender, Race, Religion, and Social Class. *Journal of Interpersonal Violence, 20*(6), 725–737. doi:10.1177/0886260505276072 PMID:15851539

Nagel, B., Matsuo, H., McIntyre, K. P., & Morrison, N. (2005). Attitudes Toward Victims of Rape: Effects of Gender, Race, Religion, and Social Class. *Journal of Interpersonal Violence, 20*(6), 725–737. doi:10.1177/0886260505276072 PMID:15851539

Schwart, M., & DeKeseredy, W. (1997). *Sexual Assault on the College Campus*. Sage Publications.

Simister, J., & Mehta, P. S. (2010). Gender-Based Violence in India: Long-Term Trends. *Journal of Interpersonal Violence, 25*(9), 1594–1611. doi:10.1177/0886260509354577 PMID:20068114

Testa, M., & Parks, K. A. (1996). The Role of Womens Alcohol Consumption in Sexual Victimization. *Aggression and Violent Behavior, 1*(3), 217–234. doi:10.1016/1359-1789(95)00017-8

Tjaden, P., & Thoennes, N. (2000). *Full Report of the Prevalence, Incidence, and Consequences of Violence against Women: Findings from the National Violence against Women Survey*. Washington, DC: U.S. Department of Justice. doi:10.1037/e514172006-001

United Nation Population Fund. (2009). *UNFPA Strategy and Framework for Action to Addressing gender based violence 2008-2011*. New York: UNFPA.

Wiener, R. L., Hurt, L. E., Russell, B., Mannen, K., & Gasper, C. (1997). Perceptions of sexual harassment: The effects of gender, legal standard and ambivalent sexism. *Law and Human Behavior, 21*, 71-93. 10.1023/A:1024818110678

Chapter 10
Girls' and Women's Rights to Menstrual Health in Nepal

Kay Standing
Liverpool John Moores University, UK

Sara Parker
Liverpool John Moores University, UK

ABSTRACT

Being able to manage menstruation safely and without stigma is a basic human right which many women and girls in Nepal are denied. Unhygienic and ineffective menstrual hygiene practices have been linked to negative consequences for women and girls, in terms of both reproductive health and social factors such as school attendance. Negative cultural attitudes and taboos around menstruation are widespread in Nepal and basic knowledge of menstruation and menstrual hygiene, especially in rural areas, is limited. The chapter begins to explore the barriers to menstrual health and right and how menstrual Hygiene Management Projects providing education on menstruation and the provision of reusable sanitary pads, are widely used by Non-Governmental Organisations (NGOs) in Nepal to address these problems, with a stated goal of improving girls' reproductive health, educational performance, employment, reducing gender based violence and other psycho-social outcomes.

INTRODUCTION

Menstruation is a natural and regular occurrence experienced by nearly all women of reproductive age. The average woman will have about 450 menstrual cycles over approximately 38 years of her life; this translates to managing menstruation for roughly 6.25 years. However, cultural taboos and stigmatisation of menstruation is almost universal (Crawford et al 2014). Being able to manage menstruation safely and without stigma is a basic human right which many women and girls are denied.

Menstrual Hygiene Management Programmes (MHMP) provide education on menstruation and are designed and implemented by a range of actors, Governmental Organisations (GOs), Non-Government Organisations (NGOs) at both the international (INGO) and national level, and smaller grassroots or-

DOI: 10.4018/978-1-5225-3018-3.ch010

ganisations. Organisations focus on health, gender and/or education and therefore an interdisciplinary approach is needed to review and evaluate the key issues surrounding this topic.

Water Sanitation and Hygiene (WASH) programmes are also an important factor when considering girls and women's' rights to menstrual health. Until recent years menstruation was neglected in WASH programmes in South Asia (Bharadwaj & Patker, 2004 cited in Mahon & Fernades, 2010).

Menstrual hygiene needs are often not considered in the design of toilets or waste disposal, or in education manuals or guidelines for health workers and gender mainstreaming. Similarly, whilst affordable production and supplies of soap and toilet construction materials have been promoted by Non-Governmental Organisations (NGOs) for poor communities, the supply of affordable and reusable sanitary pads has not been routinely part of WASH programmes. However, recently there have been reports of organizations such as Oxfam and WaterAid providing case studies and teaching resources focused on the issues of menstrual hygiene using Pakistan and Afghanistan as examples (Shafi 2011; House & Mahon 2014). This chapter will focus on the experiences of menstrual health in Nepal based on our research their working with a number of NGOs and educationalist given our longitudinal connection to Nepal[1].

In Nepal, unhygienic menstrual hygiene practices have been linked to negative outcomes for women and girls in relation to reproductive health and social factors such as school attendance (Hennegan & Montgomery, 2016; IRIN, 2010). Taboos around menstruation are widespread while basic understanding of menstrual hygiene is limited, especially in rural areas (Adhikari, 2007; Sapkota, 2013). Menstrual taboos and stigmatisation exist across many countries (WHO 1981) but there is little research on this in the South Asian context. This chapter outlines the current situation in Nepal in terms of attitudes, education and approaches to menstrual health in Nepal and begins to explore the barriers to menstrual health and menstrual rights, the negative impact these barriers can have on women and girls' everyday lives. Further the chapter presents initial findings from a pilot project evaluating the distribution of reusable sanitary pads in Nepal.

Menstrual Taboos in Nepal

The effective and safe management of menstruation is essential to women and girls' right to live healthy and dignified lives, to access education and employment, freedom of movement, family life and for their reproductive health. This requires access to safe, affordable and hygienic sanitary material (cloths, pads, menstrual cups etc), clean water, having spaces for privacy to change cloth or pads and somewhere to dispose of them and/or wash and dry reusable pads. Crucially it also means access to education and information on the menstrual cycle and how to manage menstruation hygienically. As well as these practical needs better awareness and understanding is needed among women and girls, and men and boys, about menstruation, in order to overcome taboos, stigma, embarrassment and negative cultural practices which restrict women and girls' rights and reinforce gendered inequalities and exclusions.

Menstruation is a taboo subject globally and taboos and rituals around menstruation in South Asia exclude menstruating women and girls from many aspects of social life. Nepal is culturally and ethnically diverse, 125 caste and ethnic groups were recorded in the last census, with 123 languages and ten religions recorded, of which Hinduism was the dominant religion (CBS, 2012). Although legal restrictions based on caste have been abolished, there are still discriminatory attitudes and practices towards indigenous groups and women (DFID, 2011). Menstrual pollution beliefs are prevalent in Nepal, especially in the Hindu community (Cameron, 1998), and vary across religion, class, social status and caste, but all women, regardless of caste, are traditionally seen as polluting through menstruation and childbirth. This leads to a number of exclusionary practices. Common practices are women and girls cannot enter temples or have any physical contact with men whilst they are menstruating (Crawford et al. 2014) and they are not allowed to look at their reflections during menstruation or use any public water supply (Mahon and Fernades, 2010). A study by Water Aid (2009) in Nepal found 89% respondents practised some form of restriction or exclusion during menstruation (Table 1).

The Chhaupadi practice, although illegal since 2005, is still practiced inparts of rural mid and Western Nepal (Bahandaree et al 2013; Ranabhat, et al 2015; UN 2011; Wateraid, 2009). Chhaupadi deems menstruating women 'impure; and polluting, and menstruating women are banished from the house, to sleep in the 'Chhaupadi goth' (often a cow shed) for the duration of their menstrual cycle until they are menopausal. During a girls' first menstruation she must sleep in the goth for 13 days, and after childbirth Chhaupadiis upheld with the mother and baby remaining in the goth for up to 11 days. Chhaupadi practice has been directly linked to reproductive health problems due to poor hygiene and unsanitary conditions (Ranabhat, et al 2015).

Whilst progress has been made in addressing Nepal's high maternal mortality rate (MMR) between 1996 and 2006, Nepal nearly halved its MMR, from 539 deaths per 100,000 live births, to 170 per 100,000 in 2010 (IRIN 2013) a number of problems remain concerning women's menstrual health. Ranabhat et al (2015) found that reproductive tract infections and uterine prolapse were the leading causes of maternal morbidity in areas that practice Chhaupadi. Chhaupadi also has a number of negative social impact for women and has been identified as a contributing factor for the high prevalence of depression amongst women in Nepal (Lamichhane et al 2012). Women and girls are also at risk of attack from wild animals, snake bites and from rape and sexual assault (UN, 2011). Social attitudes towards menstruation therefore provide a significant barrier to any initiatives introduced aimed at improving the situation for women and girls in Nepal (Milne et al 2015).

Menstruation taboos are not isolated to areas practicing Chhaupadi and menstruation remains a taboo subject across Nepal, resulting in negative health and social impacts. There is a high rate of uterine prolapse in Nepal, 60% of women in mid and Western regions of Nepal suffer from the condition, and the taboo nature of menstrual health, combined with the lack of education, means women and girls are

Table 1. Types of restriction during menstruation in Nepal

Restriction	%
None	10.8
Don't attend religious functons	67.6
Don't go to school	3.4
Don't cook	46.1
Don't do household work	20.6
Don't touch males	23.5
Don't play	9.8
Don't eat certain foods	13.2
Sleep separately	28.4

Source WaterAid 2009

Figure 1. Woman in chaupadi goth
(Photo credit Chitraker, 2014)

often ashamed to seek medical advice for menstrual health complications (Ranabhatet el 2015). Menstrual taboos alsoaffect income for women, especially as employment in rural Nepal revolves around agriculture. Often a week's wages can be lost per month (Care International, 2015). Menstruation often affects school attendance, even in non Chaupadi regions. Lack of private toilets or access to a water supply means that many girls do not attend school due to poor facilities or embarrassment (Mahon & Fernandes, 2010). We discuss education and the role of schools later in the chapter.

There is evidence that attitudes are changing in urban areas there is less evidence of this in more remote rural regions. Crawford et al (2014) qualitative research study with educated middle class women in Kathmandu found women had experienced stigmatisation, lack of education and preparation for menarche and adherence to rituals and 'pollution reducing' restrictions continued into adulthood, but that attitudes were changing, and women were not passing these restrictive attitudes and practices on to their daughters. However, Archarya et at (2001) conducted a study with 149 adolescent girls from a cross section of areas in Nepal and found that whilst socio-cultural practices varied from one area to another, almost all of the respondents (99.3%) reported to having some form of activity being forbidden to them during their menstruation. For example they reported they were forbidden to participate in religious activities such as lighting of holy lamps or worshipping. Many responded s that "all these are part of our culture and disobedience to the mothers / elders is a sin" (Archarya et al 2011: 118). Many of the respondents perceived menstruation negatively using terms like "disgusting, shameful, dirty and untouchable" though some "perceived it positively as the indication of maturity, femininity and reproductive capacity" (Archarya et at 2011: 123). Likewise a study by Sapkota et al (2013)in rural Nepal found several exclusionary beliefs around menstruation as polluting still existed. More than half of the respondents (55.7%), reported that menstruating women were are not allowed to do household chores, 41% said that menstruating women are not allowed to attend religious functions and go to temples. Almost one in five respondents (16.4%) reported that still there is practice of keeping menstruating women and girls outside the house or in a corner of room. However, of the 61 girls in their study, only 19% of these actually practised any restrictions, leading Sapkota et al (2013)to argue the girls in their study saw menstruation as a normal process and not a matter of fear of shame.

Education, Awareness, and Understanding

Education is key to challenging taboos around menstruation and enabling women and girls to make informed choices about managing menstruation and their reproductive health, and participate fully in social activities, education, employment and family life. Knowledge of menstruation is poor amongst women and girls in Nepal. Studies show that while girls in Nepal are aware of menstruation before menarche (their first menstrual period), a significant number do not, and many do not understand the physical process of menstruation (Mahon and Fernandes, 2010). For example, Water Aid (2009) reported 92% of girls knew about menstruation but the majority were not prepared for its onset, whilst Adhikari et al (2007) found in their research with 150 girls aged 13-15 years in Chitwan, only 6% knew menstruation was a physiological process and only 36% that it was hormonal. Knowledge and understanding varies across regions, Sapkota et al (2013) found that the girls in their study had significantly higher knowledge of the physiological process of menstruation (62%) and attributed this to the inclusion of menstrual health education in the curriculum. However, this seems to be an exception, with studies consistently report that the majority of girls learn about menstruation from their mothers, sisters or female friends (Mahon & Fernades 2010; Water Aid 2009). In the Water Aid (2009) study teachers were only mentioned as source of knowledge by one fifth of the respondents. Even when education was included in the school curriculum, very little education was given around the biological and physiological process of menstruation. Girls reported that the information and education they received was mainly about the use of cloths, and rituals and restrictions around menstruation, the concept of pollution and warnings about behaviour around boys and men. The girls emphasized instead the need for emotional support and assurance that menstruation was normal and healthy, not bad, frightening, or embarrassing. There is a need in Nepal for compulsory sex education and health education on menstrual hygiene.

Menstruation also impacts on education and school attendance. Over half of the respondents in Mahon and Fernandes (2010) Nepal study reported being absent from school at some time, owing to menstruation. Lack of privacy for cleaning and washing was the main reason given (41%), with other key factors being the lack of availability of disposal system and water supply. Whilst there is no comprehensive data on water and sanitation facilities in schools, evidence suggests it is inadequate. Menstrual hygiene guidelines recommend changing sanitary pads/cloths every two to six hours dependent on blood flow, thus facilities, toilets and access to water, are needed both at home and in schools. Open pit toilets or toilet without disposal facilities mean blood or used sanitary products reveal when a woman is menstruating resulting in embarrassment and stigma.

Women in Nepal are already managing their menstruation, but a lack of access to, or affordable, sanitary material means the majority of women use old saris or cloth rags. Repeated use of unclean cloth or improperly washing, drying and storing cloths before reusing them results in harbouring of microorganisms which cause unitary tract infections. There is evidence that there is a demand for alternatives, for example Sapkota et al (2013) found the majority of their respondents (67%) stated sanitary pads were the best thing to use, only half of the girls (54%) actually used them

The Water Aid (2009) study found the use of sanitary pads was, unsurprisingly, higher in urban schools (50% in comparison to 19% in rural schools). The survey found that 41% of girls lacked awareness of sanitary pads, but the main reasons girls didn't use them were the high cost (39%), lack of availability (33%) and lack of disposal facilities (24%). This suggests there is a need and demand for re-usable pads and a more sustainable option.

Responses: Reusable Sanitary Pads

Challenging menstrual taboos is very difficult as it is so heavily entwined in the culture of the areas that practice it. However, there are a number of international and local grassroots organisations working to improve reproductive health for women and girls in Nepal through MHMPs, education and sustainable menstrual hygiene products. WaterAid ran a participatory visual project in collaboration with Nepal Water for Health in 2016 which highlighted the taboos women faced. This project has received media attention and has served to raise awareness and start a debate about the social practices and their impact on the lives of girls and women (Bakshi 2016; Narany, 2016). The resulting work has been used in campaign and advocacy activities as demonstrated by the image below from WaterAid:

Menstrual Hygiene Management Projects (MHMP), providing education on menstruation and the provision of reusable sanitary pads, are now widely used by Non-Governmental Organisations (NGOs) in Nepal, with a stated goal of improving girls' reproductive health, educational performance, employment, reducing gender based violence and other psycho-social outcomes (Croft & Fisher, 2012; Oster & Thornton, 2011). In particular, in the aftermath of the 2014 earthquakes in Nepal a significant number of INGOs, NGOs and local women's organisations began distributing dignity kits and re-usable sanitary products. Reusable sanitary pads are made from waterproof, antibacterial and antifungal material which can be cleaned with soap, creating a sustainable alternative to expensive (and often unobtainable) disposable pads. Bobel (2010) argues these are forms of menstrual activism which challenge taboos and improve women and girls' education and social, as well as reproductive health, outcomes.

To date there has been little research or evaluation of the impact and effectiveness of MHMPs and much of the existing research is from East Africa (Dolan et al 2013, Wilson et al 2012) and therefore not directly comparable to a South Asian context. The provision of re-usable sanitary pads is viewed as a positive initiative by NGOs but there is little academic evaluation of the impact of these initiatives

Figure 2. Water Aid project
WaterAid/Mani Karmacharya, 2016

in rural Nepal, nor research assessing the effectiveness of such projects, particularly in the context of rural Nepal and across different types of communities (Mahon et al, 2010; Oster & Thornton, 2009). Hennegan and Montgomery's (2016) systematic review of the literature on MHMPs found only eight studies globally on MHMPs and interventions into improving girls' education, work and wellbeing, with only three assessing the provision of different types of sanitary products.

The rest of the chapter presents initial findings from an initial exploratory pilot project study to begin to explore the social impact of MHMP on women and girls' everyday lives. Future research is planned using a mixed methods approach, questionnaires, and focus groups, to capture the impact of MHMPs and assess the nuances of girls' experiences and observations of reusable padprogrammes.

PILOT STUDY FINDINGS AND DISCUSSION

A short survey was conducted in two districts in Nepal, Kavre and Solukhumbu where re-usable sanitary pad kits from the international organisation Days for Girls had been distributed in schools and villages by NGOs. The kits contain two pairs of underwear, two re-usable sanitary towels and eight spare pads, a washcloth, soap, a ziplock bag for storage, and instructions for use of the kits and washing and drying.

Kits had been distributed to women and girls of menstruating age in Kavre, and to girls in years 5 to 10 in Solukhumbu. A total of 133 surveys were completed by women and girls, mainly from the Tamang and Sherpa populations. The pilot study highlighted the need for further research, more in depth qualitative questions and the need to engage with different ethnic groups and communities across Nepal. It is important to note that different organisations distribute different kits in terms of where they are made, locally in Nepal or internationally, the materials the pads are made from and also the packaging they come in. In addition the information given with the distribution of the kits varies, some include

Figure 3. Re-usable sanitary pad kit
Source: Days for Girls 2016

Girls' and Women's Rights to Menstrual Health in Nepal

the instructions for use, whilst others are more strongly linked into health education classes in schools, health centres and spaces whereby females can talk about and share stories of their own experiences. Kits are thus distributed in a variety of ways utilizing health workers, teachers, NGO workers or via women's groups. An examination of the different approaches practiced by the different organisation is needed in order to assess the effectiveness of the distribution process and the education which women receive as part of this.

Initial findings were in line with previous research (WaterAid 2009) in that the majority of respondents used old cloth and saris before the distribution of the Days for Girls kit. However, 14 respondents stated they bought sanitary products from the market. We found that there was a high demand for the kits, and high levels of satisfaction were reported. The main benefits of the re-usable pads were comfort, no leakage, easy to use and they felt secure, they could walk in it and it didn't fall down. An indication of how respondents felt is indicted buy these quotes;

I don't feel that I have periods while using it, it's clean and comfortable so I like it

I felt very comfort and I recommend all the women of our neighbour to use it at the time of periods because it has no harm and it is more comfortable than others

I am very happy to get it and I wish others could get it as well. We learnt many things from it and I am very interested to give and teach it to single women every women and sister should be clean and safe while in periods so I recommend to use this kit

Figure 4. Distribution of sanitary pads, Tara Nepal women's group
photo credit Tara women's group

When asked for recommendation to improve the pads the majority of respondents wanted longer or thicker pads, with the inclusion of more cloth pad inserts and pads of difference sizes and thickness to manage different stages of the menstruation cycle and heavier bleeding.

All of the respondents talked about their periods and/or the pads with female family and friends, mainly mothers and sisters (Archarya et al 2011). Whilst this is positive, and can help to break down stigma, it also brings into focus the need for MHM education for all women, as studies show that the majority of girls also receive education about menstruation from their mothers who held several myths and misconceptions around menstruation (Sapkota et al 2013). None of the women and girls in our survey talked to any male members of their family, education is also needed for boys and men, however, Adhikari et al (2007) found that girls didn't want to talk to their fathers about menstruation. These are areas to be explored further in the follow up research, as the general consensus was that talking to female relatives and friends was useful, but qualitative research is needed to delve deeper into the details of the impact and nature of these discussions with their family.

The survey also asked about the availability of water to wash the pads. Lack of water was an issue for two-thirds of respondents. This presents a cause for concern, as the correct washing and drying of the pads is crucial for menstrual hygiene and to prevent infections. Over half of the school aged girls in Solumkumba region expressed a lack of confidence in using the toilets at schools due to the lack of water, lack of locks on toilet doors and lack of a separate room for girls. This lack of facilities, including safe water and clean, private toilets, coupled with the taboos and embarrassment associated with menstruation, mean that many women and girls do not have anywhere to change their cloths and are not always able to wash themselves regularly (water aid 2009). Our study didn't directly ask about school attendance, but 5 out of 45 girls in years 5 to 10 stated they leave school when they have their period, saying:

I feel pain and I don't like to sit in class

it's difficult [to manage] with the blood flow when in class

One respondent said:

I use the pad all the times during my menstrual cycle so I am regular at school.

It is important that further research follows up on this feedback and utilises qualitative methods to gain more insight into the wider impacts of supplying the sanitary pads.

However, encouragingly 34 out of the 45 girls took the sanitary pad kits with them when they had their period, and a further three stated they got one of the pads from a female teacher in school if their period started at school, and eight said they would '*share my problem to*' or '*seek help from*' a female teacher. Evidence as to if the provision of sanitary products increase school attendance is inconclusive. Oster and Thornton (2009, 2011) found that the distribution of sanitary products (moon cups) to school aged girls in the Terai were very popular, improved their management of menstruation, increases girls mobility and reduced laundry time, but made no difference to school attendance, however Wilson et al (2012) study in Kenya found the distribution of re-usable sanitary pads did reduce school absenteeism. More research is needed to establish if there is a correlation between availability of sanitary products and school attendance, as factors other than menstruation also prevent girls attending school, but initial findings from the pilot study show the provision of pads in schools encourages girls to talk to teachers.

When asked how they felt when they had their period the majority of women and girls responding by giving physical symptoms, eg stomach ache, back pain, tiredness, weakness and being uncomfortable. Two respondents said it was:

a sign of good health

I feel happy as timely menstruation is a sign of good health.

Further research needs to include questions that probe into the feelings of women during their period in a cross section of cases to enable a deeper insight into the experiences of women and their ability to access their right to menstrual health knowledge and support.

CONCLUSION

This chapter has shown that are many taboos and practices associated with menstruation in Nepal which limit women and girls' rights to fully participate in society, and have negative consequences for their reproductive health. It has highlighted some interesting and innovative projects being run to address these issues, and argues there is need for the work of organisations to be mapped and evaluated to demonstrate examples of good practice. There needs to be more in-depth evaluation of ongoing projects, both quantitative and qualitative in nature, in order to highlight the key successes and challenges that projects aimed at improving menstrual health face. Current research highlights a difference between rural and urban areas, but also differences within communities stressing the importance of undertaking cross sectional research in a range of locations throughout Nepal.

Education is central to empowering girls and women and to changing attitudes and this needs to be considered by Government as well as Non-Governmental Organisations. There is a need for schools and sites of non-formal education to examine how they engage with girls and women to provide education on menstrual health and to address the taboos surrounding menstruation A gendered perspective is needed at all levels. Therefore we support Archarya et al (2011: p123) in stressing that "it is important to educate the adolescent girls regarding menstruation for the purpose of developing positive attitudes towards menstruation. Basic knowledge and information regarding menarche and menstruation should also be propagated through media. There should be school as well as community based programs to educate adolescent girls on menarche and menstruation and provide spaces to discuss on related issues and problems". However the whole community, including men and boys, needs to be involved in initiatives challenge the social norms that exclude and marginalise women and girls.

As we have noted there has been a rise in programmes distributing menstrual hygiene kits and our research with these organisations suggests that there is a need for more systematic in-depth evaluation of these programmes so that the successes can be built upon, challenges identifies and key lessons shared. Government and Non-Governmental Organisations, the education and health sectors need to work together to address the need for women to access their right to menstrual health.

REFERENCES

Adhikari P, Kadel B, Dhungel S, Mandal A (2007). Knowledge and practice regarding menstrual hygiene in rural adolescent girls of Nepal. *Kathmandu University Medical Journal, 5*(3), 382-386.

Archarya, I., Shakya, M., & Sthapit, S. (2011). *Menstrual Knowledge and Forbidden Activities among the Rural Education and Development.* Academic Press.

Bhandaree, R., Pandey, B., Rajak, M., & Pantha, P. (2013). Chhaupadi: Victimising women in Nepal. In *Second International Conference of the South Asian Society of Criminology and Victimology.* SASCV.

Bakshi, G. (2016). *Girls in Nepal photograph menstrual taboos affecting their lives Brought to you by: WaterAid.* Retrieved from https://www.globalcitizen.org/en/content/girls-in-nepal-photograph-menstrual-taboos-affecti/

Bobel, C. (2010). *New Blood: Third wave feminism and the politics of menstruation.* Rutgers University Press.

Central Bureau of Statistics Nepal. (2012). *National Population and Housing Census 2011, National Report.* Available at: http://unstats.un.org/unsd/demographic/sources/census/wphc/Nepal/Nepal-Census-2011-Vol1.pdf

Chitrakar, N. (2014). *Nepal's chaupadi tradition banishes menstruating women- in pictures.* Available at: http://www.theguardian.com/global-development/gallery/2014/mar/08/nepal-chaupadi-tradition-banishes-menstruating-women-in-pictures

Crawford, M., Menger, L. M., & Kaufman, M. L. (2014). "This is a natural process": Managing menstrual stigma in Nepal. *Culture, Health & Sexuality, 16*(4), 426–439. doi:10.1080/13691058.2014.887147 PMID:24697583

Crofts, T., & Fisher, J. (2012). Menstrual hygiene in Ugandan schools: An investigation of low-cost sanitary pads. Journal of Water. *Sanitation and Hygiene for Development, 2*(1), 50–58. doi:10.2166/washdev.2012.067

Days for Girls International. (2016). *Every Girl. Everywhere. Period.* Available at: http://www.daysforgirls.org/

Department for International Development. (2011). *Nepal Operational Plan Gender Equity and Social Inclusion Annex.* Available at: https://www.gov.uk/government/uploads/system/uploads/attachment_data/file/67545/nepal-2011-annex.pdfAccessed 18 May 2016.

Dolan, C. S., Ryus, C. R., Dopson, S., Montgomery, P., & Scott, L. (2013). A blind spot in girls education: Menarche and its webs of exclusion in Ghana. *Journal of International Development, 26*(5), 643–657. doi:10.1002/jid.2917

Hennegan, J., & Montgomery, P. (2016). *Do Menstrual Hygiene Management Interventions Improve Education and Psychosocial Outcomes for Women and Girls in Low and Middle Income? A Systematic Review.* Available at http://eprints.whiterose.ac.uk/43906/1/Irise_report_-_Dec_2012_%5BSAJ%5D_v2_(1).pdf

House, S., & Mahon, T. (2014). *Menstrual Hygiene Matters: A Resource for Improving Menstrual Hygiene Around the World WaterAid*. Available at www.wateraid.org/~/media/Files/Global/MHM files/Module5_HR.pdflast

IRIN. (2013). Nepal's maternal mortality decline paradox. *IRIN News*. Available at http://www.irinnews.org/analysis/2013/03/18/nepal%E2%80%99s-maternal-mortality-decline-paradox

Lamichhane, K. B., Asis, B., Chakraborty, P., Sathian, B., Subba, S. H., & Jovanovic, S. (2012). Psychological study of depression amongst women in western region of Nepal. *Asian Journal of Medical Science*, *3*(4), 39–46.

Mahon, T., & Fernades, M. (2010). Menstrual hygiene in South Asia: A neglected issue for WASH (water, sanitation and hygiene) programmes. *Gender and Development*, *18*(1), 99–113. doi:10.1080/13552071003600083

Narany, S. (2016). *Nepali Girls Snap Exclusion During Menstruation News Deeply Women and Girls Hub*. Retrieved from https://www.newsdeeply.com/womenandgirls/nepali-girls-snap-exclusion-during-menstruation/

Oster, E., & Thornton, R. (2011). Sanitary products, and school attendance: Evidence from a randomized evaluation. *American Economic Journal. Applied Economics*, *3*(1), 91–100. doi:10.1257/app.3.1.91

Ranabhat, C., Kim, C., Choi, E., Aryal, A., Park, M., & Ah Doh, Y. (2015). Chhaupadi Culture and Reproductive Health of Women in Nepal. *Asia-Pacific Journal of Public Health*, *27*(7), 785–795. doi:10.1177/1010539515602743 PMID:26316503

Shafi, M. (2011). *Gender, WASH and Education Case Study: Enhancing Girls' Participation in Schools in Pakistan*. Retrieved from http://policy-practice.oxfam.org.uk/publications/enhancing-girls-participation-in-schools-inpakistan-142170

United Nations Development Programme (UNPD). (2015). *Human Development Reports Nepal*. Available at: http://www.hdr.undp.org/en/countries/profiles/NPL

United Nations Resident and Humanitarian Coordinator's Office. (2011). *Field Bulletin Chaupadi in the Far West*. Available at: http://www.ohchr.org/Documents/Issues/Water/ContributionsStigma/others/field_bulletin_-_issue1_april_2011_-_chaupadi_in_far-west.pdf

United Nations Resident and Humanitarian Coordinator's Office. (2011). *Field Bulletin Chaupadi in the Far West*. Available at: http://www.ohchr.org/Documents/Issues/Water/ContributionsStigma/others/field_bulletin_-_issue1_april_2011_-_chaupadi_in_far-west.pdf

WaterAid in Nepal. (2009). *Is menstrual hygiene and management an issue for adolescent girls? A comparative study of four schools in different settings of Nepal WaterAid in Nepal*. Kathamndu.

WaterAid in Nepal. (2009). *Seen But Not Heard? A Review Of The Effectiveness Of Gender Approaches In Water And Sanitation Service Provision*. Available at: www.wateraid.org/~/.../gender-approach-water-sanitation-provision.pdf

Wilson, E. F., Reeve, J. M. K., Pitt, A. H., Sully, B. G., & Julious, S. A. (2012). *INSPIRES: Investigating a reusable sanitary pad intervention in a rural educational setting—evaluating the acceptability and short term effect of teaching Kenyan school girls to make reusable sanitary towels on absenteeism and other daily activities: a partial preference parallel group, cluster randomised control trial.* Research Report ScHARRReport Series (27) School of Health and Related Research, University of Sheffield. 2012. Available: http://eprints.whiterose.ac.uk/43906/

ENDNOTE

[1] Both authors have been involved in British Council funded links between Liverpool John Moores University and the Women's College, Padma Kanya College, Tribhuvan University since 2003. They have recently secured a British Academy Small Grant to further their research into Menstrual Hygiene projects and their impact which is due to Start in November 2016.

Section 3
Vulnerability and Women

Chapter 11
More Than Body Parts:
Theorising Gender Within African Spaces

Manase Chiweshe
Chinhoyi University of Technology, Zimbabwe

ABSTRACT

This paper questions the reduction of human experience and identity to anatomical determinism in which the category of 'woman' or 'man' becomes a universal concept. Through a review of literature on African gender, feminist and masculinity studies, it highlights how people are more than their body parts. It notes how identities are shaped by an intersectionality of various factors such as education, employment status, class, age, physical condition, nationality, citizenship, race and ethnicity. These factors can be spatial and temporal producing differing experiences of gendered lives. African scholars have built up a rich collection of work that repudiates the univerlisation of gender identities based on Western philosophical schools of thought. This work explores in detail current and historical debates in African gender studies.

INTRODUCTION

The concept of gender is widely used in Africa. What this concept precisely denotes remains fraught in contestations. This chapter is an analysis of gender scholarship and academic debates in Africa. It traces the tendencies and applications of the concept by governments, policy makers, academics, non-governmental organisations and African feminists. This paper questions the essentialising tendencies of many feminist scholarship which tends to promote western binary views of gender that reduce women to their vaginas and univerlise them into an underclass of victims under the overwhelming oppression of patriarchy. The existence of patriarchy in many societies in Africa is not disputed and that it subjugates women and relegates them to the private sphere is well documented. What is missing though is a nuanced understanding of how gender interlinks and interplays with various other forms of identity such as class, age, ethnicity, religious affiliation, nationality and status to determine our lives. To proclaim gender as the overarching factor in all situations is to hide various fascinating modes of identities which are constantly being created and recreated by active agents in their everyday lives. People are not only

DOI: 10.4018/978-1-5225-3018-3.ch011

their gender and there is no benefit to a binary understanding of men and women as opposing poles especially in Africa where women are so differentiated by many factors such as age and class that it is neither desirable nor possible to define them as a singular group. Distortions of binarism borrowed from western gender studies has been replicated in a 'copy and paste' of concepts and processes to explain African realities which are totally different. Chapter focuses on the fragility of the ways gender is inscribed on bodies and the ways in which power is expressed, negotiated, and ever present in gendered practices. This is important because not only gender studies but all other academic fields in Africa have to strenuously wade off the global division of labor in knowledge production. In this system Africa exists only as a 'field' to studied, analysed and understood; and never as a laboratory of vivid ideas and knowledges from indigenous people rooted in their life experiences. As Oyewumi (2004) argues, the study of Africa must start with Africa.

Gender is an all encompassing concept which affects not only how we live but how we see and perceive our world. Whilst gender is a fundamental element of our lives, it is not our whole identity. We are more than our body and to reduce us to our anatomical basis masks varying layers of multiple and competing forms of identities which define who we really are. Gendered lives in this way end up defining men as oppressors and women as the oppressed without understanding the context and local conditions which define and determine how women and men interact between and amongst themselves. People in all situations and locations, do not always interact according to gender. The argument that all women have been oppressed by all men throughout time and across all cultures is pessimistic, politically unpalatable, and scientifically unsound; it has created an easy target for a sexist backlash against more reasoned feminist positions (Stamp 1989). The chapter ultimately illustrates that in gender studies Africans need to focus more on the interplay of various context specific factors that determine a women's and men's position in society. Distinction between biology and social in understanding gender in Africa was pioneered by the work of Ifi Amadiume (1987) on the Igbo and Oyeronke Oyewumi (1997) on the Yoruba (Boris 2007). These studies question Western epistemologies which are based on the Enlightenment which privileges sight over other senses. Oyewumi (1997:79) blames colonisation and differentiates Yoruba ontology from Western thus, 'The social category woman – anatomically identified and assumed to be a victim and socially disadvantaged – did not exist.'

BACKGROUND

Gender has become a catch phrase when discussing policy or academic issues across Africa. The type of gender being peddled however is problematic as it lacks a clear definition and fails to speak to the realities of women on the continent. Mohanty (1986) uses the concept of colonisation to note how women of colour in United States were critiquing the appropriation of their experiences and struggles by hegemonic white women's movements. Such appropriation of knowledge has led to an understanding of gender from a western point of view. Oyewumi (1997) notes that the entire western episteme bases its categories and hierarchies on visual modes and binary distinctions: male and female. Such binaries falsify the experiences of black women and how they are defined by other factors beyond their biological make up. In their book Cole et al (2007:3) agree that there is need 'to move the discourse on gender in Africa beyond simple dichotomies, entrenched debates, and the polarizing identity politics that have so paralyzed past discussions.' It is thus important to understand the micropolitics of context, subjectivity, and struggle that shape women in Africa the knowledge that not all women are the same, nor are their contexts. In an interview with Salo (2001:61), Amina Mama argues that, 'The constant tirades against 'white feminists' do not have the same strategic relevance as they might have had 20 years ago...Westerners have not only listened to the critiques...they have re-considered their earlier simplistic paradigms and come up with more complex theories.' That said this chapter is not another tirade against western feminist theories. It is an outline of feminist thinking in Africa and how western concepts of gender are still being peddled by governments, donors and academia.

Coping and pasting of Western concepts of gender has a problem of obscuring the origins, meanings, and consequences of historical events and processes. Africa gender studies require a nuanced analysis of lived experience and the structures of subordination and power. Mwale (2002) notes that African feminism faces risks of obscurantism, vulgarism, inauthenticity, and irrelevance by continued use of a model of conscientisation of women that is foreign to Africa. Grounded and situated knowledges that seek to build on agency and victimology of women are required. As Bennet (2008:1) notes that the most important challenge for, 'African feminists remains the need to create knowledges which both emerge from the diverse and complex contexts in which we live and work and speak to such contexts with sufficient resonance to sustain innovative and transformative action.' Gender as widely understood at the moment in Africa is broadly understood from borrowed concepts which have little resonance to experiences on the content. Stamp (1989) argues that radical feminism, rests on the assertion that the oppression of women is biologically based and supersedes all other forms of oppression. Boris (2007:192) notes that Africa scholarship allows a 'reconsideration of gender as a category of analysis: an unsettling of the relationship between the biological and social that reinforces trends within feminist thought; a questioning of the privileging of gender over other social attributes, especially age, lineage, kinship, and wealth, thus complicating understandings of 'intersectionality'; and a revealing of gender as an expression of power through historical struggles over colonisation and liberation.

For Oyewumi (2003a) African women and feminism are at odds because despite the adjectives used to qualify feminism, it is Western feminism that inevitably dominates. Experiences of white middle class women become the barometer of measuring women's experiences all over the world. Experiences of other women are denied; they are objectified and become a field of study. On the other hand Bakari-Yusuf (2003:) argues that any theory of gender needs to, 'specify and analyse how our lives intersect with a plurality of power formations, historical encounters and blockages that shape our experiences across time and space. This account must also recognise the concrete specificity of individual gendered experience, and how this connects to and is different from the experiences of others.' Women and men are thus more than their body parts. Gendered lives are a performance influenced by many factors which include naming and locating various contested identities. Analysis of gendered lives within African spaces refuses and rejects univerlisation of experiences and seeks a situated and context specific understanding of a person's identity. It realizes that there is always a complex interplay of competing and complimenting factors.

METHODOLOGY

This research utilises desk research approach which reviews books, documents, newspapers, magazines, articles and journals to understand the nature and extent of the problem under discussion. Desk research is the analysis of information that already exists, in one form or another. This information was easily available since it had been already collected over the years for purposes other than that of this project.

This secondary research technique involves a literature review or analysis. The researcher is involved in mining already existing data: "pull out" relevant data or information; summarize it; logically analyze and/or statistically treat it; and report results. In many instances, the issue, problem, question, etc. which prompted the idea for a research project is resolved or answered by studying previous research reports in the literature or analyzing, either statistically or logically, or both, data drawn from existing databases. There are a number of shortcomings associated with desk research. It is easy to find and collect secondary data, however, you need to be aware of the limitations the data may have and the problems that could arise if these limitations are ignored. Firstly, secondary data can be general and vague and may not really help. The information and data may not be accurate thus sources of the data must be double checked. In some cases the data might be old and outdated. In this research however there was a process to carefully search and list the most relevant and up-to-date material on the topic at hand. Due care was taken to use work that has been published in scholarly journals and from reputable organisations.

WESTERN FEMINIST THOUGHT

History and Strands of Feminism

Western feminist thought is a differentiated field with competing and polarised theoretical premises. This study does not seek to view western feminism as a singular field that rather 'draw attention to the similar effects of various textual strategies used by particular writers that codify 'Others' as non-Western and hence themselves as (implicitly) Western' (Mohanty 1986, 334). The rise of feminism in the West is often described in the various waves since the nineteenth century which saw the development of a distinct body of theory and activism towards women's issues. Freedman (2003) notes that first wave of feminism rose of the nineteenth and early twentieth century movement for voting and political rights of women in the United States of America and Britain. It also fought for the promotion of equal contract, marriage, parenting, and property rights for women. In America, although women of color continued to participate and representatives such as Ida B. Wells (1862–1931) and Mary Church Terrell (1868–1954) also strove to show how the linkage of sexism and racism functioned as the main means of White male dominance, the first wave of feminism consisted largely of White, middle-class, well-educated women (Campbell 1989). The birth of feminist theory thus is entrenched deeply Western thought.

The second wave of feminism, which emerged in the 1960s to 1970s in postwar Western welfare societies, when other "oppressed" groups such as Blacks and homosexuals were being defined and the New Left was on the rise. Second-wave feminism is closely linked to the radical voices of women's empowerment and differential rights and, during the 1980s to 1990s, also to a crucial differentiation of second-wave feminism itself, initiated by women of color and third-world women (Krolokke 2006:1). Within this second wave school, cultural and political inequalities are intrinsically linked and encourage women to understand aspects of their personal lives as deeply politicized and as reflecting sexist power structures (Echols 1989). The catch phrase of the time became, "The Personal is Political"[1]. Third-wave feminism began in the early 1990s as a response to perceived failures of the second wave and to the backlash against initiatives and movements created by the second wave. Krolokke (2006) notes that Third-wave feminism manifests itself in "grrl" rhetoric, which seeks to overcome the theoretical question of equity or difference and the political question of evolution or revolution, while it challenges the notion of "universal womanhood" and embraces ambiguity, diversity, and multiplicity in transversal theory and politics. Third-wave feminism seeks to challenge or avoid what it deems the second wave's essentialist definitions of femininity, which, they argue, over-emphasize the experiences of upper middle-class white women. Some scholars such as a Modleski (1991) and Jones (1994) talk of a post feminist era in which feminism, especially in the west is no longer an important factor.

Western feminisms developed into various theoretical standpoints which advocate for different things. There are many strands which stand for diverse views such as Liberal feminism which seeks individualistic equality of men and women through political and legal reform without altering the structure of society. They do not seek to address poverty and inequalities that exist in society. Krolloke (2006) notes that liberal feminists maintained that the discontent experienced by many middle-class women in postwar Western societies was due to their lack of social power and political influence. The solution they advocated was not necessarily paid work outside the home; indeed, one of their demands was payment for housewives and representation in public institutions, and so on. Echols (1989) argues that radical feminism is a critique of liberal feminism. Radical feminism seeks the overthrow of the male-controlled capitalist hierarchy as the defining feature of women's oppression and the total uprooting and reconstruction of society as necessary. Marxist feminists feel that overcoming class oppression overcomes gender oppression. Liberal and socialist/Marxist feminism shared a basic belief in equity and equal opportunities for women and men, but the latter focused particularly on working-class women and their involvement in class struggle and socialist revolution (Krolloke 2006, 7). Postcolonial feminists argue that colonial oppression and Western feminism marginalized postcolonial women but did not turn them passive or voiceless (Narayan 1997). Postmodern feminists argue that sex and gender are socially constructed that it is impossible to generalize women's experiences across cultures and histories, and that dualisms and traditional gender, feminism, and politics are too limiting (Butler 1999). Post-structural feminism uses various intellectual currents for feminist concerns (Johnson 2002). Many post-structural feminists maintain that difference is one of the most powerful tools that women possess.

Western Feminism: Binarism, Univerlism, and 'Othering'

In her book *The Invention of Women: Making an African Sense of Western Gender Discourses,* Oyewumi (1987) argues that in Western thinking gender is not socially constructed in reality. Gender as a social category cannot exist without sex (biological category) since the body squarely at the base of both categories. Within the African context there are many social categories that do no rest on physical distinctions of gender such as Amadiume's (1987) work on 'female husband' of Igbo culture. Oyewumi (2004) notes that Western feminism is entangled with the history and practice of European and North American where global feminism forms a part of Europology (which universalises European phenomenon). Gender thus becomes an essentialized ontology and pseudo-universals derived from Western culture and exported worldwide. Western feminist thought in general has not escaped the alterity associated with grand theories. The process of 'Othering' has meant pathologising of African women as victims of all forms of abuse. These women are stripped of all agencies and placed into one group despite their circumstances. The dichotomy is that you are either a man or a woman; if you are a man you are an oppressor and if you are a woman then you are the oppressed. Such simplistic and essentialising tendencies are the hallmark of western theories steeped into Enlightenment tradition of seeking things that are verifiable. As such biology, which can be proved by physical checks, becomes the main signifier of gender. You are either a man or a woman.

Chikwenye Ogunyemi in her seminal work, "*Womanism: The Dynamics of the Contemporary Black Female Novel in English*", offers a radical critique of the extent to which white and western women have ignored the realities and locations of African women. Using the term "womanism" as an alternative to feminism, she argues that African women and men have been united in a common struggle against colonialism. Lewis (2004) however argues that the congruence of African men and women's struggles can become tricky when a critique of colonialism and neo-colonialism and white feminists' dominance is *pitted against* an analysis of gender hierarchies in Africa. It is thus not plausible to privilege one form of oppression over the other. There is also a possibility to critique western feminist discursive dominance while simultaneously disavowing patriarchal oppression in Africa (Lewis 2004). In an attempt to circumvent the binary constructions of Western ideologies which have essentialized African women, Catherine Acholonu (1995) uses the concept of motherism. In her work entitled, *Motherism: the Afrocentric Alternative to Feminism* which elucidates a multidimensional Afrocentric theory which emphasises the essence of African womanhood. This approach is different to Western feminist thought in that it celebrates the African woman as a mother who is intimately involved in the care of her children and home. The fight therefore is not for women to be like men but to promote an African idea of a woman. Others like Mikell (1997) have gone further to argue that African feminism is distinctly heterosexual and pro-natal.

Western feminist thinking is premised on the ideas of universal concepts of female oppression. Feminist thought was thus a way of fighting and freeing these women from oppressive systems and customs. As Oyewume (2003b, 28) notes

...political activism and academic theorising are often a long distance "affair" carried out as anthropological studies and "Women in Development" projects in African, Asian and Latin-American societies. Feminism, like imperialism, discovered its social mission, which was in global scope, and like the white's man burden of the nineteenth century, the white woman's burden of the twentieth century was born. The burden, from these feminists' vantage point, entailed rescuing the exploited, helpless, brutalized, and down-trodden African woman from the savagery of the African male and from a primitive culture symbolized by barbaric customs.'

White women saw their societies as the epitome of civilisation thus could not conceive societies in which women fared better. They saw themselves as a way to measure other women across the world. This superiority and ethnocentric view created women of other cultures as 'Others'. African feminists fall in the same trap as their Western counterparts when they become 'knowers' and start speaking as and for poor, rural women. Middle class African women who are educated and have careers experience life differently from poor rural women. African female scholars should thus be careful not to expropriate the experiences of poor and rural women. They should avoid 'othering' other women and use their 'privilege' position to theorise and speak for women in lower social strata. In her work entitled 'Cartographies of Struggle', Mohanty (2003) argues that the ways in which the term 'Native', constructed in anthropology in the early twentieth century, drew on racial and sexual stereotypes to provide the epistemological basis of the term 'Third World Woman'. This analysis offered a valuable examination of the paralysing power of binary forms of 'othering', creating in this case a distinction between the 'West' and the rest of the world. Weedon (1999: 184) describes the conceptualization of gender in Western thought as a 'set of polarized binary oppositions' in which the privileged male is the normative standard against which the subordinate female is measured. This thinking cannot be applied to the reality of all Africans across spatial and temporal spans.

AFRICAN FEMINIST THOUGHT AND GENDER THEORIES

Feminist theory has consisted of writings by Westerners attached to an intellectual tradition that until recently had misunderstood its own concrete historically constructed gender systems as universal. Boris (2007) notes that in the early 1980s the feminist epistemology was being challenged from within by black, lesbian and black lesbian women whose identities appeared with a modifier that branded them as 'other' to the white, middle-class heterosexual standpoint. A second critique developed from those labelled as 'Third World women' who decried the partial knowledge available and protested their objectification as victims of backward gender relations and sexual oppression in need of saving by Western feminists (Boris 2007). Western feminism thus has this heroine attitude to it black women oppression becomes a 'white woman's burden' (Oyewumi 2003, 25). There have been a variety of approaches have sought to address the political implications of sex difference in Africa which include: those approaches that draw attention to hierarchical differences between men and women, and those that stress their socially equivalent and complementary status (Bakari-Yusuf 2003). It is appropriate here to borrow Adesina's (2006) distinction between three types of scholarships within the African social sciences: 'regurgitation', 'protest scholarship', and works of distinct epistemic significance. Most works within women's and gender studies in Africa can be classified as 'scholarship-as-regurgitation imposes received categories (concepts, theories, and paradigms) on local conditions. While the data and the sociologist may be local the narrative and analysis function as extensions of Euro-American discourses' (Adesina 2010, 3). What Zeleza (2006, 202) notes as articulating the tenets of African culture and ideas in western academic terms" These works deploy local data without challenging the received theories and conceptual frameworks; they reinforce rather than alter the terms of international division of intellectual labour (Adesina 2010, 3).

Clenora Hudson-Weems (2004) proposes a different view of Africana feminist theory which is concerned with self naming (nommo) and self defining as an essential for authentic existence. It is a call on Africana women worldwide to reclaim, rename and redefine themselves. The theory prioritizes the tripartite plight of race, class and gender for all women of African descent. Hudson-Weems (2004) is critical of feminist theory, arguing that it invariably includes anti-male sentiments, gender exclusivity or at the least the prioritization of gender issues over all other critical issues especially race. Within this framework the family remains central and it prioritizes race empowerment. This debate over the applicability of Western concepts to African realities is central to contestations around 'womanism' or 'feminism'. Arnfred (2004:86) notes that defenders of 'womanism' such as Mary Kolawole argue that the Western concept of feminism does not thoroughly accommodate African women's emphasis on the bonds of the family and the importance of being a mother. She notes, 'The African woman's conceptualisation of freedom is not based on the erosion of her feminine attributes and outlook, but in asserting her feminine qualities...The African woman cherishes her role as a home-maker as well as her status as a mother or a potential mother' (Kolawole 1997: 28-31). Whilst this claim generalises women across the continent it however shows there are many contested outcomes of women's struggle in Africa. What these goals and aims entail must be determined and articulated by women themselves.

Dosekun (2007) felt the need to defend African feminism against what she called claims that it was 'un-African'. She invokes Adeleye-Fayemi who notes that because Africa has some of the oldest civilisations in the world, it has the oldest patriarchies, and therefore the oldest traditions of resistance to patriarchy. To believe otherwise is to falsely imply "that for centuries African women have crossed their arms and accepted being battered and depersonalised by patriarchy." This is the direct implication of the argument that feminism is un-African because it is not part of our culture (Dosekun 2007). It implies, as Amina Mama (1995) indicates "the 'real' African woman…is content with her subordinate position as wife, mother and beast of burden. She is passive in the face of abuse, tolerant of all forms of infidelity; her only real ambition is to retain respectability by labouring for the maintenance of a stable marriage and family and seeing to the satisfaction of her husband's desires." In a paper in 2001, Amina Mama engages postcolonial theory and identity issues as they relate to Africa. She posits that post colonial theories have chosen to ignore gender and how it relates to our understanding of nationalism and national identity. Mama (2001, 69) criticises Oyewumi (1999), stating that, 'Equally problematic are those who would deny that gender has any relevance to matters authentically African by inventing an imaginary pre-colonial community in which gender did not exist.' The debates between the two Nigerian luminaries in African thinking have been well documented yet their ideas not highlight the diverse ways of viewing the experiences of African women. What is particularly interesting is that they both agree on the need to avoid coping and pasting western concepts into African contexts. They have fought all to ensure African women have a voice in defining themselves. As Mama (1997, 5) herself notes, 'The task we face as African intellectuals is that of developing our own applications of given theories, and more radically, of taking our own realities as the starting point for articulating perspectives, or even entirely new theories that emanate organically from our particular conditions and concerns.'

Partriachial societies have a history of female subordination[2] however we need to go beyond the general assertions how patriarchy apportions women various often contradictory roles within the system that at one point a woman is fighting it and another she is defending its interest. Taking social organisation among most Shona people is Zimbabwe a married woman is taken as married through *lobola* (bride wealth) and her sexual and productive rights move from her father to her husband. Within this partriachial system she becomes daughter in law, a mother, wife, sister, aunt, grandmother and ultimately mother in law. Each of these positions means which relates differently to other females and in cases has power over them. As a mother in law she has the potential to make her daughter in law's life a living hell and as aunt patriarchy offers her certain privileges when discussing family issues and decision making. As daughter or daughter in law or wife the same woman is faced with a different side of patriarchy. Gives analogy is an example of how complex relations between and among women are within patriarchy that to simply state that women are victims without offering a grounded and nuanced analysis will overshadow how women oppress other women in the name of custom. As Nzegwu (in Oyewumi 2004, vii) notes there is a myth of sisterhood among women, what pertains is actually a 'sisterarchy'. On another point, Nzegwu (2001) argues that the West has always embraced a mono-sex system that privileges what is male, judging equality by characteristics shaped by men's live so that equality as equivalence stacks the odds against women. But an African dual-sex system emphasises complementarity based on separate but equally significant contributions to the society (Boris 2007:195). As Arnfred (2002) notes this system like kinship is relational while Western hegemonic binary male/female is absolute.

Nzegwu (2004) talks about gender imperialism by which structures of whiteness in academia deny and subjugate African women's identities and personhood. These imperial identities have been imposed on Africans and distort a true understanding of conditions on the continent. Universal concepts produced by Westerners become markers of understanding gender across the world. In such imperialistic projects, knowledge of the locals is completely ignored as they are exoticised into 'subjects' of research and 'othering'. Gender as defined by such concepts forgets that Africa is a kaideloscope of many cultural, social and political landscapes such that experiences of gender differ from region to region. As such it is difficult to translate the various terms and concepts from the West into local systems. For example in most African societies, gender is not a function of biological sex. Amadiume (1987, 15) notes that, 'The flexibility of Igbo gender construction meant that gender was separate from biological sex. Daughters could become sons and consequently males. Daughters and women in general could be husbands to wives and consequently males in their relation to their wives.' Sex thus is not the only basis for gender roles which are highly contextual. Gender is thus a situated concept which can only be understood within the specific social contexts. It is impossible to have a universalised understanding of how gendered experiences. For example the impact of HIV and AIDS is not similar for African and Western women. Poverty and cultural factors among many other factors influence infection and access to treatment.

Mojubaolu Olufunke Okome (2003, 82) argues, 'In both its colonial and post-colonial forms, the African State has discriminated consistently against women'. At independence in most African states women were simply co-opted into the structures of the new ruling elites. There are studies which show the process of co-optation of women's movements by the state in Ghana (Tsikata 1997, 393); Gaidzanwa in Zimbabwe and South Africa (1992). In Kenya Tripp (2000, 9-10) highlights how Kenyan African National Union steadily increased its grip on women's organisations to turn the dominant *Maendeleo ya Wanawake* into a party wing and Lazreg (1994) shows how a similar situation in Algeria where women involved in Algeria's armed struggle were later confined by the patriarchal agendas of post-independent Algerian nation-building (Lewis 2004). The post colonial state in Africa has thus largely been partriachial and co-opting women through gender mainstreaming programmes which do little to transform structures that place women in inferior positions. Reading the work of people such as Meena (1992), Mblinyi (1992), McFadden and Tsikata (1997) examined ways in which 'good governance', structural adjustment, patriarchal state building, and elite consolidation have led to neo-imperial states acting in collusion with the donor community and international capital to orchestrate token policymaking for gender transformation (Lewis 2006). In Uganda Christianity introduced new gender identities within the church in which women were surbodinated as 'sisters' to males who were 'fathers' (priests). Christianity ensured that women lost their leadership in religious matters. Celibacy by Roman Catholic priests and nuns means that in Buganda they occupy a unique gender role which is neither male nor female (Nannyonga-Tamusuza 2009).

Obioma Nnaemeka (2003) introduces the concept of nego-feminism (the feminism of negotiation; no ego feminism). She notes that 'Aware of a practice (feminism in Africa) that is as diverse as the continent itself, I propose *nego-feminism* not to occlude the diversity but to argue, as I do in the discussion of "building on the indigenous" ...' (Nnaemeka 2003:361). In her arguament she interrogates positionality intersectionality as they relate to understanding one as an active subject without essentialising meaning. In this way intersectionality of race, gender, class, ethnicity, sexuality, religion, culture, national origin, and so forth from ontological considerations (being there) to functional imperatives (doing what there) and speak to the important issues of equality and reciprocity in the intersecting and border crossing (Nnaemeka 2003:361). Perreira (2003) on the other hand refuses generalisation of African women into singular homogenous group. In her rebuttal to McFadden's (2003) treatise on the relationship between sexual pleasure and power, she cautions against McFadden's generalization that African women – regardless of the diversity of cultures within the continent, and in spite of age and class differences – are sexually repressed (Undie and Benaya 2008:129). Whilst 'to some extent [for] many categories of women' this is true; the nuances of inconsistencies and convolutions that gender provokes in the African context should not be overlooked (Pereira 2003:1). Situatedness is thus important as context defines experiences and understandings of gendered practices.

DEFINING GENDER: AFROCENTRIC ENTERPRISE

Africa is a continent has multiple indigenous, colonial and national pasts (Boris 2007). Such diversity complicates any tendency to flatten gender analysis to a single presentation, illuminating even while questioning gender as we as it is variously defined. Gender is a "whole system of social meanings that specify what is associated with men and women" in a particular society at a particular time (Wood 2005, 34). Gender thus denotes socially constructed roles of femininity and masculinity. Boris (2007) notes that within Western feminist thought by the 1980s 'gender' as a category had come to distinguish the biological (male/female) from the cultural (feminine/masculine). The body thus generates gender identities in terms of specific historical and social contexts. Africanist scholars have for long accused Western gender scholarship of using biological sex as a precondition for gender; however Boris (2007) argues that it might be an exaggeration. She notes that Western scholars have for over two decades known what, 'African have known all along that gender is socially, not biologically, created and it evolves over the life cycle' (Herbet 1993,19). Oyewumi (1997) has questioned the salience of gender as an analytical category among the Yoruba in Nigeria. Yoruba language, as other African countries does not recognise gender as a grammatical marker. Mierscher (2007) notes that Oyewumi declares gender Western import thus African scholars need to develop analytical concepts such as lineage, seniority and motherhood that are more rooted in African context. Gender thus can only be understood in human culture and social patterns. Miller (1993:4) conceptualises gender as being 'based partly on biological characteristics and partly arbitrary.' Biological and cultural factors thus shape gender identities, roles and relations to other genders.

WHY DOES 'GENDER' DENOTE WOMEN?

Whilst gender is routinely defined as the social construction of femininity and masculinity, the term has become associated with women. Gender has become synonymous with women. In any and every discussion at policy or academic level there is tendency to confuse gender to mean women issues. Gender programmes by non-governmental organisations only concern women. Gender was largely seen as a matter of and for women; men were generally seen as invisible and ungendered representatives of all humanity. This happened not only in the western world but also in Africa (Ruspini 2007). Nathanson and Young (2006) criticize gender for being a discipline that excludes males from analysis as it only philosophizes, theorizes and politicizes on the nature of the *female* gender as a social construct. The term 'gender' in gender studies is thus reduced to a mere synonym for 'women'. This separation of women from all other social processes makes it difficult to understand how different genders relate and interact in everyday situations. It also leads to a universal victimology of women and pathologisation of African males as brutal perpetrators of various forms of violence on women. An important question that arises from this debate is whether men can be gender activists or feminists? Gender as it is organises leave men at the periphery of both discussion and engagement but how possible is it that men become active participants in gender forums?

The separation of women and men studies claiming that masculinities studies may make it seem that men and women are equally victimized. This will have an effect of mystifying and undermining genuine concerns by women. It is also interesting is to understand the extent to which men (however defined) can act against their own collective material interests, and pro-feminist men have been critiqued for presuming themselves to be innocent of blame, finding fault instead in a category of men that somehow excludes them. In an volume edited by Ouzgane and Morrell (2005) entitled *African Masculinities: Men in Africa from the late Nineteenth Century to the Present* contributors analyze how African boys are socialized to become men in specific historical and cultural contexts, why men behave the way they do in order to identify or to be seen and respected as masculine, and what aspects of cultures of masculinity need to be challenged or deconstructed in order to make more effective interventions toward sexual health or against male violence against women. Uchendu (2008, 1) portrays that nineteenth- and early twentieth-century European traders, missionaries and colonizers who operated on the African continent left a rich store of records, telling the world that Africa and its peoples, especially its men, were morally bankrupt, inept, barbaric, backward and doomed. Thus Europeans did not only understand social construction of maleness in traditional societies but did not recognise it as such to a point that Robert Powell said that dogs were more intelligent than Africans (Uchendu 2008).

More Than Body Parts: Intersectionality of Experience

As African and black feminist theories emerged Boris (2007) argues that Intersectionality and transnationalism became the new catchwords of gender analysis in response to these critiques. This however still had problems as theory remained abstract, subject to timelessness and prone to essentialism. Gender should be viewed as a product of location, negotiated by women and men with discursive and perfomative vocabularies that they deploy but do not command into existence. It is however imperative at this very moment to outline what Intersectionality approach entails and how we can be a starting point in discussing gender in Africa. Crenshaw (1994) provides a theoretical orientation that explains the interplay of various factors in explaining an individual's position. The theoretical basis of Intersectionality approach involves viewing societal knowledge as being located within an individual's specific geographic and social location. This theory also analyzes how various social and culturally constructed categories interact on multiple levels to manifest themselves as inequalities within society. Race, gender, and class mutually shape forms of oppression in society. To reduce analysis of women's lives to gender alone is to strip them of racial and class historical antecedents that characterise their marginal position within most African societies. Intersectionality is of the view that difficulties arise due to the many complexities involved in making multidimensional conceptualizations that explain the way in which socially constructed categories of differentiation interact to create a social hierarchy. For example, Intersectionality holds that knowing a woman lives in a sexist society is insufficient information to describe her experience; instead, it is also necessary to know her race, sexual orientation, class, as well as her society's attitude toward each of these memberships. It is only through analysing how these complex concepts intertwine and interlink that we are able to understand gendered experiences of both men and women in different contexts.

Identity is created and recreated through interaction, contestation, struggle and discourse. Krolokke (2006, 23) introduces the concept of transversity which, 'presents feminists with a theoretical and practical means by which we, as differently situated women, can simultaneously acknowledge our diverse positions and work across national, ethnic, racial, and gender lines... [it is] a sophisticated theoretical framework within which to understand both the fragility of the ways gender is inscribed on bodies and the ways in which power is expressed, negotiated, and ever present in gendered practices.' Boris (2007, 194) argues that gender tends to overshadow other markers of social identity and individual subjectivity that exists in tandem to form the category 'woman' or 'man' and forge actual women and man thus women are 'not only gendered or raced but racialized and gendered in specific culturally and historically determined ways: class, age, sexuality, ethnicity, disability, and a host of other attributes combine with racialized gender...' Privileging gender thus reduces women's oppression to one factor yet not all women are oppressed and those who are oppressed are not oppressed in the same way. Other factors such as age and seniority in Africa affect how gender identities are created and performed. Among the Akan in Ghana seniority has been as crucial to the construction of identity as gender. Both women and men could become elders but each had a different understanding of how they wield their power (Miescher 2007). Nnaemeka (2003:361) sees 'beyond a historicization of the intersection that limits us to questions of origins, genealogy, and provenance to focus more on the history of now, the moment of action that captures both being and becoming, both ontology and evolution.'

BEYOND BINARISM IN AFRICAN GENDER STUDIES

Debates about gender in Africa have been couched in western binaries of gender that separates men and women without giving space for alternative gender types. From the "*mahu*" and "*aikane*" of Polynesia to the "*berdache*" of Native American tribes; from the "*sekhet*" of prehistoric Egypt to the "*eunouchos*" of ancient Greece and Rome; from the "*saris*" of the Israelites to the "*mu'omin*" or trusted men of the Syrians; from the traditional third-gender roles of aboriginal tribes in Africa such as among the Mbo people of Zaire to the palace and harem guards of the Arabs and Chinese; from the cross-dressing entertainers of Manila and Bangkok to the "*hijra*" and "*jogappa*" dancers and temple priests of North and South India; right down to our own modern gay and transgendered communities in across the world, persistent and unmistakable "third" or alternative gender subcultures have always naturally existed in one form or another. In traditionally African societies biology was not the ultimate determining factor in the social creation of gender. Biology is neither the only determinant of gender across African societies. There has however been a tendency of biologizing of difference to the primacy of vision in European intellectual history which privileges the visual and facilitates an emphasis on appearance and visible markers of difference.

In medical and biological understanding of sexual development, each child is born either male or female. However some people born with a DSD, such as a gonadal dysgenesis, or "ambiguous genitalia" (referred to in the past as hermaphrodite) or a chromosome disorder (such as Klinefelters Syndrome) identify with both sexes[3]. Notwithstanding these biological facts, gender remains a social construct built on cultural, religious, political and economic circumstances facing societies. The problem in Africa is that gender has now been taken as a given very little interrogation of the concept in terms of its relevance and applicability to the African situation (Bakari-Yusuf 2004). In defining gender we have imported the western binary dichotomies which have proved inadequate in understanding the everyday lived realities on the continent. Most traditional African societies had distinct gender roles which were socially defined in which the third gender has a well defined social space. There are many examples of across Africa and some of them are outlined below. Historically inscribed pottery shards discovered in Egypt, dating from the Middle Kingdom (2000-1800 BCE), contain a listing of three genders of humanity: males, eunuchs, and females (Serth 1926:61). In the Egyptian story of the creation of the archetypal beings (gods), the first being is male and female, and its name is Atum. Through asexual reproduction, Atum divides and creates two other beings, Shu and Tefnut. These two in turn produce another pair, Geb and Nut. Finally, Geb and Nut, the earth and the sky, combine and produce the two pairs of Isis and Osiris, and Seth and

Nephthys. Isis exemplifies the reproductive female, Osiris the reproductive male, Seth the nonreproductive eunuch, and Nephthys the unmarried virgin (Gender Tree, n.d.).

The entire western episteme bases its categories and hierarchies on visual modes and binary distinctions: male and female, white and black, homosexual and heterosexual (Oyewumi 1997). Thus in African we have various instances of a third gender which is neither male nor female but falls somewhere in between the two genders. This is what is referred as the third gender (intermediate gender) which has a separate gender identity. The third gender thus has nothing to do with people born with male and female sexual organs. There are many documented cases of third gender identities in African societies. A good example among the Swahili, male transvestites known as *mashoga* act as drummers and musicians at women's festivals (http://www.glbtq.com/social-sciences/africa_pre.html). The mashoga were often associated with homosexuality is often associated with *mashoga*. These men were neither viewed as men nor women but occupied their own defined social space which was accepted by society. Among the Ovimbunde and the Tswana woman-woman sexual behaviour was prevalently as some women took on male roles and became 'social men' who had women under them. Robert Brain provides a similar case from Cameroon where a woman could befriend the sister of a Bangwa chief. Through this arrangement they could become husband and wife whilst the woman could have kids with men. The "androgynous princess" lived with her wife and the wife's daughter addressed the princess as 'father' (Color World, n.d.).

There is a curious silence in Africa on the existence and rights of the third gender. The African Union ratification on Gender Equality recognises only two genders in Africa (male and female). This problem is apparently across the continent where the cutting and pasting of western ideas that places gender into fixed categories. Gender within Africa is a fluid concept based on socio-cultural context and not biology. With the adoption of male/female dichotomy there has been widespread pathologization of people who do not fit into these categories. The rights of such people have not been recognised and they have been viewed as queer or strange. Everything in Africa is organised within fixed binaries of the two main genders without recognition for different categories of gender existent on the continent. We have people being forced to choose between these two binaries as shown by the shameful manner in which Caster Semenya was treated by international athletics body and the South African athletic authorities. The debate about which sex she belonged to raged on as her life was unfairly scrutinised in the public and various forms of violence were performed on her body as she was pathologised for not fitting into the 'normalised' binary of female/male. There are many examples of discrimination and 'silencing' of third gender identities across Africa as shown by the extreme laws against homosexuality in various countries. Constitutions, laws, institutions and policies are all created on the basis of two sex categories. There are many examples of discrimination against and 'silencing' of third gender identities across Africa, as is evident from the extreme legislation against homosexuals in various countries, including Uganda, Zimbabwe and Malawi. Those who do not fit into these categories are not recognised as lawful citizens, which leave them vulnerable to a variety of discriminative acts. On personal documents such as passports and identity cards, people are forced identify as one of the two sexes. In school science curriculums only two genders are taught. All sporting activities are organised along the two gender binary poles and the socialisation of children follows this distinction without question.

Nannyonga-Tamusuza (2009) notes that not all males are men and neither are all females women. In Buganda gender is a construction and that the gendering process, based partly on biological factors and partly on arbitrary and cultural traits, relates dialectally with social, cultural and political forces that have shaped Buganda's society. Whilst gender refers a set of socially constructed meanings that are associated with each sex, is difficult to explain it as a universal concept because each culture through language conceives what 'men' and 'women' mean. Luganda term *ekikazikazi* denotes a womanly-male, who is biologically male but behaves as a 'woman' and the tame *nakawanga* denotes 'she cock' or manly female (female who behaves as a man) (Nannyonga-Tamusuza 2009). Gender is thus not only biologically determined but all human creations place cultural and social rules arbitrarily to define genders. There are therefore more than two distinct genders. Binarism hides and ignores the fluidity and contested nature of gender. Nannyonga-Tamusuza (2009, 372) indicates that the palace princess whilst biologically female, were gendered as male. Which meant that being in the ruling class subverted their femaleness and as such took up male roles and paid bride price for their marriage partners.

GENDER ACTIVISM AND CAREER MOVEMENT

Gender activism and scholarship has been co-opted into global processes which has stifled the movement fighting against the impoverishment of the poor especially rural women by a global system which favours powerful multi-national corporations. This neo-liberal co-optation of feminist movements is global and it is an overwhelming feature of contemporary ostensibly 'postfeminist' liberal-democratic societies. The hegemony of global imperialism is increasingly eroding feminism and radical cultural expression and discourses in civil society at an international level. In many ways gender activism has become a career path for most educated middle class women within academia and non-governmental organisations who are using experiences of rural women and poor urban women as a platform to built careers and make a living. Feminist scholarship has become a market commodity within research houses and organisations where knowledge about and for poor rural women is used for fundraising and project making without fundamental challenge to the structures that keep these women in poverty. Gender activism as promoted by western NGO does not speak to the needs and experiences of a differentiated class of women on the continent, yet the money and benefits have led many scholars to buy into ideas and efforts that make little impact. Lewis (2006) argues that the present context of limitless information, globalised power relations, transnational media oligarchies, and commoditised academic knowledge mystifies patriarchal and neo-imperial injustice through the rhetoric of 'liberalisation' and 'legitimate' paternalist protection and patriotism. Feminist demands under such a framework are co-opted, dismissed and marginalised. The major problem is the tendency by many gender activists of 'coping and pasting' concepts, programs and analysis from Westerners and implementing them in Africa.

TOWARDS A NEW THEORY FOR AFRICAN WOMEN STUDIES?

Bakare-Yusuf (2003) notes that African feminism requires a theoretical account of embodied gender differences that is grounded in the complex realities of African women's everyday experiences. African gender theory should be fully grounded in and informed by our various local realities, and insofar as it is committed to their amelioration. It is a theoretical and practical way of speaking on, in, of and for our continent and its peoples. This way of conceptualising gendered experiences seeks to transform society in its totality, for the betterment of all, not just women or even a certain type or group of women. Gender theory in Africa inextricably linked with anti-imperialist, anti-elitist and anti-racist politics. Amina Mama state that such a theory presents a praxis that directly opposes the hegemonic interests of multinational corporations, international financial and development agencies and nation-states. As Achola A. Pala (1977, 13) wisely advices:

African scholars, and especially women, must bring their knowledge to bear on presenting an African perspective on prospects and problems for women in local societies. Scholars and persons engaged in development research planning and implementation should pay attention to development priorities as local communities see them.

Any theory, concept or analysis about Africans has to be steeped in their lived experiences and not in universal proclamations. Nnaemeka (2003) argues on the necessity and prudence of 'building on the indigenous' in the construction of African feminist theory[ies]. The key question that arises is how African scholars can ground feminist practice in the historical experiences of cultural categories as tools for the development of a new consciousness without falling into the trap of cultural essentialism that could be used to further consolidate gender power difference. Theoretical debates on gender must be inextricably linked with practice.

CONCLUSION

Gender is Africa remains a contested enterprise. This paper has outlined the major debates and thinking. African gender theory has grappled with decolonising itself from Western binary notions which tend towards biological determinism. It has shown that there are many contradictory views among African gender and feminist theorist. The entire western episteme bases its categories and hierarchies on visual modes and binary distinctions: male and female, white and black, homosexual and heterosexual. As such coping and pasting such concepts into African spaces leads to confusing, contradictory and often contested outcomes. Gender can only be defined and understood within its own specific context. The need for a gender theory steeped in African ideologies is far more apparent now as a host of Western donor driven programmes on gender have proliferated but arguing for an idea of gender which does not speak to the realities on the continent.

REFERENCES

Acholonu, C. (1995). *Motherism: The Afrocentric Alternative to Feminism*. Owerri, Nigeria: Afa Publications.

Adesina, J. (2006a). Sociology, Endogeneity and the Challenge of Transformation. *African Sociological Review*, *10*(2), 133–150.

Adesina, J. (2006b). Sociology Beyond Despair: Recovery of Nerve, Endogeneity, and Epistemic Intervention. *South African Review of Sociology*, *37*(2), 241–259. doi:10.1080/21528586.2006.10419157

Adesina, J. (2010). Re-appropriating Matrifocality: Endogeneity and African Gender Scholarship. *African Sociological Review*, *1*(14), 1–19.

Adeleye-Fayemi, B. (2005). Creating and Sustaining Feminist Space in Africa: Local and Global Challenges. In The 21st Century' in Feminist Politics, Activism and Vision: Local and Global Challenges. London: Zed Books.

Arnfred, S. (2002). Simone De Beauvoir in Africa: 'Women-The Second Sex?' Issues of African Feminist Thought. Jenda: A Journal of Culture and African Women's Studies, 2(1).

Bakare-Yusuf, B. (2003). Beyond Determinism: The Phenomenology of African Female Existence. *Feminist Africa*, (2).

Bakare-Yusuf, B. (2004). "Yoruba's don't do gender": A Critical Review of Oyeronke Oyewumi's, The Invention of Women: Making an African Sense of Western Gender Discourses. In S. Arnfred, B. Bakari-Yusuf, E. W. Kisiang'ani, D. Lewis, O. Oyewumi, & F. C. Steady (Eds.), *African Gender Scholarship: Concepts, Methodologies and Paradigms* (pp. 61–81). Dakar: CODESRIA.

Boris, S. (2007). Gender after Africa!. In Africa after Gender?. Bloomington, IN: Indiana University Press.

Bujra, J. (2000). Targeting Men for a Change: AIDS Discourse and Activism in Africa. *Agenda (Durban, South Africa)*, *44*(44), 6–23. doi:10.2307/4066430

Butler, J. (1999). *Gender Trouble: Feminism and the Subversion of Identity*. New York: Routledge.

Cleaver, F. (2001). Do men matter?. *New Horizons in Gender and Development*. Available: http://www.id21.org/static/insights35editorial.htm

Cole, C.M., Manuh, T., & Miescher, S.F. (Eds.). (2007). *Africa after Gender?*. Bloomington, IN: Indiana University Press.

Dosekun, S. (2007). Defending Feminism in Africa. *Postamble*, *3*(1), 41–47.

Echols, A. (1989). *Daring to Be Bad: Radical Feminism in America, 1967–1975*. Minneapolis, MN: University of Minnesota Press.

Gender Tree. (n.d.). *Egyptian Third Gender*. Retrieved from: http://www.gendertree.com/Egyptian%20third%20gender.htm

Freedman, E. B. (2003). *No Turning Back: The History of Feminism and the Future of Women*. Ballantine Books.

Gaidzanwa, R. (1992). Bourgeois Theories of Gender and Feminism and their Shortcomings with Reference to Southern African Countries. In Gender in Southern Africa: Conceptual and Theoretical Issues. Harare: SAPES Books.

Hanisch, C. (2006). *Hanisch, New Intro to "The Personal is Political" - Second Wave and Beyond*. The Personal Is Political.

Hudson-Weems, C. (2004). *Africana Womanist Literary Theory*. Asmara: Africa World Press Inc.

Johnson, B. (2002). *The Feminist Difference: Literature, Psychoanalysis, Race and Gender*. Harvard University Press.

Jones, A. (1994). Postfeminism, Feminist Pleasures, and Embodied Theories of Art. In New Feminist Criticism: Art, Identity, Action. New York: HarperCollins.

Kisiang'ani, D., & Lewis, O. (2004). African Gender Scholarship: Concepts, Methodologies and Paradigms. Dakar: CODESRIA.

Kroløkke, C. (2006). Three Waves of Feminism. In C. Kroløkke & A. S. Sørensen (Eds.), *Gender Communication Theories and Analyses: From Silence to Performance*. Sage Publications Inc.

Lazreg, M. (1994). *The Eloquence of Silence: Algerian Women in Question*. London: Routledge.

Lewis, D. (2004). African Gender Research and Postcoloniality: Legacies and Challenges?. In S. Arnfred, B. Bakari-Yusuf, E. W. Kisiang'ani, D. Lewis, O. Oyewumi, & F. C. Steady (Eds.), *African Gender Scholarship: Concepts, Methodologies and Paradigms* (pp. 27–41). Dakar: CODESRIA.

Lindsay, L. A., & Miescher, S. F. (Eds.). (2003). Men and Masculinities in Modern Africa. Portsmouth: Heinemann.

Mama, A. (2002). Editorial. *Feminist Africa, 1*. Retrieved from http://www.feministafrica.org/fa%201/101-2002/editorial.html

Mama, A. (2001). Challenging Subjects: Gender and Power in African Context. *African Sociological Review*, 2(5), 63–73.

Mama, A. (1995). Women. In *Studies and Studies of Women in Africa during the 1990s*. Retrieved from http://www.gwsafrica.org/knowledge/index.html

McFadden, P. (2003). Sexual pleasure as feminist choice. *Feminist Africa, 2*. Retrieved from http://www.feministafrica.org/fa%202/2level.html

Miescher, S. (2007). Becoming as Spanyin: Elders, Gender and Masculinities in Ghana since Nineteenth Century. In Africa After Gender?. Bloomington, IN: Indiana University Press.

Miller, B. D. (1993). *The Anthropology of Sex and Gender Hierarchies. In Sex and Gender Hierarchies*. Cambridge, UK: Cambridge University Press.

Modleski, T. (1991). *Feminism without Women: Culture and Criticism in a "Postfeminist" Age*. New York: Routledge.

Mohanty, C. (1991). Under Western Eyes: Feminist Scholarship and Colonial Discourses. In C. Mohanty, A. Russo, & L. Torres (Eds.), *Third World Women and the Politics of Feminism*. Indianapolis, IN: Indiana University Press.

Mohanty, C. (2003). Cartographies of Struggle: Third World Women and the Politics of Feminism. In C. T. Mohanty (Ed.), *Feminism without Borders: Decolonizing Theory, Practicing Solidarity* (pp. 43–84). Durham, NC: Duke University Press. doi:10.1215/9780822384649-003

Narayan, U. (1997). *Dislocating Cultures: Identities, Traditions, and Third-World Feminism*. New York: Routledge.

Nathanson, P., & Young, K. K. (2006). *Spreading Misandry: The Teaching of Contempt for Men in Popular Culture*. Montreal: McGill-Queen's University Press.

Nnaemeka, O. (2003). Nego-Feminism: Theorising, Practicing and Pruning Africas Way. *Signs (Chicago, Ill.), 29*(2), 357–385. doi:10.1086/378553

Nzegwu, N. (2001). Gender Equality in a Dual-Sex System: The Case of Onitsha. *Jenda: A Journal of Culture and African Women's Studies, 1*(1).

Olufunke-Okome, M. (2003). What women, whose development? A critical analysis of reformist evangelism. In African women & feminism: Reflecting on the politics of sisterhood. Africa World Press.

Ogunyemi, C. (1984). Womanism: The Dynamics of the Contemporary Black Female Novel in English. *Signs (Chicago, Ill.), 11*, 1.

Ouzgane, L., & Morrell, R. (2005). *African Masculinities: Men in Africa from the late Nineteenth Century to the Present*. New York: Palgrave MacMillan. doi:10.1057/9781403979605

Oyewumi, O. (1997). *The Invention of Women: Making an African Sense of Western Gender Discourse*. Minneapolis, MN: University of Minnesota Press.

Oyewumi, O. (2003). Introduction: Feminism, Sisterhood, and Other Foreign Relations. In O. Oyewumi (Ed.), *African Women and Feminism: Reflecting on the Politics of Sisterhood*. Asmara: Africa World Press Inc.

Oyewumi, O. (2004). Conceptualising Gender: Eurocentric Foundations of Feminist Concepts and the Challenge of African Epistemologies. In African Gender Scholarship: Concepts, Methodologies and Paradigms. Academic Press.

Pereira, C. (2003). 'Where angels fear to tread?' Some thoughts on Patricia McFadden's 'Sexual Pleasure as Feminist Choice'. *Feminist Africa, 2*. Retrieved from http://www.feministafrica.org/fa%202/2level.html

Ruspini, E. (2007). Book Review: African Masculinities: Men in Africa from the Late Nineteenth Century to the Present. *Sexualities, 10*(2), 267–268. doi:10.1177/136346070701000212

Sethe, K. (1926). Die Aechtung feindlicher Fürsten, Völker und Dinge auf altägyptischen Tongefäßscherben des mittleren Reiches. In *Abhandlungen der Preussischen Akademie der Wissenschaften* (p. 61). Philosophisch-Historische Klasse.

Sooriyakumaran, P. (2010). *"Gender and Development": Do men and masculinities need to be considered?*. Retrieved from http://www.theadr.com.au/wp/?p=273

Stamp, P. (1989). *Technology, Gender, and Power in Africa*. Ottawa: International Development Research Centre.

Tsikata, D. (1997). Gender Equality and the State in Ghana. In Engendering African Social Science. Dakar: CODESRIA.

Tripp, A. (2000). *Women and Politics in Uganda*. Kampala: Fountain Publishers.

Uchedu, E. (2008). Introduction Are African Males Men? Sketching African Masculinities. In E. Uchendu (Ed.), *Masculinities in Contemporary Africa*. Dakar: CODESRIA.

Undie, C., & Benaya. (2008). The State of Knowledge on Sexuality in Sub-Saharan Africa. *QUEST: An African Journal of Philosophy / Revue African Philosophy*, 119–154.

Weedon, C. (1999). *Feminism, theory and the politics of difference*. Malden, MA: Blackwell.

GLBTQ. (n.d.). Retrieved from: http://www.glbtq.com/social-sciences/africa_pre.html

Color World. (n.d.). *Same sex relationships and gender identities among non-whites*. Retrieved from: http://www.colorq.org/articles/article.aspx?d=2000&x=qcolor

ENDNOTES

[1] The feminist activist and author Carol Hanisch coined the slogan which became synonymous with the second wave.
[2] See the works of literary works of Tsitsi Dangarebga and Yvonne Vera in Zimbabwe.
[3] This is contained in a Fact Sheet: What is Intersex? Produced by CBC Documentaries.

Chapter 12
Unveiling Barriers and Challenges of Brothel-Based Sex Workers in Private and Public Sphere of Bangladesh

Kuntala Chowdhury
Begum Rokeya University, Bangladesh

ABSTRACT

The value of our society is constructed through different patriarchal organization. Sex workers or prostitutes whatever we call them literally they are stigmatized in our society. Double standard of our society influences us to play double role where a man act like a saint in front of society and at the night they are the regular visitor of a brothel but society respects them and abuse those women who provides sexual pleasure to that men. Most of the sex workers are engaged in this profession because of trafficking, blackmailing or they did not have any other way to earn. They are working in this profession as well as they are serving to the customers to fulfill their sexual demand. However the fact is that stigmatization, challenges and barriers are literally faced by those women who are working as sex workers. The intensity of their life struggle is too much among brothel based sex workers where they are confined to maintain all obligations imposed by Sordarni (Madam) or customers. Though challenges and barriers can be varied from chukri (new girls in brothel) to sordarni (experienced sex workers who control new girls), I tried to put intersectional lenses to understand their challenges. Sex workers in brothels are subjects of different kinds of violence in their public and private sphere and they are objectified as sex object. This chapter is going to show the condition and position of women by examining their barriers in public and private sphere of Bangladesh. This chapter also intends to recommend a few ways to redress these kinds of violence against brothel based sex workers.

DOI: 10.4018/978-1-5225-3018-3.ch012

INTRODUCTION

Sex workers are often deprived of basic human rights due to legal ambiguities and patriarchal conservative society .They are victims of an exploitative industry that leaves them exposed to cruel conditions, extortion, violence, obligatory drug use and insufficient access to water, sanitation, and health services. While sex worker are correctly portrayed as victims, many older and experienced sex worker also continue the exploitative system. (Sabet & Ahmed, 2012, pp. 1)

They were almost completely ignored by government and civil society in the beginning of mid 1990s. Various initiatives has been taken by donor funded organization to improve the life of sex workers and the welfare of their children during the last two decades. However the standard of their life is not improving. According to a study which was conducted among brothel based and street based sex worker shows that 107333 women are working in street across the Bangladesh. Moreover the number of brothel based sex workers in Bangladesh would perhaps not exceed 60000, a number that corresponds with the conservative unofficial estimates of care Bangladesh officials. In Bangladesh, it is estimated that approximately 100000 people are involved in sex work. So this data represent a large number of people. These statistics are showing the increasing number of sex worker in this profession within 4 years. (Sabet & Ahmed, 2012, pp. 1) Yet they are not recognized as citizen of our country and unofficially they are deviant of this society. They are living their life in miserable way.

There also exist a debate among intellectuals about the recognition of them as sex worker or not. If we call them sex worker there will be a possibility to increase the percentage of taking this as a profession. If they are not recognized like now, they will be forced or be trapped to do this kind of work. (Tahmina & Moral, 2004, pp.7-10) which can increase the intensity of exploitation. As a sex worker they are facing different barriers and challenges from their community as well as from the mainstream society.

Identification of Research Problem

Sex work is running continuously in our society. The number of girls are being trafficker or used for pornography because they are trapped by someone. After writing their name in this profession there is no way to look behind. They have to leave their families and home. According to land of this Bangladesh, "Sex work is legal, Soliciting is not. Sex work is legal, running brothel is not." This is the law of the land. According to these laws illegal sex worker are legally exploited by the laws enforcement agencies. Police violently evicted Tanbazar and Nimtoli brothels on 23rd July 1990. The high court of Bangladesh issued a judgment after a written petition submitted by NGOs on 14th March 2000.This rule is the first step to recognize sex workers as citizens of our country. The High Court declared that sex workers are citizens of Bangladesh and they have enforceable rights under article 31(Right to the protection of law) and 32(Right to life and liberty) of the constitution. (Terre des homes Italia [TDH],2005) On the other hand exploitation of sex workers, their children and society's attitude towards them are not changing.

In Bangladesh context, religious and conservative values push the industry underground and marginalize sex workers while also creating demand for their services. Although many people in society would prefer a purely abolitionist approach to prostitution, Bangladesh policy reflects elements of both abolitionism and regulationalism. Although sex work is recognized as a legitimate trade and partially legalized, it is still predominantly defined by exploitation and abuse. Moreover these kinds of double standard are also accelerating the process of exploitation against sex workers. Modern day slavery can be clearly seen in the system of bonded sex workers from chukri to sordarni. Also of concern, is the high number of underaged sex workers came to this profession when they might lack of knowledge and maturity for meaningful informed consent The eviction of Brothels is continuous process. So the numbers of floating sex workers are increasing day by day. They are the victim of poverty and social stigma. Sex workers are one of the most disadvantaged group among other citizen of Bangladesh. Even they are not enjoying basic human rights. They have not right to move, right to join assembly. They are stigmatized and criticized if their identity is disclosed. However this experience can be different from brothel to street. Patriarchy is controlling their whole life and poverty imposes them not to leave the profession. They have created safe homes and women's organization which run by the sex workers president in brothel. Nevertheless the condition has not been improved a lot.

Background of the Study

The history of prostitution mainly focuses on the causes of prostitution and it also gives overview of today's prostitution. If we want to know the lifestyle of sex worker and their children, it is necessary to know the beginning of prostitution. There are diversities of prostitution in different historical period. Prostitution was different in primitive races. And it also differs from time to time, place to place, context to context. Religious prostitution was available in the ancient society where the brothel is treated as a temple. (Sanger,2013,pp. 35) On the other hand one thing was common in civilized society that prostitute was criticized publicly but supported and encouraged to do her work privately which always create a dilemma for her. The suppression of prostitute has been started when prostitution came as a profession. They are subjected to various forms of oppression and torture in our civilized society after taking it as a profession. If we look at different society we will see that there are many laws which prevent prostitute from making social anarchy and annoyance as if they are the disturbing being in our society. Such as: The Law of Metropolitan police act and Burgh Police Act 1829 in Scotland (Lyman,1964). However we are not able to provide strong evidence of law which will prevent society to deprive and stigmatize them

Justification of the Study

There are many studies which have been conducted on Brothel based sex workers and floating sex workers separately. Brothel based sex worker has also a hierarchical process. They are bound to maintain the hierarchical status in their society. The new sex worker of this society is called as chukri. Moreover the old sex worker is called as Mashi and Sordarni and they are free to choose their customer and the number of their customer. Mashi and Sordarni are powerful status after getting promotion in their profession. There are also some permanent stakeholders in Brothel. (TDH, 2005) This chapter will represent the struggle of brothel based sex workers and their children in private and public life, NGOs and governmental intervention and way forward to redress the situation. Here I have adopted idea from different secondary sources about the living condition of the sex worker and their children. I have also obtained idea about Kandapara brothel which is my study area. Approximately 839 sex workers live in Kandapar brothel,300 chukris live in bondage under the 158 Sordarnis. The sex worker of Tangail have recently bought their own graveyards and different facilities. I have seen various works which has done on commercial sex workers. Actually the CSW in Bangladesh have been the focus of research for STIS and HIV/AIDS. The CSW are stigmatized in society of Bangladesh. In the society of Bangladesh CSW are subjected to physical and psychological abuse. The low social and economic statuses of CSW as well as the stigma are the main reasons for violence against them. Governmental and non-governmental organization is taking various steps to prevent sexually transmitted infections and HIV AIDS among sex workers. A group of researcher conducted a study on the sex workers in Rajshahi city where a sizable proportion of the sample stated that they badly scarred on their body (58.7%), followed by frequent scar and bites on their breasts. (Hossain,Habib and Imam:2004).So I selected this study as a document because it provides the actual summary of the female sex works in Bangladesh which will provide me a overall understanding about them. They did not notice or show anything about the sex worker children. Moreover this study also shows that the profession of the clients of CSWs are from lower class such as: Laborers, Mastans, Peon, Police, Hotel boy, Students, Rickshaw pullers etc . They are also at risk of sexual abuse from clients, police and Mastans. After giving birth of a child women face more challenges in their life. Children of prostitute are not safe. So they are not from rich background and do not like to use condom. As a result CSW are mostly affected by HIV AIDS. (Hossain,Habib and Imam:2004)..Actually this book mainly shows the attitudes and the factors and consequences and kinds against commercial sex workers. Moreover it will supplement my study by giving idea of them. They just conducted their research on CSW. I am going to show the barriers and challenges among brothel based sex worker. Government is evicting brothels. Whereas it will be quiet impossible to reduce trafficking, pornographic abuse which is the main cause of prostitution. The main culprit who brings a women in this profession, do not get punishment rather the sex worker is getting punishment. Evictions of brothel as well as existence of this profession in Bangladesh for a long time are creating barriers and challenges for sex workers.

PROMINENT THEORIES: INSIGHT FROM FEMINIST PERSPECTIVES

Sexual Objectification Theory

Objectification theory provides an important framework for understanding, researching, and intervening to improve women's lives in a socio-cultural context that sexually objectifies the female body and only connect this body with sexual function. Objectification theory (Fredrickson & Roberts, 1997) provides a framework for understanding the experience of being female in our society that sexually objectifies the female body. This theory helps us to include different perspective in feminist lenses. This lenses support psychologists to realize the ways how sexual objectification impact women's lives and the problems that they bring to therapy as well as how they adapt and find way out from this sexual objectification experiences (American Psychological Association [APA], 2007a). Additionally, they encourage psychologists to examine issues of diversity and oppression under patriarchy at micro-social and macro-social levels. Objectification theory (Fredrickson & Roberts, 1997) postulates that many women are sexually objectified and treated as an object to be valued for its use.

CONCEPTUAL UNDERSTANDING OF THE STUDY

Sex Work or Prostitution? / Defining Sex Work

Generally A sex worker is a person who works in the sex industry. The term is used in reference to all those in all areas of the sex industry including those who provide direct sexual services as well as the staff of such industries. Some sex workers are paid to engage in sexually explicit behavior which involve varying degrees of physical contact with clients (prostitutes, escorts, some but not all professional dominants). In Bangladesh a woman who sells sex for her living is commonly called by such abusive words like *Potita,Beshya,Gonika,Bajarer Meye,or Khanki* in Bangla. These terms are abusive which indicates a fallen woman. She is seen as deviant women whose services are enjoyed by many men, a women who belongs to the market, her body being a commodity. (Tahmina & Moral, 2004, pp 3-22). Our society like to use abusive word for sex worker. Moreover pornography models and actors engage in sexually explicit behavior which are filmed or photographed in western society. Phone sex operators have sexually-oriented conversations with clients, and do sexual role play. Other sex workers are paid to engage in live sexual performance, such as web cam sex and performers in live sex shows. Some sex workers perform erotic dances and other acts for an audience (striptease, Go-Go dancing, lap dancing,)

It is the issue of agency or the ability to consent to paid sex, that has been centerpiece of a global debate. Falling squarely in the regulationalist camp, advocates who view sex work as a legitimate occupation have sought to shake off the negative connotation of the word "Prostitute" in favor of the term "sex worker . Bindman (1997) showed that the term "sex work" and "sex worker" have been coined by sex workers themselves to redefine commercial sex, not as a social or psychological characteristics of a class of women, but as an income generating activity or form of employment for women and men .As such it can be considered along with other forms of economic activity. (as cited in (Sabet & Ahmed, 2012, pp. 4). But I have mentioned earlier that there was a debate about "sex work or prostitution." The regulationist camp argued to permit women to choose to engage in sex work and not to criminalize legitimate sex work in the name of protecting women from victims of trafficking. The abolitionist camp argued against the notion of consent. From their perspective, prostitution itself is a violation of a woman's rights. The prominent Advocate Salma ali argued that "Work that is not productive or creative cannot be regarded as professionals. I do not know what to call them in Bangla. *Potita or* fallen is a derogatory connotation but I feel this term is more acceptable than sex worker. We must look for a term that connotes forced into prostitution. The term has to reflect their reality as victims of exploitation and torture." (.as cited in Tahmina &Moral, 2004, p. 15).

On the other hand,the ex-president of Bangladesh Women's Health Coalition, Khondker Rebaka Sunyat (2004) argued that, " I am not saying that prostitution be encouraged as a chosen profession. But those who are already in the trade, for all sorts of reasons, need legal recognition. Otherwise the whole thing become complicated and obscure." (.as cited in Tahmina &Moral, 2004, p. 24). She feels that *sex-trader not sex worker* to be the term appropriate for these women. She explained that "The nature of sex of their job is closer to independent business ventures. However, the way they join the trade, their compulsions, and the inherent corruption, crime and torture allow them little independence." (.as cited in Tahmina &Moral, 2004, p. 26).

TERMINOLOGICAL DEFINITIONS AND CONCEPTS

Sex worker and their children are struggling a lot in our society. They are stigmatized in society. In each and every single step they have to face bad behavior from society. The sex workers of Brothel have vote rights but they are not treated as citizen of our country

Brothel Based Sex Worker

Brothel is a house or other place where men pay to have sexual intercourse with sex workers.

Brothel based sex workers are those who live in Brothel and have to maintain a hierarchical life circle where Sordarni is the most powerful women. Mainly the retired and aged sex workers are called Sordarni. Brothels are establishments specifically dedicated to prostitution. Sex tourism refers to travelling, typically from developed to underdeveloped nations, to engage in sexual activity with prostitutes. Brothel based sex workers are those whose clients contact at the recognized brothels, that is buildings or residential homes where people from outside the sex trade know that workers live and work. Typically, a brothel is a place where a small group of sex workers is managed by a Madam (Sordarni) or an agent. They have to do affidavit as a sex workers in the brothel. (TDH, 2005)

Intersectionality

Intersectionality is a perspective by which I would be able to know the different layers of struggles of sex worker. Intersectionality theory might be "the view that women experience oppression in varying configurations and in varying degrees of intensity" (Ritzer, 2007, pg. 204).

And it can also be defined as a theory to analyze how social and cultural categories intertwine. The relationship between gender, race ethnicity, disability, sexuality, social class and nationality are examined. The word intersection means one line cuts through another line. Intersectionality is a feminist ideology to understand the different layers of the marginalization. According to Mc Call, *"Intersectionality is the modalities of social relation among multiple identities."*(MC call, 2005). Here I will try to explore how one identity of sex workers intersects another identity. It's a interplay of struggle between their private and public life which reinforce the exploitation against them.

Patriarchy

Patriarchy is a social system in which the male gender role as the primary authority figure is central to social organization where fathers hold authority over women, children, and property. Traditionally patriarchy exists in the social, legal, political, and economic organization. Patriarchy literally means the rule of the "father" or "chief of a race, patriarch". Historically, the term patriarchy was used to refer to dominating rule by the male head and subordinating role of a family. From this perspectives we can also see the patriarchal position of male and female in brothels. To establish the identity of their children they need a Bandha babu or regular customer. Here the shopkeepers who live inside the brothels are Bandha babu. They sometimes live with them whereas the Bandha Babu is regarded as father of the sex worker children. Most of the time sex worker's children have no identity of father which creates stigmatized situation for them in our society. Furthermore the necessity of the identity of a father controls the children's whole life. Patriarchy controls women's life in different process like controlling women's autonomy, controlling women's sex, controlling women's access to resources, controlling women's mobility, controlling women's productive or labor power, controlling women's reproduction etc. (Bhasin, 2006, pp. 3-9)

All of the controlling system are truly applicable for sex worker women. Moreover this patriarchy shapes their lives through the family, the religion, the legal system, the economic system and economic institutions, political systems and institutions, media and educational systems and institution. (Bhasin, 2006, pp. 9-12)

METHODOLOGY OF DATA COLLECTION

The method of my research is divided into two processes. The first phase includes primary data collection and the second phase includes secondary data collection. The study is mainly a qualitative one. Because this study mainly focuses on the barriers and challenges of sex workers. My study area is Tangail Kandapara brothel which is one of the largest brothel in Bangladesh.

Design of the Study

I have used qualitative research design in this study. Because qualitative design can bring out one's mentality, one's perception. I am working on the barriers and challenge of sex worker. It is impossible for anyone to express this perception by giving the yes or no answer of quantitative question. So I preferred here to conduct the qualitative research process. Moreover I have also adopted feminist standpoint epistemology to understand the experiences of brothel based sex workers.

Study Area of Brothel Based Sex Worker

In the heart of Tangail district town, close to the police station we reach the brothel. After going there I noticed that there are several women who are waiting for the clients with painted face. This brothel is special because it's the first brothel in Bangladesh to have its own graveyard.

I have chosen Kandapara brothel as my study area which is located in Dhaka division in Tangail and it dates back to 150-200 years ago. They established a cooperative called Nari Mukti Shongho in 2005. When I went there I talked with their president to know about the living standard and actual number of sex workers. According to their calculation 863 sex workers are working there. Among them the number of Bariwalis is 52 to 56 whereas 100 children are living in safe home. The actual number may well be more since child prostitution is controversial issue and mothers and madams try to keep it hidden (TDH,2005). Most of the sex workers in the brothel are poor and illiterate with little education and no commercial skills.

Who Are Being Researched

The study is conducted among the sex workers of Tangail brothel. I went to the field and I made a good friendship with the leader of Nari Mukti Songho. I have also collected the brothel based sex workers from Tangail brothel by the help of the president, Nari Mukti Songho. Her name is Madam *Rozy*. I have selected my respondent among them. I passed a lot of time with the respondent. So that I was able to establish a good rapport with them. Some of them come to me after making intercourse with customer. It was so tough for them to provide time for me.

Sampling

The sampling method was purposive sampling. A purposive sample is a sample selected in a deliberative and non-random fashion to achieve a certain goal. To get the actual barriers and challenges I purposively selected 5 sex workers who were from brothel and was willing to talk about their life, their community, their livelihood. I observed them in their daily work even I talk with them after giving service to client.

Data Collection Tools

I have adopted in-depth interview and observation to conduct this research. I explored their feel, emotion and experiences through qualitative interviewing process. Now I am going to give a brief discussion about my experiences in applying these tools. There were mainly two tools. Such as:

- Observation
- In-depth study

Observation

I used observation method to understand their activities in brothel. After going to my field, Tangail I felt bewildered for two days. Because my socio-cultural understanding took some time to understand their behavior. I went for first time in brothel. I noticed that a lots of women are standing in front of the gate of Kandapara brothel, Tangail with their painted face and they are doing also erotic movement when clients are going near to them. Some of them painted their face with using black color because it is a symbol of not getting customer for a long time. If anyone feel pity for them, they will go to their to take their service and pay them. It is the rules of the brothel. I feel astonished after knowing this. So I was little bit nervous. I tried my level best to be normal. Then I met with the president of Nari Mukti Songho. She offered me tea with cordial behavior. Then I walked with her in their territory. Moreover I also noticed that several sex workers was waiting for their clients. Among them I also noticed teenage sex workers who may not go through their pubertal change. So I got so upset. After communicating and making good relation with the president, I told my study objectives then she showed me information about 10 women. I observed them and selected five of them for in-depth interview.

In-Depth Interview

Respondent for in-depth interviews were chosen from observation. In brothel based field I had communication with the president of Nari Mukti Songho. So I seek her help to find out my respondent who are spokesperson and their experiences will be relevant with my study. I tried to look for diversity while choosing respondent for this interview. I have selected different criteria as the factor of diversity such as: age, beauty, livelihood style, income are key factor among those thing .So I selected three adult women where age was the main factor to determine the level of violence. I stayed in Tangail for almost one week to conduct my study. From the very beginning I just noticed their daily activities with the help of the president of Nari Mukti Songho. After that I collected my respondent from the participant observation. Among them two were Sordarni and another three were chukri. So here I also used intersectional lenses. It was my tension that is it possible to win their trust? But after some time I feel that they are communicating with me like a friend. Then I got courage and asked them various question which is related with their private and public life. I noticed that they got relief after sharing and expressing their experiences.

METHOD OF ANALYSIS FROM FEMINIST PERSPECTIVE

After collecting my data I read different books and magazines to understand the different sufferings of sex worker. I have used feminist method to understand the analytical framework of my study. Here I mainly focused on the feminist standpoint. I am going to explore different understanding and experience of sex workers in brothel. Here I have tried to achieve strong objectivity by maximizing my reflexivity. And it was a tough thing for me. My research ethics restricted me to show the original identity so I used pseudo name according to their request.

Tangail: The Brothel With Multidimensional Barriers

In the heart of Tangail district town, close to the police station Tangail brothel is situated. Their private and public life has been collapsed by various factors. Here I will use the intersectional lenses to understand the hierarchy among sex workers and how this hierarchy and age factor leads to violence. My main aim is to discuss the chain of exploitation, violence and tortured situation among them and barriers and challenges of brothel based sex workers in their private and public life. In addition I will show how it can intersect or can be different from various perspectives.

Barriers in Private Life

The sex workers of Tangail brothel are vastly exploited and victim of violence in private sphere.

Now I am going to use some indicator which is an easy process to understand the barriers and challenges of sex workers.

Expensive Life Expenditure

Sex workers have to cope with several expenditures. The room rent as well as household facilities such as water and electricity is very high. Brothel landowners rent out the room to bariwali who in their turn do the same. Everyone gains his own percentage from the rent. In Babu Bazar brothel, the local powerful bariwali rents the room from the local landlords for 100 taka and in her turn she rents out the room to gharwalis and bharatias for 130 taka. The sex workers have to cope with the high price of consumer goods. They often purchase necessaries from local hawkers at a price, which is double than the outside rate. Their restricted freedom of movement confines them inside the brothel. The money that they usually send to their family and children represents the main expenditure. The second main expenditure is the food, followed by rent and drugs or alcohol. (TDH, 2005) Similarly, there are many sex workers who are not provided with electricity or it is included in the room rent. Sometimes they get tips and try to send it to their family. The young sex workers earn a lot. However all of the income goes to Madam. Their madam has house which is not neat and clean. But it takes too much cost to bear. One of my respondents Shilpi said that,

Living in brothel is so tough for us because we have to spend lots of money. The costs of goods are so high. Many of us tried to save some money for their home and family. However it is just a imagination for them .We have to give 3000 room rent .After passing one year we are able to spend the money. But we did not get any single penny to spend in our beginning. And we have to cook .So we have to spend money for fuel, for our children. Some of the sex workers children are also living in safe home. We have to bear some cost also. At the end of the day we had nothing to save just a lot of tension about our future when we will not be able to work. (Personal Communication, March 16,2013)

So expenditure is one of the main problems and barriers of brothel based sex workers in their private life. Another of my respondent Rani said that,

I could not deal with the customer 10-15 times a day. I felt so weak .Sometimes I have been suffered from fever .I could not maintain my own expenditure. Then they decided to send me back .Because I was not useful for them. (Personal Communication, February 10,2013)

This statement shows that brothel based sex workers have to maintain different types of expenditure. However the expenditure cost is so high. Though beautiful sex workers earn a lot but cannot spend their money by themselves and cannot maintain good livelihood standard.

Income Depends on Age

The sex work is a profitable business comparing with other professions such as garment worker or housemaid. Nevertheless, the sex workers cannot benefit from at least in appearance look like remunerative work. Most of them are economically exploited by a large group of society from law enforcing agency to stakeholders. Sex workers as well customers have to pay the police some money (400/500 taka) if they want to spend the night together. The local thana police usually shut down the brothels at 10 o'clock. (TDH, 2005) Generally the sex workers rely only on the proceeds of their sex trade. Few of them were able to save money and invest it in other profitable business such as grocery or tailoring shops. They are generally shordarnis or bariwalis. The income of a brothel-based sex worker depends on her age and beauty. The younger sex workers get more customers than the older ones. Here we can also getting the intersectional lenses to understand the age, hierarchical factor. Chukris is a group that entertains more clients with highest rate for intercourse. They are forced by their owners to get more customers as possible. The average number is 15/20 customers per day. The rate of income is very high when they are below 18 years old and this demand decrease when they are cross 25 years old. The average income of a bharatia is 345 taka per day and they used to get 3 or 4 customers per day. Most of the times they are between 18 and 25 years old. (TDH, 2005) It is interesting to highlight that the second highest income category gathers those who are above 35 years old and sometimes they are bound to satisfy high level influential customers. Indeed, they are shordarnis or bariwalis and hence they benefit from their bonded girls' income. However, few sex workers can become shordarni and most of the times they need a considerable amount of money and powerful lobbying with goon and law enforcing agency.

One of my respondent whose name is Chumki (40) told that,

I was a high demandable chukri in my early period. I earned a lot. But now we cannot income more .Now I travel from brothel to brothel .Now I am Sordarni. Now a day we do not deal with more customers. But we can earn money from bonded girl or chukris. Actually income depends on the age of sex worker .When she will be 18 her income will raise .After 25 her income will be down.It's trend of sex workers.

After being aged the sex workers passed a miserable life which cannot be described in word. Even in some cases the daughter of a sex worker does not like to look after her mother. (Personal Communication, March 12, 2013)

So here we are also seeing that age is a indicator which determines the income. From intersectional perspectives it's true that age is creating barriers and challenges for sex workers.

Taking Loan and Imagination of Saving

Debt is a huge problem inside the brothel. Sex workers usually start their trade with a debt towards their owners and this plague affects them for a considerable part of their life. An agent on behalf of the brothel landlords comes almost every day in order to collect the money. If they are in delay with the rent, they face the risk of violence, torture and finally eviction. It should be mentioned that several sex workers, who would like to leave the brothel, couldn't because of their debts. According to a study which was done by Terre Des Homes Italia Out of 344 sex workers, the 58% incur a loan or debt. In Kandapara brothel the 80% of the sex workers interviewed incurred a loan. (TDH, 2005) They borrow money from other sex workers inside the brothel such as shordarnis and bariwalis or from the local people outside who are influential in their community. Afterwards, they have to pay high interest rates for the money they have borrowed. Former sex workers who cannot afford their living expenditures such as food, medicines and rent represent the most affected group. Another common way to incur a loan is the purchase of girls. Because of their huge expenditures, it is very hard for a sex worker to save money.

According to Bristi,

Actually saving is an unimaginable thing in our life where we are busy to manage the daily thing. And sometimes we are unable to maintain the regular goods for us. So we did not think about savings when we were Chukri. We had debt to our roommate, Sordarni(Madam).Or sometimes we are also bound to take debt to Mahajan(Influential people in the community) with high interest .So it is tough to save money. (Personal Communication, February 9,2013)

So loan and saving is an indicator of their private life which indicates the life standard of the sex worker. Who were taking loan are passing their life with tension to repay loan with interest .So this is one of the barriers and challenges in their private life.

Miscarriage/Abortion

Abortion is very common inside the brothel. If anyone of them get pregnant, they are bound to do abortion .Abortion is hardly a free choice for a sex worker. They are forced by poor living conditions, lack of fathers for their child and many times by other sex workers such as shordarnis or bariwalis. A bharatia can at least think about keeping the child, chukris are forced to get abortion by their owners. A pregnant chukri represents a lower income for her shordarni and hence just a burden to feed. Most of the time pregnancy is ia sign of decreasing business indicator for the sex worker. Besides, they are generally forced to come back to work as soon as possible .One of my respondent Liza said that,

I have a dream of becoming a mother. But this is not possible in brothel .In each and every single sphere we have no power to decide this kind of thing .So our madam decide that we will be pregnant or not. I have aborted my baby for two times. (Personal Communication,March 19, 2013)

And same thing is also applicable for Rani. She said that "I have also aborted my baby for this reason. Because brothel authority does not want that we will be pregnant. It hampers their business." (Personal Communication, February 9,2013)

So brothel based sex workers are passing a serious situation in their own life. They are victim of three or four time abortion in their life time which causes a serious health hazard.

Economic Crisis

They have no freedom to save money. They have to maintain different kinds of hierarchy in a brothel. And they have to give all of their earned money to Sordarni.Sometimes they also get tips. But they are not able to keep it.Chukri is the most oppressed category of sex worker.

It is not like that she is very helpful or loves me so much, her behavior to me depends on customers if I can handle 3 to 4 customers in the day time and 2 to 3 customers in the night, then she is satisfied other than that she won't even give me any food to eat, in short her behavior had changed basis on how well I work or not and the amount of money I could give her. My daily income is 3 to 4 thousand taka which I used to gave "Sordarni"(Madam). But she don't give me any percentage from that income. (Personal Communication, March 11,2013)

Economic crisis is common barriers and challenges among sex workers. And most of them are not economically solvent. They are treated as sex machine. At the end of day they earn nothing except exploitation.

Identity Crisis

They have no freedom to make their own family. They cannot hide their identity if they wish. In each and every single step it has the possibility to be known. They are not also well expected by their family member. The school authority does not want to take their children in school. One of my respondent liza said that,

I have done M.R for two times when I was in Naraynganj .Actually,what will I do with this children? If my daughter can know what will happen? I cannot give a proper identity to my child. Society stigmatize us.I am educating my daughter.And they are happy now. If I tell her about my private life she will not look at me with dignity. I am not bad by my selves. I am doing my body business like truck driver and rickshaw puller. So what is the problem with the society? (Personal Communication, March 19,2013)

Sex workers always suffer from the problem of identity crisis. If their identity is disclosed in the eyes of general people, they will be stigmatized in front of their family victim of public violence.

Reproductive Health Hazard

Sometimjes taking more customers can create health hazard for sex worker. Sometimes the customers do not use condoms though they know there is high risk of being pregnant or getting affected by STD diseases. According to the brothel based sex worker Shilpi

If we did not get customer they beat us, gave kick to our vagina. I was bound to take 15- 20 customer a day. My ovaries have been damaged by doing this work repeatedly. Then I have to do operation on my tube. However doctor predicted that I will never be able to be a mother. I got damaged in my tube after giving birth of my first child. I have given birth of a baby after taking great risk in one tube. Actually I want to use contraceptives. If they don't like to use, they beat us. That's why I got STI from them which is a great stigma for anyone. One of my customer forced me to intercourse with him again and again. After that I have been so sick and he did not give me single money . I have been raped for two months and left me without giving me money. His friend also forced me to do intercourse with them. And they bite me like a beast. I was being victim of continuous rape." (Personal Communication, March 16,2013)

Cheated by Loving Partner

A sex-worker's need for protection and emotional security often leads to her getting attached to a man,from amongst the brothel muscleman or from her clients. They often lives with her as a regular partner, called bharua or babu of the women.Babu depends upon the sex workers money. They do not marry the sex worker. Rather they exploit them a lot in the name of love. They have a family but they are keeping sex worker as their entertainment in a brothel. Only the *sordarnis* r the independent sex workers can afford such a lover. The *babus or bharuas* take money from the women investing in businesses or other ventures. If a sex-worker has some savings and wants to buy property outside the brothel or to start a business for future security, she can't do it herself because of the social stigma. No one is willing to deal with them whether it's about business or selling land. She has to trust a chosen man as her deputy. In almost all the cases the men take the money and leave them. One of my respondent who is working as Sordarni, chumki said that,

While I am staying in Tanbazar,I have also an affair with a person who did not like that I talk with another people .He did not give me opportunity to income .He loves me a lot. But he was unwilling to marry me. I could not save money this time. He beat me a lot and took my all money. Actually they face challenges from our bandhababu.I could not save my money at this time. After this situation, I came to kandapatti para with empty hand (Personal Communication, March 12,2013)

This is a common trend among brothel based sex workers. They find out a loving partner and most of the time they are deceived by them.

Socialization of Children

They face a great challenge to hide their identity. Sometimes they also face great challenge for the socialization of children. When their children come out from the brothel they are also neglected in the society. They are stigmatized as beast. Because people do not like to treat them as human being. That's why they also lost their courage and enthusiasm to go to school. Sometimes they have no place to stay (Rahman & Sultana 2012). And it is so much embarrassing for sex workers to do work/sex in front of her little child .That's why these types of incidence also creates psychological impact on their child. They want to bring out their child from this situation. But it is so tough for their child to hide identity. Another of my respondent shilpi said that,

I am 5 months pregnant and don't know who is the man. It happens just because some people don't want to use condoms whether they educated or not and for money reason I let them do without condom. Now most of my known person told me for abortion but I know abortion is just like killing someone why would I do that? So I have decided not to abort. Moreover this is not the first time I am doing this. I had four child earlier two of them are dead and two of them are adopted by good family because I would not be able to provide a better life to this child that's why I have decided to give this child to a family who can provide a better future than me. I know that avoiding condoms are harmful for health and it causes many diseases but some people just don't understand. (Personal Communication, March 16,2013)

Sex workers children cannot go to mainstream school and colleges'. Though the sex worker mother has dream that her children will be educated, give her relief from this situation. NGOs are running safe home for them which is not enough. So they are facing also barriers and challenges to bear the cost and to maintain the mainstreaming socialization process of their children.

BARRIERS IN PUBLIC SPHERE

Negative Attitude of Customer

The main problem of brothel based sex workers are the negative attitude from their customer. Moreover they are bound to tolerate this attitude. Sometimes they do not pay money after taking their service. They also tortured a lot. They tortured the sex worker for giving pleasure. But they do not understand that it is impossible for a human being to do intercourse by 15-20 times. They like to do sex with us whereas they are not introduced with the term making love. They just want to make sex where no emotion, no feel exist. The main aim of this customer is orgasm. After getting orgasm they just don't care about sex workers. In the meantime they literally fuck for one or two hour's. According to Shilpi, "

Sister they tortured us a lot. They just think about their satisfaction. We try several times to stop them. After that they beat us. So we tolerate their activities though we feel that we will be died. But we have no way. Nothing to do. They are hard fucker. They like to fuck us. And we are bound to be. (Personal Communication, March16, 2013)

Reluctant of Using Contraceptives: Challenge of Overcoming HIV/AIDS

Today, several NGOs are running programmes aimed at preventing the threat of HIV/AIDS spread. Almost all the sex workers are aware of such diseases, but they told the survey team that generally customers do not want to use condoms. It should be mentioned that, compared to other Asian countries, in

Bangladesh the sex workers have the highest number of clients and hence they are at high-risk. (TDH, 2005) Anyway, they are still not completely comfortable talking about that issue. According to Shilpi,

Actually I want to use contraceptives. If they don't like to use, they beat us. That's why I got STI from them which is a great stigma for anyone. I went to doctor and examined my blood. The doctor was so good to us. I did not do MR in my lifetime. Actually I used to eat a tablet when I got any type of problem in menstruation. (Personal Communication, March 16,2013)

They have no agency to decide whether they take contraceptives or not. That's why they are bound to do anything according to others will.

Hierarchical Structure Leads to Different Forms of Violence

The hierarchy is high in brothel. Everyone in this brothel is bound to maintain hierarchy. And it will be quiet impossible for them to sustain by breaking hierarchy. So every sex worker specially chukri is bound to do anything according to the decision of Sordarni. The brothel is a place with its own rules and hierarchies. The sex workers have adopted their own expressions to identify their related social status and type of sexual exploitation. Chukris are the bonded girls and they occupy the lowest ranks inside the brothel society. They generally are victims of trafficking (deceitful love affairs or allurement of well paid jobs) and enter the brothel after being sold to a shordarni (landlady). Afterwards they start as forced prostitutes and come under the overall control of their owner. Their shordarnis get an affidavit on behalf of them before a notary public stating that they are above 18 years, consenting with the sex trade and very poor. (TDH, 2005) According to Rani,

When I went to brothel, I were 19 or 20.Once I had been pregnant, I was almost death and so tired and I could not do any type of work after the death of my baby so they decided to send me back because they thought if they do not send me, they can be trapped. The sordarni hurt me a lot and I was almost death. They spent 60000 or 70000 for me. My customer was mainly driver, rickshapuller. Actually all of them are lower class people. I was married and my husband left me out. I attended 10 -12 people in a day. Although Sordarni (Madam) was not satisfied. Because they need to pay 400 to 500 room allowance. I could not save any money. They did not also give the tips. (Personal Communication, March 10,2013)

According to Bristy, "They can torture and beat as they want. I was very young and controlled by the elder sister also known as Sordarni or Madam. All of the chukris are under control of sordarni. They have to bear torture and beated by sordarni several times." (Personal Communication, March 9,2013) So we can see hierarchical structure in brothel where exploitation varies according to the power relation .Moreover this is also an intersectional issue.

Violence and Torture in a Brothel

Brothel-based sex workers used to face several abuses, harassments and violence, especially by police, local mastans and shordarnis. Police who have regular access in many brothels, police allow customers to spend the night inside only on demand of bribe Many sex workers told the me that at patrolling officers raid the brothel and if they find some customers, they are forced to pay as well as the sex workers. In addition, they can take them to custody, too. In Doulatdia brothel, no customers can enter the brothel after 9 p.m. without taking a ticket from police. Besides, some police officers forcefully enjoy sex with them. (TDH,2005) It should be mentioned that mostly the sex workers reported at least one forceful intercourse, but they do not have a clear idea about rape as a crime. If they were raped, they generally denied such violence, but afterwards they admitted to be several times forced to have sex what actually defines rape.. That means rape. Similarly, they kept from filing a complaint against their rapist because they did not know that her customer committed an offence. They are mainly tortured and violated by police, mastan, pimps and local community people. One of my respondent shilpi said that,

They beat me a lot. After going there they cut my hair. Because hairstyle is necessary to be a sex-worker. We stood on the narrow road for "Babu." If we did not got customer they beat us, gave kick to our vagina. Bitch why don't you work? I bought you after spending 2& half lakh taka. You have to do work. Sister, If I got menstruation, they impose us to do intercourse with customer. (KAJ Korbina ken ey magi tore aray lac taka diya kinchi,tui kaj korbina ke,kaj kora lagbo, latthay apa, amonki apa amra masik hoyleo kaj kori.)Whether I am sick or not this is not the fact, I have to do work this is the main fact .If I did not call customer they would beat us. We were not free outside the brothel and we did not wear good dress because they think that we can escape. (Personal Communication, March 16,2013)

Lack of Independence/Autonomy

They did not get any type of independence when they worked as a chukri in a brothel. They are bound to stay in brothel until they did not escape. They are sealed as sex worker. They have no freedom to start their life according to their will. They have no freedom to take decision how many times will they provide their sex service. They are not free to go outside from brothel. According to Rani

I did not know that I have been sold. I was not interested to do more work. So they beat me. If I worked with 4 or 5 people, they beat me. Because they were earning money by our work. They did not give me enough food in my earlier life. I stayed brothel for four or five years. When I came to brothel, I were 19 or 20." (Personal Communication, March 10,2013)

The sex worker women cannot practice their agency in private and public sphere. They have no autonomy.They are bound to do anything according to the decision of their hierarchy.

Institutional Health Hazard From Hospital

The hospital authority does not want to take them as patient. They have the possibility to be pregnant. After getting abortion in several times, they get several health risks. They have the risk to be the victim of AIDS .And hospital authority always like to treat them as sex worker. But they do not treat them as a patient. So the doctors of the hospital always like to pinch them here and there. According to Chumki,

Actually we do not get recognition from the society. We do not get same care from hospital. I have syphilis .And I do not get good care from hospital this time. (Personal Communication, March 12,2013)

Another of my respondent Liza said that, "I want the payment from the customer. That's why they beat me. My Brother –in-law took me to medical and they pinch my breasts in Sorwardi hospital. He pinch me here and there. I did not get any difference with them to a customer" (Personal Communication, March 19,2013)

They have also been victim of sexual object in the eyes of doctor who are treated as god in the eyes of general people. Everybody of this society try to take the benefit from this sex worker.

Treated as Sexual Object

They are bound to give free sex services to powerful people. Actually they are treated as sexual object. No one try to understand that they are also human being. Our patriarchal society like to stigmatize them. And the customer also likes to exploit them. Sex worker are exploited in each and every sphere of the world. So this is a great challenge for them. They are providing sex service. Whereas patriarchal society is treating them as sex servant which is the violation of human rights. According to Shilpi,

We got so much disturbance by pimp. And police also arrest us and get free service because we are bound to do that. I have been victim of continuous rape for several times Where I will go to seek justice they will treat us a sexual object. There main aim is to exploit me. So there is no court for us. We are just the sex objects. I want to share a fact with you. I went to a house to work as a maiden. But they treat me as their home sex worker. Everybody used me. When I refused to do intercourse with them they sent me to jail. So I decided to take that work as my profession and come back to this brothel again. (Personal Communication, March 16,2013)

Sex workers women are treated as sexual object in the eyes of patriarchal society. They are just a sex machine in the eyes of them .So they did not treat them with humanity.

Eviction of Brothel Can Cause to Serious Trouble

After talking with several sex workers I understood that they suffer a lot in a brothel. But it is also true that they suffer a lot after the eviction of brothel. They have no place to stay. Because they are stigmatized in society. So they have to go different places where they are not accepted. So they start their business again and it has a adverse effect on their life. One of my respondent shilpi said that,

We have done a lot of movement when they evict brothel. I can mention about various organizer who went their and took different kinds of video. A brother who came from India, he pay heed to us. We did a lot of movements but it did not work out. Then we have been scattered. I came to Dhaka by a pimp women. She promised me a work but sold me to a officer. I stayed with him for two months in a contractual period. After coming back from him; I got so much sickness in my body. I got so many problems in my uterus. He made intercourse with me including his all friends. And he did not give money properly. So it was a miserable time for me which cannot be explained in words. After that I came back to that brothel again where I have at least a place to stay and a community. (Personal Communication, March 16,2013)

The eviction of brothel can cause serious trouble for the sex workers. When government evicted brothel in the name of rehabilitation, they had no place to go. Because their family does not support them. They are stigmatized in their society. So they face this kinds of barriers in their public life.

JUSTIFICATION OF FINDINGS FROM MULTIDIMENSIONAL LENSES

Intersectional Hierarchy Related Barriers and Challenges Among Sex Workers

We are saying that intersectionality has different layers. In this layer we can also see the life experiences of sex workers. Because there is life cycle in Brothel such as: Chukri, Varatia, Sordarni, Mashi, Bariwali .The decision making power can be varied from their position. When they are chukri they have no decision making power. They are coerced to do sexual relation 10-12 times a day. Sometimes they have no time to sleep and eat. And they do not face economic empowerment under Sordarni. When they are free from Sordarni after spending 1 or two years they can choose their customers, they can decide the number of their customers. They are not able to send their children at schools. And they are always afraid of local mastans, local police who exploits them. Sometimes they wear masks to get relief from the police.

Occupational Hazard Leads to Social Change

Sex workers are facing serious occupational hazard. They are bound to do anything under the rule of dominant patriarchal society. So they are changing from their mind. They are from different background. They have different educational status, different demand and different lifestyle from any general women of the society. So it is tough for them to be same as general society. And their expectation is also different from the general people. I talked with several brothel based sex worker who were the victim of different forms of violence. Moreover perpetrators can be police, Goons, Pimp, Husband. All of them are the representative of patriarchal society. Almost all of the street based sex workers has been victim of rape by these people. Almost all of the brothel based sex workers has been victim of forced sex or 10-15 time sex a day. So it's a great burden and challenge for them. So their sexual identity has been changing day by day. After being oppressed by several men, they are not interested about them. Some of them told me that they did not feel any attraction for men. They only feel attraction for women. Because they believe that a woman can share everything with a women. So their sharing and caring relationship has been turned into a sexual relationship. And they also think that this relationship is not oppressive. So they are dreaming of a society where women can pass life with women. A few women want to get women as their life partner. The sexual identity of the sex worker has been changing day by day. I got that a few sex worker are mentally homosexual because of sharing and caring attitude of their women friend. Nodi claimed that we can connect with each other sorrow. Actually we are dealing with men for our professional behavior and for emotional attachment we are also attracted to their women friend. (Personal Communication, March 16, 2013). There we are seeing that a social change is occurring among sex workers. And their sexual identity is also changing because of the adverse situation. And they are also demanding the recognition of sex work profession. Because they think that they are proving service like another occupation .Why their profession will not be recognized .And they are doing different movement by incorporating with international organization. And they are dreaming of sex liberal society which is turning the society into a changing situation.

Sexual Objectification of Sex Worker

Most of the time sex workers are treated as sex object. And objectification of sex worker as sex object is the main reason of exploitation. They only treat women as a being with womb and vagina. So she will be ready to provide sex at any time, any places. Our society like to think the birth of a women is supplementary to a men. And her one and only duty is to provide services for men. And this service can be any type of services. And they are just treated as sexy beast that is bound to maintain the thrust of sex.

Patriarchy Controls Whole Life of Sex Worker

Patriarchy always has an invisible hand on the lifestyles of women. Patriarchy controls each and every spheres of women's life. Patriarchal institution control women's autonomy, women's mobility, women's reproductive capability, women's access to resources, women's productive or labor power, women's reproductive capability etc. And women who are living in brothel are in patriarchal control. The domination of patriarchy is different from place to place. They will not be able to take decision by themselves where sordarni (Madam), the leader who is maintaining brothel, she is also bearing patriarchal mentality to control and to exploit sex worker. Actually they are maintaining patriarchy by chain of command. Women of the brothel cannot go outside. Because they are stigmatized in society. So the society is also controlling their autonomy and mobility. And Bandhababu who is the symbol of dominant male is also controlling the reproductive ability of his women. And sometimes they also get damaged of their sexual organ which is most pathetic result of patriarchy.

Agency of Sex Worker

Sex worker cannot practice her agency. In each and every single thing she is bound to take permission of Madams and Sordarni (Madam). She is earning because she has beauty. She is selling her body. But in a long run Babu or Bandhababu(Ragular Customer) is getting benefitted. They are earning a lot. But they cannot practice their agency. They cannot send money to their family, their children are staying unfed, and they cannot save money. They have debt/bondage. They have no way to come out from this profession. Their life is bound with the chain of brothel. They are the victim of continuous rape by goons and continuous rape by police.

Recommendation

Women in the brothel are engaged in an illegal activity and they are regularly harassed. Though, running a brothel is also illegal, the owners of these brothels are never punished. The women who live in these brothels, though, are harassed and live in continual fear of eviction. The human rights of all sex workers are grossly violated and they do not have a voice in society. The voices that are heard are always against them and come from the mouths of people who regularly enjoy their services.

Recognition as Human Being

We are not treating them as human being. And we are stigmatizing them. They are treated as animal in our society. Their main aim is to be recognized in the eyes of society. Their life should be livable. They just want if authority want to stop this business they have to create alternative income generating activities. Otherwise they will be continuously deprived from the society.

Safer Working Condition and Respect From Society

Sex workers want safer working conditions and respect, not forced rescue by feminists, and their demands are no longer as easy to ignore as they used to be. Some of them do not want to come out from this profession. Rather they demand safe working environment. Because our society cannot stop this work. In the light of day they are criticizing the sex worker. But in night they are taking their service at night. The ex-president of Durjoy, Shanaz Begum told me that

We do not want to increase the number of sex worker. But we want the legalization of sex work. If society legalizes it, everyone can use their will to take it as a profession or not. But I feel if government legalizes the profession the trafficking will be decreased" (Personal Communication, February 16, 2013)

Creation of Alternative Earning Source

I have found this recommendation from several sex workers that the creation of alternative earning source is necessary. Otherwise it will be quiet impossible for any sex worker to leave this job. Most of them come to this profession unwillingly or forcefully. If society cannot create alternative money earning sources for them, they would not be able to stop the sex work. Sex workers are not vagabond. So it is necessary to stop all practice of vagabond laws in the name of rehabilitation of the sex worker. When government is giving rehabilitation facilities for them, government should create some space for the sex worker to live their life as independent. Otherwise they will feel that they are the burden of society. (FHI 360, 2014) They will lose their respect again and again. But I guess if the government cannot manage alternative money creating source, they will not be empowered and rest of the life they will live in miserable way.

Improvement of Human Rights Situation

United Nations declaration "Universal Human Rights Charter" should be enacted /implemented truly. Non-governmental organization, development agencies should come to ensure sex worker and their children basic rights and not to drop the project in middle. The sex workers are earning a lot of money, dressing up, eating whatever they wish to eat and sometimes they go out willingly but what is not visible is the constant fear among the sex workers of Bangladesh. (TDH, 2005) To solicit in the streets and to run a brothel is totally illegal. As a result the sex workers do not have any livelihood security and they are haunted by the fear of random arrest by the law enforcement agencies. The sex workers also feel that once their work identity is disclosed they will not get a proper burial. They feel that they should be treated like normal human beings and should have the right to a proper burial after their death.

Implementation of Responsible and Transparent Law Enforcement Agency

Law enforcement authority specially the behavior of police and attitude must have to change about sex worker. According to the law of Bangladesh, the profession of sex work is discouraged and there are laws that criminalize the sex workers. After the eviction many of them are usually engaged in street based sex work. The street based-sex workers can be arrested under Section-54 of the Metropolitan Act and also under Sections 74 and 76, which says that their movement was 'suspicious' or had a 'bad body language.' (Tahmina &Moral, 2004, pp 26-30). They cannot be arrested for being sex-workers. They are often physically and mentally harassed and abused only because they are into sex work. Sex workers are not treated equally in front of the law and they often do not get justice. The police coming on rounds often beat the sex workers or just pick them up and keep them in the lock ups. They need to bribe the law enforcing authorities to get out and if they are unable to pay, they go to jail for a couple of months. So these kinds of double standard law and manipulation according to law enforcing agency should be supervised and initiatives should be taken to overcome this kinds of exploitation

Establishment of Community Engagement and Motivation Program

Sex workers are not sex worker by themselves. They are the victim of patriarchal society. But our traditional and gender stereotyped society like to stigmatize them. They do not think that most of the women do not choose this profession willingly. Because they have got this idea from traditional patriarchal attitude. So community mobilization program is necessary. Here I want to mention an example. I went to Tangail brothel and to fulfill my personal curiosity I also went to SOS safe home which has been established for the children of sex worker. The children of this sex worker told that before establishing the safe home for children they were not well accepted by the society. But they are comparatively well accepted now .And they claim that they are also welcomed by the civil society member. And they think after giving motivation by different NGOs to society, the scenario has been changed. (Rozy, personal Communication,, March, 19,2013). But we know that NGOs cannot take initiative in a broader level. So the government steps can reduce these kinds of problem. And I guess this steps can reduce the stigmatization of society against them.

Incorporation of Mass Media

Mass media and informal communications can be selectively used at all levels of program readiness and development. They can promote different drama, movies to show the vulnerability against sex workers. And they can also play this drama by community people. Or they can arrange training in every area to reduce the stigmatization against sex workers.

Reviewing Policy and Effective Measure

Strict steps must be taken against pimps, traffickers and other agents related this work. Our law is just for the victim of violence who have been trafficked and forced to take this work as profession. (Rahman & Sultana 2012)But sate policy is technically ignoring the law enacting agency that are exploiting the law and using it. So strict steps should be taken against them.

Special Policy for the Up Gradation of Sex Workers

We know that government take various policies for the disadvantaged people. I suggest the sex worker children should be grown up as mainstream children. So they will be capable to adapt with the society. the children of sex worker. If government provides special facilities for children of sex workers, they will not be imposed to be child sex worker. They will not be bound to join this profession as their mother. After taking education they can be empowered. And that's why the allocation of national budget towards the up gradation of sex workers should be ensured to improve the livelihood standard of the sex worker and their children.

CONCLUSION

The objective of this research was twofold: To develop a clear understanding of barriers and challenges of sex worker in Tangail Brothel by allowing the women to frame their own needs. The study has built on previous research by analyzing secondary material as well as primary data collected through fieldwork. In terms of barriers and challenges sex worker continue to be subjected to varying degrees of violence, harassment, stigma and torture. Their suffering can be varied from place to place and forms of the suffering can be different. However the vulnerability is a common thing among sex workers. Moreover I noticed different vulnerabilities among them and they are extremely violated in their private and public sphere. Every patriarchal institution in our society is not treating them as human being rather they are treated as sexual object. They are victim of violence and torture from their private to public life. Sex workers want recognition from the society and from government. However there is debate about recognition of sex worker among civil society. So I guess there is a scope of further work about recognition of sex work.

REFERENCES

Sabet, M.D., & Ahmad, S. (2012). Legitimacy, Legality and Consent: Sex Workers and Their Children in Bangladesh. *Sex Workers and Their Children in Bangladesh: Addressing Risks and Vulnerabilities,* 1-8.

Tahmina, A. Q., & Moral, S. (2004). Sex-Workers in Bangladesh Livelihood: At What Price?. Society for Environment and Human Development (SEHD).

Terre des hommes Italia. (2005). *Brothel –based and Floating Sex Workers in Bangladesh Living Conditions and Socio Economic Status.* Dhaka: Terre des hommes Italia.

Sanger, W. W. (2013). *The History of Prostitution.* Harper & Brothers Publishers.

Lyman, J. (1964). The Metropolitan Police Act of 1829: An analysis of Certain Events Influencing The Passage and Character of the Metropolitan Police Act in England. *The Journal of Criminal Law, Criminology, and Police Science, 55*(1), 141–154. doi:10.2307/1140471

Hossain. (2004). *Commercial Sexual Behaviour and Risk Factors in Bangladesh: An Invesigation of Female sex Workers in Rajshahi City.* Higher Education Link Programme.

Fredrickson, B. L., & Roberts, T. A. (1997). Objectification theory: Toward understanding womens lived experience and mental health risks. *Psychology of Women Quarterly, 21*(2), 173–206. doi:10.1111/j.1471-6402.1997.tb00108.x

American Psychological Association, Task Force on the Sexualization of Girls. (2007). *Report of the APA Task Force on the Sexualization of Girls.* Washington, DC: American Psychological Association. Retrieved 15 December 2016, from https://www.apa.org/pi/women/programs/girls/report-full.pdf

McCall, L. (2005). The complexity of Intersectionality. *Signs (Chicago, Ill.), 30*(3), 1771–1800. doi:10.1086/426800

Bhasin, K. (1993). *What is Patriarchy?*. New Delhi: Kali for Women.

Rahman, M. M., & Sultana, F. B. U. (2012). Institutional Protection Mechanisms, Potentials of Mainstreaming and Readiness of the Society: Unveiling Struggles of Children of Sex Workers in Bangladesh. *Sex Workers and Their Children in Bangladesh: Addressing Risks and Vulnerabilities*, 181-201.

Binagwaho. (2010). *Developing human rights-based strategies to improve health among female sex workers in Rwanda.* Retrieved from http://www.ncbi.nlm.nih.gov/pubmed/21178192

Heissler, K. (2001). *Background Paper on Good Practices and Priorities to Combat Sexual Abuse and Exploitation of Children in Bangladesh.* Bangladesh: UNICEF.

James, J. (1978). *Juvenile Female Prostitution - Final Report.* Retrieved from https://www.ncjrs.gov/App/Publications/abstract.aspx?ID=78277

O'Neill, M. (2001). Community Safety, Rights and Recognition: Towards a Coordinated Prostitution Strategy?. *Community Safety Journal, 6*(1), 45-52. Retrieved from http://www.google.com.bd/url?sa=t&rct=j&q=article%20on%20sex%20worker.doc&source=web&cd=7&cad=rja&ved=0CEoQFjAG&url=http%3A%2F%2Fmyweb.dal.ca%2Fmgoodyea%2Ffiles%2Fuk%2FMaggie%2520Oneill%2520paper%2520Csj%2520article%25203.doc&ei=UztXUeHxEouMrgfQsYHIDg&usg=AFQjCNHkzcC_YekCvHuSETuYYDwPp93SGQ&bvm=bv.44442042,d.bmk]

Rahman, M. (2012). *Amader GolpobShishder Dekha Shishu Odihikar Poristhithi.* Save The Children.

Rahman, M. (2012). *State of Children in Bangladesh 2011: In the eyes of Children.* Save The Children.

Svedin, G. C., & Back, K. (1996). *Children who don't speak out About children who being used in child pornography.* Swedish Save The Children. Radda Barnen.

Thipthrope, E., & Ahmed, I. (2005). *There is Hope:An Action Based Research Children victims of Sexual Abuse and Explotation.* Aparajeyo-Bangladesh.

Chapter 13
Women's Commuting Environment in Public Buses in Dhaka City:
A Case of Men's Perspectives

Arunima Kishore Das
Western Sydney University, Australia

ABSTRACT

The constitution of Bangladesh aims to ensure a discrimination free world guaranteeing women equal access to political and public life. The ratification of CEDAW, adaptation of both MDG and SDG by the government also promote this goal. Dhaka requires an efficient transportation system to ensure the freedom of mobility for all. However, the public buses of Dhaka are insecure, unreliable, congested and unsafe. As a result, the women and children suffer the most while boarding a bus. They have to face both physical and emotional pain. This consequently restricts women's mobility rights. As men are responsible for creating a gender insensitive commuting environment inside public buses, their perceptions on the fact is to be explored. This chapter with the help of the researcher' research data (for Masters' thesis) from 2015-2016, highlights on men's perceptions of commuting environment women experience in public buses in Dhaka city. How these perceptions are shaped as an outcome of hegemonic masculinity is also analysed in this chapter using Connell's theory of hegemonic masculinity.

INTRODUCTION

A city transport system that can offer its residents a safe, affordable, quick, comfortable, reliable and sustainable access to their destinations (e.g.; jobs, education, recreation and such other needs) can be entitled as an effective one. Dhaka, the capital city of Bangladesh is one of the fastest growing megacities of the world. The currents population of the city is twelve million and is expected to grow around 20 million in 2020, transforming it into the third largest city (in terms of population) in the world (World Bank, 2007). This enormous growth has led to increasing demand for the public transportation system.

DOI: 10.4018/978-1-5225-3018-3.ch013

However, any experience of travelling on a public bus in Dhaka has never been a delightful experience for a woman. Buses as modes of public transport are considered as insecure, unreliable, congested and unsafe. To demonstrate the questionable situation of bus services, Hasnine (2011, p. 218) claims, "the environment of public transport in Dhaka City is characterized by traffic congestion and delays, inadequate traffic management, unaffordable and inaccessible public transport for majority of the people". Because of unsatisfactory bus services, inter-city travelling has become no less than a nightmare for the travellers of Dhaka city. Nevertheless, the women and children are the ones who suffer the most while boarding a bus. They have to go through both physical and emotional pains as a part of their everyday experience of commuting environment which hampers the mobility rights women are entitled with. As men are the one primary responsible (in form of both bus staffs and male commuters) for creating a gender insensitive commuting environment inside public uses, their perception of the fact is to be explored. As a result, this chapter intends to shed light on men's perceptions of commuting environment accessible to women inside public buses in Dhaka city.

The constitution of Bangladesh and its ratification of the Convention of the Elimination of all Forms of Discrimination Against women (CEDAW) offer women equal access to public spheres irrespective of their age, class, sex and religion. Article 27, 28 (1,2,3,4) and 29 (1) of the constitution of Bangladesh ensures free and equal access to women in public and social spheres (Mahtab 2012). CEDAW promotes a discrimination-free world for women guarantying their equal access in political and public life. Besides that, the Millennium Development Goal (MDG) goal 3 (promote gender equality and empower women) as well as recently adopted Sustainable Development Goal (SDG) goal 5 (achieve gender equality and empower all women and girls) both promote removing mobility constraints by ensuring safe and reliable transport system for women to ensure the mobility rights of women.

Dhaka's transport scenario has been deteriorating visibly under fast growing population over the last few years. Buses being the most easily accessible and cheapest means of transportation in the city, both male and female commuters[1] use it for travelling from one place to another. It is worth noting that the labour force participation and the percentage of female education is gradually increasing in Bangladesh. From 2002-03, only 10.3 million women participated in the labour force, by 2010 this figure reached to 17.2 million (Labor Force Survey 2010). The literacy rate of 15-24-year-old women is currently 78.86% (Bangladesh Planning Commission 2014). Therefore, economic and educational participation of women are considered as indicators of women's socio-economic empowerment. Hannan (2007) highlighted the need to have equal access to urban facilities (transportation, sanitation, water etc.) to ensure equality and empowerment of women. Employed women use buses to have a convenient and comfortable journey to their jobs. In addition, students of schools, colleges and universities travel from one corner of the city to the other in buses to attain a better quality of education. However, the nature of commuting offered by public buses for women today remains questionable. The commuting environment of buses is very often defined as unsafe, unreliable, congested and prone to incidents of sexual harassment. "Women bus riders have long endured groping and verbal abuse every day" (Rahman, 2010, p.18).

This study aims specifically to establish the link between gendered space and women-friendly commuting by shedding light on the perceptions of male bus commuters of Dhaka. The study endeavours to understand how common men perceive women's commuting experience in public buses in Dhaka by interviewing the male travellers, drivers and helpers of public buses of the Dhaka city. Analyzing scholars' views (eg; Connell 2005, Imtiaz 2014, Messerchmidt 1999) on hegemonic masculinity, this paper also aims to explain how male perceptions on commuting environment are encouraged and shaped by the ideology of hegemonic masculinity. In other words, this study is designed to have an analytical gaze at the social and cultural relations of urban life for individuals and communities from the critical perspective of gender, sexuality and feminist epistemology. Actually, this paper draws mainly on the researcher's most recent research data (for Masters' thesis) from 2015-2016 collected using a mixed method approach combining in-depth interviews, questionnaire surveys and participant observation. During this study, the researcher observed the passengers of public buses of three selected routes of the city (a. Mirpur 12-Asadgate-Sciencelab-New Market-Azimpur; b. Mirpur12-Farm gate-Shahbag-Motijhil and c. Mirpur 2-College Gate-Shyamoli-Dhanmondi-Mohammadpur-Sciencelab-Shahbag) for two months. In addition to that, six male commuters, two drivers, and a helper were sampled for in-depth interviews and survey questionnaires were filled up by 50 male commuters and 50 female commuters.

COMMUTING ENVIRONMENT IN BUSES: A TERRIFYING EXPERIENCE FOR FEMALE COMMUTERS OF DHAKA

Dhaka being the administrative, political, economic and social life of the country, it should accommodate an efficient transportation system. Buses can be a good example of such a transportation system that can provide services to every corner of the city for the people of all socio-economic standing. Mannan and Karim (2001) found that urban dwellers in greater Dhaka have the access to 4792 public buses as a vehicle in the fleet with the capacity of 249184 seats resulting in 70.1 buses with 3656.9 seats for per 100000 populations. In such circumstances, it becomes difficult for women commuters to avail the opportunity to get into a public bus and have a seat during office hours, starting at 9 am and ending at 5 pm. ''Often the bus is so crowded that it becomes impossible for older people or women or children to get a room inside the bus'' (Rahman & Nahrin, 2012, p.99). All these odds of availing the facility of buses hamper the mobility rights of women hindering their economic empowerment.

In Dhaka, transport related difficulties faced by both working women and female students are very apparent. Recent evidences (Rahman 2010; Rahman & Nahrin 2012; Zohir 2003) strengthen this argument by suggesting that women are facing multiple problems (e.g.; unwanted touch, sexual comments, limited sitting arrangements etc.) in the current transport environment in Dhaka. Shefali (2000) captured the gender dimension of DUTP (Dhaka Urban Transport Project) showing the transport services provided currently by the public and private buses in Dhaka city are insecure, unreliable, congested and unsafe, in other words not gender friendly for women. Rahman and Nahrin (2012) in a quantitative study of 175 bus passengers explored the dimensions of difficulties faced by the bus commuters in the city. For example, several complications like long waiting cues, low frequency of buses, overcrowded buses, shortage of seats, and uncomfortable environments inside the bus, poor standard of bus quality along with a special focus on the sexual harassment and ill-treatment of bus staffs towards women have been highlighted in the study.

While inadequate transport services adversely affect everybody of the city, women commuters face particular mobility constraints. The transport services currently provided by bus are insecure and unsafe for women. (Rahman, 2010, p.18)

As most passengers of the bus are male and the sitting arrangements remain mainly male centered, it becomes hard for the female commuters to compete with men to have a seat. As a result, in most public buses during office hours, we see the helpers showing their apathy to female passengers saying there is no female seat available. Zohir (2003) while analysing Dhaka Urban Transport Project indentified the lack of information about the commuting environment, overcrowding, lack of security, bad behaviours of drivers and conductors, long wait and long lines, unfriendly fare and ticketing systems as the main concerns of female bus commuters of the city. Shefali (2000, p.1) summarised such problems as:

The public and private buses running in Bangladesh at present offer insecure, unreliable or unsafe transport services. They remain overcrowded. Women can hardly compete with men for the limited space on the buses. This occurs mainly because of the cultural background in Bangladesh. Bus operators are indifferent about the specific needs of women which are necessary for making their journeys more comfortable and secure.

Some unique difficulties harass women commuters while boarding public transports. In the first place, a woman finds it really hard to buy tickets competing with men in an gender insensitive ticketing system. Secondly, after cutting a ticket it is even more difficult to board a bus, especially during office hours. During office hours, men may somehow manage to grab the door handle and may jump inside whereas it is simply impossible for women to attempt such a move. In addition to that, they face unwelcoming behaviour from bus drivers and bus conductors. 'They just cannot chase after the bus on its run while keeping an eye out for oncoming traffic, squeeze past passengers hanging halfway at the door and risk groping from some uncouth men' (Masani 2016). Even if they somehow manage to step into the bus, there awaits a completely gender insensitive commuting environment for them. While grabbing seats women are to face rude behaviour from men who occupy seats reserved for women. In addition, sexual harassments that include groping, unwanted touch, sexual comments, staring all appear every now and then. During the occurrences of such incidents, many of the passengers, in fact, talk against women holding them guilty for their dress up and even presence inside the bus. All these indicate that the environment in a bus does not actually provide a gender-sensitive vibe.

COMMUTING ENVIRONMENT INSIDE THE BUSES FROM MEN'S VIEWPOINTS

Visibility of Female Commuters

Dhaka offers accommodation to almost 12 Million people. Dhaka's "proportion of road surface to the built-up area is hardly 7% as against 25% recommended for a good city" (Rabbani & Mahmud 2012, p. 1). As a consequence of this, lately, Dhaka's transport scenario has been deteriorating visibly. Nevertheless, the increasing population of the city is creating huge pressure on the transportation system. "Among the public transport modes available in Dhaka City, the bus is the cheapest, which also provides the highest passenger km travel of the city" (STP, 2005). The table provided below strengthen this argument:

The table demonstrates the popularity of buses as a mode of transport among the middle and lower class folks of the Dhaka city. As a result, it is clear from the table that most of the working women as well students who generally earn less than 4999 USD prefer the bus to travel long distances.

However, in spite of being a cheaper mode of transport, because of the hazardous environment a woman has to go through during bus travel; most women prefer using rickshaw and non-motorized transports. This is because they believe in non-motorized transports like rickshaws, they will not come in contact with male commuters. According to Mannan and Kabir (2001, p. 6), "after pedestrians, the

Table 1. Mode choice by income category in greater Dhaka (BDT = Bangladeshi Taka)

Average household income (BDT/month)	Rickshaw (%)	Taxi (%)	Bus (%)	Auto-tempo (%)	Car (%)	Motor-cycle (%)	Bicycle (%)	Water Transport (%)
<1,500	23.6	0.9	43.5	4.4	0.0	0.0	5.1	22.6
1,500-1,999	26.4	1.2	38.6	5.5	1.5	0.6	5.8	20.4
2,000-2,999	33.0	1.8	36.3	5.2	1.6	0.5	5.0	16.7
3,000-4,999	40.9	1.4	39.3	4.8	0.7	2.1	3.0	7.9
5,000-9,999	52.0	2.8	28.1	4.7	2.5	3.6	1.7	4.6
10,000-29,999	57.6	4.6	16.8	2.8	9.9	5.2	0.8	2.4
>29,999	40.9	7.0	7.0	1.0	39.1	4.2	0.2	0.7

- 1 USD = 55 BDT

(Mannan and Kabir, 2001, p.7)

rickshaw is the second largest mode of transport in Dhaka. However, some 40% of loaded rickshaws are used either by women, children or people with goods".

The above data is reinforced also by the perceptions of general bus travellers revealed from the researcher's research data from the three selective routes of Dhaka city. 60% Men responded seeing less than 20% women commuters in public buses. And, the perceptions of most of the female commuters (58%) also support them. On an average, women spend fewer hours in bus travels each day. Only 20% women admitted that they spend more than 2 hours on buses, 32% men admitted spending more than 2 hours in buses. 8% men argued that they had to spend more than 3 hours in buses whereas only 2% women said they travel more than 3 hours in buses each day

When the male respondents were asked in the in-depth interview whether the visibility of female respondents are increasing or not, most of them (5 among the six interviewees) believed the number is on rise. They identified the main reason as the increase of population.

The population of the country is rising and that is why I think the number of women boarding on the bus is showing a gradual rise. (Ramzan, a 19 years old bus conductor)

Unlike Ramzan the respondents who were educated to a certain level added the significant upturn in women's work force participation along with population increase as the primary causes behind women's visibility.

The population rate is undoubtedly growing. Besides, women are adamant to be self-dependant now-a-days and work hand in hand with men in different sectors. As a result, we now see a lot of women boarding in buses in comparison to last couple of years. (Aminur Rahman, a 20 years old student)

Again there are some respondents as well who are found conscious of the fact that the underdeveloped infrastructure and conservative behavioural pattern are somehow affecting women's mobility choices. According to Sarowar (a 25-year-old student):

Figure 1. Respondents (both male and female) response to the gradual increase of female commuters in buses

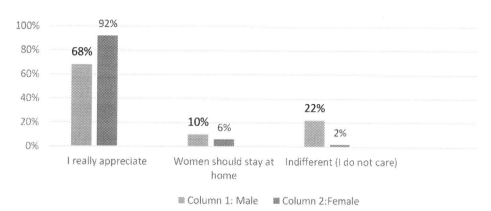

The number of female commuters is showing a positive growth. However, it is not increasing at a rate it should have been. It is because of the infrastructural deterioration as well as our conservative outlook of the society towards women's mobility.

When questions about how the respondents feel about women's increasing access to public buses were asked in survey questionnaires, most of the male respondents (both male and female) argued that they really appreciate it.

How Do You Perceive the Gradual Increase of the Number of Women Commuters in Public Buses?

This bar graph demonstrates a comparison between men and women commuters' response towards increasing number of women boarding the buses. Though 68% of male respondents appreciated women's gradual increase in bus travel, it is relatively low in comparison to female respondents (92%) who made the same choice. During the in-depth interview, it was admitted by most of the respondents that the female commuters are mainly employed women and students. The outcome of participant observation also supports this argument. Another interesting finding of this study is that 22% male were totally indifferent to the fact of women's presence in public buses. They felt that they should not be bothered with women's commuting concerns in public buses. Again a few numbers of male (10%) were in favour of keeping women confined within the household. When one of them was approached with an in-depth interview, he suggested:

Women should stay at home. Even if they need to come out, they should be under a veil. Allah has created men for doing outside work and household chores are women's responsibilities and maintaining purdah is mandatory according to our religion. (Delowar Hossain, a 45-year-old respondent)

Actually, this perception of this respondent can be explained by relating it with the concept of hegemonic masculinity's thirst of power. The power lies in the central position in conceptualizing hegemonic masculinity. According to Connell (1987, p. 179):

Understanding of hegemonic masculinity as a concept depends on the question of how particular groups of men inhabit power and wealth and how social relations are reproduced and legitimized by them to generate their domination.

Hegemonic masculinity as a concept has a special bonding with masculinity crisis. It is owing to the fact that the men fighting in favor of hegemonic masculinity consider it to be a defeat to their masculinity if women deny accepting the conventional gender norms that ask women to be busy with household chores. Actually, the concept of hegemonic masculinity always opposes women's empowerment to keep women in the lower position of the power hierarchy. It always encourages confining women within the four walls of their house so that male supremacy of power can sustain. This is why, men exercising hegemonic masculinity face a certain kind of masculinity crisis seeing women's success and women's empowerment (Imtiaz 2014, Messerchmidt 1999). As a result, men like Delowar Hossain (who support hegemonic masculinity), are sceptical about women's free movement in buses and try to control women's mobility by keeping them inside veil.

Reserved Seats Opportunity for Women

It is really hard for a woman to board an overcrowded bus, even harder is to get a seat. As most passengers of buses are male and the sitting arrangements remain mainly male centered, it becomes hard for the female commuters to access seats inside the bus. The in-depth interview data of the research also highlighted the fact:

During office hours and in the evening, it is especially tough for women to grab a seat because the buses generally get overcrowded from the first stoppage. Sometimes the male leaves the seats for women. Nevertheless, it varies from person to person. (Abul Kashem, a 28 years old respondent)

Bangladesh Road and Transport Authority in 2008 with the aim of creating a gender friendly commuting environment initiated a policy that ensured 9 seats reserved in public buses women and disabled. Whether or not this rule is followed by the buses were asked to the respondents in this study. The result showed tremendous difference between the perceptions of male and female respondents.

Though both the male and female respondents were selected from three specific bus routes, their perceptions on the availability of reserved seats inside the bus seem different. Whereas most of the women (52%) believed the buses do not have any reserved seats only 15% men agreed with them. This perception actually reflects the apathy of the male commuters regarding the inconvenience female passengers have to face.

Though the women have the rights to access reserved seats, many a time they fail to enjoy this right. The researcher's Master's research indicated that even male commuters notice violation of this mobility rights of women. 46% of the male respondents argued that most of the time these seats are availed by women only. Approximately one-third of the total respondents (34% women and 30% male) believed that the reserved seats are never occupied by women. So, one thing is pretty clear from this data that there are certain problems faced by a woman for availing a reserved seat. Naznin (2015) identified the same problem "some time they sit on the women's reserved seat without any hesitation. Some women raise their voice and some remain quiet". A better understanding of the situation has been revealed from the research data when the male commuters are asked if they have ever occupied a reserved seat. 24%

Figure 2. Availability of reserved seats in public buses

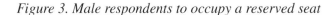

male commuters admitted that they always take possession of reserved seats and 60% argued that they sometimes grab those seats.

The inadequate number of reserved seats opportunities give birth to disputes among the commuters. In most cases, when a male commuter occupies a reserved seat, he refuses to leave it even when a female commuter requests him. This leads to unnecessary quarrels and arguments. This is why, this research showed that 48% women commuters agreed that the men would quarrel with them if requested to leave the reserved seats.

Figure 3. Male respondents to occupy a reserved seat

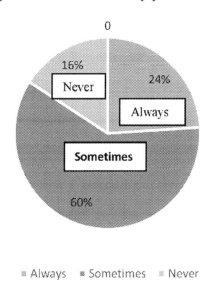

Many a time, male passengers sit on the reserved seats even though there are empty seats for them to sit. They promise to leave the reserved seat as soon as women passenger gets in but once a woman passenger gets on the bus they start a verbal dispute with that woman. This can be connected with Sharmin's (2014) argument,

Moreover, male passengers often occupy these nine reserved seats in the city transport. When they are asked to empty the seats by women passengers, they verbally humiliate the ladies. This kind of humiliation happens even when women try to occupy seats other than the reserved ones.

The problem of availing reserved seats remains only the headache of women. The male commuters are not really interested to be bothered about it. Hence, the research data showed that though all of the respondents agreed on the need to increase the seat numbers, some people do not even know the actual number of reserved seats a bus must have.

Buses must increase the number of reserved seats. Only six reserved seats for women and disabled are not enough. (Sarowar, a 25 years old respondent)

Moreover, a good number of male respondents participated in questionnaire surveys again denied the need for reserved seats. Approximately one-third of total male respondents (16% yes and 18% strongly agree, total 34%) voted against reserved seats opportunities.

When approached for in-depth interview one of them clearly uttered:

Women can also avail regular seats. It is not like they do not have the right to sit there. We must not forget about the hassles of male commuters also. And the number of female commuters, for whom the seats

Figure 4. Male commuters' reaction when asked to leave the reserved seats

Figure 5. View of male respondents on reducing reserved seats for women

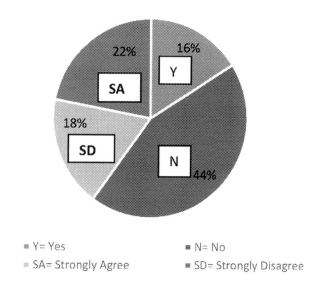

were reserved are relatively low. So, instead of just increasing reserved seats I think the total number of seats should be increased (Sultan Mahmud, a 24 years old respondent)

The aggression of hegemonic masculine attributes that wants to create mobility constraint for women to minimise their empowerment exercise is reflected from this comment of this respondent. Actually, this passenger wanted to gain masculine privilege by using masculinity as a gender capital which can be further connected with Huppatz and Goodwin's (2013) description of Bourdieu's capital theory. Huppatz and Goodwin (2013) used the concept of Capital by Bourdieu and modified it to form gender capital in order to explore how male, masculine and feminine embodiments can operate as capitals which may be accumulated and transacted, perpetuating horizontal gender segregation in the workforce but also vertical segregation within occupations in the context of Australia. In the same way, Sultan wanted to have the seat number increased using masculinity or male bodily difference as a capital to attain masculine privilege.

Again, there is also a respondent who thinks out of the box. He was not only sympathetic about the limitations of reserved seats but also thought about the location of those seats.

Most of the buses provide reserved seats that are located on engine covers. Because of the high temperatures of the running bus, it is really uncomfortable for women passengers to sit on them. (Sarowar, a 25-year-old respondent)

This type of ideology is a clear demonstration of masculine attributes that are far from the characteristics of hegemonic masculinities that try to control women's mobility instead of encouraging mobility options. Connell (2005) while showing a more clarified and modified model of hegemonic masculinity, encouraged the majority of people to practice the characteristics that go against hegemonic masculine attributes. He believed this is the only way to get rid of the negative impacts created by traditional hegemonic masculine attributes. In relation to his argument, it may be said that if most people inside the buses hold the thought like Sarwoar, the miseries of women travellers caused by insensitive hegemonic masculine practices of many would be minimised to a great extent.

Drivers and Helpers' Behaviour Towards Female Passengers

The unfriendly behaviour of the bus staffs is a concern for many scholars working on women's mobility constraint. Rahman (2010, p.19) explained the fact as:

Neither the driver nor the conductor makes an attempt to make them available for women. Moreover, often the conductor announces 'no seats for women are available' to avoid women passengers. The conductors are often reluctant to give changes to the women while purchasing tickets.

Many a time especially during peak hours the bus drivers and conductors do not allow the female passengers to get in even if some seats are available. They consider that it is better not to accommodate women inside bus because they are slow movers, they would create a chaos if someone slightly touches them. Some buses even deny to sale tickets to women during some busy hours of the day. Some respondents during in-depth interview even justified this fact:

The women are basically slow movers so sometimes the bus drivers and helpers do not prefer to stop buses for women. (Sarowar, 25 years old respondent)

If women stand in doors in an overcrowded bus, it is problematic so the drivers avoid having female passengers. (Abul Kashem, aged 25)

Both the arguments project a gender stereotype norm which is perceived true in our society where a false impression of 'bodily difference' between men and women is emphasized. Huppatz and Goodwin's (2013, p.300) embodiment of specific gender stereotype theorization shows that men is using maleness or masculinity as a 'gender capital'. This can again be connected with Imtiaz (2014, p.181) portrayal of hegemonic masculinities' characteristics. By using this specific form of gender capital some people without even being reflexive are encouraging a hegemonic masculine practice that imposes restrictions on women's mobility.

Many men were able to address this gender-insensitive behaviour offered by drivers and helpers to some extent. When the respondents were approached though survey questionnaires to share their opinions on the attitude of the drivers and helpers, majority of respondents (40% men and 44% women) agreed that they provide a hostile attitude. Again a good proportion of women (24%+26%=50%) believed the helpers and drivers' attitude is devoid of any special attention to women's specific mobility needs. Male respondents' inattentiveness to certain issues of drivers and helpers' attitude is also unveiled in this study because whereas only 6% women considered bus drivers and helpers friendly 36% male considered them to be friendly.

Although, the fact that the female commuters often get physically humiliated by conductors while boarding are addressed by a number of men during in-depth interviews. When a driver and a conduc-

Figure 6. Respondents' (both male and female) standpoint of the attitude of bus staffs to women

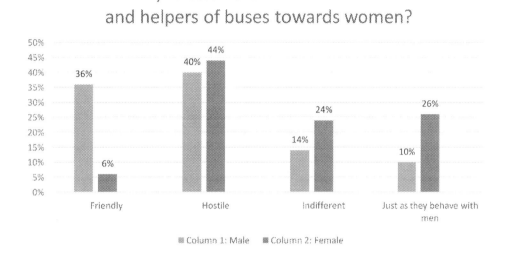

tor was asked about the fact of unfriendly behaviors by male commuters, they simply denied the fact. Rather they argued they are really friendly and helpful. They even tried to justify their indecent actions by saying that they make sure none of the women passengers fell off.

As the buses collect passengers stopping every now and then in the middle of the road while on the go, it is highly possible that a woman can slip during boarding. To prevent such an accident, we the conductors and helpers hold women passengers. (Ramzan, a 19 years old Helper)

Whilst participant observation data suggest that conductors and other passengers intentionally humiliate female commuters and justify themselves by saying they are only protecting them, some helpers are again found complaining directly against women travellers:

Women in the morning are so enthusiastic to get inside they just push me. I cannot stop them even if I want to. (Ramzan a helper, aged 19)

This declaration of Ramzan is again a clear projection of how hegemonic masculinity work silently. Being less educated Ramzan is not even reflexive about the fact that subconsciously he also nurtures an urge to restrict women's mobility. The feeling that he got pushed by women who are thought to be physically vulnerable (again using the bodily difference as gender capital) created a feeling of crisis in the masculinity for him.

Women-Only Bus Services

Women in Dhaka city face certain hurdles while travelling by buses. This can be reduced to some extent if women-only bus service is offered:

Women face difficulties like sexual harassment, 'misbehave of conductor/driver', 'problems of getting in (boarding) and off (alighting) the bus', 'overcrowded and no seat is available', and 'long waiting time', etc. 'Women only bus' service could tackle almost all the above mentioned problems (Rahman, 2010, p. 19).

Women only bus services, an initiative of BRTA, fail to draw attention of male commuters. Most of them while interviewed for the study, acknowledged that they have a relatively low knowledge about the presence of women only bus services. Nevertheless, almost all of them (5 among the six male respondents) agreed on the necessity of introducing some new buses. Only one respondent was of the opinion that it will not be beneficial in present condition:

If some more women-only buses are introduced, BRTA will have to face a financial loss because of the limited number of female commuters. Rather the development of infrastructure, as well as inclusion of some more seats in normal buses, would do the trick for now. (Aminur Rahman, aged 24)

Again, an interesting outcome was the male respondents' abhorrence towards this bus services. 36% male believed that if women have the opportunity to board on women-only bus services they should reject boarding on public buses.

This is again a clear indication of hegemonic masculine practice. The number of women-only buses is relatively low and inadequate to meet the demand of growing female commuters. However, by uttering the need to restrict their mobility by using other public buses, the male respondents are indirectly encouraging hegemonic masculinity that offers a mobility constraint for women.

Sexual Harassments: Occurrences and Responses

Recent evidences show that gender based violence incidents have taken a serious turn in Bangladesh. A report of BRAC (the largest NGO, according to NGO Advisor) demonstrated that, between 2014 and 2015, the incidents of violence against women in Bangladesh increased by 74% (Hossain, 2016, p.1). As a result a horrifying experience that almost every woman boarding on public buses has to go through is sexual harassment. Sexual Harassment in buses starts from the very beginning of getting into a crowded bus by both helpers and passengers. Even inside the bus, a woman has to experience staring, unwanted touches, sexual comments, groping. This study also reveals that whereas no men have ever experienced sexual harassment inside a bus, almost 40% women acknowledged suffering from such incidents. Gruber (1992, p.452) claims that 'sexual harassment falls into three distinct forms: remarks, requests, and nonverbal displays'. However, the male folks of the society many a time fail to identify these three distinct forms of sexual harassment. This is why this study showed that whereas 56% women agreed on witnessing incidents of sexual harassment at some point inside buses, only 28% men did so.

An important explanation of such unawareness of occurring sexual harassment may be because most of the commuters see sexual harassment as nothing serious. Sometimes they even feel that women folks are just over-reacting.

It is really common to face difficulty while boarding on an over-crowded bus. It is nothing like people intentionally push female travellers. Nevertheless, there might be some difference. (Abul Kashem, an in-depth interview participant; aged 28)

Figure 7. Perceptions of men on the argument "Women should not board public buses because they have women-only buses"

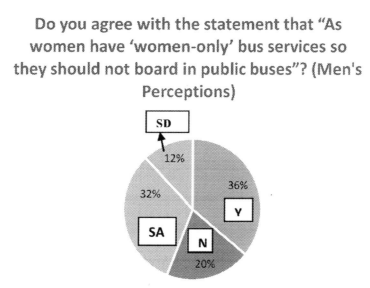

Figure 8 demonstrated that 72% of male commuters denied of ever witnessing any sexual harassment incidents. When approached a driver to have a further discussion on this matter, he argued:

I do not know about other buses but in my bus, we never detected any occurrences of sexual harassment because we strongly protest against the perpetrators. (Delowar Hossain, a 45-year-old bus driver.

Figure 8. Male and female respondents' proportion of witnessing incident of sexual harassment in buses

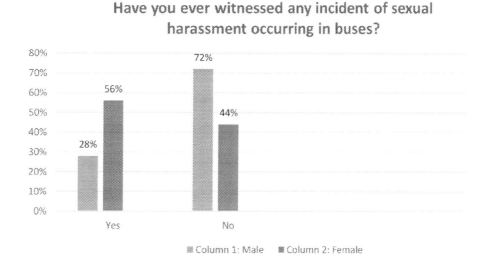

Figure 9. Types of sexual harassments identified (both male and female respondents' perceptions)

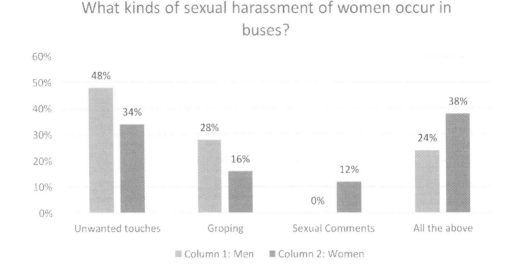

It is not like Delowar Hossain is an exception. In fact, both the two drivers and a helper participated in the in-depth interview failed to acknowledge the occurrences of sexual harassments to some extents. Ramzan, a 19 years old helper of Bihongo bus argued:

We behave very gently with the female commuters. It is really uncommon in our bus to detect any types of sexual harassments. However, some vicious and cunning men might do so in an overcrowded bus. But the numbers are relatively low.

The participants were asked to identify the forms of sexual harassment in survey questionnaires. Just beyond one-third of the total female respondents identified all these four types of sexual abuse on women whereas only 24% men could identify all the four forms.

Approximately 16% participants of survey questionnaire admitted being involved as perpetrators in sexual harassment incidents.

When participants of the in-depth interview were asked to shed light on the reasons behind these sexual harassments, a variety of responses were suggested. But most of them believed the cunning and vicious perpetrators involve in sexual harassments because they find it enjoyable.

Some people try to molest women commuters in an overcrowded bus. They look for chances to touch women's sensitive body parts, stare at them and even sometimes press themselves against standing women commuters. They do it just out of fun. (Md. Aminur Rahman, a 24 years old student)

The number of sexual harassment incidents can be reduced if they receive a strong protest from both victims as well as general passengers. Nevertheless, the perpetrators of sexual harassments sometimes are not at all protested rather receives support from other passengers. When the participants of survey questionnaires were asked how they themselves responded during occurrences of sexual harassments, only 48% male passengers voted to protest whereas 62% female passengers said they would protest. On

Figure 10. Male respondents acting as perpetrators of sexual harassment

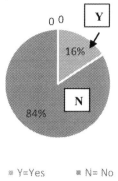

the contrary, the percentage of both men and women who preferred to stay quiet are the same (18%men and 18% women).

However, during the in-depth interview, all of the male respondents argued that they take an opposing stand against the male perpetrators and protest in favour of female commuters. Even the ones who earlier denied of having witnessed any particular incident of sexual harassment also uttered that they would protest if any incident of sexual harassment happens in front of them. However, the researcher's observation findings go against this. If women complain of sexual abuse, they get offensive remarks, like

Why does the daughter of a millionaire not use her own car?

If you feel bad, why do you travel by public transport?

Figure 11 even depicts that a good number of men, 16% of them, also preferred to be in the side of the perpetrators. These biases towards perpetrators can be easily understood because many of the in-depth interview participants blame women for incidents of sexual harassments. They believe the gesture, posture and appearance of female commuters are provocative.

Men are mostly responsible for sexual Harassment of women, but women are also responsible to a certain extent. They nowadays prefer wearing provocative dresses so men get attracted….. (Md. Rony, a 25 years old driver)

This philosophy of again supported by survey questionnaire data where 10% men answered in positive and another 10% strongly agreed that women themselves are responsible for their sexual harassment.

Imtiaz (2014) elaborated Connell's conceptualization of hegemonic masculinity by linking it with hegemonic masculinity in crisis theory. He portrayed how sexual harassment is used as a tool by certain agents of hegemonic masculinity to control women's mobility. This would, in the long run, help hegemonic masculinity to sustain its dominating power over the women folks in the long run. Hence, this ideology of blaming women for sexual harassments or trying to suppress women's voice to protest against sexual offenses is a clear demonstration of the aggression of hegemonic masculinity.

Figure 11. Respondents' (both male and female) way of reacting during sexual harassment incidents

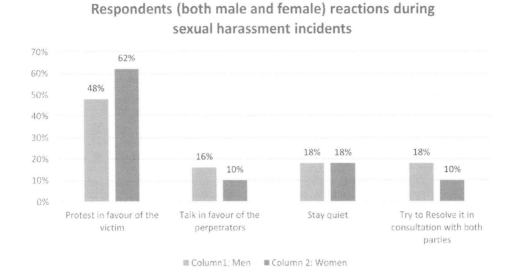

Men Trying to Define the Overall Commuting Environment

When men were asked to define the overall commuting environment of public buses, most of the respondents replied it to be hostile. Almost 40% men argued it is in a word hostile for female commuters. Again another 28% of them believed the environment to be gender friendly and 16% thought the environment is just balanced.

This type of mixed response is again demonstrated in the in-depth interview findings. Most of the travellers feel that the overall commuting environment is fairly all right. Sometimes problems and chaos might occur among the male and female commuters and bus staffs but this is nothing serious.

The environment in public buses I believe is roughly fine (Md Aminur, a 24 years old respondent)

We offer a very friendly commuting environment in my bus (Falgun). Sometimes problems might occur, it is normal, nothing serious. I have never detected any kind of sexual harassments in my bus (Md Rony, a 25 years old driver)

The commuting environment inside buses is not friendly for anyone, let alone for women and children. The women are basically slow in movements so the bus staffs rudely behave with them. Sexual harassments also occur.........Our attitude and underdeveloped infrastructure continue to this insensitive commuting environment. (Sarowar, a 24-year-old respondent)

This outlook of the male commuters directly or indirectly encourages hegemonic masculine practice. As no special attention is provided to women's specific gender needs inside of a bus, the problem of women's mobility concern would be reinforced offering hegemonic masculine attributes more power over women.

Figure 12. Men's response to the fact that "women themselves are responsible for sexual harassment"

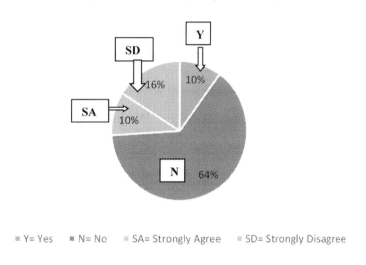

Figure 13. Men's perception of the overallcommuting environment in public buses

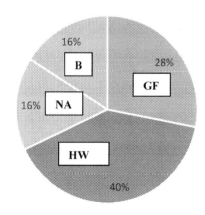

MALE PERCEPTIONS VIOLATING WOMEN'S MOBILITY RIGHTS: AN OUTCOME OF HEGEMONIC MASCULINE PRACTICE

Availability of gender sensitive atmosphere in a public bus is mandatory to ensure freedom of mobility for women. UN Women (2012) identified this need, 'safe public transit for women and girls must be based on the recognition of women's and girls' distinct roles, needs and experiences'. However, enactment of hegemonic masculine attributes (shaped by male perceptions) in public buses of the city deteriorates the condition of public buses in terms of a friendly commuting environment violating overall mobility rights of women.

Unavailability of reserved seats opportunities, unfriendly behaviour of bus staffs, prevalence of sexual harassments, non-cooperative nature of mass commuters during sexual harassment incidents, incomplete and gender biased perceptions of men about overall commuting environment of buses, ignorance of men about the special needs of women in buses are all indicators of how public transports (eg; buses) restrict women's mobility rights. How men's perceptions of commuting environment after being shaped by hegemonic masculine practices reinforce a gender insensitive environment in buses can be explained from the study findings stated above.

The survey questionnaire data revealed that only two-third (68%) of the male commuters said that they really appreciate the increase in women's participation in public buses. The rest one-third male respondents who are not really positive about women's bus travel is undoubtedly a serious threat to gender-sensitive commuting environment that instigate to restrict women's mobility.

Imtiaz (2009, p.15) while highlighting the main features of hegemonic masculinity depicted how particular groups of men occupy power and wealth and create a hierarchical social relation system in order to generate and sustain their dominance over others. As a result, many times it is seen that a specific group of men try to suppress another group by exercising certain stereotypical norms. Introducing mobility constraint on women in the name of religious practice can be a good example of such. It is again true for the male participants of this study. Approximately 10% of the male respondents hold the thought that women should stay at home and should not come outside of the four walls of their houses, let alone board on public buses. The findings of the in-depth interview again opened a new window to explore how again mobility constraint of women is strengthened by imposing the decision of veil on them by some men. According to Sultan Mahmud, a 24 years old participant of in-depth interview

Women should not go against Islamic tradition of maintaining veil. If they maintain purdah, the incidents of sexual harassment would reduce

In this way, a gender stereotypical norm imposed on women to make sure that women's mobility is restricted and so they get limited opportunity to participate in social lives. Because women's less participation ensures sustainability of hegemonic masculine power practice over women.

Hegemonic masculinity favours men only and overlooks the importance of women's special needs and experiences. As a result survey questionnaire data revealed the fact that a good number of men were against the reserved seats options. 16% men replied positively that they want to omit reserved seats and another 18% also strongly agreed on the fact. One driver when approached with in-depth interview argued:

Women do need reserved seats but I would say it is better if instead of increasing the number of reserved seats, we increase the total number of seats because most of our passengers are men. (Delowar Hossain, a 45 years old participant in interview)

The bus staff's (driver and helper) unwelcoming behaviour towards women commuters is another indicator of gender-insensitive commuting environment women face. Very often the drivers and helpers are found showing apathy to let female commuters get in. From observation, it is seen that helpers often shout out:

Mohila seat nai (There is no seat for women)

Even many a times the bus conductors even deny taking student fare from the female commuters saying:

We will not accept student fare from girls; only boys will be counted as students

This type of reactions from bus staffs clearly indicates how hegemonic masculine beliefs sustain in the viewpoints of mass people of our country where they are not even ready to count women as students, let alone provide them with the opportunities of enjoying equal rights (e.g; mobility rights) to be empowered.

When the bus staffs were asked about how they perceive the commuting environment, all the drivers and helpers replied that they offer a very comfortable setting to the women. It is because most of the bus staffs and even a few commuters see appearance of sexual harassment in buses as a very ordinary matter. These perceptions reflect the fact that sometimes men just do not know that they themselves are by their actions and perceptions are reinforcing hegemonic masculinity that disadvantages women. This is again another characteristic of hegemonic masculinity as argued by Imtiaz (2014, p. 181).

A number of scholars strongly supported the argument that sexual harassment has a strong bonding with the aim to restrict women to take part in the power practice. Sexual harassment occurring in public buses creates a fear of terror among the mass women. As a result, they fear to enter public domain and their mobility and freedom get restricted. In the long run, this results in women being left out of the power structure (Valentine 1989, Imtiaz 2014 and Harrison 2012). As an outcome of which men get exclusive access to a hierarchy of power and hegemonic masculinity is re-established. This is also true for this specific study. The conventional gender norm establishes a fixed gender role for men and women where women are portrayed in domestic realm of the home and family, maintaining their dependence on men. But when women try to break this gender norm and talk about equality, the men folks get confused. Women's gradual increase in visibility in public transportation has increased their chances of being an active participant in social development. As a result, the male-dominant power structure has got shaken. As there is a lack of measures like awareness programs or policies to encourage men to accept this change, men consider opposing women's advancement is the ultimate way to sustain male rule. As a result, they adopt the heinous activity of sexual harassment. In this study, also 16% male commuters proudly accepted that they participated in sexual harassments as perpetrators

The conservative Bangladeshi society consider women (the victim) responsible for sexual harassment. Instead of taking strong actions against incidents of sexual harassment, they prefer imposing mobility constraint on women. Valentine (1989) explored how violence against women serves the purpose of maintaining a gender hierarchy. Accordingly, spatial expression of patriarchy saying violence against women in public space results in the inability of women to enjoy independence and freedom. This consequently allows men to appropriate this space by creating a vicious cycle of fear that ensures patriarchy's power exercise over women. This power exercise of men over women is termed as hegemonic masculinity by Connell (2005). Some men in order to control women and to ensure hegemonic power exercise over women support perpetrators of sexual harassment holding women themselves responsible for it (Imtiaz 2014, p.181). This is true for this study where we find 20% male participants of survey questionnaire (10% said yes and 10% said that they strongly agree with the fact) blamed women for sexual harassments and again 16% told that they would support the perpetrator. A better understanding of such view is revealed in the in-depth interviews where a number of respondents were found believing that women's attitudes, dressing sense are causing problems for women.

I do not think only men are responsible for a bad environment inside the bus. Women's behaviour, their gesture, posture and how they dress up nowadays also contribute to it.

This study also revealed how some women nurture hegemonic masculine ideologies by considering women themselves responsible for sexual harassment (4% said yes and 4% said they strongly agree with the fact). This in the long run contribute to the restriction of mobility rights of the women.

CONCLUSION

A gender sensitive atmosphere in a public bus is a prerequisite to ensure the mobility rights of women. Dhaka the capital of the country fails to offer a safe and reliable transportation experience to most of the women commuters of the city. However, lack of reserved seats opportunities, unfriendly behaviour of bus staffs and male commuters, occurrences of sexual harassments, men showing indifference to the special needs of women in buses all characterizes the present gender insensitive commuting environment a woman experiences in public buses. Man, are the one to be blamed for the prevalence of such a gender insensitive commuting environment. This is why, how the commuting environment inside public buses is perceived by the mass male commuters play an important role to the gender sensitivity level of the commuting environment. Hence, this chapter aims to explore men's perceptions of different aspects of women's mobility concerns, especially in relation to boarding public buses. In doing so, the chapter identified the problems a woman commuter faces in their day to day life travels and justified the arguments presented using scholarly references. The findings from the researcher's Master's thesis have been also presented here to make the readers understand male standpoints towards women's access to commuting environment. In this way, the chapter manages to outline the issues necessary to ensure a gender sensitive commuting environment overlooked by male commuters. Finally, these viewpoints of the male respondents are also explained using the theoretical underpinnings of hegemonic masculinity. This will help to develop a critical gaze on gendered space, mobility and commuting experience. In addition to that, the interconnection between hegemonic masculinity and commuting environment, will leave a space for the readers to ponder over how the negative aspects of hegemonic masculinity can be tackled to ensure a gender friendly commuting environment for all.

REFERENCES

Bangladesh Bureau of Statistics. (2015). *Labour force survey 2010*. Dhaka: BBS.

Bangladesh Ministry of Communications. (2005). *Urban transport policy: the strategic transport plan (STP) for Dhaka*. Retrieved February 22, 2016, from http://lib.pmo.gov.bd/legalms/pdf/draft-urban_transport_policy.pdf

Bangladesh Planning Commission. (2014). *Millennium Development Goals: Bangladesh Progress Report 2013*. Dhaka: Bangladesh Planning Commission.

Connell, R. W. (1987). *Gender and power: society, the person and sexual politics*. Stanford, CA: Stanford University Press.

Connell, R. W., & Messerschmidt, J. W. (2005). Hegemonic masculinity: Rethinking the concept. *Gender & Society*, *19*(6), 829–859. doi:10.1177/0891243205278639

Gruber, J. E. (1992). A typology of personal and environmental sexual harassment: Research and policy implications for the 1990s. *Sex Roles*, *26*(11/12), 447–464. doi:10.1007/BF00289868

Hannan, C. (2007). *Promoting gender equality and empowerment of women in cities*. Paper presented at Global City Strategies for Implementing Policies on Gender Equality Conference, Seoul, South Korea.

Hasnine, M. S. (2011). Evaluation and development of bus based public transport in Dhaka city. *Proceedings of 4th Annual Paper Meet and 1st Civil Engineering Congress*. Retrieved February 23, 2016, from http://www.iebconferences.info/391.pdf

Hossain, M. (2016, March 30). Ekbochore nari nirjaton bereche 74 shotangsho. *Prothom Alo*.

Huppatz, K., & Goodwin, S. (2013). Masculinised jobs, feminised jobs and mens gender capital experiences: Understanding occupational segregation in Australia. *Journal of Sociology (Melbourne, Vic.)*, *49*(2-3), 291–308. doi:10.1177/1440783313481743

Imtiaz, S. M. S. (2009). *Understanding masculinities: men's perspectives and gender studies curriculum in Bangladesh*. Dhaka: Department of Women and Gender Studies.

Imtiaz, S. M. S. (2014). *Rongin shohorer torunera*. Dhaka: CMMS.

Mahmud, M., & Rabbani, A. (2012). *Travel mode choice preferences of urban commuters in Dhaka: a pilot study*. Dhaka: International Growth Center.

Mahtab, A. (2012). *Women, gender and development contemporary issues*. Dhaka: A. H. Development Publishing House.

Mannan, M. S., & Karim, M. M. (2001). Current state of the mobility of the urban dwellers in greater Dhaka. *Proceedings of the 94th Annual Conference and Exhibition of Air and Waste Management Association*. Retrieved October 14, 2016, from http://www.eng-consult.com/pub/mobility-paper.PDF

Masani, A. M. (2016, January 29). Havoc of public transport. *The Independent*. Retrieved from http://www.theindependentbd.com/printversion/details/31952

Messerchmidt, J. W. (1999). Making bodies matter: Adolescent masculinities, the body, and varieties of violence. *Theoretical Criminology, 3*(2), 197–220. doi:10.1177/1362480699003002004

Rahman, M. S., & Nahrin, K. (2012). Bus services in Dhaka city - users' experiences and opinions'. *Journal of Bangladesh Institute of Planners, 105*, 93–105. Retrieved from http://www.bip.org.bd/SharingFiles/journal_book/20130820140314.pdf

Rahman, M. S. U. (2010). Bus service for 'women only' in Dhaka city: An investigation. *Journal of Bangladesh Institute of Planners, 3*, 17–32. Retrieved from http://www.bip.org.bd/SharingFiles/journal_book/20130722133425.pdf

Sharmin, S. (2014, February 2). The saga of women commuters. *The Daily Observer*. Retrieved from http://www.observerbd.com/2014/02/02/3442.php

Shefali, M. K. (2000). *Study on gender dimensions in Dhaka Urban Transport Program (DUTP)*. Dhaka: Nari Udyog Kendro. Retrieved May 30, 2015, from http://siteresources.worldbank.org/INTGENDERTRANSPORT/Resources/bangurbantransport.pdf

UN Women. (2012). Safe *Public Transit for Women and Girls*. Retrieved February 28, 2016, from http://www.endvawnow.org/en/articles/252-safe-public-transit-for-women-and-girls-.html

Valentine, G. (1989). The geography of women's fear. *Area, 21*(4), 385–390. Retrieved from https://genderland.files.wordpress.com/2012/05/2-valentine.pdf

World Bank. (2007). *Dhaka: Improving living conditions for the urban poor*. Bangladesh: World Bank. Retrieved May 28, 2015, from http://siteresources.worldbank.org/BANGLADESHEXTN/Resources/295759-1182963268987/dhakaurbanreport.pdf

Zohir, S. C. (2003). *Integrating gender into world bank financed transport programs: Case study Bangladesh*. Retrieved May 30, 2015, from http://siteresources.worldbank.org/INTGENDERTRANSPORT/Resources/DhakaUrbanTransport.pdf

ENDNOTE

[1]   This study uses female commuters to indicate the female students, working women who use buses as their mode of transportation.

Chapter 14
Disaster, Vulnerability, and Violence Against Women:
Global Findings and a Research Agenda for Bangladesh

Khandakar Josia Nishat
University of Queensland, Australia

Md. Shafiqur Rahman
Helen Keller International, Bangladesh

ABSTRACT

Studies of natural disasters have adequately focused on gendered aspect of disaster and women's vulnerability and offered suitable suggestions though only few of these have focused on the issue of the relation between disaster and violence against women. By undertaking meta-analysis of cross-cultural studies, this paper aims to provide an overview of connections between disaster, women's vulnerability and violence against women and to highlight the importance and the relevance of similar researches in Bangladesh. Natural threats are real and moderated by existing socio-economic arrangements and cultural norms in Bangladesh where gender relationships are unequal and violence prone. Therefore it is expected that the lessons of international experiences and insights will help to develop a gendered research framework to understand 'how violence against women is increasing following disasters' in the context of Bangladesh. And finally, that would pave the way for policy options to form a better co-existence for both men and women which would be more equal, dignified and violence free.

INTRODUCTION

The people of Bangladesh have been at the mercy of natural disasters since their birth. Almost every year Bangladesh faces different types of disasters attack which are gradually intensifying by climatic changes and becoming more threating for people especially for women. From 1971 to 2005, 171 disasters were happened and more women died than men indisasters because of their lower economic status and

DOI: 10.4018/978-1-5225-3018-3.ch014

social capital (Women's Environment and Development Organization, 2008). Only in the 1991 cyclone in Bangladesh 90 per cent of the victims were female (Ikeda, 1995). During this cyclone, 'one desperate father, unable to hold on to both his son and daughter, let go of his daughter, acknowledging that he did so because his son had to carry on the family line (Fothergill, 1998). Not only in Bangladesh but also worldwide girls and women are 14 times more likely to die or be injured in a disasterthan boys and men due to gender based inequalities (Chew & Ramdas, 2004). Though disasters affect both women and men but the burden of coping with disasters falls heavily on women. During and aftermath of a disaster women and girls face a heavier load of domestic works as they are responsible for providing the family with its basic nutrition, yet they rarely have access to and control over the resources (Nasreen, 1995, 2008). In rural areas they are even more vulnerable since they are highly dependent on local natural resources for their livelihood. Consequently women suffer more than men from poverty, hunger, malnutrition, economic crises, environmental degradation; health related problems, insecurity and become victim of violence (Nasreen, 2012). The main aim of this literature review is to see 'how disaster influences violence against women' and to understand 'to what extent it is necessary to do similar researches in Bangladesh'. From past few decades a number of significant researches have already been done to understand the gendered perspective of disaster in Bangladesh and proposed effective suggestions as well as strategies to mitigate and to cope with such situation though only few researches have focused on "understanding the relation between disaster and violence against women in Bangladesh". Though some global researches have proved that- violence against women is increasing following disasters in developing countries(Enarson,2000, 2012; AusAID, 2008; Molin Valdés, 2009;Dasgupta, Siriner, &Partha,2010;Parkinson, 2011). At the same time researches on 'violence against women' have adequately focused on revealing causes, reasons of violence and on finding out effective ways to reduce violence but still one in every three women face violence in their life time throughout the world (World Health Organization, 2016).In this circumstances this topic presents a valuable connection for practical and academic exploration, and also representing a space where the gap of studying 'disaster' and 'violence against women' jointly manifest, and both create and reveal the way forward to reduce women's vulnerability to reduce/stop violence against women.

OPERATIONAL DEFINITIONS

Disaster: Disaster is a difficult concept to define; existing definitions tend to be either too broad or too narrow. However this paper will mainly focus on natural disasters. Natural disasters refer to disasters of certain magnitude caused by natural forces affecting whole populations. For example: cyclone, tornado, flood, riverbank erosion, coastal erosion, landslide, drought, heavy rainfall, bushfire, heatwave etc.

Vulnerability: Vulnerability to natural disasters is a composite of numerous social and biophysical variables, and it is established long before disasters strike in infrastructure, preparedness planning, economic status, education level, social networks, and other available systems, with each capable of being shaped by gender (Fordham, 1999, pp.15-36).

Violence against Women: Any act of gender-based violence that results in, or is likely to result in, physical, sexual or mental harm or suffering to women, including threats of such acts, coercion or arbitrary deprivation of liberty, whether occurring in public or in private life' is called Violence against women (United Nations, 1993). Throughout the paper, unless specified differently, the term "women" refers to females of all ages, including girls.

WOMEN'S ROLE AND VULNERABILITY IN DISASTERS

Disasters magnify both the strengths and the weaknesses in society so the way gender is constructed influences how women and men are affected by disaster (Domeisen, 1998; Enarson, 2000). Historically women are considered as the 'vulnerable among vulnerable' (Ariyabandhu & Foenseka, 2006) and disasters intensify their vulnerability at a great extent. Especially the women in developing countries such as Bangladesh are the worst sufferer of natural disasters than men due to their social status, cultural norms, lack of access to and control over resources, and lack of participation in decision-making processes (Khan, Ali, Asaduzzaman, Bhuyan, & Harunur, 2010).

Evidently during and aftermath of disasters women are more likely to die and to suffer ill health effects. Globally, for every one adult male who drowns in a flood, there are 3-4 women who die (Aguilar, 2008). Though women's life expectancy is higher than that of males, but some countries natural disasters narrow the gender gap in life expectancy. A study conducted by London School of Economic proves-taken a sample of up to 141 countries over the period 1981 to 2002, natural disasters and their following impacts kill more women than men or kill women at an earlier age than men related to women's lower socio-economic status (Neumayer & Plümper, 2007). Likewise a study on cyclone Sidrin Bangladesh shows that the women: men ratio of deaths from Sidr was 5:1 (Ahmad, 2011). In a patriarchy dominated society such as Bangladesh women face different types of cultural barriers as well. For instance a study conducted by Bangladesh Centre for Advanced Studies reveals that 'the aspects of gender inequalities as social phenomenon that doubly jeopardizes women by contributing to natural phenomenon like climatic disaster; came up with some interesting findings as how gender roles and responsibilities change in pre, during and post disaster scenario and how even traditional dresses like 'sari' increase women's vulnerability' (Bangladesh Centre for Advanced Studies, 2010). Other supportive studies were also found who shows that traditional dresses like sari and obligations to wear vail increase women's vulnerability during disaster and may cause more death (Ikeda 1995; Paul 2009).

Worldwide women used to work at home during disaster which is often not the safest place and causes severe death of women than men during disasters such as earthquakes, floods, cyclone or tsunamis. During flood in Bangladesh, many women have been facing greater difficulties as the female head of the household evacuate herself only after she has safeguarded all other family members and assets (Nasreen, 1995). Not only in Bangladesh, the same scenario has been observed during the 2005 earthquake of Pakistan, 73,000 people were died– women were mostly injured and died as they were at home while their adult male family members were working in the fields (Brookings-Bern Project on Internal Displacement, 2009). To understand women's higher mortality in disasters than men, Fothergill in 1998, provided an explanation based on both developed and developing countries, that their husbands had the decision-making powers and they did not dare leave without their husband's permission' and that 'women were left responsible for property and [could have been] afraid of blame and punishment'. Though all the women do not face all the vulnerabilities in same way, for some disaster vulnerabilities are even more severe. For example, Henrici, Helmuth, & Braun found pregnant women more vulnerable among all vulnerable women, they said:

Women who are pregnant or recovering from childbirth have limited mobility and face additional difficulties during disasters. Women also make up a greater proportion of the elderly, typically one of the groups with the highest mortality rates during disasters ... Women also face a high risk of gender-based violence (Henrici, Helmuth, & Braun, 2010, p. 2).

Furthermore in recent years, women in saline inundated areas have suffered frequent miscarriages, which local doctors attribute to drinking saline water (Ahmed et al., 2007). Another most vulnerable group in disaster is young girls. During 1998s flood perinea rashes and urinary tract infections were increased in a large number among adolescent girls because they were not able to properly wash and dry their menstrual rags (WHO, 2005). Consequently they may suffer from genital injury, including bleeding, infection and other complications. Sometimes the female members of the family are forced to stay close to the community; as a result, they have to drink unhygienic water form polluted tube wells which may increase gynaecological problems among all ages of women. In the context of Bangladesh Neelormi, Neelopal and Ahmed (2009) spotted this problem rationally:

Women living in marooned and slippery conditions fall victim to unhygienic reproductive health condition and increasing trends of gynaecological problems as reported. Schools become inoperative, which drastically reduces women's opportunity to become self-reliant. As a consequence of absence of land-based productive system, the poverty situation becomes so dire that the social fabric is about to be torn apart. The study suggested that the state must consider gender-specific measures to either build resilience of women or reduce their overall vulnerability by draining out stagnant water from the area – even if the cost of institutional adaptation is staggering. The cost of people's suffering must be weighed against the cost of adaptation.

Also in shelters women and girls usually feel ashamed to use public latrines and bathrooms or to be seen by men when in wet clothing (Rashid & Michaud, 2000).

Women's vulnerability is not limited to these, disasters also increase gender division of work and lead women to bear more physical burden than men due to their gender specific tasks. Usually women are responsible for household chores such as preparation of food, caring child and old people in the family, fetching water, collecting firewood and waste disposal which become double/ triple during and aftermath of disasters. In Bangladesh many girls leave schools or to be forced to leave school to help their mother in domestic chores and to take care of the younger brothers and sisters. Also sometimes due to damage of school infrastructure and road, inconvenient communication system, girls have to leave school and most of the times they do not start school again. However the irony is that- most of the time in rural areas parents try to marry off their underage school going girl, just to reduce a hungry face from the family or to get some money (Alston, Whittenbury, Haynes, & Godden, 2014). They also said that the curse of dowry demands become higher in such situation. An Old man form the study area said:

Problems are mostly around marriage and dowry. Say if there had been no dowry in the country, we would live more peacefully.

Also women and girls face serious health hazards and nutrition deficiency during and aftermath of disasters as they eat the rest of the foods, last of all the family members and sometimes they want to keep some for next meal. Globally it is the fact that women buffer the household impact of crisis especially the impact on children, through decreasing their own food consumption (International Food Policy Research Institute, 1995; Quisumbing et al., 2008; & Holmes, Jones, &Marsden, 2009). As a result, they suffer

Disaster, Vulnerability, and Violence Against Women

from malnutrition which limits their capacity to fight against disasters which causes high mortality of them. Not only physical health hazards, women are also likely to suffer from mental strain, trauma and psychological disorder during and aftermath of disasters, especially because of loses of farms, crops and age old business. In addition women also face discrimination in receiving medical treatments as most of the time women and girls are ignored by the family members to take them to hospitals. Sometimes women deny taking medical treatments to give priority to other family members and sometimes to be scared of hospitals.

Nevertheless economic insecurity and the patriarchal social structure both contribute to increased vulnerability for women in a time of disaster as women's financial situation is frequently hindered further by caring responsibilities and inequitable access to financial aid (Phillips, Jenkins, & Enarson, 2010). Enarson pointed out how disaster increases women's economic vulnerability 'first, women's economic insecurity increases, as their productive assets are destroyed, they often become sole earners, their household entitlements may decline, their small-businesses are hard-hit, they lose jobs and work time, and gender stereotypes limit their work opportunities. Second, women's workload increases dramatically. They often take on more waged or other forms of income-generating work; engage in a number of new forms of "disaster work," including emergency response and political organizing; and have expanded responsibilities as caregivers. Third, women's working conditions in the household and paid workplaces deteriorate, for example through lack of child-care and increased work and family conflicts. Fourth, women recover more slowly than men from major economic losses, as they are less mobile than male workers, likely to return to paid work later, and often fail to receive equitable financial recovery assistance from the government and/or external donors' (Enarson, 2000). Enarson focused on developing countries women especially women in rural areas. For example in Bangladesh many rural women rely on food processing, cattle, and chickens for their cash income which may hamper because of losses of harvest and livestock in disasters. This sudden loss makes them more vulnerable to disasters. Also due to scarcity of jobs after disasters, male members often leave their family to go to cities for earing money and they usually do not come back to take the responsibility of the disaster vulnerable family. In this situation, women have to come forward to maintain the family with their lower average literacy, limited access to productive employments and with limited/no control over resources which increases female headed households and lead them to be the poorest of the poor. On the other hand, in most of the cases women's well-being were undermined because of their dependence on economic activities linked to the home (Khondoker, 1996). In addition to make women's vulnerability more severe their inferior economic power contributes directly to male violence (True, 2012) especially domestic violence against women (VicHealth, 2007). Weak security system in disaster shelters, women's vulnerability to socialize, women's responsibility to collect food and fuel, existing gender roles, lack of social security and many other reasons intensity women's risk to be a victim of violence during and aftermath of disasters. In Haiti after the 2010 earthquake numerous cases of rape and sexual assault in camps were reported by media and NGOs. But the disaster affected police and other security forces could not take any actions and many of the sexual and gender-based violence was unreported (Amnesty International, 2010). In several camps, women reported to Amnesty International that it was a common practice for many girls to exchange sex for food or material goods.

THE NEXUS: DISASTER, VULNERABILITY, AND VIOLENCE AGAINST WOMEN

A Global Perspective

Violence against women is a global epidemic. Worldwide, almost one-third (30%) of all women who have been in a relationship have experienced physical and/or sexual violence by their intimate partner, in some regions this is much higher (WHO, 2016). A girl faces different types of violence on her way to be a woman or even as a woman. Moreover children who grow up in families where they suffer a range of behavioural and emotional disturbances, in future they practice such behaviours on others. Explanations for increased violence against women are different, and many researchers found strong association between disaster and violence against women. In this regard Rees et al. argued that:

Natural disasters do not exist in isolation from the social and cultural constructs that marginalize women and place them at risk of violence. In fact, there is evidence that violence against women increases in the wake of colossal disasters and that the increased risk is associated with gender inequality and the limited representation of women in disaster responses (Rees, Pittaway, &Bartolomei, 2005, p. 1).

Fothergill reviewed 100 studies from both developed and developing countries and found domestic violence such as wife battering, divorce and child abuses are increasing following disaster. He said that after Hurricane Andrew, domestic violence was increased to 50 per cent. The following statement was published in 1998 but a decade later, little had changed:

…the research on woman battering in post-disaster communities is still almost non-existent. In the disaster research community, many question whether rates of woman battering increase in a disaster. Thus, although this question has been frequently asked, it remains largely unanswered (Fothergill, 2008, p. 131).

At the same time Wilson and et al. showed that after the earthquake in Dale country domestic violence increased to 600 per cent (Wilson, Philips, & Neal, 1998). The increase of domestic violence was also faced by hurricane Katerina affected areas women (Anastario, Shehab, & Lawry, 2009) and many women reported their continuous stress, post-traumatic stress disorder and other psychological problems during and aftermath of the disaster. Likewise after the deadliest tornadoes in U.S. history in 2011, the residents of Joplin, Missouri realised that natural disasters create personal crises as domestic violence cases increased by 40 percent and the demand for beds in women's shelters doubled. Disasters increase the demand for women's shelters, not just because women's homes are ruined, but because of domestic violence (UN Women, 2013). In addition money problems not only added to the multiple stressors and potential triggers which increased the likelihood and severity of domestic violence (Jenkins &Phillips, 2008), but also it forced many women and girls to involve in prostitution. The same problem was faced by the Fijian women and girls after the Fiji floods, due to the economic burden, many girl children were being kept home from school either to earn money at night through sex work or to take care of young children in the family (UN Women, 2013).

Disasters affect the whole social structure and ruin peoples daily life style, many of them become homeless, wealth less, farm less, jobless that lead them to frustration and increase use alcohol and drugs in the aftermath of disasters (Fothergill, 2008; Enarson, 2012). A strong association between alcohol

Disaster, Vulnerability, and Violence Against Women

and violence has been identified in the domestic violence literature (Abramsky et al., 2011; Braaf, 2012; &Livingston, 2011). Many women in these studies observed that alcohol changed their partner's personality, and making them violent to their wives and children. On the other hand, moreover, men's feelings of inadequacy in meeting gender-based expectations in either disaster or the failure of the family farm result in some men reverting to a form of hyper-masculinity and using violence (Enarson & Scanlon, 1999; Alston & Whittenbury, 2013). It is reported that after the two cyclones in Fiji in 2012, number of women were forced into sex by their husband though there is crowd and lack of privacy in the relief centres (UN Women, 2013).

A UNFPA report on 'humanitarian relief in emergency settings' has described how sexual violence is associated with disasters:

Sexual violence is common in humanitarian settings. It may become more acute in the wake of a natural disaster and occurs at every stage of a conflict. The victims are usually women and adolescents, who have often been separated from their families and communities and whose care-taking roles increase their vulnerability to exploitation and abuse. Breakdowns in law and order and in protective societal norms mean that most perpetrators abuse with impunity.

In many conflicts, women's bodies become battlegrounds, with rape used as a method of warfare to humiliate, dominate or disrupt social ties. In the aftermath of natural disasters, women and young people may be left unaccompanied – out in the open or in temporary shelters – at the same time that security lapses lead to increased lawlessness and chaos. The impact of sexual violence, especially rape, can be devastating. Physical consequences include injuries, unwanted pregnancies, fistula and HIV. Widespread sexual violence is also endemic in many post-conflict situations, where it can perpetuate a cycle of anxiety and fear that impedes recovery (UNFPA, 2006).

Nevertheless natural disasters lead to decreased rainfall which creates freshwater shortages especially in water-stressed countries such as Middle East, North Africa, and South Asia and others. Water shortages often create more burdens to women than men as women are mostly responsible for the household chores. Often women were left with the sole responsibility for the family and property because socially determined roles mean that women are likely to be separated from a male in a disaster (Raphael, Taylor, & McAndrew, 2008). Therefore, women have to collect water and foods from distant places which increase insecurity and cause rape or other violence. For instance, in 2007 after the tsunami approximately 10,000 people were displaced and many women were raped in Solomon Islands. Also during the flood in 2014, women in Solomon Islands faced unusual and unwanted sexual contact as there was lack of gender- separated toilets and bathrooms (UN Women, 2013). Both domestic violence and sexual assault were widely reported to increase in the aftermath of the 2004 Indian Ocean tsunami. Examples from Sri Lanka cited by researchers include women battered because they resist their husbands' sale of their jewellery or disputed their use of tsunami relief funds and mothers blamed by fathers for the deaths of their children. One NGO reported a three-fold increase in cases brought to them following the tsunami (Fischer, 2005).

Also after any disaster such as earthquakes and tsunamis, floods or famine crises, economic, and security challenges lead women and children to seek better living places which make them potential targets of human traffickers (Hodge & Lietz, 2007).A report on gender-based violence in Aceh, Indonesia, following the 2004 South Asian tsunami found significant increases in trafficking of women and girls in the tsunami aftermath and noted that women and girls in the refugee camps were at particular risk (United Nations Development Program, 2010).In addition due to breakdown of local security and safety nets and increase levels of stress, women started to the neglect their children (Bartlett, 2008)and sometimes they sell their children to traffickers for some money. An NGO working to assist people caught in the 2013 Uttarakhand, India, flooding warns that 'trafficking of young girls happens here due to poverty, and families are often coerced into accepting money from traffickers who marry their daughters to older men in other states, rather than pay a large dowry for them. After the floods, this is likely to worsen as people are poorer and more desperate'(Bhalla,2013). The US State Department states that natural disasters exacerbate vulnerabilities and allow traffickers to flourish. Furthermore the rate of rape was found to be 53.6 times higher than the highest baseline state rate (International Federation of Red Cross and Red Crescent Societies, 2007). Evidences also found Australia as a violence prone country after disasters such as bushfires (Parkinson, 2011) and drought (Alston & Whittenbury, 2013). In addition the service providers in Queensland- a state in Australia reported an increase in requests for assistance from women who had experienced intimate-partner violence following the 2010 and 2011 floods (The Taskforce, 2015). Also in Victoria, women's service providers reported that increased violence against women in the aftermath of the 2009 bushfires (Parkinson, 2011). However, the threats of natural disasters are even more devastating in developing countries. As an example, following the Nepal earthquakes it has been clearly seen that Nepali women experience men's violence at a greater rate than before. Also women from disadvantaged castes such as Dalit women, or women with disabilities, widows and those living in remote regions experience many further disadvantages that make them even more vulnerable to discrimination, poverty and violence during and aftermath of disasters (Hawker, 2015). Also a UNHCR reports show that during the 2010 flood in Pakistan many women suffered from phobic or panic attacks, depression and anxiety which is linked to losing homes and all means of livelihood in the floods (Integrated Regional Information Networks, 2010).

'Violence against women is increasing following disaster'-acknowledgement of this statement is getting more attention though the process is so slow according to its sensitivity. Moreover it is difficult to study due to lack of data and information. If we look at the overall database about sexual violence- these are seriously limited, so in a disaster context, would be even more challenging to collect such data in a systematic way. On top of that some violence including domestic violence is un-recognised and un-recorded in the context of disaster (Phillips, Jenkins, & Enarson, 2010). As a result most of the policy makers often ignore 'disaster and violence' aspect during making and implementing disaster management policies. To address this gap World Health Organization characterizes most information about violence in disaster contexts as anecdotal which indicate that intimate partner violence, child abuse and sexual violence are highly prevalent after disasters(WHO,2005). Following this gap the main purpose of this study is to see to what extent it is necessary to study similar researches on 'disaster' and violence against women' in Bangladesh.

Disaster and Violence Against Women in Bangladesh

In this section some relevant recent (past five years) studies have been reviewed to see the existence of the relation between 'disaster' and 'violence against women' in Bangladesh, if there is any.

Disaster, Vulnerability, and Violence Against Women

Flood-Induced Vulnerabilities and Problems Encountered by Women in Northern Bangladesh by AbulKalam Azad, KhondokerMokaddem Hossain & MahbubaNasreen, 2013

This study findings show that in northern Bangladesh women suffer from physical injuries, and often they are also evicted from their dwellings due to floods. In addition they face difficulties in finding adequate shelter, food, safe water, and fuel for cooking, as well as problems in maintaining personal hygiene and sanitation and these disrupts their usual roles at home. Women also suffer from domestic violence and are subject to harassment when taking shelter or refuge at community centres. According to the researchers word:

Approximately 35 percent of women were harassed during and after floods over the last five years. Out of 64 women who reported problems with harassment, identical percentage reported similar treatment by neighbours. Near 5 percent of the women indicated that they were harassed by unacquainted persons, 6 percent by boys or youth, and 3 percent by brothers-in-law. Harassment during and after floods was frequent, and included mental, physical, and sexual dimensions. For example, around 33 percent of women encountered mental torture and more than 59 percent suffered verbal abuse. More than 34 percent of the women encountered physical abuse and 39 percent were beaten by their husband.

Not only this study but also previously the researcher found that during and aftermath of disasters women suffer more than men from poverty, hunger, malnutrition, economic crises, environmental degradation; health related problems, insecurity and become victim of violence (Nasreen, 2012).

Are Climate Challenges Reinforcing Child and Forced Marriage and Dowry as Adaptation Strategies in the Context of Bangladesh? By Margaret Alston, Kerri Whittenbury, Alex Haynes, &Naomi Godden, 2014

This paper presents a link between 'child and forced marriage', and also 'dowry and climate changes' in the context of Bangladesh. They argue that climate crises are creating as well as increasing the existing economic vulnerabilities. And to mitigate these vulnerabilities, many families demand dowry as a compulsory part of marriage which is actually a source of capital for the groom. In the study areas, researchers found that during and aftermath of disasters, the demands of dowry become a curse. The bride's family is bound to fulfil the dowry demands otherwise the girl will remain unmarried. The sufferings are not limited to these, also the rate of dowry increases and becomes more threatening and obligatory with the age of the girl. The authors also said that child marriage and forced marriages also increase as dowry is cheaper at that time.

...Of note is that 45% (276) of respondents to our survey reported that girls were now being forced into child marriages as a direct result of climate events and subsequent poverty. This view was reinforced in interviews and focus groups in the three regions. A key driver for child marriage in disaster sites is the link to the economic situation of families and the stark reality of living in extreme poverty. Many families take loans to buy food. In these circumstances girls are viewed as an economic burden and a threat to ongoing food security and food availability. The marriage of young girls reduces pressure on the family's food supplies.

This sort of marriage does not bring a smooth life for these girls, for the life time they become vulnerable to this relationship and consequently face different types of violence. Sometimes if the bride's family become late or deny to fulfil the dowry demands, the girl/ woman face immense sufferings in the in law's house. One woman form the study area expressed her daughter's sufferings like that:

But my daughter says, "No." she says, "death is a better option than being there in that [husband's] house again. I won't go there. I won't go to live there. I'll rather face whatever iswritten in my fate."

Women in Natural Disasters: A Case Study From Southern Coastal Region of Bangladesh by KhurshedAlam, &Md. Habibur Rahman, 2014

This research mainly focused on the preparedness, risk and loss, cultural and conditional behaviour, adaptability and recovery capacity of women of southern coastal region in a disaster situation. They said that women face loss of livelihood opportunities, deprivation from relief materials, sexual harassment during and after disaster. They have found that women including pregnant women and adolescent girls face harassment, unwelcome body touch, urges to physical touch, unwanted physical contact, taking advantage of physical proximity of a young girl, look intently at female organs etc. The authors divided the whole disaster period into three stages- pre, during and post to understand women's vulnerability in disasters as well as their capacity to fight against disaster. They found that during the disaster, in cyclone centre almost 60 per cent of pregnant and adolescent girls said that they faced sexual harassment, 22.86 per cent said no and rest 17.14 per cent remain silent.

Coping With Coastal Risk and Vulnerabilities in Bangladesh by S.H.M. Fakhruddin, &Juma Rahman, 2015

The main focus of this paper was "understanding gender differentiated impacts on different livelihoods in a disaster situation and how they affect the formulation of policies, programs or projects" in coastal areas of Bangladesh. After analysing the field data they found that in disaster situation women face social, cultural, economic vulnerabilities and violence against women. They described in the following manner:

During extreme events such as drought, floods and other climate related disasters, women face further risks, due to gender inequities that result in a disproportionate burden of disaster impacts. For instance, women are often discouraged from learning coping strategies and life saving skills, such as climbing trees or swimming. Some cultural norms prevent them from evacuating their homes without consent from the men, guardians in their families or communities. Often codes of dress, household work and responsibilities, and childcare may inhibit their mobility during crises, resulting in higher mortality during disasters. Furthermore intimidation, gender-based violence, sexual harassment and rape tend to increase during such events. Sometimes during climate-induced disasters they become the victims of human trafficking. Gender-based violence, sexual harassment and rape tend to increase during such events. Sometimes during climate-induced disasters they become the victims of human trafficking.

Furthermore researchers also concern about that women who are evacuated and abandoned in disasters may be forced to prostitution, human trafficking, and other exploitative acts (Ahsan and Hossain 2004).In this support, another report of the Bangladesh government guide book on 'gender and social inclusion' states that "women are often vulnerable to sexual harassment in pre and post disaster situations" (Rashid & Shafie, 2009).

Climate Change, Disaster, and Gender Vulnerability: A Study on Two Divisions of Bangladesh by Md. Sadequr Rahman, 2013

This study focused on two disaster prone division- Barisal and Rajshahi in Bangladesh. The author said that women's weakness, work pressure and stress are multiplied by their lack of personal safety. As a result many women are more at risk of rape and sexual harassment during disasters. He also said that "the shame attached to leaving the house and moving in public", making women less likely to go to shelters during disasters. However, if they go to shelters they eventually face eve-teasing, domestic and public sexual harassments.

The above researches are just selected randomly to see the violence proximity to disasters in Bangladesh among all the researches on gender and violence. Though these five studies are not particularly focused on 'disaster and violence against women', these are mainly proving women's vulnerability in disasters. But all of their field's data are indicating that women are facing different types of violence during and aftermath of disasters. To address this gap now it is a pre-requisite to identify such specific issues rather than focusing on gender as whole to make a better disaster management policy. So this literature review is a small contribution to provide a food for thought to the researches on relevant issues to come forward and to recognise the importance of this issue to stop violence against women in Bangladesh.

CONCLUSION: FUTURE RESEARCH DIRECTIONS FOR BANGLADESH

In this literature review we note that Bangladesh is affected by climate change from different perspectives and historically women in Bangladesh are deprived and supressed by the patriarchal society. We argue that to accelerate women's vulnerability and deprivation, the inevitable natural disasters are fuelling to increase violence against women in Bangladesh. To understand the relation between disasters and violence against women global literatures have been reviewed and it has been clearly seen that globally many researches are now focusing on the issue that 'how disaster is related to violence against women'?. So this paper will not be concluded rather than it would be an opening of a new research path for the researchers in Bangladesh as well as all over the world to stop or at least reduce violence against women and to decrease women's vulnerability, and also to ensure a better living for women and girls which would be safe and violence free.

REFERENCES

Abramsky, T., Watts, C. H., García-Moreno, C., Devries, K., Kiss, L., Ellsberg, M., Jansen, A.H., & Heise, L. (2011). *What factors are associated with recent intimate partner violence? Findings from the WHO multi-country study on women's health and domestic violence*. Academic Press.

Aguilar, L. (2008). *Acknowledging the Linkages: Gender and Climate Change*. Paper presented at the World Bank's workshop on social dimensions of climate change. Retrieved from http://siteresources.worldbank.org/EXTSOCIALDEVELOPMENT/Resources/244362-1170428243464/3408356-1170428261889/3408359-1202746084138/Gender_Presentation022808.pd

Ahmad, N. (2011). *Gender and climate change: myth vs reality*. Retrieved from http://blogs.worldbank.org/endpovertyinsouthasia/gender-and-climate-change-myth-vs-reality

Ahmed, N. (2012). Gender and Climate Change in Bangladesh: The Role of Institutions inReducing Gender Gaps in Adaptation Program. *The World Bank*. Retrieved from http://www-wds.worldbank.org/external/default/WDSContentServer/WDSP/IB/2012/04/04/000333038_20120404010647/Rendered/PDF/678200NWP0P1250C0in0Bangladesh0web2.pd

Ahsan, R. M., & Hossain, M. K. (2004). Woman and Child Trafficking in Bangladesh: A Social Disaster in the Backdrop of Natural Calamities. In R. M. Ahsan & H. Khatun (Eds.), *Disaster and the Silent Gender: Contemporary Studies in Geography* (pp. 147–170). Dhaka: The Bangladesh Geographical Society.

Alam, K., & Rahman, M. H. (2014). Women in Natural Disasters: A Case Study from Southern Coastal Region of Bangladesh. *International Journal of Disaster Risk Reduction*, 8, 68–82. doi:10.1016/j.ijdrr.2014.01.003

Alston, M., & Whittenbury, K. (2013). Introducing Gender and Climate Change: Research, Policy and Action. In A. Margaret & W. Kerri (Eds.), *Research, Action and Policy: Addressing the Gendered Impacts of Climate Change* (pp. 3–14). London: Springer. doi:10.1007/978-94-007-5518-5_1

Alston, M., Whittenbury, K., Haynes, A., & Godden, N. (2014). Are climate challenges reinforcing child and forced marriage and dowry as adaptation strategies in the context of Bangladesh? *Womens Studies International Forum*, 47, 137–144. doi:10.1016/j.wsif.2014.08.005

Amnesty International. (2010). *Haiti after the Earthquake: Initial Mission Findings*. Author.

Anastario, M., Shehab, N., & Lawry, L. (2009). Increased Gender-based Violence Among Women Internally Displaced in Mississippi Two Years Post-Hurrican Katrina. *Disaster Medicine and Public Health Preparedness*, 3(1), 18–26. doi:10.1097/DMP.0b013e3181979c32 PMID:19293740

Ariyabandu, M. M., & Foenseka, D. (2006). Do Disasters Discriminate?. In D. Nivaran (Ed.), South Asia Network for Disaster Mitigation: Tackling the Tides and Tremors (pp. 23–40). Islamabad: South Asia Disaster Report.

AusAID Office of Development Effectiveness. (2008). *Violence against women in Melanesia and East Timor Building on Global and Regional Promising Approaches*. Canberra: Office of Development Effectiveness.

Azad, A. K., Hossain, M. K., & Nasreen, M. (2013). Flood-Induced Vulnerabilities and Problems Encountered by Women in Northern Bangladesh. *International Journal of Disaster Risk Science*, *4*(4), 190–199. doi:10.1007/s13753-013-0020-z

Bangladesh Centre for Advanced Studies. (2010). *Report on Gender and Climate Change Issues in the South Central and South West Coastal Regions of Bangladesh*. Dhaka, Bangladesh: Author.

Bartlett, S. (2008). *Climate change and urban children Impacts and implications for adaptation in low- and middle-income countries. In Human settlements discussion paper, Series theme: climate change and cities.* International Institute for Environment and Development.

Bhalla, N. (2013). *Women, children at risk of trafficking after Uttarakhand floods.* Thompson Reuters Foundation. Retrieved from http://in.reuters.com/article/2013/07/05/uttarakhand-floods-women-childrentraffi-idINDEE96402V20130705

Braaf, R. (2012). *Elephant in the room: Responding to alcohol misuse and domestic violence.* Australian Domestic & Family Violence Clearing House. Retrieved from http://trove.nla.gov.au/work/169482645?q&versionId=184708568

Brookings-Bern Project on Internal Displacement. (2009). *Protecting and Promoting Rights in Natural Disasters in South Asia: Prevention and Response*. Retrieved from http://www.brookings.edu/~/media/Files/rc/reports/2009/0701_natural_disasters/0701_natural_disasters.pdf

Chew, L., & Ramdas, K. N. (2005). *Caught in the Storm: The Impact of Natural Disasters on Women*. San Francisco: The Global Fund for Women.

Dasgupta, S., Siriner, I., & Partha, S. D. (Eds.). (2010). *Women's Encounter with Disaster*. London: Frontpage Publications.

Domeisen, N. (1998). Community Life and Disaster Reduction. *DHA News: Women in Emergencies.* Retrieved from http://www.reliefweb.int/ocha_ol/pub/dhanews/issue22/communit.html

Enarson, E., & Scanlon, J. (1999). Gender patterns in flood evacuation: A case study in Canadas Red River Valley. *Applied Behavioral Science Review*, *7*(2), 103–124. doi:10.1016/S1068-8595(00)80013-6

Enarson, E. (2000). *Gender issues in natural disasters: Talking points and research needs*. Paper presented at the ILO in Focus Programme on Crisis Response and Reconstruction Workshop, Geneva. Retrieved form https://www.scribd.com/document/253509365/Ilo-Talking

Enarson, E., & Phillips, B. (2008). Invitation to a new feminist disaster sociology: integrating feminist theory and methods. In B. Phillips & B. H. Morrow (Eds.), *Women and Disasters: From Theory to Practice* (pp. 41–74). International Research Committee on Disasters.

Enarson, E. (2012). *Women confronting natural disaster: from vulnerability to resistance*. Boulder, CO: Lynne Reinner Publishers.

Fakhruddin, S. H. M., & Rahman, J. (2015). Coping with coastal risk and vulnerabilities in Bangladesh. *International Journal of Disaster Risk Reduction*, *12*, 112–118. doi:10.1016/j.ijdrr.2014.12.008

Fischer, S. (2005). *Gender Based Violence in Sri Lanka in the Aftermath of the 2004 Tsunami Crisis*. Retrieved from http://www.gdnonline.org/resources/fisher-post-tsuami-gbv-srilanka.doc

Fordham, M. (1999). The intersection of gender and social class in disaster: Balancing resilience and vulnerability. *International Journal of Mass Emergencies and Disasters*, *17*(1), 15–36. PMID:12295202

Fothergill, A. (1998). The neglect of gender in disaster work: an overview of the literature. In E. Enarson & B. H. Morrow (Eds.), *The Gendered Terrain of Disaster: Through Women's Eyes*. Westport, CT: Praeger Publishers.

Fothergill, A. (2008). Domestic Violence after Disaster: Voices from the 1997 Grand Forks Flood. In B. D. Phillips & B. H. Morrow (Eds.), *Women and Disasters: From theory to practice* (pp. 131–154). International Research Committee on Disasters.

Henrici, J. M., Helmuth, A. S., & Braun, J. (2010). *Women, Disasters, and Hurricane Katrina*. Washington, DC: Institute for Women's Policy Research.

Hawker, C. (2015, November 23). Why men's violence against women skyrockets after natural disaster. *The Daily Life*. Retrieved from http://www.dailylife.com.au/news-and-views/take-action/why-mens-violence-against-women-skyrockets-after-natural-disaster-20151120-gl3sid

Hodge, R. D., & Leitz, A. C. (2007). The International Sexual Trafficking of Women and Children: A Review of the Literature. *Affilia*, *22*(2), 163–174. doi:10.1177/0886109907299055

Holmes, R., Jones, N., & Marsden, H. (2009). Gender vulnerabilities, food price shocks and social protection responses. Overseas Development Institute Background Note.

Ikeda, K. (1995). Gender differences in human loss and vulnerability in natural disasters: A case study from Bangladesh. *Indian Journal of Gender Studies*, *2*(2), 171–193. doi:10.1177/097152159500200202

Integrated Regional Information Networks. (2010). *Pakistan: Minorities test aid impartiality*. Retrieved from available at: http://www.refworld.org/docid/4c8df239c.html

International Federation of Red Cross and Red Crescent Societies. (2007). *World Disaster Report: Focus on discrimination*. Retrieved from http://www.ifrc.org/Docs/pubs/disasters/wdr2007/WDR2007-English.pdf

International Food Policy Research Institute. (1995). Women: the key to food security: Looking into the household. Washington, DC: Author.

Jenkins, P., & Phillips, B. (2008). Battered Women, Catastrophe, and the Context of Safety after Hurricane Katrina. *NWSA Journal*, *20*(3), 49–69.

Khan, I. A., Ali, Z., Asaduzzaman, M., Bhuyan, R., & Harunur, M. (2010). The social dimensions of adaptation to climate change in Bangladesh. Development and climate change discussion paper. Washington, DC: World Bank; Retrieved from http://documents.worldbank.org/curated/en/920271468174884196/pdf/588990NWP0Bang10Box353823B01public1.pdf

Khondoker, M. H. (1996). Women and floods in Bangladesh. *International Journal of Mass Emergencies and Disasters*, *14*(3), 281–292.

Livingston, M. (2011). A longitudinal analysis of alcohol outlet density and domestic violence. *Addiction (Abingdon, England)*, *106*(5), 919–925. doi:10.1111/j.1360-0443.2010.03333.x PMID:21205052

Maplecroft. (2011). *Climate Change Vulnerability Index*. Retrieved from Ihttps://maplecroft.com/about/news/ccvi.html

Molin Valdés, H. (2009). A gender perspective on disaster risk reduction. In E. Enarson & P. G. Dhar-Chakrabarti (Eds.), Women, gender and disaster: Global issues and initiatives (pp. 18-28). Los Angeles, CA: Sage.

Nasreen, M. (1995). *Coping with Floods: The Experience of Rural Women in Bangladesh* (Unpublished doctoral dissertation). Messey University, New Zealand.

Nasreen, M. (2008). *Impact of Climate Change on Food Security in Bangladesh: Gender and Disaster Perspectives*. Paper presented at the International Symposium on Climate Change and Food Security in Bangladesh.

Nasreen, M. (2012). *Vulnerable or resilient? Women and girls*. Dhaka: Dhaka Institute of Disaster Management and Vulnerability Studies.

Neelormi, S., Neelopal, A., & Ahmed, A. U. (2009). *Gender Perspectives of Increased Socio-economic Risks of Waterlogging in Bangladesh Due to Climate Change*. Retrieved from http://www.ioiusa.net/view/article/141603

Neumayer, E., & Plümper, T. (2007). The Gendered Nature of Natural Disasters: The Impact of Catastrophic Events on the Gender Gap in Life Expectancy, 1981-2002. *Annals of the Association of American Geographers*, *97*(3), 551–566. doi:10.1111/j.1467-8306.2007.00563.x

Oxfam International. (2011). *Owning Adaptation Factsheet: Bangladesh*. Retrieved from https://www.oxfam.org/sites/www.oxfam.org/files/bp146-owning-adaptation-130611-summ-en.pdf

Parkinson, D. (2011). Gender disaster and violence: literature review. *Women's Health Goulburn North East*. Retrieved form http://www.whealth.com.au/documents/environmentaljustice/women-disaster-violence-lit-review.pdf

Paul, B. K. (2009). Why relatively fewer people died? The case of Bangladeshs Cyclone Sidr. *Natural Hazards*, *50*(2), 289–304. doi:10.1007/s11069-008-9340-5

Phillips, B., Jenkins, P., & Enarson, E. (2010). Violence and disaster vulnerability. In B. Phillips, D. Thomas, A. Fothergill, & L. Blinn-Pike (Eds.), *Social vulnerability to disasters*. CRC Press.

Quisumbing, A., Meinzen-Dick, R., Bassett, L., Usnick, M., Pandolfelli, L., Morden, C., & Alderman, H. (2008). Helping women respond to the global food price crisis. International Food Policy Research Institute Policy Brief, 7.

Rahman, M. S. (2013). Climate Change, Disaster and Gender Vulnerability: A Study on Two Divisions of Bangladesh. *American Journal of Human Ecology*, *2*(2), 72–82. doi:10.11634/216796221302315

Raphael, B., Taylor, M., & McAndrew, V. (2008). Women, catastrophe and mental health. *The Australian and New Zealand Journal of Psychiatry*, *42*(1), 13–23. doi:10.1080/00048670701732707 PMID:18058439

Rashid, A. K. M., & Shafie, H. A. (2009). *Facilitators Guide: Practicing Gender and Social Inclusion in Disaster Risk Reduction. Directorate of Relief and Rehabilitation*. Dhaka: Ministry of Food and Disaster Management.

Rashid, S. F., & Michuad, S. (2000). Female adolescents and their sexuality: Notions of honour, shame, purity and pollution during the floods. *Disasters*, *24*(1), 54–70. doi:10.1111/1467-7717.00131 PMID:10718014

Rees, S., Pittaway, E., & Bartolomei, L. (2005). Waves of Violence - Women in Post-Tsunami Sri Lanka. *Australasian Journal of Disaster and Trauma Studies*, 2.

True, J. (2012). *The Political Economy of Violence against Women*. New York: Oxford University Press. doi:10.1093/acprof:oso/9780199755929.001.0001

The Taskforce. (2015). *Not now, not ever: Putting an End to Domestic and Family Violence in Queensland*. Retrieved from https://www.qld.gov.au/community/documents/getting-support-health-social-issue/dfv-report-vol-one.pdf

United Nations. (1993). *Declaration on the Elimination of Violence Against Women*. Retrieved form http://www.un.org/documents/ga/res/48/a48r104.htm

United Nations Development Program. (2010). *Gender and Disasters*. Retrieved from http://www.undp.org/content/dam/undp/library/crisis%20prevention/disaster/7Disaster%20Risk%20Reduction%20-%20Gender.pdf

United Nations Population Fund. (2006). *Women are the fabric, Reproductive health for communities in crisis*. Retrieved form https://www.unfpa.org/sites/default/files/pub-pdf/women_fabric_eng_0.pdf

UN Women. (2013). *The 2012 Fiji Floods: Gender Sensitivity in Disaster Management, A Qualitative Review of Gender and Protection Issues in Disaster Management*. Retrieved from http://www.pacific-disaster.net/pdnadmin/data/original/FJI_FL_UNWomen_2012_gender_sensitivity.pdf

VicHealth. (2007). *Preventing violence before it occurs: A framework and background paper to guide the primary prevention of violence against women in Victoria*. Victorian Health Promotion Association.

Wilson, J., Phillips, B. D., & Neal, D. M. (1998). Domestic Violence after Disaster. In E. Enarson & B. H. Morrow (Eds.), *The Gendered Terrain of Disaster: Through Women's Eyes*. Westport, CT: Praeger Publishers.

Women's Environment and Development Organization. (2008). Case Study: Gender, Human Security and Climate Change: Lessons from Bangladesh, Ghana and Senegal. New York: Author.

World Health Organization. (2005). *Factsheet: Gender and Health in Disasters*. Retrieved from http://www.who.int/gender/gwhgendernd2.Pdf

World Health Organization. (2016). *Violence against women, Intimate partner and sexual violence against women, Fact sheet*. Retrieved from http://www.who.int/mediacentre/factsheets/fs239/en/

Section 4
Equality and Empowerment

Chapter 15
Engaging Men in Women's Economic Empowerment in Butiama District, Mara Region, Tanzania

A. N. Sikira
Sokoine University of Agriculture, Tanzania

T. Matekere
Sokoine University of Agriculture, Tanzania

J. K. Urassa
Sokoine University of Agriculture, Tanzania

ABSTRACT

The chapter addresses women's income poverty using men as active participants in empowering women economically. Butiama district was used as a study area, using 120 women and their husbands who were beneficiaries of the programme dealing with loan provision. As an outcome of the study, men had little participation in women's economic activities, hence, women's economic empowerment was at medium level. Unlike men, women's income was used for fulfilling basic needs of the family, therefore, had little impact on their economic empowerment. By conclusion, men as decision makers have high impact on women's economic empowerment. It is recommended that, awareness creation among men would enhance their participation in empowering women. Improvement of women's access to and control over production resources would improve their income. It is recommended that lobbying and advocacy approaches should be applied to enable women's control over the production resources.

DOI: 10.4018/978-1-5225-3018-3.ch015

BACKGROUND INFORMATION

It is estimated that women account for two thirds of the 1.4 billion people currently living in extreme poverty and they make up 60% of the 572 million poor people in the world (DFID, 2000). In Sub-Saharan Africa women are more likely to live in poverty than men in 22 out of the 25 countries (Folbre, 2012). The high proportion of women living in poverty highlights the importance of focusing on women's economic empowerment (WEE) (Garry, 2009). Similarly, the situation of women in Tanzania does not differ much from other women in Africa and in the world at large (Morse, 1991). Unlike women in the male headed households, poverty level is higher in the female headed household as take care of the twin burden of mother and father by providing the family's daily needs for survival while husbands are working in cities or searching for greener pastures far from home (Vuuren, 2000; Kuzilwa, 2005). About 60% of the women live in absolute poverty in Tanzania (URT, 2000). Lack of access to credit and other financial services is one of the causes for women's high poverty levels. Moreover, lack of knowledge and skills resulting from low level of education has been reported as one of the reasons for women's failure to make viable choices for their lives (Kabeer, 2009; URT, 2005). Women's poverty in Tanzania as in other African countries, is partly, caused by gender inequality between men and women as a result of unequal distribution of income and control over resources (including property, assets and financial capital (OECD, 2008).

Generally, women's economic empowerment (WEE) is believed to be the solution towards elimination of poverty among women. The term women's economic empowerment is derived from the word empowerment. According to Batliwala (1994) and Gary (2009), empowerment is the process by which the powerless (marginalized) gain greater control over their life circumstances. It includes the control over resources (physical, human, and intellectual, financial) and over ideology (beliefs, values and attitudes). This means that empowerment entails a process of change by which those who have been denied the ability to make choices (women) acquire such ability (Malhotra *et al.*, 2002). Similarly, women's economic empowerment is the process of increasing women's real power over economic decisions that influence their lives and priorities in society (Kabeer, 2009). Economic empowerment approaches and intervention usually focus on income-generating activities, which allow women to independently acquire their income (Eyben, 2008). Income-generating activities encompass a wide range of areas, such as small business promotion, cooperatives, and job creation schemes (Kabeer, 2005).

Many researchers are working towards economic empowerment of women as crucial element for both realization of women's rights and to achieve broader development goals such as economic growth and poverty reduction (ICRW, 2011). Empirically research data indicates that women's economic empowerment is not just a work, earning income, or even, ownership, unless it involves control over production resources (Duflo, 2012) such as land, livestock, forest leading to: (1) gain more equality and control over their own lives while also (2) contributing: (a) directly to their children's human capital (nutrition, health and education) and thereby indirectly to their nation's income growth; (b) directly to the wealth and well-being of their nations, and (c) indirectly to their country's national income growth through their own – and their educated children's' lower fertility (Blumberg, 2005).

The government of Tanzania in collaboration with donor agencies has for a long time been working to implement financial rural programs with the goal of empowering women. Some of these efforts include Savings and Credit Cooperative Organizations (SACCOs. Despite remarkable achievement of these initiatives women continue to live under control of men (Kato *et al.*, 2012). According to TGNP (2005), the overall equality in economic power in Tanzania decreased by 10% in the year 1995 and 2000.

This was attributed by the decrease in access to resource by 50% among women (TGNP, 2005). It has been reported that men might have a specific role in relation to women's economic empowerment as they are the gatekeepers for production resources necessary for economic advancement, hence leading to gender equality. It is anticipated that once men are willing to open the gates for major reforms gender equality will be achieved (Cornell, 2005).

The role of men as key players in dealing with gender inequality cannot be overemphasized. According to Chant (2007) men have an important role if alteration of household gender-inequalities is to be achieved. Generally, empirical evidence has shown that excluding men in WEE initiatives weaken women's position in the family and increases gender based violence as men are become unnecessarily hostile toward their spouses (Goetz & Gupta, 1996; Makombe *et al.*, 1999). Evidence also shows that a significant proportion of women's loans from WEE programs are controlled by male relatives (including spouse) and some invest the same unwisely while women's position are worsened (Goetz & Gupta, 1996). Men have traditionally been treated as generic and untendered representatives of all humanity (Goetz & Gupta, 1994). When men speak for all members of their communities, they perpetuate masculine norms and widen the gender inequality gap. Normally, men control the resources required to implement women's claims for justice (Garry, 2009). However, more broadly, gender inequalities are based on gender relations, in the complex webs of relationships that exist at every level of human experience. Therefore, men are important actors when it comes to reconstructing gender relations and equality (Mayoux, 1999). Hence, excluding men in the battle against poverty among women/WEE programs by itself cannot overcome patriarchal systems at the household and community levels (UN, 2011). Therefore, there is a need for a more effective way of addressing gender inequality resulting from the existing patriarchal system.

While there are number of studies on economic empowerment of women, this chapter presents a unique gender perspective by determining the role of men in realizing women's economic empowerment in the study area. Previous studies, for example that by Makombe (2006) reported that women's economic empowerment can be achieved through entrepreneurship development; while, Sikira's (2010) reported that gender based violence in the community is a stumbling block towards women's empowerment in Serengeti district, Mara Region. Another study is that by Kato et al. (2013), the study looked at the role of microfinance in empowering Tanzanian women. However, useful the above may be it is unclear as to how men could influence intra-household decision making to enable women's economic empowerment.

THEORETICAL APPROACHES

Women in Development (WID) Theory

Women Economic Empowerment approaches are guided by different theories. The main argument is on how women can be integrated into ongoing development initiatives without compromising the existing structures in which the sources of women's subordination and oppression are embedded (Gershuny & Sullivan, 2003; Folbre, 2012). The theory argues that modernization is impacting women in an unfavorable manner; hence the need for a solution to effectively include women in the economic system (Chodorow, 1989). Generally, most of the WEE approaches guided by WID theory have been focusing on increasing women's participation in economic activities with the goal of empowering them (Chant, 2000).

Gender and Development Theory

Gender and Development (GAD) paradigm centers on gender relations between men and women as the object of change (Moser, 1993). The GAD approach recognizes that gender relations differ within and between cultures. Women are seen as agents of change rather than passive recipients of development efforts. The GAD theory further acknowledges that women's weakness in socio-economic and political structures as well as their limited bargaining power puts them in a disadvantaged position (CIDA, 1997). Generally, Women are subject to inequality not only in the public sphere but also within the private sphere. Based on the GAD theory, including men in the process of women's economic empowerment is critical. This approach does not blame men for the patriarchal systems in which they were raised; rather, it focuses on men's commitment to be the champions towards transformation of the structures of male privilege and authority (Wyss, 1995).

RESEARCH METHODOLOGY

Description and Justification of the Study Area

The chapter is based on the research that was carried out in Butiama District, Tanzania. Butiama District was selected due to its ideal patriarchal social life (Chiragi, 2013). This is associated with the fact that most of the economic resources in the district are planned, managed, administered and distributed by men (Chiragi, 2013). In addition the study area was chosen based on presence of WEE program. This study used a cross-sectional research design; generally the design allows data to be collected at one point in time (Bernard, 2006).

Sampling and Sample Size

The study sampling frame involved all married women who were beneficiaries of WEE program. A total of 120 married women and their spouses constituted the sample selected at random. A questionnaire was used to collect quantitative data collection whereas; checklist of questions was used to collect qualitative data. The study conducted two FGDs in each village, one for men and the other for women. In order to capture qualitative data FGDs was conducted involving 10 participants per FGD. Qualitative data was collected from in-depth interviews and focus group discussion using a checklist of questions and FGD guide. In addition to the above, secondary data were extracted from reports and other documentary materials that were of relevancy to the study. Other methodological issues are presented in details in the subsequent sections.

Data Management and Analysis

Analysis of Qualitative and Quantitative Data

The qualitative data were coded and summarized and analyzed using the content analysis approach. Quantitative data were analyzed using the Statistical Data Package for Social sciences (SPSS). Descriptive statistics were determined specifically frequencies, percentages, and mean values of individual variables. Attitude of men towards WEE was also analyzed descriptively. Inferential statistics included in the study were chi square, ordinal regression and multiple regressions.

Determination of Women's Empowerment Levels

In order to measure women's empowerment levels, a Cumulative Empowerment Index (CEI) was developed. Three indicators were used to develop the CEI which determined the level of women's economic empowerment; these indicators include women's economic decision making, women's control of savings and income and women's ownership of assets and land. The CEI was developed based on the composite assigned values for 16 indices (explaining variables) covering all the three dimensions, the cutoff point (mean index) was used for determining the levels of empowerment. Categories of empowerment were made on the basis of CEI. The CEI was also partitioned into three categories for the purpose of determining empowerment levels among women (low, medium and high)

Determination of Men's Participation Index

In order to measure men's participation in women's economic empowerment, seven variables were used in developing men's participation index. These were husband cooperation which included; helping with household chores; involvement in spouse's economic activity; contributing to a spouses capital; purchasing food for the family; meeting educational cost for children; looking after children and respecting spouse's loans and savings. A three point rating scale was adopted a score 3 was given for 'high participation' 2 for 'average participation' and 1 for "low participation.

Ordinal Regression

Ordinal logistic regression model was used to establish relationship between empowerment levels and factors affecting women's empowerment. The model was used because the dependent variable in this study is categorical representing women's empowerment level as Low, Medium and High empowerment. The independent variables are age, education, type of marriage, men level of support men contribution to startup capital, women's income, type of asset owned and duration in economic activity.

$$Y_1 = \alpha + b_1 X_1 + b_2 X_2 + b_3 X_3 \ldots\ldots\ldots\ldots b_n X_n \sum i \ldots\ldots\ldots\ldots\ldots\ldots \quad (1)$$

Where:

α= constant while Y_1= Time taken to survive in businesses Y_1= Women empowerment levels

b_1, b_2, b_3, b_n =Regression coefficient

X_1= Age of women, X_2= Men Religion, X_3=Type of marriage, X_4= Men's attitude

X_5=Men education level, X_6=Women average income per month, X_7=Women contribution in household income, X_8=Women duration in economic activity, X_9=Women type of economic activity, X_{10}=Men level of participation and εi= Error term

RESULTS AND DISCUSSION

Demographic Characteristics of the Respondents

Age and Education of Respondents

The minimum and maximum age of respondents ranged from 26 to 60 years. Results in Table 1 show that more than half of both male and female were aged above 25 years. In Tanzania, a person is considered an adult after attaining the age of 18 years; this implies that all the respondents were adults. Furthermore, the results in Table 1 indicate that more than half (56.6) and (53.3%) of men and women respectively were aged between 36 - 45 and 26 - 35 years. The result implies that the age of women has a great influence on their ability to take part in economic activities can be shared and influencing benefit from the economic activities (Fakir, 2008).

Table 1 further show that majority (82.7%) and (78.3%) of men and women respectively had primary education level. Also the results show that about 11.3% and 7.5% of men and women respectively had had secondary school education while the percentage of women was slightly lower. This implies that still there is a gender gap in attainment of secondary school education. This can be attributed by the boy child favoritism syndrome, high school dropout and early marriage which reduce girl's chances to attain their secondary education. Generally, the boy child favoritism syndrome denies girl's education attainment particularly when resources are scarce.

Table 1. Social demographic characteristics (n=120)

Variables	Categories	Male (%)	Female (%)
Age	26 – 35	5.8	53.3
	36 – 45	56.7	29.3
	46 – 55	27.5	15.8
	Above 55	10.0	3.2
Education level	No formal education	3.5	9.2
	Adults education	2.4	5.8
	Primary education	82.8	78.3
	Secondary education	11.3	7.5
Type of marriage	Polygamy	40.0	11.7
	Monogamy	60.0	87.3

Type of Marriage

Marriage is almost universal which is a tradition and social institution and is highly valued for social and economic reasons. The institution of marriage greatly influences gender relations, even after a marriage ends through divorce (URT, 2010). In patriarchal societies married women with children are more respected. According to Sikira (2010) most important social status that a woman achieves is that of being a wife and mother. Results in Table 1 show that all women were married of which women (87.3%) were under monogamy. The above findings are in-line with Makombe *et al.* (2009) who found that the majority of women in the savings groups were under monogamy. Interestingly, about 60% and 40% of men were under monogamy and polygamy respectively. This implies that men are likely to have more informal extra marital relationship. In most of the polygamous households, women are the main breadwinners; there is always pressure on their small resources to keep the household going, which ultimately decreases their time in participation in economic activities and the level of engagement in other productive activities.

One woman FGD participants said that:

I am a third wife I was married three years back I found my husband with four children of his two former wives, I have to take care of all these children, it is very difficult for me to engage in economic activities.

This implies that women's workload is still higher among rural women which, in turn impacts negatively on their economic empowerment.

Type of Economic Activities Preferred by Women

The findings as presented in Table 2 show that about 43.7% and 25.3% of women were engaged in selling of dried fish and firewood respectively. Whereas 11.2% of women were engaged in operating a grocery shop, and only 9.8% were engaged in food vending. The nature of the above economic activities that women engage in provides them with little return and can contribute little to their economic empowerment.

During the FGDs women revealed that they prefer selling dried and smoked fish because through this business they also get food. One of the female discussants said:

During food deficit at home, I normally exchange fish with flour to enable my family to get food.

Women also revealed that sometimes they are forced to temporarily put a hold on their income generating activities because of farming activities. Involvement in selling firewood as one of the income generating activity was only preferred by few women due to the fact that it entails walking long distances to the forestry which is risky and more time consuming and in most cases, it entails leaving early in the morning.

The Role of Men in Women Economic Activities

Results in Table 2 show that men play various roles in supporting their wives in economic activities. More than half (55%) contribute the startup capital, whereas more than a third (34.5%) directly participate in the economic activities especially when the wife is engaged in household chores. One of the key

Table 2. The role of men and Type of women economic activities (n=120)

Type of Economic Activity	Percent
Dried and smoked fish business	43.7
Firewood business	11.2
Grocery shop	25.3
Food vendor	9.8
Role of Men	**Percent**
Providing capital for economic activity	55.0
Contribute to household income	8.5
Attend household chores	2.0
Engaging in women economic activities	34.5

informants revealed that very few men consider helping their wives in the domestic chores as a result women spend less time in economic activities. Generally, most of the men prefer giving their wives money as a startup capital rather than participating in their income generating activities. The findings suggest that men's status has not changed from masculinity to care-giving while women have changed from just a housewife to becoming notable breadwinners. Normally, very little of caring takes place in the daily lives of men.

Capital Contribution by Men to Women's Economic Activities

Table 3 present data on amount of capital that men contribute to their wife's economic activities for the last year. Capital contributions among men varied. About 60.3% of the men contributed between TZS 10 000 to 30 000, while 17.1% contribute between 30 000 and 60 000 and only 0.7% contributes more than 90 000. Although WEE program aim at providing women with loans as startup capital, in most

Table 3. Men's capital contribution to women's economic activities and their support to household needs (n=66)

Type of Economic Activity	Percent
Between 10 000 - 30 000	60.3
Between 300 000 - 60 000	17.1
Between 60 000 - 90 0 000	11.9
More than 90 000	0.7
Type of Support Provided by Spouses/Men	**Percent**
Buying food	66.0
School expenses	26.4
Medical costs	7.5

cases the amount is spent on household needs and women end up requesting additional funding from their husband/spouse to be able to establish the intended economic activities. One woman in Mugango village said:

When I wanted to start my kiosk business I took a 50,000= Tanzanian Shillings (Tsh) loan, I could not take more because this was the limit according to my savings. However, the amount was not enough to start the economic activity I had envisaged. So I requested my husband to provide me an additional of Tsh 50 000/=.

During the FGDs in Kwibara men revealed that, although women take loans, their investment is always small because their savings are also small, as a result they need support from men to continue running their business. Men FGD participants further revealed that women's income is used mostly on food and other household expenses. Therefore, although women are expected to have more power on the income they earn, it makes very little difference to their empowerment. Furthermore, women have less access to financial services than men; in particularly rural women face strong barriers when it comes to borrowing money due to lack of collateral (property). They have less power and ability to do activities as it is for men; in addition, they have no meaningful authority to initiate and run any viable business without seeking permission from their husbands/spouses. Therefore, women continue depending on men (husband) economically, as men are traditionally considered assertive and the breadwinners of the family. Sometimes women use their husband's income in loan repayment or to support their Income Generating Activities (IGA's).

Men's/Spouses Support to Household Needs

In many African cultures husbands play a role of ensuring the family has its basic needs. However, in recent years women have been taking a leading role in ensuring a family gets its basic needs. The reasons for women being breadwinners mainly emanates from a majority of men not fulfilling their traditional role. The findings as presented in Table 3indicate that majority (66%) of men support their families by purchasing food while 26.4% spent their income on school expenses and only 7.5% spend on medical costs.

On the other hand, Women FDGs participants pointed out that some husbands do not buy food for the family resulting into women using their loans in meeting their family needs, and when it comes to repaying the loans some husbands/spouses are not cooperative. The women further revealed that some of their fellows have decided not to be part of the program because each time they took loan to start and income generating activity they ended up spending it on other family needs.

Men's/Spouse's Average Support on Food Per Day

The findings in Table 4 show that 46.7%, 36.7% and 16.6% of men contribute only TZS 2,000, 3,000 and 4,000 respectively for food. As it was reported by women FGD participant, men's contribution to food is not provided on a regular basis. During the men FGDs, it was pointed out that men do also face financial constraints and limited sources of income. For example, in one of the FGD's participants said:

Table 4. Men average support on food per day (n=120)

Average Amount	Percent
Less than 2000	46.7
Between 2000 – 3000	36.7
Between 3000 – 5000	16.6

Nowadays we don't get much from fishing as it was the case in the past. Sometimes fishing is restricted and since it is our only source of livelihood then at such times the situation becomes worse.

Although men also indicated a need for diversifying their livelihood activities one key informant revealed that in most cases men are less willing to buy food for the family when their spouse earns an income.

Men Support in Women's Usage of Loans

The findings as presented in Table 5 indicate that men never asked their wives to divert their loans for unintended activities. Even if they do so, the wife has a room to agree or to refuse. However, 84.5% said they have never asked their spouses to give them their credit while 15.5% agreed to have asked their spouse to give them their loans (Table 5). Also 42.5% convinced their spouse to use money for unintended use while 52.5% had never convinced their spouse on the same. This implies that women had the decision making power in relation to how they use their loans. These findings are contrary to Makombe (1999) who reported women's credit to be controlled by their husbands/spouses.

On the other hand findings in Table 5 show that more than half (62.5%) invest their loans on economic activities, while about a third (31.2%) use loans to meet other household expenses including purchasing food. Very few (6.8%) spend accessed loan on education. In cases where the money has been used for household expenses women were not able to repay their loans on time. One village leader pointed out

Table 5. Men support in women usage of loans (n=120)

Category	Percent (%)
Men responses on their spouse loans	
Ever asked for spouse loan	15.5
Never asked for spouse loan	84.5
Un-intentional use of loans	
Convince their spouse	42.5
Never convinced their spouse	52.5
Uses of loans	
Purchasing food for the family	31.2
Investing in economic activities	62.5
Spending on school expenses	6.8

that there have been issues of delay in repaying loans by women borrowers. The above is generally due to a high proportion of the loan being used for consumption and the fact that income earned from most of the income generating activities is small then, women are left with no option but to request their husbands/spouses to assist them in loan repayment. As a consequence of the above, women continue to be dependent on men and hence lowering their likelihood of being economically empowered.

Levels of Men's Participation in Women's Economic Activities

In order to assess men's participation in women's economic activities, a participation index was developed by combining six participation indicators as indicated in the earlier methodology sub-section. Cumulative participation index varied from 21 to 72, whereas 21 indicate the lowest participation level and 72 means the highest participation level. Results as presented in Table 6 indicate that the majority (71.6%) of men belong to low participation category with the score ranges between 21-37, whereas 22.6% fall under average participation level with the score range between 38-54 and very few (5.8%) belong into high participation level with the score ranges between 55-72. The result shows that men do not offer enough support in their spouses' economic activities. Therefore, women are faced with a double burden of performing the domestic chores as well as income generating activities in most cases the latter, is compromised in favour of the former. This suggests that men's contribution to women economic activities is very minimal and does not contribute to significant improvement of women's economic empowerment. Generally, women's income is important for achieving economic growth (Kabeer, 2009). However, when women do not receive enough support from their spouses their economic empowerment is hindered.

Factors Affecting Men Participation in WEE

Multiple linear regression model was used to determine factors that influence men participation in WEE. Men participation in WEE was based on the Cumulative Participation Index (CPI), and factors restricting men participation such as men attitude, age, education level, type of marriage, and religion. Table 10 presents the results from estimated parameters determining the factors constraints men participation in WEE. Through its R-square value, the model shows that 51.6% variation in men's participation is due to fitted predicators and the remaining 48.4% cause by predicators not included in the model. The statistical tests of the model itself show that the explanatory power of the model was significant ($p<0.001$).

The result in the model on Table 7 indicate that age was statistically significant at $p<0.005$ with a positive influence in men's participation. Most men in the study were in the active age category. This implies that their participations to economic strengthening depend on people who are active and health since most women economic activities are traditional and labour intensive.

Table 6. Levels of men participation in WEE activities (n=120)

Levels	Percent (%)
Low	71.6
Average	22.6
High	5.8

Table 7. Regression analysis on factors affecting men participation in WEE (n=120)

Independent Variable		Estimate	Standard Error	Wald	Sig
Constant		0.397	0.158	2.505*	0.000
Age of men		0.022	0.001	0.236	0.002*
Attitude of men	Positive	0.053	0.020	0.582	0.021
	Negative	-0.164	0.020	-0.638	0.000**
	Neutral	0.366	0.340	3.743	0.413
Education level of men	No formal education	-0.268	1.890	5.743	0.315
	Adult education	0.850	0.010	-0.935	0.629
	Primary education	0.249	0.008	-2.584	0.012
	Secondary education	0.371	0.082	1.510	0.015
Men support in food	High support	0.249	0.173	2.130	0.003*
	Medium support	0.107	0.777	1.255	0.352
	Low support	1.164	0.013	4.643	0.413
Religion	Christians	0.517	0.002	2.436	0.114
	Muslims	2.278	2.090	1.880	0.104
	Traditional	-0.178	1.792	-2.004	0.000**
Type of Marriage	Polygamy	-0.050	0.193	-0.489	0.836
	Monogamy	0.250	0.264	-2.503	0.015
R^2=51.6%	Adjusted R^2=0.495				
*** significant at 0.1%	** significant at 1%	* significant at 5%			

The findings reveal that men's attitude was found to have a significant relationship at p<0.001 on men's participation. It was found that most men had negative attitude towards WEE. Majority agreed that women do not need men's support in their economic activities. This implies that men believe that they have no role to play in supporting their wife towards economic empowerment; as a result in most cases women are less empowered.

Findings show that low support on food was found to be significant at p<0.001 with a negative influence on men's participation. Men are regarded as breadwinner and are supposed to provide for the family. Men with low support to food believe that their spouse has money so even though they are not participating in economic empowerment activities, the wife will still make it in his absence.

Furthermore the result in Table 31 indicate that traditional religions, was statistically significant p<0.001with a negative influence men's participations. Men with traditions religions still hold strong norms and culture with in most cases are discriminatory to women. This influences their participations in WEE.

Indicators for Women Economic Empowerment

Results in Table 8 indicate that majority 65.4% of women were able to make decision regarding purchasing household assets such as mattresses, bed and cattle. This implies that high economic decision by women is attributed by their ability to control income from their economic activities. The results are

Table 8. Indicators for women economic empowerment (n=120)

Indicators for WEE	Percentage (%)		
	Husband	Husband and Wife	Wife
Ownership of land	74.6	20.3	5.1
Economic decision making	11.5	23.1	65.4
Control of savings and income	7.2	9.7	83.1
Control of loans	21.5	15.2	63.3
Ownership of assets	9.4	57.2	33.4

similar to Kabeer (2009) who contends that having income increase women participation in economic decision especially in societies where women are marginalized. Additionally, the result indicated in Table 8 show that majority 83% of women control their savings implying that women participation in economic activities has provided a safe place for women to save their money Although women earn income from their economic activities, the amount is very little for building up their capital as a result they end up using it to meet the immediate household need. This study agrees with what was pointed out by Parveen (2005) that women used their earning for family welfare such as buying nutritious food, paying school fees for children and other household necessities rather than on their personal need or economic activities. Inversely, majority of men spend more on their personal needs such as alcohol, and gambling. As a result majority of the women continue to be involved in traditional and more feminine economic activity instead of starting larger enterprises. It is well-established in literature that an economically active woman with her own independent savings and greater income share within the household has more economic power (Duflo, 2005).

Results in Table 8 further show that the majority (63.3%) of women had the power to control of loans. This implies that women can make decisions on how much loans to take and use in starting an economic activity without consulting their husband. Again 21.5% of men agreed that they control women's loan, this implies that husbands determine how loans can be used which in most cases is used for household consumption. The findings are in line with Rahman (1999) who found that some men compel their wives to hand over loans to them, which tends to increase marital conflicts and poverty among women as they must repay the loan from other unintended sources such as selling labor.

Men may allow their wives to use household assets as collateral with the intention of controlling their spouse's loans. The courage of men to convince their spouse to use the loan can be associated with the support they receive from them. The findings are similar with the study by Goetz and Gupta (1996) who pointed out that credit programs pay insufficient attention to their impact from a gender perspective and, as consequence, may weaken rather than strengthen women's position in the family.

Productive assets enable women to earn more income compared to non-productive asset. Result in Table 8 indicates that slightly more than half 57.6% of assets are controlled by both husband and wife. During the FGDs few women revealed that they owned productive assets like cattle, goats and poultry as well as non-productive assets such as bed, mattresses and kitchen utensils. Result in Table 8 further show that about three quarters (74.6%) of land is owned by men, while only 5.1% of women own land. Land ownership among women was very low due to male dominancy under the patriarchy system. The findings are in line with Chiragi (2013) who found that patriarchal nature of society in Mara region, provide women fewer chances to own property.

Cumulative Empowerment Index (CEI)

In order to assess women's economic empowerment, the CEI was constructed combining three key empowerment indicators including economic decision making, control over income and savings and ownership of assets and land. Results in Table 9 show that more than half (57.1%) fall under medium empowerment category, while under a third (31.2%) falls under low empowerment category and few (11.7%) were highly empowered. The results suggest that participation in the empowerment program has increased women economic empowerment as majority of the women were in the medium level. The result is in-line with Bali and Wallentin (2009) who found that members are empowered by participating in WEE program in the sense that they have a greater propensity to resist existing negative gender norms and culture that restrict their ability to develop and make choices.

CONCLUSION AND RECOMMENDATIONS

Based on the findings it can be concluded that women participate in various income generating activities in order to fulfill their family needs. It can also be concluded that men play a minor role in women's economic empowerment, generally, after providing startup capital to their spouses their participation becomes minimal in their spouses economic activities. As a result of the above rural women's empowerment is curtailed.

Based on the women's empowerment indicators that were used to determine the levels of women empowerment, it can be concluded that that more than half of women in the study area attained medium level of empowerment. It can further be concluded that though women do control their savings, income, loans and other resources land is a men's preserve as a result women fail to use it as collateral in seeking loans. Generally, lack of ownership over land increases women's vulnerability and hence their higher poverty levels. Additionally, it can be concluded that there was a positive relationship between the level of women's empowerment and men's support and that women's economic empowerment increases with increased support from their spouses.

Based on the Multiple Regression results it can be concluded that factors such spouse's (men's), age, negative attitude, low support in food and their traditional beliefs were important predictors of the men's participation in WEE. The above significantly affected the spouses participation in WEE. Lastly, it is concluded that traditions and norms continue to hinder men's participation and attitude towards women's economic empowerment.

Table 9. Cumulative Empowerment Index (CEI)

Empowerment Level	Percent
Low	31.2
Medium	57.1
High	11.7

Recommendations

1. Based on the conclusions made above, it is recommended that enhancing awareness among men on WEE will improve women's economic gain therefore leading to WEE. Through awareness creation of gender roles and improvement of intra-household relationship men are likely to change. It is therefore recommended that the major intervening institutions, namely government organizations (GOs), non-government organizations (NGOs) and women's organizations (WOs), private institutions, civil society, etc.) as well as entire communities need to ensure men's involvement in women's empowerment activities at all stages of the development programs. More specifically lobbying by traditional leaders could greatly reduce some of the cultural barriers that are patriarchal and which have been holding back men from involvement in women's activities and their empowerment in general.
2. Women's economic decision making, control over resources and income, women's ownership of land are indicators for women economic empowerment. It is also recommended that for WEE there is need to improve women's access and control over resources in particular land. Therefore, there is need for all stakeholders interested in WEE to create awareness and educate communities on the importance of the above.

REFERENCES

Batliwala, S. (1994). *The meaning of Women's Empowerment: Population Policies Reconsidered*. Harvard Series on Population and International Health.

Bernard, H. R. (2002). *Research Methods in Anthropology: Qualitative and Quantitative Approaches*. Oxford, UK: Altamira Press.

Blumberg, R. (2005). *Women economic empowerment as a magic portion of development*. Paper Presented at the 100 Annual Meeting of the American Sociological Association, Philadelphia, PA.

Chant, S. (2007). Dangerous Equations? How Female-Headed Households Became the Poorest of the Poor: Causes, Consequences and Cautions. In A. Cornwall, E. Harrison, & A. Whitehead (Eds.), *Feminisms in Development: Contradictions, Contestations and Challenges* (pp. 35–47). London: Zed Books.

Chant, S. (2007). Dangerous Equations? How female-headed households became the poorest of the poor: causes, consequences and cautions. In *Feminisms in Development Contradictions, Contestations and Challenges* (pp. 35–47). London: Zed Books Publishers.

Chant, S., & Gutmann, M. (2007). *Mainstreaming Men into Gender and Development: Debates, Reflections and Experiences*. Oxford, UK: Oxfam.

Chirangi, M. (2013). *Afya Jumuishi: Towards interprofessional collaboration between traditional and medicinal practitioner in Mara Region of Tanzania* (Dissertation). University of Laiden.

Chodorow, N. J. (1989). *Feminism and Psychoanalytic Theory*. New Haven, CT: Yale University Press.

CIDA. (1997). *Guide to Gender Sensitive Indicators*. Canadian International Development Agency. Retrieved from http://acdi-cida.gc.ca

DFID. (2000). *Eliminating World Poverty. Making Globalisation Work for the Poor.* London: Her Majesty's Stationery Office.

Duflo, E. (2012). Women Empowerment and Economic Development. *Journal of Economic Literature, 50*(4), 1051–1079. doi:10.1257/jel.50.4.1051

Eyben, R. (2008). *Conceptualizing Empowerment and the Implications for Pro-poor Growth.* Brighton, UK: Institute of Development Studies, University of Sussex.

Fakir, M., & Folbre, N. (2006). Measuring care: Gender, empowerment, and the care economy. *Journal of Human Development, 7,* 2.

Folbre, N. (2012). *The Care Economy in Africa: Subsistence Production and Unpaid Care.* Paper for the AERC Biannual Research Workshop.

Gary, B., & Jennifer, S. (2010). *Engaging Men as Allies in Women's Economic Empowerment: Strategies and Recommendations for CARE Country Offices.* Washington, DC: ICRW.

Gershuny, J., & Sullivan, O. (2003). Time use, gender, and public policy regimes. *Social Politics, 10*(2), 205–227. doi:10.1093/sp/jxg012

Goetz, A. M. and Sen Gupta, R. (1994). *Who Takes the Credit? Gender, Power, and Control over Loan Use in Rural Credit Programmes, Bangladesh.* Retrieved from http://www.gdrc.org/icm/references/microfinance.html

Goetz, A. M., & Sen Gupta, R. (1996). Who Takes The Credit? Gender, Power and Control over Loan Use in Rural Credit Programs in Bangladesh. *World Development, 24*(1), 45–63. doi:10.1016/0305-750X(95)00124-U

ICRW. (2011). Determination of family task sharing: A study of husbands and wives. *Journal of Marriage and the Family, 46,* 345–355.

International Center Research on Women. (2011). *Understanding and Measuring Women's Economic Empowerment Definition.* Washington, DC: International Center Research on Women.

Kabeer, N. (2005). Gender equality and women's empowerment: A critical analysis of the third millennium development goal. *Gender and Development, 13*(1), 13–14. doi:10.1080/13552070512331332273

Kabeer, N. (2009). *Women's Economic Empowerment: Key Issues and Policy Options. SIDA Background Paper.* Sussex, UK: Institute of Development Studies.

Kato, M., & Kratzer, J. (2013). Empowering women through Microfinance: Evidence from Tanzania. *Journal of Entrepreneurship Perspective, 2*(1), 31–45.

Kuzilwa, J. A. (2005). The Role of Credit for Small Business Success: A Study of the National Entrepreneurship Development Fund in Tanzania. *Journal of Entrepreneurship, 14*(2), 131–161. doi:10.1177/097135570501400204

Makombe, I. A. M. (2006). *Women Entrepreneurship Development and Empowerment in Tanzania: Thecase of SIDO/UNIDO-Supported Women Microentrepreneurs in the Food Processing Sector* (Doctoral dissertation). University of South Africa, South Africa.

Makombe, I. A. M., Temba, E. I., & Kibombo, A. R. M. (1999). *Credit Schemes and Women's Empowerment for Poverty Alleviation*. The Case Study of Tanga Region. Research Report No. 1. Research for Poverty Alleviation.

Malhotra, A. (2002). *Measuring women's empowerment as a variable in international development*. Paper prepared for the World Bank workshop on poverty and Gender; New Perspective.

Moser, C. (1991). *Gender planning in the third world: Meeting practical and strategic needs*. Retrieved from http://www.china-up.com:8080/international/case/.../1296.p

OECD (2008). *Gender and Sustainable Development Maximizing the Economic, Social and Environmental Role of Women, USA*. Retrieved from http://www.oecd.org/../sustain abledevelopmentkeyreports

Parveen, S., & Leonhauser, I. (2005). *Empowerment of rural women in Bangladesh: A Household Level Analysis*. Paper presented on Conference on Rural Poverty Reduction through Research for Development and Transformation, Berlin, Germany.

Rahman, A. (1999). Micro-credit Initiatives for equitable and sustainable development: Who pays? *World Development Research*, 27(1), 67–82. doi:10.1016/S0305-750X(98)00105-3

Sikira, A. (2010). *Gender bases violence and women empowerment: A case study of Serengeti District* (PhD Thesis). Sokoine University of Agriculture, Morogoro, Tanzania.

Soomro, G. Y. (2000). A re-examination of fertility transition in Pakistan. *Pakistan Development Review*, 39(3), 247–261.

TGNP. (2005). African Gender and Development Index Dar es Salaam, Tanzania. population policies considered: *Health. Empowerment and Rights*, 1, 127–138.

United Nations. (2011). *Gender Equality in the Contemporary World*. New York: United Nations, Department of Economic and Social Affairs, Division of Social Policy and Development.

URT. (2000). *National Micro-finance Policy*. Dar es Salaam, Tanzania: Ministry of Finance.

URT. (2005). *A country Report on the Implementation of the Beijing Platform for Action and Outcome*. Dar es Salaam, Tanzania: Ministry of Community Development Gender and Children.

URT. (2010). Tanzania Gender Indicators Booklet 2010: Ministry of Finance and Economic Affairs, Poverty Eradication and Economic Empowerment Division. Research and Poverty Alleviation.

Vuuren, A (2000). *Female headed household: Their survival strategies in Tanzania. De-Agrarianisation and Rural Development Network*. Africa studiescentrum.

Wyss, B. (1995). *Gender and economic support of Jamaican households: Implications for children's living standards* (Doctoral Dissertation). University of Massachusetts, Amherst, MA.

Chapter 16
Empowering Women Entrepreneurs in India With ICT Applications

Ananya Goswami
Birla Institute of Technology, India

Sraboni Dutta
Birla Institute of Technology, India

ABSTRACT

In a developing nation like India where the "Gender Digital Divide" is still prevalent, ICT is emerging as a powerful catalyst for women's economic, social and political empowerment. Empowering women entrepreneurs with ICT in this globally competitive environment can have a ripple effect in bettering the social fabric of the nation. Incorporation of ICT has created new opportunities for women entrepreneurs by contributing to knowledge sharing, networking and electronic commerce activities. This study investigates the factors which influence the women entrepreneurs to incorporate ICT in their business firms. It also provides an insight on the barriers towards adoption of ICT applications by these women entrepreneurs. It has been observed that both Government and Non-Government Organizations are working towards ICT awareness programmes, i.e., ICT-related education, training and technical support for the women entrepreneurs so that they can tap the benefit of the applications.

INTRODUCTION

Information and Communication Technology (ICT) has contributed significantly to the social and economic upliftment of nations worldwide by generating greater employment and productivity to attain a better quality of living. ICT integrates electronic technologies and techniques to produce, store, process, distribute and exchange information. ICT generates many affirmative effects on our daily lives – improved access for communities in rural or remote areas, upgraded health care system, data sharing, storage, interpretation and management. ICT develops business, education system and employment opportunities for countries. Furthermore, ICT enables communication between people, since it increases

DOI: 10.4018/978-1-5225-3018-3.ch016

societal interaction. Information and communication technologies (ICT) provide new opportunities for employment and also create improved ways for expanding existing ones. With respect to small and micro enterprises, studies have shown that that ICTs have not just helped the firms perform better but has also improved the living conditions of the people involved (USAID, 2005). Through networked economy, ICT has enabled to link the businesses with their suppliers and customers on a real time basis. ICT has also slashed the mammoth expenditure on coordination, communication and information processing (Ssewanya & Busler, 2007).

Women using ICTs for business has initiated a shift in perception about the role of women in the development of the society. ICTs are most useful tools at helping women owned firms in saving time and accessing new markets. Technologies like mobile phones permit women to eradicate travel, multitask and coordinate business with household responsibilities.

In the context of developing countries, ICTs have become very useful business tools especially for women entrepreneurs. ICT is an enabler in unlocking the potentials of women entrepreneurs. The innovative use of ICT can fasten the growth of the economy by providing the women with a various business opportunities and subsequently leading to their economic empowerment. E-commerce opportunities ushered in by modern ICT platforms can highly benefit women entrepreneurs. The fast development of the Information and Communication Technology (ICT) sector has positioned India on the global platform by creating novel avenues and opportunities in the development process (OECD, 2010).

Although women have been engaged in different types of jobs in traditional sectors as well as in a number of self-employment activities, they are less likely to reap the benefits from existing or new technologies. The 'gender-divide' in accessing ICTs has pushed the women entrepreneurs far behind their male counterparts and addressing these bottlenecks have become very essential to uplift the status of the women entrepreneurs in the modern economy (Rahman, 2016).

There have been massive investments by the private and government sectors in the development of the communications industries in India (International Centre for Research on Women, 2012). For example, Self-Employed Women's Association (SEWA) in India has integrated ICTs effectively into their on-going production and training activities and has derived benefits from more efficient and wider marketing through ICT platforms (Joshi, 2012). There are also a number of other cases where women's groups are utilizing ICTs for various types of business purposes successfully in a number of developing counties (Joshi, 2011; Maier & Nair-Reichert, 2007).

The objective of the chapter is to understand the importance of ICT in women empowerment, and the factors that induce the women entrepreneurs to adopt ICT in their businesses. The study has also highlighted the barriers that are being encountered to implement ICT by the women entrepreneurs and the role of Government and other institutions in promoting ICT tools amongst the women entrepreneurs.

PREVALENCE OF ICT IN INDIA AND GLOBAL ECONOMY

Over the past two decades, ICT has played a revolutionary role in the socio-economic advancement of India. The ICT sector, which comprises of telecom operators, hardware developers, software developers, internet service providers, content developers, application providers and equipment manufacturers, now plays a very promising role in the development of the global economy today. Various researches across the world have consistently established the fact that investment in ICT positively affectsGDP growth, jobs, productivity and innovation (Intel, 2010). Figure 1 outlines the benefits of ICT in economic development.

Empowering Women Entrepreneurs in India With ICT Applications

Figure 1. ICT in economic development

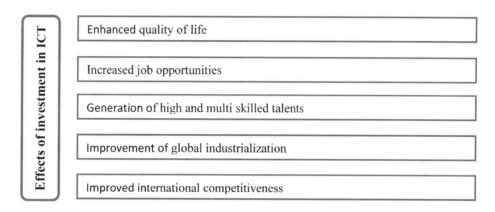

Figure 2 clearly depicts that there is a direct association between ICT development and the overall economic growth of a country. The countries having the top ranks in terms of ICT development have the highest GDP levels. This clearly shows that the incorporation of ICT in a country enhances the overall economic growth.

Hence, it is clear that ICT sector plays an important role in fostering productivity, providing employment opportunities and serves as a growth catalyst for the economy. Economic developments apart, ICTs bridge the gap between the rural and urban masses. It fosters societal development which includes better health, education system and boosts the citizen participation in the society (EY, 2015).

Figure 3 highlights the worldwide mobile-cellular penetration rate. The developing countries have a very low penetration rate of 89% as compared to developed countries with penetration rate as high as128%which shows that the developing countries are lagging behind in terms of mobile usage.

Figure 2. ICT development Vs GDP per capital
Source: EY, 2015

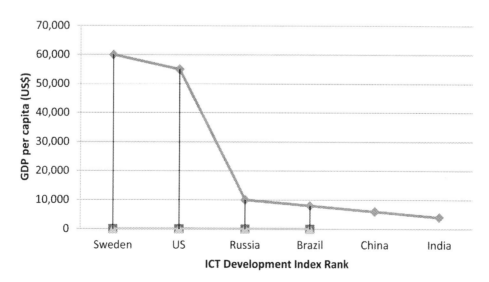

Figure 3. Mobile cellular penetration, 2013
Source: ITU, 2013

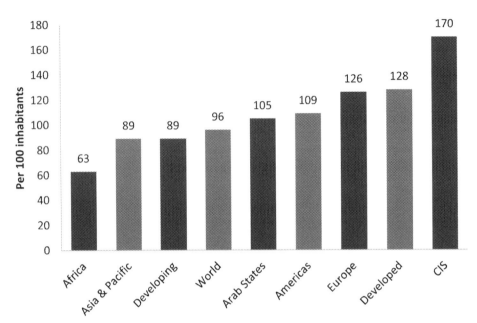

Men use Internet more than women. Figure 4 shows that globally, 37% of all women are online, compared with 41% of all men which is 1.3 billion women and 1.5 billion men (ITU, 2013). Jackson et al. (2001) found that women use emails more than men whereas men use web-portals more than their women counterpart. Similarly, Jones *et al.* (2009) found that males are repeated users of Internet and as a result, their usage of ecommerce sites is also very high.

Figure 4. Internet users: Gender gap
Source: ITU, 2013

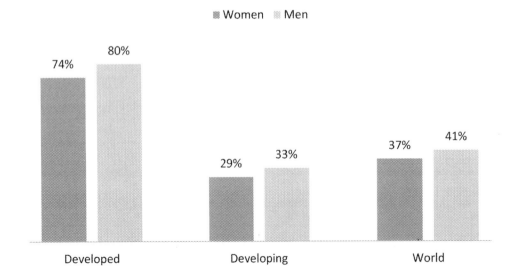

Empowering Women Entrepreneurs in India With ICT Applications

Figure 5 highlights that in 2013, over 2.7 billion people are accessing Internet which corresponds to 39% of the world's population. In the developing world, 31% of the total population strength are accessing Internet as compared to the 78% in the developed world and the difference is quite higher. This is due to the reasons that the individuals in the developing countries have lesser access to ICT.

WOMEN'S USAGE AND EMPOWERMENT THROUGH ICT

Women's empowerment is focused on increasing their ability to take independent decisions that might shape their lives. ICT provides a host of avenues for women empowerment through maximising their access to health, education and other human development opportunities. The sustainable livelihoods of women can be enhanced by expanding the access of the market for the women producers and traders and providing them with education, training and employment opportunities. The economic empowerment of women can be augmented by various ICT interventions such as:

- Creating business and employment opportunities for women.
- Formulating training programmes where women feel comfortable in engaging themselves in village or community development initiatives.
- Formulating and implementing ICT-based tools that specifically address women's issues on literacy programmes, ICT training, business course, trading information and e-commerce initiatives.

In several countries, various ICT projects have been initiated that have led to women empowerment. The Multimedia Caravan project in Senegal provided an opportunity to the rural women todevelop their own concept and ideas on how ICT can be used to meet their development needs and goals (Jain,

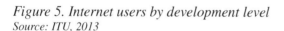

Figure 5. Internet users by development level
Source: ITU, 2013

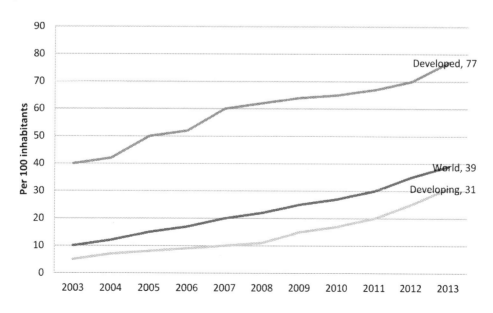

2015). Weavers in Kenyawere trained to use the Internet and learn innovativeways of weaving and gain information on more sensible prices for their finished goods (United Nations, 2005). In Uganda, the Uganda Media Women's Association established a radio programme—Mama FM—where women can take part and learn about developmental issues such as human rights, governance, children, health and nutrition etc. (Jain, 2015).The UNDP/Japan Women in Development Fund has supported number of programmes in India, Bhutan, Egypt Rwanda, Cameroon and Ukraine to maximize the ICT access by the rural women (United Nations, 2005). The women's radio clubs in Zimbabwe facilitated women to develop network with other rural women to contribute in state politics. In Ukraine, a project called "Sustaining Women Farmers" hasapproximately trained 2,000 prospective women entrepreneurs on ICT (United Nations, 2005).

The Asian Women's Resource Exchange (AWORC) is an internet-based programme for women to provide necessary information for women's empowerment (WomenAction, 2000). A UNESCO project in Nabanna, India, on "Networking Rural Women and Knowledge" have distributed knowledge to the poor women in the rural areas on the innovative uses of databases, websites and web based partnerships with other organizations which are located outside the territory. In Baduria ICT Centre of West Bengal, women have confirmed that they gained more respect in their social life due to their acquired ICT skills. Younger women felt that they are able to approach the job market with high confidence level (United Nations, 2005). Studies in Information Technology Applications (SITA) is a training programme on computer skills sponsored by World Bank and the Women's e-Cooperative Mitramandal is also another initiative which has four wings – Professional Wing is to train the trainers, Earning Wing is to train on the use of IT skills to generate income, Learning Wing is to implement the learning strategy and Public/Private Organizations is to provide work (Singh & Sahay, 2006).

WOMEN ENTREPRENEURS AND ICT USAGE IN BUSINESS

ICTs are rapidly changing the global scenario, serving a strong force in shaping the way people work, live and communicate. As the trend in both the public and private sector is towards digitization, any firms without access to technologies have a clear disadvantage. ICTs are consistently believed to be one of the most effective instruments for economic development. In Bangladesh the women entrepreneurs are provided with more than 55,000 phones to access market information, dealing with the traders and customers under the Grameen Bank's Village Phone Program (Maier & Reichert, 2007). Singh and Sahay (2006) have discussed that the project named as Free and Young for Taiwan offers 4 level of courses for the women entrepreneurs. Level 1 is for beginners who want to implement ICT networks in the firms. Level 2 is for women entrepreneurs who want to move into e–business. Level 3 is for those who are already into business and training is being provided on the development plans, managerial skills, legal issues and ICT strategies. Level 4 is for the women who are into politics but have no knowledge on the economic issues to support women entrepreneurs. Digital Filipino.com is an initiative in Philippines for women entrepreneurs to assist them on training, e-commerce strategy, internet marketing and social networking (Singh & Sahay, 2006). In Gujarat, India, women dairy producers use the Dairy Information System Kiosk (DISK), which gives information about the dairy sector (Goswami & Dutta, 2015).

E-commerce initiatives can directly connect women producers with traders, at all levels – local regional, national and even at global levels. An NGO named RODEMU in Argentina trained young women from the rural areas on ICT for marketing their handicrafts in the global world through e-portals.

Elsouk, an e-commerce website was set up in assistance with the World Bank to help the women artisans from Lebanon, Morocco, Jordan, Egypt and Tunisia and to sell their finished products and develop B2B network (Maier & Reichert, 2008).

MOTIVATIONAL FACTORS TO USE ICT

In the context of globalization, information is the soul for enterprise creation, growth and survival and ICT is easing out the information gaps in the business sector (Mokaya & Njuguna, 2010). ICT enhances the firm's efficiency, reduces costs, widens market reach – locally and globally which results in job creation, revenue generation and overall economic growth of the country. ICT applications are important for women oriented firms as it eases out the inter and intra firm activities. The World Bank (2010) has identified that women empowerment is the key to reduce poverty and sustainable development. Women's equal access to ICT can enhance their capabilities and thus improve the quality of life (Matangi & Kashora, 2013). The use of ICT by women entrepreneurs has led to higher productivity of the firms and also given added value to the products or services that is fetching increased revenue share. Women business owners are increasingly using ICTs to offer customers a more convenient and efficient experience. Technology assists in generating various reports that are being used by the businesswoman for addressing various issues and is impetus for important strategic decisions. ICT is also instrumental in streamlining, optimising and automating various internal processes that reduces red tapism, human error and complexity of internal procedures (Marius, 2013). The information, communication and services provided by a mobile phone are enabling women entrepreneurs in saving time and money, improving productivity and return on investment. They feel more connected to the business world. It also helps the women business owners to sell their products in the most profitable markets and determine the optimum timing of scale (Maier & Reichert, 2007). External pressure like pressure from trading partners and competitors are the important predictors that have strong influence on adoption of ICT. According to Kirby & Turner (1993) when major supplier/customers adopts IT, women owned small firms are also likely to adopt. The small business firms are often forced to use ICT by the large firms. This is a driving factor to use technology if their trading partners force them to use it.

BARRIERS TO USE ICT

While there is recognition of the potential of ICT as a tool for the promotion of gender equality and the empowerment of women, a "gender divide" has also been identified, reflected in the lower numbers of women accessing and using ICT compared to men. However, if the gender disparities —in terms of access and use of ICT and building employment opportunities are explicitly recognized and dealt with, ICT can be an influential catalyst for political and social empowerment of women, and thus, promoting gender equality. A UNESCO Report on 'Gender Issues in the Information Society' highlighted that the ability of a woman to use technology is highly dependent on the societal factors i.e mobility, geographic location, literacy level and social classes (Natasha, 2003). The digital divide is often characterized by low levels of access to technologies. Poverty, low level of literacy level, lack of computer knowledge and linguistic issue are among the factors that create obstacles in accessing ICT infrastructure, particularly in developing countries. Martinez & Nguyen (2014) studied that women in developing countries are technically not sound and have less access to training to fully deploy ICT into their businesses. Social norms that generally support men do not permit women to connect with the world outside their neighbourhood (Martinez & Nguyen, 2014). Women are found to be less likely to own mobile phones than men in low and middle income countries (Cherie Blair Foundation, 2012) and less likely to use mobiles for business activities (Ilavarasan & Levy, 2010).

The cost of adoption is an important factor in the implementation and exploitation of ICT. Generally, the women owned SMEs will intend not to adopt ICT if the primary set up cost is high (Dixon et al, 2002). Seyal and Rahim (2006) found that there is a direct association between cost and implementation of technology. The lower the cost of adoption the higher will be the rate of adoption. ICT knowledge and skills is also definitely increasing the opportunity of ICT adoption amongst the women-owned SMEs. Reynolds (1994) found that small business owners are unlikely to implement modern technologies into their business processes if they are unfamiliar with the basic methods and techniques. This is because the employees are not technically skilled in handling the modern applications. Allison (1999) pointed that a skilled and knowledgeable workforce is closely linked with the successful implementation of ICT. It has been observed that employees of small firms generally lack the desired competency level to operate IT in their businesses (Spectrum, 1997).

GOVERNMENT AND INSTITUTIONAL SUPPORT

ICT can deliver potentially useful information to the women entrepreneurs related to the market knowledge in small and micro enterprises. ICT training can cater to the need of the women entrepreneurs to build up the capacity in accessing information and technical knowledge. Investment in content development on the local information is the key to increase women's access to use ICT.

In the Indian context, the Kerala government has initiated an e-commerce project called Kudumbashree to facilitate women's micro enterprise to establish suitable contacts to procure business deals (Goswami & Dutta, 2015).The e-Seva Centres in Andhra Pradesh are staffed and run by women. They provide wide range of services – bill payments, issuance of land/birth certificates, browsing, online auctions, filing complaints and grievances and matrimonial services (Maier & Reichert, 2008). FOOD (The Foundation of Occupational Development) is an NGO in Tamil Nadu, that promotes the selling of indigenous products such as sarees, leather goods and other handicraft items made by rural women artisans (Maier & Reichert, 2008). It enabled the rural artisans to market their products locally, nationally and globally and ensuring higher profits. Goswami and Dutta (2015) studied that the Cottage Industry – Global Marketplace (CIGM) was initiated by the Communication, Culture and Technology (CCT) program at Georgetown University and was funded by the World Bank. They have involved the women artisans of North India to sell online hand-woven shawls to American and European customers. Government of India promotes continuous training programmes and awareness workshops on the use and potential of ICT throughout the country. Aamagaon Soochna Kendra (My village's information centre) is a project undertaken by the Government of Odisha, for setting up 73 Information and Communication Technology (ICT) kiosks in the 12 rural districts of Odisha. The Government has partnered with Mission Shakti to train the women self help group members on computer fundamentals and Internet basics at the IT Kiosks at a very nominal fee (Suresh, 2011). The 'Inter-city Marketing Network of Women Entrepreneurs' project in Chennai has set up a communication network amongst women's community-based organizations (CBOs) to market their products. The CBOs are supplied with cellular phones, and women have been trained to market their products through telephones and sell the same not only in their neighbourhood but also in potential markets in the city. With the use of this technique, poor women from CBOs who were refrained by pressure of time and mobility are able to assess and aggregate market demand by communicating with their peer CBOs (Suresh, 2011). The All India Society for Electronics and Computer Technology (AISECT) is an educational business operational in 28 Indian states which generates opportunities for rural women to manage IT kiosks that sell e-commerce, e-governance and educational products and services to rural clients by means of mobile phones, Internet and computers (International Centre for Research on Women, 2012).

The Union of Kazakhstani Women Entrepreneurs and the mobile phone company JSK Kcell, have provided training on the use of mobile phones for women entrepreneurs. The union was responsible in organizing the groups and sessions and Kcell in imparting the training. Almost 250 women entrepreneurs were trained and coached in the cities of Taraz, Aksu, and Karaganda in 2013. According to Kcell, the women found the training very useful and the company regards the program a success (Martinez & Nguyen, 2014).The Women of Uganda Network (WOUGNET), an NGO which promotes and supports the women entrepreneurs in using ICT to ensure that they are benefitted from the opportunities presented by ICTs (UNCTAD, 2014). African Government initiated PesaPata which is a micro loan facility that can be purchased from kiosks set up for the micro-women entrepreneurs (STOA, 2015).

CONCLUSION

Nowadays, mobile phones, computers, and the internet, are the vital ICT tools to develop the trade and commerce and to enhance the competitiveness of firms. As a business tool, ICT has eased up the information access that assists the entrepreneur to develop or expand the business firms. ICT provides facts and figures on markets, suppliers, and producers that help the women entrepreneurs to develop their business plan. It reduces the cost of transportation and enables an easy access to financial services. ICT tools also provide business related support services such as training, guidance and advisory services. It also facilitates the provision of business related government services.

ICT is a potent instrument to support women entrepreneurs and lessen women-specific constraints to their businesses. These technologies can help to beat time and mobility constraints; ease access to financial services; improved access to information, skills training and facilitate participation in business networks. Simultaneously, women entrepreneurs are being faced with lot of challenges in terms of implementing ICT in their firms.

The study proposes policy interventions to promote ICT tools to generate and develop women's entrepreneurial activity. The Government & other Institutions should create an enabling environment where women owned firms can use ICT effectively by

- Setting up women-friendly ICT access points.
- Implementing women-targeted ICT programmes to build ICT related skills.
- Providing support for easy access to financial services by facilitating loan applications, disbursement and repayment.
- Support affordable ICT infrastructure.
- Implement of awareness raising campaigns to remove the social and cultural barriers.
- Developing financial schemes to encourage the women entrepreneurs to use ICT.

ICT is a fastest growing area that can provide vast opportunities to catalyse womens' participation in the global economy. The function of the internet, mobiles, e-commerce, social sites and the new opportunities associated with the use of ICT are just a few examples of the growing landscape. Simultaneously, barriers to ICT usage by the women entrepreneurs should be identified and minimized so that advancement of ICT does not widen the gender gap. Women's increased participation in business firms empowers them from all spheres and promotes equal opportunity for both men and women, which, eventually, contributes to economic development.

REFERENCES

Allison, I. K. (1999). Information systems professionals' development: A work-based learning model. *Journal of Continuing Professional Development*, *2*(3), 86–92.

Cherie Blair Foundation. (2012). *Women & Mobile: A Global Opportunity: A study on the mobile phone gender gap in low and middle-income countries*. Available at http://www.Cherieblairfoundation.org/wp_content/uploads/2012/07/women_and_mobile_a_global_opportunity.pdf

Dixon, T., Thompson, B., & McAllister, P. (2002). *The value of ICT for SMEs in the UK: a critical literature review*. Report for Small Business Service research programme. The College of Estate Management. Available: www.sbs.gov.uk/SBS_Gov_files/researchandstats/value_of_ICT_for_SMEs_UK.pdf

Goswami, A., & Dutta, S. (2015). ICT in Women Entrepreneurial Firms -A Literature Review. *IOSR Journal of Business and Management*, *17*(2), 2319–7668. <ALIGNMENT.qj></ALIGNMENT>10.9790/487X-17243841

Ilavarasan, P., & Levy, M. (2010). *ICTs and Urban Microenterprises: Identifying and Maximizing Opportunities for Economic Development*. Available at http://www.idrc.ca/uploads/userS/12802403661ICTs_and_Urban_Microenterprises_104170-001.pdf

International Centre for Research on Women. (2012). *Connectivity – How mobile phones, computers, and the Internet can catalyze women's entrepreneurship – India: A Case Study*. Author.

Jackson, L. A., Ervin, K. S., Gardner, P. D., & Schmitt, N. (2001). Gender and the Internet: Women Communicating and Men Searching. *Sex Roles*, *44*(5/6), 363–379. doi:10.1023/A:1010937901821

Jain, S. (2015). *ICTs and Women's Empowerment : Some Case Studies From India*. Academic Press.

Jones, S., Johnson-Yale, C., Millermaier, S., & Pérez, F. S. (2009). US College Students Internet Use: Race, Gender and Digital Divides. *Journal of Computer-Mediated Communication*, *14*(2), 244–264. doi:10.1111/j.1083-6101.2009.01439.x

Joshi, S. (2011). President launches unique ICT scheme for women. *The Hindu*. Retrieved from http://www.thehindu.com/news/national/article1517932.ece

Kirby, D., & Turner, M. (1993). IT and the small retail business. *International Journal of Retail & Distribution Management*, *21*(7), 20–27. doi:10.1108/09590559310046022

Maier, S., & Reichert, U.N. (2007). *ICT-Based Business Initiatives: An Overview of Best Practices in E-Commerce / E-Retailing Projects.* MIT Press.

Marius, M. (2013). 4 Ways ICT/Technology can improve your business. *ICT Pulse – ICT Issues From a Caribbean Perspective.* Retrieved from http://www.ict-pulse.com/2013/09/4-ways-icttechnology-improve-business/

Martinez, I., & Nguyen, T. (2014). *ADB Briefs: Using Information and Communication Technology to Support Women's Entrepreneurship in Central and West Asia.* ADB.

Matangi, E. S., & Kashora, P. (2013). Empowerment and Information and Communication Technology (ICT) prospects and challenges for women in Zimbabwe. *International Journal of Education and Research, 1*(5), 1–10.

Mokaya, S. O., & Njuguna, E. W. (2010). Adoption and Use of Information and Communication Technology (ICT) By Small Enterprises in Thika Town, Kenya. *Scientific Conference Proceedings*, 498–504. Retrieved from http://elearning.jkuat.ac.ke/journals/ojs/index.php/jscp/article/view/730

Natasha, P. (2003). *Gender Issues in the Information Society.* Paris: United Nations Educational, Scientific and Cultural Organization (UNESCO).

Organization for Economic Co-operation and Developement (OECD). (2010). *The Information and Communication Technology Sector in India: Performance, Growth and Key Challenges.* Retrieved from http://www.oecd.org/dataoecd/55/56/45576760.pdf

Rahman, S. M. A. (2016). Leveraging ICTs For Empowering Women Entrepreneurs in Bangladesh: A Review of Recent Developments and Way Forward. *European Journal of Business and Social Sciences, 5*(3), 1–15.

Reynolds, W., Savage, W., & Williams, A. (1994). *Your Own Business: A Practical Guide to Success.* ITP.

Sanou, B. (2014). ICT Facts and Figures. *The World in 2014: ICT Facts and Figures,* 1–8. Retrieved from http://www.itu.int/en/ITUD/Statistics/Documents/facts/ICTFactsFigures2014-e.pdf

Science and Technology Options Assessment. (2015). *ICT in the developing world.* Available at http://www.europarl.europa.eu/RegData/etudes/STUD/2015/563482/EPRS_STU(2015)563482_EN.pdf

Seyal, A. H., & Rahim, M. M. (2006). A Preliminary Investigation of Electronic Data Interchange Adoption in Bruneian Small Business Organisations. *The Electronic Journal of Information Systems in Developing Countries, 24*(4), 1–21.

Singh, N. P., & Sahay, A. (2006). ICT for women Entrepreneurs. In Entrepreneurship: Education, Research and Practice, (pp. 151-159). Academic Press.

Spectrum. (1997). *Moving into the Information Society.* HMSO.

Ssewanyana, J., & Busler, M. (2007). Adoption and Usage of ICT in Developing Countries : Case of Ugandan Firms. *International Journal of Education and Development Using Information and Communication Technology, 3*(3), 49–59.

Suresh, L. B. (2011). Impact of Information and Communication Technologies on Women Empowerment in India. *Systemics, Cybernetics and Informatics, 9*(4), 17–23.

The Economic Benefits of Strategic ICT Spending. (2010). Intel.

The World Bank Annual Report. (2010). Retrieved from http://siteresources.worldbank.org/EXTANNREP2010/Resources/WorldBank-AnnualReport2010.pdf

UNCTAD. (2014). *Empowering Women Entrepreneurs through Information and Communications Technologies.* Retrieved from http://unctad.org/en/PublicationsLibrary/dtlstict2013d2_en.pdf

United Nations Division for the Advancement of Women. (2005, September). Gender equality and empowerment of women through ICT Gender equality and empowerment. *Women 2000 and Beyond.*

WomenAction. (2000). *Asia & Pacific.* Retrieved from: http://www.womenaction.org/asia.html

Chapter 17
Advocating the Woman Affirmative Action and Women Empowerment in Rural Cross River State of Nigeria:
The Role of the Civil Society and the Media

Endong Floribert Patrick Calvain
University of Calabar, Nigeria

ABSTRACT

Most media initiatives (particularly radio and television programs) bordering on women empowerment and the woman affirmative action tend to give less attention to the rural woman to the advantage of her urban counterpart who, to a high extent is already abreast of the feminist concept. This more or less "accidental" discrimination is causing the grassroots women to stay somewhat in ignorance and to further be victimized by the viscous patriarchal system which prevails in traditional circles. Based on a documentary analysis and semi structured interviews with experts, this chapter explores the role of the local media and the civil society in the sensitization of the rural woman towards emancipation and socio-economic empowerment in Cross River State of Nigeria. The chapter equally assesses the effectiveness of the advocacy strategies employed by local media houses and NGOs for such purposes. It assesses civil society's use of the media for the women affirmative action in rural Cross River State of Nigeria as well as the local media potential to push this affirmative action in the grassroots.

INTRODUCTION

The global struggle against patriarchy and chauvinism – manifested by issues such as the discrimination against women, gender inequality and the relegation of women to a subordinate status in the society – has engendered a variety of strategies and paradigms geared towards women emancipation and women

DOI: 10.4018/978-1-5225-3018-3.ch017

empowerment. Some of these strategies include (i) the Beijing Conference, (ii) the Vienna Declaration of All Forms of Discrimination Against Women [1979], (iii) the Declaration on the Protection of Women and Children in Emergency and Armed Conflicts [1974], and (iv) the Optional Protocol to the Convention on the Elimination of Discrimination Against Women [2000] among others. To keep pace with this global mobilization against women marginalization, the Nigerian Federation has ratified the above mentioned declarations as well as a multitude of other international conventions pertaining to women emancipation. In addition to its signing of these international conventions, the Nigerian Federation has adopted gender sensitive schemes such as the Women in Development (WID) and recently the Women Affirmative Action which is described as a paradigm conceived "to promote power sharing and to protect groups [notably women] considered to be relatively disadvantaged" in the Nigerian socio-economic sphere (Jibril, 2006).

In principle, the Affirmative Action is a program or policy seeking to redress pass social discriminations through the elaboration of strategic actions to ensure equal opportunities in such areas of development as education, law, politics and employment. Neologisms such as the Africanization policy (of the 1940s), the Indigenization policy (adopted since 1960), and the quota system represent various facets of the Affirmative Action in Nigeria. These forms of Affirmation Action have been adopted at different periods in the history of Nigeria. As a neologism and socio-political (development) paradigm, the Women Affirmative Action is progressively becoming popular in today's Nigeria. It has come to be supported by the 1999 Nigerian Constitution, as revealed in its three components including: (i) anti-discrimination clause, (ii) the federal character principle and (iii) the federal character commission (Jibril, 2006).

Despite all these colossal (non-)governmental efforts, women marginalization is still strongly perceptible in almost all the spheres of the Nigerian economy. Illiteracy among women is still high and the role of women in development is still relatively insignificant. As observed by The British Council Nigeria (2012), the local implementation of the various documents aimed at enabling the Women Affirmative Action "has remained weak" (p.54). Though the course for women emancipation and empowerment is getting remarkable momentum in the political sphere, the plight of the Nigerian women continues to be grossly deplorable in the socio-economic sphere of the country. The various advocacy strategies aimed at pushing the women affirmative action are still very patchy and yet to yield the awaited results, especially in the grassroots. In effect, most women-based and feminist initiatives by governmental and non-governmental organizations in Nigeria tend to focus principally on the situation of the urban/modern woman (the woman in the town) paying relatively little attention to her counterpart in the grassroots. Similarly, most media initiatives (especially radio and television programs) bordering on the woman affirmative action tend to give less attention to the rural woman to the advantage of her urban counterpart who, to a relatively high extent, is already at breast of the feminist concept. This more or less "accidental" discrimination is causing the grass roots women to stay somewhat in ignorance and to further be victimized by the viscous patriarchal system which prevails in traditional(ist) circles. Based on a documentary analysis and semi structured interviews with experts (from local support organization and media houses), this chapter has as principal objective to critically explore the role of the local media and the civil society in the sensitization of the rural woman towards emancipation in Cross River State of Nigeria. The chapter will equally attempt to assess the effectiveness of the advocacy strategies employed by local media organizations and NGOs for the purpose. It will thus assess civil society's use of the media for the women affirmative action in rural Cross River State of Nigeria as well as will examine local media's potential to push this affirmative action in the grassroots.

THEORETICAL FRAMEWORK

This paper is anchored on two theories namely (media) advocacy and the development media theory. Being somehow broad theoretical concepts, it will be expedient in this section to carefully highlight the specific keystones (of these theories) that will be considered in this study.

Media Advocacy Theory

The description of the advocacy theory largely depends on how one construes the phenomenon of advocacy. Therefore, before delving into an explanation of this theory it will be expedient to define the term "advocacy". Advocacy is a process whereby individuals, groups or other social forces embark on activities geared towards influencing public policy and interest. It can also be apprehended as a situation where an individual or group deploys well coordinated communication strategies/initiatives aimed at influencing resource allocation decision in a socio-political system. Such initiatives could be motivated by moral ethical or faith principles aimed at protecting an asset or interest. Advocacy may be reflected in media campaigns, public speaking commissioning and publishing research or poll. In tandem with this, the media advocacy theory stipulates that the media have great potential to serve as platforms in which series of actions could be taken and vital issues highlighted, to change the "what is" (socio-political *dysnomia*) into a "what should be" (an ideal situation), as a decent social value.

The mass media are seen as constituting a veritable platform to advance a common cause because of their pivotal role in the society. Information and communication are fundamentals in contemporary societies. As a unique feature of society, mass media development has orchestrated an increase in the scale and complexity of societal activities. The technological innovations in the domains of information and communication have set the pace for more aggressive media advocacy in Nigeria and as in other parts of the world in general. This paradigm shift is manifested in information accessibility with the emerging new media and internet technologies. Media advocacy can be as a counter voice of discrimination against women in Nigeria as in other parts of the globe.

Development Media Theory

The second theory considered in this study is the development media theory. Often considered the fifth theory of the press, the development media theory principally underscores the role of the mass media in general (and broadcasting in particular) in achieving nation building, particularly socio-economic and political development in the society where it (the development concept) operates. Also called "Developmental Concept", the development media theory stipulates that the utility of the mass media is exclusively determined by their ability to support developmental efforts – by the government and other influential development partners/authorities – in a given country. In line with this, the media of mass communication are considered relevant only if they strive at all times to ensure the progress and development of the country or community in which they operate.

It is hinging on this theory that Nigerian government officials and pro-government critics have abundantly argued that the media should key into governmental schemes towards nation building, particularly rural development in Nigeria which include women empowerment/emancipation among other imperatives. In accordance with the development media theory, media organizations should go beyond mere story engineering or construction and entertainment to be eloquent advocates of a better developed Nigeria. They should strive to be veritable partners in the socio-cultural and political development of the country. A number of principles of development media theory have been formulated by critics. These principles include the following:

- The media should "volunteer" to support all nation-building efforts by the government and other important nationalist institutions. This will entail executing special development tasks such as national integration, socio-economic modernization, promotion of literacy, gender equality and cultural creativity.
- Being fully guided by nationally established policies, the media should carry out positive development task, without neglecting their traditional functions in the society.
- The media should give a modicum of attention to their foreign news reportage and their transmission of cultural information to international audiences, thereby ensuring that a good link and entente are established with other countries sharing a similar socio-cultural orientation or socio-political aspiration.

THE WOMAN AFFIRMATIVE ACTION IN NIGERIA

As earlier alluded to, the women affirmative action is envisaged as a series of policies geared towards redressing past discriminations against women. Such a redress is done through the adoption of measures aimed at ensuring equality of opportunities between men and women in varied domains including education, employment and politics. Such policies equally ensure equal opportunities for sexes in access to public contract and health programs. It entails taking positive steps to increase the representation of disadvantaged social groups – notably women – in areas such as employment, business and education; areas from which they have historically been excluded. In tandem with this, popular conceptions or postulations have associated the Women Affirmative Action with the various constitutional efforts aimed at empowering women and enhancing their participation in decentralized government bodies (Angya 2010, p.9; Ihemeje 2013, p.60). However, the Women Affirmative Action paradigm aims not only to ensure women's access to, and full participation in the power structures and decision making processes of their societies but it equally seeks to increase the capacity to participate in decision-making. Viewed from this perspective the Women Affirmative Action is in accord with the theory of "Politics of Presence" which stipulates that disadvantaged groups can secure fair representation only if they are present in elected assemblies. In line with this, both genders should equitably be represented at decision making levels locally, regionally and nationally, particularly in domains or sectors where vital resources are allocated. The British Council Nigeria (2012) insightfully notes that "allocation is more effective and efficient, and ultimately produces superior human development outcomes, in countries where women are more broadly represented" (p.53). It is equally argued that women's way of allocating resources often vary significantly from that of men. Women tend to proffer a redistributive agenda, and devote more resources to children's education, social services and health, which are not always the priorities for men. With this, an association between gender representation and social spending becomes imperative.

Gender-based affirmative action has visibly been adopted in Nigeria around the year 2000, under the administration of General Olesugun Obasanjo. The policy was predicated on a number of cardinal human right instruments, among which should be counted the Beijing Platform for Action, the Convention on the

Elimination of All Forms of Discriminations Against Women (CEDAW), the National Policy on Women and the Third Millennium Goal among others. The Women affirmative Action came to systematically correct or redress the early models of affirmative action which rather created a breeding ground for male domination and patriarchy. In effect, the policy has sought to redress, imbalances, discrimination and under-representation of women which have prevailed in different sectors of the Nigerian economy since the 1070s. It must be emphasized here that the 1970's Nigerian Constitution glaringly overlooked gender imbalance. As explained by Ikpeze (2002), the above mentioned Constitution merely provided the concept of Federal Character which has remained part of Nigerian national discourse and has not perfectly been implemented till date. However, this concept "is deficient because it did not take into cognizance gender balance. Based on that, quota application to the feminine gender has suffered negatively" (Ikpeze, 2002, p.165). The Women Affirmative Action was thus implemented as from 2000, to tentatively correct this "abnormally". Since the year 2000, successive Nigerian governments have employed various systems of quotas to show and materialize their affiliation to the Women Affirmative Action paradigm. President Olesegun Obasanjo proffered a 15% affirmative action for women while his successors, Musa Yar Adua and Goodluck Jonathan respectively advocated a 30 and 35%.

The gender-based affirmative policy was equally adopted as a strategy to counter poverty and enable socio-economic development. As Ikpeze (2002) insightfully observes, this policy places emphasis on women empowerment; this due to the fact that inequality between genders in relation to economic, social and political emancipation seems to have seriously intensified poverty and boosted socio-economic underdevelopment in the Nigerian nation. The Women Affirmative Action paradigm has thus aimed to tackle gender inequality which remains "the instrument of increased poverty and squalor in our society. For the poverty of the women folk equates to the poverty of any nation" (Ikpeze, 2002, p.164).

The Women Affirmative Action can be said to have theoretically liberalized the political space in Nigeria; creating more opportunities for the participation of women in politics. However, it is observed that since 1999, there has not been significant improvement in the position of women in politics in Nigeria (as shown in Table 1 below). Women are still grossly underrepresented in the legislative and executive arms of the government. They are thus marginalized in the country democratization process, irrespective of the fact that Nigeria's national policy on women insists on a 35% affirmative action for women. In effect, party programs and manifestoes glaringly overlook women issues. According to available statistics, only eight (8) out of the 109 Senators in the current National Assembly are women, while only 24 out of the 360 members of the House of Representatives are women (Eme & Onyishi, 2014; Faroye, 2015). This statistics evidently illustrate a lopsided membership of the legislatures in favor of men. A similar scenario is observed at the local level, where only a few women function as Chairpersons or Councilors in local government councils. Discrimination against women continues to be so obvious that administrative posts such as the country's Presidency and Vice-Presidency are virtually considered no go zones for women. History also has it that only one case of female governor has so far been registered in the whole history of the Nigerian Federation. This female governor (late Dame Virgy Etiaba) came to power after the impeachment of her boss (Governor Peter Obi of Anambra State) on the second of November 2006 and functioned in this capacity for only six months. According to a 2016 report released by Nigeria's National Bureau of Statistics, women representation in the Nigerian civil service has remained one of the most serious concerns raised in various government and non-governmental platforms. However, the lack of reliable data on such female representation has made it difficult to properly address the problem of gender disparity in the Nigerian civil service. The report equally underscores that at the level of State civil service, up to 65.3 percent of senior positions have been occupied by men compared to 34.7 per-

Table 1. Women elected in public office in Nigerian since 1999

Office	1999 Seats Available	1999 Women	2003 Seats Available	2003 Women	2007 Seats Available	2007 Women	2011 Seats Available	2011 Women
President	1	0	1	0	1	0	1	0
Vice President	1	0	1	0	1	0	1	0
Senate	109	3 (2.8)	109	4 (3.7)	109	9 (8.3)	109	7 (6.4)
House of Representatives	360	7 (1.9)	360	21 (5.8)	360	27 (7.5)	360	25 (6.9)
Governor	36	0	36	0	36	0	36	0
State House Assembly (SHA)	990	24 (2.4)	990	40 (3.9)	990	57 (5.8)	990	68 (6.9)
SHA Committee Chairpersons	829	18 (2.2)	881	32 (3.6)	887	52 (5.9)	887	-
LGA Chairpersons	710	13 (1.8)	774	15 (1.9)	740	27 (3.6)	740	-
Councilors	6368	69 (1.1)	6368	26 (4.2)	6368	235 (3.7)	6368	-

Adapted from British Council Nigeria (2012:55) and Eme and Onishi (2014:5-6).

cent by women for the period between 2010-2015. At the junior level and across cadre, similar pattern have been maintained (National Bureau of Statistics 2016, p.19). The proportion of men employed from 2010-2015 in the country has consistently been higher than that of women.

A myriad of socio-political and economic factors strongly militate against the effective participation of women in politics. Some of these factors include "thuggry" and monetization of politics. Not to be forgotten is the fact that entrenched patriarchal attitudes – illustrated in the myth of gender inequality – have discouraged many women from participating in politics. Decades of neglect of women issues have facilitated the growth of patriarchy which, today, continues to hamper the effective implementation of the Women Affirmative Action in Nigeria. Because of Nigerians' affiliation to patriarchal religious dogmas and chauvinistic cultural fixations, women participation in politics is mainly considered a taboo and rare are women who will "dare" go against "this natural order of things". Most religious vitalities – be it animist, Christian or Muslim – teach that the women's right place is in the home or the kitchen and not in an administrative office. Such religious dogmas tend to criticize women participation in politics on the arguable ground that women are to be led by men. This is not to categorically insinuate that there are not quarters and segments of the Nigerian society that are supportive of women participation in politics. What is clearly said here is that such enthusiastic and sincere support for women's participation in politic is arguably weak in the Nigerian society. Minds are certainly changing but at a seemingly slow pace.

At the household front, the women are confronted to an unequal division of labor manifested in the fact that chores such as child-care and kitchen chores are principally assigned them. Similarly, old cultural beliefs and popular imaginations/myths brand politics a men's business. Such popular beliefs and imaginations have been so rooted in peoples' sub-conscious that any alteration of such belief is seen as a social deviancy. With this, women participation in politics is likely seen as bad leadership. In tandem with this, social narratives stipulate that while the place of the woman is in the kitchen, that of the man is in politics.

The prohibitive effects of religion and culture have motivated most critics to always underscore the need to supplement constitutional provisions and gender policies with a rich network of actions in the field. Such actions may include aggressive advocacy and sensitization in favor of women emancipation and empowerment. Such an advocacy and sensitization by both governmental and non-governmental organizations may facilitate the effective implementation of the Women Affirmative Action. As Eme and Onyishi (2014) pointedly argue,

Despite unprecedented human development efforts, a widespread inequality between genders still persists in access to political terrain. This is as a result of decades of neglect to focus on gender issues. Gender mainstreaming has become the catch phrase for narrowing the gender gap and should provide the significant impetus for political development that will correct generations of social injustice in gender relations in Nigeria. (p.9)

A number of NGOs and local support organizations have taken up the cause of advocating women empowerment and particularly the Women Affirmative Action in Nigeria. However, the fruits of their efforts are still patchy. Their initiatives are still mainly confined in urban areas, to the detriment of the rural woman. Such confinement of women empowerment and emancipation initiatives in the urban areas is not without serious consequences on the situation of the rural woman. This will be discussed in greater details in subsequent sections of this book chapter.

THE MYTH OF GENDER INEQUALITY IN NIGERIA AS BARRIER TO THE WOMEN AFFIRMATIVE ACTION

The postulation stressing that gender roles are culturally rather than biologically produced seems verifiable and true to the Nigerian context. In effect, the philosophy of patriarchy – which prevails in the whole country (particularly in the grassroots) – is fuelled by a mix of societal forces including culture, education, the law, the family/marriage (as an institution) among others. These forces otherwise referred to as ideological state apparatuses are greatly responsible for the negative stereotyping and relegation of women to subordinate roles in the Nigerian society. Such stereotyping and relegation of women immensely contribute to discourage women participation in politics, thus representing a threat to the effective implementation of the Women Affirmative Action in Nigeria. It has for instance been abundantly argued that many Nigerian communities still stick to some harmful, old but revered customs and traditions which exalt male domination to the detriment of the women folk. These customs and traditions particularly dehumanize the women, instituting gender inequality and women discrimination as a norm or a veritable "religion". Olateru-Olagbegi and Afolabi (2011) insightfully note that some of these customs and traditions have been practiced for so long that they are today "embedded in the societal perception almost as a legal norm. Such that, the laws of the land and international instruments which protect the rights of women, are flagrantly infringed in the guise of these age long cultural and/or religious beliefs" (p.56).

Okafor (2012) similarly captures this critical situation in her observation that "from a disadvantaged beginning, the Nigerian girl's child journey into adult life becomes one long battle against harmful traditional and cultural practices that threaten her life and put her down generally" (p.110). Some of these harmful and dehumanizing cultural practices include female genital mutilation (aimed at controlling women's sexuality), disproportionate emphasis made on marriage as the only acceptable status for a woman (which puts a tremendous psychological pressure on women) and a wide range of unjust widow rites which, besides exposing women to both physical and psychological violence (torture), ultimately "rib" them of their late husbands' proprieties. In some ethnic groups notably the *Igbos*, the widow is often subjected to such humiliating cultural practices and burial rites as the obligation of shaving of her hair (to signify that she is morning her husband), the drinking of the water used to bath the corpse of her late husband (often as a test to prove her innocence over the death of her husband), spending the night with the corpse of her husband among others (Makama, 2013; Okafor, 2012; Ojiakor, 1997). The marginalization is even accentuated by the fact that such arbitrary and repugnant treatments are reserved exclusively to women. Men are totally exempted from such debasing treatments by the culture. With this, it may not be an overstatement to posit that most customary laws in the country seem to principally protect the man sometimes to the detriment of the woman.

Cultural beliefs push some Nigerians to have a preference for the male child. For the sake of having a male child (merely to please their husbands), some women often expose themselves to too much child bearing, sometimes risking their lives. Furthermore, from his tender age, the male child is often exempted from domestic chores arguably considered a feminine obligation. As such, household chores are popularly believed to be the sole responsibility of the girl child. While the place of the girl child is believed to be in the kitchen, that of the male child is by anticipation in the office. The "male child preference syndrome" also motivates most family to prioritize male child's education over that of his sister(s). In the advent of limited financial resources, the girl child's education is likely to be discontinued to permit her brothers to further their own education. Agu (2007) aptly captures this disheartening bias when she notes that:

High-powered education is available for the women [in Nigeria] but how many of them have access to it? In poor families, priority will be given to boys' education at the expense of the girls and socio-cultural fixations discourage them from pursuing disciplines that will enable them benefit from the education they have acquired but simply queue up in the unemployment line. The resultant effect is what has been called "genderization of poverty". (p.17)

It goes without saying that such partial nay total exclusion of the girl child from education systematically lays the foundation for the marginalization of women in terms of life's opportunities and access to resources. Despite the adoption of the laudable National Gender Policy, Government is yet to have a deliberate policy to encourage and assist women in the domain of competitive education (Angya, 2014, p.15). Through myths and societal dogmas that stress the imperativeness of marriage, from early stages of their lives, women are socialized into thinking that finding a husband is a do or die affair, due to the presumed scarcity of men in the Nigerian society. In line with this, not being married is regarded as a stigma which most women are desperate to escape from as they progressively get older. "Indeed, so constraining is society's emphasis on marriage for the female gender that an unmarried, a divorced or spinster is a monstrosity" (Okafor, 2012, p.110). Most Nigerian societies have equally so overemphasized on the virtue of virginity that the phenomenon of child marriage has become rampant in Nigerian communities. In line with this, little girls are married off to men who are often old enough to be their fathers. Societal beliefs have equally shaped power relation in marriage to be in favor of the men folk. Ojiakor (1997) notes that irrespective of the level of education or enlightenment, husband-wife relations are a power-based system where the woman expects orders and gives in return total obedience. The man's prerogative to command and eventually redress his wife includes employing violence (beating her) and denying her sexual rights. Such a violent treatment reserved for women is even somewhat favored by some customary laws and other legal instruments (notably the penal code), considered in the country. In tandem with this observation, Section 55 of *The Nigerian Penal Code* provides that: "Nothing is an offence which does not amount to infliction of grievous hurt upon any person which is done by a husband for the purpose of correcting his wife, such husband or wife being subject to native law or custom in which such correction is recognized as lawful".

Such gender bias provisions (characterizing the Nigerian legal system) coupled with similar customary laws exacerbate discrimination against women and the latter's stereotyping in the Nigerian socio-cultural ecology. Based on this premise, most gender-sensitive projects including feminist or gender sensitive media communications have concentrated on countering these stereotypes. In Okafor and Abdulazeez's (2007) language, such projects are basically "chasing shadows of social realities at the expense of real facts" and subsequently instead exalting the phenomenon of patriarchy and its attendant consequences (p.236).

THE PLIGHT OF THE RURAL WOMAN IN NIGERIA

Though a national problem, women marginalization is more accentuated in the rural areas of the country. Though this may partially be predicated on the fact that patriarchal social fixations are predominant in the these rural regions, the principal reason for this state of things rests in the fact that most governmental and non-governmental initiatives aimed at pushing feminism and women empowerment tend to be more concentrated in urban centers than in grassroots zones. Most NGOs and local support organizations involved in advocating gender equality and women emancipation seem to principally target urban women who, from many indications, are more abreast of the feminist and women affirmative concepts, compared to their counterparts from the grassroots. Corroborating this position, the Civil Society Legislative Advocacy Center [CSLAC] (2015) notes that there is most often limited access to justice among rural women due partially to high legal fees and lack of capacities for asserting rights. This is principally – if not exclusively – due to the fact that most organizations providing free legal services are principally based in urban centers and restrict their actions in these urban centers. The CSLAC (2015) further enumerates the following challenges as negative resultants of such a reduced action of the civil society and governmental initiatives in the grassroots:

- Limited access to information as a result of inadequate power supply, inadequate knowledge and skill about information technology is a major impediment to the advancement of women in rural communities.
- Lack of equal access to land and opportunities to contribute to decision making processes at the community level.
- Traditional beliefs – that the use of certain modern technologies – hinder women's progress in farming at the rural level.
- Women, generally do not participate in decision making at the community level, except they are members of Traditional Village Council or Community Development Committees. However, at the household level, women participate more in decision making because of increase in female headed household. (Society Legislative Advocacy Center 2015, p.10)

In view of all these challenges, there has always been a greater necessity to predominantly target rural women communities in regional and national campaigns aimed at women empowerment. In tandem with this, Kinuthia-Njenga (2010) recommends that advocacy strategies deployed to push the Women Affirmative concept be intensified more in the grassroots. She insightfully argues that: "As the level of government closest to citizens, local authorities can play a vital role in addressing gender inequality and in building the capacities of women by involving them in local decision making, planning and management" (p.235). This is in line with the fact that the importance of grassroots' administrative structures was recognized by the International Union of Local Authorities as well as by the 1998 World Wide Declaration on women in local government. Increasing the participation of women [including those in rural areas] in politics and decision making was the central theme of the Beijing Platform for Affirmative Action (1995), and re-affirmed in 2000 in the third Millennium Goal, to "promote gender equality and empower women".

LOCAL MEDIA AND THE CIVIL SOCIETY AS ADVOCATES OF THE WOMEN AFFIRMATIVE ACTION/WOMEN EMPOWERMENT IN RURAL CROSS RIVER[1]

Many civil society organizations based in Cross River State are becoming more and more conscious of the fact that women marginalization is more intensified in the grassroots. Some of these organizations therefore consider the rural women as the main targets of their women emancipation schemes. As earlier noted, contrarily to her counterpart from the metropolis, the rural woman is hardly – or not sufficiently – exposed to concrete and substantial women empowerment programs through education, capacity building and the media. This scenario often causes her to be abandoned to herself and made to be further victimized by multiple forms of patriarchal systems and other social strictures prevailing in the rural areas. Corroborating this fact, Atim Ita, coordinator of the Blossom Women Organization asserts that,

The rural woman is now considered our major target. The urban woman is more enlightened than the rural woman. She is already abreast with gender sensitive issues. So, we have our field workers who go to these rural areas. Through their various community heads who bring them together for us to talk to them [...] We train them in various skills acquisition and encourage them to train their girl child and family planning.

The local NGOs' use of the media for their women's emancipation programs seems to be aimed principally at ensuring massive turnout in sensitization campaigns and training workshops in the hinterland. Most, if not all, of the NGOs being interviewed, pointedly attested to this point. Nkanu Evelyn (coordinator of the Women Action Organization) for instance notes that "each time we place announcements on radio or television, the turnout is always encouraging. Most times we create awareness on gender issues by producing jingles which are aired on the television and radio and this is of a great positive impact to people". The media therefore serve as complementary tools of multi-dimensional communication strategies by the NGOs geared at women empowerment. Some NGOs activities in the rural communities have attracted media attention. Such a media coverage (which is visibly rare and whose impact is yet to be measured) has enabled some of these NGOs to occasionally relay messages about the plight of the rural woman and on simple women emancipation strategies. Ekwelle mentions and commends the media coverage of such women emancipation programs in the grass root. She underlines the invaluable role the media may play in the advocacy for women affirmative and women empowerment in the grassroots, noting that:

We broadcast our programs on NTA and CBRC. Last December, we brought women together, held a seminar and they conducted various drama pieces relating to gender issues. NTA came and covered our program. It was on [the] news and we used that opportunity to relay our message and pour our hearts to the male folk. In fact, we also involved our men in that program and we told them our heart which is to empower the woman and carry her along.

This suggests that the rural woman attracts the attention of the media, mostly occasionally. It is only on particular occasions (for instance on the outcome of giant women empowerment campaigns in the grass root) that the media in Cross River may endeavor to address issues bordering on the plight of the rural woman. Given the reduced number of women programs on local radio and television, it can be argued that the rural woman is almost forgotten. Media programs seldom devote attention to her. Some of the local media houses considered for this study (the Nigerian Television Authority [NTA] Calabar and Cross River State Broadcasting Corporation [CRBC]) do not even have a single program conceived exclusively for the rural women. Izumana Odock, female producer with CRBC notes that,

We don't have any special programs for the rural women on [the] women affirmative action; but we have programs like "The Girl Power Initiative" and a few others that are gender sensitive issues. If the rural woman has access to radio and television, then she stands a chance of watching or listening to the programs.

Similarly, Mgbepe Pasmond, (who is program manager with NTA) further corroborates this point asserting that: "in NTA Calabar, we don't have any specific program on women's affirmative action that involves the rural woman, though we have other related programs like "Women in Focus" which is being relayed from NTA network centers. We have booster stations in Ogoja and Ikom which are supposed to cover those rural areas". As can be noted in this assertion, Calabar based audio-visual media houses often reserve the duty of producing women affirmative programs (aimed principally at the rural women), to their booster stations which they think may enjoy proximity to the rural women. Meanwhile, these stations also shy away from such an assignment either because of the heavy financial sacrifices needed for their production or because of lack of creativity. Ewa Henshaw, a producer with NTA somehow corroborates this position thus:

Honestly, for now we don't have programs on women affirmative Action [...] Even in our booster stations in Ogoja and Ikom[2], which are nearer to this rural areas, we don't have any; except occasionally. We have jingles, announcements brought in by NGOs on gender sensitive issues. May be, when these jingles run, they [the rural women] watch, that is for those who are able to get our signals. But if we get sponsorship by the government like the Ministry of Women Affairs, we may be equipped enough to produce such programs.

One of the excuses commonly advanced by these media houses to justify their reduced attention to the rural woman (as evidenced by their programming) is the lack of fund for the production of such women affirmative action programs, involving the rural woman. In effect producing local programs involving or directed at the rural women entail enormous financial sacrifices which both the local support organizations and the local media may not afford. Only well established civil society organizations such as the Girl Child Initiative have been able to do the necessary financial sacrifice to produce and air gender-related issues on local media. Another excuse advanced particularly by the producers working with this local media houses (NTA and CRBC Calabar) is the reach of their respective media. Ebe Margrate, another female producer with NTA notes that,

As a producer, I would love to produce programs for the rural woman, but how can I reach the rural woman in the interior Obudu, Bekwara, Obanliku, Yala, Yakuur, Abi and so forth. If my reach - as in the signal - cannot get them. Not to rule out the rural woman completely, the rural woman in Akpabuyo, Nyangasang[3] can have access to programs on NTA Calabar. If we have sponsors, we will build programs on Affirmative Action for women.

The few programs aired over the stations considered for this study are dominantly presented in Standard English. Such programs are seldom punctuated with expressions the Nigerian Pidgin English. This clearly indicates that local media's target audiences are theoretically female audiences based in urban areas; who theoretically are literate or at least semi-literate in their majority, contrarily to their counterparts from the grassroots (who are mostly proficient in their mother tongues or in indigenous languages). The choice of English as the exclusive language of presentation of the women programs over CRBC and NTA can be viewed as another form of marginalization against the illiterate rural woman. NTA female producer Ebe Margaret explains that:

Here in NTA, we have "Women in Focus", a program that encourages women to stand up and follow their dreams. It showcases successful women in their various carriers. The rural women in Akpabuyo and Nyangasang can watch these programs. But what about the language, it could be a barrier, because it is not all of them that understand English. But if we can get sponsors, we can even go as far as producing programs in their various local languages.

From the findings presented in this study, it remains clear that most of the advocacy efforts of the civil society organizations in favor of women empowerment in the rural areas are conceived as those aimed at the urban women. No special effort is done to properly address issues that directly concern the rural woman. All these are evidences that both the civil society and the local media need to re-strategize. In effect, starting with the language in which the programs are conceived and presented and going to the issues raised in these programs through programming, local media must give greater attention to the rural women.

CONCLUSION

This chapter argued that most women-based and feminist initiatives by both governmental and non-governmental organizations in Nigeria tend to focus principally on ameliorating the situation of the modern woman (the woman in urban centers) paying relatively little attention to her counterpart in the grassroots. Similarly, most media initiatives (especially radio and television programs) bordering on the woman affirmative action (women empowerment) tend to give less attention to the rural woman to the advantage of urban counterpart who, to a relatively high extent is already abreast of the feminist concept. This more or less "accidental" discrimination is causing the grassroots women to stay somewhat in ignorance and to further be victimized by the viscous patriarchal system which prevails in traditional circles.

This chapter explored the role of the local media and the civil society in the sensitization of the rural woman towards emancipation and socio-economic empowerment in Cross River State of Nigeria. It argued that the local media seem less devoted to pushing the women affirmative action in rural areas as most of their programs are designed to address issues not connected with women empowerment in the grassroots. The civil society's use of the local media for women empowerment is likewise minimal given the fact that most local support organization (NGOs) involve in women empowerment depend on very limited financial resources to pilot media programs dedicated to the cause of the rural woman. Based on these observations, arguments and conclusions, the following recommendations may be made:

1. The government and individual media houses should design working systems that will ensured gender parity at decision taking levels in the various local media houses. Such a system may be a pre-requisite for the programming styles adopted by these media houses to reflect women's aspirations in general and the rural women's aspirations in particular.
2. A clear and fair percentage of programs aimed at the rural women should be defined as a form of positive discrimination, in favor of the rural woman.
3. The Nigerian government should create more booster stations to enable a greater media reach in the hinterland. This will enable the rural women in the far hinterland to be reached with well conceived women empowerment messages.
4. The local support organizations (NGOs) should be fully empowered to deploy the media for the women affirmative action. Airtime charges should be revised and reduced for them. This may enable them create a diversity of programs that will singularly focus on the plight of the rural woman.
5. The NGOs, should equally synergize to surmount high airtime charges. Furthermore, they should create inter-organization radio programs that will address issues concerning the rural woman.

REFERENCES

Abu, E. (1997). *Women in broadcasting: An African perspective in deregulation of broadcasting in Africa*. Lagos: National Broadcasting Commission.

Adebayo, F. (2011). Promoting children's right through the new media: The Nigerian experience. *Journal of Communication, 2*(2), 57–65.

Adesina, L. A. (2010). Audience perception of portrayals of women in the Nigerian home video. *JMCS: Journal of Media and Communication Studies, 2*(9), 200–207.

Agba, A. M. O. (2010). Sociological Analysis of Marital Stress and Women Effectiveness in Grassroot Socio-Economic Transformation in Nigeria. *Global Journal of Human Social Science, 10*(2), 38–46.

Agu, S. (2007). Gender equality, education and women empowerment: The Nigerian challenge. *Multi-disciplinary Journal of Research Development, 8*(2), 1–7.

Angya, A. (2014). *Achieving affirmative action for gender mainstreaming: The journey so far*. Paper presented at the Center for Women, Gender and Development Studies, Federal University of Technology, Owerri.

Civil Society Legislative Advocacy Center. (2015). *Policy brief on gender equity and empowerment towards achieving the MDGS*. Lagos: CSLAC and TY Danjuma Foundation.

Davis, M. (2016). Emancipation of women. *Page Hub*. Retrieved 30 July, 2016, from http://hubpages.com/politics/Emancipation-Of-Women

Eme, O. I., & Onyishi, T. (2015). Women and politics in Nigeria: Strategizing for 2015. *Kuwait Chapter of Arabian Journal of Business and Management Review*, *3*(12), 1–13. doi:10.12816/0019113

Endong, F. P. C. (2012). Femininity versus feminism in feminine Christian communication: A case study of "The Christian Woman Morror". *CAJOLIS: Calabar Journal of Liberal Studies*, *16*(1), 15–34.

Eya, R. (2005). *Gender and culture: What needs to change in the society and in the Church. In Gender equality from a Christian perspectives* (pp. 23–35). Enugu: Ifendu publications.

Faroye, E. (2014). Nigerian women in politics: Achieving the 35% affirmative policy. *Royal Time Newspaper*, *35*, 16–18.

Ifemeje, S., & Ikpeze, O. (2012). Global trend toward gender equality: Nigeria's experience in focus. *Kuwait Chapter of Arabian Journal of Business and Management Review*, *2*(3), 51–63.

Ihemeje, G. (2013). The need for participation of women in local governance: A Nigerian discourse. *International Journal of Educational Administration and Policy Studies*, *5*(4), 59–66.

Ikpeze, O. V. C. (2002). Understanding affirmative action as aid to women's human rights in Nigeria. In H. Ibrahim (Ed.), *Bar perspective: A quarterly publication of the Nigerian bar Association* (pp. 540–580). Abuja: Nigerian Bar Association.

Kinuthia-Njenga, C. (2010). *Local government for gender*. Retrieved September 20, 2016, from http://www.capacity.com

Makama, G. A. (2013). Patriarchy and gender inequality in Nigeria: The way forward. *European Scientific Journal*, *9*(17), 115–144.

National Bureau of Statistics. (2016). *2015. Statistical report on women and men in Nigeria*. Abuja: National Bureau of Statistics.

National Women Law Center. (2000). Affirmative action and what it means for women. *Resources*. Retrieved 30 July, 2016 from https://nwlc.org/resources/affirmative-action-and-what-it-means-women/

Ocheni, S., & Nwankwo, B. C. (2012). Analysis and critical review of rural development efforts in Nigeria, 1960-2010. *Studies in Sociology of Science*, *3*(3), 48–86.

Okafor, A. C. (2010). Gender inequality in Nigeria. *OASIS Journal*, *1*(1), 104–113.

Okafor, E., & Abdulazeez, Y. (2007). Gender-sensitive projects for sustainable development in Nigeria: A critical assessment. *Journal of Sociology and Social Science*, *23*(3), 235–248.

Olateru-Olagbegi, B. A., & Afolabi, A. (2013). *Actual women situation in Nigerian*. Retrieved September 26, 2016, from: http://www.widaf-ao.org/spip.php

Shepherd, K. E. (2016). *Applicability of the lobbying act to grass root communications*. Office of the Commissioner of Lobbying of Canada. Retrieved July 30, 2016, from https://lobbycanada.gc.ca/eic/site/012.nsf/eng/00874.html

United Nation Organization. (2005). *Improvement of the situation of women in rural areas. report of the secretary-general*. Geneva: UNO.

Willis, B. (2015). What is grassroots advocacy and why should I know about it?. *Votility*. Retrieved July 30, 2016, from http://www.votility.com/blog/bid/261018/What-is-Grassroots-Advocacy-Why-Should-I-Know-About-It

KEY TERMS AND DEFINITIONS

Civil Society: A community of citizens, linked by a common interest and having the same activity. This community comprises organizations which are non-governmental and non-profit in nature, and which work for the interest of citizens. Examples of civil society organizations include churches, labor unions, NGOs, and other non-profit organizations which work for the common good, providing very important services in a society; this for very little or nothing in return.

Community Journalism: This is journalism designed to serve distinct communities, particularly small towns, suburbs or urban neighborhoods, as well as specific communities and short term goals. The communities concerned in a context of community journalism are usually "small" in some respects and have a number of characteristics which differentiate then for the larger population. Given their "small" size, the news that serve them (these communities) tend to be small and the journalists producing this news enjoy strong connections to the communities in question.

Community Media: A term used to refer to any form of media created and controlled and influenced by a community. Such a community may be geographic (a small town) or virtual (interest and identity) in nature. Community media are equally participatory in nature. They are created or envisaged out of the need to enable the expression by a specific community of its opinions/views in a systematized, strategic and influential way. Community media are therefore to be contrasted with state-owned media, public broadcasting and commercial media.

Cross River State: It is one of the 36 States of the Nigerian Federation. It is located in the south-eastern zone of the country and has as capital city Calabar.

Grassroots Communications: This is communication strategies developed for mobilization and sensitization in the grassroots (localities often viewed as the rural and agricultural zones of a country). Grassroots is equally used to refer to the totality of people living in the rural areas of a country, as a socio-economic or political force. Viewed from this angle, grassroots communication is seen as emanating from rural communities and aiming at advocating specific issues. It therefore occurs when, for payment and on behalf of a client or employer, individuals (particularly civil society organizations) appeal to rural communities to communicate with public office holders about an important/vital topic, through such means as advertisements, websites, organization of a letter writing campaign, or through social media tools such as (but not limited to) Facebook or Twitter.

Women Affirmative Action: A term used to refer to various government policies or programs aimed particularly at increasing the proportion of women in various sectors historically considered to be male dominated. These sectors include employment and education among others. This definition is by analogy with the term affirmative action which is a government program, conceived to encourage the increased representation of minority, disadvantaged or marginalized social groups at key sectors of a country. In countries such as India the movement us known as reservation while in UK, it is called positive discrimination.

Women Emancipation: The term "emancipation" is often associated with the value of freedom. It implies freedom from legal, political or social restrictions. It is equally a process which enables the powerless social groups to gain access and control of resources in a given society. In tandem with this, woman emancipation is inextricably linked to efforts or social schemes aimed at setting the women free from all types of bondage and sociopolitical and economic exploitation. The term "woman emancipation" is thus generally used to refer to the process by which women in general and poor women in particular are made to gain access and control of all forms of resources in a nation. It is a movement which aims at ensuring freedom of self-fulfilment and self-development for women, as well as equal access to domestic and community resources.

Women Empowerment: Women empowerment is a term used to refer to struggles by women (particularly poor women) to achieve full and equal human rights. It is equally used to refer to the totality of social, political and economic mutations/changes needed by women to realize their full human right. In tandem with this, there are over three interrelated forms of women empowerment namely political empowerment (through participation in elections and government), economic empowerment (which entails women having authority to make decision regarding their access to and use resources) and social empowerment (often through public policy and education).

ENDNOTES

[1] Cross River is one of the 36 States of the Nigerian Federation. It is situated in the South Eastern part of the country.

[2] Ogoja and Ikom are rural localities within Cross River State. They are located very far from Calabar the capital city, where the media houses considered for the study (CRBC and NTA) are based.

[3] Obudu, Bekwara, Obanliku, Yala, Yakur, Abi, Akpabuyo and Nyangasang are rural localities within Cross River State.

Chapter 18
Role of Women Empowerment in Public and Corporate Leadership

P. Lakshmi
Indian Institute of Technology Madras, India

S. Visalakshmi
VIT University, India

ABSTRACT

The present study attempts to highlight the social and economic benefits of leadership of Indian women based on past evidence; current trends; challenges faced and the path forward in the public and corporate arena. Women empowerment has been a vital issue that has come to limelight in the recent years. Despite numerous government schemes and policy decisions, women in India remain deprived of equal opportunities in terms of education, employment and skill development. Many social scientists have derived that economic independence plays a vital role in ensuring that women get equal opportunities in the society and thereby enjoy and benefit from their other rights. This makes women empowerment as much of an economic issue as a social one. In corporate and public life, success of policies is determined by decisions that incorporate the viewpoints of both men and women. Hence, it becomes essential to understand the nature and extent of gender equality especially in public and corporate leadership and decision making roles. The outcomes of this study from these perspectives will serve to help both sectors in narrowing the gender bias in leadership roles.

INTRODUCTION

"Empowering Women, Empowering India"

Empowerment means decentralisation of authority and power. Women empowerment aims at getting increased participation of women in decision-making process. In spite of initiation of profound measures to ensure gender equity, India still finds it hard to answer the questions on women empowerment raised by Mahatma Gandhi way back in 1930:

DOI: 10.4018/978-1-5225-3018-3.ch018

Has she not greater intuition, is she not more self-sacrificing,

has she not greater powers of endurance,

has she not greater courage?

Women empowerment refers to boosting women to be self-supporting, obligate positive self-esteem, economically independent, create confidence to face any problematic situation and provoke active participation in various socio-political development endeavours. In corporate and public life, success of service delivery is driven by decisions that integrate the perspectives of both men and women. The extent of under-representation of women in most decision-making bodies is an issue of serious concern considering its overall impact on inclusive growth. History has much evidence to signify the role of women leaders. The increased emphasis of this issue by policy makers and international organisations is a sufficient proof for gender equity not occurring as a natural phenomenon even in developed countries (Mason, 2005). Equal leadership of men and women in public and corporate life is inherent not only from the perspective of gender equity and unbiased governance but also ensures inclusive growth of an economy. Hence, it becomes essential to understand gender equality in public and corporate leadership and decision-making roles especially in the context of an emerging economy like India striving towards inclusive growth.

Need for Women Empowerment

The UNDP has made gender equity and women empowerment as the third goal in the Millennium development goals (MDG). Women Empowerment leads to an overall development of the society. Women Empowerment spawns more economic benefits not to the individuals but to the society as well. Women are participating in the national development process by making the nation proud by their outstanding enactments in almost every domain.

Women population constitutes around 50% of the world population. Women are equally talented as men. Earlier, women were not permitted for higher education like men and hence their abilities were unexploited. However, presently they are allowed to pursue higher studies and it inspires women to show their talents, which will not only benefit her individually but to the whole world at large. Traditionally, women had four fold status-role sequences as a daughter, wife, housewife (homemaker), and mother. But, modern women are inclined towards social issues, and are trying hard to improve the social status of women at large. Industrialization and technological change have opened vast opportunities of employment for women in different sectors of the national economy.

WOMEN EMPOWERMENT IN PUBLIC LEADERSHIP ROLES IN INDIA

Women's public/ political empowerment is based on gender equality, right to full development, right to self-representation and self-determination. In India, several measures have been initiated from time to time to provide welfare and representation of women in the constitutional/ institutional frameworks.

(Parida & Nayak,2009).These include ensuring voting rights for women as early as 1929, setting up of the committee on the status of women in India in 1971 to ensure increased participation of women in public life. Amendments to the constitution are in place to make 33% reservation for women in representing the houses of parliament.

Indian women have made their presence felt in public leadership roles, right from the time of India's struggle for independence from the British colonial rule. With respect to their presence in the parliament, Vijayalakshmi Pandit was the first Indian woman to hold a cabinet post in pre-independent India. The first woman cabinet minister of independent India was Ms. Rajkumari Amrit Kaur. Though she was the only woman in the cabinet (health ministry), she made a remarkable imprint in her role by initiating the launch of several prominent institutions like the All India Institute of Medical Sciences (AIIMS) in New Delhi, Tuberculosis Association of India and the Central Leprosy Teaching and Research Institute (CLTRI), Chennai which have grown outstandingly since inception. But, subsequent governments had only a sparse representation of women in the cabinet. These include prominent faces like Maneka Gandhi, Sarojini Mahishi, Nandini Satpathy, Sushila Rohatgi, Saroj Khaparde and Mohsina Kidwai. However, till the 10th cabinet, women's representation ranged only between 0-7%. For the first time since independence, the cabinet headed by Dr. Manmohan Singh (2004-2009) welcomed more than one woman union minister. Thus, Meira Kumar, Ambika Soni and Panabaka Lakshmi took women's cabinet representation to 10% (knowledge@ Wharton, 2009).

The present cabinet headed by Mr. Narendra Modi which came to power in 2014 has the maximum women representation in the cabinet. Six out of a total of 23 ministers are women handling some of the most challenging portfolios. For example, Ms. Sushma Swaraj is in charge of the External Affairs ministry, which makes her a part of the Cabinet Committee on Security (CCS), the top decision-making body on national security. Other prominent faces of the cabinet include Ms. Maneka Gandhi, Smriti Irani and Najma Heptulla heading child development, human resource development and minority affairs respectively. The current representation has taken the women leadership to 25% in the country's largest decision making body, which is a very promising sign of reversal of past trends (Shubhojit, 2014; Kounteya Sinha, 2015).

Women in the Houses of Parliament

Out of a total of 543 seats, the representation of women in the Lok Sabha has never gone beyond 12%. Figure 1 presents the percentage of women MPs in Lok Sabha between 1952 and 2014. In the upper house (Rajya Sabha) the number is slightly higher at 15% till 1990 (out of the total 245 seats) but is declining in the recent years (See Figure 2 for trends in women MPs in RajyaSabha from 1952-2014).

Thus, it can be observed that in spite of a wide range of support for the 33% representation for women, the actual numbers stay far behind. In the Indian Civil Services, which is considered as the highest in public administration, there are only three women IAS officers for every 20 men in the same cadre. Since 1974, it has a representation of 687 women whereas more than 3,000 men have been selected (scroll.in, 2017). Nevertheless, women have played a remarkable role in their public life exercising considerable influence over the region they represented and the decision-making process. Table 1 lists the top ten most influential women politicians in India and their achievements as of 2015.

Figure 1. Women MP's in Lok sabha
Source: Kuldeep Fadia (2014)

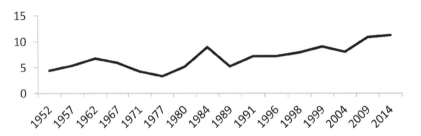

Figure 2. Women MP's in Rajya sabha
Source: Kuldeep Fadia (2014)

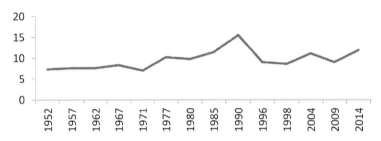

Table 1. Ten most influential women political leaders in India

S.No.	Name of the Indian Leader	Achievement
1.	Sonia Gandhi	Longest tenure as All India Congress President
2.	Sushma Swaraj	Seven times Member of Parliament, three times Member of Legislative Assembly, holds External Affairs Ministry
3.	Sheila Dikshit	Chief Minister of Delhi from 1998 to 2013, senior member of the Congress party
4.	Mamata Banerjee	First woman Chief Minister of West Bengal, dethroned 34-year-old left front government in the state, first woman Railway minister
5.	Jayalalitha	Five times chief minister of Tamilnadu, general secretary of All India Anna Dravida Munnetra Kazhagam (AIADMK), initiated the most popular women self-help groups (SHG) for rural women employment and empowerment
6.	Mayawati	Most powerful Dalit leader in India, four times chief minister of Uttar Pradesh
7.	Vasundhara Raje Scindia	Rajasthan's first woman Chief Minister
8.	Ambika Soni	Served as Union Minister of Information and Broadcasting, senior member of Congress party
9.	Supriya Sule	Lok Sabha MP, major part of new generation Indian politicians
10.	Agatha Sangma	Youngest minister of state for rural development from Meghalaya

Source: India Today (September 2015)

The Challenges Faced by Women Politicians

The sparse representation of women in Indian politics is dominated by various factors such as acute barriers in the entry level and odd working hours making it difficult to balance private and public life. Apart from this, political factors such as campaign financing, internal party preferences and biases, male dominance in decision-making and limited encouragement and support from the society and family also hinder their willingness to take active political careers.

The Way Forward

It is imperative that implementation of gender equality in public leadership roles fosters better governance and inclusive growth. For ensuring progress, international bodies like OECD have come up with a set of recommendations that address the challenges in women empowerment. Accordingly, member nations are encouraged to promote gender diversity in parliamentary and executive committees, disclose quotas, impose penalties for non-compliance through regulatory and voluntary measures in their respective regions. Additionally, members are urged to embed political commitment through introduction of appropriate measures in appointments to judicial and public services, ensuring work-life balance, family-friendly work culture, mentoring, promoting women role models and regular monitoring of practices of gender balance in leadership roles. Additionally, regular recording of evidences on the implementation of gender diversity measures is a transparent way of measuring progress towards achieving these objectives (Background Report OECD, 2016).

WOMEN EMPOWERMENT IN CORPORATE LEADERSHIP ROLES IN INDIA

Women play a substantial role in economic, social and political development of India as it heads towards the 21st century. Now in almost every sector, women are increasingly occupying decision-making roles and have silently begun challenging the conventional male ideas that had shaped the policies earlier. In recent years, India has been taking numerous measures to introduce gender equality to the workplace, but women still make up only 7% of board positions of publically traded companies whereas only 11% percent of Indian firms have women participating in ownership. Table 2 provides the list of India's most powerful women in business.

Extant Scenario of Women Empowerment in Banking Sector

Banks are one of the primary pillars of Indian economy and are therefore an ideal agent to play a pivotal role as far as women empowerment is concerned. A latest report in "The Wall Street Journal" has exposed that in spite of India's issues with women's rights, more women are escalating to top positions in the banking industry. In Fortune's 50 Most Powerful Women International list, India's top women bankers, SBI chairman Arundhati Bhattacharya is ranked 2nd, ICICI head Chanda Kochhar in on the 5th spot and Axis Bank CEO Shikha Sharma is on the 19th position.

Bhattacharya's profile has elevated SBI as India's largest bank during her three-year tenure. She continued her high-profile battle with the bank's bad loans, while persuading overseas partners to in-

Table 2. India's Top Most Powerful women in Business

2016 Ranking	Name / Designation & Company	2015 Ranking	Name / Designation & Company	2014 Ranking	Name / Designation & Company
1	Arundhati Bhattacharya (Chairman, State Bank of India)	1	Arundhati Bhattacharya (Chairman, State Bank of India)	1	Arundhati Bhattacharya (Chairman, State Bank of India)
2	Chanda Kochhar (MD and CEO, ICICI Bank)	2	Chanda Kochhar (MD and CEO, ICICI Bank)	2	Chanda Kochhar (MD and CEO, ICICI Bank)
3	Shikha Sharma (MD and CEO, Axis Bank)	3	Shikha Sharma (MD and CEO, Axis Bank)	3	Shikha Sharma (MD and CEO, Axis Bank)
4	Zia Mody (Co-Founder, AZB Partners)	4	Nishi Vasudeva (Chairman &MD, HPCL)	4	Nishi Vasudeva (Chairman &MD, HPCL)
5	Aruna Jayanthi (CEO, Capgemini India)	5	Zia Mody (Co-Founder, AZB Partners)	5	Zia Mody (Co-Founder, AZB Partners)
6	Yasmine Hilton (Chairman, Shell India)	5	Aruna Jayanthi (CEO, Capgemini India)	6	Mallika Srinivasan (Chairman & CEO, TAFE)
7	Mallika Srinivasan (Chairman & CEO, TAFE)	7	Suneeta Reddy (MD, Apollo Hospitals)	7	Aruna Jayanthi (CEO, Capgemini India)
8	Kiran Mazumdar-Shaw (Chairman & MD, Biocon)	8	Mallika Srinivasan (Chairman & CEO, TAFE)	8	Preetha Reddy (MD, Apollo Hospital)
9	Suneeta Reddy (MD, Apollo Hospitals)	9	Yasmine Hilton (Chairman, Shell India)	9	Kiran Mazumdar-Shaw (Chairman & MD, Biocon)
10	Chitra Ramakrishna (MD&CEO,NSE)	10	Chitra Ramakrishna (MD& CEO, NSE)	10	Shobhana Bhartia (Chairperson, HT Media)

(Source: Fortune India, 2016)

vest in the stressed assets. She also arranged SBI's merger with its five associate banks in April, 2017. ICICI Bank MD Chanda Kochhar, is viewed by rival bankers as a "visionary". She has revamped the nation's consumer retail business after 7 years at the helm of India's largest private sector lender with consolidated assets of USD 139 billion. Although bad loans took a toll on income growth, she involved turnaround experts to ditch those distressed assets. She has taken strenuous efforts to boost the bank's digital growth and enable female employees to work from home for a year. Shikha Sharma has grown Axis from an underrepresented bank to the nation's fastest growing private sector lender, with revenue up 15 per cent to USD 7.9 billion in 2015 and nearly 3000 branches across 1,800 cities and towns. Ms. Sharma deserves honours for publicising a 'watch list' to monitor 4% of the bank's potentially-troubled assets (Aboli, 2015; The Economic Times, 2016).

Extant Scenario of Women Empowerment in IT Sector

Women leaders represent a new emerging segment of women CEOs at IT companies. Aruna Jayanthi is the CEO of Capgemini India, one of the major business units of Capgemini group. Aruna is liable for operations across all the business units like Consulting, Technology and Outsourcing services in India with a focus to upsurge the integration and performance of over 40,000 growing employee base. The only woman on Capgemini's global leadership board, Jayanthi was part of the team that oversaw iGate's integration with Capgemini. The exercise took Capgemini's headcount to 83,000, and elevated Jayanthi to a global position as the head of the French company's BPO division. Capgemini acquired iGate in a $4 billion deal in 2015. Besides chairing the board of Capgemini Sweden, Jayanthi serves on the boards of the Michelin Group and SBI Capital Markets, and is an executive council member of the IT industry body Nasscom. Vanitha Narayanan is the MD of IBM India Private Limited, and the Regional General Manager for India/ South Asia (ISA). Since 2009, she is serving as the Sales & Distribution Leader and recently as the Managing Partner for Global Business Services (GBS). She is the executive sponsor for developing the women's leadership pipeline and also leads several leadership development & diversity initiatives for ISA.IBM has opened up the API (application programming interface) of IBM Watson to developers, companies, and governments to innovate on its cognitive computing or machine learning platform. Vanitha seeks to drive volumes in cloud environments and harness IBM's industry knowledge, particularly in financial services, health care and retail. Kirthiga Reddy is the MD of Facebook India, leads the Global Marketing Solutions teams in India and plays a crucial role in building and maintaining strategic relationships with top regional agencies and clients. In July 2010, Kirthiga joined as the first Facebook India employee and also the Vice Chairman of Internet and Mobile Association of India (IAMAI). Kirthiga has been featured in Fortune India's Top 50 Most Powerful Women, Business Today's hottest young executives, Fast Company's 100 Most Creative People in Business 2013, Impact's 100 Icons of India Digital Ecosystem among other recognitions (Arun Prabhudesai, 2013).

The Challenges Faced by Women Professionals

Gender wage gap, managing work-life balance, having children while pursuing career options and harassment are some of the challenges faced by women across corporate career and leadership roles. Corporate leadership positions demand long working hours creating additional stress apart from child and family responsibilities (Sinha et al.,2012) In addition, cultural apprehensions on gender specific roles also hider women's career growth.

The Way Forward

Removing the socio-cultural inhibitions in gender equality requires strategic planning and an overall transformation in organisational culture and management practices that foster trust, self-respect, motivation and a strong network. OECD Guidelines on Corporate Governance commends that jurisdictions should stimulate measures such as voluntary targets, disclosure requirements and private initiatives that augment gender balance on boards and in senior management of listed companies. These measures are generic and are adaptable by non-OECD countries as well.

CONCLUSION

Women play a pivotal role in public and corporate as these sectors develop a pipeline of women leaders paving way for inclusive growth. Both sectors need to scale up efforts to create a result oriented framework and robust accountability mechanism to effectively deliver their commitments to gender equality at the top. This could be achieved through political commitment in introduction of appropriate measures in appointments to judicial and public services, ensuring work-life balance, family-friendly work culture, mentoring, promoting women role models and regular monitoring of practices of gender balance in leadership roles. Corporate organisations should encourage measures such as voluntary targets, disclosure requirements and private initiatives that augment gender balance on boards and in senior management of listed companies. Overall, the study emphasises that Indian policy makers and corporate management trustees should initiate appropriate measures to customize and implement appropriate policies in ensuring gender equality taking into consideration the atypical aspects in culture, family and societal setup. Only, this will create a radical shift towards increasing the presence of women in public and corporate leadership roles.

REFERENCES

Aboli. (2015, August 31). *Top 8 Most Influential Women in Indian Banking*. Retrieved from https://letstalkpayments.com/top-8-most-influential-women-in-indian-banking

Fadia, K. (2014). Women's empowerment through Political participation in India. *The Indian Journal of Public Administration, LX*(3), 537–548. Retrieved from http://www.iipa.org.in/New%20Folder/13--Kuldeep.pdf

India, F. (2016). *Annual ranking of India's most powerful women in business*. Retrieved from http://fortuneindia.com/mpw/2016

IndiaToday.in. (2015, Sep 4). *10 most powerful female politicians in India*. Retrieved from http://indiatoday.intoday.in/education/story/women-politicians/1/465444.html

Knowledge@Wharton. (2009, May 21). *What Is the Role of Women in Indian Politics? Growing Stronger...* Retrieved from http://knowledge.wharton.upenn.edu/article/what-is-the-role-of-women-in-indian-politics-growing-stronger/

Mason, K. O. (2005). Measuring Women's Empowerment: Learning from Cross-National Research. In D. Narayan (Ed.), *Measuring Empowerment: Cross-Disciplinary Perspectives* (pp. 89–102). Washington, DC: The Word Bank.

OECD Background Report. (2016, March 8). *Conference on improving women's access to leadership*. Retrieved from https://www.oecd.org/daf/ca/OECD-Women-Leadership-2016-Report

Parida, S. C., & Nayak, S. (2009). *Empowerment of women in India*. New Delhi, India: Northern Book Centre.

Prabhudesai, A. (2013, Jan 15). *10 Indian women in Technology who made it big*. Retrieved from http://trak.in/tech/top-10-indian-successful-women-in-technology/

Scroll.in. (2017, May 21). *Three women IAS officers for 20 men: Five charts reveal profile of India's civil servants*. Retrieved from https://scroll.in/article/720183/three-women-ias-officers-for-20-men-five-charts-reveal-profile-of-indias-civil-servants

Shah, B. (2016, April 9). *8 Indian women in the Asia's 50 Power Businesswomen 2016 list*. Retrieved from https://yourstory.com/2016/04/forbes-power-businesswomen-2016/

Shubhojit. (2014, July 1). *Women Cabinet Ministers in India*. Retrieved from http://www.elections.in/political-corner/women-cabinet-ministers-india/

Sinha, B., Jha, S., & Negi, N. S. (2012). Migration and empowerment: The experience of women in households in India where migration of a husband has occurred. *Journal of Gender Studies, 21*(1), 61–76. doi:10.1080/09589236.2012.639551

Sinha, K. (2015, March 15). *India has more women ministers than its neighbours*. Retrieved from http://timesofindia.indiatimes.com/india/India-has-more-women-ministers-than-its-neighbours/articleshow/46521090.cms

The Economic Times. (2016, Sep 13). *Arundhati Bhattacharya, Chanda Kochhar, Shikha Sharma among most powerful women outside US in Fortune list*. Retrieved from http://economictimes.indiatimes.com/news/company/corporate-trends/arundhati-bhattacharya-chanda-kochhar-shikha-sharma-among-most-powerful-women-outside-us-in-fortune-list/articleshow/54304638.cms

Section 5
Gender and Media

Chapter 19
Structuring the "Expected":
New Social Media Platforms and the Role of Women in Urban Spaces

Devanjan Khuntia
Jawaharlal Nehru University, India

ABSTRACT

This paper based on empirical research attempts to deal with the question of media imagination and the marginalization of women migrants in Indian Megapolis. Foregrounding on the emerging social fact regarding the urban settings catering to one-third of country's population as migrants of which more than two-thirds are women categorically from non-urban rural areas. Further, in the backdrop of the internet and the new media penetration of rural population by half of total usage in India by 2020, the functions of the mediated imageries of the sexes need to be re-examined within the rural-urban continuum for a better clarity of media-gender relationship. The popular media imageries many of which disseminate unrealistic, stereotypical, and restrictive perceptions resulting in portrayal of women in stereotypical ways contradicts the general perception of non-urban women-emancipation through consumption of media texts which is highly urban centric. Such contestation of media effects raises a need to investigate how women migrant to the urban setting consider, analyse, internalize and utilize such portrayal of themselves in the media thus reflecting the actual consumption pattern of media texts and gender roles fixations. This paper particularly looks at an unexplored area of new media consumption within the non-urban migrants to Indian metropolis. It is an attempt to locate affordable alternative communication technology to understand the renewed social interactions of women migrants via virtual social networks in urban centres and how it infers and shape their social identity formation.

INTRODUCTION

Understanding urban space in India in the context of providing home to one-third of country's population as 'migrants' of which more than two-thirds are women categorically from rural areas indicates two annotations. First, that the spaces and essence of contemporary megacities in the global-south like that of Delhi, for example, have developed into a different urban meaning with reference to classical theories

DOI: 10.4018/978-1-5225-3018-3.ch019

of urbanism and second, as much as the city has changed, so have the imageries engulfing the urban dwellers especially women migrants. In other words, the transforming media conceptualize, construct and finally deliver these images to the migrants. The broad argument I wish to present is that the valency of voluminous media sources processed by informal accessibility via unrestricted virtual portability leads to an increase in spontaneous dissemination of corresponding mediated messages within an urban space has become a constitutive frame for a distinctive mode of social experience for non-native city dwellers such as rural women migrants. However within this system of creating an urban experience, the media watchful of not disturbing the market forces and the state, and generates a coverage that simultaneously propagates existing power relations and confines alternatives to the dominant social system. I argue that rather than perceiving media as something separate from the city, the medium which 'represents' urbanity by transforming it into an image, the spatial experience of contemporary social life in urban setting arises over a complex course of co-constitution between urban structures, social practices and media feedback. Thus, for having a holistic understanding of women migrants' social experience in the city and the corresponding construction of her social identity formation, an investigation covering mediated imageries and its relationship with rural women migrants is a must.

Migrants: The Backbone of Megapolis

In India, the urban and semi urban areas consisting megapolis, metropolis and other major urban setting absorbs most of the secondary and tertiary sector's activities. Such urban concentrated process of economic development has initiated one of the biggest internal migration in the country in recent years. As per the UNESCO report of Social Inclusion of Internal Migrants in India 2013 at least two-thirds of city-dwellers are migrants. Most of these migrants to the major urban settings are from the rural areas or the regions with less developed status of their economy, directing increased out-migrants than receiving, hence rural areas are net loser of their population. Such a trend of declining rural population due to migration to urban areas is currently a fact with 27 Indian states are likely to begin seeing shrinking rural populations in the current decade (Rajadhyaksha, 2013). Such a monumental demographic change suggests that the alternative income opportunities have been substantially more effective in bringing a voluminous pattern of mobility to cities. (Rao 2011 ; De Haan and Rogaly 2002; Mitra 2003). This trend of declining rural population can be accorded with an increase in the proportion of the urban population, and subsequently, an increase in the proportion of the unorganized workforce. Post initiation phase of the liberalization of economic policies in India, the urban centres especially metropolitan cities saw a huge influx of urban infrastructural development, in-city industrial growth, commercial diversification, affordable alternative communication technologies, increased transportation development and even in social development activities. All of such institutional and allied developments increased migrants' flow to the Delhi NCR region for capping the related jobs which were mostly located in the informal sector of economy, thus marking a progression in the sector. Over the period since economic liberation, the pattern of involvement of workers in the economy has transformed particularly in the primary sector. The involvement of workers in the primary sector who were mainly farmers or related agriculture activities has reduced from 66.0 percent in 1983-1984 to 53.2 percent in 2009-2010 (RBI 2011). This decline of workforce associated with the primary sector has accompanied with the rise of secondary and tertiary sector employment. The expectations of alternative employment with higher remunerations availability in secondary and tertiary activities have led to the migration of rural workers towards towns and cities. This trend could be associated with the increasing levels of urbanization in the country having an

Structuring the "Expected"

increase from 27.7 percent in 2001 to 31.1 per cent in 2011, an increase of 3.3 per cent point over 2001 census. The latest census of 2011 reveals a good picture of the urbanization and net rural-urban ordering. The rural to urban migration can be seen increasing from 42.0 percent in 1991-2001 to 56.0 percent in 2001-2012 (Kundu 2011). The rising trend of a large number of new urban centres (towns) in 2011 does indicate an increase in mobility as a component of urban growth. Certainly, all these factors were mainly responsible for an increase in the proportion of the unorganized workforce and an increase of informal activities. In fact by 2001-02 the unorganized sector contributed nearly 60 per cent of the Net Domestic Product (NDP) in the country (National Commission for Enterprises in the Unorganised Sector, 2008). This could be marked as a reference point in visualizing current status of the contribution of the unorganized sector in context of increase in amassing of rural migrants into urban informal workforce in the near past. In fact three quarters of the labour workforce comprises of unorganized sector workers forming the backbone of urban economy in the country (Chandrasekhar, 2014). However, no matter how lucrative the urban centres look to offer employment to the rural workers but informal activities do not provide a regular employment nor it offers any job security or social security and the rural poor remains poor and vulnerable throughout their working and social life. At the same time job opportunities for the rural unskilled and semi-skilled workers remain shrunk in the organized sector, and the employment generated during the period of economic reform remains largely informal. Therefore the requirement of the informal labour for the economic growth of urban centres, more labour force is required resulting in continuous influx of migrants to the Indian cities resulting in the increase in the population density of migrants residential colonies and development of newer residential areas to cater their residential needs. It is also important to observe that migrants prefer staying close to each other having similar socio economic background, in Delhi linguistic association is decisive in finalizing the residing locale. Therefore it becomes important to analyse the use of social media platforms by the migrants in an hyper mediated urban environment, where the only way to counter alienation is to be connected to their people and interests is via social media platforms apart from a neighbourhood.

The Tripartite: Rural Women Migrants, New Media and Identity Formation

One of the most important phenomena which have been overlooked is the gender question of migrants and the formation of their social identity in the urban centres. Referring to the fact that the highest percentile of growth in terms of total time consumed on 'Google Search' has been undertaken by women in India. This growth in particular terms of the time spent on search overtakes the percentile growth of men by 123% (IANS, 2016). Also looking at the increasing numbers of women use social media, this newest form of media is being considered as a substantial agent of participatory democracy and civic empowerment. But does the volume of women online users of new social media platforms connotes the actual representation of women social empowerment? Exploring this overriding question through this paper, the present sociological study stresses on how new social media platforms especially instant messaging applications usage among the rural women migrants of metropolitan cities appropriates social behaviour outcomes through mediating gender norms. This paper also debates the general perspectives on the relationship between women and media and point towards higher degree of technological usage among women in metropolis doesn't amount to attainment of social empowerment. Further this paper also deals with the notion that the variance in the approach of women and men route for expressing personal opinions, predominantly with reference to the feedback they receive on Instant Messaging (IM) applications plays a noteworthy part towards identity formation among women. This identity formation among women through Instant Messaging Applications is principally an outcome of the prevailing social norms which are reflected in their conversations through IMs. The paper critically locates how women migrants in the urban centres opined their participation in public discussions being often subjected to be disregarded, belittled or censured and thus recapped by the society about the traditional gender roles. This reluctance of sharing personal opinions or sharing any specific content by these women in public in an alien land – city (away from their rural social setup) is seen towards a greater participation of women in new social media platforms such as WhatsApp, an Instant Messaging platform. The argument is that the greater acceptance of WhatsApp among the women migrants could be associated with its 'gated' platforms which enable participants especially rural women migrants, participate in communication exchanges with a reduced specific group/s rather than using much open public interaction at their working locales or residential locales thus reducing the chance of receiving adverse responses. Such social interaction within WhatsApp which is more intimate, highly responsive and less perpetual reflects more intuitively the way interactions among women have been sanctioned traditionally in rural setups thus not challenging social norms. Interestingly the study contrary to its hypothesis found the interacting groups and content of the interactions that are being exchanged by the women users within WhatsApp are found to be source of gender stereotyping as-well-as strengthening the repetitive performances of gender. This paper concludes how culturally constructed gender roles are constituted as valid and reconstituted by the new social media platforms i.e. Instant Messaging Applications.

METHODOLOGY

The study is based on qualitative interviews which were carried out in the state of Delhi. To locate our field, we categorically focused on the North-East District where the population density of rural migrants is the most. The sampling was based on Maximum Variation Sampling as we were interested in knowing varied categories of women migrants using Instant Messaging Applications. The categories were divided among school going girls, women pursuing higher education, married working women1, unmarried working women, married non-working women2 and, unmarried non-working women. In-depth interviews were employed for recording the data from the respondents. Other than field work, secondary data was collected from various sources like NSSO, Census of India, NCRB etc.

RESULTS

Mediated Urbanism and Construction of Gender Roles

One of the recurrent themes that came up with all the respondents was of exchanging those messages which clearly demarcates gender roles. The category of respondents belonging to school and college level indicated their preference of exchanging private and personal information in WhatsApp. Since this category of respondents is teenagers and young adults, they focus much on understanding their gender roles and identity in their life world. This category of respondents stressed more on differentiating accepted gender roles by their parents and those expected out of the urban space where they reside and operate. A clear contestation is visible in the behavioural outcome of the respondents when their family expects expression of traditional rural values in their daily social acts but the urban setup and the constant media consumption confuses them. Such contestations and sometimes reprimands on non-conformity to parental expectations leads to the realization among the young respondents of 'correct' social expected behaviour of women in public and that has a big role in forming her identity. In the categories of unmarried - working women and nonworking women and married - working women and nonworking there was an interesting variation. While unmarried working women and unmarried nonworking women exhibited focus on their 'identity formation' but married working women and married nonworking women were more focused on 'sustaining' their identity and not much into experimenting with it. For example one of the respondent, unmarried working in organized sector age 27 years said:

I always keep my eyes open for something which could be useful for me. When I travel in metro to my work place, I always look for those travellers who are better than me in terms of their appearance, clothing, accessories, and body language. I sometimes click their photo and text (WhatsApp)it to my brother. I am really close to him and seek his advice to know if something suits me or not. He sometimes gets surprized that how do I manage to have such nice formal wear. Trust me there is no place better than office going crowd in metro. You could see all the latest designs and trends. I guess wearing formal skirts is in trend these days. So many girls wear skirts to their office. They look so nice and confident. Recently I bought an amazing skirt too but I don't think can wear it.

Here we could see how our respondent is correlating collectivization of feminine clothing habits to 'confidence'. Although its normal for her to associate skirts with confidence but it's the socially sanctioned feminine clothing that gives her the confidence of not getting reprimanded for being a deviant of gender roles. She even takes advice of her brother or rather seeking his approval of her clothing indicates power relation in the context of gender roles. Her buying of the skirt but not sure of wearing it indicates the restriction of clothing choices by women in a traditional family of migrants. This process of reinstating gender roles speed up with the instant messaging applications as continuous exchange of gender role specific messages constantly socialize women. For the married categories of our respondents, most part of information exchanged over WhatsApp were found to be relating to family healthcare, parenting, food recipes, spirituality, women health issues. For unmarried categories most part of information exchanged devoted to relationships, personality development, health, lifestyle and hobbies. Interestingly all the respondents spent at least 2 hours daily on WhatsApp interacting with their close friends. Their preference in the information exchanged while understanding, developing or sustaining their identities indicate that they are more concerned for those issues while are in-line of gender roles set by the governing society. Such attitudes and gender roles perceived by social actors could be understood by relating with what the mid-century functionalists argued. Their argument could be summarized as claiming that sex role differences remain static for the reason of promoting social stability. However the functionalists did not elaborate whether this was an intentional (manifest) or unintentional (latent) function of sex role differences (Lindsey, 2015). The primary locus of functionalist understanding was the 'corresponding roles' executed by women and men as they function to keep society running efficiently. One of the most important part of functionalism tradition is Talcott Parsons' (Parsons and Bales, 2014) views of women and men's 'complementary roles' that are considered as the key statement of functionalist ideas about gender. Arguing in the 1950s, Parsons argued that social life in modern societies, along-with the division of labour in modern organization of work as distinct from family or place of residence, confer that somebody was needed to stay at home to nurture the young ones and the elderly along-with undertaking the process of initial socialization of human infants (ibid). However for highly debatable and not entirely clear reasons associated with the workings of social groups, this socially conferred 'nursing and nurturing' domestic role is assigned to women and the socially conferred 'rational and instrumental' role of work which includes wages or salary is associated with men. Such variance in conferred sex roles became the 'natural' social norms and Parsons carefully describes how children become socialized into them. Therefore, Parsons's outlook towards social norms and family is very much sociological in looking not to nature but to social groups and social processes such as socialization to define women's and men's different social positions as perceived by the society. Parsons work also presented more of an explanation for current gender expectations than a clarification of the inequalities accompanying the differing sex roles. Our respondents consider gender roles as the requirement for social stability and alterations to socially constructed gender roles is considered as threatening to the status quo and social stability. The idea that 'stability' may not be beneficial to women constrained within traditional roles did not seem to occur to the respondents.

Conforming "Womanhood"

All of our respondents agreed that they are expected to have knowledge of domestic work attributes like cooking, housekeeping, decorating home, nursing, along with having a pleasant personality with having soft skills. Interestingly all the categories of our respondents emphasised upon discussing either of these attributes mentioned above in all of their conversations in the WhatsApp. Although when asked why do they discuss such expected attributes on regular basis? The answers were varied but indicated gender socialization as major reason behind this. The school going and college going respondents pointed towards possessing workable knowledge of cooking and housekeeping as they were always expected to be with their mothers or other female member of the house during such activities being undertaken and especially during special occasions and festivals. One of our college going respondent age 21 said:

I always knew how to make sweets at home, as from the early age I used to accompany my mother to the local market to buy ingredients and have always helped her in preparing the sweet dish. Especially during festivals I come as an extra hand as we need to make so much of sweets for our relatives. Although lately we (the respondent and her mother) have started experimenting with the sweets as my maternal grandmother has a smartphone. Now we regularly discus (on WhatsApp) different types of sweets with her.

This clearly shows appropriation of gender roles through socialization by exposing the respondent about culinary knowledge and other domestic work such as buying things from the market at an early age. Our respondent did not mention her father or any other male members of the family in sweet making process. This indicates how men are excluded from domestic work especially in managing kitchen and housekeeping. Married category of working respondents said they partly or fully take part in domestic activities at home as it is expected from them. Married categories of nonworking women said they undertake domestic activities as they do not have any other option to do. When asked if the same thing applies to nonworking men, they simply rejected the idea as it's not their (natural) work. Unmarried working women expressed their knowledge of undertaking domestic work makes them more skilful and they will not find any problem in case of settling out of home alone or when married. Unmarried nonworking women said if they do not have knowledge of domestic work their identity is nil as they do not work outside. Their domestic work is their true identity. To understand the association of Indian women with domestic work could be explained by the gender expectations as part of the larger culture which emphasise more on the betterment of the larger caste community and expects women to respect the same and voluntarily contribute to that community welfare and to consider individual goals as secondary. Thus caring roles at home are still promoted as the proper course for many less privileged women (Kodoth and Eapen, 2005; Mukhopadhyay and Seymour,1994). Also, university graduates of both sexes are encouraged to seek a suitable job at the end of their degree. However, early gender socialization paves way for later inclination towards jobs and it the choice of subjects they take in doing their degrees are likely to differ and, therefore, their job options will differ. Our respondents in school and college told us about discussing issues relating to humanities and arts and giving a miss to more technical issues and subjects in their daily conversation. Such daily practice of ignoring science or technological subjects is not something they do out of their choice but how the girls have been socialized from the beginning. The result is that while making a choice in study streams in school or college, women are more inclined towards humanities and arts. Have a look around a social science class and there are more women than men. The same can be seen in an English or History classes. But such a sight dramatically changes if one visits subjects like physics or engineering where men outnumber the women. These gender differences in choice of subject will affect what sorts of jobs graduates will be able to get.

Out of 20 women respondents who are working (married and unmarried), 13 expressed probability of leaving their paid employment. 7 married working women expressed their desire to leave their jobs as it was getting difficult for them to manage their family and work together. 6 unmarried working women suspected loss of their job within 2 years as they might get married. Our respondents displayed their phase of constant analysis on resignation from their work with taking suggestions from their family and friends through instant messaging application WhatsApp. Although real-time feedback seems to diffuse any confusion but managing too many responses at a time on WhatsApp could be more confusing as well. Interestingly the suggestions from their sources were more in the forms of links to newspaper articles or blogs which discussed women's life after leaving their jobs. And most of these links discussed serious repercussions of job loss. Although our respondents expressed their knowhow about life after employment loss but somehow they also discussed alternative employment opportunities at home. Such a pattern is not something unusual as in most of South Asia, the Middle East and North Africa, women's economic participation rate is only around 30 per cent, compared to around 45 per cent in OECD (high income) countries (World Bank, 2006). This means that in most cases women are less likely to have an income based employment in comparison to men. Even in the sectors where women constitute majority of the workforce they receive less pay than their male counterparts. Such gendered division of labour in terms of 'men's jobs' and 'women's jobs' have contributed to the 'domestication' of women. In fact such dilemmas in continuing with their jobs as expressed by our respondents have contributed to the gendered vertical division of labour i.e. women are evidently rare in the higher positions across the sectors.

DISCUSSION

Decoding Gender Socialization

The terminology 'Sex' indicates a physiological variance within the biological categories of females, males and intersex persons. This also includes both their primary and secondary sex characteristics. On the other hand the term 'Gender', specifies social (which includes cultural) variances allied to given biological sex categories (Strong et al.: 2011). This process of assigning 'social variance' of boys or girls begins at the time of birth with family classifying the primary sex characteristics. Interestingly intersex babies are usually assigned one category or another between boys or girls and this is being done as per the prevailing social and cultural norms (Sharma, 2013) of a particular time and space. Therefore the process of 'gender construct' is a social construct and not natural. From the beginning a child is reared by the family and society as per the collective authorization of gender roles and gradually socialized to conform to socially 'expected' gender roles which have been assigned to their biological sex and the gender.

Portion of socialization process for a child is to classify and assimilate to socially authorized gender roles. With time the child acquires workable knowledge to understand 'gender role' and learns how boys and girls are expected to act and behave by family in general and society in particular. Although gender roles are grounded upon the collectivized authorization of traditional norms by a given society but across cultures and societies, masculine roles have been sanctioned to take the form of strength, aggression, and dominance, while feminine roles have been sanctioned to take the form of passivity, nurturing, and subordination (Lee and Ashcraft, 2005; Beal, 1994).

The process of appropriation of gender roles for a child begins with the time of its birth. Interestingly from day one gender roles are imposed on the child. In this post-modern society, we have been socially trained to pass on the information, behaviours, attitudes associated with gender differentiations. Parents are spontaneous while applying 'colour coded' gender labels while selecting clothing for male new-borns in 'boy specific' colours like green or blue, and 'girl' specific colours like red or pink. Interestingly these gender specific colour associations are social and not natural but due to prevailing norms in the society such appropriations are assumed to be natural(Paoletti, 2012). I use the term 'prevailing' social norms because many of these benchmarks change with time for example, till early 20th century, colour pink which is currently being associated with girls was then socially authorized as more masculine in nature hence voluntarily associated with boys, while colour blue which is currently being associated with boys was then socially authorized to be more feminine hence voluntarily associated with girls. This process of shifting colour coded gender labels within less than a time span of a century illustrates socially constructed gender associations are not always fixed or natural but indeed dynamic and social in nature.

Under the progression of gender socialization doesn't takes place only at the family level but occurs through other levels of four major agents together i.e. family, education, peer groups, and media (Kane, 2013). Each of these agents not only introduces and familiarizes a new entrant to the society i.e. a child to the gender specific roles and expected behaviour outcomes but also reinforces societal gender norms by developing and maintaining a status quo of normative expectations for gender-specific behaviour. Apart from these agents which have primary responsibilities of exposing a child to gender expectations, other secondary agents, such as religion, the workplace and public spaces also have their role in socializing a child (Green and Neusner, 1996). Continuous and repeated exposure to these agents through lifetime of a child/person strengthens and legitimizes the social actions of people as natural based on their gender roles.

As we have just discussed about children learning through various agents to differentiate between assigned gender roles to them and others at a very young age. Some research studies have very well described that children start reciprocating to their learning's of the gender socialization process by exhibiting their awareness about differentiating gender roles as early as age two or three. By the child attains the age of five, most of the children have internalized the gender socialization and thus conclusively inherited culturally appropriate gender roles (Kane, 1996). To understand how the whole process of gender socialization gets initiated the following example is well suited. Family members often provide male child with some toys to play with like those of cars, aeroplanes, guns, and superhero gear etc. Since these toys replicate the workability characteristics of the original self, hence share the essence of the workable know how and physical or emotional association of the toy with the child. Consequently the aggression, power and technicalities of the replicating ideas associated with the toys are passed to the male child playing with it. Contrary to the toys given to the male child, on the other hand, female child is more often provided with those toys which are delicate and more associated with love, passion and care like those of dolls, soft toys, kitchen accessories and dress-up apparels which consequently endorse the essence of nurturing, social propinquity, and role play. But mere playing with toys doesn't propagate the idea of gender differentiation among children. In fact the actual gender socialization comes into play when parents along-with providing 'gender-appropriate' toys discourage their child playing with cross gender toys thus promote gender-normative behaviour (Cherney et al., 2003).

Although gender socialization is not only limited to early childhood, in fact it's a life-long process and results into manifold results. As boys are (gender) socialized in a particular way, this defines a platform for their adulthood position, at the time of choosing their career they are socially aligned more with particular professions such as law enforcement, the defence services, and politics hence male dominated. Whereas girls are (gender) socialized in a particular way leading to their 'natural' (social) inclination towards choosing professions such as childcare, healthcare, and social work thus female dominated (Jackson and Scott, 2002). Such peculiar variation while selecting occupational roles between women and men is most vocal examples of typical gendered behaviour outcomes of cultural tradition. Hence it won't be incorrect to say about occupational selections as not natural outcome of sex but gender which is socially constructed. Adherence to these gender roles establishes realization of social expectations but not necessarily personal preference (Diamond, 2002).

The prevailing social attitudes and gender expectations in terms of the corresponding roles are not typically based on any essential or natural gender variances; rather it is grounded on gender stereotypes. There are overgeneralised ideas regarding the attitudes, personalities, and behaviour outlines of women and men. These oversimplified gendered ideas form the basis of gender stereotypes which further strengthens the basis of sexism which considers prejudiced beliefs that value males over females as a priori (Dolan, 2014). Such beliefs still pervades every society in today's world despite women empowerment and development and expecting women to be the primary caretakers of the household remains one of the most important parts of gender-role expectations. Gender role expectations of women have always included some traits such as friendly nature, passivity, and nurturing. Such traits are always considered as inherent to women. They are expected to carry these traits forever with them or they should be ready to get penalized by the society on the count of flouting such social expectations. If found guilty, a gender role 'deviant' women may be socially ostracized (Rudman, 1998). On the other hand, a gender role 'deviant' man acting in an equally insistent manner might be perceived as resilient or even gain respect in some circumstances.

Socially constructed gender differentiations and corresponding stereotyping values have penetrated the society at various levels in varied degrees such as in employment ratio of men and women, education, property ownership, parliamentary representation etc. (Roscigno, 2007). In Indian context, women too face discrimination at workplaces catering to male-dominated professions such as defence services, engineering, aviation, etc. (Booroah et al., 2015). In many areas of the country, women are devoid of adequate nutrition, healthcare, and education as boys due to gender discrimination.

Gender roles not only conform and appropriate behaviour outcomes of an individual by providing guidelines to be followed by each gender, but also by awarding penalties for those who flout the norms. While the society which safeguards its authorized gender norms somewhat has lately sanctioned women to deviate to a hairline width of masculine characteristics without being much reprimanded (such as wearing male clothing), but men have not been sanctioned to deviate towards feminine characteristics (such as wearing skirts) (Thompson and Gibbs, 2016). Such deviance may carry threat of heavy penalty of harassment and/or violence. This socially approved threat of punishment for deviating from the expected gender norms could be better understood from the mistreatment been extended towards third gender who do not comply to socially approved identification of gender duality as male or female. As most of the societies believe in the binary of gender existence i.e. female or male, socially 'other' sexual categories beyond accepted gender categories like those of transgender and other gender-nonconforming people are highly discriminated and frequently suppressed through the means of violence and deprived of societal benefits like property ownership, parliamentary representation and electoral rights to name a few for not adhering to society's traditional gender roles (Soble and Power, 2008).

The New Public-Ness: Behind the Closed Doors

The newest media or the internet has changed the way we interact and connect with other social actors within our society. Social media has proved to be most important part of social life in the modern society (Partridge, 2011). But lately the exchange of messages in virtual public realm is fast altering. Past couple of years have become a witness to majority of 'open' social activity been gradually shifting to private virtual spaces or groups and messaging apps. This represents a significant alteration in what "social media" was thought to be. The mainstream social media platforms like Facebook or Twitter enabled social interaction and message communication through the timelines and news feeds which were 'open' and accessible by the public. But gradually such message exchanges are now being challenged by target specific closed communication messages on Instant Messaging (Banerjee, 2016). Such alteration in message exchanges over virtual social spaces is challenging much of the things we've learned about social media over the past decade or so.

How much challenge the mainstream social media are facing could be sensed from the statement given by the founder of Facebook, Mark Zuckerberg in November 2014, he said: *"Messaging is one of the few things that people do more than social networking"* (Rowan, 2015). Since 2014, Facebook having realized potential of instant messaging have made huge investments in the messaging space by acquiring WhatsApp worth US $19 billion and developing a strong approximately 900 million users worldwide. A social media giant Facebook acquiring Instant Messaging Application WhatsApp and Dark Social Channels was considered by many as a simple investment strategy but it has considerable sociological importance for us. We will start with discussing some of the media coverage on WhatsApp. As per an article in The Economist:

A quarter of all downloaded apps are abandoned after a single use. Only instant messaging bucks the trend. Over 2.5 billion people have at least one messaging app installed. Within a couple of years, that will reach 3.6 billion, about half of humanity. The market's leading duo, Facebook Messenger and WhatsApp, which is also owned by Facebook, are nearing one billion monthly users each. Many teenagers now spend more time on smartphones sending instant messages than perusing social networks. WhatsApp users average nearly 200 minutes each week using the service (The Economist, 2016).

Hence it is astonishing to visualize that by 2018 half of the humanity will be interacting with each other through a mediation i.e. through cloud computing service of instant messaging applications in which

Structuring the "Expected"

WhatsApp is currently the largest of the service provider with 1 billion active monthly users (Statista, n.d.). It is evident that Instant Messaging is dominating all types of online message sharing from the fact that almost 70% of all online activities happen in the dark social3 which includes messaging apps, emails and private browsing. Instant Messaging not only dominates social sharing, but it has surpassed message sharing through social networking websites in terms of monthly active user numbers too.

The transition of activities taking place in public platforms to closed platforms (instant messaging platforms) could be the biggest change in social interactions and communications. Hence it becomes essential to understand the sociological relevance of mediated interactions through such applications. It becomes even more important to discuss instant messaging platforms as some of the largest business corporations in the world are using the same platform to disseminate their ideation regarding their products and services. But as we know women are quite often presented in the forms of advertorials involving lifestyle products, healthcare products, consumer durables, investments and corresponding issues for the promotion of business products (Byerly & Ross, 2006) hence corporations infiltrating personal discussions through personalized interacting spaces like WhatsApp have more tendency to strengthen culturally constructed gender roles as valid.

Regarding the corporates infiltrating the gated communities of instant messaging could be understood from the below example who have started to experiment with dark social, and marketing through instant messaging platforms. Adidas, the German sportswear giant has been recently using WhatsApp to build hyper-local communities in cities across the world. As per Florian Alt, senior director of global brand communications for Adidas "There is excitement about the opportunity dark social presents and how it can help Adidas become the most personal brand" (Seb, 2016).

Having staged to be the 'most personal brand' Adidas has started focusing on one-to-one messaging rather than one-to-many messaging marketing strategy. The company is also en route to track communications that are shared privately in WhatsApp. There's a reason for referring to dark social as dark reason being the difficulty in operational technicalities to track private conversation trends in gated virtual communities. For this reason of difficulty but extremely useful method is making Adidas to use WhatsApp to develop hyper local communities in cities across the world (Seb, 2016). But an incident in 2015 underlines an issue. Adidas came under heavy criticism from across the globe and had been referred to as 'sexist' and ' gender discriminatory' as their Manchester United women's kit featured a T-Shirt with heavy plunging neckline and different design from the men's kit (Sheen, 2015). Such cases underlines the issue of company thought process in-line with existing social gender norms. In such case while establishing personalized interactions with consumers on closed personal instant messaging platforms like WhatsApp, these corporations have the tendency to pass on traditionally accepted gender norms through their product's general ideation.

CONCLUSION

In this section before summing up our observations, findings and analysis I would like to start with quoting a sociological thinker who has been perceived to overlook the question of Gender. Interestingly unlike thought otherwise, Marx looked at the question of 'social differences' between women and men. Although Marx has been critiqued for having a blind eye for women condition of his time, but one has to look at the applicability of his writings to our understanding of today's concept of Gender as the word gender was not known to them in its present usage. In his Economic and Philosophical Manuscripts,

Marx argued that women's position in society could be considered as a reference point or the measure of the progress of society as a whole. Through a dialectical argument, Marx directly related to his overall theory of society. In order for society to frame beyond its capitalist arrangement, a need for a renewed structure of social relations would have to be considered which goes further than an alienated construction of value. Social actors need to acknowledge each and every person in the society having their individual values rather than serving as worthy enough in context of exchange value only. In such an arrangement existence of women derives a different meaning and significance altogether. But for having such conditions women and men both need to attain certain pre-requisites in which the society need to reach a point of development where an individual is valued for who they are, rather than any abstract category of man, woman, etc. In our research findings we sensed that women did realize such a requisition but they admitted they couldn't escalate their need to their family and especially to male members. Although they were quite active on WhatsApp discussing the same with their women colleagues or friends but their conversations are more towards functioning as a catharsis agent. The ease of connecting with anybody at anytime due to WhatsApp has certainly made women more vocal than earlier but rather than collectivizing towards identifying their problems and finding a solution to their issues they are utilizing the communication space for appropriating their current situations. Although Marx appeared to be indicative towards the direction of gender as a dynamic rather than a static category but he emphasized upon women themselves capable of changing their position. Interestingly our respondents acknowledged the gender role discrimination but did not displayed any urgency for a change and seem to accept the causation of gender role differentiation as 'natural'. However Marx in his writings - In the Manuscripts (Marx and Engels 2011) and in The German Ideology (Marx and Engels 1998), gave a strong argument on the alternative to the traditional dualistic views of the nature/society dualism. He stressed upon the fact that unlike a generalized perception in which it is considered that nature and society exists as two distinctive entities that complement each other without fundamentally changing the essence of it-self or the other, Marx argues that the two are dialectically related. As human beings form a point of connection with the nature through its labour, both the individual and nature subject to change. This occurs because human beings exist as part of nature, and the labour process offers the means for such a unity in a provisional form. Since both nature and society are not static units, Marx argued that it's problematic to undertake an assumption about what is 'natural' by the means of transhistorical notions (as perceived by our respondents about gender roles) and could only possibly be understood for a specific historical circumstances. Although one should not draw too close a parallel between the nature/culture dualism and the man/woman dualism since doing so could lead to a reification of these interpretations that we seek to understand. This discourse of nature/culture dualism can also be found in Marx and Engels's argument of the gender division of labour in The German Ideology. Here, they both discuss the division of labor in the family which is not completely 'natural' as considered. In their discourse on mapping the development of the family, they point out that such gendered division of labor is valid as 'natural' for very undeveloped productive relations, where women's bodily variance would make it difficult if not impossible for them to undertake 'some particular' physically demanding tasks. Hence division of labour in family which is gendered could possibly change as society changes.

Although there are important arguments which were discussed to show how instant messaging platforms appropriate gender roles via ease of communication but unintentionally the findings tend to cast women as victims of large social processes including technological innovations in communications. Women in numerous circumstances may lack control over their own lives, but this does not prove they are entirely

Structuring the "Expected"

without choices, or totally lack in power to bring about change. The ability to make choices and changes is referred to as agency. Materialism has been periodically critiqued for overlooking agency because of its determinist tendencies and focusing too much on material factors such as economic resources and thus entirely determines how people live their lives. The post structuralist at this juncture try filling up the void by trying to understand what kind of meanings people give to their own actions. In order to understand this, it is necessary to understand the role of ideas in the social construction of gender. And for the same reason this study focuses more on what the women perceive of gender roles through their daily interaction especially in today's world of virtual social networks.

REFERENCES

Beal, C. R. (1994). *Boys and Girls: The Development of Gender Roles*. McGraw Hill.

Borooah, V. K. (2015). Caste, Discrimination, and Exclusion in Modern India. *Sage (Atlanta, Ga.)*.

Byerly, C. M., & Ross, K. (2006). *Women and Media: A Critical Introduction*. Blackwell Publishing. doi:10.1002/9780470774908

Chandrasekhar, C. P. (2014). India's informal economy. *The Hindu*. Retrieved from: http://www.thehindu.com/opinion/columns/Chandrasekhar/indias-informal-economy/article6375902.ece

Cherney, I. D., Kelly-Vance, L., Gill Glover, K., Ruane, A., & Oliver Ryalls, B. (2003). The Effects of Stereotyped Toys and Gender on Play Assesment on Children Aged 1847 Months. *Educational Psychology*, *23*(1), 95–106. doi:10.1080/01443410303222

Diamond, M. (2002). Sex and Gender are Different: Sexual Identity and Gender Identity are Different. *Clinical Child Psychology and Psychiatry*, *7*(3), 320–334. doi:10.1177/1359104502007003002

Dolan, K. (2014). *When Does Gender Matter? Women Candidates and Gender Stereotypes in American Elections*. Oxford University Press. doi:10.1093/acprof:oso/9780199968275.001.0001

Eagly, A. H., & Carli, L. L. (2007). *Through the Labyrinth: The Truth About How Women Become Leaders*. Harvard Business School Press.

Funny or Die. (2016). 21 best GIFs of all the time of the week #168. *Funny or Die*. Retrieved from: http://www.funnyordie.com/slideshows/7e240c15c2/21-best-gifs-of-all-time-of-the-week-168

Green, W. S., & Neusner, J. (1996). *The Religion Factor: An Introduction to how Religion Matters*. Westminster John Knox Press.

IANS. (2016). Women outnumber men in using Google Search in India. *The Indian Express*. Retrieved from: http://indianexpress.com/article/technology/social/google-search-women-outnumber-men-happy-international-womens-day/

Jackson, S., & Scott, S. (2002). *Gender: A Sociological Reader*. Routledge.

Kane, E. (1996). *Gender*. Culture and Learning.

Kane, E. W. (2013). *Rethinking Gender and Sexuality in Childhood*. Bloomsbury.

Kodoth & Eapen. (2005, July 23). Looking Beyond Gender Parity: Gender Inequities of Some Dimensions of Well-Being in Kerala. *EPW*.

Lee, J. W. (2005). *Gender Roles*. Nova Biomedical Books.

Lindsey, L. L. (2015). *Gender Roles: A Sociological Perspective*. Routledge.

Marx, K., & Engels, F. (1998). *The German Ideology*. Prometheus Books.

Marx, K., & Engels, F. (2011). *Economic and Political Manuscripts of 1844*. Wilder Publications.

Mukhopadhyay, C. C. (1994). *Women, Education, and Family Structure in India*. Westview Press.

National Commission for Enterprises in the Unorganised Sector. (2008). *Contribution of the unorganised sector to GDP report of the subcommittee of a NCEUS task force*. National Commission for Enterprises in the Unorganised Sector Working Paper. Retrieved from: http://nceuis.nic.in/Final_Booklet_Working_Paper_2.pdf

Paoletti, J. B. (n.d.). *Pink and Blue: Telling the Boys from the Girls in America*. Academic Press.

Parsons, T., & Bales, R. F. (2014). *Family: Socialization and Interaction Process*. Routledge.

Partridge, K. (2011). *Social Networking*. H.W. Wilson.

Rajadhyaksha, N. (2013). Rural India in decline. *LiveMint*. Retrieved from: http://www.livemint.com/Opinion/hYkJxMUgidtc69y1eWivVJ/Rural-India-in-decline.html

Roscigno, V. J. (2007). *The Face of Discrimination: How Race and Gender Impact Work and Home Lives*. Rowmann and Littlefield Publishers Inc.

Rowan, D. (2015). Facebook Messenger: Inside Zuckerberg's app for everything. *Wired*. Retrieved from: http://www.wired.co.uk/article/inside-facebook-messenger

Rudman, L. A. (1998). Self-Promotion as a Risk Factor for Women: The Costs and Benefits of Counter-stereotypical Impression Management. *Journal of Personality and Social Psychology, 74*(3), 629–645. doi:10.1037/0022-3514.74.3.629 PMID:9523410

Seb, J. (2016). Adidas spotlights 'dark social' to be the 'most personal brand'. *The Drum*. Retrieved from: http://www.thedrum.com/news/2016/03/05/adidas-spotlights-dark-social-be-most-personal-brand

Shambhu. (2016). WhatsApp: Unlocking The Goldmine. Educreation Publishing.

Sharma, R. (2014). Parents prefer male child in intersex operations in Gujarat. *The Times of India*. Retrieved from: http://timesofindia.indiatimes.com/india/Parents-prefer-male-child-in-intersex-operations-in-Gujarat/articleshow/29879738.cms

Sheen, T. (2015). Manchester United and Adidas branded 'sexist' and 'discriminatory' as women's shirt features plunging neckline and different design. *Independent*. Retrieved from: http://www.independent.co.uk/sport/football/premier-league/manchester-united-sexist-kit-causes-outrage-as-womens-short-features-plunging-neckline-10433277.html

Soble, A., & Power, N. P. (2008). *The Philosophy of Sex: Contemporary Readings*. Rowman and Littlefield Publishers Inc.

Statista. (n.d.). Number of consumer cloud-based service users worldwide in 2013 and 2018 (in billions). *Statista*. Retrieved from: https://www.statista.com/statistics/321215/global-consumer-cloud-computing-users/

Strong, B. (2011). *The Marriage and Family Experience: Intimate Relationships in a Changing Society*. Wadsworth Cengage Learning.

The Economist. (2016). Bots the next frontier. *The Economist*. Retrieved from: http://www.economist.com/news/business-and-finance/21696477-market-apps-maturing-now-one-text-based-services-or-chatbots-looks-poised

Thompson, W. E., & Gibbs, J. C. (2016). *Deviance and Deviants: A Sociological Approach*. Wiley Blackwell.

ENDNOTES

[1] Working Women - Women who are engaged in paid employment.
[2] Non-Working Women – The women not earning an income through their work at home.
[3] Facebook – 23%, Dark Social - 69%, All other Social – 8%.

Chapter 20
The Role of Media in Perpetuating or Obstructing Gender Equality in the Context of Developing World

Prabartana Das
Jadavpur University, India

Media engineers subtle ways in which gender bias can persist in society and ensures the perpetuation of women subjugation in the society. In this chapterI want to excavate the various factors which contributes to the augmentation of gender biases by the media and how the media in developing countries strengthens the cause patriarchy masquerading in the façade of preserving traditions and customs? I also intend to unravel how perennial problems like illiteracy and abject poverty further dents the projectof women empowerment and how deeply entrenched patriarchal values manipulate the media to withhold emancipation in true sense. How women even after being qualified suffers from several negative effects undermining her own status? It will also be interesting to delve into the ways in which gendered media is far more subversive and ubiquitous in the developing world than developed world. And lastly how the gender bias in media can be curbed in the light of social and political awakening in women in particular and the development of humaningenuity and consciousness in general.

THE BASIC UNDERSTANDING OF MEDIA BIASES TOWARDS GENDER ROLES

In the era of globalization, media has emerged as the most powerful medium of communication with an unimaginable capacity to galvanize, shape and influence public opinion. The accentuation of a globalized era facilitated free flow of ideas, perspectives and opinion which made the role of media all the more vital. The media today plays a preponderant role in shaping and molding our outlook which has a great impact in our daily life and its impossible to repudiate the colossal authority that media exercises today. Media eventually became an indispensable element of our life and emerged as the most pertinent link between the world and the people. As far as the role of media is concerned, there are two aspects that we must keep in mind. Firstly, media has a traditional role of reporting news reports objectively and present-

DOI: 10.4018/978-1-5225-3018-3.ch020

ing facts before the people so that they can judge the veracity of those facts by themselves. Secondly, we deal with media role of dissecting, analyzing and assessing an issue and this is how it plays a pivotal role in nurturing, shaping and galvanizing public opinion and reorienting ideas of people. Media thus has the potential not only influence but can also reconstruct and dominate the mindset of a society as a whole. In developing countries, mass media manages to use gender stereotypes to induce or appease consumer. Media acts as a mirror to the society and reflects what a society desire to see.

Media and gender projections have become one of the most debatable and vexed issue which needs a close and nuanced perusal. Gender stereotypes and its perpetuation has become one of the most intractable hurdle in the path of women empowerment. Gender bias against women has perennially plagued the project of women emancipation in the true sense in our society. The all-pervasive patriarchal mindset triumphantly dominates the common sense of the society. Despite all the high octane sermons on gender equality, women empowerment has largely been a mere symbolic gesture. In this context, it is important to delve into the two types Of equality which persists in the academic discourses. Firstly, gender equality is largely a phenomenon of "formal equality". Nivedita Menon (1999) explains that the "formal equality" is the form of gender equality which persists in the society as a mere formality without any practical implementation. For instance, the Convention on the Elimination of all Forms of Discrimination Against Women (CEDAW) is an international treaty adopted in 1979 by the United Nations General Assembly which guarantees the well being of women worldwide. Further, the political and judicial institutions of most of the countries assure adequate safeguards against the vilification of women and so walks an extra mile by underlining equal rights and privileges for women. But the biggest regret remains that the formal equality as the name suggests is confined to the tenets of tokenism which is utopian and lacks practical implementation. This gives rise to "substantive equality" which implies real equality which embodies a qualitative and tangible change in the condition of women in the society which enables them to enjoy equality in the true sense of the term. While formal equality is readily available for superficial assurances of gender equality, it is the lack if substantive equality which remains a matter of great concern. The well entrenched shackles of patriarchy and male chauvinism impedes the fructification of "substantive" gender equality.

The prejudices related to women is reflected vividly in the projections of mass media of various kind. Advertisements, movies, television shows, social networking sites, print and electronic media portrays the hegemony of men over women and unfortunately enough media rather than empowering women tries to demean women. Suppression of women may not be ideal for this present era, which claims to be liberal in nature but the reality is paradoxical. Media is the medium to generate transformation in the society. Contradictory to this view, it acts as a barrier to gender equality. Media remains to be the protector of status quo. It is very disheartening to see how media now have become a business enterprise and increasing their TRP is the only goal. Money being the necessary evil have turned the media into a hungry monster. A monster who is always in search of mouthwatering news. It possess the power to attract the customers so that it can sell their products like a hot chocolate cake. Their obsession for 'Breaking news' makes media crave for sensational events, so that they can spice it up and present it in the market. But what media often tends to forget is that it is the only source which carries information to the mass and can mould existing perception of many.

While media bias against women is ubiquitous and rampant, it has been observed that developing societies plays a much more hostile role to denigrate the existence of women than the developed countries. The developed nations armed with adequate technological and industrial growth as well as due to strong espousal of liberal values and the virtue of equality have made concerted effort to improve the position of women in the society. And as media resonates the modus operandi of the society works to some extent for the emancipation of women in the developed world. On the other hand, the developing world still languishes in the vestiges of Colonial regressive mindset. The unflinching deep-rooted patriarchal values debilitates the development of women in the developing world. Media plays a vicious role in furthering the prejudices against women. Media is illustrative of the traditions and culture of a society. Therefore, the media make incessant endeavors to perpetuate the traditional role of women in the society by continuous projection of gender stereotypes. Media sometimes implicitly and many a times explicitly supports the retrograde and archaic principles of the so called orthodoxy. Furthermore, media leaves no stone unturned in order to ascertain that women are not empowered to challenge the sinister gender biases in the society. Media in many nefarious ways aims to indoctrinate the viewer with the submissive nature of women who are solely dependent on their male counterparts in every walk of life. Media defines a perfect women as one who is beautiful, fair, thin, a loving wife, a caring mother. Even if women are projected as employees and working professionals by the media, their profession and its work is considered to be a corollary of their domestic chores. A woman has to be a class apart, playing dual role and balancing her heels between her office and household works. She has to be the one sacrificing her own identity for the sake of her household and sometimes even for her family. Media in developing countries thus represent a women less as an individual and more to 'wow-men'. The impediments in the path of women emancipation are numerous in the developing societies. The inflexible patriarchal valves which further stems the sense of immense male superiority, abject poverty of women send their complete financial dependence on men for their sustenance remains perennial causes behind rampant gender biases in the media against women. Simmering conditions of widespread illiteracy among women obstructs any chance for women to prosper and progress in their lives. The lack of education has traditionally led the women to a world of ignorance, subjugation and lack of confidence which is reflected and furthered by the media. But it would be simplistic on our part, if we ascribe media biases against women in developing world only to poverty and illiteracy. The subtle sense of over-arching male superiority has debilitated even the growth of educated and distinguished womenfolk which is inadvertently reflected by the media propaganda. Now a question may come to ones mind that what is the real reason behind media being so biased in case of gender in developing countries? A simple answer to this might be illiteracy and abject poverty of women! But again a question may arise as many women are now working and educated. What about them? Do they face the same problems as other illiterate, poverty stricken women? Well the answer might be complex and require us to further extrapolate the nature of gender biases and gender roles in the society by studying the nuances of media projections vis-a-vis gender. So considering the fact that media affects various different sections of women differently, it is imperative on our part to ponder over it with adequate attention.

THE ROLE OF VARIOUS FORMS OF MASS MEDIA AS FACILITATOR OR IMPEDIMENT IN THE PATH OF GENDER EQUALITY

Advertisements

It has been an age old audio-visual techniques to drive consumers for selling their products. It helps the viewers to know about the upcoming products, their prices in the market and do comparative analysis before consumption. So advertisement is basically a medium which analyses the market, its phenomena,

The Role of Media in Perpetuating or Obstructing Gender Equality

and demands before showcasing the commodities in the market. This survey often leads to a situation where the Advertisement agencies tries their best to stick to the customs and traditions of that particular society. The intention behind such activity is often less related with quality and quantity and at times becomes more about satisfying the viewers.

In order to tune viewers in front of television, advertisement portrays a women as one who is always confined either to childcare or kitchen, now that in modernized era it is expected a women to be a superwomen working both in kitchen and doing office work equally. In India, if one takes the example of 'Airtel' advertisement where a woman in office is shown as a boss ordering her employee to work late and finish his work on time, who is also her husband. She leaves the office. Going back home she prepares dinner for her husband and later calls her husband telling him that she is anxiously waiting for him to come back and have dinner with her. It shows her waiting for her husband to come back home. This triggers the gender stereotype mentality showing that a women may become the Boss in her office but back at home she is the wife bounded by many household duties. Duties which the society expects her do, duties which a wife have towards her husband.

Similarly, advertisement of any detergent or cooking utensils always present a woman in the ad so that the society can relate with it. In advertisement like 'Vim' concentrated gel challenge, its shows a woman in her kitchen is given challenge by man who is the host. The man challenges the women on washing all her kitchen utensils with one spoon of vim liquid. Finally concluding the women with a grin on her face as if it's every woman's ultimate achievement in her life to find a product for cleaning utensils.

Advertisement of all kind of cosmetics for women ensures that women should always look fair with glowing skin. Women should always do makeup to look pretty. Women should always dye their hair to look younger. Aged women should use products like Olay and Lakmi to stay wrinkle free. All such ideas are infused in minds of women that to get socially accepted because being natural is not enough. Society teaches her that she needs make-up, she needs to glow and stay young for time immortal. On other hand, 'Wild Stone' talcum advertisement distinguishes men and women by showing that a man uses a ladies talcum powder and by doing so he is warned that now he might look like women, behave like women and act like women where the actor is shown weeping. And finally, it says "If you smell like women, you will become women" so in the interest of mankind, men should use 'Wild Stone' products. Here being women is portrayed inferior than men.

Interestingly enough even the food industry is taking advantage of the situation by selling products like 'Oats and Kellogg's K' for women to stay slim. Does looks really matters so much? Noami Wolf (1990) explains, "A culture fixated on female thinness is not an obsession about female beauty, but an obsession about female obedience. Dieting is the most potent political sedative in women's history; a quietly mad population is a tractable one." Why is that in a developing country were people are educated enough to understand that looks should not judge people still believes in such stereotypical images?

Mostly men are featured in all kind of banking, savings and investment plans or in sports brands like 'Nike' and 'Adidas'. Women are equally active in sports but the viewers hardly get to see them in any advertisements. The above examples are emblematic of the glaring gender biases which are being propagated by the media deepens gender inequality and further shrinks the image of women.

The relevance of such mentality can be seen in 'Kinder Joy' advertisement where the product has been wrapped in pink and blue to make it distinct for the consumer based on colours. Pink containers are for girls carrying Barbie dolls in it whereas the blue containers are for boys carrying rockets and superheroes. Discrimination emerges with birth of a new born and video games are another medium which advertises boys playing games like Ninja and FIFA, going for adventure and conquering the world! And the world of a girl starts and ends with pink pony.

While we engage ourselves in expressing our displeasure over gender biases enunciated by the media, we tend to lose sight of the positive roles played by the media through the prism of advertisements. The recent media campaigns encouraged by the government against abusive practices like female infanticide, genital mutilation and promotion of girl child education and proper healthcare facilities for girls shows the constructive role played the media to obliterate the gender equalities which plague the lives of womenfolk in the developing world. Moreover, various advertisements express in subtle manner the urgency to recognize the inherent right of women to lead a free, independent and carefree life regardless of social obligations and regressive traditions. Media also reinforces the need to eradicate poverty which engulfs the lives of women in developing countries like India, Bangladesh and many others. Thus, media helps in establishing the importance of social, cultural, political and most importantly economic independence of women through various innovative advertisements.

Serials

Television dramas which are also known as 'daily soaps' engrosses the audience, especially women. In developing countries, these dramas are made based on daily lives of people, synthesis of culture and traditions. Portrayal of ideal women maintaining traditional family values. Television being considered as the best leisure is engulfing human mind negatively. It paralyzes the thought process of a society and infuses certain image of women leading to gender bias.

This regressive action in the name of entertainment leads to preservation of culture. Daily soaps portray a woman who is a perfect wife, perfect mother and perfect sister. A educated women is always shown happily getting married in a posh family. She marries with certain expectation and end up suffering in hand of in-laws or her husband. The mother-in-law becomes the 'monster-in-law' and does not leave a single opportunity to humiliate her daughter in law. And interestingly enough each and every serial runs on this same line which bounds the society to believe that 'saas-bahu' relation is bound to be like this and all women should accept the ugly truth without retorting.

Conservatism is given a stronger base by showing the new bride covering her head when she is in front of her in-laws. She is characterized as submissive and one who's priority begins and ends with her family. They r sometimes shown as sacrificing and leaving their job due to household works or family pressure. This effects progressive development of a society negatively. The stereotypical nature to appease audience shows men at the superior position. Men are the fountainhead and majority of the dramas are perfect blend of values and norms emphasizing the patriarchal values in the existing society. A woman, on other hand have the most passive role to play. She will get educated, attain certain degrees and will be daydreaming about her prince charming to come. Her parents will find a man for her. She will marry him, follow him, flatter him, change her judgements for him, sacrifices her job to have babies and if not sacrifice then she has a duel role to play. Duality is not a curse, it's a bliss- Society proclaims! After all, they believe empowering of women lies in illustration of women at the epitome.

The present scenario of the television dramas can be analyzed through the book The Female Man by Joanna Russ (1975) where she said, "Men succeed. Women get married. Men fail. Women get married. Men enter monasteries. Women get married. Men start wars. Women get married. Men stop them.

The Role of Media in Perpetuating or Obstructing Gender Equality

Women get married." When the whole universe is ratiocinating then why is it limited only to men? The only compulsion of women is to get married.

Television dramas hold the power to propagate gender equality and it is gradually challenging social taboos. Daily soaps like Angoori in Pakistan, Balika Vadhu in India have motivated community and educated people with certain women rights. The taboo of a dark complexion and fat women cannot get married have also been worked upon in this industry. But the biased mentality of developing nation did not free the viewers with doubts in their mind. Serials have a natural predilection to reflect the traditional moorings of the society. The serials telecasted in the developing world reiterates the traditional gender roles of men and women and projects homely women as ideal sources of inspiration. On the other hand, outspoken modern girls who drink and smoke, who have got tattoos and dyed hair are indiscriminately projected as women of bad character and in many superstitious shows goes to the extent to comparing such girls with vamp and witches. Women many a times, are also associated with witchcraft. Such projections are not only regressive but also extremely reprehensible.

However, there are certain television shows which entails the progressive, talented and brighter projection of women who is not only present in various fields of work but also thrives in which ever work they undertake. Such serials strengthen the image of women in the heart of the viewers and also infuses confidence in the womenfolk.

Cinema

The Oxford Dictionary acknowledges *Cinema* as "Films as an art or an industry." The most fascinating aspect of motion picture is that it is a grand art form which encapsulates all the arts of literature, photography, music. This makes film making a quintessential piece of unique art. But as rightly said by an Indian actress, Vidya Balan in her film Dirty Picture " films do well only because of three reasons... entertainment, entertainment, entertainment...and I am entertainment." Portraying the reality of the universe that cinema as the modern world understands is the most widespread and popular audio-visual means of entertainment and women are the only mode of entertainment.

Casting of women in the film industry is general in nature but with the image she is showcased with in public is what should particularly be delve upon. This industry, for centuries have managed to attract and keep the viewers happy. Sometimes with its pool of talent and sometimes by objectifying women. In a patriarchal society, the film industry shows what a society wants to see. So if one particularly observes that except the women centric films, its mostly the men who are the main speakers. Best dialogue holders are mostly men, and women get dialogues like "one pinch of vermilion is the crown of a married woman one pinch of vermilion is the dream of every women". Developing countries, being very conservatives in nature the film industry makes effort to make family films to sell their tickets in theaters but over years the conception is changing and now most of the films focuses less on story plots and more on the actress and her features. Most of the women actors are seen wearing sexually revealing cloths and getting partially nude as opposed to men. Noami Wolf (1990) says, "To live in a culture in which women are routinely naked where men aren't is to learn inequality in little ways all day long".

Film industry is becoming the industry of image. An industry which exploits women to earn money. Most recently in this industry, item numbers are taking over which specifically is not necessary in films. It shows a woman dancing and wooing other male partners with their seductive moves. Such roles strip away her dignity and subject her to male gaze making her a mere object to promote the film. Women are portrayed in the film in typical stereotypical image as one who is delicate, talkative, emotional, desirous for security, dependent and cries a lot. Whereas men as independent, decisive, tough and security provider to women.

There are handful of actors who have been in film industry for years and are still wearing the crown of best actors. Their age does not stop them from leaving their hallmark in big bannered films. On the other hand, women actors who were equally talented once are now hard to find in lead roles. As their glamour faded away, so did they with time and are mostly seen sitting in the award ceremony, either applauding for her husband or son/daughter or colleagues while they are on stage receiving awards. And it is also sad on the part that they have accepted the present scenario. When a male actor after getting married can manage to balance both work and family then what about the women actors? Most of them ended up marrying business man or their co-actors and sometimes directors of films. Marrying someone of the same profession ensures that their partners would be cooperative with their lifestyle and work routine. Instead we see our Diva staying with her in-laws, taking break from her profession for years and rearing child. When media asks her about her comeback, she takes pride in answering that she is taking time and concentrating on her family and once she gets a suitable role, she will be back on the big screen. Which most of the time remains illusion in nature.

The film industry is a small world in its own. Unfortunately enough, the world consists of more men than women. From Script writers to makeup artists, directors to videographer most of the backstage crew are men. Women in this industry also claim to get less paid than male for the same piece of work. Women are less trusted with production work than men.

Perceptions are changing, and many directors are taking the initiative in making films like Neerja, Akira, Pink, NH10, Kahaani, Queen are now breaking the ice by highlighting the current mindset and gender bias which have continued for generations. These stories of every woman who suffers in rigid patriarchal society and how they finally stand up giving befitting message to all male chauvinists are finally empowering women. These films may not bring a dynamic change in our so called reformed society but it is surely a little step towards the change that every woman craves for.

PRINT AND ELECTRONIC MEDIA'S APPROACH TO GENDERED VIOLENCE

It is appalling is see that how media sensationalizes the heart wrenching incidents of gendered violence. It has been observed that a section of media demeans and humiliates the victims of sexual assault by throwing vituperative pejoratives at the already shattered victims. It has become the modus operandi of the media to embarrass the victims and their family members after the occurrence of some unfortunate tragedy. Such inhumane and insensitive behavior on the part of media exposes the diabolical commercial nature of media which stoops down to any extent in order to further their publicity stunts. Such apathy and indifference towards a rape victim or an acid attack survivor makes media totally antagonistic towards the poor victims. Media also sets distasteful examples by posing uncomfortable and painful questions to the victims without taking into consideration the mental state of the girl or woman in question. This shows how media tries to encash on the misfortune of women by violating the privacy and jeopardizing the reputation of the victims. Nevertheless, there is a section of media which brings to the forefront the female abuses responsibly and acts as a panacea to the wounds of the victims by pressing upon the authorities to take swift action against the culprits by repeated telecasts and by exposing the complacency and reluctance of the system. Media should expand its positive role in order to initiate and expedite the process of gender justice.

AND OTHERS

Assemblage of all the above mentioned factors which contributes to the argument of gender bias by the media gives birth to the factor social media which indirectly affects the society. With the emergence of science and technology, the world sails towards the ocean of network and connectivity. The social media negates the traditional media and have facilitated some of the most well-known online social networking sites like Facebook, Whatsapp, Twitter, Instagram, YouTube, etc.

Social media is the new platform to foster advertisements, films and serials other than communication. Previously, it was only the television which use to affect mindset of the society now it is the social media which have successfully percolated in the mind of youths and have made the new generation especially girls aware of the upcoming trend. The trend of consuming less food to stay slim and be fair. As soon as she posts her picture, she anxiously waits to see how many 'Likes' she gets in Facebook or Instagram. The more the number of 'Likes', the more is she socially accepted which gladden her with inner peace. Surprisingly enough with the arrival of new editing applications in the market, it has become much easier for women to keep intact with their obsession of looking good. Globalization may prioritize quality over quantity but the developing countries still have fasten itself with traditional outlook.

In developing countries, where illiteracy is the cause and abject poverty is the effect often leads to narrowing down the lane for further development of status of both men and women. But taking a ride through this lane from a different angle, a question triggers that what defines a educated man? Does education successfully make a man think beyond patriarchal norms and values set by the society? It remains a delusion.

The author finds rape cases, marital rapes, cyber stalking of women, passing lucid comments are not only done by illiterate men but educated men are equally found guilty. So education or literacy is sometimes not about holding a good job and earning money, it is more about conscience. Another factor which is pornography maybe a mode of entertainment to millions have strengthen the vilification of woman. Problem does not arise with watching of porn, It arises only with few developing nations which have a narrow perception on women and their status. Portrayal of women as the sex object denigrates the very existence of woman and reduces women to mere tools of gratification. The practise of sado-masochism often makes a viewer think of women in a poor light and this sometimes leads to violence and disrespect towards women.

MEDIA'S MULTIFARIOUS APPROACH TOWARDS GENDER AND THE ROAD AHEAD

It would be a lopsided proposition if the author only harps on the cascading effect that media has on the project of gender equality. But it is imperative that the people doesn't lose sight of the other side if the story which exhumes optimism, hope and good will. Reiterating the point that media is the living embodiment of the ongoing trend of the society, it is interesting and also very satisfying to observe that there is a tectonic shift that is taking place in the mindset of the people regarding gender roles. People today are slowly but surely moving out of the shackles of nefarious and obnoxious patriarchal values and gradually embracing a more liberal point of view as far as gender roles are concerned. There is a perceptible transformation in the air today which finds resonance in the propaganda of the media. Media is playing a highly positive role in furthering the cause of gender equality and women empowerment and vociferously condemning every act of violence against women. This is illustrative of the growing realization that women are also integral part of the society and they are at par with men. There is also greater recognition of the fact that women deserve dignity and respect and any act which outrages the modesty of women and denigrates their existence must be vehemently deplored. Media is also attentive to the rights of women and carries out remarkable campaign to protect and preserve the rights of women and such high decibel media campaign helps in a number of ways to mould and refine the outlook of the society. In the light of the growing suzerainty of the media in the heart and mind of the people, it is not a trivial issue. Such positive propaganda campaign has the propensity to usher in transformational change in the perspective of the society. Media's unflinching support for gender equality can be a huge impetus in the process of eradicating the age-old menace of women subjugation.

Media is rapidly changing its demeanor of being biased against women to being the most significant instrument of women emancipation. Media's vigilantism against assault on women has gained considerable momentum over the years. It has become a unanimous objective of the media cutting across all sections that any act of violence against women must be brought to the limelight which had hitherto been ignored by the society as such case were lost in the oblivion. Recently, media's hyperactive stance on any rape cases or regarding any other crimes against women has been one of the most spectacular brouhaha over the electronic and social media. Media's relentless campaign condemning such acts compels the people to extend there empathy for the female victims and propels them to criticize such acts in the strongest possible words. This creates awareness about such heinous crimes among the people and enables the women to get adequate safeguards against such attacks. Such furor that media over these issues creates tremendous pressure on the governmental and judicial authorities to bring the culprits to justice. Media can be credited for making the system more effective and responsive as far as fighting the menace of women exploitation is concerned. But it would be naive for the author to believe that media's activism is uniform and proportionate. An intricate study on media's response to gendered violence reflects glaring discrepancies and inconsistencies. It has been noticed with some clinching evidences that media is more forthcoming in reporting cases on female abuses in the urban centre than in rural areas. Recent past is replete with such incidents which indicates the innate media bias towards urban areas. The sexual abuse of an distinguished educated working woman gets easy attention of the media which in turn induces strong reaction from the urban citizenry. Such high-profile propaganda naturally ensures somewhat speedy justice to the victim. On the contrary, such zealousness is not exhibited by the media when gruesome sexual crimes takes place in some remote Sub-urban rural centre against illiterate, suppressed and subjugated village girl. In the developing world, such glaring disparities wreck the equilibrium of the discourse of gender equality and women empowerment as undertaken by the media. This makes the author wary of the suspicious urban-relativity as furthered by the media in popularizing its propaganda.

There is another aspect which in the author's opinion is an important tenet in studying media's approach to gender in developing countries. It is indeed a matter of pride to observe that the developing countries have witnessed a steady rise of women leaders who have reached the helm of affairs by their undaunting determination and firm resolve. The media portrays the rise of such women leaders with such awe and appreciation. The developing world right from its inception has produced charismatic leaders like Indira Gandhi who rose to become the most pragmatic Prime Minister of independent India and one of the notable personalities of the world. Indira's authoritative, charismatic and decisive leadership which eclipsed the presence of her political opponents who in spite of being "experienced political stalwarts" could not undermine the overwhelming dominance of Mrs. Gandhi. Such insurmountable aura of Indira

The Role of Media in Perpetuating or Obstructing Gender Equality

was appreciated and buttressed by the media. Despite the initial vitriolic campaign against Mrs. Gandhi's "excesses" during the emergency period of 1975-77, media gradually hailed Indira's indispensability in Indian politics. It is particularly very interesting to observe that after Indira's defeat in 1977 elections in the aftermath of the controversial emergency, the media projected her as a victim or a sacrificial lamb in the hands of the" chaotic and vindictive" Janata government. This campaign of media went greatly in India's favour which drew her immense sympathy from all over the world and facilitated her political comeback in 1979. Media has a tendency of creating personality cults out of women leaders. In India, it started with Indira ad "mother godess", then the dalit leader Mayawati has been projected as the "messiah" of the dalits. Jayalalita in Tamil Nadu is venerated as "Amma" who commands habitual obedience from her people. Mamata Banerjee of West Bengal is or projected by the media as the saviour of poor and toiling classes. Such larger than life personality cults are made out of wine women politicians by the media which immediately strikes the cord with the local people which works remarkably well with the people of the developing world where people seeks refuge in their leaders. Despite the high-octane Islamic orthodoxy holding its sway in Pakistan, Benazir Bhutto became the Prime Minister of Pakistan whom the media projected as" apostle of democracy" in the country. Bangladesh similarly exonerates women leaders like Khalida Zia and Sheikh Hasina who are the two towering political personalities of the country. Media's projection of these women as" larger than life" legendary figures helps them to consolidate their image among the masses. Such projections show media's affinity towards powerful women and thus acts as a facilitator to perpetuate the influence of the women leaders and enable them to buttress their status.

Another area which is a matter of grave concern is the pre-emptive bias against the problems faced by men in the society. While media reports are replete with cases of mental and physical harassment of women, the plight of the male counterparts are widely underreported in the developing countries. This is also due to the well-entrenched traditional views which considers men to be powerful, self-sufficient and invincible as well as strong. Such self-evident conceptions make the weaknesses of men a social taboo. Men apprehending the fear of social stigma and humiliation never report incidents of abuse and torture in the public. This renders the male victims in terrible pain and depression. Media's insensitivity towards male predicaments can be reflected how the problem of sexual impotency in men and homosexuality are issues of mockery and ridicule in the media. Moreover, in the light of rape cases, media pre-emptively gives verdict against the male accused in the case and subjects him to unimaginable humiliation without confirming the veracity of such allegations. This also reflects the other side of the story which exposes media's periodic insensitivity towards men.

All said and done, it is an absolute no-brainer to understand that media plays a pivotal role in determining the trajectory of gender equality in the developing countries. Media which undoubtedly plays a preponderant role in influencing the common sense of the public has an innate responsibility of reporting news in such a manner that gender biases are not further percolated in the society which is already fraught with innumerable fissiparous and invidious elements. Media though has gradually emerged as a guarantor of women's rights must do more to remove inherent prejudices against women and make more assertive campaign to safeguard the rights of women. On the other hand, media must also exhibit more compassion todays men and establish gender equality in true sense.

REFERENCES

Cinema. (n.d.). In *Oxford English dictionary.* Retrieved from https://www.oxforddictionaries.com/

Menon, N. (1999). *Gender and politics in India.* Oxford, UK: Oxford University Press.

Russ, J. (1975). *The female man.* New York: Bantam Books.

Wolf, N. (1990). *The beauty myth.* New York: Chatto & Windus.

Section 6
Emerging Challenges and Inclusion of Men on Women's Issues

Chapter 21
Migration, Muslim Women, and Social Reproduction of Gender Inequality:
International Migration and Social Remittances in Gender Relations in Bangladesh

Ishret Binte Wahid
London School of Economics and Political Science, UK

Mohammed Kamaruzzaman
BRAC, Bangladesh

ABSTRACT

Does international migration have a role to reproduce unequal gender relation in a patriarchal society? How does it make such role? How does it further implicate people's religious as well as cultural practices? These are the questions have been addressed in this paper. It takes the case of Bangladesh, a South Asian Muslim-majority country with millions of international labour migrants to different Middle East and Gulf countries including Saudi Arabia, United Arab Emirates, and Bahrain. This international migration makes very positive financial contributions to the migrants and their families at origins, mostly in rural villages. The paper makes it focus on social outcomes, especially on household level gender relations with such migration. Taking up the idea of 'social remittances', it argues that these migrants, mostly men, experience with a range of 'Islamic' norms and practices in destinations, and send back those to origins for religious obligations. These norms and practices largely include discouraging female household members, especially wives, to earn or go outside without purdah in line with the perceived 'Islam'. The paper explains that such 'social remittances' encourage the female household members to be 'good' Muslim women along with the reproduction of gender inequality between women and men.

DOI: 10.4018/978-1-5225-3018-3.ch021

INTRODUCTION

In the era of globalization, people have gained greater access to mobility than ever, often leading to the expansion of transnational communities. The term 'transnational communities' comprises of migrants and their friends and families maintaining a strong chain of socio-cultural connection (Fries, 2012). The contemporary trend in the globalized world gives a sense of this expansion. According to latest data, the total number of migrants is about 247 million (KNOMAD, 2016, p.6) of which 48 percent is women (Ratha, Plaza, & Ozden, 2016, p.3). Their contributions to the global economy are noteworthy, as the amount of remittances in the current year is roughly $601 million in which developing countries take the share of $441 million (Ratha, Plaza, & Ozden, 2016, p.6). The amount of remittance compared to debt of these developing countries is three times higher than their total debt (Ratha, Plaza, & Ozden, 2016, p.6). The United States, followed by Saudi Arabia, Germany, the Russian Federation, the United Arab Emirates, the United Kingdom, France, Canada, Spain, and Australia remain the top migrant receiving countries (Ratha, Plaza, & Ozden, 2016, p.6). Despite the growing number of migrants in the global North, the South-South migration trend is on the upsurge. It stands for 38 percent of the aggregated migration and is larger in number than South-North migration which stands for 34 percent (Ratha, Plaza, & Ozden, 2016, p.6). The paper makes it focus on social outcomes, especially on household level gender relations with such migration. Taking up the idea of "social remittances", it argues that these migrants, mostly men, experience with a range of "Islamic" norms and practices in destinations, and send back those to origins for religious obligations. These norms and practices largely include discouraging female household members, especially wives, to earn or go outside without purdah in line with the perceived "Islam". The paper explains that such "social remittances" encourage the female household members to be "good" Muslim women along with the reproduction of gender inequality between women and men.

BACKGROUND

Bangladesh, one of the top five of migrants sending countries (United Nations, Department of Economic and Social Affairs, Population Division, 2016, p.16) and ranks tenth as recipients of remittance in this year (KNOMAD, 2016, p.29). It has shown remarkable growth as its current GDP growth rate is 7.11 percent ("GDP - Bangladesh Bureau of Statistics-Government of the People's Republic of Bangladesh", 2016) which is twice than the global GDP growth rate of 3.1 percent (International Monetary Fund, 2016, p.6). Such migration from Bangladesh constitutes the labour force in the destination countries, the very reason they are called "labour migrant" (Siddiqui, 2003). There are seven million Bangladeshi labour migrants working in more than twenty countries of which Oman is the highest recipient in the year of 2016 ("Overseas Employment in 2016", 2016). As mentioned earlier, women accounts for 48 percent of the global migrants (Ratha, Plaza, & Ozden, 2016, p.3) whereas in Bangladesh their share in the migrant population is about 13 percent (United Nations, Department of Economic and Social Affairs, Population Division, 2016, p.29). In the current year, the amount of remittance has been about 11million USD ("Overseas Employment & Remittance from 1976 - 2016", 2016). Remittance consists more than 7 percent of the country's GDP ("Personal remittances, received (% of GDP) | Data", 2016) and stands higher compared to the aggregate contribution of agricultural, industrial and service sector which is about 6.5 percent (Bangladesh Bank, p.4). Remittance has a significant role in country's poverty reduction and building human capital (Hatemi-J & Uddin, 2013). A recent study by Bureau of

Manpower Employment and Training (BMET) suggests that remittance has significantly contributed poverty reduction in Bangladesh and poverty ratio fell to 50 percent in 2000 from 70 percent in 1970 (Bureau of Manpower Employment and Training, 2016). The recent transition of Bangladesh in the list of middle-income countries ("World Bank Country and Lending Groups – World Bank Data Help Desk", 2016) clearly directs us towards the fact that the country's economy is on the upward move.

FOCUS AND METHODOLOGY

Applying the Levitt's notion of "social remittances" (Levitt 2005), the paper explores the relationship between international migration and gender equality in the contexts of Bangladesh. It focuses on both female and male migrants to various Middle East and the Gulf Countries, the "social remittance" they 'earn'(define) and send back to origins, and the consequences of such remittance in gender relations. It takes two different districts in the country—one is Dhaka, the capital city of Bangladesh with developed communication and along with various state and non-state support services while the other one is Noakhali, far from the capital with less developed communication and infrastructure with, fewer support services but significant for huge number of international migrants compared to that of other districts. Noakhali has also a contrast to Dhaka considering people's attitude—it is considered as one of "conservative" (Faisal, 2005) areas while Dhaka as the capital city is much more open in terms of women's mobility (Kabeer, 2000) in public place for example. As part of the qualitative methodology, a total of 15 case stories including 11 women and four men and two FGDs, one with male migrants and the other with female migrants were conducted as sources of primary data analysis. The respondents were selected purposively based on the criteria, like - minimum two years of stay in Gulf countries, returnee migrants (during the time of interview) and age ranging from 25 to 40. The primary data was collected during the period of January to April in 2015. A range of literature including government's statistical documents was reviewed as secondary data.

Gender, Migration, and Social Remittance: The Conceptual Linkage

The term "social remittance" was first introduced by Levitt in 1998 (Levitt, 1998). She identified three major types of social remittances – (i) normative structure (ii) systems of practice and (iii) social capital into the discussion of social remittances (Levitt, 2005). 'Normative structure' refers to social values, beliefs, ideologies, attitudes; it influences people's practices and is well reflected in their actions. 'Social capital' is also based on the normative structure and is a kind social remittance itself; it may include respect, honour from society (Ibid). Markley revisited and reinforced Levitt's concept of 'social remittance' and defined her concept of remittance from two dimensions – "economic" and "beyond economic remittances" (Markley, n.d.). The later one has an exclusive connection to Levitt's "social remittance". This kind of remittance focuses on the socio-economic status of migrants. Their "economic remittance" is often considered to determine such status without considering their differential gender, racial and class positions within a society. The differences might be significant in society and the construction of these differences can strongly be rooted in a traditional cultural system and reinforced by similar kind of social remittances. Levitt and Schiller pointed out the significance of considering the cases where migrants reinvent and re-enforce gender divisions and hierarchies which are stiffer in the country of destination rather than their country of origin (Levitt and Schiller, 2006).

Levitt focused also on the 'transnational perspective of migration' where she asserted transnational migrants have a strong influence on their non-migrant family members. She shed light on how the impact of social remittance varies based on gender, class or the life-cycle of the recipient (Levitt, 2005). Her arguments, in the context of Guzrat, also reveal that the non-migrants' power and resources determine to what extent such remittance will be accepted or rejected (Levitt, 2005). Social remittance has a strong connection with gender which constructs or reconstructs the perception about women and men and gender roles in society. Thus migration led social remittances may have both positive and negative associated impact dynamics (Levitt, 1998). A more contemporary thought of Dannecker and Sieveking focused on remittance and female migrants arguing that it often victimizes them due to the working conditions of comparatively 'new sector' (Dannecker & Sieveking, 2009). Their arguments are important where increasing female migration has been conceived as the pathways of their empowerment.

The Trade-Off Between the Material Significance and Social Cost

There are micro and macro-level studies which looked into the causal effect of remittance and development (Ratha, Plaza, and Ozden, 2016; Hugo, 2011). There is a tendency of countering the economic impact of migration which is reflected in most of the studies (Ratha, Plaza, and Ozden, 2016; United Nations, Department of Economic and Social Affairs, Population Division, 2016; Nath and Mamun, n.d.). In order to understand the complex nexus of migration and development in North and the South, one needs to go beyond the simplistic scenario and explore the social, political and distributional impact of it (Piper, 2009). An important aspect of this nexus is that the debt-led pressure hanging on the shoulder of the developing countries pushes them to promote international migration which appears as an easy mean to reduce the debt amount without considering the socio-cultural impact of such rapid migration (Sassen, 2010). The economy of developed countries is moving upward on the back of these migrant workers, often low-paid and deprived of their rights. A case study of the Latin American female domestic workers in Spain presents strong evidence of this fact (Gil Araujo and González-Fernández, 2014). Some mentioned rapid economic growth in the cost of 'brain-drain' from the countries of origin (Ratha, Plaza and Ozden, 2016) whereas other studies brought up the issues associated with immigration of low skilled labour paired with the outflow of higher-skilled labour ('brain drain'), greater mobility for migrant workers (Hugo, 2011), funding for public projects in home country from migrants (Aparicio and Meseguer, 2012). A study conducted Bangladesh perspective suggests that there are macro and micro-level impacts of remittance for instance – increased savings and investment, increased foreign exchange, better living conditions, infrastructural development, income opportunities (Ahmed, 2014; Arifeen, 2013). On the other hand, improved food intake and health conditions, increased education level, enhanced socio-economic status of the family, greater involvement in the political organization and at times reducing family structures are the impacts of remittance in the household (micro) level, which have greater social implications (Ibid). Several studies identified the impact of migration and remittance on women, and suggested that women gain less control on remittance, their bargaining power declines, their role stays limited within the household, they do not take important decision-related asset management (de Haas and van Rooij, 2010; Agarwal, 1994; Francis, 2002). Similar kind of gender perspective applies while the gender equality implications of international migration are largely ignored in Bangladesh. Dannecker emphasized that migration and remittance, to some extent, have reproduced unequal gender relations between men and women in Bangladesh though her exploration of such inequality confined to power relation associated with utilization of economic remittance mainly (Dannecker, 2005; Dannecker and

Sieveking 2009). A study conducted on the Bangladeshi migrant workers reveals that male migrants returning from Malaysia perceived female migrant workers negatively (Dannecker, 2005). They would to avoid any contact with the female migrants due to the reason that they were violating 'purdah' and thus create the construction of 'otherness' (Ibid). Acknowledging the very positive roles of female migrants both in the household and the state economies; this paper questions these roles from gender equality perspective. These questions have recently been significant in line with the idea of 'inclusive growth' which puts emphasis on gender perspective of economic growth (Kabeer, 2012).

Although Bangladesh has made significant achievements in many areas of development goals, for example, achieving gender parity into school enrolment as targeted in the UN-led MDGs, the country's poverty situation is still complex with increasing income inequality and multifaceted vulnerabilities of various sections of people including women (Ferdousi and Dehai, 2014). According to BBS Household Income and Expenditure Survey the percentage of men and women in lower poverty line in rural areas is respectively 29 percent and 23.6 percent (BBS, 2011). Unemployment and underemployment have been identified as the critical areas that forced many, especially youth to be the overseas migrants. The problem is critical in rural parts due to declining role of agriculture in employments, lack of industrialization as well as a stuck in business and growth. In this context, the international migration plays a very significant role in providing employments to rural youth as well as earning incomes. It also contributes to the national economy as a form of the reserve with the Central Bank. The Bank's latest figures in March 2015 reveal the reserve of 1338.31 USD comes from remittances. Thus this international migration has become an important part of the country's poverty reduction efforts. Due to its significance, the government set a separate ministry named Ministry of Expatriates' Welfare and Overseas Employment supported by some other state-run agencies like Bureau of Manpower, Employment and Training (BMET), Bangladesh Overseas Employment & Services Ltd. (BOESL), Wage Earners' Welfare Board (WEWB) etc. Not the state only, many private agencies also, for example, Bangladesh Association of International Recruiting Agencies (BAIRA), have come forward to support various services on international labour migration. Even many non-government organizations like BRAC, the country's largest NGO have started work to secure migrants' rights, especially with the females. Both the government and non-government sectors identify international migration as opportunity—for poorer people who face unemployment in the country but potential to enhance its economic growth.

Bangladesh: Society, Culture, and Making a Choice for Migration

The Bangladeshi society is identified 'patriarchal' in nature which defines a set of rules for women and men in line with gendered norms and values. This local context of patriarchy has explored in many studies, and introduced it as 'corporate patriarchy' (Kabeer, Mahmud & Tasneem 2011). Traditionally men become the household head and take major decisions on family matters, incomes and expenditures in particular (Rouf, 2013). In this context, women are confined to carry out household chores only including rearing children. Not the division of work only, it also limits women's access to material resources and incomes and puts a barrier into mobility to the public place of their own choice (Kabeer, Mahmud & Tasneem 2011; Parvin, A. G. et al. 1998). Gardner and Kotalova identify this mobility as 'institutionalized restraint' (Gardner & Kotalova, 1995). Women are absorbed into their husbands' patrilineage through a marriage system that not only cuts their original kin identity but also makes them dependent on husbands or male family members (Kabeer, Mahmud, & Tasneem, 2011). They also have restrictions on equal access to inheritances. This kind of patriarchy strongly motivates people for son preference for economic reasons (Kabeer, Mahmud, & Tasneem, 2011). Although there is a change with women's lives taking place in recent times (World Bank, 2008), e.g. women's increasing access to paid work, the situations are still complex for multifaceted vulnerabilities including violence in different aspects of their lives (Solotaro & Pande, 2014). For example, women's employment rates are still very low, even by South Asian standards; despite growth in employment, the labor market is highly segmented along lines of gender; women are still concentrated in domestic services and home-based work, for which many do not report (World Bank, 2008). This patriarchy affects not women's economic participation only, but also their other non-economic aspects of lives. For example, violence against women is extreme and a national survey report in 2013 reveals intimate partner violence as 87% while 65% married women have experienced physical violence by current husbands in their life time (BBS, 2013, p. xvi). Child marriage in Bangladesh is higher, ranks 8th in the world and according to latest data, it is 52% under age 18 (UNICEF, 2016, p. 150). In the case of education, high drop-out of girls is still a concern. It gets higher in upper levels, for example, 23.37% at grade XI-XII, known as college education ("BANBEIS-Educational Database", 2016). Therefore, the patriarchal norms in Bangladesh also affect younger girls, the new generation, in spite of lots of progress over years.

This local form of patriarchy is mixed up with as well as reinforced by the norms and values which produced and delivered by Islam as religion and has been historical as well as political. History shows that Islam was invented to this region in the 7th century by the Arabian traders who also converted lots of local people into Islam (Abecassis, 1990). The process not only gave a new religious identity to the locals but also a spiritual attachment with Mecca, the origin of Islam. This spiritual attachment gradually developed a sense of ummah led global citizenship among the locals and built a social psychology of people (Kamruzzaman, 2009). This sense of ummah refers to Muslim-hood, connected them with the Middle East, particularly Saudi Arabia and that is emotional too embedded in cultural cum religious practices in local contexts. Looking at the political perspective of Islam in contemporary Bangladesh, Hashmi argues that women's status, rights, and opportunities are strongly connected to this religion; it (Islam) plays an important role in politics, socio-cultural norms and political culture of the people in the country (Hashmi, 2000).

Within the circumstances, the Bangladeshi people's international migration, to the Middle East in particular, can't be explained merely from the economic perspective. They migrate for economic reasons but in many cases, their choices are cultural where a religion led dichotomy of 'good' and 'bad' works when they chose destinations. Kamruzzaman explores that the rural Muslims tend to imagine the Middle East and the Gulf countries as 'Islamic', more specifically Saudi Arabia which is perceived as a sacred place because of having Kaba house there and provides an opportunity not to earn only but also achieving spiritual gains through performing hajj there (ibid). This is the non-economic context that motivates many rural Muslims to choose the Middle East countries, particularly Saudi Arabia for migration. Until March 2015, around 2,646,110 migrants from Bangladesh went to Saudi Arabia which is the highest in choosing the destination by country.

Economic Remittances and the Gender Equality Implications

As indicated before, material significance, the economic remittances, matters both for the country and the person in Bangladesh. But there have also been focused that such migration, as well as the flow of economic remittances, makes a significant sense for non-economic aspects of lives. Many of contemporary literature argue a change in social dynamics, women's empowerment, in particular, connecting it to the idea of 'feminization of migration' (Dannecker & Sieveking, 2009) although many focuses on female migrants' empowerment have been derived from "economic remittances" as well as market-led growth. The gendered pattern of females' migration does reveal certain things. Dannecker argues that the rapid increase in the number of female migration represents their global mobility (Dannecker, 2005). This is very significant in the context of Bangladesh that rarely allowed women to engage in paid work outside the home (Kabeer, Mahmud & Tasneem, 2011). Looking at gender dimension, a recent study by International Organization for Migration (IOM) explores several challenges the women face during the migration period (Bruyn, 2006). In spite of the challenges, studies found that female migrants regularly send higher remittances in comparison to men (Global Commission on International Migration, 2005). This is important for the poorer households in rural Bangladesh as poverty often pushes them to migrate out (Siddique 2003). Apart from the migrant identities on their own, the women can also be seen as non-migrant receiver of both 'economic' and 'beyond economic remittances' (Markley, n.d.). The IOM study also reveals the socio-economic impact of migration on non-migrant wives of migrant husbands. It found that there is a notion of protection of the women imposed by their overseas migrant husbands. It was evident that migration revises the structured gender roles compared to that of the pre-migration stage. Sometimes, it led to female managed households in absence of their husbands who often experience an increase in their decision-making power. While 'voice' has been an important area for women's empowerment (Malhotra, Schuler, & Boender, 2002), such decision-making power is critically important from a gender perspective. It includes gaining control over the remittances sent by their husbands though it is mostly temporary in nature; in many cases, their education level increased. The economic remittances changed the standard of their living often ending to increase in resources and assets. Several studies reveal negative consequences—the women had to suffer from socio-economic vulnerabilities like insecurity, losing honour, restricted mobility etc. along with the obligation to wear burkha in many cases. There are experiences of heavy workload too for women due to the absence of their husbands. The finding was quite contradictory in the sense that along with their improving living standard, their health condition was detrimental (de Haas & van Rooij, 2010; Silliman & Agarwal, 1996; Francis, 2002; Bruyn, 2006). But in most cases, the arguments put economic remittances or resources as central into the exploration while a perspective of social remittances largely undermined.

Gender and Transmission of Social Remittances: Evidences From the Ground

The empirical data reveals a range of social remittances those are transmitted to the origins in line with the international migration. Most of them are attached to people's perceived religious values; however, there are some non-religious elements too which have connections to gender relations. The types of remittances also vary from destination to destination –how they are experienced there. The paper here considers three key areas—(i) sense of identity (Muslim-hood) (ii) cultural constructions and reconstructions of gender (and women's purity) and (iii) decision making with own incomes—to describe the transmission of social remittances.

Desire to be a 'Good Muslim'

Transmission of social remittances into constructing people's sense, as the paper argues, is strongly connected to perceived religion, here Islam, therefore, desires to be a 'good' Muslim has been a significant area of such transmission. The migrants perceive the destination as 'Islamic country', experience

Migration, Muslim Women, and Social Reproduction of Gender Inequality

a range of perceived Islamic norms and values, and that influence their sense of duty or responsibility to be a 'good' Muslim.

The following case of Alimuzzaman, who is 40 years old, illustrates his own experiences in Saudi Arabia and its implications for the origin:

The people of that country are really good and honest. It's very difficult to live in Bangladesh. I spent 10 years in Saudi Arabia of my 43 years life. I feel those 10 years was the best time of my life. They have a rule that every shop has to be shut instantly when it's time of prayer otherwise police will arrest them and beat. Nowadays, in Bangladesh in prayer time I think I should shut my shop and I do it. I still have that habit. On Friday after 10.30am every shop except hospital and pharmacy is closed. I try to follow that lifestyle here. Nowadays people respect me more; they also invite me in different social meetings. I learned more about our religion there. I have read about Quran and Hadith. I paid for my father's hajj too (interview, Dhaka, Bangladesh, 21 January 2015).

The meaning of 'good' Muslim as the case illustrates is associated with performing religious activities, the everyday prayer in particular. It further produces a value of the person in that socio-cultural context because of its historical formation. Such value does not limit to one-to-one respect only, it implicates creating a symbolic as well as social capital as becomes true for Alimuzzaman. The transition of social remittances helps him to be a socially significant person dealing with community events which may not have any connection to religion. Not males only like Alimuzzaman, but the females interviewed in this research also have same experiences in Saudi Arabia. The following statements come from Tanu Begum to whom the local Arabian people are good in practicing Islam and she likes it:

I hadn't faced any kind of problem there by the grace of Allah. Arabian people are good at all. Their wage scale is good, behavior is also good. I went there with a visa valid for 2 years. In Bangladesh, some people know them as good people some as bad. I went there and saw everyone is good people. They follow the Holy Quran, the message from Allah and the Prophet Muhammad. To see the hands or legs of a woman by an unknown man was illegal to them (interview, Dhaka, Bangladesh, 21 January 2015).

The idea of 'goodness' here is necessarily mixed up with performing religion. The issues of wage at work, human behavior etc. may not necessary to have a connection with one's religion. But the migrants interviewed, tended to connect the sense of goodness with religion. 'Goodness' as part of the universal value is desired for them and they then tend to be a 'good' Muslim because of the experiences. Such experiences implicate or influence both the perceptions and practices of not the individual migrants only, but also their family members because of the cultural context in origin where family membership produces some set of obligations including obeying to the directions to the head of a family.

This reflects into the daughters of Alimuzzaman as he narrates:

My daughters weren't used to wear burkha but they do now. They also perform their prayers regularly (interview, Dhaka, Bangladesh, 21 January 2015).

Burkha for Muslim women and girls has been a symbol in terms of 'protecting' their prestige and honour at the community level. Burkha is nothing but a full covered dress for women but from cultural perspectives it is significant to a family, men, in particular, to 'save' a family woman from social critique.

There are so many critiques with burkha from development as well as feminist perspective (Rozario, 2006). In the case of Bangladesh's political and development contexts the issue of burkha has been much debatable (Ibid). The practices of wearing burkha in recent Bangladesh are still popular. Even in urban areas, girls attending schools, colleges or universities are found wearing burkha. Many popular write-ups argue that the urban girls and women wear burkha not for religious obligations but as part of securing their bodies amid increasing insecurity in recent Bangladesh. However, among the migrants in this research burkha is a cultural element and it is reinforced by the experiences gained in the destination, the perceived 'Islamic countries' like Saudi Arabia.

The idea of 'good Muslim' also implicates interactions between women and men those don't belong to the same family. The migrants experienced that there have restrictions in the destinations between a non-kin woman and man to interact, even talk to them. These experiences are almost similar to the traditional village cultures in origin where women and girls have some sort of taboo to interact with men and boys those are unknown and don't belong to same family or lineage.

The following narratives come from Kona, aged 40, a woman who was in Saudi Arabia and became familiar with the women-men interaction there:

When women try to talk to men they beat them up. Sometimes Bangladeshi women come out of the house to dry the clothes in sunshine and meet with the Bangladeshi men. If they talk to a man, he gets fired or even imprisoned. Even if anyone has close relatives there, they can't help them in fear of losing their own job (interview, Noakhali, Bangladesh, 14 March 2015).

The village cultures in the past had extreme restrictions for non-kin women and men to talk or gossip. That was perceived as part of 'Islamic values' although it was equally practiced among Hindus (Frederick Littrell & Bertsch, 2013). According to the social practices, a woman, especially the never married younger girl, was not allowed to interact with other non-kin boys or men with the fear that it might create a love as well as a sexual relationship between them. The village cultures in Bangladesh over the years have changed a lot and nowadays many girls and women do not face many restrictions like before (Mahmud, Shah, & Becker, 2012). The interaction, however, is conditional and in many cases follow patriarchy led Islamic norms and values. Parents or guardians, especially for girls, often become attentive to the interaction to avoid further complexities. The sense of 'purity' strongly works for girls and women that in turns produce social rules—what they can (should) do and what not—in terms of interactions and behavior with men and boys. It becomes much true when they are in public place. The migrants have been used to such norms and replicates in their personal lives too in origins. As Kona states:

Women of that country {Saudi Arabia} don't talk to men and they maintain burkha. I also wish to wear burkha. Still, do it when getting out of the house, I wear a long scarf. I haven't changed almost anything since came back ... (interview, Noakhali, Bangladesh, 14 March 2015).

Practicing of these social norms may have a connection to the 'safety' issue for girls in recent Bangladesh. Insecurity, as well as physical assaults including rape, has been a serious concern in recent time (Barkat et. al. 2012) and many tend to connect these situations with increasing mobility of girls to the public place. It's a popular notion that veil can be a safeguard for girls when they are in public places. This popular notion, in many cases, is based on the arguments that women in Saudi Arabia don't face such problems as they wear the veil and don't talk to men while in public places. This reflects in the perceptions of Alimuzzaman:

The people of that country are really good and honest. There's no crime in our country. It's very difficult to live in Bangladesh (interview, Dhaka, Bangladesh, 21 January 2015).

Women and girls' safety issue in recent Bangladesh may be associated with increasing mobility to the public place and attending schools. There has been a remarkable progress over years in girls' enrolment and education. The situation is gradually changing and now more girls are intending to complete education to enter into job markets instead getting married early. According to the latest data, net attendance in secondary school for girls in rural areas is 50.8% in rural areas (BBS, 2015, p. 123). While lots of girls have been in public place competing men, it may not be unusual to feel concern about their safety as the society is still patriarchal and men tend to have arrogant attitudes in many incidents. So, when the migrants compare Bangladesh with Saudi Arabia, then they find a better situation about women's safety in public place and they prefer that situation. This preference for the cultural ground is embedded into the perception of religion. They wish to replicate that form of safety in origins, and because of cultural connections, by applying Islamic norms and values.

Kohinoor, aged of 37, was a female migrant to Saudi Arabia and closely observed system of women's safety there:

We were used to meeting other Bangladeshi women in marketplaces. We never went there alone ... women can go there ... social safety there is good enough. The house was by the side of the factory. We got time for prayers (interview, Dhaka, Bangladesh, 26 April 2015).

While Saudi Arabia has been a 'very good Islamic country' to the migrants, some other countries in the Middle East, like United Arab Emirates (UEA) is ranked 'less good' to them because of 'flexible Islamic' rules and practices there. It produces a sense of dissatisfaction to the migrants. Boktiar, aged of 34 from Dhaka has experienced in both countries but likes Saudi Arabia most because of its 'more Islamic' images. He states:

In Saudi Arab women don't come out of the house but in Dubai it's common. I was in Saudi Arab and in Dubai ... I liked Saudi Arabia most ... in Saudi Arabia you can't do anything you wish but in Dubai, it's very easy. In Saudi Arabia, there is huge restriction ... foods, people's behavior... everything I liked most (interview, Dhaka, Bangladesh, 22 March 2015).

He also states:

I didn't like the behavior of people in Dubai but saw something different when I was in Saudi Arabia; Women of all ages wear burkha. It was not seen frequently in Dubai. Drugs were available in Dubai. For this, I like Saudi Arabia most (interview, Dhaka, Bangladesh, 22 March 2015).

Migrants' sense of 'good' Muslim, therefore, also connects the notion and process of Westernization. Generally, the rural people have an anti-Western sentiment as the 'West' is often interpreted as part of Christianity and that contrasts to Islam. The migrants experience a reflection of the flexible Western culture in Dubai which allows women and men to interact or wish and according to them this is not Islamic; therefore, don't like.

Not that all the elements they experienced are religious or come from the spiritual ground. To be a 'good' Muslim they tend to include many things –both religious and non-religious although frame into religion from a moral or cultural perspective.

To Alimuzzaman 'honesty' is the desired thing that he saw among people in Saudi Arabia. The meaning of 'honesty' is necessarily connected to women's behavior there. He narrates:

Women always wear burkha in Saudi Arabia; they seldom work outside of home ...they are conservative and honest (interview, Dhaka, Bangladesh, 21 January 2015).

Kamruzzaman (2005) explores people's perceptions towards the association of purdah and Islam in the case of rural Bangladesh is higher among international migrants those migrant to the Middle East and the Gulf States. He argues that rural people have different kinds of identity—from lineage to spiritual—and all make sense to their everyday life. Connecting this everyday form of life with international migration, he explores that local socio-cultural practices are reinforced by migrants' experiences in overseas, especially in Saudi Arabia. Thus a sense of spiritual community-hood, Muslim-hood in this paper, develops with the migration.

Cultural Reconstruction of Gender in Origin

Lots of studies on females' migration identified a range of opportunities for women. Momsen explores that migration offers education and career opportunities for women; it includes the opportunities for getting domestic work in other households for an income rather than to be an unpaid domestic in their own household (Momsen, 1999). Carling makes focus on remittances saying that migration as a transforming experience, can improve or worsen the position of women in families and society (Carling, 2005). As indicated before, husband's migration offers wife to manage household matters in absence of the husband further to an increase in her decision-making power. This paper explores that the international migration to the Middle East countries, especially Saudi Arabia reinforces the existing gender norms in origin. Income poverty in households is the key reason that makes them migrants. The females migrate because of poverty that exists in their households. But they usually do the same household chores that they did in origins. In addition, they experience more patriarchal forms of gender relations in destinations where one husband has more wives, women always wear burkha, some forms of restrictions work for the women etc. These experiences are historically located in the traditional society too in the origin. This traditional society practices a culture which reconstructs identical gender relations. Therefore, the women find a cultural attachment with the gender relations in the destinations. These altogether reinforce to reproduce cultural constructions of gender in the origin.

Reconstruction of Women's 'Purity'

The idea of 'family' in the Bangladesh's patriarchal society, especially in rural parts, not only defines women's roles and responsibilities within a family, but also frames their relationship through a marriage system (Gardener & Kotalova, 1995). This relationship goes even beyond personal defines—what a woman should do (and should not do) and with whom—at the community level. This framing very critically questions migrant women's sexual purity when they come back from the destination. Rozario explores women's purity issue in the context of rural Bangladesh and argues how this reinforces gender inequality (Rozario, 2001). The issue of "women's purity" becomes critical and in many cases produces a high level of discomfort for individual migrant women along with their husbands and/or male partners; also creates conflict into the family relationship.

Anwara, aged of 38 from Noakhali went to Dubai but had to come back as she was not paid her salary for most of the time in her two and half year's life there. The local employer did not allow her to communicate to family in the origin. When she came back, the villagers started to make gossip with her—what she did actually in Dubai and why she had to come back. As she stated:

The people surrounding me asked questions. They wanted to know, why I was sent back to home or did the owner harass me sexually or not etc. People here say that women go abroad to be used sexually by men employers. After I came back my husband was not happy. He used to beaten me up because I was unable to send any money to him. He said I am a bad woman and he does not want to live with me. After that, I am staying at my father's house (interview, Noakhali, Bangladesh, 17 January 2015).

Like Anwara, many men went to overseas for work, often reported they did not receive salary or/and face different kinds of problems including torture. But for men, society does not ask any question about their sexual 'purity' in line with the patriarchal rules. For Anwara the situations were extreme but not that the all migrant women faced such degree of crisis in their personal lives. Mayesha, another migrant woman went to Abu Dhabi of UAE and experienced very positive behavior with the employer. She lived there for three years and faced the problem with foods only. She used to receive her salary regularly and that was sent to her family by the employer himself. In spite of that, she faced questions about her sexual purity and needed to explain it to her husband. The following statements come from Mayesha, the woman aged 36 years:

After coming back home, some foul-mouthed people of my surroundings talked badly about me. They said, I'm a bad woman and I did many bad works back there. But I didn't bother. Some people still comment badly about me. Once I went to the hospital to adopt birth control system. People talked worst about me then. They said, "Oh! This woman went abroad and did wrongdoings back there!" They indicated that I had an illegal sexual relationship with others. My husband also had to hear bad comments about me, when I was abroad. But when I came back, I explained everything to him (interview, Dhaka, Bangladesh, 7 February 2015).

Not the interviews only, the focus group discussions (FGDs) data also support these situations. One returnee woman migrant says:

I could not stay long. People said bad things about me. There were many rumors ... My husband got married again (FGD, Noakhali, Bangladesh, 7 February 2015).

While some argue that gender norms and role expectations for women in Bangladesh are not static (for example, Blunch & Das 2014), this paper explores that the traditional norms about women's 'purity' have not been changed yet. This is a very sensitive 'private' issue for a woman's life in Bangladesh, produces an extreme level of discomfort for the family she belongs to and may hinder to pursue income activities outside the home. This study reveals that such crisis discourages women not to migrate again despite financial necessity. Tanu Begum went to Saudi Arabia and had very positive experiences there. She also is afraid of such critiques although people know her very religious. She says:

... here in our country, many rumors are established about those countries. So I didn't want to go there but I realized that everything wasn't true. My opinion changed from then and in everywhere in the world, there are good and bad people (interview, Dhaka, Bangladesh, 26 April 2015).

Not only the researched communities, it seems to have a bigger effect on the national level. The Bangladesh government has the intention to send female workers to abroad to earn remittances, and recently they made a G2G (government to government) agreement with the Royal Saudi government to send female domestic workers there as the Bangladeshi women have the highest demand in the Saudi labour markets. This highest demand of Bangladeshi women has been in line with declining demands of women from other countries, particularly the Philippines, India and Sri Lanka on wage ground. The latest newspaper reports reveal that the Bangladesh government is not getting the expected response from the country's women to take the works there. Many reports also reveal that many families do fear with the women's jobs there that making them discouraged to respond to the G2G agreement.

It seems there is a trade-off between women's virginity ('purity') and incomes, and society always prefers virginity than making incomes. Therefore, the labour market phenomenon is more than economic and strongly associated with gender norms and values located in the cultural contexts. While the state authority has the intention to increase the country's economic remittances through the efforts, the social structures and practices act differently paying higher value to 'purity' led prestige of women. This patriarchal ideology of womanhood not only affects women's access to incomes but also girls' schooling in Bangladesh (Yance, 2015).

Rethinking Women's Paid Work for Empowerment

Women's access to outside paid work has been identified as one of the important pathways of their empowerment in contemporary literature (Kabeer, Mahmud, & Tasneem, 2011). It is argued that women in many societies are undervalued as they do not have access to formal outside employments. These arguments are empirically based on women's economic roles in informal work, for example, household work, which is non-paid in nature (Mahmud & Tasneem, 2011). There are plenty of literature which show that women's engagements in outside formal work, as well as incomes, can contribute to their empowerment (Kabeer, Mahmud, & Tasneem, 2011). This paper, however, suggests to be careful to the generalization of such arguments and puts emphasis on considering specific cultural contexts before drawing any conclusion. It becomes much true in the case of Bangladesh, the country which has made significant progress over years. The percentage of females in the labour force was 4.1 in 1974; it was 33.5% as the latest (BBS 2015, p. xii). More than four million workers, of which about 80% are women, are working in the readymade garments' sector (Rahman & Siddiqui 2015, p. 1). Women are also coming in Small and Medium Enterprises (SME) and data says about 3.8 and 5.2 billion taka disbursed as credit among the women entrepreneurs in 2012 and 2013 respectively (Bakht & Basher 2015, p. 29).

Women's participation in parliament was 12.7% in 1991-1995 while it became 19% in the 2014 national election (Jahan 2014, p. 70). In the case of the civil administration about 8.5% women as against 91.5% men in 1999 while it goes up 15% for women as against 85% for men in 2006 and 19% as the latest. In case of education, the gender gap has closed in primary education and reduced at secondary level, and according to the latest data the net enrolment for girls in primary education is 98.8% compared to 97.1% for boys (BBS 2016, p. 432); the gross enrolment in secondary school is higher among girls than boys; it is 55% for girls against 50% for boys (UNICEF 2016, p. 134). At the same time, there are some critical issues which question such progress. Violence against women is extreme and a very recent national survey report reveals intimate partner violence as 87%; 65% married women have experienced physical violence by current husbands in their lifetime (BBS 2013). Child marriage in Bangladesh is higher, ranks 8th in the world and according to latest data, it is 52% under age 18 (UNICEF, 2016, p. 150). A study by Jahan (2010) indicates that female civil servants in Bangladesh face numerous problems such as negative work environment as well as problems of dual responsibilities at both home and at work. A recent World Bank study explores that religious and social norms become crucial factors that reinforcing unequal gender relations (Solotaro and Pande, 2014). As indicated earlier, the female migrants are an important contributor to the national economy; they, being paid workers, play a very significant role in household incomes; but as the data (Gil Araujo and González-Fernández, 2014) reveals these economic contributions rarely make any sense for gender equality in their own lives. Their employments in a religious mixed patriarchal structure very often interact with particular norms and values which act against gender equality and reinforce inequality.

Towards a Gender Responsive Migration Policy Framework

The empirical evidence from the ground portraits the precarious situation of the migrant workers, more specifically that of women. The Government in Bangladesh is not ignorant of it and acknowledges the problems faced by the women labour migrants, like – lack of gender sensitive and right based approach to employment, lack of access to information, heavy concentration on low paid and unskilled employment opportunities, lack of skill (Islam, 2013). The circular from the Government following the newly adopted strategies include- skill building, safe house in Bangladeshi Mission abroad, monitoring, special briefing, awareness campaign, and accountability of the Recruiting agencies for women labour migrants.

The Overseas Employment and MigrantsAct 2013 is the revised legal instrument to promote opportunities for overseas employment, to facilitate safe migration, and to ensure rights and welfare of the migrant workers and their families in Bangladesh. It reassured strict control of state over foreign employment by bringing the Recruiting agencies under regulation. It officially recognized the rights of the migrant workers in terms of getting employment contract, proper information, legal aid, and also right to return home.

Ministry of Expatriates' Welfare and Overseas Employment, Policies 2016 covers a broad range of issues focusing on labour migrants, again specially on the women migrants in the country. Acknowledging that migrants have significant contributions to the national economy in spite of many obstacles, it aims to ensure equal and fundamental human rights for the labour migrants. It encourages gender sensitivity and elimination of discrimination against women. It also focuses on ensuring the decent work environment and safety at the workplace. In addition, encourages female migration and promoting women to new occupations. The revised one also proposes to include the provision of protecting migrants and their families from socio-economic deprivation; terms on migrants' welfare including their health facilities, timely/regular wage, setting minimum wage etc., and importantly to ensure safety from forced labour, child labour, and human trafficking.

One of the limitations of the new policy framework is that it does not take in establishing account gender equity to leverage safe migration for women migrants. It also ignores the fact that it is a pre-requisite to emphasize on building agency of the women labour migrants. The findings of this study suggests that the migrant women remain unable to take decisions or negotiate about many significant issues related to their life. Having access to services and resources might not be fruitful enough to reduce their vulnerabilities both in origin and destination. The resource itself, in the case of 'employment' of female migrants, is not enough if it cannot be capitalized well in favour of women (Kabeer 1999). Achieving gender equality is an outcome which requires a number of steps into their empowerment process (Ibid). Encouraging and promoting them in non-conventional employments is very important, but it may be too generalizing and simplifying, if any policy or law, claims to be gender responsive and ends up overlooking the wider patriarchal processes and structures. Then there is a risk of reproducing inequality in spite of women's increasing access to outside employments as well as incomes.

CONCLUSION

Migration pattern in Bangladesh is mainly South-South including labour migrants, more men though recently women's migration have increased. In the last 40 years, the number of migration has gradually increased. Female labour migration is a recent phenomenon compared to male labour migration though the former plays vital role. The output of such migration is crucial in both economic and social term. On one hand, the country's economic growth is benefitted from it and on the other hand the migrants, live life full of discriminations. To frame the later, as a result of the increasing international labour migration from Bangladesh, this chapter took Levitt's concept of "social remittance", not a very widely used term in the existing literature in Bangladesh perspective. This chapter is an attempt to draw the connection between the theoretical regime and the empirical evidence. The findings suggest that the attitudes and norms perceived by the male labour migrants have reinforced the idea of becoming a "good Muslim" primarily for women and they have also emphasized on maintaining burkha for women. The sense of women's purity remains dominance in the society and their mobility is restricted. For female migrant labours, migration has reconstructed gender relation in an unequal manner, reproducing discriminatory gender norm and roles. While there is a growing dependency on the remittance as it contributes to the national economy, the South-South migration led to more precarious condition for women migrant workers. The response from the Government of Bangladesh has been slow yet positive. The recent changes in the laws and policy framework signals the progressive attitude towards these migrants though it requires further improvement. This micro study is only an attempt to open a new horizon and put the call forward for further macro level research in this sector.

REFERENCES

Abecassis, D. (1990). *Identity, Islam, and human development in rural Bangladesh* (1st ed.). Dhaka, Bangladesh: University Press.

Agarwal, B. (1994). Gender and command over property: A critical gap in economic analysis and policy in South Asia. *World Development, 22*(10), 1455–1478. doi:10.1016/0305-750X(94)90031-0

Ahmed, C. (2014). Impacts of Remittance on the Socioeconomic Condition of Bangladesh: An Analysis. *IIASS, 7*(3), 23–43. doi:10.12959/issn.1855-0541.IIASS-2014-no3-art02

Aparicio, F., & Meseguer, C. (2012). Collective Remittances and the State: The 3×1 Program in Mexican Municipalities. *World Development, 40*(1), 206–222. doi:10.1016/j.worlddev.2011.05.016

Arifeen, A. (2013). Understanding the contribution of remittances at the macroeconomic and household levels and exploring how these transfers could be better leveraged for development in Bangladesh. Lecture, Dhaka. *BANBEIS- Educational Database*. Retrieved 14 November 2016, from http://192.254.190.210/~banbeis/data/index.php

Bangladesh Bank. (2016). Retrieved from https://www.bb.org.bd/pub/annual/anreport/ar1415/full_2014_2015.pdf

BBS. (2011). *Report on Household Income and Expenditure Survey Bangladesh 2011*. Dhaka: Bangladesh Bureau of Statistics.

BBS. (2013). *Report on Violence against Women (VAW) Survey 2011*. Dhaka: Bangladesh Bureau of Statistics.

BBS. (2015). *Report on Labor Force Survey (LFS) Bangladesh 2013*. Dhaka: Bangladesh Bureau of Statistics.

BBS. (2016). *Statistical Yearbook 2015*. Dhaka: Bangladesh Bureau of Statistics.

Bakht, Z., & Basher, A. (2015). Strategy for Development of the SME Sector in Bangladesh. Dhaka: Bangladesh Institute of Development Studies (BIDS).

Barkat, A., Osman, A., Ahsan, M., & Kumar, A. P. (2012). Situational Analysis of Sexual Harassment at Tertiary Level Education Institutes in and around Dhaka. Dhaka: Human Development Research Centre (HDRC).

Bruyn, T. (2006). Dynamics of Remittance Utilization in Bangladesh. In *Remittances and Expatriates: Development in Bangladesh*. The Hague: Bangladesh Support Group (BASUG). Retrieved from https://www.academia.edu/8017098/Dynamics_of_Remittance_Utilization_in_Bangladesh

Bureau of Manpower Employment and Training (BMET). (2016). Retrieved from http://www.bmet.gov.bd/BMET/resources/Static%20PDF%20and%20DOC/publication/Remittance%20and%20its%20impact.pdf

Carling, J. (2005). Migrant Remittances and Development Cooperation. Oslo: PRIO Report 1/2005, International Peace Research Institute.

Dannecker, P. (2005). Transnational Migration and the Transformation of Gender Relations: The Case of Bangladeshi Labour Migrants. *Current Sociology, 53*(4), 655–674. doi:10.1177/0011392105052720

Dannecker, P., & Sieveking, N. (2009). Gender, Migration and Development: An Analysis of the Current Discussion on Female Migrants as Development Agents. *COMCAD, 69*(2009). Retrieved from https://www.uni-bielefeld.de/tdrc/ag_comcad/downloads/Workingpaper_69_dannecker+sieveking.pdf

Das, N., Yasmin, R., Ara, J., Kamruzzaman, M., Davis, P., & Behrman, J. (2013). *How Do Intrahousehold Dynamics Change When Assets Are Transferred to Women? Evidence from BRACCs Challenging the Frontiers of Poverty Reduction Targeting the Ultra Poor Program in Bangladesh.* SSRN Electronic Journal. doi:10.2139/ssrn.2405712

de Haas, H., & van Rooij, A. (2010). Migration as Emancipation? The Impact of Internal and International Migration on the Position of Women Left Behind in Rural Morocco. *Oxford Development Studies, 38*(1), 43–62. doi:10.1080/13600810903551603

Faisal, I., & Kabir, M. R. (2005). An Analysis of Gender-Water Nexus in Rural Bangladesh. *Journal of Developing Societies, 21*(1-2), 175–194. doi:10.1177/0169796X05054623

Ferdousi, S., & Dehai, F. (2014). Economic Growth, Poverty and Inequality Trend in Bangladesh. *Asian Journal of Social Sciences & Humanities, 3*(1). Retrieved from http://www.ajssh.leena-luna.co.jp/AJSSHPDFs/Vol.3(1)/AJSSH2014(3.1-01).pdf

Francis, E. (2002). Gender, Migration and Multiple Livelihoods: Cases from Eastern and Southern Africa. *The Journal of Development Studies, 38*(5), 167–190. doi:10.1080/00220380412331322551

Frederick Littrell, R., & Bertsch, A. (2013). Traditional and contemporary status of women in the patriarchal belt. Equality, Diversity And Inclusion. *International Journal (Toronto, Ont.), 32*(3), 310–324. doi:10.1108/edi-12-2012-0122

Fries, L. (2012). Book Review: Transnational Communities: Shaping Global Economic Governance. *Organization Studies, 33*(8), 1091–1094. doi:10.1177/0170840611431656

Gardner, K., & Kotalova, J. (1995). Belonging to Others: Cultural Construction of Womanhood Among Muslims in a Village in Bangladesh. *Journal of the Royal Anthropological Institute, 1*(2), 445. doi:10.2307/3034740

Global Commission on International Migration (GCIM). (2005). *Migration in an interconnected world: New directions for action.* Retrieved from http://www.queensu.ca/samp/migrationresources/reports/gcim-complete-report-2005.pdf

GDP - Bangladesh Bureau of Statistics-Government of the People's Republic of Bangladesh. (2016). Retrieved 12 November 2016, from http://bbs.gov.bd/site/page/dc2bc6ce-7080-48b3-9a04-73cec782d0df/Gross-Domestic-Product-(GDP)

Government of Bangladesh. (2016). Probasi Kollayan O Boideshik Kormosangstahn Niti 2016. Dhaka: Ministry of Expatriates' Welfare and Overseas Employment. (in Bengali)

Gil Araujo, S., & González-Fernández, T. (2014). International migration, public policies and domestic work. *Womens Studies International Forum, 46,* 13–23. doi:10.1016/j.wsif.2014.01.007

Hatemi-J, A., & Uddin, G. (2013). On the causal nexus of remittances and poverty reduction in Bangladesh. *Applied Economics, 46*(4), 374–382. doi:10.1080/00036846.2013.844331

Hossain, N., Nazneen, S., & Sultan, M. (2011). National Discourses on Women's Empowerment in Bangladesh: Continuities and Change. *IDS Working Paper, 2011*(368). 10.2139/ssrn.2026729

Hugo, G. (2011). Migration and Development in Malaysia. *Asian Population Studies, 7*(3), 219–241. doi:10.1080/17441730.2011.608983

International Monetary Fund. (2016). Retrieved from http://www.imf.org/external/pubs/ft/weo/2016/update/01/

Islam, M. (2013). Gender Analysis of Migration from Bangladesh. Dhaka, Bangladesh: Bureau of Manpower, Employment and Training. Retrieved from http://www.bmet.gov.bd/BMET/resources/Static%20PDF%20and%20DOC/publication/Gender%20Analysis

Jahan, I. (2014). *Obstacles to Women's Participation in the Politics of Bangladesh* (Master's dissertation). Department of Political Science, University of Dhaka.

Kamruzzaman, M. (2005). *Community Well-being and Religious Form of Organisations (Postgraduate).* Dhaka, Bangladesh: North South University.

Hashmi, T. (2000). *Women and Islam in Bangladesh* (1st ed.). Houndmills, UK: Palgrave. doi:10.1057/9780333993873

Kabeer, N. (1999). Resources, Agency, Achievements: Reflections on the Measurement of Womens Empowerment. *Development and Change, 30*(3), 435–464. doi:10.1111/1467-7660.00125

Kabeer, N. (2000). *The power to choose.* London: VERSO.

Kabeer, N., Mahmud, S., & Tasneem, S. (2011). *Does Paid Work Provide a Pathway to Women's Empowerment? Empirical Findings from Bangladesh* (IDS Working Paper 375). IDS, University of Sussex.

Kabeer, N. (2012). *Women's economic empowerment and inclusive growth: labour markets and enterprise development* (SIG Working Paper 2012/1). International Development Research Centre (IDRC).

KNOMAD. (2016). Retrieved from http://siteresources.worldbank.org/INTPROSPECTS/Resources/334934-1199807908806/4549025-1450455807487/Factbookpart1.pdf

Gardner, K., & Kotalova, J. (1995). Belonging to Others: Cultural Construction of Womanhood Among Muslims in a Village in Bangladesh. *Journal of the Royal Anthropological Institute, 1*(2), 445. doi:10.2307/3034740

Levitt, P. (1998). Social Remittances: Migration Driven Local-Level Forms of Cultural Diffusion. *International Migration Review, 32*(4), 926. doi:10.2307/2547666 PMID:12294302

Levitt, P. (2005). *Social remittances - Culture as a development tool.* Presentation, International Forum on Remittances.

Levitt, P., & Schiller, N. (2006). Conceptualizing Simultaneity: A Transnational Social Field Perspective on Society1. *International Migration Review, 38*(3), 1002–1039. doi:10.1111/j.1747-7379.2004.tb00227.x

Mahmud, S., Shah, N., & Becker, S. (2012). Measurement of Womens Empowerment in Rural Bangladesh. *World Development, 40*(3), 610–619. doi:10.1016/j.worlddev.2011.08.003 PMID:23637468

Mahmud, S., & Tasneem, S. (2011). The Under Reporting of Women's Economic Activity in Bangladesh: An Examination of Official Statistics. *BRAC Development Institute Working Paper, 01*(February).

Malhotra, A., Schuler, S. R., & Boender, C. (2002), *Measuring Women's Empowerment as a Variable in International Development*, Background Paper Prepared for the World Bank Workshop on Poverty and Gender: New Perspectives.

Markley, E. (n.d.). *Social remittances and social capital: Values and practices of transnational social space*. Retrieved 23 October 2015, from http://www.revistacalitateavietii.ro/2011/CV-4-2011/02.pdf

Momsen, J. (1999). *Gender, migration, and domestic service* (1st ed.). London: Routledge.

Nath, H., & Mamun, K. (n.d.). Workers' Migration and Remittances in Bangladesh. *Journal of Business Strategies, 27*(1). 10.2139/ssrn.1592764

Overseas Employment and Migrants Act 2013 (Act No. VLVIII of 2013) (Bangladesh). (n.d.). Retrieved from http://asianparliamentarians.mfasia.org/phocadownload/resources/policies/bangladesh%20overseas%20employment%20and%20migrants%20act%202013%20_english_.pdf

Overseas Employment in 2016. (2016). Retrieved 12 November 2016, from http://www.bmet.gov.bd/BMET/viewStatReport.action?reportnumber=29

Overseas Employment & Remittance from 1976 - 2016. (2016). Retrieved 12 November 2016, from http://www.bmet.gov.bd/BMET/viewStatReport.action?reportnumber=20

Parvin, A. G. (1998). Women Empowerment Performance of Income Generating Activities Supported by Rural Women Employment Creation Project (RWECP): A Case Study in Dumuria Thana, Bangladesh. *The Journal of Geo-Environment, 4*, 47-62.

Personal remittances, received (% of GDP) | Data. (2016). Retrieved 12 November 2016, from http://data.worldbank.org/indicator/BX.TRF.PWKR.DT.GD.ZS?locations=BD

Piper, N. (2009). The complex interconnections of the migration-development nexus: A social perspective. *Population Space and Place, 15*(2), 93–101. doi:10.1002/psp.535

Rafiqul, I. M. (2011). Rural Women's Empowerment through Self-income Generating Activities: A Study on NGOs Credit Programs in Bangladesh. *Journal of Global Citizenship & Equity Education, 1*(1), 96–123.

Rahman, H., & Siddiqui, S. A. (2015). Female RMG worker: Economic Contribution in Bangladesh. *International Journal of Scientific and Research Publications, 5*(9), 1–9.

Ratha, D., Plaza, S., & Ozden, C. (2016). *Migration and Development*. New York: World Bank Group. Retrieved from http://pubdocs.worldbank.org/en/468881473870347506/Migration-and-Development-Report-Sept2016.pdf

Rouf, K. A. (2013). Religious patriarchal values obstruct Bangladeshi rural women's human rights. *Journal Research in Peace, Gender and Development*, 3(5), 75–79. Available online http://www.interesjournals.org/

Sassen, S. (2010). Strategic Gendering: One Factor in the Constituting of Novel Political Economies. In S. Chant (Ed.), *The International Handbook of Gender and Poverty* (pp. 29–34). Chelteham, UK: Edward Elgar Publishing Ltd. doi:10.4337/9781849805162.00012

Siddique, T. (2003). *Migration as a livelihood strategy of the poor: the Bangladesh case*. Dhaka, Bangladesh: Presentation.

Silliman, J., & Agarwal, B. (1996). A Field of Ones Own: Gender and Land Rights in South Asia. *Land Economics*, 72(2), 269. doi:10.2307/3146971

Solotaro, J., & Pande, R. (2014). Violence against Women and Girls: Lessons from South Asia. New York: World Bank. Retrieved from https://openknowledge.worldbank.org/bitstream/handle/10986/20153/9781464801716.pdf?sequence=1

UNICEF. (2016). *The State of the World's Children 2016: a fair chance for every child*. New York: United Nations Children Fund.

United Nations, Department of Economic and Social Affairs, Population Division. (2016). Retrieved from http://www.un.org/en/development/desa/population/migration/publications/migrationreport/docs/MigrationReport2015_Highlights.pdf

Wilce, J. M. Jr. (1994). Purity and Communal Boundaries: Women and Social Change in a Bangladeshi Village. *American Ethnologist*, 21(4), 986–987. doi:10.1525/ae.1994.21.4.02a01000

World Bank. (2008). *Whispers to Voices: Gender and Social Transformation in Bangladesh, Bangladesh Development Series, paper No. 22*. The World Bank.

World Bank Country and Lending Groups – World Bank Data Help Desk. (2016). Retrieved 12 November 2016, from https://datahelpdesk.worldbank.org/knowledgebase/articles/906519-world-bank-country-and-lending-groups

Yance, T. (2015). *The Multidimensionality of Schoolgirl Dropouts in Rural Bangladesh* (Master's thesis). University of San Francisco.

Chapter 22
Towards a More Gender-Inclusive Climate Change Policy

Farah Kabir
ActionAid Bangladesh, Bangladesh

ABSTRACT

Climate change is a reality, and poses a serious long term threat to society and to the environment. Much has been written on the negative effects of climate change across the globe focusing on the greater vulnerability of least developed countries and developing countries. Numerous studies back up the argument that "countries that are most vulnerable to the effects of climate change tend to be poorer with a wider gender gap. In contrast, countries that rank high in environmental performance and gender equality, are among the richest nations of the world" (Samy, 2011, p. 100). Women are often denied of their basic rights due to discriminatory social practices and gender blind policies. Impacts of climate change affect life and livelihood of women, and diverse work responsibilities of women augment their exposure to climate hazards. Due to less access or rights to financial and productive resources, information and services that may help them cope with impacts of stresses and shocks, are not present as a result of the gaps in policies, development agendas, thus leaving women in a greater vulnerable condition. Primarily, these are the reasons slowing the progress on achieving overall gender equality. The objective of this paper is to look at the Post 2015 Arrangements. These are numerous international frameworks and agreements ie SFDRR, SDG and the Paris Agreement, that will determine sustainable development for humanitarian response and climate politics as well as policies for the next fifteen years. They focus on development from a climate change and gender equality point of view, in particular how the policies are enabling 'gender equality', taking common but differentiated responsibilities, and equity, justice and fairness as principles.

INTRODUCTION

When we think of climate the tendency is to think of weather. Climate is usually defined as the "average weather" in a place. It includes patterns of temperature, precipitation (rain or snow), humidity, wind and seasons. Climate patterns play a fundamental role in shaping natural ecosystems, and the human economies and cultures that depend on them. Rising levels of carbon dioxide and other heat-trapping

DOI: 10.4018/978-1-5225-3018-3.ch022

gases have warmed the earth and are already causing wide-ranging impacts, from rising sea levels, to melting snow and ice, to more drought and extreme rainfall. Scientists project that these trends will continue and in some cases accelerate, posing significant risks to human health, our forests, agriculture, freshwater supplies, coastlines, and other natural resources. Nation state and societies around the globe need to reduce human-caused greenhouse gas emissions to avoid worsening climate impacts and reduce the risk of creating changes beyond our ability to respond and adapt.

Climate change is a reality, and poses a serious long term threat to society and to the environment. Much has been written on the negative effects of climate change across the globe focusing on the greater vulnerability of least developed countries and developing countries. Numerous studies back up the argument that "countries that are most vulnerable to the effects of climate change tend to be poorer with a wider gender gap. In contrast, countries that rank high in environmental performance and gender equality, are among the richest nations of the world" (Samy, 2011, p. 100).

Gender equality is a basic human right for all women and men, and it refers to equality between the two sexes. "Gender equality refers to equal rights, responsibilities and opportunities for women and men, girls and boys…Gender equality implies that the interests, needs and priorities of both women and men are taken into consideration, recognising the diversity among different groups of women and men."

Women's vulnerability often linked with unequal power relations in societies, which pervades all aspects of their lives and denies their basic rights, from access to education to participation in community governance ((Turnbull, Sterret, & Hilleboe, 2012). Women in general are found more vulnerable than men to climate change especially in time of disasters due to their socially constructed roles and responsibilities in addition to lack of adequate power and assets (Neelormi & Uddin, 2012). The 1991 Cyclone the death toll (Bern et al., 1993) was 138,000 where an astonishing 90 percent of the deaths were that of women (Global Humanitarian Forum Geneva, 2009). Gender inequality is one of the major factors contributing to the increased vulnerability of women and girls in disaster situations where women and children are 14 times more likely to die than men during a disaster (United Nations, 2009). Since the change in climate will increase the frequency and intensity of hydro-metrological shock and hazards[1], analysis suggests that women's vulnerability will, therefore, be increased.

The objective of this paper is to look at the Post 2015 Arrangements. These are numerous international frameworks and agreements, i.e., SFDRR, SDG and the Paris Agreement, that will determine sustainable development for humanitarian response and climate politics as well as policies for the next fifteen years. They focus on development from a climate change and gender equality point of view, in particular how the policies are enabling 'gender equality', taking common but differentiated responsibilities, and equity, justice and fairness as principles.

Women are often denied of their basic rights due to discriminatory social practices and gender blind policies. Impacts of climate change affect life and livelihood of women, and diverse work responsibilities of women augment their exposure to climate hazards. Due to less access or rights to financial and productive resources, information and services that may help them cope with impacts of stresses and shocks, are not present as a result of the gaps in policies, development agendas, thus leaving women in a greater vulnerable condition. Primarily, these are the reasons slowing the progress on achieving overall gender equality. Adding climate change to the scenario makes it even more difficult as the women living in poverty are taking on extra burden every day. In order to address the problem, over the last 15 years (MDGs in 2000), progress has been made at policy level as well as on implementation level. However, many have seen the progress yet to be gender sensitive as women's role remains limited to participation level only.

There is much evidence on how men and women can act as active agents of change with different capacities in responding to climate change. In particular, women are playing a significant role in disaster preparedness and humanitarian response. However, women are seldom engaged by the policy makers at local and national levels in decision-making processes. As a result their concerns are less likely to be addressed in relevant policies. It is opined that exclusion of women, especially from rural communities is a factor that significantly adds to their vulnerability. It reiterates the crucial importance of having women in decision making to influence both policy making processes and accountability mechanisms.

"Women can and have led the preparedness and response to emergencies in today's world-backtracking from it is not an option"

Policy responses at international and national level did not echo the reality of women properly. For over twenty years 'Gender' related discussion was absent from global process of United Nations Framework Convention for Climate Change (UNFCCC). Since 2001 with a provision on gender and representation in the Marrakech decision, the Conference of the Parties has been slowly taking actions towards the goal of gender equality; the Conference of the Parties has been slowly taking actions towards the goal of gender equality. Decision 36/CP.7 - improving the participation of women in the representation of Parties in bodies established under the Convention or the Kyoto Protocol urged 'Parties to take the measures necessary to enable women to participate fully in all levels of decision making relevant to climate change' and invited Parties to give active consideration to the nomination of women for elective posts in any body established under the Convention or the Kyoto Protocol. Since then a number of COP decisions have built on the initial early decision (including for example, decisions 1/ CP.16, 6/CP.16, 7/CP.16, 2/CP.17, 3/CP.17, 5/CP.17, 6/ CP.17, 12/CP.17 and 13/CP.17) culminating in Decision 23/CP.18.[2]

Following the COP since Bali 2007, we find that the emphasis on gender mainstreaming picked up at Cancun, Mexico (COP 16) under the presidency of the Government of Mexico. COP 18 in Doha, Qatar, 2012- is defined as the 'Gender COP', with the first ever 'Gender Day' raising awareness on the millions of women who struggle to overcome the challenges of climate change every day. Countries at the UNFCCC agreed on Decision 23/CP.18. This decision adopts the goal of gender balance and to ensure that 'gender and climate change' will be a standing item on the agenda at future COPs. This decision marks an important step forward in advancing gender-sensitive climate policy by ensuring that women's voices are represented in the global discussion on climate change. It does this, for example, by setting a goal of gender balance in the bodies of the Convention and the Protocol and by inviting Parties to strive for gender balance in their delegations. At COP 19 significant steps were taken towards the meaningful implementation of the COP18 Gender Decision. And at COP 20 in Lima, Peru, 2014, failed to move substantially forward towards the ultimate goal of agreeing on a plan to avert climate catastrophe, although in the final hours it agreed to an outcome in order to keep work moving towards Paris next year. Hence, 'Lima Work Programme on Gender', establishes a two-year plan that includes a review of gender mandate implementation, training on gender-responsive climate policy, guidelines for implementing gender considerations in climate change activities, and the appointment of a gender focal point within the UNFCCC Secretariat. Representatives from several countries championed the inclusion of women's and human rights in various parts of the Lima and Paris texts.

Gender mainstreaming is a more successful way of addressing gender inequality; in practice it risks reducing attention to women unless changes occur in departmental cultures, and gender mainstreaming accountability measures are introduced at international and national levels. Hence, "Gender mainstreaming is essential in ensuring that not only climate policies and programs are comprehensive, but so too are women-focused policies designed to ensure that women are supported and empowered to take action on their own behalf" (Alston, 2014). Positive side of these post 2015 agendas are that it emphasis on research issues more than previous era. So, we should consider scientific research on gender to mainstreaming it in policy and programme. However, more work will be needed to ensure policy makers get it — and more still to make sure they take action to improve women's lives in a climate-changed world.

Gender in Post-2015 International Development Agendas/ Framework/ Agreements/ Policy Instruments

In 2015, world adopted the Post 2015 Framework with promise to 'Leave No One Behind'. This section will briefly evaluate how women and their roles are seen in the agreements mostly the Sendai Framework for DRR, SDGs and COP21 outcome.

Therefore, this study aims to conduct light touch review of three high profile international policy/ agreements/ frameworks (i.e. Sendai Framework for Disaster Risk Reduction (SFDRR)-2015 and Sustainable Development Goals (SDGs)-2015 through the lens of gender, to explore how gender is incorporated in international and national climate change policies and strategies, whether these policies incorporate research findings on gender and climate change, and to identify gaps and suggest recommendation to bridge these gaps to inform policies on climate change, so that they reflect a more nuanced understanding on the link between gender and climate changes.

Sendai Framework for Disaster Risk Reduction 2015-2030

In March 2015, representatives from 187 countries adopted the 'Sendai Framework for Disaster Risk Reduction 2015-2030' (SFDRR), making it the first major agreement of the post-2015 development agenda during the Third UN World Conference on Disaster Risk Reduction (WCDRR) held in Sendai, Japan in March 2015.

With an overarching intended outcome of "The substantial reduction of disaster risk and losses in lives, livelihoods and health and in the economic, physical, social, cultural and environmental assets of persons, businesses, communities and countries", the framework aims to "Prevent new and reduce existing disaster risk through the implementation of integrated and inclusive economic, structural, legal, social, health, cultural, educational, environmental, technological, political and institutional measures that prevent and reduce hazard exposure and vulnerability to disaster, increase preparedness for response and recovery, and thus strengthen resilience".

Since, the *Women Major Group*[3] has started the discussion and have pointed out that 'SFDRR repeats the gender perspective in all policies and practices and gender needs in multi-hazard early warning systems, but it takes the agenda forward by focusing on the 'critical' role of women in 'designing, resourcing and implementing gender -sensitive DRR policies, plans and programmes'. Thus, Sendai Framework emphasized that "women and their participation are critical to effectively managing disaster risk and designing, resourcing and implementing gender-sensitive disaster risk reduction policies, plans and programmes; and adequate capacity building measures need to be taken to empower women for preparedness as well as build their capacity for alternate livelihood means in post-disaster situations." Leadership role of women in DRR finds specific mention in at least three separate places in SFDRR mentioning 'all-of-society engagement and partnership'; 'equitable and universally accessible response, recovery rehabilitation and reconstruction approaches'; and 'capacity building for alternate livelihood means'.

UNISDR adopted a Gender Policy in 2011 for gender mainstreaming in DRR to provide guidance to stakeholders and to promote gender equality and empowerment of women internally. To support governments and partners efforts on promoting gender in DRR, UNISDR developed a Twenty-Point Checklist on Gender-Sensitive DRR.

Paris Agreement/ COP21 (From 2020)

The Paris Agreement is an agreement within the framework of the United Nations Framework Convention on Climate Change (UNFCCC) governing greenhouse gases emissions mitigation, adaptation and finance from 2020. Gender responsive climate change policy and action for post 2020 has been considered, however, gender considerations in provisions that crystallise decisions in all the thematic areas of the global climate response: mitigation, adaptation, loss and damage, finance, technology development and transfer, capacity building and transparency of action and support should be taken with highest priority. However, Parties to the Convention must do more than focus on increasing women's participation in decision-making, and commit to gender equality as a guiding principle of post-2020 climate policy and action. Stronger steps need to be taken for real gender parity in climate policies, including strong monitoring and evaluation of the process. Additionally, it is important to improve monitoring of gender-specific data and introduce accountability for gender-specific targets.

In the Paris agreement, the use of "gender-responsive" has been seen as big step forward, even though the agreement fails to recognise women's existing capacity and skills. Rather, women are seen as victims of climate change in need of capacity building.

At least 50% of the 160 parties of the COP21 who made gender references in their Intended National Determined Contributions (INDCs) were from the industrialized countries, and they should be held accountable.

If we look at a section from the draft agreement's article on 'Adaptation', for example:

- **Article 7/ Adaptation:** *5. Parties acknowledge that adaptation action should follow a country-driven, gender-responsive, participatory and fully transparent approach, taking into consideration vulnerable groups, communities and ecosystems, and should be based on and guided by the best available science and, as appropriate, traditional knowledge, knowledge of indigenous peoples and local knowledge systems, with a view to integrating adaptation into relevant socioeconomic and environmental policies and actions, where appropriate*
- **Article 11/Adaptation:** *2. Capacity-building should be country-driven, based on and responsive to national needs, and foster country ownership of Parties, in particular, for developing country Parties, including at the national, sub national and local levels. Capacity-building should be guided by lessons learned, including those from capacity-building activities under the Convention, and should be an effective, iterative process that is participatory, cross-cutting and gender-responsive*
- **Draft decision -/CP.21 are:** *Acknowledging that climate change is a common concern of humankind, Parties should, when taking action to address climate change, respect, promote and consider their respective obligations on human rights, the right to health, the rights of indigenous peoples, United Nations FCCC/CP/2015/L.9 Distr.: Limited 12 December 2015 Original: English FCCC/CP/2015/L.9 2 local communities, migrants, children, persons with disabilities and people in vulnerable situations and the right to development, as well as gender equality, empowerment of women and intergenerational equity*

FACILITATING IMPLEMENTATION AND COMPLIANCE (PAGE 14)

103. Decides that the committee referred to in Article 15, paragraph 2, of the Agreement shall consist of 12 members with recognized competence in relevant scientific, technical, socio-economic or legal fields, to be elected by the Conference of the Parties serving as the meeting of the Parties to the Paris Agreement on the basis of equitable geographical representation, with two members each from the five regional groups of the United Nations and one member each from the small island developing States and the least developed countries, while taking into account the goal of gender balance.

These are undeniably important guiding principles. The paragraphs are also exceptionally vague.

Nevertheless, it is necessary to increase women's participation in the negotiation, and achieving balanced representation of women and men from developing countries and developed countriesto ensure the formulation of climate policy that would be gender sensitive as well as gender responsive. It will helps to bring a greater variety of views and more representative perspectives of society, and facilitate the adaptation of climate policy that addresses people's diverse interests and priorities.

Sustainable Development Goals

The Sustainable Development Goals (SDGs), officially known as Transforming our world: the 2030 Agenda for Sustainable Development are an intergovernmental set of aspiration 17 Goals with 169 targets. The Goals are contained in paragraph 54 United Nations Resolution A/RES/70/1 of 25 September 2015. The Resolution is a broader intergovernmental agreement that, while acting as the Post 2015 Development Agenda (successor to the Millennium Development Goals), builds on the Principles agreed upon under Resolution A/RES/66/288, popularly known as The Future We Want.

Although, Out of 17 Goals 'Goal 5' is directly about 'Gender Equality'. In relation to disaster and climate change there are several direct or indirect goals. Of which the SDG 13 is about taking urgent action to combat climate change and its impacts. It has five targets of which 3 targets are directly related to climate change and disaster. Goal 5 is known as the stand-alone gender goal because it is dedicated to achieving these ends. Women have a critical role to play in all of the SDGs, with many targets specifically recognizing women's equality and empowerment as both the objective, and as part of the solution.

However, there are some progresses in achieving women empowerment, e.g. regarding women and education. However, much more is needed to dismantle the more resilient structures of inequality in the market place and the political sphere. The key lesson from MDGs is the broader challenge is addressing the structural causes of gender inequality is that "technocrats can only go so far when the problems to be tackled are symptoms of deeply entrenched, often hidden structures of power. We need to pay more attention to the substance of the changes we want to see, not just their form, to the quality of the solutions we achieve, not just their quantity, and we need to pay more attention to the process by which we achieve our goals, to questions of participation, inclusion and accountability, because this is how we can achieve substance, quality and structural transformation" (Kabeer, 2015).

"For feminists, the SDG agenda has been described as a bitter-sweet victory. It incorporates the two-track strategy that feminists fought hard for: a stand-alone goal on gender equality, women's empowerment and women's rights (under threat by those who wanted it subsumed under 'social inequalities' more generally), and integration of gender equality concerns in other key goals. But it is a watered-down version of feminist demands since the rights perspective is largely missing. What the goal does incorporate are some of the key issues that feminists have sought recognition for: the unfair gender division of unpaid productive and reproductive activity that curtails women's ability to participation in the public sphere of market and politics; violence against women and girls, the issue that appears to have the support of feminist organisations across the world; and reproductive and sexual health and reproductive rights. The odd phrasing of the third issue reflects the fact that yet again, we have failed to get sufficiently strong international support for sexual rights, thus failing all those who are oppressed by repressive forms of sexuality – not only the LGBTI community but also many heterosexual men and women. The other bitter aspect of the SDGs is the unwavering commitment to economic growth and the private sector to generate the resources necessary to translate these goals into concrete outcomes, rather than seeking redistribution of gross global and national inequalities in wealth and income. This makes a mockery of the commitment to the reduction of inequality and means that the agenda has been largely left to the vagaries of market place and the whims of unaccountable global corporations" (Kabeer, 2015).

Bangladesh Scenario

Over the last few years Bangladesh has given much more emphasis on women and gender issues in context of disaster and climate change at institutional level. This has been reflected in several Policy documents including political commitments. Bangladesh was the first to formulate a Climate Change Strategy and Action Plan in 2009.

Bangladesh Climate Change Strategy and Action Plan (BCCSAP) 2009

Bangladesh had prepared NAPA in 2005 through a consultative process; Moreover, Bangladesh prepared response to Bali Action Plan and submitted it to UNFCCC in March 2008. BCCSAP is based on NAPA- finalised as a national document in 2009.

Table 1. National policy mechanisms

o National Adaptation Plan of Action (NAPA) (Developed in 2005, revised in 2009) o Bangladesh Climate Change Strategy and Action Plan (BCCSAP) 2009 o Climate Investment Funds (CIF) Strategic Program for Climate Resilience (SPCR), 2010 o Reducing Emissions from Deforestation and Forest Degradation (REDD+) o The National Strategy for Accelerated Poverty Reduction (NSAPR, FY 2009-11) - General Economic Division, 2009 o 6th Five-Year Plan (2011 – 2015), 2011 o 7th Five Year Plan (2015-16 to 2019-20) o National Plan for Disaster Management (NPDM), 2010 – 2015 o Establishment of National Climate Funds	o The National Policy for Women's Advancement (NPWA) within the framework of CEDAW and a follow up of Beijing Conference on Women and aimed at eradicating gender disparities and mainstreaming of gender issues; o The National Action Plan (NAP) as a follow-up to the Beijing Platform of Action; o The establishment of the MoWCA, a Parliamentary Standing Committee for MoWCA, an Interministerial o Coordination and Evaluation Committee and WID Coordination Committees at district and Upazila Levels; o The Poverty Reduction Strategy Paper (PRSP); o The establishment of the National Council for Women and Child Development (2009); o Gender Responsive Budget to ten ministries in 2009-2011 o The National Policy for Women's Advancement 2008, the National Education Policy, 2010, Domestic/ Family Violence (Prevention and Protection) Act, 2010, Prevention of Cruelty to Women and Children Act, Acid Crime Control Act, Child Marriage Restraint Act and Dowry Prohibition Act, o National Women Development Policy, 2011, o the National Health Policy, 2011; and o Steps Towards Change: NSARP-II, Vision 2021, etc.

BCCSAP includes the Climate Change Action Plan "a 10-year program (2009 – 2018) of the country to meet the challenge of climate change. [The BCCSAP states that] ... the needs of the poor and Vulnerable, including women and children, will be mainstreamed in all the activities under the Action Plan." NAPA was the major impetus to mobilize Climate Change and Adaptation Policy in Bangladesh, it is important to consider the structural mechanisms which ensure gender is integrated in nationally implemented adaptation plans. Through the NAPAs, the UNFCCC recognizes that men and women have different roles in securing livelihoods in the developing world. The Adaptation Fund supports activities that are demonstrably gender-sensitive, and funding proposals are reviewed to ensure that they support participatory processes and monitoring in projects/programmes that disaggregates data on specific indicators by gender (UNFPA and WEDO, 2009)

The six pillars (Themes) in BCCSAP emphasised the integration of gender and climate change concern into policies and national documents, increase women's participation in decision making process for efficient water management and better social security/protection, community risk assessment (CRA), vulnerability and capacity assessment activities, disaster risk reduction planning, monitoring and capacity development activities etc.

BCCSAP (2009) has given more importance on research and data management to ensure 04 securities inviolate on food, water, energy and livelihood (including health). Hence, five Task Forces have been set up, comprising government officials, academics, professionals and representatives of NGOs for guiding countries responses to impacts of Climate Change and support Bangladesh Government in regarding CC Talks. Additionally, BCCSAP studied, investigated and played active role in IPCC process in 2nd, 3rd, 4th & 5th assessments.

Under Research & Knowledge Management pillar, it is clearly mentioned to establish Centre for knowledge management & training on CC, Climate change modelling at national and sub-national levels, preparatory studies for adaptation against sea level rise, monitoring of ecosystem and biodiversity changes and their impacts, Macroeconomic and sectoral economic impacts of CC, Monitoring of Internal and external migration of adversely impacted population, and Monitoring of Impact of various issues related to management of tourism in Bangladesh

However, Findings reveal that the climate change and differentiated gender impacts are not recognized. Policy objectives related to climate change and gender are generally addressed as mutually exclusive issues; existing policies do not consider gender-specific operational activities. The only policy that includes gender-based considerations for climate adaptation is the Poverty Reduction Strategy paper (2005); however operational activities under this policy have not yet fulfilled these objectives. Climate change policies generally recognize women as vulnerable but operational responses are not established. In policies related to gender and reproductive health, the impact of climate change is not considered, with the exception of the National Women Development Policy, which briefly promotes women's role in environmental management and the importance of ensuring facilities for and the security of pregnant women in the event of natural disasters. (Shabib and Khan, 2014, p.332)

Under the Reducing Vulnerability to Climate Change (RVCC), gender issues were promoted through the participation of women in the management committees. Furthermore in monitoring schemes there are mechanisms to ensure equitable outcomes, particularly in livelihood activities. Thus, the unique role of women in livelihood activities is recognized under the RVCC, but their unique health needs due to the impact of climate change is not addressed. Moreover, Climate change policies consider women as vulnerable, weak and burden to society (not considered as contributor to economic development); there are numbers of example where women have showed their capacity-but those are not recognized. (e.g. Women Leadership in Emergency Response is not recognized by the government). In independent NGO activity and top-down initiatives such as the CDMP and CDMP II, gender is excluded from operational plans. This indicates the need to integrate gender into the culture and lexicon of Climate Change and Adaptation Programming. (Shabib and Khan, 2014, p. 333)

Due to lack of appropriate governance and resources, existing development policies are not implemented on the ground. Very few policies i.e. social safety net, provide safeguard for women in stress due to disaster or climate change. Although women, poverty and gender nexus are focused in the PRSP, the implementation of the strategies remains difficult, especially in disaster situation. Higher budget goes to agricultural subsidies or NGOs usually work on 'women empowerment' – that sometimes tends to ignore the power dynamics between men and women within the family structure. Overall, the Acts and Policies are not adequate to even protect women in current climate and disaster context. These are certainly not adequate to ensure women's rights and dignity in climate change context.

In the National Environment Policy (1992), the coastal zone policy (2005), and the NAPA (2005), Bangladesh climate change strategy and action plan (2008) there is no clear indication about the problems of population displacement. For instance, it is written in coastal zone policy, 2005 that susceptibilities of coastal communities will be addressed as these people are very dependent on natural resources for their livelihood. However, how will their sufferings be addressed? There is no action plan with a timeframe in the national policy to address the problem' (Akter, 2009, p. 11)

The National Plan for Disaster Management 2010-2015 generously sprinkled the word women in the document but utter absence of any gender analysis is quite obvious. The core principle of the plan said: 'Result oriented and focused on outcomes that will benefit vulnerable communities, especially women, the poor and socially disadvantaged.' In page 48 it reads 'The Plan is to be used to: ii. Demonstrate a commitment to address key issues: risk reduction, capacity building, information management, climate change adaptation, livelihood security, issues of gender and the socially disadvantaged, etc." It even includes in action agenda Revision of Standing Orders on Disaster (SOD) in line with Comprehensive DRR and Emergency Management with special emphasis on gender and diversity group. All of which is clear evidence of attempt to include the word gender without any seriousness or commitment.

At the national level the Ministry of Environment and Forest produced 'Climate Change and Gender Action Plan' (CCGAP). The objective is "to mainstream gender concerns into climate change-related policies, strategies and interventions ensuring access to, participation in, contributions towards and benefits for the diverse group of stakeholders for the sustainable and equitable development of Bangladesh". It defines the role that the MoEF would play in initiating and facilitating efforts internally, as well as with strategic partners at the national, regional and international levels. It seeks to mainstream gender in climate change and facilitate transformational change in climate action as per the BCCSAP and other policy instruments.

In the current 7th Five years plan, emphasis has been given on gender to ensure women's advancement as self-reliant human beings and reduce discriminatory barriers by taking both developmental and institutional measures. For the 7thFYP a Background document has also been prepared on 'Climate Change and Disaster Management' for the first time with a wide range of gender dimension. Gender equality and women's empowerment agenda for the 7th FYP is based on pursuing strategies and actions that not only enhance women's capabilities and access to resources and opportunities but also address the barriers in structures and institutions and aim at changing social norms and protecting their rights are critical to integrate within the plan. Establishing monitoring, oversight and accountability mechanisms is equally important.

GoB has highlighted gender sensitivity as an important issue in climate change adaptation and supported the Ministry of Women and Children Affairs (MoWCA) to take initiative under the BCCTF to integrate gender sensitivity in their respective project designs.

However, hitherto intra-ministerial coordination, intra- agencies coordination is missing in this particular issue. Government should take leadership to reduce the gap between policy and practice/implementation. It is important to see 'GENDER & CLIMATE CHANGE' as holistic, not in a separated segment. Thereby, more scientific research is required in different issues and dimension to identify innovative ways of delivering DRR projects and policies is important. One area where innovation is needed is on how risk, uncertainties, and transformation interact in the lives of poor women and men, not just in community level, but across the globe. This implies engaging more with the perspective of different gender groups and grassroots organizations.

RECOMMENDATION

1. Recognize the value of women contribution in community based adaptation and mitigation where relevant.
    a. Monetize the value of women works in the home and community particularly in regards to natural resource management and green practices.
    b. Institute reward systems for contributions of women to CBA. This will act as an incentive to further women's contribution and leadership.
    c. Celebrate women leaderships regarding existing solutions as well as innovation to address climate change vulnerabilities.
2. Recognize gender gaps in policy, planning and budget.
    a. It is imperative that GoB takes into consideration the numerous policy reviews by academics and non government organizations available to identify gender gaps regarding climate change planning, finance, and implementation. We are seeing certain changes in recent times which are reassuring.
    b. Undertake research for policy reform to improve the system of developing climate change adaptation plans and finance linked with gender priority. This requires to be on a holistic approach and not in silos/sectors/or specific dimensions.
    c. Incorporate gender lenses in climate finance and in selection of projects for BCCTF and BCCRF.
    d. Review the present gender budgeting policy and incorporate climate change and gender diversity in the analysis and planning. Annual budget preparation on gender budgeting for ministries works together with MoEF and Ministry of Planning to maximize the incorporation of gender lenses and dimension in addressing Climate Change.
3. Ensure social protection programmes are established for women vulnerable to climate change.
    a. At present Bangladesh has social protection programmes therefore increase coverage of these schemes to climate change vulnerable communities was something we had lobbied for and is now reflected in the 7th Five Year Plan.

    b.   Reduce and remove impediments in regard to the access of social protection programme for women and girls.

    c.   Ensure that at the Union Paris had level women and children welfare committee as well as DRR committee with women membership plays a decision making role in developing social protection programme.

4.   Ensure greater coordination for developing and implementing gender sensitive budget and plans.

    a.   By way of inter-ministerial coordination between MoWCA and MoEF for climate change and gender.

    b.   A steering committee established on CC and Gender equality that bridges MoEF and MoWCA planning and implementation of target initiatives. It is important to create a mechanism for inter ministerial coordination and co-operation to further both adaptation and mitigation.

5.   Establish effective implementation and monitoring mechanism.

    a.   Monitor the systems and institutions for policy Implementation.

    b.   Monitoring and supporting development of climate finance for gender sensitive interventions and development programmes through regular data collection, evaluation and impact assessment.

    c.   Modify existing programmes especially in response to gender priority articulated by communities particularly women. This requires women participating in planning and implementation at national and local level.

    d.   Reporting on gender sensitive plans and programmes to address climate change, community based adaptation and mitigation plans.[4]

REFERENCES

Akter, T. (2009). *Climate change and flow of environmental displacement in Bangladesh acknowledgement.* Available at: http://bdresearch.org.bd/home/climate_knowledge/cd1/pdf/Bangladesh%20and%20climate%20change/Climate%20change%20impacts%20,vulnerability,%20risk/Climate_Change_and_Flow_of_Environmental_displacement.pdf

Alston, M. (2014). Gender mainstreaming and climate change. *Women's Studies International Forum, 47.*

Bern, C., Sniezek, J., & Mathbor, G., Siddiqi, Ronsmans, C., Chowdhury, A., Choudhury, A., ... Noji, E. (1993). Risk factors for mortality in the Bangladesh cyclone of 1991. *Bulletin of the World Health Organization, 71*(1), 73–78. PMID:8440041

Disaster Management Bureau and Disaster Management and Relief Division. (2010). *National plan for disaster management government of the people's republic of Bangladesh national plan for disaster management 2010-2015 disaster management bureau disaster management & relief division.* Available at: http://www.lcgbangladesh.org/derweb/doc/Final%20Version%20Nataional%20Plan%20for%20Disaster%20(2010-2015).pdf

Global Humanitarian Forum Geneva. (2009). *Human impact report the anatomy of A silent crisis the anatomy of A silent crisis.* Available at: http://www.ghf-ge.org/human-impact-report.pdf

Kabeer, N. (2015). Gender equality, the MDGs and the SDGs: Achievements, lessons and concerns. *International Growth Centre.* Available at: http://www.theigc.org/blog/gender-equality-the-mdgs-and-the-sdgs-achievements-lessons-and-concerns/

Kabir, F. (2014). *Policy Brief on Local Adaptation to Climate Change: The Gender Perspective.* Available at: http://www.icccad.net/wp-content/uploads/2014/07/CCG_Policy-Brief_June-2014.pdf

Ministry of Environment and Forest. (2013). *Bangladesh Climate Change and Gender Action Plan.* Available at: http://ngof.org/wdb_new/sites/default/files/iucn__bangladesh_climate_change__gender_action_plan__1.pdf

Neelormi, S., & Ahmed, A. (2012). Loss and damage in a warmer world: Whither gender matters?. *Gender Perspectives on the Loss and Damage Debate.*

Oxfam International. (2016). *Women & Climate Change.* Available at: https://www.oxfam.org/sites/www.oxfam.org/files/gender_copenhagen_media_briefing_oxfam_international.pdf

Samy, K. (2011). Women and climate change: An opportunity to address gender inequality. *Yale Journal of International Affairs, 6*(1), 99–101.

Shabib, D., & Khan, S. (2014). Gender-sensitive adaptation policy-making in Bangladesh: Status and ways forward for improved mainstreaming. *Climate and Development, 6*(4), 329–335. doi:10.1080/17565529.2014.951017

Turnbull, M., Sterrett, C. L., & Hilleboe, A. (2012). *Toward Resilience: A Guide to Disaster Risk Reduction and Climate Change Adaptation.* Available at: http://reliefweb.int/sites/reliefweb.int/files/resources/ECB-toward-resilience-Disaster-risk-reduction-Climate-Change-Adaptation-guide-english.pdf

UNFPA & WEDO. (2009). *Making NAPAs work for women.* Available at: https://www.unfpa.org/sites/default/files/pub-pdf/climateconnections_4_napas.pdf

United Nations. (2009). *Making disaster risk reduction gender-sensitive policy and practical guidelines.* Available at: http://www.unisdr.org/preventionweb/files/9922_MakingDisasterRiskReductionGenderSe.pdf

ECB Project. (2013). *Towards Resilience: A Guide to Disaster Risk Reduction and Climate Change Adaptation.* Author.

Neelormi, S., & Uddin, A. (2012). *Loss and Damage in a warmer world: Whether Gender Matters?.* Academic Press.

Bern, C. (1993). Risk factors for mortality in the Bangladesh cyclone of 191. *Bulletin of the World Health Organization, 71,* 73–28. PMID:8440041

Forum, G. H. (2009). *The Anatomy of a Silent Crisis.* Geneva: Author.

UNISDR. (2009). Making Disaster Risk Reduction Gender Sensitive, Policy and Practical Guideline. Author.

World Metrological Organisation. (n.d.). *Climate Information for Disaster Risk Reduction.* Retrieved from https://www.wmo.int/gfcs/site/documents/HLT_DRR_EN.pdf

Islam, T., & Neelim, A. (2010). *Climate Change in Bangladesh: A Closer Look into Temperature and Rainfall Data.* Academic Press.

Oxfam Monash Partnership Project. (n.d.). *Gendered impacts of climate variability in Bangladesh in 2010-2013.* Author.

FAO. (2014). *Bangladesh Nutrition Country Profile.* Retrieved from http://goo.gl/Nbkiy6

Mahbuba, N. (2008). *Violence Against Women during flood and post-flood situations in Bangladesh.* ActionAid Bangladesh.

Norwegian Refugee Council (NRC). (2015). *Community Resilience and Disaster Related Displacement in South Asia.* Author.

ENDNOTES

[1] World Metrological Organisation(Undated) Climate Information for Disaster Risk Reduction https://www.wmo.int/gfcs/site/documents/HLT_DRR_EN.pdf.

[2] See Appendix 2.

[3] Women Major Group formed for the 3rd World Conference in Disaster Risk Reduction/3WCDRR held in Japan.

[4] Kabir, Farah, June 2014, Policy Brief on Local Adaptation to Climate Change: The Gender Perspective, published by Climate Change Governance(CCG).

APPENDIX 1

Research on Gendered Impacts of Climate Variability

Women's vulnerability often linked with unequal power relations in societies, which pervades all aspects of their lives and denies their basic rights, from access to education to participation in community governance (ECB Project, 2013). Women in general are found more vulnerable than men to climate change especially in time of disasters due to their socially constructed roles and responsibilities in addition to lack of adequate power and assets (Neelormi & Uddin, 2012). The 1991 Cyclone the death toll (Bern et al, 1993) was 138,000 where an astonishing 90 percent of the deaths were that of women (Global Humanitarian Forum, 2009). Gender inequality is one of the major factors contributing to the increased vulnerability of women and girls in disaster situations where women and children are 14 times more likely to die than men during a disaster (UNIDSR, 2009). Since the change in climate will increase the frequency and intensity of hydro-metrological shock and hazards (WMO, n.d.). analysis suggests that women's vulnerability will, therefore, be increased.

In Bangladesh, impact of climate change is very much visible. Temperature, rainfall, wind pattern and solar radiation mainly characterize the climatic systems in Bangladesh and determine the seasons and based on data from 31 weather stations in different places, it was found that in average winter days are much warmer; so are the summer days (Islam & Neelim, 2010). Such changes have already impacted peoples' lives and livelihood particularly of women.

Climate change has had a range of detrimental impacts on livelihoods, and has exacerbated existing gender inequalities. In particular, declining yields from agriculture and fisheries has driven a significant number of men to out-migrate for employment, leaving women to cope with and adapt to the changes occurring in their communities. This out-migration has also changed family relationships and has led to increases in domestic violence against women. Meanwhile, women have suffered disproportionately from food shortages and from reduced availability of fuel and drinking water. Finally, girls' access to education has been put under pressure by increasing financial hardship, with families increasingly unable to support their ongoing education, and with some families pulling their daughters out of education in favour of early marriage (Oxfam, n.d.).

Malnutrition rates are among the highest in the world, more than 50% of women suffering from chronic energy deficiency (FAO, 2014).

Women's vulnerability results from highly embedded and normalized social practices and structural inequalities. Social customs hinders the ability of women in Bangladesh to disaster respond and disaster preparedness. Their capacity restricted by their lesser access to the resource- financial, knowledge, natural. Many women reported that they are not able to go shelter without the permission of their husband; not receiving early warning, there being no women's toilet in shelter; threats of violence; a lack of privacy; not being consulted or provided with information; and being responsible for on-going unpaid care work and livelihoods.

ActionAid Bangladesh has conducted a study in drought prone Naogaon District where water is the scarcest natural resource. In addition, accesses to water bodies and sources are restricted by resource owners including government. Women reported number of mental and sexual harassment cases while fetching water. In floodplain area of Faridpur or coastal areas such as Khulna or Haor area Sunamganj, ecology and hazard context have less problem with water availability. However, lack of affordability and undrinkable quality (especially for saline prone Khulna) compel women to travel distant places where similar to Naogaon, women reported sexual and mental harassment cases. While on the road towards or at the location of water reservoir and fuel collection, women often face physical and mental harassment. In all areas, improper sanitation system was found serious threat to women's health. During the time of disaster such as dense cyclone and dense fog water, sanitation and health related hazards increases manifold – reported by women during consultation. Women also shared experiences and stories of increased mental and physical assault in comparing to regular days while fetching water or collecting fuels for household.

Violence against women increases during and after disasters as there are number of reports indicated that during disaster sexual harassment takes place while women are staying at cyclone or flood shelter. Many women and girls don't go to the shelter due to lack of security (Mahbuba, 2014). Women also informed the study that after disaster, during humanitarian response phase, they often hesitate to go for relief as mental and physical harassment. In Khulna, women claimed rape cases were reported after cyclone Aila where the men from same community denied such incident during FGD.

Bangladesh in last 10 years suffered more disasters in compared to any past decades (as far as the record goes) and if the warming continues, the impact will be severe particularly for Bangladesh in terms of more stresses on water for daily use to irrigation, and there will be more disasters. Riverbank erosion and seasonal floods displaces as many as 400,000 people each year in Bangladesh. In the period 2008 to 2013, about 4 million people of Bangladesh have been displaced by sudden onset disaster (NRC, 2015).

APPENDIX 2

[There are 29 Articles mentioned in the Paris Agreements. (COP21)]
Gender in COP21:
Draft decision -/CP.21

Acknowledging that climate change is a common concern of humankind, Parties should, when taking action to address climate change, respect, promote and consider their respective obligations on human rights, the right to health, the rights of indigenous peoples, United Nations FCCC/CP/2015/L.9 Distr.: Limited 12 December 2015 Original: English FCCC/CP/2015/L.9 2 local communities, migrants, children, persons with disabilities and people in vulnerable situations and the right to development, as well as gender equality, empowerment of women and intergenerational equity

Facilitating Implementation and Compliance (Page 14)

103. Decides that the committee referred to in Article 15, paragraph 2, of the Agreement shall consist of 12 members with recognized competence in relevant scientific, technical, socio-economic or legal fields, to be elected by the Conference of the Parties serving as the meeting of the Parties to the Paris Agreement on the basis of equitable geographical representation, with two members each from the five regional groups of the United Nations and one member each from the small island developing States and the least developed countries, while taking into account the goal of gender balance;

Table 2.

Article 7/ Adaptation	5. Parties acknowledge that adaptation action should follow a country-driven, gender-responsive, participatory and fully transparent approach, taking into consideration vulnerable groups, communities and ecosystems, and should be based on and guided by the best available science and, as appropriate, traditional knowledge, knowledge of indigenous peoples and local knowledge systems, with a view to integrating adaptation into relevant socioeconomic and environmental policies and actions, where appropriate
Article 11	2. Capacity-building should be country-driven, based on and responsive to national needs, and foster country ownership of Parties, in particular, for developing country Parties, including at the national, sub national and local levels. Capacity-building should be guided by lessons learned, including those from capacity-building activities under the Convention, and should be an effective, iterative process that is participatory, cross-cutting and gender-responsive

Research in COP21:

Technology Development and Transfer (Page 09)

67. Decides to strengthen the Technology Mechanism and requests the Technology Executive Committee and the Climate Technology Centre and Network, in supporting the implementation of the Agreement, to undertake further work relating to, inter alia: (a) Technology research, development and demonstration; (b) The development and enhancement of endogenous capacities and technologies;

Table 3.

Article 7	7. Parties should strengthen their cooperation on enhancing action on adaptation, taking into account the Cancun Adaptation Framework, including with regard to: c) Strengthening scientific knowledge on climate, including research, systematic observation of the climate system and early warning systems, in a manner that informs climate services and supports decision making;
Article 10	5. Accelerating, encouraging and enabling innovation is critical for an effective, long-term global response to climate change and promoting economic growth and sustainable development. Such effort shall be, as appropriate, supported, including by the Technology Mechanism and, through financial means, by the Financial Mechanism of the Convention, for collaborative approaches to research and development, and facilitating access to technology, in particular for early stages of the technology cycle, to developing country Parties.

Chapter 23
Women Painters of Mithila:
A Quest for Identity

Sudha Jha Pathak
Amity Law School, India

ABSTRACT

The region of Mithila has become synonymous with the beautiful and vibrant Madhubani paintings which are very much coveted by the connoisseurs of art the world over. The women from Mithila have been making these paintings and it is admirable that they have been able to carve out a space and name for themselves amidst the patriarchal set-up of society. Indeed, there is no other parallel anywhere else in the world of a folk-painting being mastered exclusively by women. The progressive commercialization of this art has resulted in the corrosion of this pristine variety of art - in form as well as content. Except a miniscule number of artists, economically the plight of the vast majority of these women painters has remained quite miserable who are forced to sell their artistic pieces for a pittance while a huge profit is earned by the middlemen. The commodification and commercialization of this traditional art form has caused much alarm to the anthropologists, art historians and connoisseurs of art who are sensitive to the cultural origins and solemnity of these art forms, and also made them empathetic to the economic deprivation of the women artists who produce them. These women artists are undermined by the patriarchal social structures of the community and family and also by the market that expropriates traditional knowledge and cultural expressions.

'Painting is in our culture - my mother used to paint and I started painting with her. - Shashikala Devi

Since the ancient period of human history, even going as far back as the primeval times, art has been an integral and inalienable aspect of human life, as revealed in the cave paintings belonging to the prehistoric period found in various parts of the world. Painting is an important medium for the expression of creative thoughts, human feelings, emotions and sentiments as well as the secular themes, religious

DOI: 10.4018/978-1-5225-3018-3.ch023

Women Painters of Mithila

beliefs and variegated mundane subject matters. As such, the study of painting concerning the genre of the folk-art helps us in understanding the deep co-relation between art and the various facets of the respective culture and civilization.

The region of Mithila has become synonymous with the beautiful and vibrant Madhubani paintings which are very much coveted by the connoisseurs of art the world over. Madhubani painting is a predominantly feminine oriented folk-art form of the Mithila region in the northern part of the state of Bihar in India and some adjacent areas of Nepal Terai. Thus, Mithila broadly refers to the geographical areas encompassing the old and undivided districts of Darbhanga (out of which the district of Madhubani was formed upon its bifurcation), Bhagalpur, Purnea and Saharsa in North Bihar and some areas of the Nepal Terai adjoining the border of Bihar. The uniqueness of this art along with a clearly specified geographical area of its practice has led to the Government of India giving it its own Geographical Identification or GI tag. These paintings have been aesthetically appreciated and also received international acclaim.

HISTORY OF MADHUBANI PAINTINGS

Mithila has had a glorious tradition in the political and cultural life of ancient India. The region also saw the rise and collapse of many kingdoms like Magadha and republics like the Licchavis, Vaisali etc. Mithila earned the distinction of being the land which witnessed the emergence of personalities like Yajnavalkya, Kapila, the founder of *Samkhya* philosophy, Kanada (the exponent of the *Vaisesika* philosophy),and Jaimini (the exponent of the *Mimansa* school).It was also the land of the *Upanishads* which embody the highest philosophical speculations about life, soul and God. Vaisali, an ancient Indian republic was a stronghold of Buddhist and Jaina religion and philosophies. The second Buddhist Council was held in the city of Vaisali. Hence Mithila has remained the cradle of Indian region and culture.

It cannot be stated with certainty as to when these *bhitticitras* (wall paintings) really began. From the fact that this art is mentioned in the ancient literature of Mithila inferences can be drawn to the fact that it is a very ancient art. The name Mithila was also usually used for the kingdom of Videha. This art form is said to date as far back as the *Ramayana* when King Janaka, who ruled over Mithila, commissioned artists to make paintings to celebrate his daughter Sita's marriage to Rama. Legends state that the ladies of King Janaka's household used to paint on the walls.

This glorious tradition continued during the medieval period in Mithila, which included the period from 1097 AD to 1550 AD under the *Karnatas* and *Oinavaras* as also under the Khandavala dynasty (Darbhanga Raj), down to the present times. The age of the *Karnatas* and *Oinavaras*, though not very significant politically, was a landmark with respect to developments in culture, art and literature in north-eastern India. There is an abundance of literary works in *Maithili* (dramas, poetry and prose), the language spoken in Mithila from about the eleventh century.

FEATURES OF MADHUBANI PAINTINGS

These paintings are characterized by loose-limbed, exaggerated vertical figures with great reserve in their forms. Foilage and flowers are stylistically arranged in the paintings to form decorative patterns. The unique feature of the Madhubani painting is that the women are the sole custodians of this art form, which is also an indicator of their fine aesthetic sense. Indeed, there is no other parallel anywhere else in the world of a folk-painting being mastered exclusively by women. As is true for any anthropologically significant art form, where it is passed on from one generation to the other, the responsibility of carrying out this process in the case of Madhubani painting has been shouldered by women of the various successive generations.

The paintings depict the way in which women have created a communicative space for themselves articulating their perspective on the social and sacred world around them by consecrating domestic rituals with sacred symbolisms. While painting, women usually draw their inspiration from various religious and folklore themes. Themes from the *Ramayana* and *Mahabharata*, various manifestations of the Mother Goddess, the *Ardhanarisvara* concept and other popular representations of Hindu deities, as also scenes from day-to-day life mostly comprise the themes and subject matter of the paintings. However, gradually, new changes and developments have been introduced in this art form also. Secular themes, such as such as environmental pollution, feminism, have been incorporated into the domain of Madhubani paintings. It is, therefore, said that Madhubani painting is no longer confined to being a folk art but has rather transformed itself into a fine art.

The *Visnudharmottara* stated that an artist or a painter should be well acquainted with literature, music and dance. The woman Mithila painter however possessed none of these attributes except singing the songs of Vidyapati and other Maithili folk songs which cannot be termed as 'classical music'. The woman painter of Mithila is indeed an enigma as she does not fit into the definition of the qualities and attributes of a painter as given in our classical works on art.

The woman-painter of Mithila was however, well-versed in line-drawing (a commendable quality according to the *Visnudharmottara*), drawing patterns and designs of the *aripana* (floor painting) which was passed on through generations by women. The Mughal, Kangra and Rajasthani styles have not influenced the Madhubani Paintings which is the creation of these women reflecting amazing beauty, virility and novelty.

These natural artists followed no set principles and instructions from art books, and were rather led and inspired by their own ideas and imagination. Since women were an integral aspect of domestic rituals they were able to obtain mastery in this art by means of traditions and legacy. The choice of colours and subject reflects the finesse of these artists. They created a magical effect with their artistic creations while providing them with aesthetic satisfaction too.

Initially, these paintings were made in Madhubani and its neighbouring villages by women as traditional murals usually on the walls, floors and outside of huts. Painting is done by artists or painters in three ways: wall painting (*bhitti chitra*), canvas painting (*pata chitra*) and floor-painting (*aripana*). Nowadays, these paintings are mostly made on paper and fabric.

Though there were many occasions on which these paintings were made, but it was more prevalent during socio-religious festivities as the birth of a child, various *samskaras* such as the *yagyopavita* (sacred-thread ceremony), *vivaha* (marriage) ceremonies and *pujas*.

Since time immemorial, these paintings have been made on the walls of houses on ceremonial occasions. The paintings known as *kohabar* were more elaborate and made during the ceremonies of marriage. *Kohabar* is an elaborate painting on the walls of the *kohabar ghar* (wedding chamber) where the bride and bridegroom spend their first four nights after the wedding ceremony. The walls of the room are painted with stories and legends from the folklore and mythology.

The characteristic attributes of Madhubani paintings are:

- Use of bright natural colours.
- Elongated stylized figures.
- A double-line border with ornate flower patterns or simple geometric patterns.
- Figures of deities or humans as well as animals and birds.
- The faces of figures have large bulging eyes and sharp nose.

Some of the expertise associated with Indian miniature paintings like juxtapositioning human figures, birds and animals along with lofty figures in order to create the impression of vastness and space can be discerned in these paintings.

Madhubani paintings are an expression of the everyday experiences and beliefs of these women artists. The features of beauty, simplicity and symbolism bind the paintings in a common bond. The paintings reflect the elements of the human and animal world, along with an understanding of spiritual beliefs. They reflect on the feelings of joys, sorrows and the mysteries related to nature and society. The symbols used by the artists have specific connotations as fish symbolizes fertility, good luck, peacocks are associated with love and religion, serpents are divine protectors. The paintings characterized by the vibrant use of colours, along with the traditional geometric designs and underlying symbolism, supporting the main theme have succeeded in carving out a niche for themselves at the international level.

According to Burke (1978) culture is "a system of shared meanings, attitudes and values and the symbolic forms....in which they are expressed and embodied." But it is also pertinent to note that culture is a multi-faceted concept and there is variation of culture according to diverse social groups. There exists a dichotomy between the cultural traditions characterized as 'elite culture' and 'popular culture' or using E.P. Thompson's phraseology between 'patrician' and 'plebian' cultures.

Over a period of time, various forms of expression can be discerned in the paintings practiced by the women, depending on their social background, besides other factors. The styles can be classified as *geru*, *kachni*, *bharni*, *gobar* and *godana*. The 'spiritual' form generally practiced by the upper-caste women and the 'secular' form usually by the lower-caste women are other parameters of differentiations in these paintings.

The *bharni* style is characterized by the use of bright colours with minimal use of lines, while the *kachni* style is marked by beautiful patterns along with the intricate use of lines. The *geru* style meanwhile has a close association with the folk-art tradition. The characteristic features of this style include a lack of ornamentation along with a prominent black line. The *Harijan* paintings are broadly categorised into two styles *gobar* or cowdung painting and *godana* or tattoo painting. The former is attributed to *Chamar* artists and the latter to artists of the *Dusadh* community.

The colours are made by women from natural sources. The women artists use a wonderful range of natural hues derived from flowers, bark, clay, berries etc. Initially homemade colours were made from plant extracts like henna leaves, flowers, *neem* etc. Red and green are used in abundance in the Madhubani paintings. Flowers are crushed and mixed with flaxseed oil to make bright colours. Scarlet and red colour is obtained from the *kusum* blossom, yellow from turmeric, soft gold from a compound of banana leaf juice, milk and lime. The earth colours are made from the soil around the villages. They make black from lamp black and soot, white from powdered rice. These natural colours are mixed with resin derived from banana leaves and gum in order to bind the paint to the medium. Thin twigs from trees as *babool* and others are tied with strings to make brushes.

Usually two kinds of brushes were used- one for filling in minute details made of bamboo twigs, and the other for filling in spaces made by attaching a piece of cloth to the twig. Though home-made paints were cheap, it was quite time-consuming; and was not able to meet the requirements. The solution was found in turning to synthetic colours and brushes which were available in plenty in the market. Now synthetic powdered colour is used which is then mixed with goat's milk.

DISCOVERY OF MADHUBANI PAINTINGS TO THE OUTSIDE WORLD

The world of Madhubani paintings was unknown to the outside world till about the 1930s. It was only post the natural calamity of earthquake which struck the district of Darbhanga in Bihar in 1934, that the then Sub-Divisional officer William J. Archer discovered the world of Madhubani paintings and looked upon these paintings as art pieces. In 1949 he wrote an article in the journal *Marg* about the tradition of Madhubani painting.

This art was also popularized to a great extent due to the efforts of Pupul Jayakar, a cultural activist and writer, who is well-known for her efforts for the revival of traditional arts and crafts as well as handlooms in post-Independence India. As Chairperson of the All India Handicrafts Board she played an instrumental role in the revival of Madhubani painting.

The agricultural economy of the region was crippled due to the drought in 1966-1968. In order to provide relief to the people of the region, an initiative was taken by Pupul Jayakar who sent Mr. Bhaskar Kulkarni, a Mumbai-based artist to Mithila in order to persuade the women to replicate their paintings on paper which would ensure an income to them for their survival.

During the 1970s many foreign art historians, curators, art collectors and promoters like Erika Moser, Yves Vacquard, Tokio Hosegawa and others made a lot of effort in bringing Madhubani painting to the limelight. Yves Vacquard, a French novelist and journalist conducted research on Mithila paintings, based on which he wrote a book and also produced a film "The Women Painters of Mithila". In the 1990's Japan also depicted an avid interest in Madhubani paintings primarily due to the efforts made by Tokio Hosegawa, who even set up the Mithila Museum in Tokamachi where regular exhibitions of Madhubani paintings are held.

Other organisations like Sewa Mithila have taken an endeavour to provide the artists of the region with a regular source of income by means of sales and exhibitions to curators and art galleries.

Shri Upendra Maharathi, an artist from Orissa also worked extensively for the revival and popularisation of this art form. Subsequently the Bihar State Cottage Industries and Handicrafts Board was formed which supported the artists and helped them in the sale of their products. This beautiful art form is indebted greatly to the efforts made by individuals like Pupul Jayakar, Mr. Bhaskar Kulkarni, Sri Upendra Maharathi, Raymond Lee Owens etc. who helped popularise it and attain international recognition.

The present form of Madhubani paintings is a culmination of the wall paintings, floor paintings onto paper. This experiment was undertaken in about the 1960s in order to create job opportunities for women who were faced with a terrible famine. In this transition to paper the efforts of the All India Handicrafts Board proved to be very fruitful.

Women Painters of Mithila

SOME EMINENT WOMEN ARTISTS

This enterprise to translate the art from walls, floors and other creative forms to paper or canvas proved to be very successful with enormous consequences for the region. It has brought income into a deeply impoverished part of Bihar; it has provided a source of income to women who previously had none, especially women of high caste; it raised a cultural product of women in a highly patriarchal society to national and international esteem; it empowered women by giving widows a means of independence and wives a source of prestige. It drew foreigners interested in culture to a part of Bihar that had scarcely seen a European since the British departed; simultaneously it detached the art from its dense ritual meanings by catering to the tastes of foreign buyers with limited curiosity about its significance; and it turned a handful of women artists into international celebrities.

These exotic paintings have in fact taken the world by storm. Leaving aside a few women artists like Jagdamba Devi, Sita Devi, Ganga Devi and others we have very little information of the other hundreds of talented women who bloom like wild flowers and fade off unseen, unheard and unsung leaving behind only their fragrance for posterity. These anonymous women artists have brought have brought fame and glory to the land of Mithila by means of their immortal artistic creations.

Madhubani paintings was appreciated and officially recognized in about 1970 when Jagdamba Devi from village Jitwarpur near Madhubani got the *Padma Shri* from the President of India in 1975. Sita Devi received the *Padma Shri* in 1981. She was also awarded the *Bharat Ratna* in 1984 and *Shilp Guru* in 2006.

Mahasundari Devi was an accomplished artist who received state and national awards. She received the *Padma Shri* from the Government of India in 2011 for her contributions in the domain of art. She was regarded as a 'living legend' in the art of painting. She also founded a co-operative society called Mithila Hastashilp Kalakar Audyogki Sahyog Samiti which looked into the development of handicrafts and artists.

Ganga Devi's work is a manifestation of the transition of an artist from traditional art to her response to a changed scenario in the world. The wide range of paintings made by her ranging from the Cycle of Life to the *Ramayana* series are a reflection of her artistic abilities. These paintings are a reflection of her evolution from a rural artist to her venturing out to a new pictorial vocabulary portraying new experiences of the modern-day world. The credit for popularising this art form goes to women artists like Jagdamba Devi, Sita Devi who have indeed done a creditable job in popularising these paintings by means of new colour combinations and designs.

Participation in national and international fairs, exhibitions, private commissions were instrumental in bringing prosperity to these artists. Some of the women have been able to improve the standard of living for themselves and their families in this predominantly poor region. These women have been able to market their traditional designs and carve out a market for their product both in India and abroad.

For women Mithila artists the elevation of their ritualistic activities to the status of an art also enhanced their social status and prestige. It also enabled them to gain recognition and respect in the outside world. Their paintings and art were looked upon as *kulin* art or high art. Madhubani paintings have great potential in the international market due to its authenticity and traditional aesthetic sensibility. Folk art conveys a sense of cultural identity by conveying the collective values of the community and a sense of aesthetics. In Mithila art we can appreciate the perfect blend of beauty, divinity and universality.

According to Choudhary (1976) 'Thus these wall paintings have an exquisite simplicity and irresistible attraction. The variety and inventiveness make them perhaps the most sophisticated and elegant of all popular paintings in India."

With the recognition received for the paintings from the world over, it has led to an enhancement in status of these women artists. According to Jain (1980) they have been transformed from the "dependent partner" into a vital contributor to family income. This fact alone has endowed the women with a certain distinction and esteem." Devaki Jain substantiated her arguments about the empowerment of women drawing examples from the lives of women like Sita Devi, Mahasundari Devi, Ganga Devi, Baua Devi etc.

COMMODIFICATION OF ART

These exotic paintings have taken the world by storm. Buoyed by promotion through national and state awards, exhibitions, cultural fairs etc., these paintings received appreciation from multifarious quarters and achieved national and international recognition. While on the one hand these paintings have left an indelible imprint in the world of art, finding place of eminence in art galleries abroad, portals of five-star hotels, walls of railway platforms to the drawing rooms of the elite etc. the genre of Madhubani paintings have also spilled over into the world of fashion, saris, material etc. These paintings have revolutionized the world of painting and carved out a niche for themselves in the world of fashion.

Madhubani literally meaning 'forest of honey' gradually became famous for the commercial reproductions of this art. The upper and middle classes, art connoisseurs and the gallery owners –all encouraged this vibrant art tradition, leading to the commercial reproductions and growth of private trade involving these paintings.

This beautiful art form and its painters is now faced with a multitude of problems-such as mass-produced imitations, sold at throwaway prices to ignorant customers. The artists are being deprived of their dues, simultaneously there has been a decline in the artistic value and authenticity of the traditional forms and styles of paintings. Modern art is in quest of new directions, techniques and themes which in turn has made the newer artists quite indifferent to the traditional styles of art forms. The use of traditional folk-stories as themes is also not considered to be a necessity either. Anything which vaguely resembles Madhubani paintings sells-this appears to be the consideration. As the noted Mithila artist Lalita Devi stated, "The traditional themes of Mithila are now broken up into fragments to make it more sellable. Those pieces don't make any sense, no stories in them, meanings are lost, but they still sell."

An alarming development is the fact that a number of artists prefer to become middlemen as they can earn more by selling the works of other artists at a commission rather than investing their own time and energy in creating these works of art. Other changes include the use of pencils and artificial colours in place of the traditional materials.

The roots of the problem of middlemen can be traced back to the drought of 1966 which brought a lot of sufferings to the people of Bihar. In order to facilitate the people to earn extra money, the Government allowed the commercialization of the art. Taking advantage of the relaxation in rules, the middlemen started making profit out of the scheme, a trend from which there was no going back. The artists were encouraged to paint not in their traditional styles, but rather to create 'bulk-quantity' art as instructed by the middlemen. The artists who got less payment for their work took on more orders to meet their needs; hence the result was production of inferior quality of paintings. The absence of a proper system of monitoring, grading, pricing and marketing also helped the middlemen. This was further accelerated by some organizations trying to create a new market based on mass-production of the paintings, selling it in the name of contemporary art. The cumulative effect of all these developments was the loss of a great art-heritage in the process of commercialization. Commenting on the dismal state of affairs, Gauri Mishra, the founder of an NGO Sewa Mithila stated that 'Preserving the traditional themes is the next big challenge for today's era."

To curb this alarming situation, efforts have been made by various organizations like Sewa Mithila with the objective of reviving the traditional folk-art of Mithila.

The demands of commercialization have put a lot of pressure on women artists to change their traditional styles and motifs. Moreover, barring a miniscule number of artists, economically the plight of the vast majority of these painters has remained quite miserable. Unfortunately, these painters have not received adequate protection from the Government and are thus forced to sell their artistic pieces for a pittance while huge profit is earned by the middlemen who obtain contracts from national and international agencies.

When the piece is displayed on a museum wall, a whole new cultural meaning is given to it. The work of art has been transformed into a very expensive commodity and is now the object of elegant connoisseurship and auction; it has got a new market and respect. The work of art as well as the artist has undergone a transformation in the entire process of commodification. An object of aesthetic and ritual value has been given a price and produced for sale; it has even achieved the status of an expensive aesthetic art object.

The commodification of Madhubani paintings and their mass production keeping in tune with the demands of the market and elite has resulted in the corrosion of this pristine art form in form and content. The meaning and dimensions of traditional art change when local forms are commercialized and brought into the international art market. According to Fergusson (1990) the constant delivery of novelty to the art world is part of a global process in which the vital cultures of socially subordinated groups are utilized for newer ideas to energize the art world based on the circulation of commodities and ideas.

The commodification and commercialization of traditional art forms has caused much alarm to the anthropologists, art and museum gallery curators, art historians and others who are sensitive to the cultural origins of these art forms and are empathetic to the reputation and feeling as well as economic deprivation of the women artists who produce them.

However, economically the plight of the majority of women painters is quite miserable. It is imperative that a co-operation of the artists is formed in order to look into their needs and to maintain the dignity and purity of this art form. Simultaneously while safeguarding this glorious tradition it is also necessary to diversify the uses of this art form and further expand its potentialities.

MARGINALISATION OF WOMEN

Marginalization has often been described as a social process whereby people are relegated to the fringes or 'margins 'of society. It restricts persons from enjoying access to resources, opportunities rights, privileges that are available to others. In general, women as a 'category' or 'group' in contrast to men have always remained relegated to the margins of society as they face all kinds of discrimination in society. The experiences of these marginalized women remain invisible and their objective remains unseen.

In Mithila's history, women's voices have largely been marginalized by the dominant and regressive patriarchal forces. The Maithils are patrilineal and women hardly enjoy any power or control over their lives and decision-making. Hence it is indeed ironical that the fame of women has surpassed that of men, for Mithila art is now known throughout the world. In Mithila's history women's voices have been marginalized by male writers and glimpses of it can be discerned only in women's folk-songs, rituals and traditions. The iniquitous traditions sustaining marginalization of women can be discerned even in the domain of Mithila art. The contribution of women to the protection and maintenance of cultural heritage is not given due recognition. Leaving aside a few women artists like Jagdamba Devi, Sita Devi, Ganga Devi, Mahasundari Devi, there has been little appreciation and recognition of the other hundreds of anonymous women artists who have brought fame and glory to the land of Mithila by means of their paintings which are now known throughout the world. It is indeed creditable for the women of Mithila that they have been able to carve out a space for themselves amidst the patriarchal set-up of society.

These paintings provide a glimpse into women's socio-cultural perspectives, moral frameworks and projection of the world around them. They are a reflection of the attempts of these women to carve out an identity for themselves in the predominantly patriarchal set-up. It is also a manifestation of the relations between the male/female in terms of the empowered and disempowered.

For these women artists the paintings are an expression of their artistic abilities and are intrinsic to their survival. It is important to realise the worth and potential of these women artists who are the chief creators and custodians of this traditional art form. These women artists are undermined by the patriarchal social structures of the community and family and also by the market that expropriates traditional knowledge and cultural expressions. It is pertinent to keep in mind the multiple layers of exploitation that women have to undergo on various fronts –the family, community and market which prevent the women from claiming their social, economic and cultural rights.

There are various factors which act as impediments in claiming material returns for the cultural creativity of women. With the opening up of the international market, the local artists have been subjected to exploitation. The painters do not receive adequate protection from the Government and are thus forced to sell their artistic pieces for a pittance. The renowned women painters like Jagdamba Devi, Mahasundari Devi and others like them literally lived from hand to mouth though their artistic pieces are sold at very lucrative prices in the cities and abroad. The benefits of the attractive prices are not being made available to these women as not all painters can get a good price for their product except for a few established names. The women are also not paid in due consideration of the time and efforts that they put in. For instance a *tussar* sari sells for Rs. 6,000-10,000 in the market outside while the artist is paid a paltry sum of Rs. 800 for 7-8 days of hard work.

The people of this region are confronted with a multitude of problems including poverty, illiteracy, poor infrastructure, apathy of the Government. Madhubani paintings remain the primary source of employment for the people of this region especially the women. The demands of commercialization have put a lot of pressure on women to change their traditional styles, motifs and meanings.

The artists also suffer on account of lack of proper space for work and luminosity. The place of work mostly has to be re-arranged within the house itself after the completion of the woman's household chores which is not properly illuminated. There is also lack of a proper storage place for the colours, paper, tools and finished paintings etc.

The government often prefers to support artists indirectly through NGOs and intermediaries. Many of the erstwhile painters have established NGOs claiming to help other artists. These NGOs are provided with a lot of funds by the government agencies to execute various programmes and organise market events. These NGOs in turn exploit the poor and talented artists as cheap skilled workers and sell their product at a premium price without sharing the profit with the artist. This is detrimental to the morale and efforts of these artists who are deprived of their due rights and price.

The intermediaries obtain contracts from national and international agencies for the artists. There exists no collective forum amongst the artists which would help them in negotiation and sale of their product which in turn is exploited by the intermediaries to their advantage. The formation of a collective forum would help the artists in negotiating for a better price for their product.

SUGGESTIONS

There is a need to preserve this priceless heritage of folk-art, and the means of livelihood of gifted artists. The future of this irreplaceable tradition as well as the artists can be safeguarded by the combined efforts of the Maithil people distributed globally, multifarious agencies including individuals, organizations, the Government and society at large. It is imperative to preserve this art form for posterity in its authentic form and content and make it financially viable to continue this great art form.

Though the Government of India and other agencies are making efforts and supporting the talented artists by arranging exhibitions, skill enhancement training and workshops, helping artists to market their paintings, providing incentives, loans and awards to artists for their work, more sustained efforts need to be taken in this direction. Poor implementation mechanisms along with a lack of awareness are obstacles in the path of empowerment of women. More significantly the concept of empowerment of women is regarded as a western hegemonizing concept which has little relevance in the Indian context; a perception which needs to be addressed and rectified.

There is a need for establishing an effective institutional framework accompanied with widespread societal change which is required if traditional artists like the women painters of Mithila are to be given meaningful protection and granted their due rights. The need of the hour is to set up an autonomous institution with members drawn from diverse sources as art experts, women's right activists, government and bureaucracy to draw up a plan with a woman-centric focus in order to protect their rights.

A group of art promoters, intellectuals, volunteers need to work together to preserve their cultural heritage. A step in this direction could also be the setting up of a museum representing the history and current scenario of Madhubani paintings. The museum could also function as a place where the artists could assemble, paint and display their skills. Gift shops could also be opened in the museum to generate funds where the artist could directly sell their paintings and other art objects. This could also serve as an additional platform where the artists could sell their work.

There could also be a research team of the museum which would focus on collecting, documenting and archiving the information as well as the paintings. In this way the proposed museum on Madhubani paintings by means of the collective efforts of the Maithil community, intellectuals, Government agencies etc. would help to safeguard the traditional ethos of the painting and be a step forward in preserving this beautiful art-form.

Guaranteeing the social and economic rights of women is imperative for the survival and growth of traditional artisan communities like the women painters of Mithila. The future of this art has to be made secure; the artists need to be given full employment and also a good price for their work. It is also necessary that a co-operative body of the artists, duly supported by the Government, is formed in order to look into their financial needs and safeguard their interests as also to maintain the dignity and purity of this art form. There is also a pressing need for vigilance on the cultural front in order to sustain this glorious tradition of art.

Paying tribute to the women painters of Mithila; Hosegawa, a Japanese art –connoisseur, having one of the largest collections of Mithila paintings in the world and even a museum of his own in Osaka has stated these women painters are 'the most spiritual beings' that he has met.' 'They can summon the gods to their paintings, draw spiritual power and bid farewell through prayer'. These talented women have made invaluable contributions to the world of Madhubani paintings with respect to its evolution, maturity, styles, techniques and innovations and in the process have gained world-wide recognition. In spite of economic deprivations these women decorate their homes, walls, enclosures on every socio-religious occasion with beautiful paintings, a fact for which they really need to be appreciated.

The experiences of these marginalized women remain invisible and their objective remains unseen. The women therefore need to locate the space for contest, to utilize it in order to resist and carve out a better place for themselves. Last but not the least, it is imperative that the women artists of Mithila should themselves play a leading role in utilizing, to the extent possible, the existing marginal space to assert their claims and contest for their rights. These paintings are not mere paintings but rather they are an anthology of an entire culture. There is still a lot to be said about women's art and eventually the women artists will say it.

REFERENCES

Anand Mulk Raj. (1984). *Madhubani Painting*. New Delhi: Publications Division.

Archer, W. G. (1949). Maithil Painting. *Marg*, *3*(3), 24–33.

Heinz, B. C. (2006). Documenting the Image in Mithila Art. *Visual Anthropology Review*, *22*(2), 5–33. doi:10.1525/var.2006.22.2.5

Peter, B. (1978). *Popular Culture in Early Modern Europe*. London: Academic Press.

Choudhary, R. K. (1976). *Mithila in the Age of Vidyapati*. Varanasi.

Ray, R. (2012, October 5). Bonding With Roots to Revive Madhubani Folk Art. *New Global Indian*.

Devaki, J. (1980). Women's Quest For Power: Five Indian Case Studies. Academic Press.

Jyotindra. (1997). *Ganga Devi: Tradition and Expression in Mithila Painting*. Academic Press.

Pupul, J. (1971). Paintings of Mithila. *The Times of India*.

Mathur, J. C. (1966). The Domestic Arts Of Mithila. *Marg*, *20*(1), 43–55.

Rekha, N. (2004). *Art and Assertion of Identity: Women and Madhubani Paintings* (Unpublished Ph.D. Dissertation). Patna University.

Rekha. (2010). From Folk Art to Fine Art: Changing Paradigms in the Historiography of Maithil Painting. *Journal of Art Historiography*, 2.

Upendra, T. (1982). *Madhubani Painting*. New Delhi: Academic Press.

Thompson, E. P. (1974). Patrician Society, Plebian Culture. *Journal of Social History*, 7, 395.

Vegetal colours on paper, depicting the Rama-Sita marriage by *Padma Shri* Jagdamba Devi

Kohbar, by the legendary *Padma Shri* Sita Devi

Ardhanarisvara by Sita Devi

Celestial Union by Sita Devi

Untitled by Baua Devi

DeviMahasundari

Chapter 24
Development Interventions and Masculinity in Transition:
A Study Among Marma Men Living in Bandarban Sadar in Chittagong Hill Tracts

Noorie Safa
Asian Institute of Technology, Thailand

ABSTRACT

Intent of the study was to trace the shifts in masculinities among three generation's indigenous Marma men due to their increased affiliation with development interventions and its impact on gender relationship in Marma community. Following qualitative methodology, total 28 in-depth interviews and 10 focus group discussions were carried out at Bandarban Sadar, Tigerpara and Balaghata areas. Study covered 70 Marma men of three different generations, where age ranged from 13 to 60 years above. It reflected that to keep pace with modernization or to fill up increased gap with Bengali settlers, indigenous men are moving from primitive non hegemonic order to hegemonic order as existing situation is forcing them to grow up with competitive mind for survival purpose. Gigantic gap among men of three generations, in terms of their perception on what it ought to be a 'real man' signifies how stereotypical gender norms, values, practices are getting engrossed in indigenous Marma communities which is putting serious impact in gender relationships by leaving indigenous women in vulnerable state.

INTRODUCTION

The study stems from the need of understanding the impact of development interventions on the construction of masculinities in three generations indigenous Marma men and its impact on gender relationship in the studied community. With a view to generating in-depth understanding regarding the fact, the paper has been divided in four broader sections. First section elaborately focused on background, justification, objective and methodology of the study. Second and third sections endeavored to capture how perception

DOI: 10.4018/978-1-5225-3018-3.ch024

concerning development interventions and conception regarding 'real men' varies from one generation to another. With regard to 'real man' concept, the study focused on participant's imaginary picture of man who they idealize as the superlative characteristic of man. Finally the fourth section comes up with the interconnection between development intervention and masculinities to map out how transitional masculinities impact on gender relationship in the studied area.

BACKGROUND OF THE STUDY

Development is not a new phenomenon in the Chittagong Hill Tracts as from British period miniature interventions took place, but the region became a site of wide range of development activities after the liberation war. Erstwhile, indigenous people over this area were solely engaged in traditional way of living which kept them completely reliant on subsistence based economy. During that period; their livelihood utterly relied on shifting slash and burn cultivation which is traditionally called *jum*. Afterwards in colonial era and Pakistan period-introduction of private ownership, nationalization of land, introduction of reserved forest, commercial extraction of timber, increased linkage with low land, improved road networks and industrial use of resources has result in severe depletion of forest resources. Deforestation and land degradation had adversely affected the livelihood of the indigenous people in CHT, as most of them were solely depended on agriculture. After liberation, Bangladesh Government sponsored in-migration of people from some of the heavily populated plains districts during the late 1970s and early 1980s. About 250,000 in-migrants (Bengalis from neighboring plains districts) were encouraged to settle during this period and they were primarily located on land that was already occupied or claimed by the indigenous residents. According to AmenaMohsin, in a resource poor and agrarian country ownership of land is associated with the power structure of the community. In the CHT the indigenous people have been alienated from their land through a state sponsored project of settlement of Bengalis into the hill (Mohsin, 2000:66). Beside Bengali settlement programs state sponsored other initiatives like-afforestation programme, militarization and commercial use of land, intensified telecommunication, road construction, electrification, and overall infrastructural facilities put severe impact on the livelihood pattern of Indigenous people. Moreover, number of Bengali settlers got higher due to infrastructural advancement which in result promoted multiculturalism in this area. The rise of Bengali population in the CHT after liberation has dramatically changed the ratio of indigenous communities and Bengalis. According to Asian Indigenous people's pact at the time of independence of India and Pakistan, the total population of CHT was only 247,053. Out of this number, only 2.5per cent were Bengali (including 1.5 percent of whom were Bengali Muslims). But after 20 years of the Pakistan period and 31 years of the Bangladesh period, the demography of CHT has significantly changed especially after the systematic illegal settlement of Bengali Muslims by the successive governments. (AIPP,2007). According to the provisional census report of 2001, the total population of the CHT was 1,342,740 (including ethnic Bengali and settlers). Of this number, 736,682 were Jumma (who are less than 0.5per cent of the population of the country) and 606,058 were Bengali.

Although the size of indigenous people in the CHT in 2001 was still larger than Bengali population, they become marginal in the city centers and most of the business has gone under the control of the Bengalis. It is to be noted that, Bengali settlers tend to depend on surplus economy which has directed them to get engage with commercial use of land which is much related to capitalist thought. Again, the life style of people from low land background is way different than the life style of indigenous people in CHT. The values and practices that Bengalis have brought in CHT are contrary to that of indigenous people.Again, from generation people of low land were not dependent on nature like indigenous people. Consequently, when Bengali settlers got in CHT, they became more attracted to the commercial use of land as they are not used to traditional use of resources. According to Phillip Gain Bengali settlers not only put pressure on land but also caused massive deforestation and ecological problem (Gain,2000:4). This capital reliance among Bengali settlers assist them to accumulate wealth within a very short period of time than people those tend to hold on tight with traditional way of life, more precisely those depend on subsistence based economy.

So, it is to be noted that the superior tag of settlers as 'Bengali' and their massive reliance on profit oriented surplus economy have made them sturdy, which in long run assisting them to get a strong grip in existing social, economical and political setting. Consequently this group of people has been grabbing outcomes of development more easily and intensively than indigenous people. Such situation is broadening gap between Indigenous people and Bengali settlers, as development initiatives those are directing towards CHT have been made indigenous people more marginalized. To keep pace with the wave of modernization or for filling up increased gap with Bengali settlers, many indigenous people may have moved on from their primitive way of living as the existing situation is constantly forcing them to grow up with competitive mind for survival purpose. So a shift in masculine attributes might have risen in such condition in CHT which should have brought under study for assuming future social, economic and political picture of CHT.

Justification of the Study

For the time being indigenous people become the victim of exploitation by state sponsored various initiatives, militarization and by Bengali settlers .The veracity of this statement is evident from various existing literatures those constantly focus on increased conflict driven situation between Bengali and indigenous people in CHT. Nevertheless, it is to mention negligible number of literatures is found relating how development interventions has increased gap between Bengali settlers and indigenous people. It is unfortunate but true that none of existing literatures have precisely mentioned how the increased gap is constantly keeping impact on reshaping attributes of masculinity among indigenous men in CHT.

According to Phillip Gain, inhabitants of CHT have undergone enormous assault and sufferings due to ill conceived development initiatives and human greed. The first large scale industrial development project that hit the CHT was the Pakistani national pride 'Karnaphuli Paper Mill' financed by external resources including World Bank Loan of US 4.2 million (Arens 1997:49 in Bahumik et ak,eds).The Karnaphuli Paper Mill came into production in 1953.Construction of the Kranaphuli Paper mill created 10,000 jobs but the hill people got only around 5% of them mainly in the lower rank (Arens 1997:49 in Bhawmil et al,eds).The same story was repeated in the case of Karnaphuli Rayon Mill,which was also constructed in 1966 with foreign funds. The Betbunia Satellite station constructed with the Canadian funds brought its benefits to the elite who could effort television and long distance telephone and to the army (Gain, 2000:33) Again, just after few years of the construction of Karnaphuli Paper Mill, the Pakistani symbol of development, and the Kaptai hydroelectric project was put into operation. Started in 1959 the US $ 100 million project was completed in 1963(van schendel et al 2000:203).The project created a 650 square kilometer upstream reservoir, submerged 40% of the most productive valley land of the CHT, many villagers and forests. It displaced around 100,000 people who constituted one quarter of the regions population. With this outright effects the project generated discontent and anger among the indigenous peoples in the CHT(Gain,2000:33).Although the Kaptai dam is still a significant source of electric power, the indigenous hill people did not benefit much from the project. According to forestall survey before the dam was built, the tribal people had attained a reasonably satisfactory way of life adequately adjusted to the limitations imposed by the physical environment (Anti-slavery society 1984:36)

After independence no significant development plan was initiated until the time of general zia who declared in 1976 that the problems of CHT originated from underdevelopment. He founded the CHT Development Board (CHTDB) in 1976 by an ordinance to solve the CHT problems through large scale development programmes. The major development interventions in the CHT since then were designed, managed or observed by the CHT Development Board (CHTDB). Although 60 percent of its board was composed of hill people, the chiefs (Rajas) and other prominent ethnic members of the CHTDB Board would not attend the board meetings for many years before the peace accord signed in December 1997. This was a protest against its undemocratic structure.

At the time of the Kaptai Dam construction, the Pakistan Government announced its intention to open up the area for economic development and encouraged poor Bengali families to settle there. This policy was even more vigorously pursued by the Bangladesh Government after independence in 1971(amnesty international,2000).Later in 1979,a BD government programme, which relocated hundreds of thousands of poor Bengalis into the hill tracts put additional stress on the situation and reduced the tribal people to minority status within the region(khan,1994).The government settlement programmes increased the number of Bengali inhabitants in the CHT from 3% of regions total population in 1947 to about 50% in 1997(US department of state, 1998).The settlers were attracted by the then Government scheme to provide five acres of hilly land, four acres of mixed forest land and 2.5 acres of cropped land for each newly settled Bengali family(Haque,2001).The people were also settled with the help of the army and army started building bases in the hill tracts. Various land grabbing activities by settlers were also taken place in CHT. Consequently, these caused outnumbering of the Jummas and evicted thousands of individual indigenous people from their ancestral lands.

The CHTDB has implemented projects and programmes for construction of roads, telecommunication, electrification and moving hill people into the model or 'cluster' villages. Although the stated goal of the CHTDB is the welfare of hill people, in reality, most villagers in the hills do not have telephones and electricity. Although the roads have been beneficial for transporting products to markets, they have first been very for fast military movements. Roads expended the mobility of the military to combat the shanty bahini and help the businessmen most of whom were Bengalis (Gain, 2000:34). The land hungry Bengalis want the land which has been the crux of the turmoil in the CHT. The rural people specially the ethnic people have limited access to service and jobs. Day laboring and small business are dominant among the Bengali people in contrast to agricultural practices among the ethnic people. (Gain, 2000:13)

The ethnic people have witnessed how the Bengalis specially the settlers have pushed them out of their land for some decades-by force and tricks. The Bengalis have also taken control of most of the business opportunities in the towns and Thana and headquarters. All those factors –especially competition for land and business opportunities contribute to the strained relationship between the Bengalis and ethnic groups. The insurgency war for two and half decades further ruined the mutual trust between the ethnic groups and Bengalis and complicated the politics of resources.(Gain,2000:11)The CHT economy is almost entirely dependent on land. In the old days there was little competition for land in CHT. But these days' tension and competition between indigenous and Bengali settlers get a hazardous form.

According to these mentioned literatures it becomes clear that Bengali settles are found to be way privileged by numerous developmental interventions than indigenous people, which in long runcreated severe gap between these two groups. Within such social hierarchy of power, it is likely that the powerful group will dominate the less powerful and at the expense of later, the powerful will attempt to gain more stabilized social position. To keep pace with the frequent social change as well as with increased Bengali settlers, a shift in masculinities could have encountered among indigenous men which is absent from all of earlier works. So, considering existing challenging perspective of indigenous people of CHT, it is highly justifiable to conduct a study to assess how transitional mode of masculinities gets operated among them.

STUDY OBJECTIVES

Justification of the study stems from the need of understanding the impact of development interventions on the construction of masculinities in three generations indigenous Marma men and its impact on gender relationship in the studied community. With a view to generating in-depth understanding regarding the fact, the study endeavored to capture how perception concerning development interventions and conception regarding 'real men' varies from one generation to another and then it tried to identify the interconnection between development intervention and masculinities .With regard to 'real man' concept, the study focused on participant's imaginary picture of man who they idealize as the superlative characteristic of man.

Methodology of the Study

As the purpose of the study was to locate shifts in attributes of masculinities among men living in Bandarban district, thus the study had been designed as a qualitative one. Making the study qualitative was helpful to take out the reality of the individuals of the respective area.

Both primary and secondary sources were employed to gather pertinent information. A great deal of time was spent to find out information in the online sources and printed versions of existing literatures of journals, news, research papers etc on masculinity, development interventions in CHT and its aftermath on indigenous people's lives.

After understanding conceptual issues and reviewing existing relevant literatures, the major work was to go to the ground and to collect relevant data which was likely to provide the true picture of the field.

Selection of the Study Areas

Bandarbansadar, Balaghata and Tiger point were chosen as study areas .These areas were selected for some specific reasons. Development intervention has massively taken place in 'BandarbanSadar' and access in Bandarbansadar helped to sketch out masculine attributes of indigenous men those are already in touch of modernization.Balaghata and Tiger point are bit distant from Bandarbansadar where light of modernization has not reached entirely like town areas. Conducting research in these areas helped to make a good comparison between men living in sadar area and men living in bit distant area.

Selection of the Samples of the Research

Study respondents were selected through the process of purposive sampling. The respondents were selected from BandarbanSadar, Balaghata, Tigerpoint and Shornamandir. The study was conducted among men population.

All the informants hailed from indigenous Marma group. Respondents were from different age group but belonged to similar socio-economic status (lower middle class). For this study, men from three consecutive generations were selected where the first one represents 60+ years old, second one represents 30-59 years old and third one represents 13-29 years old. The age brackets for three generations have been selected considering the historical significance of the nation. It is to mention that the birth of Bangladesh is closely intertwined with the history of Bengal and history of India sub-continent. While fixing age brackets of three mentioned generations, prime focus was given on getting three different groups where the first one would have vibrant experience with both British and Pakistan ruling period; 2nd one would have experience with Pakistan period, and with the immediate independent Bangladesh; and third one would have experience with more stabilized Independent Bangladesh.

Methods of Data Collection

The study employed both Focus Group Discussion and In-depth Interview. The primary information about the interviewees was taken from focus group discussions. Latterly, further information was gathered from the in-depth interview sessions.

Focus Group Discussions (FGDs)

Ten focus group discussions had been conducted in three different study areas. Having seven persons in each discussion from different families, the number of respondents of the focus group discussions was seventy; The groups were mixed men in different age. The respondents were selected through purposive sampling. After initiating the discussions it took some time for breaking the ice between the respondents and the researcher. Afterwards the researcher let the respondents share the views of their own. During study period, a checklist had been kept to keep the conversation on track. The focus group discussions helped the conductor of the research to get an overall view of the existing social situation, basic information about the respondents. Some common issues about the changing trend of masculine attributes were sorted out through the group discussions.

In-Depth Interviews

While conducting focus group discussion importance was given to sort out interesting and informative respondents. So, after completion of the conversation total twenty eight respondents were chosen as interviewees. The primary information about the interviewees was taken from focus group discussions. Latterly, further information was gathered from the interview sessions. The interviews were open ended so no particular questionnaires were set. Some indications were given to carry on the interviews. The interviews were person specific and in-depth. Through interviews the researcher tried to understand transition in masculine attributes by examining their perception on masculinity and various development interventions those are taking place in CHT over time.

Limitations of the Study

Due to time constraint, the study could not include indigenous women as well as Bengali population of the respectivearea. Initially language barrier was a crucial factor which was later alleviated by employing an indigenous Marma boy as interpreter. Literature on the focused area was limited which initially posed difficulties in accumulating secondary based data.

Perceiving Development: Across Three Generations

Under this broader headline, perceptions of three chronological generations with regard to development intervention getillustrated. Throughout the discussion, first generation represents aged Marmamen(60+ years old),second generation represents middle aged Marma men(30-59 years old) and the 3rd generation represents young aged Marma men(13-29 years old)

Different perceptions were found regarding development intervention among three generations which is described below-

First Generation (Old Aged Marma Men)

It is widely perceived that development initiatives are directed towards people's welfare so people are bound to take such intervention positively. But interestingly, completely negative picture was reflected in opinions of some indigenous people. Some people think that, the primitive condition of CHT was way better than that of todays. According to them previous environment in CHT helped them to generate innovative strategies for their survival purpose which is seemed by them as prerequisite for broadening someone's inner potential. During in-depth interview a respondent said-

When I was a teenager, a negligible development took place in CHT. Consequently the place where I lived was like a jungle. Such environment literally helped me as well as my siblings to grow up with an adventurous mind which had assisted us to be instant problem solver. During that time we had high attachment with natural resources so the importance of such strategies or techniques was inevitable for our survival purpose. (Bo Cho MongMarma, a 68 years old respondent)

Indigenous people are generally known as industrious and diligent because of their higher ability of getting engaged with heavy workload. But some respondents think that they are about to lose such eminence as enduring development interventions has already made them lazy. In this regard one respondent said-

I still remember that in earlier period, at a stretch we could walk miles after miles which still keeps our body fit! But at present because of contemporary NGO and government based diversified development interventions, people have learnt to follow short cut way for making profit instead of working hard. Consequently by destroying their strength level, the system is turning them into sluggish being. I am very much worried about my future generation as I am cent per cent much sure that they will not be able to reach at the age where I am now and by any chance if they reach, with such poor strength level, will not be able to move around the way I do today. (MongMarma, a 81 years old respondent)

Development Interventions and Masculinity in Transition

Though ongoing development programs have commenced many projects those are supposedly for benefiting local people, but the extent to which these projects have improved the socio economic conditions of the intended beneficiaries is open to question. Such vagueness has constructed suspicious thoughts and worries among some indigenous people as they could not came to a decision whether development interventions had benefitted them. But some respondents were too confident with the fact that they are actually being more marginalized because of such interventions instead of being privileged. One of respondents was found saying during focus group discussion –

I think projected development initiatives in CHT have been directed to make indigenous people more marginalized and you can get a clear idea about this fact if you just give a look over 'BandarbanSadar'. Nowadays this place has become a site of a wide range of development activities which has made it a place of trade and business, more precisely a place for commercial deals. By this time you must have observed that 90% population of this 'sadar' are Bengali settlers. I would suggest you to go at main market and main bazaar in Sadar and I can assure you the picture that you are going to observe will compel you to decide who the main beneficiaries of extensive development initiatives. This is none other but Bengali settlers who are blessed to occupy 95% of trades in Sadar. I think because of advantaged social, economical and political condition of Bengali settlers they are more likely to grab outcomes of development initiatives. A new comer in Bandarbansadar can never assume the actual ratio of indigenous and Bengali settlers (which accounts almost 50:50 unless make a visit in remote areas in Bandarban. Prevailing discriminatory situation has compelled indigenous people to get in remote places as they are constantly being failed to catch the fruit of development. (AungPrueMarma,a 62 years old respondent)

Some of respondents claimed that increased development intervention in CHT is promoting multiculturalism which fosters interaction between indigenous people and Bengali settlers. They think because of such interaction, indigenous people are about to lose their intrinsic nature, traditional culture, thoughts and beliefs and their simplicity. During in-depth interview one respondent said in this concern -

We would be the ultimate loser if Chittagong Hill Tracts Development Board takes more initiatives to construct broad roads in our area. Over years we have witnessed how improved communication system had encouraged Bengali settlers to have a direct access to most of hilly areas especially in sadar area. The area where I live is still underdeveloped so still today I can live with my family calmly but I am pretty sure if this area is brought under development intervention, I could not be able to stay peacefully (Ba Cho MongMarma, a 68 years old respondent)

Second Generation (Middle Aged Marma Men)

Although only afew delivered negative statements regarding development interventions, majority respondents from this group delivered neutral perception in this regard. Analyzing general perspective it comes forth neither they had welcomed nor they had denied the importance of such initiatives. During focus group discussion, a state of neutrality with regard to development interventions got visible among this generation. To get a glimpse of such condition following statement of a respondent is quoted below-

The position of mine lies in between two generations. I have experienced life with modernity as well as life without modernity. But to be very clear, none of these lifestyle was good for me as the primitive way of life tortured me physically and the present one has been torturing me psychologically (ChingThowaiMarma, a 58 years old respondent)

According to them, they are bound to accept frequent infrastructural change of the region not only for getting adjusted with the trend of modernity but also for ensuring their survival. A sense of struggle was highly noticeable throughout the entire FGD session. Some of respondents of this group agreed that modernity has both positive and negative impacts. They find it good as it has been broadening scopes to some extent and find it bad as it is facilitating the mode of competition which ultimately makes them more marginalized. This group of people is found to be worried about their future generation as their suspicious mind always strikes their inner soulwhether their future generation would be able to survive with the increased competitiveness. Driven by such survival threat, they always feel the pressure of ensuring secured life for the future generation and deep inside they believe chances are there for them to break down if cannot get the hold on power like Bengali settlers.

Third Generation (Young Aged Marma Men)

Some respondents of this group delightfully accept development intercession in CHT as they think such initiatives have made them civilized. They believed that if they were not blessed by modern facilities, their condition would be just like their ancestor who had to work whole day long by delivering highest possible physical strength yet got minimum output. According to most of respondents, such confined way did not let their ancestor make profit, and they had to depend on fate or luck at the time of facing any challenge.

During in-depth interview one respondent said-

To keep pace with this modern world the importance of development initiatives is unavoidable. I feel pity for my ancestor when I hear various stories about their uncivilized way of living. They did not even know what is going on just outside their own web. They were so tightly confined with backwardness which did not assist them to enlarge their outlook .Moreover they hardly knew about the word 'saving', so in case of dealing with any problem they had to merely depend on fate (U.S Singh,a 22 years old respondent)

Some respondents were pleased with the outcome of development as they think it helps them a lot to enlarge their outlook. They feel this broader outlook has oriented them about the importance of saving which was completely ignored by their ancestor. They also think that their increased affiliation with Bengali settlers has taught them to apply several strategies for making maximum output with minimum effort. They strongly believe that they could not grasp advanced strategies if they were not a part of this modern competitive world. During the FGD and interview sessions several times they referred to their ancestor to clarify the gradual generational change. In this regard one respondent said during in-depth interview-

Development Interventions and Masculinity in Transition

From my childhood I am habituated to see the struggling life of my parents. Their reliance on traditional shifting agriculture hardly left space to make profit. Definitely I am not going to repeat the same mistake as my parents (ProshenjitMarma, a 24 years old respondent)

He delivered an interesting reply when he was asked what he wants to be in future life. He said-

I have been so overwhelmed seeing one of my Bengali friend's father, who has made big profit by playing the role of 'mediator'. Just over mobile he makes big deal with various multinational companies. Yesterday I listened from my friend that he had made a big contract with British American Tobacco. Though I am little bit confused with his role as mediator but with no doubt he is my idol. I have tried to build up a personal relationship with him so that I can learn all of his techniques which would assist me to be an independent mediator' in my future life (ProshenjitMarma, a 24 years old respondent)

Almost all of respondents of this group think increased educational facilities have uplifted their standard of life. Furthermore they think achieved knowledge has made them conscious about their own worth which in long run helps them to build the level of confidence. Again they think the power of knowledge has made them different from any backward portion of society. According to one respondent-

I am a HSC candidate and I am the only one in my family who is literate. Definitely this distinct identity of mine has made me different from any member of my family. My parents always come to me for solving any problem instead of going to my brother who is presently working in agricultural sector and who do not have any formal education. I think it happens as I have the ability to think everything rationally am pretty sure without education I would not be able to attain such quality. (KashengshoiMarma, a 19 years old respondent)

He also added-

I have lots of Bengali friends in my school and by interacting them I have learnt pure Bengali. Having fluency over Bengali is power in order to keep pace with this modern world. Without proper interaction with Bengali people I think I would not be able to learn it as none of my family members can speak it properly (KashengshoiMarma, a 19 years old respondent)

So it becomes clear from the discussion that perception regarding development varies from one generation to another as older aged Marma men see development from negative aspect, middle aged Marma men see it from neutral perspective and young aged Marma men perceive development from positive aspect.

Construction of Masculinities: Across Three Generations

The term 'masculinity' was not familiar among the study respondents, thus they were asked to give their opinion regarding what a 'real man' should be like. By 'real man' respondents were asked to create an imaginary picture of man who they idealize as the superlative characteristic of man. In response they expressed their views differently. The concept of ideal man varied from person to person and from age to age although few commonalities were observed in every generation. I tried to reflect views of three different generations which is likely to help readers to identify sequential changes in masculinities across three generation's Marma men. Beside this, the studyalso included their perception regarding gender relationship. Throughout the discussion, first generation represents agedMarma men(60+ years old),second generation represents middle aged Marma men(30-59 years old) and the 3rd generation represents young aged Marma men(13-29 years old) .

First Generation (Old Aged Marma Men)

According to this group, a real man has to be honest, benevolent, and helpful .They believes, a person without such attributes is similar to beast. Furthermore they think real men should have strong ethical standpoint which would not let them get engage with any kind of violence. According to few aged respondents a real man should be cultural minded as well as should entails the sense of humor .They give priority over strong physical structure of male as it would help them to carry heavy work load.

I think a real man is someone who is always ready to dedicate himself for the welfare of others as such behavior undoubtedly represents the essence of humanity (MongMarma,a 80 years old respondent)

Another respondent said-

A good physical structure can make someone real men. I had a relative who was six feet high as well as had strong muscle. As a result of this he could work in field the whole day long but the most amazing part is he did not get tired consequently he could keep large influence in his family's income. He was my idol and I always dreamt to be like him (AungPrueMarma,a 62 years old respondent)

2nd Group (Middle Aged Group)

Like primitive group they also gave emphasize on strong physical structure of men. Most of respondents from this group believe that a man who can provide full financial support to his family should be considered real man.

They think taking responsibility of family members supposed to be the real duty of a man. They show bit importance over honesty or benevolence. According them, these positive behavioral attributes are required as these make any person human being, however, in spite of having these qualities, if someone fails to earn money to feed the family properly, should be considered as failure. In this regard one respondent said-

A real man is someone who is able to understand the need of his family members and can satisfy them by providing financial support (KaneiSeiMarma, a 51 years old respondent)

3rd Group (Young Generation)

According to this group, a real man is considered as someone who is likely to think everything rationally as this power helps him to construct strategic planning. They believe that for the survival purpose as well as for keeping pace with this competitive world, the importance of strategic planning cannot

Development Interventions and Masculinity in Transition

be denied. Beside this, they put emphasize on men's role as bread earner. They believe that a strategic mind can earn maximum output with a very minimum input so this is not a well structured body rather a deliberate, planned and strategic mind which make a man the real one. Like other two generations, some of them think that a real man can also possess traits like benevolence, honesty and so on as long as these do not create any hindrance towards fulfilling their desired goals. One of respondents said during in-depth interview –

A man who can cope up with this competitive world and can adapt himself with the momentum of modernity is seemed to me as real man. I think such man can hold the ability to think everything realistically. By the grace of such ability he can find the most suitable as well as the easiest way to make profit which can assist the person to perform his main duty as bread earner. Instead of focusing on well body structure a man should emphasize on building up a developed and strategic mind which can help him to be a real man (U.S Singh, a 22 years old respondent)

So the concept of masculinity is perceived by three generations differently .The preferred masculine attributes by old aged Marma men is honesty, benevolence, ethical, cultural minded, and they put emphasize on strong physical structure. According to middle aged Marma men the highest possible masculine man has the ability to provide full financial support to family members. Honesty and benevolency are seemed as secondary required attributes to them. Yet again according to young aged Marma men, preferred masculine traits are –rationality, ability to make strategic plan. They prefer mind rather than body and to them secondary required masculinity attributes are benevolence and honesty but they reject these if qualities like these create hindrance towards fulfilling desired goal. Reflected different perceptions on masculinities arelikely to create ripple effects in gender relationship. So, with a view to getting a glimpse on how transitional mode of masculinities are impacting on gender relationship, the study intended to unveil three generational perceptions regarding what ought to be the position of women in society.

The findings show that according to most of respondents of first generation, men and women are equal. They believe that men and women have the same ability to work. They denied the issue of public private dichotomy and they think by the virtue of being human being both men and women entail the same ability to work together.

In our society both men and women use to work equally, nevertheless, women are found to work harder than men to some extent

But some respondents of this group believe that there are few differences between these two groups where they mainly focused on men and women's biological differences. But most of the respondents denied the fact by referring to their women counterpart's strong energy to work both inside and outside the home. They believe core biological difference between men and women does not impact on women's energy level if they are habituated and are trained to work hard from the very early hood.

Like the first generation, respondents of second generation believe that men and women are almost equal although they put emphasize over the issue of public private dichotomy. In spite of seeing their mothers to work outside the home they want their wives to work inside the home as they believe contemporary social context cannot ensure security for women. Beside this, some respondents had emphasized on issues related to children's future as they believe women's engagement in private sphere is important for the purpose of nurturing children in order to make them ideal human being.

I want my wife to get engage with domestic sphere. In order to take proper care of my kids I think this engagement is obligatory

Some of respondents were found bit flexible as they think like men, women can also work outside the home although they think this condition is applicable only when the male member of a family cannot ensure full financial support for the welfare of all members.

However, on the contrary to members of other two generations, majority respondents of third generation believe that men and women are different as they find men as rational being and women as emotional being. They think an emotional being cannot perfectly adjust with public sphere or more precisely with the place that is full of competition. They strongly support public private dichotomy as they believe women are born to get engage in private sphere on contrary men are for public sphere.

Yet again, like the members of second generation, few respondents think women should not engage with public life as the condition of present society cannot ensure women's security. Interestingly one respondent was found whose perception regarding men women's relationship was same as group one men's perception. He said-

I think men and women have the ability to bear the same work load although in some cases women can bear more than men

Being bit interested when he was asked to share his background he told that he hailed from a very remote area in Bandarban where negligible development interventions had been carried out and where all of members of family (father, mother, grandmother, grandfather, brother, sister) work together . Just a day ago for the first time he had come at Bandarbansadar with his uncle as his father passed away a month ago. By hearing his response I realized may be it is not too far for this person to get involved in a massive transformation which would make him an ideal third generation respondent!

So a shift in gender relationship has been observed. According to first generation, men and women are equal and both of them have the same ability to get engage in same types of works. Moreover some respondents of this group think women can work more than men to some extent. They placed men and women in same position and opposed the importance of public-private dichotomy. Middle aged Marma men think women should not come out of private sphere as long as the male member of the family can provide full financial support to his family. They emphasized on the security aspect of women. Again, respondents from third generation think that women should not come out of home as they find them emotional being which they think unfriendly for keeping pace with this competitive world.

INTERCONNECTION: BETWEEN DEVELOPMENT INTERVENTION AND MASCULINITIES

The study reflected a strong interconnection between development interventions and masculinities. Considering first generation it is observable that primitive subsistence economy based way of living did not let first generation men get acquainted with the word 'saving'. Moreover, extreme reliance on simplicity literally could not help them to be up to date. Being failed to inject coping mechanism to adjust with sudden flow of modernity, they got fallen from their age long steadfast position.

However, observing first generation's inability in making savings for the future security purpose, men from second generation become much aware which grows a sense of responsibility to protect their family. But, in spite of struggling hard most of the time they got challenged due to socio economic reality, which so often creates fear and frustration among them. It becomes visible that although men from second generation believe in gender equality as like their prior generation, but in reality they cannot transform their ideology into practice considering the blooming social insecurity.

In contrast to these two generations, radical ideological shift has been observed in the third generation's participants. Backed by competitiveness, their constant thrives for getting adapted with changing socio cultural scenario indicates a sharp transition in masculinities, which is graving alarming impact in gender relationship. Unlike first two generations, third generation's attitude of considering men and women as two polar categories has reflected how power dynamics driven by patriarchy escalates hegemonic masculinities which ultimately makes powerless portion more vulnerable.

To put the whole discussion in a nutshell it can be said that amid competitive socio cultural setting, the overarching tension among Marma men for ensuring their survival ultimately results in shifting trend in masculinity followed by non hegemonic masculinity to hegemonic masculinity, more precisely to dominant form of masculinity within the gender hierarchy. Needless to mention, depending on position within the social hierarchy of power, hegemonic masculine people enact kind of practices that supports gender inequality in a given space and time. It got observable that in the studied area at intra community level gender based discrimination has been fostering alarmingly as a consequence of ongoing transitional masculinities, which in result not only creating constraints for women to realize their potential and dignity but also hindering them to participate with men the way they used to do before.

It stands to reason that, Influenced by dominant Bengali culture, if indigenous Marma community gets deviant from their robust cultural value, that would certainly be a threat for ensuring gender equality in the concerned community. Ongoing development interventions in the studied area is problematic, as the process is not only doubling gap between indigenous and Bengali setters but also putting severe negative impact in indigenous community's intrinsic moral values and practice. Addressing this concern, proper measures should be undertaken both by Government and NGO interventions and in this respect starting from project plan to implementation, gender concerns needs to be mainstreamed.

REFERENCES

AIPP. (2007). *A brief account of Human right situation of indigenous peoples in Bangladesh*. AIPP.

Connell, R. W., & Messerschmitt, J. W. (2005). Hegemonic masculinity: Rethinking the Concept. *Gender & Society*, *19*(6), 830. doi:10.1177/0891243205278639

Connell, R. W. (1987). *Gender and Power: society, the person and sexual politics*. University of California Press.

Connell, R. W. (1995). *Masculinities*. Berkeley, CA: University of California press.

Connell, R. W. (2000). *The men and the boys*. Cambridge, UK: Polity Press.

Connell, R. W. (2002). *Gender*. Cambridge, UK: Polity Press.

Connell, R. W. (2005). *Masculinities* (Vol. 1). Cambridge, UK: Polity Press.

Giddens, A. (2005). Sociology (2nd ed.). Cambridge, UK: Polity Press.

Harding, G. S. (1987). *Feminism and Methodology: social science issues Women's studies social sciences*. Indiana University Press.

Huq, M. M. (2000). *Government Institutions and Underdevelopment: A Study of the Tribal People of Chittagong Hill Tracts, Bangladesh*. Dhaka: Center for Social Studies, Dhaka University.

Mohsin, A. (1997). *The Politics of Nationalism: The Case of Chittagong Hill Tracts, Bangladesh*. Dhaka, Bangladesh: The University Press Limited.

Rasul, G., & Thapa, G. (n.d.a). *State Policies, Praxis and Land-use in the Chittagong Hill Tracts of Bangladesh*. Asian Institute of Technology.

Rasul, G., & Karki, M. (n.d.b). *Political Ecology of Degradation of Forest Common in the Chittagong Hill Tracts of Bangladesh*. Kathmundu: International Centre for Integrated Mountain Development.

Roy, R. (2000). *The Chittagong Hill Tracts: Life and Nature at Risk*. SEHD.

Compilation of References

Abbas, Q., & Hussain, U. (2008). *Globalization, Privitization and Collective Bargaining of Labour: A Time Series Analysis of Pakistan 1973- 2004. 8th Global conference on Business and Economics*, Florence, Italy.

Abbey, A. (2002). Alcohol-Related Sexual Assault: A Common Problem among College Students. *Journal of Studies on Alcohol. Supplement*, (14): 118–128. doi:10.15288/jsas.2002.s14.118 PMID:12022717

Abdel Hameid. (1998). *The attitude of university women students towards the selection of a spouse* (Unpublished Masters dissertation). Ahfad University for Women.

Abdel Rahman, W. A. (1999). *Employed Women and Domestic Responsibilities: Perceptions, Challenges and Strategies* (Unpublished Masters dissertation). Ahfad University for Women.

Abecassis, D. (1990). *Identity, Islam, and human development in rural Bangladesh* (1st ed.). Dhaka, Bangladesh: University Press.

Aboli. (2015, August 31). *Top 8 Most Influential Women in Indian Banking*. Retrieved from https://letstalkpayments.com/top-8-most-influential-women-in-indian-banking

Abramsky, T., Watts, C. H., García-Moreno, C., Devries, K., Kiss, L., Ellsberg, M., Jansen, A.H., & Heise, L. (2011). *What factors are associated with recent intimate partner violence? Findings from the WHO multi-country study on women's health and domestic violence*. Academic Press.

Abu, E. (1997). *Women in broadcasting: An African perspective in deregulation of broadcasting in Africa*. Lagos: National Broadcasting Commission.

Acholonu, C. (1995). *Motherism: The Afrocentric Alternative to Feminism*. Owerri, Nigeria: Afa Publications.

ADB. (2008). *Rleasing Women's Potential Contribution to Inclusive Economic Growth, Country gender Assesment Pakistan*. ADB.

Adebayo, F. (2011). Promoting children's right through the new media: The Nigerian experience. *Journal of Communication*, *2*(2), 57–65.

Adeleye-Fayemi, B. (2005). Creating and Sustaining Feminist Space in Africa: Local and Global Challenges. In The 21st Century' in Feminist Politics, Activism and Vision: Local and Global Challenges. London: Zed Books.

Adesina, J. (2006a). Sociology, Endogeneity and the Challenge of Transformation. *African Sociological Review*, *10*(2), 133–150.

Adesina, J. (2006b). Sociology Beyond Despair: Recovery of Nerve, Endogeneity, and Epistemic Intervention. *South African Review of Sociology*, *37*(2), 241–259. doi:10.1080/21528586.2006.10419157

Adesina, J. (2010). Re-appropriating Matrifocality: Endogeneity and African Gender Scholarship. *African Sociological Review*, *1*(14), 1–19.

Adesina, L. A. (2010). Audience perception of portrayals of women in the Nigerian home video. *JMCS: Journal of Media and Communication Studies*, *2*(9), 200–207.

Adhikari P, Kadel B, Dhungel S, Mandal A (2007). Knowledge and practice regarding menstrual hygiene in rural adolescent girls of Nepal. *Kathmandu University Medical Journal*, *5*(3), 382-386.

Adnan, S. (2004). *Migration, land alienation and causes of poverty in the Chittagong Hill Tracts*. Dhaka, Bangladesh: Research and Advisory Services.

Afshar, H., & Barrientos, S. (1999). *Women, Globalization and Fragmentation in the Developing World*. London: Women Studies at York. doi:10.1057/9780230371279

Agarwal, B. (1994). Gender and command over property: A critical gap in economic analysis and policy in South Asia. *World Development*, *22*(10), 1455–1478. doi:10.1016/0305-750X(94)90031-0

Agarwal, B. (1997). Bargaining and Gender Relations: Within and Beyond the Household. *Feminist Economics*, *3*(1), 1–51. doi:10.1080/135457097338799

Agba, A. M. O. (2010). Sociological Analysis of Marital Stress and Women Effectiveness in Grassroot Socio-Economic Transformation in Nigeria. *Global Journal of Human Social Science*, *10*(2), 38–46.

Agrawal, T. (2013). Are there glass-ceiling and sticky-floor effects in India? An empirical examination. *Oxford Development Studies*, *41*(3), 322–342. doi:10.1080/13600818.2013.804499

Aguilar, L. (2008). *Acknowledging the Linkages: Gender and Climate Change*. Paper presented at the World Bank's workshop on social dimensions of climate change. Retrieved from http://siteresources.worldbank.org/EXTSOCIALDEVELOPMENT/Resources/244362-1170428243464/3408356- 1170428261889/3408359-1202746084138/Gender_Presentation022808.pd

Agu, S. (2007). Gender equality, education and women empowerment: The Nigerian challenge. *Multidisciplinary Journal of Research Development*, *8*(2), 1–7.

Ahmad, N. (2011). *Gender and climate change: myth vs reality*. Retrieved from http://blogs.worldbank.org/endpovertyinsouthasia/gender-and-climate-change-myth-vs-reality

Ahmed, N. (2012). Gender and Climate Change in Bangladesh: The Role of Institutions inReducing Gender Gaps in Adaptation Program. *The World Bank*. Retrieved from http://www-wds.worldbank.org/external/default/WDSContentServer/WDSP/IB/2012/04/04/000333038_20120404010647/Rendered/PDF/678200NWP0P1250C0in0Bangladesh0web2.pd

Ahmed, C. (2014). Impacts of Remittance on the Socioeconomic Condition of Bangladesh: An Analysis. *IIASS*, *7*(3), 23–43. doi:10.12959/issn.1855-0541.IIASS-2014-no3-art02

Ahmed, S., & Maitra, P. (2015). A distributional analysis of the gender wage gap in Bangladesh. *The Journal of Development Studies*, *51*(11), 1444–1458. doi:10.1080/00220388.2015.1046444

Ahsan, R. M., & Hossain, M. K. (2004). Woman and Child Trafficking in Bangladesh: A Social Disaster in the Backdrop of Natural Calamities. In R. M. Ahsan & H. Khatun (Eds.), *Disaster and the Silent Gender: Contemporary Studies in Geography* (pp. 147–170). Dhaka: The Bangladesh Geographical Society.

AIPP. (2007). *A brief account of Human right situation of indigenous peoples in Bangladesh*. AIPP.

Compilation of References

Akter, T. (2009). *Climate change and flow of environmental displacement in Bangladesh acknowledgement*. Available at: http://bdresearch.org.bd/home/climate_knowledge/cd1/pdf/Bangladesh%20and%20climate%20change/Climate%20change%20impacts%20,vulnerability,%20risk/Climate_Change_and_Flow_of_Environmental_displacement.pdf

Al Fatih, T. (2005). *Participation in Decision Making Processes in the Local Government after the Comprehensive Peace Agreement of 2005: Case Study pf South Kordofan and Upper Nile States (PhD Proposal)*. Ahfad University for Women.

Ala Uddin, M. A. (2009). Cultural assimilation and survival strategy of ethnic people in Bangladesh: Bengali dress on ethnic physic in Chittagong Hill Tracts. *Canadian Social Science*, *5*(1), 16–23.

Alam, K., & Rahman, M. H. (2014). Women in Natural Disasters: A Case Study from Southern Coastal Region of Bangladesh. *International Journal of Disaster Risk Reduction*, *8*, 68–82. doi:10.1016/j.ijdrr.2014.01.003

Alarabi. (2001). *Ahfad University Students' Opinions on Sexual Harassment* (Unpublished Masters dissertation). Ahfad University for Women.

Ali, W. (2008). A Brief Overview on Women Economic Participation and Employment. In *Sudanese Women Profile and Pathways to Empowerment*. Ahfad University.

Alim, L. O. (1999). *Women executive managers in the Sudanese banking system: Experience and challenges* (Unpublished Masters dissertation). Ahfad University for Women.

Alim, L. O. (1999). *Women Executive Managers in the Sudanese Banking System: Experience and Challenges* (Unpublished Masters dissertation). Ahfad University for Women.

Ali, M., & Haq, U. (2006). Women's Autonomy and Happiness: The Case of Pakistan. *Pakistan Development Review*, *45*(1), 121–136.

Allison, I. K. (1999). Information systems professionals' development: A work-based learning model. *Journal of Continuing Professional Development*, *2*(3), 86–92.

Alston, M. (2014). Gender mainstreaming and climate change. *Women's Studies International Forum*, *47*.

Alston, M., & Whittenbury, K. (2013). Introducing Gender and Climate Change: Research, Policy and Action. In A. Margaret & W. Kerri (Eds.), *Research, Action and Policy: Addressing the Gendered Impacts of Climate Change* (pp. 3–14). London: Springer. doi:10.1007/978-94-007-5518-5_1

Alston, M., Whittenbury, K., Haynes, A., & Godden, N. (2014). Are climate challenges reinforcing child and forced marriage and dowry as adaptation strategies in the context of Bangladesh? *Womens Studies International Forum*, *47*, 137–144. doi:10.1016/j.wsif.2014.08.005

American Psychological Association, Task Force on the Sexualization of Girls. (2007). *Report of the APA Task Force on the Sexualization of Girls*. Washington, DC: American Psychological Association. Retrieved 15 December 2016, from https://www.apa.org/pi/women/programs/girls/report-full.pdf

Amnesty International. (2010). *Haiti after the Earthquake: Initial Mission Findings*. Author.

Anand Mulk Raj. (1984). *Madhubani Painting*. New Delhi: Publications Division.

Anastario, M., Shehab, N., & Lawry, L. (2009). Increased Gender-based Violence Among Women Internally Displaced in Mississippi Two Years Post-Hurrican Katrina. *Disaster Medicine and Public Health Preparedness*, *3*(1), 18–26. doi:10.1097/DMP.0b013e3181979c32 PMID:19293740

Angya, A. (2014). *Achieving affirmative action for gender mainstreaming: The journey so far*. Paper presented at the Center for Women, Gender and Development Studies, Federal University of Technology, Owerri.

Anker, R., & Hein, C. (1985). Why Third World urban employers usually prefer men. *International Labour Review, 24*(1), 73–90. PMID:12269173

Anker, R., & Hein, C. (1986). *Sex Inequality in Urban Employment in the Third World*. London: Macmillan Press. doi:10.1007/978-1-349-18467-5

Aparicio, F., & Meseguer, C. (2012). Collective Remittances and the State: The 3×1 Program in Mexican Municipalities. *World Development, 40*(1), 206–222. doi:10.1016/j.worlddev.2011.05.016

Appadurai, A. (1990). Disjuncture and Differences in the Global Cultural Economy. In M. Featherstone (Ed.), *Global Culture: Nationalism, Globalization and Modernity* (pp. 295–310). Newbury Park, CA: Sage.

Archarya, I., Shakya, M., & Sthapit, S. (2011). *Menstrual Knowledge and Forbidden Activities among the Rural Education and Development*. Academic Press.

Archer, W. G. (1949). Maithil Painting. *Marg, 3*(3), 24–33.

Ardhanarisvara by Sita Devi

Arfken, D. E., Bellar, S. L., & Helms, M. M. (2004). The ultimate glass ceiling revisited: The presence of women on corporate boards. *Journal of Business Ethics, 50*(2), 177–186. doi:10.1023/B:BUSI.0000022125.95758.98

Arifeen, A. (2013). Understanding the contribution of remittances at the macroeconomic and household levels and exploring how these transfers could be better leveraged for development in Bangladesh. Lecture, Dhaka. *BANBEIS- Educational Database*. Retrieved 14 November 2016, from http://192.254.190.210/~banbeis/data/index.php

Ariyabandu, M. M., & Foenseka, D. (2006). Do Disasters Discriminate?. In D. Nivaran (Ed.), *South Asia Network for Disaster Mitigation: Tackling the Tides and Tremors* (pp. 23–40). Islamabad: South Asia Disaster Report.

Arnfred, S. (2002). Simone De Beauvoir in Africa: 'Women-The Second Sex?' Issues of African Feminist Thought. Jenda: A Journal of Culture and African Women's Studies, 2(1).

Arnold, J. (2005). *Work Psychology: Understanding Human Behavior in the Workplace* (4th ed.). London: Prentice Hall Financial Times.

Arthur, J. A. (2009). *African women immigrants in the United States: crossing transnational borders*. New York: Palgrave Macmillan. doi:10.1057/9780230623910

Asian Development Bank. (2010). *Women thrive in local business*. Retrieved from: http://www.adb.org/features/women-thrive-local-business

Asian Development Bank. (2013). *Closing the gender gap*. Retrieved from: http://www.adb.org/themes/gender/overview

Asjarraj, A., & Abdel Mageed, A. (2008). *Sudanese women owned large scale enterprises: opportunities and perspectives* (Unpublished Masters dissertation). Ahfad University for Women.

Astin, H. S. (1984). The Meaning of Work in Womens Lives: A sociopsychological model of career choice and work behavior. *The Counseling Psychologist, 12*(4), 117–126. doi:10.1177/0011000084124002

Aurat Foundation, Pakistan NGO Alternative Report on CEDAW, 2012. (2012). Aurat Publication and Information Service Foundation.

Compilation of References

AusAID Office of Development Effectiveness. (2008). *Violence against women in Melanesia and East Timor Building on Global and Regional Promising Approaches.* Canberra: Office of Development Effectiveness.

Austen, S. E., & Birch, E. R. (2000). *Family Responsiblities and Women Working Lives.* Discussion Paper Series 00/3. Women's Economic Policy Analysis Unit, Curtin University of Technology.

Ayub, N. (1994). The Self-Employed Women in Pakistan: A Case Study of the Self-Employed Women of Urban Informal Sector in Karachi. Karachi, Pakistan: Association for Women's Studies & News.

Azad, S. K. (2006). *Sexual Harassment at Work: Experiences with two development organizations in Bangladesh.* Working Paper Series: 1. Department of Women and Gender Studies, University of Dhaka, Bangladesh.

Azad, A. K., Hossain, M. K., & Nasreen, M. (2013). Flood-Induced Vulnerabilities and Problems Encountered by Women in Northern Bangladesh. *International Journal of Disaster Risk Science, 4*(4), 190–199. doi:10.1007/s13753-013-0020-z

Badawi, Z. A. (2003). *Gender sensitivity in Sudanese labour and employment laws: working women views and experiences* (Unpublished Masters dissertation). Ahfad University for Women.

Badawi. (2010). *Factors affecting women's promotion into top managerial positions in the Sudan.* Population Council Final Dissemination Conference on Gender and Work in the Mena Region, Cairo, Egypt.

Badri, A., & Elfatih, T. (2008). Sudanese girls and Women Educational Attainment. In Sudanese Women Profile and Pathways to Empowerment. Ahfad University for Women.

Badri, B. (2008a). Introducing Sudan. In Sudanese Women Profile and Pathways to Empowerment. Ahfad University for Women.

Badri, B. (2008b). Feminist Perspectives in Sudan. In Sudanese Women Profile and Pathways to Empowerment. Ahfad University for Women.

Badri, L. I. (2002). *Agency and negotiating restrictions in creating space for women within the household.* Preliminary PhD proposal.

Badri, N. (1998a). *State Power over the Female Body* (Unpublished Masters dissertation). Ahfad University for Women.

Badri, N. (2008b). Sudanese Women Health Profile. In Sudanese Women Profile and Pathways to Empowerment. Ahfad University for Women.

Bakare-Yusuf, B. (2003). Beyond Determinism: The Phenomenology of African Female Existence. *Feminist Africa*, (2).

Bakare-Yusuf, B. (2004). "Yoruba's don't do gender": A Critical Review of Oyeronke Oyewumi's, The Invention of Women: Making an African Sense of Western Gender Discourses. In S. Arnfred, B. Bakari-Yusuf, E. W. Kisiang'ani, D. Lewis, O. Oyewumi, & F. C. Steady (Eds.), *African Gender Scholarship: Concepts, Methodologies and Paradigms* (pp. 61–81). Dakar: CODESRIA.

Bakht, Z., & Basher, A. (2015). Strategy for Development of the SME Sector in Bangladesh. Dhaka: Bangladesh Institute of Development Studies (BIDS).

Bakshi, G. (2016). *Girls in Nepal photograph menstrual taboos affecting their lives Brought to you by: WaterAid.* Retrieved from https://www.globalcitizen.org/en/content/girls-in-nepal-photograph-menstrual-taboos-affecti/

Baldwin-Edwards, M. (2005). *Migration in the Middle East and the Mediterranean.* Geneva: Global Commission on International Migration.

Bal, V. (2004). Women scientists in India: Nowhere near the glass ceiling. *Economic and Political Weekly, 38*(32), 3647–3653.

Bangladesh Bank. (2016). Retrieved from https://www.bb.org.bd/pub/annual/anreport/ar1415/full_2014_2015.pdf

Bangladesh Bureau of Statistics (BBS). (2004). *Report on the Labour Force Survey, Bangladesh 2002-2003*. Dhaka: Planning Division, Ministry of Planning, Government of the People's Republic of Bangladesh.

Bangladesh Bureau of Statistics (BBS). (2011). *Report of the Labour Force Survey*. Author.

Bangladesh Bureau of Statistics. (2015). *Labour force survey 2010*. Dhaka: BBS.

Bangladesh Centre for Advanced Studies. (2010). *Report on Gender and Climate Change Issues in the South Central and South West Coastal Regions of Bangladesh*. Dhaka, Bangladesh: Author.

Bangladesh Ministry of Communications. (2005). *Urban transport policy: the strategic transport plan (STP) for Dhaka*. Retrieved February 22, 2016, fromhttp://lib.pmo.gov.bd/legalms/pdf/draft-urban_transport_policy.pdf

Bangladesh National Labor Force Survey. (2002-2003). Bangladesh Bureau of Statistics.

Bangladesh Planning Commission. (2014). *Millennium Development Goals: Bangladesh Progress Report 2013*. Dhaka: Bangladesh Planning Commission.

Bangladesh. (2010). Dhaka: Planning Division, Ministry of Planning, Government of the People's Republic of Bangladesh.

Bangladesh-1999-2000. (n.d.). Dhaka: Planning Division, Ministry of Planning, Government of the People's Republic of Bangladesh.

Barbezat, D. (2003). Occupational Segregation around the World. In Women, Family, and Work: Writings on the Economic of Gender. Blackwell Publishing.

Barkat, A., Halim, S., Poddar, A., Osman, A., Khan, S. M., Rahman, R., ... Bashir, S. (2009). Socio-Economic baseline survey of Chittagong Hill Tracts. United Nations Development Program.

Barkat, A., Osman, A., Ahsan, M., & Kumar, A. P. (2012). Situational Analysis of Sexual Harassment at Tertiary Level Education Institutes in and around Dhaka. Dhaka: Human Development Research Centre (HDRC).

Bartlett, S. (2008). *Climate change and urban children Impacts and implications for adaptation in low- and middle-income countries. In Human settlements discussion paper, Series theme: climate change and cities*. International Institute for Environment and Development.

Bashier, M. A. (2000). *The Position of Women Unionists in the High Echelons of the Sudanese Trade Unions* (Unpublished Masters dissertation). Ahfad University for Women.

Basow, S., & Minieri, A. (2011). You Owe Me: Effects of Date Cost, Who Pays, Participant Gender, and Rape Myth Beliefs on Perceptions of Rape. *Journal of Interpersonal Violence, 26*, 479.

Batliwala, S. (1994). *The meaning of Women's Empowerment: Population Policies Reconsidered*. Harvard Series on Population and International Health.

BBS. (2011). *Report on Household Income and Expenditure Survey Bangladesh 2011*. Dhaka: Bangladesh Bureau of Statistics.

BBS. (2013). *Report on Violence against Women (VAW) Survey 2011*. Dhaka: Bangladesh Bureau of Statistics.

BBS. (2015). *Report on Labor Force Survey (LFS) Bangladesh 2013*. Dhaka: Bangladesh Bureau of Statistics.

Compilation of References

BBS. (2016). *Statistical Yearbook 2015*. Dhaka: Bangladesh Bureau of Statistics.

Beal, C. R. (1994). *Boys and Girls: The Development of Gender Roles*. McGraw Hill.

Beck, D., & Davis, E. (2005). EEO in senior management: Women executives in Westpac. *Asia Pacific Journal of Human Resources, 43*(2), 273–288. doi:10.1177/1038411105055063

Beneria, L. (2001). The enduring debate over unpaid labour. In L. Beneria & S. Bisnath (Eds.), Gender and Development: Theoretical, Empirical and Practical Approaches. Edward Elgar.

Bergmann, B. (1974). Occupational segregation. Wages and profits when employers discriminate by race or sex. *Eastern Economic Journal, 1*(2), 103–110.

Bernard, H. R. (2002). *Research Methods in Anthropology: Qualitative and Quantitative Approaches*. Oxford, UK: Altamira Press.

Bern, C. (1993). Risk factors for mortality in the Bangladesh cyclone of 191. *Bulletin of the World Health Organization, 71*, 73–28. PMID:8440041

Bern, C., Sniezek, J., & Mathbor, G., Siddiqi, Ronsmans, C., Chowdhury, A., Choudhury, A., ... Noji, E. (1993). Risk factors for mortality in the Bangladesh cyclone of 1991. *Bulletin of the World Health Organization, 71*(1), 73–78. PMID:8440041

Bhalla, N. (2013). *Women, children at risk of trafficking after Uttarakhand floods*. Thompson Reuters Foundation. Retrieved from http://in.reuters.com/article/2013/07/05/uttarakhand-floods-women-childrentraffi-idINDEE96402V20130705

Bhandaree, R., Pandey, B., Rajak, M., & Pantha, P. (2013). Chhaupadi: Victimising women in Nepal. In *Second International Conference of the South Asian Society of Criminology and Victimology*. SASCV.

Bhasin, K. (1993). *What is Patriarchy?*. New Delhi: Kali for Women.

Bhasin, K. (2000). *Understanding Gender*. New Delhi: Kali for Women.

Bhattacharya, R. (2007). Gender and Employemnt in the Context of Globalization: Some Facts and Figures. In R. Ghadially (Ed.), *Urban Women in Contemporary India*. Sage.

Bihagen, E., & Ohls, M. (2006). The glass ceiling – where is it? Womens and mens career prospects in the private vs. the public sector in Sweden 19792000. *The Sociological Review, 54*(1), 20–47. doi:10.1111/j.1467-954X.2006.00600.x

Biko, A. (2015, 6 October). *Access to justice for Kenyan domestic workers*. Retrieved from https://kituochasheria.wordpress.com/2015/10/06/access-to-justice-for-kenyan-domestic-workers/

Billing, Y. (2000). Organizational Cultures, Families and Careers in Scandinavia. In L. Haas, P. Hwang, & G. Russell (Eds.), *Organizational Change and Gender Equity*. Thousand Oaks, CA: Sage.

Binagwaho. (2010). *Developing human rights-based strategies to improve health among female sex workers in Rwanda*. Retrieved from http://www.ncbi.nlm.nih.gov/pubmed/21178192

Black, M. C., Basile, K. C., Breiding, M. J., & Smith, S. G. (2011). *The national intimate partner and sexual violence survey(NISVS):2010 summery report*. Atlanta, GA: National Center for Injury Prevention and Control, Centre for Disease Control and Prevention. Available at www.cdc.gov/violence prevention/pdf/misvs_executive_summeryapdf

Blair, S. L., & Lichter, D. T. (1991). Measuring the division of household labor: Gender segregation of housework among American couples. *Journal of Family Issues, 12*(1), 91–113. doi:10.1177/019251391012001007

Bloom, S. (2008). *Violence against Women and Girls: A Compendium of Monitoring and Evaluation Indicators*. Chapel Hill, NC: MEASURE Evaluation.

Blumberg, R. (2005). *Women economic empowerment as a magic portion of development*. Paper Presented at the 100 Annual Meeting of the American Sociological Association, Philadelphia, PA.

Bobel, C. (2010). *New Blood: Third wave feminism and the politics of menstruation*. Rutgers University Press.

Boris, S. (2007). Gender after Africa!. In Africa after Gender?. Bloomington, IN: Indiana University Press.

Borooah, V. K. (2015). Caste, Discrimination, and Exclusion in Modern India. *Sage (Atlanta, Ga.)*.

Boserup, E. (1970). *Women's Role in Economic Development*. New York: St. Martin's Press.

Bozionelos, N. (2004). Mentoring Provided: Relation to Mentors Career Success, Personality, and Mentoring Received. *Journal of Vocational Behavior*, 64(1), 24–46. doi:10.1016/S0001-8791(03)00033-2

Braaf, R. (2012). *Elephant in the room: Responding to alcohol misuse and domestic violence*. Australian Domestic & Family Violence Clearing House. Retrieved from http://trove.nla.gov.au/work/169482645?q&versionId=184708568

Braunstein, E. (2007). *The Efficiency of Gender Equity in Economic Growth: Neoclassical and Feminist Approaches*. The International Working Group on Gender, Macroeconomics, and International Economics, Working Paper Series. Retrieved from www.genderandmacro.org

Braunstein, E. (2009). *Women's Employment, Empowerment and Globalization: An Economic Perspective*. Retrieved September 23, 2010, from World Survey on the Role of Women in Development, Expert Papers EC/WSRWD/2008/EP.3: http://www.un.org/womenwatch/daw/ws20 09/first_experts.html#expert1

Briggs, J., & Sharp, J. (2004). Indigenous knowledge and development: A postcolonial caution. *Third World Quarterly*, 25(4), 661–676. doi:10.1080/01436590410001678915

Brookings-Bern Project on Internal Displacement. (2009). *Protecting and Promoting Rights in Natural Disasters in South Asia: Prevention and Response*. Retrieved from http://www.brookings.edu/~/media/Files/rc/reports/2009/0701_natural_disasters/0701_natural_disasters.pdf

Brumley, K. M. (2014). The gendered ideal worker narrative professional womens and mens work experiences in the new economy at a Mexican company. *Gender & Society*, 28(6), 799–823. doi:10.1177/0891243214546935

Bruyn, T. (2006). Dynamics of Remittance Utilization in Bangladesh. In *Remittances and Expatriates: Development in Bangladesh*. The Hague: Bangladesh Support Group (BASUG). Retrieved from https://www.academia.edu/8017098/Dynamics_of_Remittance_Utilization_in_Bangladesh

Bryman, A., & Bell, E. (2011). *Business research methods*. Oxford, UK: Oxford University Press.

Bujra, J. (2000). Targeting Men for a Change: AIDS Discourse and Activism in Africa. *Agenda (Durban, South Africa)*, 44(44), 6–23. doi:10.2307/4066430

Bureau of Manpower Employment and Training (BMET). (2016). Retrieved from http://www.bmet.gov.bd/BMET/resources/Static%20PDF%20and%20DOC/publication/Remittance%20and%20its%20impact.pdf

Butler, J. (1999). *Gender Trouble: Feminism and the Subversion of Identity*. New York: Routledge.

Byerly, C. M., & Ross, K. (2006). *Women and Media: A Critical Introduction*. Blackwell Publishing. doi:10.1002/9780470774908

Compilation of References

Cain, M., Khanam, S. R., & Nahar, S. (1979). Class, Patriarchy, and Womens Work in Bangladesh. *Population and Development Review*, *5*(3), 405–438. doi:10.2307/1972079

Carling, J. (2005). Migrant Remittances and Development Cooperation. Oslo: PRIO Report 1/2005, International Peace Research Institute.

Celestial Union by Sita Devi

Central Bank of Sri Lanka. (2016). *Central bank of Sri Lanka annual report 2015*. Colombo: Central Bank of Sri Lanka.

Central Bureau of Statistics Nepal. (2012). *National Population and Housing Census 2011, National Report*. Available at: http://unstats.un.org/unsd/demographic/sources/census/wphc/Nepal/Nepal-Census-2011-Vol1.pdf

Centre for Integrated Program and Development. (n.d.). Retrieved from: <http://www.cipdauk.org/index.php/about-cipd>

Chakma, B. P. (2010). *The economy of the Indigenous people of CHT: some myths and realities*. Paper presented at the Conference on Development in the Chittagong Hill Tracts, Rangamati, Bangladesh.

Chakma, K. (2011). *(In)equality and (In)difference: indigenous women of the Chittagong Hill Tracts in post-colonial Bangladesh*. Paper presented at a workshop on Gender, militarization and endemic conflict: new research agendas, Radcliff Institute of Harvard University.

Chakma, G. K., Chakma, B., & Tripura, S. P. (2007). *The occupation of shifting cultivation and indigenous peoples: a case study in the Chittagong Hill Tracts, Bangladesh*. Dhaka, Bangladesh: ILO.

Chakma, H. (2013). *Indigenous women's role in the market economy*. Prothom Alo.

Chakma, K. G. (2010). *'Shifting cultivation as traditional livelihood and impacts of climate change in Bangladesh', Traditional Livelihoods and Indigenous Peoples*. Thailand: Asian Indigenous Peoples Pact Foundation.

Chakma, K., & D' Costa, B. (2013). The Chittagong Hill Tracts: diminishing violence or violent peace?. London: Routledge.

Chakma, K., & Hill, G. (2013). Indigenous women and culture in the colonized CHT of Bangladesh. In K. Visweswaren (Ed.), *Everyday Occupations: Experiencing Militarism in South Asia and Middle East*. University of Pennsylvania.

Chakraborty, E. (1993). *Marginality, modes of insecurity and indigenous women of Northern Bangladesh*. Retrieved from http://calternatives.org/resource/pdf/Marginality,%20Modes%20of%20insecurity%20and%20Indigenous%20Women%20of%20Northern%20Bangladesh.pdf

Chakraborty, E., & Sarkar, C. (2014). *BangladesherAdibashiNari: shamajikobosthan o biponnotarchalchitro*. Dhaka: Banglaprakash.

Chammartin, G. (2002). The feminization of international migration. International Migration Programme: International Labour Organization, 37-40.

Chandrasekhar, C. P. (2014). India's informal economy. *The Hindu*. Retrieved from: http://www.thehindu.com/opinion/columns/Chandrasekhar/indias-informal-economy/article6375902.ece

Chant, S. (2007). Dangerous Equations? How Female-Headed Households Became the Poorest of the Poor: Causes, Consequences and Cautions. In A. Cornwall, E. Harrison, & A. Whitehead (Eds.), *Feminisms in Development: Contradictions, Contestations and Challenges* (pp. 35–47). London: Zed Books.

Chant, S. (2007). Dangerous Equations? How female-headed households became the poorest of the poor: causes, consequences and cautions. In *Feminisms in Development Contradictions, Contestations and Challenges* (pp. 35–47). London: Zed Books Publishers.

Chant, S., & Gutmann, M. (2007). *Mainstreaming Men into Gender and Development: Debates, Reflections and Experiences*. Oxford, UK: Oxfam.

Chaudhury, S. (2010). *Women's Empowerment in South Asia and South East Asia: A Comparative Analysis*. MPRA- Munich Personal RePEc Archive. Retrieved from http://mpra.ub.uni-muenchen.de/1968611/

Chaudhury, S. (2009). *Economic Development and Women's Empowerment*. University of Wisconsin- Eau Claire.

Cha, Y. (2010). Reinforcing Separate Spheres: The Effect of Spousal Overwork on Mens and Womens Employment in Dual Earner Households. *American Sociological Review*, *75*(2), 303–329. doi:10.1177/0003122410365307

Chen, M. (2008). Informality and social protection. Theories and realities. *IDS Bulletin*, *39*(2), 18–27. doi:10.1111/j.1759-5436.2008.tb00441.x

Cherie Blair Foundation. (2012). *Women & Mobile: A Global Opportunity: A study on the mobile phone gender gap in low and middle-income countries*. Available at http://www.Cherieblairfoundation.org/wp_content/uploads/2012/07/women_and_mobile_a_global_opportunity.pdf

Cherney, I. D., Kelly-Vance, L., Gill Glover, K., Ruane, A., & Oliver Ryalls, B. (2003). The Effects of Stereotyped Toys and Gender on Play Assesment on Children Aged 1847 Months. *Educational Psychology*, *23*(1), 95–106. doi:10.1080/01443410303222

Chew, L., & Ramdas, K. N. (2005). *Caught in the Storm: The Impact of Natural Disasters on Women*. San Francisco: The Global Fund for Women.

Chirangi, M. (2013). *Afya Jumuishi: Towards interprofessional collaboration between traditional and medicinal practitioner in Mara Region of Tanzania* (Dissertation). University of Laiden.

Chitrakar, N. (2014). *Nepal's chaupadi tradition banishes menstruating women- in pictures*. Available at: http://www.theguardian.com/global-development/gallery/2014/mar/08/nepal-chaupadi-tradition-banishes-menstruating-women-in-pictures

Chittagong Hill Tracts Commission. (1991). *Life is not ours: Land and human rights in the Chittagong Hill Tracts*. Retrieved from: http://www.iwgia.org/iwgia_files_publications_files/0129_Life_is_not_ours_1-108.pdf

Chittagong Hill Tracts Development Facility United Nations Development Program. (2010). *Economic Development*. Retrieved from: http://www.chtdf.org/index.php/focus-areas/economic-development

Chodorow, N. J. (1989). *Feminism and Psychoanalytic Theory*. New Haven, CT: Yale University Press.

Choudhary, R. K. (1976). *Mithila in the Age of Vidyapati*. Varanasi.

Chou, W. G., Fosh, P., & Foster, D. (2005). Female managers in Taiwan: Opportunities and barriers in changing times. *Asia Pacific Business Review*, *11*(2), 251–266. doi:10.1080/1360238042000291153

Chowdhury, K. (2008). Politics of identities and resources in the Chittagong Hill Tract, Bangladesh: Ethnonationalism and/or Indigenous identity. *Asian Journal of Social Science*, *36*(1), 57–78. doi:10.1163/156853108X267567

Chow, E., & Lyter, D. (2002). Studying Development With A Gender Perspective: From Main stream Theories to Alternative Frame Works. In E. Chow (Ed.), *Transforming Gender and Development in East Asia* (pp. 25–30). New York: Routledge.

Cianni, M., & Wnuck, D. (1997). Individual Growth and Team Enhancement: Moving toward a New Model of Career Development. *The Academy of Management Executive, 11*(1), 105-111.

CIDA. (1997). *Guide to Gender Sensitive Indicators*. Canadian International Development Agency. Retrieved from http://acdi-cida.gc.ca

Cinema. (n.d.). In *Oxford English dictionary*. Retrieved from https://www.oxforddictionaries.com/

Civil Society Legislative Advocacy Center. (2015). *Policy brief on gender equity and empowerment towards achieving the MDGS*. Lagos: CSLAC and TY Danjuma Foundation.

Clarke, G. (2001). From ethnocide to ethno development? Ethnic minorities and indigenous peoples in Southeast Asia. *Third World Quarterly, 22*(3), 413–436. doi:10.1080/01436590120061688

Cleaver, F. (2001). Do men matter?. *New Horizons in Gender and Development*. Available: http://www.id21.org/static/insights35editorial.htm

Cole, C.M., Manuh, T., & Miescher, S.F. (Eds.). (2007). *Africa after Gender?*. Bloomington, IN: Indiana University Press.

Color World. (n.d.). *Same sex relationships and gender identities among non-whites*. Retrieved from: http://www.colorq.org/articles/article.aspx?d=2000&x=qcolor

Combs-Lane, A. M., & Smith, D. W. (2002). Risk of Sexual Victimization in College Women: The Role of Behavioral Intentions and Risk-Taking Behaviors. *Journal of Interpersonal Violence, 17*(2), 165–183. doi:10.1177/0886260502017002004

Connell, R. W. (1987). *Gender and power: society, the person and sexual politics*. Stanford, CA: Stanford University Press.

Connell, R. W. (1987). *Gender and Power: society, the person and sexual politics*. University of California Press.

Connell, R. W. (1995). *Masculinities*. Berkeley, CA: University of California press.

Connell, R. W. (2000). *The men and the boys*. Cambridge, UK: Polity Press.

Connell, R. W., & Messerschmidt, J. W. (2005). Hegemonic masculinity: Rethinking the concept. *Gender & Society, 19*(6), 829–859. doi:10.1177/0891243205278639

Coyle, A. (1988). Continuity and Change: women in paid work. In Women and Work: Positive Action for Change. Macmillan London

Crawford, M., Menger, L. M., & Kaufman, M. L. (2014). "This is a natural process": Managing menstrual stigma in Nepal. *Culture, Health & Sexuality, 16*(4), 426–439. doi:10.1080/13691058.2014.887147 PMID:24697583

Crenshaw, K. (1991). Mapping the margins: Intersectionality, identity politics, and violence against women of color. *Stanford Law Review, 43*(6), 1241–1299. doi:10.2307/1229039

Crofts, T., & Fisher, J. (2012). Menstrual hygiene in Ugandan schools: An investigation of low-cost sanitary pads. Journal of Water. *Sanitation and Hygiene for Development, 2*(1), 50–58. doi:10.2166/washdev.2012.067

Dainty, A. R. J., Bagilhole, B. M., & Neale, R. H. (2000). A Grounded Theory of Womens Career Under-achievement in Large UK Construction Companies. *Journal of Construction Management and Economics, 18*(2), 239–250. doi:10.1080/014461900370861

Dainty, A. R. J., & Lingard, H. (2006). Indirect Discrimination in Construction Organizations and the Impact on Womens Careers. *Journal of Management Engineering, 22*(3), 108–118. doi:10.1061/(ASCE)0742-597X(2006)22:3(108)

Dannecker, P., & Sieveking, N. (2009). Gender, Migration and Development: An Analysis of the Current Discussion on Female Migrants as Development Agents. *COMCAD, 69*(2009). Retrieved from https://www.uni-bielefeld.de/tdrc/ag_comcad/downloads/Workingpaper_69_dannecker+sieveking.pdf

Dannecker, P. (2005). Transnational Migration and the Transformation of Gender Relations: The Case of Bangladeshi Labour Migrants. *Current Sociology, 53*(4), 655–674. doi:10.1177/0011392105052720

Dasgupta, S., Siriner, I., & Partha, S. D. (Eds.). (2010). *Women's Encounter with Disaster*. London: Frontpage Publications.

Das, N., Yasmin, R., Ara, J., Kamruzzaman, M., Davis, P., & Behrman, J. (2013). *How Do Intrahousehold Dynamics Change When Assets Are Transferred to Women? Evidence from BRACCs Challenging the Frontiers of Poverty Reduction Targeting the Ultra Poor Program in Bangladesh*. SSRN Electronic Journal. doi:10.2139/ssrn.2405712

David, M., & Woodward, D. (1998). Introduction. In M. David & D. Woodward (Eds.), *Negotiating the glass ceiling: Careers of senior women in the academic world* (pp. 2–22). London: Routledge.

Davis, M. (2016). Emancipation of women. *Page Hub*. Retrieved 30 July, 2016, from http://hubpages.com/politics/Emancipation-Of-Women

Days for Girls International. (2016). *Every Girl. Everywhere. Period*. Available at: http://www.daysforgirls.org/

de Haas, H., & van Rooij, A. (2010). Migration as Emancipation? The Impact of Internal and International Migration on the Position of Women Left Behind in Rural Morocco. *Oxford Development Studies, 38*(1), 43–62. doi:10.1080/13600810903551603

De Janasz, S. C., & Sullivan, S. E. (2004). Multiple Mentoring in Academe: Developing the Professorial Network. *Journal of Vocational Behavior, 64*(2), 263–283. doi:10.1016/j.jvb.2002.07.001

Demetriou, D. (2015). 'Tied Visas' and Inadequate Labour Protections: A formula for abuse and exploitation of migrant domestic workers in the United Kingdom. *Anti-Trafficking Review, 5*(2015).

Department for International Development. (2011). *Nepal Operational Plan Gender Equity and Social Inclusion Annex*. Available at: https://www.gov.uk/government/uploads/system/uploads/attachment_data/file/67545/nepal-2011-annex.pdfAccessed 18 May 2016.

Derks, B., Van Laar, C., & Ellemers, N. (2016). The queen bee phenomenon: Why women leaders distance themselves from junior women. *The Leadership Quarterly, 27*(3), 456–469. doi:10.1016/j.leaqua.2015.12.007

Devaki, J. (1980). Women's Quest For Power: Five Indian Case Studies. Academic Press.

Devanarayana, C. (1997). *A review of Sri Lanka's free trade zone*. Ja-Ella: Dabindu Collective.

DeviMahasundari

Dewan, A. (2002). *Woven textiles as art: an examination on the revival of weaving in the Chittagong Hill Tracts* (Master thesis). Concordia University, Montreal, Canada.

Dewan, I. (2010). Women in Hill society. In *Between Ashes and Hope: Chittagong Hill Tracts in the Blind Spot of Bangladesh Nationalism* (pp. 190–191). Dhaka: Drishtipat Writers Collective.

DFID. (2000). *Eliminating World Poverty. Making Globalisation Work for the Poor*. London: Her Majesty's Stationery Office.

Dhali, H. H. (2008). Deforestation and its impacts on indigenous women: A case from the Chittagong Hill Tracts in Bangladesh. *Gender, Technology and Development, 12*(2), 229–246. doi:10.1177/097185240801200204

Compilation of References

Diamond, M. (2002). Sex and Gender are Different: Sexual Identity and Gender Identity are Different. *Clinical Child Psychology and Psychiatry*, *7*(3), 320–334. doi:10.1177/1359104502007003002

Dicken, P. (2007). *Global shift: Mapping the changing contours of the world economy*. London: Sage.

Disaster Management Bureau and Disaster Management and Relief Division. (2010). *National plan for disaster management government of the people's republic of Bangladesh national plan for disaster management 2010-2015 disaster management bureau disaster management & relief division*. Available at: http://www.lcgbangladesh.org/derweb/doc/Final%20Version%20Nataional%20Plan%20for%20Disaster%20(2010-2015).pdf

Dixon, T., Thompson, B., & McAllister, P. (2002). *The value of ICT for SMEs in the UK: a critical literature review*. Report for Small Business Service research programme. The College of Estate Management. Available: www.sbs.gov.uk/SBS_Gov_files/researchandstats/value_of_ICT_for_SMEs_UK.pdf

Dixon, B. R. (2001). Women in agriculture: counting the labour force in developing countries. In L. Beneria & S. Bisnath (Eds.), *Gender and Development: Theoretical, Empirical and Practical Approaches* (Vol. 1). Edward Elger Publishing Limited.

Dolan, C. S., Ryus, C. R., Dopson, S., Montgomery, P., & Scott, L. (2013). A blind spot in girls education: Menarche and its webs of exclusion in Ghana. *Journal of International Development*, *26*(5), 643–657. doi:10.1002/jid.2917

Dolan, K. (2014). *When Does Gender Matter? Women Candidates and Gender Stereotypes in American Elections*. Oxford University Press. doi:10.1093/acprof:oso/9780199968275.001.0001

Domeisen, N. (1998). Community Life and Disaster Reduction. *DHA News: Women in Emergencies*. Retrieved from http://www.reliefweb.int/ocha_ol/pub/dhanews/issue22/communit.html

Dorsey, R. W., & Minkarah, E. (1992). *Women in Construction. A report to The Construction Industry Institute*. The University of Texas at Austin.

Dosekun, S. (2007). Defending Feminism in Africa. *Postamble*, *3*(1), 41–47.

Dousa, M. H. (1999). *Gender Identity Formation and its impact on the status of women in Zaghara tribe* (Unpublished Masters dissertation). Ahfad University for Women.

D'Souza, A. (2010). *Moving towards decent work for domestic workers: an overview of the ILO's work*. Geneva: ILO.

Duflo, E. (2012). Women Empowerment and Economic Development. *Journal of Economic Literature*, *50*(4), 1051–1079. doi:10.1257/jel.50.4.1051

Duraisamy, M., & Duraisamy, P. (2016). Gender wage gap across the wage distribution in different segments of the Indian labour market, 1983–2012: Exploring the glass ceiling or sticky floor phenomenon. *Applied Economics*, *48*(43), 4098–4111. doi:10.1080/00036846.2016.1150955

Eagly, A. H., & Carli, L. L. (2007). *Through the Labyrinth: The Truth About How Women Become Leaders*. Harvard Business School Press.

ECB Project. (2013). *Towards Resilience: A Guide to Disaster Risk Reduction and Climate Change Adaptation*. Author.

Echols, A. (1989). *Daring to Be Bad: Radical Feminism in America, 1967–1975*. Minneapolis, MN: University of Minnesota Press.

Elrahman. (2001). *The Sudanese Islamic Movements' Perceptions to Womens Rights* (Unpublished Masters dissertation). Ahfad University for Women.

Elson, D. (1999). Labour Markets as Gendered Institutions: Equality, efficiency andempowerment issues. *World Development*, *27*(3), 611–627. doi:10.1016/S0305-750X(98)00147-8

El-Tahir, G. H. (1999). *Children games: Towards different gender roles* (Unpublished Masters dissertation). Ahfad University for Women.

Eme, O. I., & Onyishi, T. (2015). Women and politics in Nigeria: Strategizing for 2015. *Kuwait Chapter of Arabian Journal of Business and Management Review*, *3*(12), 1–13. doi:10.12816/0019113

Enarson, E. (2000). *Gender issues in natural disasters: Talking points and research needs*. Paper presented at the ILO in Focus Programme on Crisis Response and Reconstruction Workshop, Geneva. Retrieved form https://www.scribd.com/document/253509365/Ilo-Talking

Enarson, E. (2012). *Women confronting natural disaster: from vulnerability to resistance*. Boulder, CO: Lynne Reinner Publishers.

Enarson, E., & Phillips, B. (2008). Invitation to a new feminist disaster sociology: integrating feminist theory and methods. In B. Phillips & B. H. Morrow (Eds.), *Women and Disasters: From Theory to Practice* (pp. 41–74). International Research Committee on Disasters.

Enarson, E., & Scanlon, J. (1999). Gender patterns in flood evacuation: A case study in Canadas Red River Valley. *Applied Behavioral Science Review*, *7*(2), 103–124. doi:10.1016/S1068-8595(00)80013-6

Endong, F. P. C. (2012). Femininity versus feminism in feminine Christian communication: A case study of "The Christian Woman Morror". *CAJOLIS: Calabar Journal of Liberal Studies*, *16*(1), 15–34.

England, P. (2005). Emerging theories of care work, Annual Review of Sociology. *Annual Reviews*, *31*(1), 381–399. doi:10.1146/annurev.soc.31.041304.122317

Ensher, E. A., Heun, C., & Blanchard, A. (2003). Online Mentoring and Computer-mediated Communication: New Directions in Research. *Journal of Vocational Behavior*, *63*(2), 264–288. doi:10.1016/S0001-8791(03)00044-7

Evetts, J. (1996). *Gender and Career in Science & Engineering*. London: Taylor & Francis.

Eya, R. (2005). *Gender and culture: What needs to change in the society and in the Church. In Gender equality from a Christian perspectives* (pp. 23–35). Enugu: Ifendu publications.

Eyben, R. (2008). *Conceptualizing Empowerment and the Implications for Pro-poor Growth*. Brighton, UK: Institute of Development Studies, University of Sussex.

Ezzedeen, S. R., Budworth, M. H., & Baker, S. D. (2015). The glass ceiling and executive careers still an issue for pre-career women. *Journal of Career Development*.

Fadia, K. (2014). Women's empowerment through Political participation in India. *The Indian Journal of Public Administration*, *LX*(3), 537–548. Retrieved from http://www.iipa.org.in/New%20Folder/13--Kuldeep.pdf

Faisal, I., & Kabir, M. R. (2005). An Analysis of Gender-Water Nexus in Rural Bangladesh. *Journal of Developing Societies*, *21*(1-2), 175–194. doi:10.1177/0169796X05054623

Fakhruddin, S. H. M., & Rahman, J. (2015). Coping with coastal risk and vulnerabilities in Bangladesh. *International Journal of Disaster Risk Reduction*, *12*, 112–118. doi:10.1016/j.ijdrr.2014.12.008

Fakir, M., & Folbre, N. (2006). Measuring care: Gender, empowerment, and the care economy. *Journal of Human Development*, *7*, 2.

FAO. (2014). *Bangladesh Nutrition Country Profile*. Retrieved from http://goo.gl/Nbkiy6

Faroye, E. (2014). Nigerian women in politics: Achieving the 35% affirmative policy. *Royal Time Newspaper, 35*, 16–18.

Ferdousi, S., & Dehai, F. (2014). Economic Growth, Poverty and Inequality Trend in Bangladesh. *Asian Journal of Social Sciences & Humanities, 3*(1). Retrieved from http://www.ajssh.leena-luna.co.jp/AJSSHPDFs/Vol.3(1)/AJSSH2014(3.1-01).pdf

Ferguson, A. (2009). Alternative economies Mexican women left behind: Organizing solidarity economy in response. In L McGovern & I. Wallimann (Eds.), Globalization and Third World Women: Exploitation, Coping and Resistance. Ashgate.

Fernandez, B. (2010). Cheap and disposable? The impact of the global economic crisis on the migration of Ethiopian women domestic workers to the Gulf. *Gender and Development, 18*(2), 249–262. doi:10.1080/13552074.2010.491335

Ferrant, G., Pesando, L. M., & Nowacka, K. (2014). *Unpaid Care Work: The missing link in the analysis of gender gaps in labor outcomes*. OECD Development Centre.

Ferree, M. M. (1991). The gender division of labor in two-earner marriages. *Journal of Family Issues, 12*(2), 158–180. doi:10.1177/019251391012002002

Fischer, S. (2005). *Gender Based Violence in Sri Lanka in the Aftermath of the 2004 Tsunami Crisis*. Retrieved from http://www.gdnonline.org/resources/fisher-post-tsuami-gbv-srilanka.doc

Fisher, B., Cullen, F., & Turner, M. (2000). *The sexual victimization of college women*. Washington, DC: US Department of Justice. Available at www.ecrs.gov/pdf files/nij/182369.pdf

Fisher, B. S., Cullen, F. T., & Turner, M. G. (2000). *The Sexual Victimization of College Women*. Washington, DC: National Institute of Justice and Bureau of Justice Statistics. doi:10.1037/e377652004-001

Flanders, M. L. (1994). *Breaking through: The Career Woman's Guide to Shattering the Glass Ceiling*. London: Paul Chapman.

Fletcher, J. K. (1999). *Disappearing Acts: Gender, Power and Relational Practice at Work*. Cambridge, MA: MIT Press.

Fleury, A. (2016). *Understanding Women and Migration: A Literature Review*. Academic Press.

Folbre, N. (2003). Caring labor [Video transcript]. Amherst, MA: Academic Press.

Folbre, N. (2012). *The Care Economy in Africa: Subsistence Production and Unpaid Care*. Paper for the AERC Biannual Research Workshop.

Fordham, M. (1999). The intersection of gender and social class in disaster: Balancing resilience and vulnerability. *International Journal of Mass Emergencies and Disasters, 17*(1), 15–36. PMID:12295202

Foreign and Commonwealth Office. (2009). *Sudan country profile*. Retrieved from: http://www.fco.gov.uk/en/travelling-and-living-overseas/travel-advice-by-country/sub-saharan-africa/sudan1?ta=all

Forum, G. H. (2009). *The Anatomy of a Silent Crisis*. Geneva: Author.

Fothergill, A. (1998). The neglect of gender in disaster work: an overview of the literature. In E. Enarson & B. H. Morrow (Eds.), *The Gendered Terrain of Disaster: Through Women's Eyes*. Westport, CT: Praeger Publishers.

Fothergill, A. (2008). Domestic Violence after Disaster: Voices from the 1997 Grand Forks Flood. In B. D. Phillips & B. H. Morrow (Eds.), *Women and Disasters: From theory to practice* (pp. 131–154). International Research Committee on Disasters.

Francis, E. (2002). Gender, Migration and Multiple Livelihoods: Cases from Eastern and Southern Africa. *The Journal of Development Studies*, *38*(5), 167–190. doi:10.1080/00220380412331322551

Franiuk, R. (2007). Discussing and defining sexual assault: A classroom activity. *College Teaching*, *55*(3), 104–107. doi:10.3200/CTCH.55.3.104-108

Frank, A. K. (2008). Key feminist concerns regarding core labor standards, decent work and corporate social responsibility. WIDE Network. Retrieved from www.wide-network.org

Fraser, N. (2003). *Redistribution or recognition? A political-philosophical exchange*. London: Verso.

Frederick Littrell, R., & Bertsch, A. (2013). Traditional and contemporary status of women in the patriarchal belt. Equality, Diversity And Inclusion. *International Journal (Toronto, Ont.)*, *32*(3), 310–324. doi:10.1108/edi-12-2012-0122

Fredrickson, B. L., & Roberts, T. A. (1997). Objectification theory: Toward understanding womens lived experience and mental health risks. *Psychology of Women Quarterly*, *21*(2), 173–206. doi:10.1111/j.1471-6402.1997.tb00108.x

Freedman, E. B. (2003). *No Turning Back: The History of Feminism and the Future of Women*. Ballantine Books.

Friedman, T. (2000). *The Lexus and The Olive Tree*. Anchor Books.

Fries, L. (2012). Book Review: Transnational Communities: Shaping Global Economic Governance. *Organization Studies*, *33*(8), 1091–1094. doi:10.1177/0170840611431656

Funny or Die. (2016). 21 best GIFs of all the time of the week #168. *Funny or Die*. Retrieved from: http://www.funnyordie.com/slideshows/7e240c15c2/21-best-gifs-of-all-time-of-the-week-168

Fussell, E. (2000). Making Labor Flexible: The Recomposition of Tijuanas. *Feminist Economics*, *6*(3), 59–79. doi:10.1080/135457000750020137

Gaidzanwa, R. (1992). Bourgeois Theories of Gender and Feminism and their Shortcomings with Reference to Southern African Countries. In Gender in Southern Africa: Conceptual and Theoretical Issues. Harare: SAPES Books.

Gain, P. (2000). *Life and nature at risk*. In The Chittagong Hill Tracts: Life and Nature at Risk (pp. 1–41). Dhaka, Bangladesh: SEHD.

Gain, P. (2000). *Women in the CHT: some facts*. In The Chittagong Hill Tracts: Life and Nature at Risk (pp. 94–95). Dhaka, Bangladesh: SEHD.

Gardner, K., & Kotalova, J. (1995). Belonging to Others: Cultural Construction of Womanhood Among Muslims in a Village in Bangladesh. *Journal of the Royal Anthropological Institute*, *1*(2), 445. doi:10.2307/3034740

Gary, B., & Jennifer, S. (2010). *Engaging Men as Allies in Women's Economic Empowerment: Strategies and Recommendations for CARE Country Offices*. Washington, DC: ICRW.

Gatrell, C. J., & Cooper, C. L. (2007). (No) cracks in the glass ceiling: women managers, stress and the barriers to success. In D. Biliomoria & S. K. Piderit (Eds.), Handbook on Women in Business and Management, (pp. 57-77). Glos: Edward Elgar Publishing Ltd.

GDP - Bangladesh Bureau of Statistics-Government of the People's Republic of Bangladesh. (2016). Retrieved 12 November 2016, from http://bbs.gov.bd/site/page/dc2bc6ce-7080-48b3-9a04-73cec782d0df/Gross-Domestic-Product-(GDP)

Geddes, D. (1998). CU report: Inequality among women in the workplace is widening. *Cornell Chronicle*. Retrieved from http://www.news.cornell.edu/Chronicle/98/2.19.98/Blau_report.html

Gender Tree. (n.d.). *Egyptian Third Gender*. Retrieved from: http://www.gendertree.com/Egyptian%20third%20gender.htm

Gerharz, E. (2001). *Ambivalences of development co-operation in post-conflict regions: ethnicity in the Chittagong Hill Tracts Bangladesh* (Diploma Thesis). Bielefeld University.

Gershuny, J., & Sullivan, O. (2003). Time use, gender, and public policy regimes. *Social Politics*, *10*(2), 205–227. doi:10.1093/sp/jxg012

Gherardi, S. (1995). *Gender, Symbolism and Organizational Cultures*. London: Sage.

Ghosh, J. (2009). 'Informalization and women's workforce participation. A consideration of recent trends in Asia. In S. Razavi (Ed.), *The gendered impacts of liberalization: towards 'embedded' liberalism?*. London: Routledge.

Giddens, A. (2005). Sociology (2nd ed.). Cambridge, UK: Polity Press.

Giddens, A. (1990). *The Consequences of Modernity*. Cambridge, UK: Polity Press.

Gikuru, C. M. (2013). *The Plight of Kenyan Domestic Workers in Gulf Countries*. San Francisco, CA: University of San Francisco.

Gil Araujo, S., & González-Fernández, T. (2014). International migration, public policies and domestic work. *Womens Studies International Forum*, *46*, 13–23. doi:10.1016/j.wsif.2014.01.007

GLBTQ. (n.d.). Retrieved from: http://www.glbtq.com/social-sciences/africa_pre.html

Global Commission on International Migration (GCIM). (2005). *Migration in an interconnected world: New directions for action*. Retrieved from http://www.queensu.ca/samp/migrationresources/reports/gcim-complete-report-2005.pdf

Global Humanitarian Forum Geneva. (2009). *Human impact report the anatomy of A silent crisis the anatomy of A silent crisis*. Available at: http://www.ghf-ge.org/human-impact-report.pdf

Goetz, A. M. and Sen Gupta, R. (1994). *Who Takes the Credit? Gender, Power, and Control over Loan Use in Rural Credit Programmes, Bangladesh*. Retrieved from http://www.gdrc.org/icm/references/microfinance.html

Goetz, A. M., & Sen Gupta, R. (1996). Who Takes The Credit? Gender, Power and Control over Loan Use in Rural Credit Programs in Bangladesh. *World Development*, *24*(1), 45–63. doi:10.1016/0305-750X(95)00124-U

Goonesekere, S. W. E. (2000). Legal education in independent Sri Lanka: 1948 to 1997. In S. Tilakaratna & H. P. M. Gunasena (Eds.), *University Education since Independence* (pp. 86–110). Colombo: University Grant Commission.

Goswami, A., & Dutta, S. (2015). ICT in Women Entrepreneurial Firms -A Literature Review. *IOSR Journal of Business and Management*, *17*(2), 2319–7668. <ALIGNMENT.qj></ALIGNMENT>10.9790/487X-17243841

Government of Bangladesh. (2016). Probasi Kollayan O Boideshik Kormosangstahn Niti 2016. Dhaka: Ministry of Expatriates' Welfare and Overseas Employment. (in Bengali)

Government of Pakistan. (2009). *Pakistan Employment Trends for Women: Series No.5*. Islamabad: Ministry of Labour, Manpower, Labour Market Information and Analysis Unit.

Green, W. S., & Neusner, J. (1996). *The Religion Factor: An Introduction to how Religion Matters*. Westminster John Knox Press.

Gross, A. M., Winslett, A., Roberts, M., & Gohm, C. L. (2006). An Examination of Sexual Violence against College Women. *Violence Against Women*, *12*(3), 288–300. doi:10.1177/1077801205277358 PMID:16456153

Gruber, J. E. (1992). A typology of personal and environmental sexual harassment: Research and policy implications for the 1990s. *Sex Roles*, *26*(11/12), 447–464. doi:10.1007/BF00289868

Guhathakurta, M. (2000). Women's survival and resistance. In P. Gain (Ed.), *The Chittagong Hill Tracts: Life and Nature at Risk* (pp. 79–93). Dhaka, Bangladesh: SEHD.

Hafeez, A., & Ahmed, E. (2002). *Factors Detremining the Labour Force Participation Decision of Educated Married Women in District of Punjab*. Islamabad: SDPI, Working Paper No. 74.

Haider, R. (2000). *A Perspective in Development*. Dhaka, Bangladesh: UPL.

Halim, S. (2007). Situation of indigenous women and ILO Convention on discrimination. *Solidarity*. Bangladesh Indigenous People's Forum.

Halim, S. (2010). Insecurity of indigenous women. In N. Mohaiemen (Ed.), Between Ashes and Hope: Chittagong Hill Tracts in the Blind Spot of Bangladesh Nationalism. Drishtipat Writers' Collective.

Halim, S., & Roy, R. D. (2006). *Lessons learned from the application of human rights-based approaches in the Chittagong Hill Tracts, Bangladesh: A case study of the village common forest project implemented by Taungya*. United Nations Development Programme. Retrieved from: http://hrbaportal.org/wp-content/files/bangladesh_forestry-sector.pdf

Hancock, P., Carastathis, G., Georgiou, J., & Oliveira, M. (2015). Female workers in textile and garment sectors in Sri Lankan Export Processing Zones (EPZs): Gender dimensions and working conditions. *Sri Lanka Journal of Social Sciences, 38*(1), 63–77. doi:10.4038/sljss.v38i1.7386

Hanisch, C. (2006). *Hanisch, New Intro to "The Personal is Political" - Second Wave and Beyond*. The Personal Is Political.

Hannan, C. (2007). *Promoting gender equality and empowerment of women in cities*. Paper presented at Global City Strategies for Implementing Policies on Gender Equality Conference, Seoul, South Korea.

Haque, T. (2009). *Household Diplomacy: Access to Income and Women's Agency in Bangladesh*. Working Paper Series: 5. Department of Women and Gender Studies, University of Dhaka.

Harding, S. (1987) Introduction: Is there a Feminist Method?. In Feminism and Methodology (pp. 1-15). Bloomington, IN: Indiana University Press.

Harding, G. S. (1987). *Feminism and Methodology: social science issues Women's studies social sciences*. Indiana University Press.

Harding, S. (1987). Rethinking Standpoint Epistemology: What is Strong Objectivity? In L. Alcoff & E. Potter (Eds.), *Feminist Epistemologies*. New York: Routledge.

Harkar, T. (2007). Consequences of work-family conflict for working women and possible solutions: A conceptual model. *Journal of Global Strategic Management, 02*, 60–72.

Harvey, D. (2005). *A brief history of neoliberalism*. Oxford, UK: Oxford University Press.

Hashmi, T. (2000). *Women and Islam in Bangladesh* (1st ed.). Houndmills, UK: Palgrave. doi:10.1057/9780333993873

Hasnine, M. S. (2011). Evaluation and development of bus based public transport in Dhaka city. *Proceedings of 4th Annual Paper Meet and 1st Civil Engineering Congress*. Retrieved February 23, 2016, from http://www.iebconferences.info/391.pdf

Hatemi-J, A., & Uddin, G. (2013). On the causal nexus of remittances and poverty reduction in Bangladesh. *Applied Economics, 46*(4), 374–382. doi:10.1080/00036846.2013.844331

Hawker, C. (2015, November 23). Why men's violence against women skyrockets after natural disaster. *The Daily Life*. Retrieved from http://www.dailylife.com.au/news-and-views/take-action/why-mens-violence-against-women-skyrockets-after-natural-disaster-20151120-gl3sid

HBR. (2005). *Harvard business review on women in business*. Boston, MA: Harvard Business School Publishing Corporation.

Hearn, J. (1992). *Men and organizational culture*. Paper given in IRRU Workshop, Warwick Papers in Industrial Relations, No. 48, University of Warwick.

Heffernan, M. (2004). *The naked truth: a working woman manifesto on business and what really matters* (1st ed.). San Francisco, CA: Jossey-Bass, A Wiley Imprint.

Heinz, B. C. (2006). Documenting the Image in Mithila Art. *Visual Anthropology Review, 22*(2), 5–33. doi:10.1525/var.2006.22.2.5

Heissler, K. (2001). *Background Paper on Good Practices and Priorities to Combat Sexual Abuse and Exploitation of Children in Bangladesh*. Bangladesh: UNICEF.

Hennegan, J., & Montgomery, P. (2016). *Do Menstrual Hygiene Management Interventions Improve Education and Psychosocial Outcomes for Women and Girls in Low and Middle Income? A Systematic Review*. Available at http://eprints.whiterose.ac.uk/43906/1/Irise_report_-_Dec_2012_%5BSAJ%5D_v2_(1).pdf

Henrici, J. M., Helmuth, A. S., & Braun, J. (2010). *Women, Disasters, and Hurricane Katrina*. Washington, DC: Institute for Women's Policy Research.

Herath, H. M. A. (2015). Place of women in Sri Lankan society: Measures for their empowerment for development and good governance. *Vidyodaya Journal of Management, 1*(1), 1–14.

Hersch, J., & Stratton, L. S. (1994). Housework, Wages and the Division of Housework time for Employed Spouses. *The American Review, 84*(2), 120–125.

Hewamanne, S. (2003). Performing dis-respectability: New tastes, cultural practices, and identity performances by Sri Lankas free trade zone garment-factory workers. *Cultural Dynamics, 15*(1), 71–101. doi:10.1177/a033109

Hewamanne, S. (2008). *Stitching identities in a free trade zone; Gender and politics in Sri Lanka*. Philadelphia: University of Pennsylvania Press.

Hochschild, A. R. (2000). Global care chains and emotional surplus value. In A. Giddens & W. Hutton (Eds.), *On the edge: living with global capitalism* (pp. 130–146). London: Jonathan Cape.

Hodge, R. D., & Leitz, A. C. (2007). The International Sexual Trafficking of Women and Children: A Review of the Literature. *Affilia, 22*(2), 163–174. doi:10.1177/0886109907299055

Holland, K. (2015). *Working moms still take on bulk of household chores*. CNBC. Retrieved from http://www.cnbc.com/2015/04/28/me-is-like-leave-it-to-beaver.html

Holmes, R., Jones, N., & Marsden, H. (2009). Gender vulnerabilities, food price shocks and social protection responses. Overseas Development Institute Background Note.

Hondagneu-Sotelo, P. (1997). Affluent players in the informal economy: Employers of paid domestic workers. *The International Journal of Sociology and Social Policy, 17*(3/4), 130–158. doi:10.1108/eb013303

Horton, S. (1996). *Women and Industralization in Asia*. New York: Routledge. doi:10.4324/9780203434369

Hossain, J. B. (2007). *Women Engineers in Construction Industry: A Comparative Study in Bangladesh and Thailand*. AIT Diss. no.GD-07-01. Asian Institute of Technology, Bangkok.

Hossain, J. B., & Kusakabe, K. (2005). Sex segregation in construction organizations in Bangladesh and Thailand. Journal of Construction Management and Economics, 23(6).

Hossain, M. (2016, March 30). Ekbochore nari nirjaton bereche 74 shotangsho. *Prothom Alo*.

Hossain, M. D. (2013). Socio-economic situation of Indigenous people in the Chittagong Hill Tracts (CHT) of Bangladesh. *Middle-East Journal of Business, 7*(3).

Hossain, N. (2012). *Women's empowerment revisited. From individual to collective power among the export sector workers in Bangladesh*. IDS Working Paper Vol. 2012. No.389. Brighton, UK: IDS.

Hossain, N., Nazneen, S., & Sultan, M. (2011). National Discourses on Women's Empowerment in Bangladesh: Continuities and Change. *IDS Working Paper, 2011*(368). 10.2139/ssrn.2026729

Hossain. (2004). *Commercial Sexual Behaviour and Risk Factors in Bangladesh: An Invesigation of Female sex Workers in Rajshahi City*. Higher Education Link Programme.

House, S., & Mahon, T. (2014). *Menstrual Hygiene Matters: A Resource for Improving Menstrual Hygiene Around the World WaterAid*. Available at www.wateraid.org/~/media/Files/Global/MHM files/Module5_HR.pdflast

Huda, S. (1999). Perspectives on Sexual Harassment in Bangladesh: Acknowledging its Existence. *Empowerment*, 6.

Hudson-Weems, C. (2004). *Africana Womanist Literary Theory*. Asmara: Africa World Press Inc.

Hughes, C. (2002). *Women's contemporary lives: Within and beyond the mirror*. London: Routledge. doi:10.4324/9780203451618

Hugo, G. (2011). Migration and Development in Malaysia. *Asian Population Studies, 7*(3), 219–241. doi:10.1080/17441730.2011.608983

Humm, M. (1989). *The Dictionary of Feminist Theory*. London: Prentice Hall.

Huppatz, K., & Goodwin, S. (2013). Masculinised jobs, feminised jobs and mens gender capital experiences: Understanding occupational segregation in Australia. *Journal of Sociology (Melbourne, Vic.), 49*(2-3), 291–308. doi:10.1177/1440783313481743

Huq, M. M. (2000). *Government Institutions and Underdevelopment: A Study of the Tribal People of Chittagong Hill Tracts, Bangladesh*. Dhaka: Center for Social Studies, Dhaka University.

Hyder, A., & B, R. (2005). The Public and Private Sector Pay Gap in Pakistan: A Quantile Regression Analysis. *Pakistan Development Review, 44*(3), 271–306.

IANS. (2016). Women outnumber men in using Google Search in India. *The Indian Express*. Retrieved from: http://indianexpress.com/article/technology/social/google-search-women-outnumber-men-happy-international-womens-day/

ICRW. (2011). Determination of family task sharing: A study of husbands and wives. *Journal of Marriage and the Family, 46*, 345–355.

Ifemeje, S., & Ikpeze, O. (2012). Global trend toward gender equality: Nigeria's experience in focus. *Kuwait Chapter of Arabian Journal of Business and Management Review, 2*(3), 51–63.

Ihemeje, G. (2013). The need for participation of women in local governance: A Nigerian discourse. *International Journal of Educational Administration and Policy Studies, 5*(4), 59–66.

IIPS. (2007). National Family Health Survey (NFHS-3), 2005–06: India Volume I. International Institute for Population Sciences (IIPS).

Ikeda, K. (1995). Gender differences in human loss and vulnerability in natural disasters: A case study from Bangladesh. *Indian Journal of Gender Studies, 2*(2), 171–193. doi:10.1177/097152159500200202

Ikpeze, O. V. C. (2002). Understanding affirmative action as aid to women's human rights in Nigeria. In H. Ibrahim (Ed.), *Bar perspective: A quarterly publication of the Nigerian bar Association* (pp. 540–580). Abuja: Nigerian Bar Association.

Ilavarasan, P., & Levy, M. (2010). *ICTs and Urban Microenterprises: Identifying and Maximizing Opportunities for Economic Development*. Available at http://www.idrc.ca/uploads/userS/12802403661ICTs_and_Urban_Microenterprises_104170-001.pdf

ILO. (1990). International standard classification of occupations: ISCO 88. Geneva: ILO.

ILO. (2011). *Decent work for domestic workers: Convention 189 and Recommendation 201 at a glance*. Geneva: ILO.

ILO. (2011). *Report of the Director General. A new era of social justice*. In International Labor Conference, 100th Session, ILO, Geneva, Switzerland.

ILO. (2013). *Domestic workers across the world: Global and regional statistics and the extent of legal protection*. International Labour Office Geneva.

ILO. (2016). Retrieved from http://www.ilo.org/islamabad/info/public/pr/WCMS_233379/lang--en/index.htm

Imtiaz, S. M. S. (2009). *Understanding masculinities: men's perspectives and gender studies curriculum in Bangladesh*. Dhaka: Department of Women and Gender Studies.

Imtiaz, S. M. S. (2014). *Rongin shohorer torunera*. Dhaka: CMMS.

India, F. (2016). *Annual ranking of India's most powerful women in business*. Retrieved from http://fortuneindia.com/mpw/2016

IndiaToday.in. (2015, Sep 4). *10 most powerful female politicians in India*. Retrieved from http://indiatoday.intoday.in/education/story/women-politicians/1/465444.html

Integrated Regional Information Networks. (2010). *Pakistan: Minorities test aid impartiality*. Retrieved from available at: http://www.refworld.org/docid/4c8df239c.html

International Center Research on Women. (2011). *Understanding and Measuring Women's Economic Empowerment Definition*. Washington, DC: International Center Research on Women.

International Centre for Research on Women. (2012). *Connectivity – How mobile phones, computers, and the Internet can catalyze women's entrepreneurship – India: A Case Study*. Author.

International Federation of Red Cross and Red Crescent Societies. (2007). *World Disaster Report: Focus on discrimination*. Retrieved from http://www.ifrc.org/Docs/pubs/disasters/wdr2007/WDR2007-English.pdf

International Food Policy Research Institute. (1995). Women: the key to food security: Looking into the household. Washington, DC: Author.

International Labor Organization. (2016). *Women at Work: Trend 2016*. Geneva: International Labor Office.

International Monetary Fund. (2016). Retrieved from http://www.imf.org/external/pubs/ft/weo/2016/update/01/

International Organization for Migration. (2015). *Migration in Kenya: A country in profile*. Nairobi: International Organization for Migration.

International Organization for Migration. (2015, December 11). *Migrant workers suffer exploitation, abuse in Middle East, North Africa: Report*. Retrieved from https://www.iom.int/news/migrant-workers-suffer-exploitation-abuse-middle-east-north-africa-report

Irfan, M. (2008). *Pakistan's Wage Structure, During 1990/91 - 2006/07*. Retrieved March 13, 2011, from PIDE: http://www.pide.org.pk/pdf/pws.pdf

IRIN. (2013). Nepal's maternal mortality decline paradox. *IRIN News*. Available at http://www.irinnews.org/analysis/2013/03/18/nepal%E2%80%99s-maternal-mortality-decline-paradox

Islam, M. (2013). Gender Analysis of Migration from Bangladesh. Dhaka, Bangladesh: Bureau of Manpower, Employment and Training. Retrieved from http://www.bmet.gov.bd/BMET/resources/Static%20PDF%20and%20DOC/publication/Gender%20Analysis

Islam, M. M., & Jannat, G. (2016). Recognition and Redistribution of Household Work: Exploring the Perception of Middle Class Women and Men. Social Science Review, 33(2), 199-214.

Islam, R. M. (2010). *Maternal morbidity and mortality among Indigenous peoples in Bangladesh: a study of the Mru community* (MPhil Thesis). University of Tromsø, Norway.

Islam, T., & Neelim, A. (2010). *Climate Change in Bangladesh: A Closer Look into Temperature and Rainfall Data*. Academic Press.

Islam, M. M. (2012). The GDP Matter: Valuing The Fulltime Homemakers Household Work Time. *Modern Social Science Journal, 1*(1), 1–20.

Itzin, C. (1995). The gender culture in organizations. In C. Itzin & J. Newman (Eds.), *Gender, culture and organizational change* (pp. 30–53). London: Rutledge. doi:10.4324/9780203427965_chapter_2

Jackson, L. A., Ervin, K. S., Gardner, P. D., & Schmitt, N. (2001). Gender and the Internet: Women Communicating and Men Searching. *Sex Roles, 44*(5/6), 363–379. doi:10.1023/A:1010937901821

Jackson, S., & Scott, S. (2002). *Gender: A Sociological Reader*. Routledge.

Jahan, I. (2014). *Obstacles to Women's Participation in the Politics of Bangladesh* (Master's dissertation). Department of Political Science, University of Dhaka.

Jahan, M. (2008). The impact of environmental degradation on women in Bangladesh: An overview. *Asian Affairs, 30*(2), 5–15.

Jahan, R. (1995). *The Elusive Agenda: Mainstreaming Women in Development*. Dhaka: UPL.

Jain, S. (2015). *ICTs and Women's Empowerment : Some Case Studies From India*. Academic Press.

Jain, N., & Mukherji, S. (2010). The perception of 'glass ceiling' in Indian organizations: An exploratory study. *South Asian Journal of Management, 17*(1), 23.

Jaiswal, R. P. (1993). *Professional Status of Women: A comparative study of women and men in science and technology*. New Delhi, India: Rawat Publications.

Compilation of References

James, J. (1978). *Juvenile Female Prostitution - Final Report*. Retrieved from https://www.ncjrs.gov/App/Publications/abstract.aspx?ID=78277

Jayawardena, D. (2010). *Narratives, lamai and female labour: (Re)narrating the untold story of HRM in Sri Lanka's apparel industry* (Unpublished doctoral thesis). University of Leicester, Leicester, UK.

Jayawardena, D. (2015). On the burden of being-qua-non-being: In between the lines of (working class) writings. In A. Pullen & C. Rhodes (Eds.), The Routledge companion to ethics, politics and organizations (pp. 150-161). London: Routledge.

Jayawardena, D. (2012). Looking through the glass of managerial femininity: A polemic. *Journal of Gender and Justice, 1*, 1–13.

Jayawardena, D. (2014). HRM as a web of texts: (Re)articulating the identity of HRM in Sri Lankas localized global apparel industry. *Organizational Management Journal, 11*(4), 289–298. doi:10.1080/15416518.2014.973794

Jayawardena, K. (2000). *Nobodies to somebodies: the rise of the colonial bourgeoisie in Sri Lanka*. Colombo: Association and Sanjiva Books.

Jayaweera, S. (2002). Women in education and employment. In S. Jayaweera (Ed.), *Women in post- independence Sri Lanka* (pp. 99–142). Colombo: CENWOR.

Jenkins, P., & Phillips, B. (2008). Battered Women, Catastrophe, and the Context of Safety after Hurricane Katrina. *NWSA Journal, 20*(3), 49–69.

Jewkes, R., Sen, P., & Garcia-Moreno, C. (2002). Sexual Violence. In E. Krug, L. Dahlberg, J. A. Mercy, A. B. Zwi, & R. Lozano (Eds.), World Report of Violence and Health (pp. 147–181). Geneva, Switzerland: The World Health Organization. Available at http://www.who.int/violence_injury_prevention/ violence/global_campaign/en/chap6.pdf

Johnson, B. (2002). *The Feminist Difference: Literature, Psychoanalysis, Race and Gender*. Harvard University Press.

Jones, A. (1994). Postfeminism, Feminist Pleasures, and Embodied Theories of Art. In New Feminist Criticism: Art, Identity, Action. New York: HarperCollins.

Jones, S., Johnson-Yale, C., Millermaier, S., & Pérez, F. S. (2009). US College Students Internet Use: Race, Gender and Digital Divides. *Journal of Computer-Mediated Communication, 14*(2), 244–264. doi:10.1111/j.1083-6101.2009.01439.x

Joshi, S. (2011). President launches unique ICT scheme for women. *The Hindu*. Retrieved from http://www.thehindu.com/news/national/article1517932.ece

Joshi. (2005). *Gender friendly environment in the workplace*. Forum for Women, Law and Development, The Asia Foundation.

Jyotindra. (1997). *Ganga Devi: Tradition and Expression in Mithila Painting*. Academic Press.

Kabeer, N. (2008). Mainstreaming gender in social protection for the informal economy. Commonwealth Secretariat, London.

Kabeer, N. (2012). *Women's Economic Empowerment and Inclusive Growth: Labor Markets and Enterprise Development*. SIG Working Paper, Supported by Dept for International Development (DFID) and International Development Research Center (IDRC).

Kabeer, N. (2012). *Women's economic empowerment and inclusive growth: labour markets and enterprise development* (SIG Working Paper 2012/1). International Development Research Centre (IDRC).

Kabeer, N. (2015). Gender equality, the MDGs and the SDGs: Achievements, lessons and concerns. *International Growth Centre*. Available at: http://www.theigc.org/blog/gender-equality-the-mdgs-and-the-sdgs-achievements-lessons-and-concerns/

Kabeer, N., Mahmud, S., & Tasneem, S. (2011). *Does Paid Work Provide a Pathway to Women's Empowerment? Empirical Findings from Bangladesh* (IDS Working Paper 375). IDS, University of Sussex.

Kabeer, N. (1994). *Reversed realities. Gender hierarchies in development thought London*. Verso.

Kabeer, N. (1997). Women, Wages and Intra-household Power Relations in Urban Bangladesh. *Development and Change*, *28*(2), 261–302. doi:10.1111/1467-7660.00043

Kabeer, N. (1999). Resources, Agency, Achievements: Reflections on the Measurement of Womens Empowerment. *Development and Change*, *30*(3), 435–464. doi:10.1111/1467-7660.00125

Kabeer, N. (2000). *The power to choose*. London: VERSO.

Kabeer, N. (2005). Gender equality and women's empowerment: A critical analysis of the third millennium development goal. *Gender and Development*, *13*(1), 13–14. doi:10.1080/13552070512331332273

Kabeer, N. (2009). *Women's Economic Empowerment: Key Issues and Policy Options. SIDA Background Paper*. Sussex, UK: Institute of Development Studies.

Kabir, F. (2014). *Policy Brief on Local Adaptation to Climate Change: The Gender Perspective*. Available at: http://www.icccad.net/wp-content/uploads/2014/07/CCG_Policy-Brief_June-2014.pdf

Kallefalla. (2000). *Towards gender sensitive policies in Sudan: A Case Study: Sudan National Comprehensive Strategy (1992-2002)* (Unpublished Masters dissertation). Ahfad University for Women.

Kalof, L. (2000). Vulnerability to Sexual Coercion among College Women: A Longitudinal Study. *Gender Issues*, *18*(4), 47–58. doi:10.1007/s12147-001-0023-8

Kalof, L., Eby, K. K., Matheson, J. L., & Kroska, R. J. (2001). The influence of race and gender on student self-reports of sexual harassment by college professors. *Gender & Society*, *15*(2), 282–302. doi:10.1177/089124301015002007

Kamruzzaman, M. (2005). *Community Well-being and Religious Form of Organisations (Postgraduate)*. Dhaka, Bangladesh: North South University.

Kane, E. (1996). *Gender*. Culture and Learning.

Kane, E. W. (2013). *Rethinking Gender and Sexuality in Childhood*. Bloomsbury.

Kang, H., & Rowley, C. (2005). Women in management in South Korea: Advancement or retrenchment? *Asia Pacific Business Review*, *11*(2), 213–231. doi:10.1080/1360238042000291171

Kargwell, S. (2008). Is the glass ceiling kept in place in Sudan? Gendered dilemma of the work-life balance. *Gender in Management: An International Journal*, *23*(3), 209–224. doi:10.1108/17542410810866953

Kato, M., & Kratzer, J. (2013). Empowering women through Microfinance: Evidence from Tanzania. *Journal of Entrepreneurship Perspective*, *2*(1), 31–45.

Kelegama, S. (2005). Ready-made garment industry in Sri Lanka: Preparing to face the global challenges. *Asia-Pacific Trade and Investment Review*, *1*(1), 51–67.

Kelley, M. L., & Parsons, B. (2000). Sexual harassment in the 1990s: A university-wide survey of female faculty, administrators, staff, and students. *The Journal of Higher Education*, *71*(5), 548–568. doi:10.2307/2649259

Compilation of References

Kemal. (1999). *Privatization in South Asia: Minimizing Social Effects Through Restructuring* (G. Joshi, Ed.) Retrieved April 19, 2011, from ILO Publications: http://www.ilo.org/public/english/region/asro/bangkok/paper/privatize/index.htm

Kemal, A., & Amjad, R. (1997). Macroeconomic Policies and their impact on Poverty Alleviation in Pakistan. *Pakistan Development Review*, *36*(1).

Khan, I. A., Ali, Z., Asaduzzaman, M., Bhuyan, R., & Harunur, M. (2010). The social dimensions of adaptation to climate change in Bangladesh. Development and climate change discussion paper. Washington, DC: World Bank; Retrieved from http://documents.worldbank.org/curated/en/920271468174884196/pdf/588990NWP0Bang10Box353823B01public1.pdf

Khan, N. A., & Rashid, M. (2006). *A study on the indigenous medical plants and healing practices on Chittagong Hill Tracts (Bangladesh)*. Academic Press.

Khandker, S. (1987). Labour Market Participation of Married Women in Bangladesh. *The Review of Economics and Statistics*, *69*(3).

Khan, F. C. (2005). Gender violence and development discourse in Bangladesh. *International Social Science Journal*, *57*(184), 219–230. doi:10.1111/j.1468-2451.2005.546.x

Khan, S. (1988). *The Fifty Percent: Women in Development Policy in Bangladesh*. Dhaka: The University Press Limited.

Khattak, S. G. (2001). *Women, Work and Empowerment*. Working Paper No. 4. Karachi: PILER & SDPI.

Khattak, S. G., & Sayeed, A. (2000). *Subcontract Women Workers in the World Economy: The Case of Pakistan*. Islamabad: SDPI.

Khisa, S. (2011). *The women of the Chittagong Hill Tracts and their experiences on climate change. In Indigenous Women, Climate change & Forests* (pp. 127–140). Baguio City, Philippines: TEBTEBBA Foundation.

Khondoker, M. H. (1996). Women and floods in Bangladesh. *International Journal of Mass Emergencies and Disasters*, *14*(3), 281–292.

Khosla, N. (2009). The ready-made garments industry in Bangladesh: A means to reducing gender-based social exclusion of women? *Journal of International Women's Studies*, *11*(1), 289–303.

Kiaye, E. R., & Singh, M. A. (2013). The glass ceiling: A perspective of women working in Durban. *Gender in Management: An International Journal*, *28*(1), 28–42. doi:10.1108/17542411311301556

Kingsbury, D. (2008). Globalization and Development. In D. Kingsbury (Ed.), *International Development: Issues and Challenges*. Palgrave.

Kinuthia-Njenga, C. (2010). *Local government for gender*. Retrieved September 20, 2016, from http://www.capacity.com

Kirby, D., & Turner, M. (1993). IT and the small retail business. *International Journal of Retail & Distribution Management*, *21*(7), 20–27. doi:10.1108/09590559310046022

Kisiang'ani, D., & Lewis, O. (2004). African Gender Scholarship: Concepts, Methodologies and Paradigms. Dakar: CODESRIA.

KNOMAD. (2016). Retrieved from http://siteresources.worldbank.org/INTPROSPECTS/Resources/334934-1199807908806/4549025-1450455807487/Factbookpart1.pdf

Knowledge@Wharton. (2009, May 21). *What Is the Role of Women in Indian Politics? Growing Stronger...* Retrieved from http://knowledge.wharton.upenn.edu/article/what-is-the-role-of-women-in-indian-politics-growing-stronger/

Kodoth & Eapen. (2005, July 23). Looking Beyond Gender Parity: Gender Inequities of Some Dimensions of Well-Being in Kerala. *EPW*.

Koggel, C. M. (2003). Globalization and Womens Paid Work: Expanding Freedom. *Feminist Economics*, 9(2-3), 163–183. doi:10.1080/1354570022000077935

Kohbar, by the legendary *Padma Shri* Sita Devi

Koss, M. P., & Cleveland, H. H. III. (1996). Athletic Participation, Fraternity Membership, and Date Rape: The Question Remains—Self-Selection or Different Causal Processes?. *Violence Against Women*, 2(2), 180–190. doi:10.1177/1077801296002002005 PMID:12295458

Koukkanen, R. (2011). Indigenous economies, theories of subsistence, and women: Exploring the social economy model for Indigenous Governance. *American Indian Quarterly*, 35(2), 215–240. doi:10.5250/amerindiquar.35.2.0215

Kroløkke, C. (2006). Three Waves of Feminism. In C. Kroløkke & A. S. Sørensen (Eds.), *Gender Communication Theories and Analyses: From Silence to Performance*. Sage Publications Inc.

Kuhn, S., & Bluestone, B. (1987). Economic Restrcturing and the Female Labour Market: The Importance of Industrial Change on Women. In L. Beneria & C. R. Stmpson (Eds.), *Women, Households and the Economy*. Rutgers University Press.

Kusakabe, K. (1998). *Women's Participation in the Market: A Case Study of Women Retail Traders in Phnom Penh, Cambodia*. AIT Dissertation No. GD-98-01. Asian Institute of Technology, Bangkok.

Kuzilwa, J. A. (2005). The Role of Credit for Small Business Success: A Study of the National Entrepreneurship Development Fund in Tanzania. *Journal of Entrepreneurship*, 14(2), 131–161. doi:10.1177/097135570501400204

Labor Force Survey Bangladesh. (2013). *Bangladesh Bureau of Statistics, Statistics and Informatics Division, Ministry of Planning, with support from International Labor Organization*. ILO.

Lamichhane, K. B., Asis, B., Chakraborty, P., Sathian, B., Subba, S. H., & Jovanovic, S. (2012). Psychological study of depression amongst women in western region of Nepal. *Asian Journal of Medical Science*, 3(4), 39–46.

Lawry, L. (2011). *Research study on sex and gender based violence*. Retrieved from www.africom.mil/news room / transcript/7957/transcript-research

Lazreg, M. (1994). *The Eloquence of Silence: Algerian Women in Question*. London: Routledge.

Lee, J. W. (2005). *Gender Roles*. Nova Biomedical Books.

Levene, M. (1999). The Chittagong Hill Tracts: A case study in the political economy of creeping genocide. *Third World Quarterly*, 20(2), 339–369. doi:10.1080/01436599913794 PMID:22523784

Levitt, P. (2005). *Social remittances - Culture as a development tool*. Presentation, International Forum on Remittances.

Levitt, P. (1998). Social Remittances: Migration Driven Local-Level Forms of Cultural Diffusion. *International Migration Review*, 32(4), 926. doi:10.2307/2547666 PMID:12294302

Levitt, P., & Schiller, N. (2006). Conceptualizing Simultaneity: A Transnational Social Field Perspective on Society1. *International Migration Review*, 38(3), 1002–1039. doi:10.1111/j.1747-7379.2004.tb00227.x

Lewenhak, S. (1992). The Revaluation of Women's Work. Earthscan Publications Limited.

Lewis, D. (2004). African Gender Research and Postcoloniality: Legacies and Challenges?. In S. Arnfred, B. Bakari-Yusuf, E. W. Kisiang'ani, D. Lewis, O. Oyewumi, & F. C. Steady (Eds.), *African Gender Scholarship: Concepts, Methodologies and Paradigms* (pp. 27–41). Dakar: CODESRIA.

Lien, B. (2005). Gender, power and office politics. *Human Resource Development International, 8*(3), 293–309. doi:10.1080/13678860500199758

Li, L., & Leung, R. W. (2001). Female managers in Asian hotels: Profile and career challenges. *International Journal of Contemporary Hospitality Management, 13*(4), 189–186. doi:10.1108/09596110110389511

Linda, W. (2004). *Breaking through the glass ceiling: Women in management (Updated)*. Geneva: ILO.

Lindsay, L. A., & Miescher, S. F. (Eds.). (2003). *Men and Masculinities in Modern Africa*. Portsmouth: Heinemann.

Lindsey, L. L. (2015). *Gender Roles: A Sociological Perspective*. Routledge.

Livingston, M. (2011). A longitudinal analysis of alcohol outlet density and domestic violence. *Addiction (Abingdon, England), 106*(5), 919–925. doi:10.1111/j.1360-0443.2010.03333.x PMID:21205052

Lorber, J. (1994). *Paradoxes of gender*. New Haven, CT: Yale University Press.

Luke, C. (1998). Cultural politics and women in Singapore higher education management. *Gender and Education, 10*(3), 245–263. doi:10.1080/09540259820880

Lyman, J. (1964). The Metropolitan Police Act of 1829: An analysis of Certain Events Influencing The Passage and Character of the Metropolitan Police Act in England. *The Journal of Criminal Law, Criminology, and Police Science, 55*(1), 141–154. doi:10.2307/1140471

Lynch, C. (2002). The politics of white womens underwear in Sri Lankas open economy. *Social Politics, 9*(1), 87–125. doi:10.1093/sp/9.1.87

MacKinnon, C. A. (1979). *Sexual harassment of working women: A case of sex discrimination*. New Haven, CT: Yale University Press.

Maddock, S. (1999). *Challenging Women: Gender, Culture and Organization*. London: Sage.

Mahalingam, A. (2010). *Conceptual Guide to the Unpaid Work Module. Gender, Work and Data base*. Retrieved from http://www.genderwork.ca/cms/displayarticle.php?sid=18&aid=56

Mahbuba, N. (2008). *Violence Against Women during flood and post-flood situations in Bangladesh*. ActionAid Bangladesh.

Mahmud, S., & Tasneem, S. (2011). The Under Reporting of Women's Economic Activity in Bangladesh: An Examination of Official Statistics. *BRAC Development Institute Working Paper, 01*(February).

Mahmud, M., & Rabbani, A. (2012). *Travel mode choice preferences of urban commuters in Dhaka: a pilot study*. Dhaka: International Growth Center.

Mahmud, S. (2002). *Informal women's groups in Rural Bangladesh:operation and Outcome. In Group Behavior and Development: Is the market destroying cooperation* (pp. 209–225). Oxford, UK: Oxford University of Press.

Mahmud, S., Shah, N., & Becker, S. (2012). Measurement of Womens Empowerment in Rural Bangladesh. *World Development, 40*(3), 610–619. doi:10.1016/j.worlddev.2011.08.003 PMID:23637468

Mahon, T., & Fernades, M. (2010). Menstrual hygiene in South Asia: A neglected issue for WASH (water, sanitation and hygiene) programmes. *Gender and Development, 18*(1), 99–113. doi:10.1080/13552071003600083

Mahtab, N. (2007). *Women in Bangladesh: From Inequality to Empowerment*. Dhaka: A H Development Publishing House.

Mahtab, N. (2012). *Women, Gender and Development: Contemporary Issues*. Dhaka: A H Development Publishing House.

Mahtab, A. (2012). *Women, gender and development contemporary issues*. Dhaka: A. H. Development Publishing House.

Maier, S., & Reichert, U.N. (2007). *ICT-Based Business Initiatives: An Overview of Best Practices in E-Commerce / E-Retailing Projects*. MIT Press.

Makama, G. A. (2013). Patriarchy and gender inequality in Nigeria: The way forward. *European Scientific Journal*, 9(17), 115–144.

Makombe, I. A. M. (2006). *Women Entrepreneurship Development and Empowerment in Tanzania: Thecase of SIDO/UNIDO-Supported Women Microentrepreneurs in the Food Processing Sector* (Doctoral dissertation). University of South Africa, South Africa.

Makombe, I. A. M., Temba, E. I., & Kibombo, A. R. M. (1999). *Credit Schemes and Women's Empowerment for Poverty Alleviation*. The Case Study of Tanga Region. Research Report No. 1. Research for Poverty Alleviation.

Malhotra, A. (2002). *Measuring women's empowerment as a variable in international development*. Paper prepared for the World Bank workshop on poverty and Gender; New Perspective.

Malhotra, A., Schuler, S. R., & Boender, C. (2002), *Measuring Women's Empowerment as a Variable in International Development*, Background Paper Prepared for the World Bank Workshop on Poverty and Gender: New Perspectives.

Malhotra, A., & Mather, M. (1997). Do schooling and work empower women in developing countries? Gender and domestic decisions in Sri Lanka. *Sociological Forum*, 12(4), 599–630. doi:10.1023/A:1022126824127

Malik, S. A. (2008). Women Political Rights, Decision Making, Representation and Good Governance. In Sudanese Women Profile and Pathways to Empowerment. Ahfad University Press.

Mallick, D., & Rafi, M. (2008). *Are the female-headed households more food secure? Evidence from Bangladesh*. Working Paper, Deakin University, Australia.

Mama, A. (1995). Women. In *Studies and Studies of Women in Africa during the 1990s*. Retrieved from http://www.gwsafrica.org/knowledge/index.html

Mama, A. (2002). Editorial. *Feminist Africa, 1*. Retrieved from http://www.feministafrica.org/fa%201/101-2002/editorial.html

Mama, A. (2001). Challenging Subjects: Gender and Power in African Context. *African Sociological Review*, 2(5), 63–73.

Mannan, M. S., & Karim, M. M. (2001). Current state of the mobility of the urban dwellers in greater Dhaka. *Proceedings of the 94th Annual Conference and Exhibition of Air and Waste Management Association*. Retrieved October 14, 2016, from http://www.eng-consult.com/pub/mobility-paper.PDF

Maplecroft. (2011). *Climate Change Vulnerability Index*. Retrieved from Ihttps://maplecroft.com/about/news/ccvi.html

Marchand, M. H., & Runyan, A. S. (Eds.). (2000). *Gender and Global Restructuring: Sightings, Sites and Resistance*. London: Routledge.

Marilyn, C., Martha, C., & Renana, J. (Eds.). (1996). *Speaking Out*. New Delhi: Vistaar Publication.

Marius, M. (2013). 4 Ways ICT/Technology can improve your business. *ICT Pulse – ICT Issues From a Caribbean Perspective*. Retrieved from http://www.ict-pulse.com/2013/09/4-ways-icttechnology-improve-business/

Markley, E. (n.d.). *Social remittances and social capital: Values and practices of transnational social space*. Retrieved 23 October 2015, from http://www.revistacalitateavietii.ro/2011/CV-4-2011/02.pdf

Compilation of References

Martin,, S. L. (1972). Sexual behaviour and reproductive health outcomes: Associations with wife abuse in India. *Journal of the American Medical Association.*

Martinez, I., & Nguyen, T. (2014). *ADB Briefs: Using Information and Communication Technology to Support Women's Entrepreneurship in Central and West Asia.* ADB.

Martin, S., Kilgallen, B., Tsui, A., Maitra, K., Singh, K., & Kupper, L. (1999). Sexual behaviors and reproductive health outcomes: Associations with wife abuse in India. *Journal of the American Medical Association, 282*(20), 1967–1972. doi:10.1001/jama.282.20.1967 PMID:10580466

Marx, K., & Engels, F. (1998). *The German Ideology.* Prometheus Books.

Marx, K., & Engels, F. (2011). *Economic and Political Manuscripts of 1844.* Wilder Publications.

Marx, B. P. (2005). Lessons learned from the last twenty years of sexual violence research. *Journal of Interpersonal Violence, 20*(2), 225–230. doi:10.1177/0886260504267742 PMID:15601796

Masani, A. M. (2016, January 29). Havoc of public transport. *The Independent.* Retrieved from http://www.theindependentbd.com/printversion/details/31952

Mason, J. (2002). *Qualitative researching.* London: Sage.

Mason, K. O. (2005). Measuring Women's Empowerment: Learning from Cross-National Research. In D. Narayan (Ed.), *Measuring Empowerment: Cross-Disciplinary Perspectives* (pp. 89–102). Washington, DC: The Word Bank.

Matangi, E. S., & Kashora, P. (2013). Empowerment and Information and Communication Technology (ICT) prospects and challenges for women in Zimbabwe. *International Journal of Education and Research, 1*(5), 1–10.

Mathur, J. C. (1966). The Domestic Arts Of Mithila. *Marg, 20*(1), 43–55.

Maume, D. J. (2004). Is the glass ceiling a unique from of inequality. *Work and Occupations, 31*(2), 250–274. doi:10.1177/0730888404263908

Mavin, S. (2006). Venus envy 2: Sisterhood, queen bees and female misogyny in management. *Women in Management Review, 21*(5), 349–364. doi:10.1108/09649420610676172

McCall, L. (2005). The complexity of Intersectionality. *Signs (Chicago, Ill.), 30*(3), 1771–1800. doi:10.1086/426800

McDowell, L. (1997). *Capital Culture: Gender at Work in the City.* Oxford, UK: Blackwell. doi:10.1002/9780470712894

McEwan, C. (2001). Postcolonialism, feminism and development: Intersections and dilemma. *Progress in Development Studies, 1*(2), 93–111. doi:10.1191/146499301701571390

McFadden, P. (2003). Sexual pleasure as feminist choice. *Feminist Africa, 2.* Retrieved from http://www.feministafrica.org/fa%202/2level.html

McIlwee, J. S., & Robinson, J. G. (1992). *Women in Engineering: Gender, Power, and Workplace Culture.* Albany, NY: State University of New York Press.

Mehta, P. S., & Simister, J. (2010). Gender Based Violence in India: Long-term Trends. *Journal of Interpersonal Violence, 25*(9), 1594–1611. doi:10.1177/0886260509354577 PMID:20068114

Menon, N. (1999). *Gender and politics in India.* Oxford, UK: Oxford University Press.

Mesh'a. (2002). The influence of traditional culture on attitudes towards work among Kuwaiti .... *Women in Management Review*, *17*(5/6), 245.

Messerchmidt, J. W. (1999). Making bodies matter: Adolescent masculinities, the body, and varieties of violence. *Theoretical Criminology*, *3*(2), 197–220. doi:10.1177/1362480699003002004

Metcalfe, B. D. (2007, January). Gender and human resource managementin the Middle East. *Int. J. of Human Resource Management*, *18*(1), 54–74.

Metcalfe, B., & Linstead, A. (2003). Gendering Teamwork: Re-Writing the Feminine. *Gender, Work and Organization*, *10*(1), 94–119. doi:10.1111/1468-0432.00005

Metthananda, T. (1990). Women in Sri Lanka: Tradition and change. In S. Kiribamune & V. Samarasinghe (Eds.), *Women at crossroads: A Sri Lankan perspective* (pp. 41–71). New Delhi: Vikas Publishing House.

MHCHD/UNDP. (1999). A Profile of Poverty in Pakistan. Islamabad: Author.

Miescher, S. (2007). Becoming as Spanyin: Elders, Gender and Masculinities in Ghana since Nineteenth Century. In Africa After Gender?. Bloomington, IN: Indiana University Press.

Mies, M. (1998). *Patriarchy and Accumulation on a World Scale: Women in the International Division of Labour*. London: Zed Books.

Mies, M. (2012). Dynamics of Sexual Division of Labor and Capital Accumulation. In S. Padmini (Ed.), *Women and Work*. New Delhi: Orient Blackswan.

Miller, B. D. (1993). *The Anthropology of Sex and Gender Hierarchies. In Sex and Gender Hierarchies*. Cambridge, UK: Cambridge University Press.

Ministry of Environment and Forest. (2013). *Bangladesh Climate Change and Gender Action Plan*. Available at: http://ngof.org/wdb_new/sites/default/files/iucn__bangladesh_climate_change___gender_action_plan__1.pdf

Mirza, J. (2002). Between Chaddor and The Market. Oxford, UK: Karachi.

Mitchell, S. (2011). Falling far from the tree: How forestry practices in Bangladesh leave women behind. *Heinonline*, *24*, 93–122.

Modleski, T. (1991). *Feminism without Women: Culture and Criticism in a "Postfeminist" Age*. New York: Routledge.

Moghadam, V. M. (2006). Maternalist policies versus women's economic citizenship? Gendered social policy in Iran. In Gender and social policy in a global context: Uncovering the gendered structure of 'the social'. Basingstoke, UK: Palgrave Macmillan and U.N. Research Institute for Social Development.

Moghadam, V. M., & Sidiqui, F. (2006). Women's activism and the public sphere: An introduction and overview. *Journal of Middle East Women's Studies*, *2*(2).

Mohamed. (2007). *Educated Sudanese Women Knowledge about Women rights in the Constitution in Khartoum State* (Unpublished Masters dissertation). Ahfad University for Women.

Mohanty, C. (1991). Under Western Eyes: Feminist Scholarship and Colonial Discourses. In C. Mohanty, A. Russo, & L. Torres (Eds.), *Third World Women and the Politics of Feminism*. Indianapolis, IN: Indiana University Press.

Mohanty, C. (2003). Cartographies of Struggle: Third World Women and the Politics of Feminism. In C. T. Mohanty (Ed.), *Feminism without Borders: Decolonizing Theory, Practicing Solidarity* (pp. 43–84). Durham, NC: Duke University Press. doi:10.1215/9780822384649-003

Mohanty, T. C. (1991). Under western eyes: Feminist scholarships and colonial discourses. In C. T. Mohanty, A. Russo, & L. Torres (Eds.), *Third world women and the politics of feminism* (pp. 51–80). Bloomington, IN: Indiana University Press.

Mohsin, A. (1997). *The Politics of Nationalism: The Case of Chittagong Hill Tracts, Bangladesh*. Dhaka, Bangladesh: The University Press Limited.

Mokaya, S. O., & Njuguna, E. W. (2010). Adoption and Use of Information and Communication Technology (ICT) By Small Enterprises in Thika Town, Kenya. *Scientific Conference Proceedings*, 498–504. Retrieved from http://elearning.jkuat.ac.ke/journals/ojs/index.php/jscp/article/view/730

Molin Valdés, H. (2009). A gender perspective on disaster risk reduction. In E. Enarson & P. G. DharChakrabarti (Eds.), Women, gender and disaster: Global issues and initiatives (pp. 18-28). Los Angeles, CA: Sage.

Molyneux, M. (2002). Gender and Silences of Social Capital:Lessons Capital:Lessons from Latin America, Developmnet nad. *Change*, *33*(2), 167–188. doi:10.1111/1467-7660.00246

Momsen, J. (1999). *Gender, migration, and domestic service* (1st ed.). London: Routledge.

Momsen, J. H. (2004). *Gender and Development*. London: Routledge.

Morrison, A. R., Schiff, M. W., & Sjöblom, M. (2007). *The international migration of women*. World Bank Publications.

Moser, C. (1991). *Gender planning in the third world: Meeting practical and strategic needs*. Retrieved from http://www.china-up.com:8080/international/case/.../1296.p

Mueller, F. (1994). Team between Hierarchy and Commitment: Change Strategies and the Internal Environment. *Journal of Management Studies*, *31*(3), 383–403. doi:10.1111/j.1467-6486.1994.tb00623.x

Mukhopadhyay, C. C. (1994). *Women, Education, and Family Structure in India*. Westview Press.

Mumtaz, K., & Shaheed, F. (1987). *Diversification of Women's Employment and Training: Country Study Pakistan, Unpublished Report*. Retrieved April 17, 2011, from www.researchcollective.org/Documents/Women_Paid_Work.pdf

Nagel, B., Matsuo, H., McIntyre, K. P., & Morrison, N. (2005). Attitudes Toward Victims of Rape: Effects of Gender, Race, Religion, and Social Class. *Journal of Interpersonal Violence*, *20*(6), 725–737. doi:10.1177/0886260505276072 PMID:15851539

Namuggala, V. F. (2015). Exploitation of empowerment? Adolescent female domestic workers in Uganda. *International Journal of Child, Youth, and Family Studies*, *6*(4), 561–580. doi:10.18357/ijcyfs.64201514288

Naqvi, Z. F., & Shahnaz, L. (2002). How Do Women Decide to Work in Pakistan. *Pakistan Development Review*, *41*(4 Part II), 495–513.

Narany, S. (2016). *Nepali Girls Snap Exclusion During Menstruation News Deeply Women and Girls Hub*. Retrieved from https://www.newsdeeply.com/womenandgirls/nepali-girls-snap-exclusion-during-menstruation/

Narayan, U. (1997). *Dislocating Cultures: Identities, Traditions, and Third-World Feminism*. New York: Routledge.

Naseef, F. U. (n.d.). *Women in Islam: A discourse in rights and obligations*. New Delhi: Sterling Publishers Pvt. Ltd.

Nasreen, M. (1995). *Coping with Floods: The Experience of Rural Women in Bangladesh* (Unpublished doctoral dissertation). Messey University, New Zealand.

Nasreen, M. (2008). *Impact of Climate Change on Food Security in Bangladesh: Gender and Disaster Perspectives*. Paper presented at the International Symposium on Climate Change and Food Security in Bangladesh.

Nasreen, Z., & Togawa, M. (2010). Politics of development. *Journal of International Development and Cooperation*, 93-97.

Nasreen, M. (2012). *Vulnerable or resilient? Women and girls*. Dhaka: Dhaka Institute of Disaster Management and Vulnerability Studies.

Nasreen, S., Shah, N. A., & Ali, A. (2012, December). Ascertaining Impact of Economic Conditions of Pakistan on Women Working in Industrial Sector of Karachi. *Pakistan Journal of Gender Studies*, 6.

Nasrin, J. (2007). *Leading Indigenous (Adivasi) Women* (J. Nasrin & B. Chakaborty, Eds.). Dhaka, Bangladesh: Oxfam GB Bangladesh Program.

Natasha, P. (2003). Gender Issues in the Information Society. Paris: United Nations Educational, Scientific and Cultural Organization (UNESCO).

Nath, H., & Mamun, K. (n.d.). Workers' Migration and Remittances in Bangladesh. *Journal of Business Strategies*, 27(1). 10.2139/ssrn.1592764

Nathanson, P., & Young, K. K. (2006). *Spreading Misandry: The Teaching of Contempt for Men in Popular Culture*. Montreal: McGill-Queen's University Press.

Nath, D. (2000). Gently shattering the glass ceiling: Experiences of Indian women managers. *Women in Management Review*, 15(1), 44–55. doi:10.1108/09649420010310191

Nath, K. T., Inoue, M., & Chakma, S. (2005). Shifting cultivation (jhum) in the Chittagong Hill Tracts, Bangladesh: Examining its sustainability, rural livelihood and policy implications. *International Journal of Agricultural Sustainability*, 3(2), 130–142. doi:10.1080/14735903.2005.9684751

National Bureau of Statistics. (2016). *2015. Statistical report on women and men in Nigeria*. Abuja: National Bureau of Statistics.

National Commission for Enterprises in the Unorganised Sector. (2008). *Contribution of the unorganised sector to GDP report of the subcommittee of a NCEUS task force*. National Commission for Enterprises in the Unorganised Sector Working Paper. Retrieved from: http://nceuis.nic.in/Final_Booklet_Working_Paper_2.pdf

National Women Law Center. (2000). Affirmative action and what it means for women. *Resources*. Retrieved 30 July, 2016 from https://nwlc.org/resources/affirmative-action-and-what-it-means-women/

Nayyar, R., & Sen, S. (1987). The Employment of Women in Bangladesh, India and Pakistan. In United Nations Economic & Social Commission for Asia and the Pacific (p. 125). United Nations Economic & Social Commission for Asia and the Pacific.

Neelormi, S., & Ahmed, A. (2012). Loss and damage in a warmer world: Whither gender matters?. *Gender Perspectives on the Loss and Damage Debate*.

Neelormi, S., & Uddin, A. (2012). *Loss and Damage in a warmer world: Whether Gender Matters?*. Academic Press.

Neelormi, S., Neelopal, A., & Ahmed, A. U. (2009). *Gender Perspectives of Increased Socio-economic Risks of Waterlogging in Bangladesh Due to Climate Change*. Retrieved from http://www.ioiusa.net/view/article/141603

Nelson, B. J., & Chowdhury, N. (Eds.). (1994). *Women and Politics World Wide*. New Haven, CT: Yale University Press.

Neumayer, E., & Plümper, T. (2007). The Gendered Nature of Natural Disasters: The Impact of Catastrophic Events on the Gender Gap in Life Expectancy, 1981-2002. *Annals of the Association of American Geographers*, 97(3), 551–566. doi:10.1111/j.1467-8306.2007.00563.x

Compilation of References

Njoroge, K. (2015, July 15). Regulations lift pay of househelps to Sh10, 954. *Business Daily, Politics and Policy*. Retrieved from http://www.businessdailyafrica.com/Regulations-lift-pay-of-househelps-to-Sh10-954-/-/539546/2776084/-/178v6nz/-/index.html

Nnaemeka, O. (2003). Nego-Feminism: Theorising, Practicing and Pruning Africas Way. *Signs (Chicago, Ill.)*, *29*(2), 357–385. doi:10.1086/378553

Norwegian Refugee Council (NRC). (2015). *Community Resilience and Disaster Related Displacement in South Asia*. Author.

Nouh, I., & Badri, B. (2008). Social Capital and Women institutions in government and Non Government bodies. In Sudanese Women Profile and Pathways to Empowerment. Ahfad University for Women.

Nyambegera, S. M. (2002, November). Ethnicity and human resource management practice in sub-SaharanAfrica: The relevance of the managing diversity discourse. *International Journal of Human Resource Management*, *13*(7), 1077–1090. doi:10.1080/09585190210131302

Nzegwu, N. (2001). Gender Equality in a Dual-Sex System: The Case of Onitsha. *Jenda: A Journal of Culture and African Women's Studies*, *1*(1).

O'Neill, M. (2001). Community Safety, Rights and Recognition: Towards a Coordinated Prostitution Strategy?. *Community Safety Journal*, *6*(1), 45-52. Retrieved from http://www.google.com.bd/url?sa=t&rct=j&q=article%20on%20sex%20worker.doc&source=web&cd=7&cad=rja&ved=0CEoQFjAG&url=http%3A%2F%2Fmyweb.dal.ca%2Fmgoodyea%2Ffiles%2Fuk%2FMaggie%2520Oneill%2520paper%2520Csj%2520article%25203.doc&ei=UztXUeHxEouMrgfQsYHIDg&usg=AFQjCNHkzcC_YekCvHuSETuYYDwPp93SGQ&bvm=bv.44442042,d.bmk]

Ocheni, S., & Nwankwo, B. C. (2012). Analysis and critical review of rural development efforts in Nigeria, 1960-2010. *Studies in Sociology of Science*, *3*(3), 48–86.

OECD (2008). *Gender and Sustainable Development Maximizing the Economic, Social and Environmental Role of Women, USA*. Retrieved from http://www.oecd.org/.. /sustain abledevelopmentkeyreports

OECD Background Report. (2016, March 8). *Conference on improving women's access to leadership*. Retrieved from https://www.oecd.org/daf/ca/OECD-Women-Leadership-2016-Report

Ogunlana, S. (Ed.). (1993). Women in the Thai Construction Industry. AIT Women Study Circle and structural Engineering and Construction Program (AIT WSC), Asian Institute of Technology, Bangkok.

Ogunyemi, C. (1984). Womanism: The Dynamics of the Contemporary Black Female Novel in English. *Signs (Chicago, Ill.)*, *11*, 1.

Okafor, A. C. (2010). Gender inequality in Nigeria. *OASIS Journal*, *1*(1), 104–113.

Okafor, E., & Abdulazeez, Y. (2007). Gender-sensitive projects for sustainable development in Nigeria: A critical assessment. *Journal of Sociology and Social Science*, *23*(3), 235–248.

Olateru-Olagbegi, B. A., & Afolabi, A. (2013). *Actual women situation in Nigerian*. Retrieved September 26, 2016, from: http://www.widaf-ao.org/spip.php

Olufunke-Okome, M. (2003). What women, whose development? A critical analysis of reformist evangelism. In African women & feminism: Reflecting on the politics of sisterhood. Africa World Press.

Omair, K. (2009). Arab women managers and identity formation through clothing. *Gender in Management*, *24*(6), 412-431.

Omar, A., & Davidson, M. J. (2001). Women in management: A comparative cross-cultural overview. *Cross Cultural Management: An International Journal*, *8*(3/4), 35–67. doi:10.1108/13527600110797272

Ondimu, K. N. (2007). Workplace violence among domestic workers in urban households in Kenya: A case of Nairobi city. *Eastern Africa Social Science Research Review*, *23*(1), 37–61. doi:10.1353/eas.2007.0005

Organization for Economic Co-operation and Developement (OECD). (2010). *The Information and Communication Technology Sector in India: Performance, Growth and Key Challenges*. Retrieved from http://www.oecd.org/dataoecd/55/56/45576760.pdf

Osman, M. E. (2008). Overview of Women's Social Positioning in Sudan. In Sudanese Women Profile and Pathways to Empowerment. Ahfad University for Women.

Oster, E., & Thornton, R. (2011). Sanitary products, and school attendance: Evidence from a randomized evaluation. *American Economic Journal. Applied Economics*, *3*(1), 91–100. doi:10.1257/app.3.1.91

Ostin, P. (2002). Examining Work and Its Effect on Health in Gita. In Engendering International Health: The Challenge of Equity. The MIT Press.

Ouzgane, L., & Morrell, R. (2005). *African Masculinities: Men in Africa from the late Nineteenth Century to the Present*. New York: Palgrave MacMillan. doi:10.1057/9781403979605

Overseas Employment & Remittance from 1976 - 2016. (2016). Retrieved 12 November 2016, from http://www.bmet.gov.bd/BMET/viewStatReport.action?reportnumber=20

Overseas Employment and Migrants Act 2013 (Act No. VLVIII of 2013) (Bangladesh). (n.d.). Retrieved from http://asianparliamentarians.mfasia.org/phocadownload/resources/policies/bangladesh%20overseas%20employment%20and%20migrants%20act%202013%20_english_.pdf

Overseas Employment in 2016. (2016). Retrieved 12 November 2016, from http://www.bmet.gov.bd/BMET/viewStatReport.action?reportnumber=29

Oxfam International. (2011). *Owning Adaptation Factsheet: Bangladesh*. Retrieved from https://www.oxfam.org/sites/www.oxfam.org/files/bp146-owning-adaptation-130611-summ-en.pdf

Oxfam International. (2016). *Women & Climate Change*. Available at: https://www.oxfam.org/sites/www.oxfam.org/files/gender_copenhagen_media_briefing_oxfam_international.pdf

Oxfam Monash Partnership Project. (n.d.). *Gendered impacts of climate variability in Bangladesh in 2010-2013*. Author.

Oyewumi, O. (2004). Conceptualising Gender: Eurocentric Foundations of Feminist Concepts and the Challenge of African Epistemologies. In African Gender Scholarship: Concepts, Methodologies and Paradigms. Academic Press.

Oyewumi, O. (1997). *The Invention of Women: Making an African Sense of Western Gender Discourse*. Minneapolis, MN: University of Minnesota Press.

Oyewumi, O. (2003). Introduction: Feminism, Sisterhood, and Other Foreign Relations. In O. Oyewumi (Ed.), *African Women and Feminism: Reflecting on the Politics of Sisterhood*. Asmara: Africa World Press Inc.

Pakistan Employment Trends. (n.d.). Retrieved from http://www.pbs.gov.pk/sites/default/files/Labour%20Force/publications/Pakistan_Employment_2013.pdf

Paoletti, J. B. (n.d.). *Pink and Blue: Telling the Boys from the Girls in America*. Academic Press.

Pape, K. (2016). ILO Convention C189—a good start for the protection of domestic workers: An insiders view. *Progress in Development Studies*, *16*(2), 189–202. doi:10.1177/1464993415623151

Parida, S. C., & Nayak, S. (2009). *Empowerment of women in India*. New Delhi, India: Northern Book Centre.

Parikh, P. P., & Sukhatme, S. P. (1993). *Women Engineers in India. A Study on the Participation of Women in Engineering Courses and in the Engineering Profession*. Bombay: Indian Institute of Technology.

Parkinson, D. (2011). Gender disaster and violence: literature review. *Women's Health Goulburn North East*. Retrieved form http://www.whealth.com.au/documents/environmentaljustice/women-disaster-violence-lit-review.pdf

Parreñas, R. S. (2005). *Children of global migration: transnational families and gendered woes*. Stanford, CA: Stanford University Press.

Parsons, T., & Bales, R. F. (2014). *Family: Socialization and Interaction Process*. Routledge.

Partridge, K. (2011). *Social Networking*. H.W. Wilson.

Parveen, S., & Leonhauser, I. (2005). *Empowerment of rural women in Bangladesh: A Household Level Analysis*. Paper presented on Conference on Rural Poverty Reduction through Research for Development and Transformation, Berlin, Germany.

Parvin, A. G. (1998). Women Empowerment Performance of Income Generating Activities Supported by Rural Women Employment Creation Project (RWECP): A Case Study in Dumuria Thana, Bangladesh. *The Journal of Geo-Environment*, *4*, 47-62.

Paul, B. K. (2009). Why relatively fewer people died? The case of Bangladeshs Cyclone Sidr. *Natural Hazards*, *50*(2), 289–304. doi:10.1007/s11069-008-9340-5

Paul-Majumder, P. (2003). *Health Status of the Garment Workers in Bangladesh*. Arambagh, Motijheel, Dhaka: Bangladesh atAssociates Printing Press.

Paul-Majumder, P., & Begum, S. (1997). *Upward occupational mobility among female workers in the garment industry of Bangladesh*. Research Report No. 153 (Dhaka, BIDS).

Pereira, C. (2003). 'Where angels fear to tread?' Some thoughts on Patricia McFadden's 'Sexual Pleasure as Feminist Choice'. *Feminist Africa, 2*. Retrieved from http://www.feministafrica.org/fa%202/2level.html

Perera, S. (2008). Rethinking working-class literature: Feminism, globalization, and socialist ethics. *Differences: A Journal of Feminist Cultural Studies*, *19*(1), 1–31. doi:10.1215/10407391-2007-015

Personal remittances, received (% of GDP) | Data. (2016). Retrieved 12 November 2016, from http://data.worldbank.org/indicator/BX.TRF.PWKR.DT.GD.ZS?locations=BD

Peter, B. (1978). *Popular Culture in Early Modern Europe*. London: Academic Press.

Peter, F. (2001). Review of Martha Nussbaum's Women and Human Development. *Feminist Economics*, *7*(2), 131–135.

Phillips, A., & Taylor, B. (1980). Sex and skills: Notes towards a feminist economics. *Feminist Review*, *6*(1), 79–88. doi:10.1057/fr.1980.20

Phillips, B., Jenkins, P., & Enarson, E. (2010). Violence and disaster vulnerability. In B. Phillips, D. Thomas, A. Fothergill, & L. Blinn-Pike (Eds.), *Social vulnerability to disasters*. CRC Press.

Piper, N. (2009). The complex interconnections of the migration-development nexus: A social perspective. *Population Space and Place, 15*(2), 93–101. doi:10.1002/psp.535

Pompper, D. (2011). Fifty years later: Mid-career women of color against the glass ceiling in communications organizations. *Journal of Organizational Change Management, 24*(4), 464–486. doi:10.1108/09534811111144629

Powell, G. N., & Butterfield, D. A. (2015). The glass ceiling: What have we learned 20 years on? *Journal of Organizational Effectiveness: People and Performance, 2*(4), 306–326. doi:10.1108/JOEPP-09-2015-0032

Prabhudesai, A. (2013, Jan 15). *10 Indian women in Technology who made it big*. Retrieved from http://trak.in/tech/top-10-indian-successful-women-in-technology/

Pupul, J. (1971). Paintings of Mithila. *The Times of India*.

Quisumbing, A., Meinzen-Dick, R., Bassett, L., Usnick, M., Pandolfelli, L., Morden, C., & Alderman, H. (2008). Helping women respond to the global food price crisis. International Food Policy Research Institute Policy Brief, 7.

Rafiqul, I. M. (2011). Rural Women's Empowerment through Self-income Generating Activities: A Study on NGOs Credit Programs in Bangladesh. *Journal of Global Citizenship & Equity Education, 1*(1), 96–123.

Rahman, M. M., & Sultana, F. B. U. (2012). Institutional Protection Mechanisms, Potentials of Mainstreaming and Readiness of the Society: Unveiling Struggles of Children of Sex Workers in Bangladesh. *Sex Workers and Their Children in Bangladesh: Addressing Risks and Vulnerabilities*, 181-201.

Rahman, A. (1999). Micro-credit Initiatives for equitable and sustainable development: Who pays? *World Development Research, 27*(1), 67–82. doi:10.1016/S0305-750X(98)00105-3

Rahman, H., & Siddiqui, S. A. (2015). Female RMG worker: Economic Contribution in Bangladesh. *International Journal of Scientific and Research Publications, 5*(9), 1–9.

Rahman, M. (2012). *Amader GolpobShishder Dekha Shishu Odihikar Poristhithi*. Save The Children.

Rahman, M. (2012). *State of Children in Bangladesh 2011: In the eyes of Children*. Save The Children.

Rahman, M. S. (2013). Climate Change, Disaster and Gender Vulnerability: A Study on Two Divisions of Bangladesh. *American Journal of Human Ecology, 2*(2), 72–82. doi:10.11634/216796221302315

Rahman, M. S. U. (2010). Bus service for 'women only' in Dhaka city: An investigation. *Journal of Bangladesh Institute of Planners, 3*, 17–32. Retrieved from http://www.bip.org.bd/SharingFiles/journal_book/20130722133425.pdf

Rahman, M. S., & Nahrin, K. (2012). Bus services in Dhaka city - users' experiences and opinions'. *Journal of Bangladesh Institute of Planners, 105*, 93–105. Retrieved from http://www.bip.org.bd/SharingFiles/journal_book/20130820140314.pdf

Rahman, R. I. (2002). *The dynamics of the labour market in Bangladesh and the prospects of economic development based on surplus labour*. Employment and Labour.

Rahman, S. M. A. (2016). Leveraging ICTs For Empowering Women Entrepreneurs in Bangladesh: A Review of Recent Developments and Way Forward. *European Journal of Business and Social Sciences, 5*(3), 1–15.

Rajadhyaksha, N. (2013). Rural India in decline. *LiveMint*. Retrieved from: http://www.livemint.com/Opinion/hYkJxMUgidtc69y1eWivVJ/Rural-India-in-decline.html

Rajar, S. R., & Parl, Y. (2000). *Postcolonial feminism/postcolonialism and feminism*. In H. Schwarz & S. Ray (Eds.), *A Companion to Postcolonial Studies* (pp. 53–71). Blackwell Publication.

Compilation of References

Ranabhat, C., Kim, C., Choi, E., Aryal, A., Park, M., & Ah Doh, Y. (2015). Chhaupadi Culture and Reproductive Health of Women in Nepal. *Asia-Pacific Journal of Public Health, 27*(7), 785–795. doi:10.1177/1010539515602743 PMID:26316503

Raphael, B., Taylor, M., & McAndrew, V. (2008). Women, catastrophe and mental health. *The Australian and New Zealand Journal of Psychiatry, 42*(1), 13–23. doi:10.1080/00048670701732707 PMID:18058439

Rashid, A. K. M., & Shafie, H. A. (2009). *Facilitators Guide: Practicing Gender and Social Inclusion in Disaster Risk Reduction. Directorate of Relief and Rehabilitation*. Dhaka: Ministry of Food and Disaster Management.

Rashid, S. F., & Michuad, S. (2000). Female adolescents and their sexuality: Notions of honour, shame, purity and pollution during the floods. *Disasters, 24*(1), 54–70. doi:10.1111/1467-7717.00131 PMID:10718014

Rasul, G., & Karki, M. (n.d.b). *Political Ecology of Degradation of Forest Common in the Chittagong Hill Tracts of Bangladesh*. Kathmundu: International Centre for Integrated Mountain Development.

Rasul, G., & Thapa, G. (n.d.a). *State Policies, Praxis and Land-use in the Chittagong Hill Tracts of Bangladesh*. Asian Institute of Technology.

Ratha, D., Plaza, S., & Ozden, C. (2016). *Migration and Development*. New York: World Bank Group. Retrieved from http://pubdocs.worldbank.org/en/468881473870347506/Migration-and-Development-Report-Sept2016.pdf

Ray, R. (2012, October 5). Bonding With Roots to Revive Madhubani Folk Art. *New Global Indian*.

Rees, S., Pittaway, E., & Bartolomei, L. (2005). Waves of Violence - Women in Post-Tsunami Sri Lanka. *Australasian Journal of Disaster and Trauma Studies, 2*.

Rege, S. (2007). More than Just Taking Women on to the Macro- Picture: Feminist Contributions to Globalization Discourses. In R. Ghadially (Ed.), *Urban Women in Contemporary India*. Sage.

Rekha, N. (2004). *Art and Assertion of Identity: Women and Madhubani Paintings* (Unpublished Ph.D. Dissertation). Patna University.

Rekha. (2010). From Folk Art to Fine Art: Changing Paradigms in the Historiography of Maithil Painting. *Journal of Art Historiography, 2*.

Reynolds, W., Savage, W., & Williams, A. (1994). *Your Own Business: A Practical Guide to Success*. ITP.

Roediger, D. (2008). *How Race Survived US History*. New York: Verso.

Roscigno, V. J. (2007). *The Face of Discrimination: How Race and Gender Impact Work and Home Lives*. Rowmann and Littlefield Publishers Inc.

Rouf, K. A. (2013). Religious patriarchal values obstruct Bangladeshi rural women's human rights. *Journal Research in Peace, Gender and Development, 3*(5), 75–79. Available online http://www.interesjournals.org/

Rowan, D. (2015). Facebook Messenger: Inside Zuckerberg's app for everything. *Wired*. Retrieved from: http://www.wired.co.uk/article/inside-facebook-messenger

Roy, R. D., & Halim, S. (2007). Populaton transfer, minoritization and ethnic conflict in Bangladesh: the case of the Chittagong Hill Tracts. In *Indigenous Communities and Settlers: Resource Conflicts in Frontier Regions of South and Southeast Asia*. Department of Social Anthropology, University of Zurich. (Unpublished)

Roy, A. D. (2005). *Indigenous Textiles of the Chittagong Hill Tracts.* Rangamati, Bangladesh: Charathum Publishers.

Roy, C. (2004). *Indigenous women: a gender perspective.* Resource Centre for the Rights of Indigenous Peoples.

Roy, R. (2000). *The Chittagong Hill Tracts: Life and Nature at Risk.* SEHD.

Roy, R. D. (2000). Occupations and economy in transition: A case study of the Chittagong Hill Tracts. In *Traditional Occupations of Indigenous and Tribal Peoples: Emerging Trends: Project to Promote ILO Policy on Indigenous and Tribal Peoples.* International Labour Organization.

Rudman, L. A. (1998). Self-Promotion as a Risk Factor for Women: The Costs and Benefits of Counterstereotypical Impression Management. *Journal of Personality and Social Psychology, 74*(3), 629–645. doi:10.1037/0022-3514.74.3.629 PMID:9523410

Ruspini, E. (2007). Book Review: African Masculinities: Men in Africa from the Late Nineteenth Century to the Present. *Sexualities, 10*(2), 267–268. doi:10.1177/136346070701000212

Russ, J. (1975). *The female man.* New York: Bantam Books.

Rutherford, M. D. (2004). The effect of social role on theory of mind reasoning. *British Journal of Psychology, 95*(1), 91–103. doi:10.1348/000712604322779488 PMID:15005870

Ryan, M. K., & Haslam, S. A. (2005). The glass cliff: Evidence that women are over-represented in precarious leadership positions. *British Journal of Management, 16*(2), 81–90. doi:10.1111/j.1467-8551.2005.00433.x

Sabet, M.D., & Ahmad, S. (2012). Legitimacy, Legality and Consent: Sex Workers and Their Children in Bangladesh. *Sex Workers and Their Children in Bangladesh: Addressing Risks and Vulnerabilities,* 1-8.

Safa, H. I. (1996). Gender Inequality and Women's Wage Labor: A Theoretical and Empirical Analysis. In V. M. Moghadam (Ed.), *Patriarchy and Economic Development: Women's Positions at the End of the Twentieth Century* (pp. 184–219). Oxford, UK: Clarendon Press. doi:10.1093/acprof:oso/9780198290230.003.0009

Samanmali, H. I. (2007). Wetup wediwenawita target ekada wediwe [When salaries go up, the target also goes up]. *Dabindu, 23,* 9.

Samy, K. (2011). Women and climate change: An opportunity to address gender inequality. *Yale Journal of International Affairs, 6*(1), 99–101.

Sanger, W. W. (2013). *The History of Prostitution.* Harper & Brothers Publishers.

Sangstha. (2012). *Annual Reflections 2011.* Khagrachari, Bangladesh: Academic Press.

Sanou, B. (2014). ICT Facts and Figures. *The World in 2014: ICT Facts and Figures,* 1–8. Retrieved from http://www.itu.int/en/ITUD/Statistics/Documents/facts/ICTFactsFigures2014-e.pdf

Sassen, S. (2010). Strategic Gendering: One Factor in the Constituting of Novel Political Economies. In S. Chant (Ed.), *The International Handbook of Gender and Poverty* (pp. 29–34). Cheltenham, UK: Edward Elgar Publishing Ltd. doi:10.4337/9781849805162.00012

Sauers, D., Kennedy, J. O., & Sullivan, D. (2002). Managerial sex-role stereotyping: A New Zealand perspective. *Women in Management Review, 17*(7), 342–347. doi:10.1108/09649420210445794

Sayeed, A. (2001). *Structural Adjustment and Its Impact on Women.* Working Paper No. 1. Karachi: PILER & SDPI.

Sayem, D. R. (n.d.). *Best practices and alternative integrated community based model in delivering primary health care service for Chittagong Hill Tracts of Bangladesh*. Retrieved from: http://www.google.com.au/url?sa=t&rct=j&q=&esrc=s&source=web&cd=1&ved=0CCkQFjAA&url=http%3A%2F%2Fwww.dghs.gov.bd%2Flicts_file%2Fimages%2FOther_publication%2FHealth_System_in_Chittagong_Hill_Tracts.pdf&ei=fWGDUrSoOoSpiAeo74CQBg&usg=AFQjCNGI9rMzv6RcKF8jPStnqNs9Okd5mw&bvm=bv.56343320,d.dGI

Schwart, M., & DeKeseredy, W. (1997). *Sexual Assault on the College Campus*. Sage Publications.

Science and Technology Options Assessment. (2015). *ICT in the developing world*. Available at http://www.europarl.europa.eu/RegData/etudes/STUD/2015/563482/EPRS_STU(2015)563482_EN.pdf

Scroll.in. (2017, May 21). *Three women IAS officers for 20 men: Five charts reveal profile of India's civil servants*. Retrieved from https://scroll.in/article/720183/three-women-ias-officers-for-20-men-five-charts-reveal-profile-of-indias-civil-servants

SDPI. (2008). *Pakistan: Country Gender Profile*. Retrieved September 12, 2010, from http://www.jica.go.jp/activities/issues/gender/pdf/e08pak.pdf

Seb, J. (2016). Adidas spotlights 'dark social' to be the 'most personal brand'. *The Drum*. Retrieved from: http://www.thedrum.com/news/2016/03/05/adidas-spotlights-dark-social-be-most-personal-brand

Sen, A. (1999). *Development as Freedom*. Knopf and Oxford University Press.

Sethe, K. (1926). Die Aechtung feindlicher Fürsten, Völker und Dinge auf altägyptischen Tongefäßscherben des mittleren Reiches. In *Abhandlungen der Preussischen Akademie der Wissenschaften* (p. 61). Philosophisch-Historische Klasse.

Seyal, A. H., & Rahim, M. M. (2006). A Preliminary Investigation of Electronic Data Interchange Adoption in Bruneian Small Business Organisations. *The Electronic Journal of Information Systems in Developing Countries, 24*(4), 1–21.

Shabib, D., & Khan, S. (2014). Gender-sensitive adaptation policy-making in Bangladesh: Status and ways forward for improved mainstreaming. *Climate and Development, 6*(4), 329–335. doi:10.1080/17565529.2014.951017

Shafi, M. (2011). *Gender, WASH and Education Case Study: Enhancing Girls' Participation in Schools in Pakistan*. Retrieved from http://policy-practice.oxfam.org.uk/publications/enhancing-girls-participation-in-schools-inpakistan-142170

Shah, B. (2016, April 9). *8 Indian women in the Asia's 50 Power Businesswomen 2016 list*. Retrieved from https://yourstory.com/2016/04/forbes-power-businesswomen-2016/

Shah, N. M. (1986). *Pakistani Women: A Socioeconomic & Demographic Profile*. Islamabad: PIDE & East-West Population Institute.

Shambhu. (2016). WhatsApp: Unlocking The Goldmine. Educreation Publishing.

Sharif, M. Y. (2015). Glass ceiling, the prime driver of women entrepreneurship in Malaysia: A phenomenological study of women lawyers. *Procedia: Social and Behavioral Sciences, 169*, 329–336. doi:10.1016/j.sbspro.2015.01.317

Sharma, R. (2014). Parents prefer male child in intersex operations in Gujarat. *The Times of India*. Retrieved from: http://timesofindia.indiatimes.com/india/Parents-prefer-male-child-in-intersex-operations-in-Gujarat/articleshow/29879738.cms

Sharma, S., & Sharma, K. (2006). *Women's Employment*. New Delhi: Anmol Publications.

Sharma, U. (1986). *Women's Work, Class and the Urban Household*. San Francisco: Tavistock Publications Ltd.

Sharmin, S. (2014, February 2). The saga of women commuters. *The Daily Observer*. Retrieved from http://www.observerbd.com/2014/02/02/3442.php

Sheen, T. (2015). Manchester United and Adidas branded 'sexist' and 'discriminatory' as women's shirt features plunging neckline and different design. *Independent*. Retrieved from: http://www.independent.co.uk/sport/football/premier-league/manchester-united-sexist-kit-causes-outrage-as-womens-short-features-plunging-neckline-10433277.html

Shefali, M. K. (2000). *Study on gender dimensions in Dhaka Urban Transport Program (DUTP)*. Dhaka: Nari Udyog Kendro. Retrieved May 30, 2015, from http://siteresources.worldbank.org/INTGENDERTRANSPORT/Resources/bangurbantransport.pdf

Shepherd, K. E. (2016). *Applicability of the lobbying act to grass root communications*. Office of the Commissioner of Lobbying of Canada. Retrieved July 30, 2016, from https://lobbycanada.gc.ca/eic/site/012.nsf/eng/00874.html

Shiva, V. (1989). *Staying Alive: women, ecology and development*. London: Zed Books.

Shubhojit. (2014, July 1). *Women Cabinet Ministers in India*. Retrieved from http://www.elections.in/political-corner/women-cabinet-ministers-india/

Siddique. (2003). Workplace environment for Women: issues of Harassment and need for interventions. *CPD Dialogue Report, 65*.

Siddique, T. (2003). *Migration as a livelihood strategy of the poor: the Bangladesh case*. Dhaka, Bangladesh: Presentation.

Sikira, A. (2010). *Gender bases violence and women empowerment: A case study of Serengeti District* (PhD Thesis). Sokoine University of Agriculture, Morogoro, Tanzania.

Silliman, J., & Agarwal, B. (1996). A Field of Ones Own: Gender and Land Rights in South Asia. *Land Economics, 72*(2), 269. doi:10.2307/3146971

Singh, N. P., & Sahay, A. (2006). ICT for women Entrepreneurs. In Entrepreneurship: Education, Research and Practice, (pp. 151-159). Academic Press.

Sinha, K. (2015, March 15). *India has more women ministers than its neighbours*. Retrieved from http://timesofindia.indiatimes.com/india/India-has-more-women-ministers-than-its-neighbours/articleshow/46521090.cms

Sinha, B., Jha, S., & Negi, N. S. (2012). Migration and empowerment: The experience of women in households in India where migration of a husband has occurred. *Journal of Gender Studies, 21*(1), 61–76. doi:10.1080/09589236.2012.639551

Sobania, N. W. (2003). *Culture and customs of Kenya*. Westport, CT: Greenwood Press.

Soble, A., & Power, N. P. (2008). *The Philosophy of Sex: Contemporary Readings*. Rowman and Littlefield Publishers Inc.

Solotaro, J., & Pande, R. (2014). Violence against Women and Girls: Lessons from South Asia. New York: World Bank. Retrieved from https://openknowledge.worldbank.org/bitstream/handle/10986/20153/9781464801716.pdf?sequence=1

Soomro, G. Y. (2000). A re-examination of fertility transition in Pakistan. *Pakistan Development Review, 39*(3), 247–261.

Sooriyakumaran, P. (2010). *"Gender and Development": Do men and masculinities need to be considered?*. Retrieved from http://www.theadr.com.au/wp/?p=273

Sparr, P. (1994). Feminist Critiques of Structural Adjustment. In P. Sparr (Ed.), *Mortgaging Women's Lives* (pp. 20–29). London: Zed Books.

Spectrum. (1997). *Moving into the Information Society*. HMSO.

Compilation of References

Spivak, G. C. (1988). Can the subaltern speak? In C. Nelson & L. Grossberg (Eds.), *Marxism and the interpretation of culture* (pp. 271–313). London: Macmillan Education. doi:10.1007/978-1-349-19059-1_20

Ssewanyana, J., & Busler, M. (2007). Adoption and Usage of ICT in Developing Countries : Case of Ugandan Firms. *International Journal of Education and Development Using Information and Communication Technology, 3*(3), 49–59.

Stamp, P. (1989). *Technology, Gender, and Power in Africa.* Ottawa: International Development Research Centre.

Standing, H. (1985). Resources wages and Power;The impact of Women's employment on the urban Bengali Household. In H. Afshar (Ed.), *Women, Work and Ideology in the third world.* London: Tavistock Publications.

Statista. (n.d.). Number of consumer cloud-based service users worldwide in 2013 and 2018 (in billions). *Statista.* Retrieved from: https://www.statista.com/statistics/321215/global-consumer-cloud-computing-users/

Strong, B. (2011). *The Marriage and Family Experience: Intimate Relationships in a Changing Society.* Wadsworth Cengage Learning.

Sultana, A. (2010). Patriarchy and Women's Subordination: A Theoretical Analysis. *The Arts Faculty Journal.*

Sultana, A. (2009). Patriarchy and women's subordination: A theoretical analysis. *Asian Journal of Social Science, 37*(4), 599–662.

Sunday Island. (1991, December 15). Shocking goings on at FTZ. *Sunday Island*, pp. 1, 3.

Suresh, L. B. (2011). Impact of Information and Communication Technologies on Women Empowerment in India. *Systemics, Cybernetics and Informatics, 9*(4), 17–23.

Svedin, G. C., & Back, K. (1996). *Children who don't speak out About children who being used in child pornography.* Swedish Save The Children. Radda Barnen.

Syed, J. (2008). A context-specific perspective of equal employemnt oppurunity in Islamic socities. *Asia Pacific Journal, 25*(1), 135–151. doi:10.1007/s10490-007-9051-6

Tahmina, A. Q., & Moral, S. (2004). Sex-Workers in Bangladesh Livelihood: At What Price?. Society for Environment and Human Development (SEHD).

Tandrayen-Ragoobur, V., & Pydayya, R. (2015). Glass ceiling and sticky floors: Hurdles for Mauritian working women. *Equality, Diversity and Inclusion. International Journal (Toronto, Ont.), 34*(5), 452–466.

Tanjeem, N., & Khan, I. J. (2009). *Impact of Hegemonic Masculinity at Work Place: An Analysis of Challenges Faced by Today's Middle Class Working Women.* Working Paper Series no. 9. Department of Women and Gender Studies, University of Dhaka, Bangladesh.

Tarafder, T. (2014). Reproductive health beliefs and their consequences: A case study of rural indigenous women in Bangladesh. *Australian Journal of Regional Studies, 20*(2), 251–374.

Taungya. (n.d.). *Activities.* Retrieved from: http://www.taungya.org.bd/Activities.aspx

Terjesen, S., & Singh, V. (2008). Female presence on corporate boards: A multi-country study of environmental context. *Journal of Business Ethics, 83*(1), 55–63. doi:10.1007/s10551-007-9656-1

Terre des hommes Italia. (2005). *Brothel –based and Floating Sex Workers in Bangladesh Living Conditions and Socio Economic Status.* Dhaka: Terre des hommes Italia.

Testa, M., & Parks, K. A. (1996). The Role of Womens Alcohol Consumption in Sexual Victimization. *Aggression and Violent Behavior*, *1*(3), 217–234. doi:10.1016/1359-1789(95)00017-8

TGNP. (2005). African Gender and Development Index Dar es Salaam, Tanzania. population policies considered: *Health. Empowerment and Rights*, *1*, 127–138.

The Economic Benefits of Strategic ICT Spending. (2010). Intel.

The Economic Times. (2016, Sep 13). *Arundhati Bhattacharya, Chanda Kochhar, Shikha Sharma among most powerful women outside US in Fortune list.* Retrieved from http://economictimes.indiatimes.com/news/company/corporate-trends/arundhati-bhattacharya-chanda-kochhar-shikha-sharma-among-most-powerful-women-outside-us-in-fortune-list/articleshow/54304638.cms

The Economist. (2016). Bots the next frontier. *The Economist.* Retrieved from: http://www.economist.com/news/business-and-finance/21696477-market-apps-maturing-now-one-text-based-services-or-chatbots-looks-poised

The Taskforce. (2015). *Not now, not ever: Putting an End to Domestic and Family Violence in Queensland.* Retrieved from https://www.qld.gov.au/community/documents/getting-support-health-social-issue/dfv-report-vol-one.pdf

The United Nations Statistics Division. (2013). *Economic activity.* Retrieved from: http://unstats.un.org/unsd/demographic/sconcerns/econchar/econcharmethods.htm#A

The World Bank Annual Report. (2010). Retrieved from http://siteresources.worldbank.org/EXTANNREP2010/Resources/WorldBank-AnnualReport2010.pdf

Thipthrope, E., & Ahmed, I. (2005). *There is Hope:An Action Based Research Children victims of Sexual Abuse and Explotation.* Aparajeyo-Bangladesh.

Thitipaisan, A. (1999). *Strategies for Improving the Construction Industry in Thailand.* AIT Thesis No. ST-99-52, Asian Institute of Technology, Bangkok.

Thompson, E. P. (1974). Patrician Society, Plebian Culture. *Journal of Social History*, *7*, 395.

Thompson, W. E., & Gibbs, J. C. (2016). *Deviance and Deviants: A Sociological Approach.* Wiley Blackwell.

Tjaden, P., & Thoennes, N. (2000). *Full Report of the Prevalence, Incidence, and Consequences of Violence against Women: Findings from the National Violence against Women Survey.* Washington, DC: U.S. Department of Justice. doi:10.1037/e514172006-001

Tripp, A. (2000). *Women and Politics in Uganda.* Kampala: Fountain Publishers.

True, J. (2012). *The Political Economy of Violence against Women.* New York: Oxford University Press. doi:10.1093/acprof:oso/9780199755929.001.0001

Tsikata, D. (1997). Gender Equality and the State in Ghana. In Engendering African Social Science. Dakar: CODESRIA.

Turnbull, M., Sterrett, C. L., & Hilleboe, A. (2012). *Toward Resilience: A Guide to Disaster Risk Reduction and Climate Change Adaptation.* Available at: http://reliefweb.int/sites/reliefweb.int/files/resources/ECB-toward-resilience-Disaster-risk-reduction-Climate-Change-Adaptation-guide-english.pdf

Uchedu, E. (2008). Introduction Are African Males Men? Sketching African Masculinities. In E. Uchendu (Ed.), *Masculinities in Contemporary Africa.* Dakar: CODESRIA.

UN Women. (2012). Safe *Public Transit for Women and Girls.* Retrieved February 28, 2016, from http://www.endvawnow.org/en/articles/252-safe-public-transit-for-women-and-girls-.html

Compilation of References

UN Women. (2013). *The 2012 Fiji Floods: Gender Sensitivity in Disaster Management, A Qualitative Review of Gender and Protection Issues in Disaster Management.* Retrieved from http://www.pacificdisaster.net/pdnadmin/data/original/FJI_FL_UNWomen_2012_gender_sensitivity.pdf

UNCTAD. (2014). *Empowering Women Entrepreneurs through Information and Communications Technologies.* Retrieved from http://unctad.org/en/PublicationsLibrary/dtlstict2013d2_en.pdf

Undie, C., & Benaya. (2008). The State of Knowledge on Sexuality in Sub-Saharan Africa. *QUEST: An African Journal of Philosophy / Revue African Philosophy,* 119–154.

UNDP. (1995). Human Development Report 1995. United Nations Development Programme (UNDP).

UNDP. (1999). *Human Development Report 1999.* United Nations Development Programme (UNDP).

UNDP. (2008a). *Human Development Indices: A statistical update 2008 - HDI rankings.* Retrieved from http://hdr.undp.org/en/statistics/

UNDP. (2008b). *Human Development Report: Sudan country factsheet.* Retrieved from: http://hdrstats.undp.org/countries/data_sheets/cty_ds_SDN.html

UNDP. (2009). *Human Development Report 2009.* Retrieved from: http://hdr.undp.org/en/media/HDR_2009_EN_Complete.pdf

UNDP. (2016). Human Development Report 2016: Human Development for Everyone. United Nations Development Programme (UNDP).

UNFPA & WEDO. (2009). *Making NAPAs work for women.* Available at: https://www.unfpa.org/sites/default/files/pub-pdf/climateconnections_4_napas.pdf

UNICEF Bangladesh. (2011). *A perspective on gender equality in Bangladesh From young girl to adolescent: What is lost in Transition? Analysis based on selected results of the Multiple Indicator Cluster Survey 2009.* Author.

UNICEF. (2016). *The State of the World's Children 2016: a fair chance for every child.* New York: United Nations Children Fund.

UNISDR. (2009). Making Disaster Risk Reduction Gender Sensitive, Policy and Practical Guideline. Author.

United Nation Organization. (2005). *Improvement of the situation of women in rural areas. report of the secretary-general.* Geneva: UNO.

United Nation Population Fund. (2009). *UNFPA Strategy and Framework for Action to Addressing gender based violence 2008-2011.* New York: UNFPA.

United Nations Development Program. (2010). *Gender and Disasters.* Retrieved from http://www.undp.org/content/dam/undp/library/crisis%20prevention/disaster/7Disaster%20Risk%20Reduction%20-%20Gender.pdf

United Nations Development Programme (UNPD). (2015). *Human Development Reports Nepal.* Available at: http://www.hdr.undp.org/en/countries/profiles/NPL

United Nations Division for the Advancement of Women. (2005, September). Gender equality and empowerment of women through ICT Gender equality and empowerment. *Women 2000 and Beyond.*

United Nations Population Fund. (2006). *Women are the fabric, Reproductive health for communities in crisis.* Retrieved form https://www.unfpa.org/sites/default/files/pub-pdf/women_fabric_eng_0.pdf

United Nations Resident and Humanitarian Coordinator's Office. (2011). *Field Bulletin Chaupadi in the Far West.* Available at: http://www.ohchr.org/Documents/Issues/Water/ContributionsStigma/others/field_bulletin_-_issue1_april_2011_-_chaupadi_in_far-west.pdf

United Nations, Department of Economic and Social Affairs, Population Division. (2016). Retrieved from http://www.un.org/en/development/desa/population/migration/publications/migrationreport/docs/MigrationReport2015_Highlights.pdf

United Nations. (1993). *Declaration on the Elimination of Violence Against Women.* Retrieved form http://www.un.org/documents/ga/res/48/a48r104.htm

United Nations. (2009). *Making disaster risk reduction gender-sensitive policy and practical guidelines.* Available at: http://www.unisdr.org/preventionweb/files/9922_MakingDisasterRiskReductionGenderSe.pdf

United Nations. (2011). *Gender Equality in the Contemporary World.* New York: United Nations, Department of Economic and Social Affairs, Division of Social Policy and Development.

Untitled by Baua Devi

URT. (2000). *National Micro-finance Policy.* Dar es Salaam, Tanzania: Ministry of Finance.

URT. (2005). *A country Report on the Implementation of the Beijing Platform for Action and Outcome.* Dar es Salaam, Tanzania: Ministry of Community Development Gender and Children.

URT. (2010). Tanzania Gender Indicators Booklet 2010: Ministry of Finance and Economic Affairs, Poverty Eradication and Economic Empowerment Division. Research and Poverty Alleviation.

Valentine, G. (1989). The geography of women's fear. *Area, 21*(4), 385–390. Retrieved from https://genderland.files.wordpress.com/2012/05/2-valentine.pdf

Varia, N. (2011). Sweeping changes? A review of recent reforms on protections for migrant domestic workers in Asia and the Middle East. *Canadian Journal of Women and the Law, 23*(1), 265–287. doi:10.3138/cjwl.23.1.265

Vegetal colours on paper, depicting the Rama-Sita marriage by *Padma Shri* Jagdamba Devi

VicHealth. (2007). *Preventing violence before it occurs: A framework and background paper to guide the primary prevention of violence against women in Victoria.* Victorian Health Promotion Association.

Vinding, D., & Kampbel, E. R. (2012). *Indigenous Women Workers with case studies from Bangladesh Working Paper, Nepal and the Americas.* International Labour Standards Department, ILO Bureau for gender Equality, Switzerland.

Vuuren, A (2000). *Female headed household: Their survival strategies in Tanzania. De-Agrarianisation and Rural Development Network.* Africa studiescentrum.

Wajcman, J. (1998). *Managing Like a Man: Women and Men in Corporate Management.* Oxford, UK: Polity Press.

Wanyama, M. (2015, July 14). To pay or not to pay your house help Sh11,000?. *The Star.* Retrieved from http://www.the-star.co.ke/news/2015/07/14/to-pay-or-not-to-pay-your-house-help-sh11000_c1168337

Ward, K. B. (1988). Women in the Global Economy. In Women and Work an Annual Review (Vol. 3). New York: Sage Publications.

Waring, M. (1988). *Counting for Nothing: What Men Value & What Women are Worth.* Allen & Unwin New Zealand Limited. doi:10.7810/9780868615714

Watch, H. R. (2015, June 30). Kuwait: New Law a Breakthrough for Domestic Workers: Guarantees Crucial Rights, but Gaps Remain. *Human Rights Watch*. Retrieved from https://www.hrw.org/news/2015/06/30/kuwait-new-law-breakthrough-domestic-workers

WaterAid in Nepal. (2009). *Is menstrual hygiene and management an issue for adolescent girls? A comparative study of four schools in different settings of Nepal WaterAid in Nepal*. Kathamndu.

WaterAid in Nepal. (2009). *Seen But Not Heard? A Review Of The Effectiveness Of Gender Approaches In Water And Sanitation Service Provision*. Available at: www.wateraid.org/~/.../gender-approach-water-sanitation-provision.pdf

Wazed, S. (2012). *Gender and Social Exclusion: A Study of Indigenous Women in Bangladesh* (Unpublished PhD Thesis). Institute of Applied Social Sciences, University of Birmingham.

Weedon, C. (1987). *Feminist practice and poststructuralist theory*. Oxford, UK: Basil Blackwell.

Weedon, C. (1999). *Feminism, theory and the politics of difference*. Malden, MA: Blackwell.

Weissbrodt, D., & Rhodes, J. (2013). United Nations Treaty Body Monitoring of Migrant Workers in the Middle East. *Middle EL & Governance, 5*(1-2), 71–111. doi:10.1163/18763375-00501003

White, L. (2009). *The Comforts of Home Prostitution in Colonial Nairobi*. Retrieved from http://www.myilibrary.com?id=207026

Wiener, R. L., Hurt, L. E., Russell, B., Mannen, K., & Gasper, C. (1997). Perceptions of sexual harassment: The effects of gender, legal standard and ambivalent sexism. *Law and Human Behavior, 21*, 71-93. 10.1023/A:1024818110678

Wignaraja, G. (1998). *Trade liberalization in Sri Lanka: Exports, technology and industrial policy*. London: Macmillan Press. doi:10.1007/978-1-349-26267-0

Wilce, J. M. Jr. (1994). Purity and Communal Boundaries: Women and Social Change in a Bangladeshi Village. *American Ethnologist, 21*(4), 986–987. doi:10.1525/ae.1994.21.4.02a01000

Wilkinson-Weber, C. M. (2001). Gender, Handicrafts, and Development in Pakistan: A Critical Review. *Pakistan Journal of Women's Studies: Alam-e-Niswan, 1&2*, 91-103, 98.

Willis, B. (2015). What is grassroots advocacy and why should I know about it?. *Votility*. Retrieved July 30, 2016, from http://www.votility.com/blog/bid/261018/What-is-Grassroots-Advocacy-Why-Should-I-Know-About-It

Wilson, E. F., Reeve, J. M. K., Pitt, A. H., Sully, B. G., & Julious, S. A. (2012). *INSPIRES: Investigating a reusable sanitary pad intervention in a rural educational setting—evaluating the acceptability and short term effect of teaching Kenyan school girls to make reusable sanitary towels on absenteeism and other daily activities: a partial preference parallel group, cluster randomised control trial*. Research Report ScHARRReport Series (27) School of Health and Related Research, University of Sheffield. 2012. Available: http://eprints.whiterose.ac.uk/43906/

Wilson, J., Phillips, B. D., & Neal, D. M. (1998). Domestic Violence after Disaster. In E. Enarson & B. H. Morrow (Eds.), *The Gendered Terrain of Disaster: Through Women's Eyes*. Westport, CT: Praeger Publishers.

Wolf, N. (1990). *The beauty myth*. New York: Chatto & Windus.

Women Resource Network. (2010). *Draft Report on the Situation of Indigenous Women in Bangladesh*. Rangamati, Bangladesh: Author.

Women's Environment and Development Organization. (2008). Case Study: Gender, Human Security and Climate Change: Lessons from Bangladesh, Ghana and Senegal. New York: Author.

WomenAction. (2000). *Asia & Pacific*. Retrieved from: http://www.womenaction.org/asia.html

World Bank Country and Lending Groups – World Bank Data Help Desk. (2016). Retrieved 12 November 2016, from https://datahelpdesk.worldbank.org/knowledgebase/articles/906519-world-bank-country-and-lending-groups

World Bank. (2007). *Dhaka: Improving living conditions for the urban poor*. Bangladesh: World Bank. Retrieved May 28, 2015, from http://siteresources.worldbank.org/BANGLADESHEXTN/Resources/295759-1182963268987/dhakaurbanreport.pdf

World Bank. (2008). *Whispers to Voices: Gender and Social Transformation in Bangladesh, Bangladesh Development Series, paper No. 22*. The World Bank.

World Health Organization. (2005). *Factsheet: Gender and Health in Disasters*. Retrieved from http://www.who.int/gender/gwhgendernd2.Pdf

World Health Organization. (2016). *Violence against women, Intimate partner and sexual violence against women, Fact sheet*. Retrieved from http://www.who.int/mediacentre/factsheets/fs239/en/

World Metrological Organisation. (n.d.). *Climate Information for Disaster Risk Reduction*. Retrieved from https://www.wmo.int/gfcs/site/documents/HLT_DRR_EN.pdf

Wyss, B. (1995). *Gender and economic support of Jamaican households: Implications for children's living standards* (Doctoral Dissertation). University of Massachusetts, Amherst, MA.

Yance, T. (2015). *The Multidimensionality of Schoolgirl Dropouts in Rural Bangladesh* (Master's thesis). University of San Francisco.

Yao, Y. (2015). Pay gap still wide between men and women despite improvements. *China Daily USA*. Retrieved from http://usa.chinadaily.com.cn/epaper/2015-03/13/content_19803414.htm

Yassin, U. E. (2006). *Women and Work: An examination of how women manage their triple roles* (Unpublished Masters dissertation). Ahfad University for Women.

Yeates, N. (2005). A global political economy of care. *Social Policy and Society*, *4*(2), 227–234. doi:10.1017/S1474746404002350

Yukongdi, V., & Benson, J. (2005). Women in Asian management: Cracking the glass ceiling? *Asia Pacific Business Review*, *11*(2), 139–148. doi:10.1080/1360238042000291225

Zafarullah, H. M., & Khan, M. M. (1989). Toward equity in public service employment: the Bangladesh experience. In Equity in public employment across nations. Lanham, MD: University Press of America.

Zaidi, A. A. (1999). Issues in Pakistan Economy. Karachi: Oxford.

Zlotnik, H. (2005). International migration trends since 1980. *International Migration and the Millennium Development Goals*, 13.

Zohir, S. C. (2003). *Integrating gender into world bank financed transport programs: Case study Bangladesh*. Retrieved May 30, 2015, from http://siteresources.worldbank.org/INTGENDERTRANSPORT/Resources/DhakaUrbanTransport.pdf

Zywno, M. S., Gilbride, K. A., Hiscocks, P. D., Waalen, J. K., & Kennedy, D. C. (1998). *Attracting Women into Engineering - A Case Study*. IEEE. Retrieved from http://www.ieee.org/

About the Contributors

Nazmunnessa Mahtab is Professor (Supernumery) in the Department of Women and Gender Studies, University of Dhaka, Bangladesh. She is one of the founding members involved in the establishment of the Department of Women's Studies in March 2000. She pursued a Masters' Degree in Politics, with specialization in Public Administration from the London School of Economics and Political Science (LSE), University of London, in 1975. She completed her PhD from the University of Delhi, India in 1982. She also did her Post-Doctoral Research as a Senior Fulbright Scholar from George Washington University, Washington D.C. in 1989 with a focus on Women in Administration. She has published two books: 1) *Women in Bangladesh: From Inequality to Empowerment* (2007); 2) *Women, Gender, and Development: Contemporary Issues* (2012). Her recent publications include: 1) "Women's Transformational Leadership in Bangladesh: Potentials and Challenges," published in *Women, Political Struggles, and Gender Equality in South Asia* edited by Margaret Alston, Palgrave Macmillan, August 2014.

Md. Mynul Islam is working as an Assistant Professor at the department of Women and Gender Studies, University of Dhaka, Bangladesh.

* * *

Shahira O. Abdel-Hameid obtained her Ph.D in Human Resource Management and Organizational Behaviour from the University of Manchester, UK in 2003 and MA in Labour and Employment studies from the Institute for Social Studies, The Netherlands in 1995. She is currently an Assistant Professor in the Higher Colleges of Technology, Abu Dhabi. Other positions held were program coordinator of the HRM Program and champion of the international accreditation ACBSP at the Emirates College of Technology, Abu Dhabi and coordinator of the MBA Program at Ahfad University for Women, Sudan. Shahira has published papers in conference proceedings and peer reviewed journals, such as Ahfad Journal: Women & Change. In conjunction with academics, she held the position of a national project director for UNFPA supported project on women empowerment and gender mainstreaming; part of the Population Development Strategy Sub-program, Sudan. Shahira has conducted consulting and training activities in the area of women empowerment and gender mainstreaming. Areas of research interests include different worldviews of women empowerment challenges and relationship between HRM, supportive organizational culture and corporate strategy.

Endong Floribert Patrick Calvain (PhD) is a research consultant in the humanities and social sciences. His areas of interest include gender, culture, media laws, international communication and religious communication. He is author of numerous articles and book chapters in the above mentioned areas.

Manase Chiweshe is a Senior Lecturer in the Institute of Lifelong Learning and Development Studies at Chinhoyi University of Technology and winner of the 2015 Gerti Hessling Award for the best paper in African studies. He is a young African scholar with interest in African agrarian studies, land, livelihoods, football, gender and youth studies. Dr Chiweshe's work revolves around the sociology of everyday life in African spaces with special focus on promoting African ways of knowing.

Kuntala Chowdhury is working as a lecturer at the Department of Women & Gender Studies, Begum Rokeya University, Rangpur. She completed her BSS and MSS degree from the Department of Women & Gender studies, University of Dhaka. Kuntala worked on several research projects focused upon the issues of sexual and reproductive health, media and culture, human rights, violence against women and women empowerment etc. She worked as researcher and trainer in different international Organizations like BBC Media Action, ICDDR, Brac before joining teaching profession. In her earlier professional period she also worked as media personnel in Radio Today and Dhaka FM so she has keen interest of analyzing the position of women from different dimension and connects this status of women with theoretical propositions. She has also presented her papers at Jaharginagar University and United International University in Bangladesh which were about contemporary issues (Modern Hijab, Menstrual Stigma) in Bangladesh.

Arunima Kishore Das is currently enrolled as a PhD fellow at the Western Sydney University's School of Humanities and Communication Arts. Prior to this, she completed both Bachelor and Masters Degrees in Women and Gender Studies from the University of Dhaka. Her research interests include gendered urbanization and space, masculinities and violence against women.

Prabartana Das is currently pursuing Masters degree in International Relations at Jadavpur University and my area of interest has always revolved around Gender or International conflicts. Thereby i would like to explore and analyze my interest through this new platform.

Sraboni Dutta is an Associate Professor in Business Management with Birla Institute of Technology, Mesra, Kolkata Campus. She is a Ph.D in Business Management from Calcutta University and has many years of teaching experience coupled with experience in the industry. She was awarded the prestigious Fulbright Scholarship of the United States India Educational Foundation (USIEF) in 2012 and has undertaken teaching and research assignments in universities in U.S.A. She has presented at numerous international conferences in India and abroad and has many publications in refereed international and national journals to her credit. Her research interests are in the fields of Entrepreneurship, Corporate Sustainability and Gender issues and has 4 doctoral research scholars under her supervision. She is interested in social work and has been involved with NGOs like Manikpur Chaitali Sangha and ASED. She has also conducted Entrepreneurship Development Programmes in association with Pragati, the Ladies Wing of Bengal National Chamber of Commerce.

About the Contributors

Ananya Goswami is a Research Scholar in Department of Management of Birla Institute of Technology, Mesra, Kolkata Campus. She has almost seven years of industry exposure in human resource area. Her research interest is in entrepreneurship and women issues.

Julaikha B. Hossain is working as an Affiliated Faculty and Senior Research Specialist in Gender and Development Studies at the Asian Institute of Technology, Thailand. Her research interests are gender and development with emphasis on the policies and programmes for mainstreaming gender and women's empowerment; Gender, laws and human rights; Organizational management and development in Asia; Gender and environment; Women. peace and security, etc. Dr. Hossain has been involved in a large number of social and gender-responsive development programs and projects funded by development agencies, including UN Women, IFAD, ADB, JICA, European Union, CIDA, and UNDP.

Vivian Innis is an MA candidate in International Development at Brandeis University. She also completed a BBA degree in Management and Economics at United Methodist University, Liberia. She is currently acting Supervisor of UNCSR 1325 Secretariat, Ministry of Gender, Liberia.

Gulay Jannat is a Lecturer in the Department of Women and Gender Studies, University of Dhaka, Bangladesh.

Dhammika Jayawardena is a senior lecturer in management and organisational behaviour in the Department of Business Administration at the University of Sri Jayewardenepura, Sri Lanka. He received his PhD from the University of Leicester, UK, in 2010. His current research interests focus on critical HRM, the formation of gender identities in the Global South, language and ethics, and the marketisation of higher education in Sri Lanka. In 2015, Dhammika won the Best Article Award for his article, entitled 'HRM as a "web of texts": (re)articulating the identity of HRM in Sri Lanka's localized global apparel industry', appeared in *Organization Management Journal* 11(4), from the Eastern Academy of Management and Routledge, Taylor and Francis, USA.

Farah Kabir has been working in the field of development and research for close to 2 decades. She has research experience and a host of publications especially on Women in Politics to her credit. At present, she is working as the Country Director of ActionAid Bangladesh since June 2007. She won the "Nawab Ali Chowdhury National Award 2012" for her significant contribution in women's empowerment in Bangladesh. She worked with British Council for close to ten years both in Bangladesh and UK. She has been an activist on women's rights, gender equity, climate justice and child rights for a long time. She is an active member of many professional societies. She is working as the Chair of the Global Board of GNDR. Farah is a member of UCEP General Assembly; Napier University, Edinburgh Scotland; Board of Trustees for Zero Tolerance, Scotland; Climate Action Network, South Asia; Campaign for Popular Education (CAMPE), Education Watch and Funding Committee of Civil Society Education Fund (CSEF). As a newscaster on both National Television and Radio for a long time, Farah built an association with the media. Farah is married with two sons. She is fond of music and reading. In her teens she was involved with amateur theatre.

Mohammed Kamruzzaman works as Senior Manager, Knowledge Management for Gender Justice and Diversity programme of BRAC in Bangladesh. He manages tasks related to monitoring, evaluation and knowledge management of various gender related projects in BRAC. Before joining his current position, he has served for more than eleven years in various academic and development research projects which included livelihoods, well-being, NGO governance and women's empowerment. Mr. Kamruzzaman has some national and international publications and his most recent co-authored publication titled "Addressing multiple dimensions of gender inequality: the experience of the BRAC Gender Quality Action Learning (GQAL) Programme in Bangladesh" in Gender & Development, 23 (2), 333-346.

Devanjan Khuntia is a Senior Research Scholar and currently pursuing PhD from the Centre for the Study of Social Systems at Jawaharlal Nehru University, New Delhi, India. His area of research includes Women and Gender Studies, Media and Communications, Urban Studies, Political Economy, Criminology and Research Methodology. His M.Phil research was on the rise of 24x7 news channels and their role in the production of contemporary discourses in India. He has contributed to some of the best of research studies undertaken in South Asia in contemporary times. He is a trained journalist and has served Indian National Media networks besides providing consultation to development sector organizations and emerging media houses.

Hina Kousar studied social work and did her Doctorate from Jamia Millia Islamia, New Delhi. She has experience in academia and NGO activity. She has also worked as researcher in YWCA Dallas on many research projects ranging from breast cancer to microcredit financing among women. Presently she is employed with as victim advocate in DARCC. She has been associated with international organizations like Taxes Muslim women foundation and Galveston women studies center of university of Taxes at Dallas. Her research interests are highly complementary ranging from mental health, trafficking, substance abuse, and women empowerment.

Anne Namatsi Lutomia is a doctoral candidate in the Human Resource Development at the University of Illinois at Urbana-Champaign. She holds a Bachelor of Education degree in Administration and French from Kenyatta University, Kenya, and a master's degree in Nonprofit Management from Hamline University in Minnesota, in the United States with a minor in Gender and Women Studies. Her research interests span organizational network collaborations, leadership, adult learning, labor mobility, and nonprofit organizations. Among other publications, she published an article and two book chapters on women's organizations and leadership.

Turphina Matekere was a Master student at the college of social sciences and humanities, she has a vast experience in social sciences, currently working as a coordinator in gender related fields.

About the Contributors

Patricia Mwesiga is an academician and researcher specialized in International Community Economic Development, Gender and general Development Studies. She holds a PhD in Development Studies, a Masters in Community Economic Development and a Post-Graduate Diploma in Poverty Analysis for Socioeconomic Security and Development as well as a Bachelor of Science in Home Economics and Human Nutrition. She has 10 years experience in community development work including research and project development. She has evaluated area development projects for World Vision International in Tanzania, Mapped and Analyzed Initiatives to Empower Women in Agriculture and Designed a way Forward. She has also conducted several scoping and baseline studies. Apart from teaching and supervising students' researches, Patricia is a consultant trainer for leadership and champions for change for transformation of African Agriculture. Currently, she is employed by the Mwalimu Nyerere Memorial Academy as a Lecturer and Head of Department of Gender Studies.

Shagufta Nasreen is an Assistant Professor at Centre of Excellence for Women's Studies, University of Karachi, Pakistan. She is a Ph.D. in Women's Studies from University of Karachi, Pakistan and has more than ten years of teaching experience. She has presented at numerous national and international conferences in Pakistan and has many publications in peer reviewed national journals to her credit. Her areas of academic and research interest are gender, development, globalization and media. She is also assistant editor of Pakistan Journal of Gender Studies.

Sara Parker is a Reader in Development Studies at Liverpool John Moores University who has long standing research links with Nepal. After volunteering in Nepal in 1992 Sara completed her PhD exploring the impact of ActionAid's participatory non formal education programme REFLECT in a remote mountainous village in Nepal. She has led a number of British Council and DFID funded Higher Education links between Liverpool John Moores University and CERID and Padma Kanya Campus, Tribhuvan University in Kathmandu as well as with Dhaka University in Bangladesh.

Sudha Jha Pathak has done her post-graduation in History from Jadavpur University, Calcutta and Doctorate from the M.S University of Vadodara, Baroda. She was also granted Junior Research Fellowship (JRF) by the Indian Council of Historical Research (ICHR). She taught at various colleges in Mumbai before joining the Amity Law School, Delhi where she currently teaches. She is a Member of the Indian History Congress as well as a Life Member of the Epigraphical Society of India. She is also trained in Indian classical dance *Bharatnatyam* and in playing the guitar.

Dorothy Owino Rombo is an assistant professor of child and family studies at the State University of New York. She holds a Ph.D in family and social science and a minor in family policy from the University of Minnesota, twin cities. Her research interests are on the ecological contexts of vulnerable populations especially women, children and international families. She has published on the impact of policy on these populations.

About the Contributors

Parboti Roy is Lecturer at the department of Political Science and Sociology in North South University. She completed her Post graduation in Women's Studies from Flinders University and did her Bachelor and Master in Women and Gender Studies, University of Dhaka. Roy has research interest in gender based violence, indigenous women, human rights and marginalized people, gender and development, climate change, migration and gender.

Noorie Safa is a Senior Sector Specialist at Gender Justice Diversity program of BRAC. Presently she is on study leave for pursuing a master degree on Gender and Development studies from Asian Institution of Technology under ADB JSP scholarship. She had her graduation from Women and Gender studies, University of Dhaka. After graduation she joined at NETZ Partnership for Development and Justice as researcher and conducted a study to assess the impacts of development interventions on women's position in gender power relationships. In addition she also had the opportunity to work in World Health Organization funded research work on Engendering Health Information System. Moreover, while being employed in Center for Men and Masculinities Studies, as research associate she worked in several projects notably Vanderbilt University funded project on Social and Environment Change in Bangladesh, Save the Children Nepal funded study titled Pathways to Violence.

Nasreen Aslam Shah is Director, Centre of Excellence for Women's Studies and Chairperson Department of Social Work, University of Karachi. She is Meritorious Professor and editor of Pakistan Journal of Gender Studies and Pakistan Journal of Applied Social Sciences. She has published many books and papers in research journals. Her areas of interest are Women and work, home-based/ self-employed women and research. Dr. Nasreen has been involved in many social and gender-responsive development programs and projects funded by national and development agencies.

Anna Sikira holds a PhD in Rural Development and an M.Sc. Agricultural Education and Extension and Bachelor of Science in Home Economics and Human Nutrition of Sokoine University of Agriculture. She holds a Diploma in Poultry production obtained from Uyole Agricultural Institute in Mbeya. She has a vast experience in research and consultancies in social research related fields. She is interested in Gender related activities

Kay Standing is a Reader in Gender Studies at Liverpool John Moores University who has worked in Nepal since 2005 and was associated with the DFiD funded DeLPHE link focusing on Mainstreaming gender within Higher Education which brought together Padma Kanya Campus, Tribhuvan University in Kathmandu as well as with Dhaka University in Bangladesh. This programme led to a Master in Gender Studies being launched in Nepal in 2010. She has also led a Big Lottery funded Tender project in schools in the UK to educate young people about healthy relationship and challenge attitudes which condone and normalise violence.

About the Contributors

Justin K. Urassa holds a PhD (Development Studies) and an M.Sc. Social research Methods (Development Studies) from the university of Sussex (United Kingdom), A Post-graduate Diploma in Poverty Analysis for Socioeconomic Security and Development from the Institute of Social Studies-The Hague, Holland in collaboration with the Economic and Social Research Foundation (ESRF)-Tanzania and Research on Poverty Alleviation (REPOA)-Dar es Salaam, Tanzania, an MSc. and B.Sc. (Agriculture) from Sokoine University of Agriculture (SUA) and a Diploma in Dairy Husbandry from Livestock Training Institute (LITI) Tengeru, Tanzania. His research interests include; Rural livelihoods and well-being; Poverty analysis; Food Security; Agricultural and rural development; Policy analysis; Social development and gender and development.

Elisabeth Wilson is an Independent academic and consultant in the U.K. After a first career as a social worker and social work manager, Elisabeth Wilson undertook her PhD, an early study of gender and organizational culture, at Liverpool John Moores University. She also has an MBA from Huddersfield University, as well as a BA from the University of East Anglia. Elisabeth has researched gender and organisation in the UK, India and Sudan. She is the author or co-author of over 25 refereed publications and book chapters, and has written about organizational culture, perception, gendered career paths, and yoga and management. The edited volume: "Organizational Behaviour Re-assessed : the Impact of Gender", published by Sage in 2000, is still in print and has become a classic reference text. Elisabeth taught at Liverpool Business School, Liverpool John Moores University, and later at the Institute for Development Policy and Management, University of Manchester, UK. She directed professional, post-experience and Masters courses at both universities, and has written learning materials for online Masters courses. In 2009 she was a Visiting Professor at Ahfad University for Women. She is a chartered member of the Chartered Institute of Personnel and Development, and member of the Higher Education Academy. Elisabeth has undertaken consultancy for the UK Department of International Development, as well as the Finnish and Tanzanian governments and UNESCO.

Index

A

African feminism 172, 175-176, 183

B

Bangladesh 37-39, 41, 44, 47, 52-60, 62-63, 65-66, 69-81, 83-84, 90-92, 95-97, 99-101, 126, 189-193, 195, 203, 208-209, 212-213, 215, 218, 224, 235-239, 242-245, 274, 326, 331, 334-348, 360-362, 367-368, 383, 385, 387
Banking sector 301
Barriers 21-23, 31, 38, 61-62, 69, 71, 73, 76-77, 156-157, 189-190, 192, 195, 197-200, 202, 206, 210, 237, 260, 269-270, 275, 278, 301, 363
barriers and challenges 189-190, 192, 195, 197, 199-200, 202, 206, 210
brothel based sex workers 189-191, 194-195, 197-198, 200-202, 206

C

Care work 14, 37-43, 46-48, 52, 367
Career 19-22, 24, 28, 31-32, 37-48, 55, 60-62, 69-74, 76, 80-85, 109, 115-116, 128, 150, 183, 303, 315, 344
chauvinism 281, 323
Chittagong Hill Tracts 90-91, 96-97, 382-383, 389
Civil Society 62, 109, 112, 118, 152, 183, 190, 209-210, 281-282, 289-290, 292-293, 295
Climate 151, 243-245, 354-363, 367-369
commodification of art 376
Community Journalism 295
Community Media 295
Commuting Environment 212-215, 218, 228, 230-232
Construction organizations 69, 71-76, 78, 80-81, 84, 86
COP 356-358
Corporate leadership 297-298, 301, 303-304
Cross River State 281-282, 290-291, 293, 295

D

Development Intervention 383, 386, 388-389, 394
Disaster 235-245, 355-357, 359-362, 367-368
Domestic Work 1-7, 12-15, 18, 111, 128, 134, 312, 344

E

Electronic Media 323, 328
emancipation 111-112, 281-283, 285, 287, 289-290, 293, 296, 322-324, 330
empowerment 4, 25, 38, 47, 52, 61, 65, 99-100, 109, 112, 117-118, 121-122, 135, 152, 173, 176, 206, 213-214, 218, 221, 252-256, 258, 260, 262-263, 265, 269-270, 273-275, 282-283, 285, 287, 289-293, 296-298, 301-302, 309, 315, 322-323, 329-330, 337, 339-340, 346, 348, 358-359, 362, 368, 376, 379
Environment 23, 52-53, 55-61, 63, 65, 67, 74-75, 80-82, 84-86, 97, 109, 124, 128, 137, 150, 208, 212-215, 218, 228-232, 236, 269, 277, 309, 347, 354-355, 362, 385, 388
Equality 37-39, 41, 47, 57, 59-62, 65, 67, 74, 76, 107, 112, 115, 117-118, 128, 137, 145, 152, 174, 177-178, 182, 213, 231, 253-254, 275, 284, 289-290, 297-298, 301, 303-304, 322-324, 327, 329-331, 336-339, 347-348, 354-356, 358-359, 362, 368, 395

F

Family Commitments 20, 22, 32
Formal Sector 54, 57, 59, 113, 125-126, 132, 134-136
Free Trade Zone 23

G

gender inequality 52, 55, 70-71, 115, 240, 253-254, 281, 285-287, 290, 325, 334-335, 345, 355-356, 359, 367, 395

Index

Gender Insensitive 212-213, 215, 230, 232
Gender Relationship 382-383, 386, 392-395
Gender Stereotype 222, 325
gender violence 144-147
Gendered Job Segregation 20
Global South 19-23, 31-32
Globalization 2, 4, 8, 95-98, 100-101, 121-125, 128-130, 136-137, 145, 275, 322, 329, 335
Government 1-3, 5-6, 13, 15, 23, 39, 53-55, 57-59, 61, 64-65, 72, 74, 76, 82-83, 95-97, 101, 108-109, 112, 114, 116-118, 125, 129, 132, 135-137, 152, 165, 190, 192, 206, 208-210, 212, 239, 245, 253, 269-270, 276-277, 283-285, 288, 290-291, 296-297, 326, 331, 336, 338, 346-348, 356, 361-363, 367, 371, 375-379, 383, 385, 388, 395
Grassroots Communication 295
Grassroots Communications 295

H

Hegemonic Masculinity 212-213, 217-218, 221, 223-224, 227, 230-232, 395
Hegemony 183, 323
Human Rights 1-5, 7-8, 10-15, 53, 55, 109, 145, 190-191, 205, 207-208, 274, 296, 347, 356, 368

I

ICT 54, 269-271, 273-278
Immigration 4, 7, 15, 337
Indian women 297, 299, 312
indigeneity 94, 101
Indigenous Community 395
Indigenous women 90-102, 382, 388
Informal Sector 53-54, 57, 111, 113, 121-122, 124-128, 130, 132-133, 136-137, 308
international migration 4, 14, 123, 334, 336-340, 344
Intersectionality 1-3, 11, 14, 18, 56, 59, 170, 172, 178, 180, 194, 206
intimate partner violence 144, 146, 148, 151-152, 242, 339, 347
Islam 38, 40-42, 76, 95, 113, 115, 118, 334-335, 339-341, 343-344, 347, 367
IT sector 302

K

Kenya 1-6, 8-10, 13-15, 18, 108, 164, 178
Khafala 4, 8, 18

L

Lamai Identity 24-29, 31-32

M

Managerial Women 19, 31-32
marginalization of women 123-124, 288, 307, 378
Masculinity 3, 70, 170, 179-180, 212-213, 217-218, 221-224, 227, 230-232, 259, 382, 384, 386-387, 391, 393, 395
Men's perceptions 212-213, 230, 232
men's role 393
menstrual hygiene 156-157, 160-161, 164-165
menstruation 156-161, 164-165, 203-204
Middle East 2, 4-5, 7-10, 12, 18, 107, 241, 313, 334, 336, 339, 343-344
Migrant 1-2, 4-5, 7-10, 14-15, 18, 23-24, 61, 307, 335, 337-338, 340, 343-345, 347-348
Mobility Rights 212-214, 218, 230-232

N

Nepal 156-160, 162-163, 165, 242, 371
New Social Media Platforms 307, 309-310

O

Organizational culture 69, 72-73, 76, 81, 84, 86

P

Pakistan 91, 95-96, 121, 125, 127-133, 157, 237, 242, 327, 331, 383, 385, 387
Paris Agreement 354-355, 358-359, 368
patriarchy 10, 19-21, 25-26, 41, 56, 111, 118, 170, 176-177, 191-192, 194, 207, 231-232, 237, 264, 281, 285-287, 289, 322-323, 338-339, 342, 395
Public Buses 136, 212-214, 216-219, 224-225, 228-232
Public leadership 298-299, 301

R

rape 97, 144, 146-149, 158, 201, 204-207, 239, 241-242, 244-245, 328-331, 342, 368
Recruiting Bureaus 2, 5, 7-8, 12-13, 18
Returnees 8, 13, 15, 18
Rural Migrants 309-310

S

sanitary pads 156-157, 161, 163-164
Self-Employment 121, 270
sexual assault 24, 144, 146, 148-152, 158, 239, 241, 328
sexual harassment 20, 24, 41, 56, 58-59, 64, 97, 114, 136, 144-151, 213-214, 224-232, 244-245, 367-368
Social Actors 24-26, 28, 311, 316, 318
Social Networking 12-13, 15, 274, 316-317, 323, 329
social remittances 334-337, 340-341
stalking 144, 146, 148, 152, 329
subjugation 322, 324, 330

T

The Gulf Countries 18, 336, 339
Third gender 181-182, 316
traditional economic activities 90-101

U

unpaid care work 42, 52, 367

V

Violence against Women and Girls 360
Vulnerability 58, 96-97, 209-210, 235-241, 244-245, 265, 354-357, 361, 367

W

Women Affirmative Action 281-282, 284-287, 290-293, 296
Women and work 110, 121-123, 127-128, 136-137
Women Emancipation 281-282, 287, 289-290, 296, 323-324, 330
Women Empowerment 121-122, 152, 265, 270, 273, 275, 281, 283, 285, 287, 289-293, 296-298, 301-302, 315, 322-323, 329-330, 359, 362
Women engineers 69, 71-77, 80, 82-86
Women Entrepreneurs 58, 269-270, 274-278, 346
Women Marginalization 282, 289-290
Women's Economic Empowerment 61, 252-256, 262, 265
Women's Employment 37, 53, 66, 71-72, 75-76, 83, 113, 121, 128, 339
Women's Subordination 19-20, 22, 25, 31-32, 144, 254
Working environment 52-53, 55-56, 58-59, 61, 63, 65, 75, 81, 84, 208

Purchase Print, E-Book, or Print + E-Book

IGI Global books can now be purchased from three unique pricing formats:
Print Only, E-Book Only, or Print + E-Book. Shipping fees apply.

www.igi-global.com

Recommended Reference Books

ISBN: 978-1-4666-9938-0
© 2016; 425 pp.
List Price: $185

ISBN: 978-1-5225-0813-7
© 2017; 345 pp.
List Price: $190

ISBN: 978-1-4666-9461-3
© 2016; 1,788 pp.
List Price: $2,150

ISBN: 978-1-4666-6433-3
© 2015; 2,121 pp.
List Price: $2,250

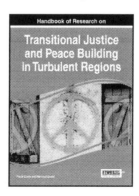

ISBN: 978-1-4666-9675-4
© 2016; 559 pp.
List Price: $295

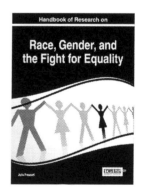

ISBN: 978-1-5225-0047-6
© 2016; 744 pp.
List Price: $320

Looking for free content, product updates, news, and special offers?
Join IGI Global's mailing list today and start enjoying exclusive perks sent only to IGI Global members.
Add your name to the list at **www.igi-global.com/newsletters**.

Publishing Information Science and Technology Research Since 1988

www.igi-global.com   Sign up at www.igi-global.com/newsletters   facebook.com/igiglobal   twitter.com/igiglobal

Stay Current on the Latest Emerging Research Developments

Become an IGI Global Reviewer for Authored Book Projects

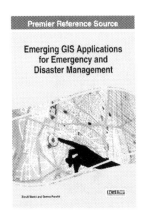 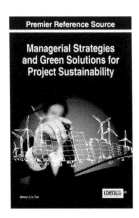  

The overall success of an authored book project is dependent on quality and timely reviews.

In this competitive age of scholarly publishing, constructive and timely feedback significantly decreases the turnaround time of manuscripts from submission to acceptance, allowing the publication and discovery of progressive research at a much more expeditious rate. Several IGI Global authored book projects are currently seeking highly qualified experts in the field to fill vacancies on their respective editorial review boards:

Applications may be sent to:
development@igi-global.com

Applicants must have a doctorate (or an equivalent degree) as well as publishing and reviewing experience. Reviewers are asked to write reviews in a timely, collegial, and constructive manner. All reviewers will begin their role on an ad-hoc basis for a period of one year, and upon successful completion of this term can be considered for full editorial review board status, with the potential for a subsequent promotion to Associate Editor.

If you have a colleague that may be interested in this opportunity, we encourage you to share this information with them.

InfoSci®-Books

A Database for Progressive Information Science and Technology Research

www.igi-global.com

Maximize Your Library's Book Collection!

Invest in IGI Global's InfoSci®-Books database and gain access to hundreds of reference books at a fraction of their individual list price.

The InfoSci®-Books database offers unlimited simultaneous users the ability to precisely return search results through more than 75,000 full-text chapters from nearly 3,400 reference books in the following academic research areas:

Business & Management Information Science & Technology • Computer Science & Information Technology
Educational Science & Technology • Engineering Science & Technology • Environmental Science & Technology
Government Science & Technology • Library Information Science & Technology • Media & Communication Science & Technology
Medical, Healthcare & Life Science & Technology • Security & Forensic Science & Technology • Social Sciences & Online Behavior

Peer-Reviewed Content:
- Cutting-edge research
- No embargoes
- Scholarly and professional
- Interdisciplinary

Award-Winning Platform:
- Unlimited simultaneous users
- Full-text in XML and PDF
- Advanced search engine
- No DRM

Librarian-Friendly:
- Free MARC records
- Discovery services
- COUNTER4/SUSHI compliant
- Training available

To find out more or request a free trial, visit:
www.igi-global.com/eresources

IGI Global Proudly Partners with

Enhance Your Manuscript with eContent Pro's Professional and Academic
Copy Editing Service

Additional Services

Expert Translation

eContent Pro Translation provides professional translation services across key languages around the world. Our expert translators will work to provide a clear-cut translation of your document, while maintaining your original meaning and ensuring that your document is accurately and professionally translated.

Professional Proofreading

eContent Pro Proofreading provides fast, high-quality, affordable proofreading that will optimize the accuracy and readability of your document, ensuring that its contents are communicated in the clearest way possible to your readers.

IGI Global Authors Save 20% on eContent Pro's Services!

Scan the QR Code to Receive Your 20% Discount

The 20% discount is applied directly to your eContent Pro shopping cart when placing an order through IGI Global's referral link. Use the QR code to access this referral link. eContent Pro has the right to end or modify any promotion at any time.

Email: customerservice@econtentpro.com

econtentpro.com

Information Resources Management Association

Advancing the Concepts & Practices of Information Resources Management in Modern Organizations

Become an IRMA Member

Members of the **Information Resources Management Association (IRMA)** understand the importance of community within their field of study. The Information Resources Management Association is an ideal venue through which professionals, students, and academicians can convene and share the latest industry innovations and scholarly research that is changing the field of information science and technology. Become a member today and enjoy the benefits of membership as well as the opportunity to collaborate and network with fellow experts in the field.

IRMA Membership Benefits:

- **One FREE Journal Subscription**
- **30% Off Additional Journal Subscriptions**
- **20% Off Book Purchases**

- Updates on the latest events and research on Information Resources Management through the IRMA-L listserv.
- Updates on new open access and downloadable content added to Research IRM.
- A copy of the Information Technology Management Newsletter twice a year.
- A certificate of membership.

IRMA Membership $195

Scan code or visit **irma-international.org** and begin by selecting your free journal subscription.

Membership is good for one full year.

www.irma-international.org

Available to Order Now

Order through www.igi-global.com with <u>Free Standard Shipping</u>.

The Premier Reference for Information Science & Information Technology

100% Original Content
Contains 705 new, peer-reviewed articles with color figures covering over 80 categories in 11 subject areas

Diverse Contributions
More than 1,100 experts from 74 unique countries contributed their specialized knowledge

Easy Navigation
Includes two tables of content and a comprehensive index in each volume for the user's convenience

Highly-Cited
Embraces a complete list of references and additional reading sections to allow for further research

Included in:
InfoSci®-Books

Encyclopedia of Information Science and Technology Fourth Edition
A Comprehensive 10-Volume Set

Mehdi Khosrow-Pour, D.B.A. (Information Resources Management Association, USA)
ISBN: 978-1-5225-2255-3; © 2018; Pg: 8,104; Release Date: July 2017

For a limited time, <u>receive the complimentary e-books for the First, Second, and Third editions</u> with the purchase of the *Encyclopedia of Information Science and Technology, Fourth Edition* e-book.**

The **Encyclopedia of Information Science and Technology, Fourth Edition** is a 10-volume set which includes 705 original and previously unpublished research articles covering a full range of perspectives, applications, and techniques contributed by thousands of experts and researchers from around the globe. This authoritative encyclopedia is an all-encompassing, well-established reference source that is ideally designed to disseminate the most forward-thinking and diverse research findings. With critical perspectives on the impact of information science management and new technologies in modern settings, including but not limited to computer science, education, healthcare, government, engineering, business, and natural and physical sciences, it is a pivotal and relevant source of knowledge that will benefit every professional within the field of information science and technology and is an invaluable addition to every academic and corporate library.

Scan for Online Bookstore

Pricing Information

Hardcover: **$5,695**   E-Book: **$5,695***   Hardcover + E-Book: **$6,895***

Both E-Book Prices Include:
- *Encyclopedia of Information Science and Technology, First Edition E-Book*
- *Encyclopedia of Information Science and Technology, Second Edition E-Book*
- *Encyclopedia of Information Science and Technology, Third Edition E-Book*

* Purchase the Encyclopedia of Information Science and Technology, Fourth Edition e-book and receive the first, second, and third e-book editions for free. Offer is only valid with purchase of the fourth edition's e-book. Offer expires January 1, 2018.

Recommend this Title to Your Institution's Library: www.igi-global.com/books

InfoSci®-OnDemand

www.igi-global.com/infosci-ondemand

Continuously updated with new material on a weekly basis, InfoSci®-OnDemand offers the ability to search through thousands of quality full-text research papers. Users can narrow each search by identifying key topic areas of interest, then display a complete listing of relevant papers, and purchase materials specific to their research needs.

Comprehensive Service
- Over 81,600+ journal articles, book chapters, and case studies.
- All content is downloadable in PDF format and can be stored locally for future use.

No Subscription Fees
- One time fee of $37.50 per PDF download.

Instant Access
- Receive a download link immediately after order completion!

Database Platform Features:
- Comprehensive Pay-Per-View Service
- Written by Prominent International Experts/Scholars
- Precise Search and Retrieval
- Updated With New Material on a Weekly Basis
- Immediate Access to Full-Text PDFs
- No Subscription Needed
- Purchased Research Can Be Stored Locally for Future Use

"It really provides an excellent entry into the research literature of the field. It presents a manageable number of highly relevant sources on topics of interest to a wide range of researchers. The sources are scholarly, but also accessible to 'practitioners'."

— Lisa Stimatz, MLS, University of North Carolina at Chapel Hill, USA

"It is an excellent and well designed database which will facilitate research, publication and teaching. It is a very very useful tool to have."

— George Ditsa, PhD, University of Wollongong, Australia

"I have accessed the database and find it to be a valuable tool to the IT/IS community. I found valuable articles meeting my search criteria 95% of the time."

— Lynda Louis, Xavier University of Louisiana, USA

Recommended for use by researchers who wish to immediately download PDFs of individual chapters or articles.

www.igi-global.com/e-resources/infosci-ondemand

www.igi-global.com

Printed in the United States
By Bookmasters